ULTIMATE
ARABIC
BEGINNER–INTERMEDIATE

By

Rajaa Aquil, Ph.D.
(Saudi Arabic lessons and basic phrases)

Sanna Dhahir, Ph.D.
(Iraqi Arabic lessons and basic phrases)

Ahmed Fekry Ibrahim
(Modern Standard Arabic lessons 5 to 15,
Appendices A to I, Glossary)

Aziz N. Ismail
(Egyptian Arabic lessons and basic phrases)

Nathalie Khazaal
(Modern Standard Arabic lessons 1 to 4,
Lebanese Arabic lessons and basic phrases)

Sara Nimis
(Modern Standard Arabic lessons 5 to 15,
Appendices A to I, Glossary)

Edited by
Zvjezdana Vrzić, Ph.D., and Rania G. Hejazeen

LIVING LANGUAGE, A RANDOM HOUSE COMPANY
NEW YORK

Published in the United States by Living Language, A Random House Company

www.livinglanguage.com

Editors: Zvjezdana Vrzić and Rania G. Hejazeen

Production Editors: John Whitman and Lisbeth Dyer

Production Manager: Heejin Kim

Interior Design: Sophie Ye Chin

First Edition
ISBN: 1-4000-2081-6
ISBN-13: 978-1-4000-2081-2
Library of Congress Cataloging-in-Publication Data available upon request.

PRINTED IN THE UNITED STATES OF AMERICA
10 9 8 7 6 5 4 3 2 1

ACKNOWLEDGMENTS

Thanks to the Living Language team: Tom Russell, Sanam Zubli,
Christopher Warnasch, Zviezdana Verzich, Suzanne McQuade, Shaina
Malkin, Denise De Gennaro, Linda Schmidt, John Whitman, Lisbeth Dyer,
Alison Skrabek, Helen Kilcullen, Heejin Kim, Fabrizio La Rocca, Guido
Caroti, and Sophie Chin.

CONTENTS

INTRODUCTION

Living Language® Ultimate Arabic Beginner–Intermediate is an enjoyable and unique course in Arabic, that teaches Modern Standard Arabic as well as four colloquial Arabic dialects. The complete course consists of this text and eight hours of recordings. You can, however, use the coursebook on its own, if you already know how to pronounce Arabic.

Below is the description of the course materials and the different sections of the coursebook.

COURSE MATERIALS

THE COURSEBOOK

Living Language® Ultimate Arabic consists of thirty-five lessons, eight review sections, and three reading passages. This course teaches both Modern Standard Arabic and four widely spoken colloquial Arabic dialects. The lessons of the course are divided into five groups: The course starts with Modern Standard Arabic (Lessons 1 to 15) and continues with Egyptian Arabic (Lessons 16 to 20), Iraqi Arabic (Lessons 21 to 25), Lebanese Arabic (Lessons 26 to 30), and Saudi Arabic (Lessons 31 to 35). At the beginning of the book, you can find the Arabic Sounds chart and the Arabic Script chart.
At the end of the book, there are Appendices containing various grammar reference charts, 250 Basic Phrases in Egyptian, Iraqi, Lebanese, and Saudi Arabic, and an Arabic–English/English–Arabic Glossary.

Here is the description of the different components of the coursebook:

ARABIC SOUNDS: This section lists the sounds, consonants and vowels, used in Modern Standard Arabic. The sounds and model words are recorded on Recording Set A.

ARABIC SCRIPT: This section gives the Arabic alphabet and additional characters and signs used in Arabic handwriting with arrows showing the stroke direction. It also provides the list of transliteration symbols used in the course. The Arabic alphabet is recorded on Recording Set A.

DIALOGUES: Each lesson begins with a dialogue presenting a realistic situation in an Arabic locale. In Lessons 1 to 15, the dialogue is in Modern Standard Arabic and in Arabic script, followed by a transliteration and an English translation. In Lessons 16 to 35, the dialogues are Egyptian Arabic (Lessons 16 to 20), Iraqi Arabic (Lessons 21 to 25), Lebanese Arabic (Lessons 26 to 30), and Saudi Arabic (Lessons 31 to 35). All dialogues in dialects are written in transliteration, followed by an English translation.

WRITING AND PRONUNCIATION: In Lessons 1 to 3, you will learn the correct pronunciation of vowels and consonants in Modern Standard Arabic. You will also learn how to read and write the Arabic script. In Lessons 16 to 35, which teach four different Arabic dialects, the sounds particular to a given dialect are discussed.

GRAMMAR AND USAGE: This section explains the major grammatical and usage points covered in the lesson and in the exercises.

VOCABULARY: In this section, you can review the new words and expressions introduced in the dialogue, listed in the order and form of their appearance. You can also learn some supplemental vocabulary.

EXERCISES: You can practice the lesson's essential vocabulary and grammatical structures by doing the exercises. Check your answers in the Answer Key that immediately follows.

CULTURAL NOTES: These brief notes put the language in its cultural context. Cultural awareness will enrich your understanding of Arabic and your ability to communicate effectively.

REVIEWS: Review sections appear after Lessons 3, 7, 11, 15, 20, 25, 30, and 35. These sections are similar to the Exercises in format, but they integrate material from all the lessons you have studied up to that point.

READING PASSAGES: The three reading passages are not translated. However, the material covered in the preceding lessons, along with the vocabulary lists that accompany the reading passages, will enable you to infer the meaning, just as you would need to do when reading a newspaper or another text abroad.

APPENDICES: The appendices provide additional information on various aspects of Arabic grammar covered in the course. They are meant to be used for quick reference when reading or writing Arabic. Appendix J is a list of about 250 basic phrases in each of the four dialects taught in the course: Egyptian, Iraqi, Lebanese, and Saudi Arabic. These handy basic phrases are recorded on the four CDs contained in Recording Set B.

GLOSSARY: A two-way Arabic–English and English–Arabic glossary is included at the end of the book. All words used in the Modern Standard Arabic Lessons 1 to 15 are listed there.

INDEX OF GRAMMAR TOPICS: The index includes a list of all the grammar topics covered in the course. The numbers point to the lessons in which they are discussed.

If you have purchased this book as part of an audio package, the course also includes eight hours of recordings, described below.

RECORDING SETS A AND B

This course provides you with eight hours of audio practice. There are two sets of complementary recordings. The first set is designed for use with the coursebook, while the second set may be used without it.

RECORDING SET A—LEARN AT HOME

Materials from all thirty-five lessons in the course, both in Modern Standard Arabic and in Egyptian, Iraqi, Lebanese, and Saudi Arabic, are on Recording Set A. This recording set contains only Arabic speech, without English translations.

The recordings start with Arabic sounds and the Arabic alphabet. The following sections are recorded in each lesson: the dialogue, the examples from the Writing and Pronunciation section, and the words from the Vocabulary section.

First, you will hear native Arabic speakers read the complete dialogue at a conversational pace without interruption; then, you'll have a chance to listen to the dialogue a second time and repeat each sentence or sentence segment in the pause provided.

Next, listen carefully to learn the sounds and words from the Writing and Pronunciation sections. By listening and repeating after the native speakers, you will gradually master all the sounds.

Finally, you will hear the new vocabulary words, listed in the Vocabulary section, pronounced by native speakers. Repeat in the pauses provided.

RECORDING SET B—ON THE GO

Recording Set B gives you an additional hour of audio practice in each of the four dialects taught in this course: Egyptian, Iraqi, Lebanese, and Saudi Arabic. This recording set works as an audio phrasebook containing about 250 basic phrases in each of the four dialects. First, the phrase is read in English and then the Arabic translation is provided, followed by a pause, so you can repeat the phrase after a native speaker. Because it includes English, this recording set is perfect to use on the go—while driving, jogging, or doing housework.

STUDY TIPS

Below are some suggestions on how to study Arabic using this book. Because there are many different individual learning styles, feel free to experiment and explore to find out what suits you best.

Start with the first fifteen lessons of the course, which teach Modern Standard Arabic. The basics of Arabic grammar and vocabulary are taught here. You will also learn how to read and write the Arabic script. After mastering the Modern Standard Arabic lessons, turn to the lessons teaching an Arabic dialect to learn the colloquial, everyday Arabic used in an area of the Arab world you're interested in.

Here are some suggestions about how you can organize your study of a particular lesson.

   Look through the Vocabulary list, found in the back of the lesson, to familiarize yourself with the new vocabulary. You may also listen to the native speaker pronouncing these words on Recording Set A.

Read the short introduction to the dialogue, so you know what the dialogue is about. In the beginning, when your Arabic vocabulary is still very small, you may even read the translation of the dialogue first. This will help you follow the dialogue better and make out words and sentences.

Listen to the dialogue once or twice, without and then, with the book, noticing the words you know from previous lessons, looking for the words you encountered in the Vocabulary list, and making an effort to get the gist of the dialogue.

Study the dialogue by comparing the text in Arabic script to the transliteration (if you're working on one of the first fifteen lessons) and by looking words up in the Vocabulary section or the Glossary. Then check the translation to make sure you understand everything. Underline or circle portions of the text, for example, constructions or word forms, that are unclear or new to you. You will probably find them explained in the Grammar and Usage section of the lesson. Go back to one of the previous lessons if you need a review.

Read about the new grammar points in the Grammar and Usage section. Study the examples carefully. Look for the discussed constructions in the dialogue.

Do the exercises. You can fill in the answers in the book, or, for more practice with writing, write them out in your assigned Arabic notebook. Check your answers in the Answer Key. If you made mistakes, reread the relevant parts of the Grammar and Usage section or look words up in the Vocabulary section.

Listen to the vocabulary again. Repeat after the recording in the pauses provided. Then listen and repeat the dialogue as many times as you find it necessary, until you understand every word and construction, and can read the dialogue aloud with ease.

Read the culture note. Explore the culture topic on your own, on the Web, by talking to people, or in the library. You're ready to move on to the next lesson!

Here's some more general advice about language learning:

Stay motivated—immerse yourself in the culture. Language is much more than vocabulary and grammar. To keep motivated, immerse yourself in the culture and the history of the people who speak Arabic: Visit Arabic Web sites, watch Arabic movies, listen to Arabic music, eat at restaurants offering Arabic food, pick up a book on Arabic history or art, and read works by Arabic authors, even if in English. The more you know about the Arabic culture, the better you will understand the language and the more you will enjoy speaking it.

Exposure, exposure, exposure. The more you hear the language, the better! Even passive listening to Arabic music, TV, movies, or the dialogues, vocabulary lists, and basic phrases on our recordings, as you go about some other business, will increase your language skills. The sounds and inflections of a language have a way of creeping into your head, even when you're not paying attention. To improve your speaking skills, look for every occasion to speak: If you don't have the opportunity to travel, go to a deli or a restaurant where Arabic is spoken, or look for an Arabic-speaking neighbor.

بالتوفيق إن شاء الله

bi t-tawfīq inshā'allāh!

May your efforts be successful!

ARABIC SOUNDS

Use this section on Modern Standard Arabic sounds for quick reference. The details of Modern Standard Arabic pronunciation are presented in Lessons 1 to 4. You can listen to all sounds and examples in this section on Recording Set A, Disc 1.

1. CONSONANTS

CONSONANTS WITH ENGLISH EQUIVALENTS				
Sound	Approximate English Sound	Arabic Letter	Example	Transliteration
ā	a in at, or a in far	ا	أراد	'arād
b	b in bit	ب	باب	bāb
t	t in tell	ت	توت	tūt
th	th in thorn	ث	أثاث	'athāth
j	j in jam	ج	جوز	jawz
d	d in dill	د	دود	dūd
dh	th in there	ذ	ذيل	dhayl
r	r, rolled, as in Scottish English roof	ر	رادار	rādār
z	z in zoo	ز	زهر	zahr
s	s in self	س	سوس	sūs
sh	sh in shell	ش	شاشة	shāsha
f	f in flower	ف	فرن	furn
k	k in kiss	ك	كركوك	karkūk
l	l, lighter, as in British English love	ل	ليل	layl
m	m in may	م	مرسم	marsam
n	n in name	ن	نيسان	nīsān
h	h in here	ه	هلاهل	halāhil
w, ū	w in way, or oo in loom	و	وفود	wufūd
y, ī	y in yacht, or ee as in feel	ي	ينوي	yanwi

The following consonants do not have equivalents in English.

CONSONANTS WITHOUT ENGLISH EQUIVALENTS				
Sound	Approximate English Sound	Arabic Letter	Example	Transliteration
H	—	ح	حوت	Hūt
kh	ch in Scottish English loch	خ	خوخ	khaūkh
S	—	ص	صوص	SūS
D	—	ض	ضار	Dār
T	—	ط	طار	Tār
DH	—	ظ	ظلام	DHalām
'	—	ع	عنب	'inab
gh	—	غ	غار	ghār
q	—	ق	قلق	qalaq
'	the sound at the beginning of English uh-oh	ء[1]	سماء سأل	samā' sa'al

Arabic consonants are divided into "sun" and "moon" consonants. "Sun" consonants are listed below. They are all pronounced in the front part of the mouth (but not at the lips). It is important to remember them, as they affect the form of the definite article when it precedes a noun starting in one of the consonants. See Lesson 3 for more details on this phenomenon.

"SUN" CONSONANTS						
n	l	DH	T	D	S	sh
ن	ل	ظ	ط	ض	ص	ش

s	z	r	dh	d	th	t
س	ز	ر	ذ	د	ث	ت

All other Arabic consonants are "moon" consonants.

---

[1] This consonant is not part of the alphabet; it is usually written as a diacritic symbol over another letter.

2. VOWELS

Modern Standard Arabic has three long vowels, three short vowels, and two diphthongs.

<table>
<tr><th colspan="5">LONG VOWELS</th></tr>
<tr><th>Sound</th><th>Approximate English Sound</th><th>Arabic Letter</th><th>Example</th><th>Transliteration</th></tr>
<tr><td>ā</td><td>a in car, or a in dad</td><td>ا</td><td>ناس</td><td>nās</td></tr>
<tr><td>ī</td><td>ee in near, or ee in meet</td><td>ي</td><td>تين</td><td>tīn</td></tr>
<tr><td>ū</td><td>oo in boot</td><td>و</td><td>دود</td><td>dūd</td></tr>
</table>

Short vowels are represented by diacritic symbols, not actual letters of the alphabet. A short vowel diacritic appears either above or under the letter it follows. The lines under and above vowel diacritics used in the following table are placeholders for consonants.

<table>
<tr><th colspan="5">SHORT VOWELS</th></tr>
<tr><th>Sound</th><th>Approximate English Sound</th><th>Arabic Letter</th><th>Example</th><th>Transliteration</th></tr>
<tr><td>a</td><td>e in net, or u in cup</td><td>َـ</td><td>رَب</td><td>rab</td></tr>
<tr><td>i</td><td>i in sit</td><td>ـِ</td><td>مِن</td><td>min</td></tr>
<tr><td>u</td><td>oo in book</td><td>ُـ</td><td>دُب</td><td>dub</td></tr>
</table>

Diphthongs are vowel sounds consisting of two vowels joined together.

<table>
<tr><th colspan="5">DIPHTHONGS</th></tr>
<tr><th>Sound</th><th>Approximate English Sound</th><th>Arabic Letter</th><th>Example</th><th>Transliteration</th></tr>
<tr><td>aw</td><td>ow in now</td><td>وْ</td><td>مَوْز</td><td>mawz</td></tr>
<tr><td>ay</td><td>i in mine</td><td>يْ</td><td>بَيْت</td><td>bayt</td></tr>
</table>

ARABIC SCRIPT

1. ARABIC ALPHABET

The Arabic alphabet has 28 consonant letters. Most letters have two or more different shapes depending on the position in the word. Letters are shown here in handwriting with arrows indicating stroke direction. The Arabic alphabet is recorded on Recording Set A, Disc 1.

Arabic Alphabet in Handwriting

Letter Name	Sound and Transliteration Symbol	Letter	Final Position	Medial Position	Initial Position
alif	ā, 'ā	ا	ـا	ـا	ا
bā'	b	ب	ـب	ـبـ	بـ
tā'	t	ت	ـت	ـتـ	تـ
thā'	th	ث	ـث	ـثـ	ثـ
jīm	j	ج	ـج	ـجـ	جـ
Hā'	H	ح	ـح	ـحـ	حـ
khā'	kh	خ	ـخ	ـخـ	خـ
dāl	d	د	ـد	ـد	د
dhal	dh	ذ	ـذ	ـذ	ذ

Letter Name	Sound and Transliteration Symbol	Letter	Final Position	Medial Position	Initial Position
rā'	r	ار	ـر	ـر	ار
zay	z	از	ـز	ـز	از
sīn	s	اس	ـس	ـسـ	اسـ
shīn	sh	اش	ـش	ـشـ	اشـ
Sād	S	ص	ـص	ـصـ	صـ
Dād	D	ض	ـض	ـضـ	ضـ
Tā'	T	ط	ـط	ـطـ	طـ
DHā'	DH	ظ	ـظ	ـظـ	ظـ
'ayn	'	ع	ـع	ـعـ	عـ
ghayn	gh	غ	ـغ	ـغـ	غـ
fā'	f	ف	ـف	ـفـ	فـ
qāf	q	ق	ـق	ـقـ	قـ

Letter Name	Sound and Transliteration Symbol	Letter	Final Position	Medial Position	Initial Position
kāf	k	كك	لك	كك	گ
lām	l	ل	ل	ل	ل
mīm	m	م	م	مـ	مـ
mūn	n	ن	ن	نـ	نـ
hā'	h	ه	ه	ـهـ	هـ
wāw	w, ū	و	و	و	و
yā'	y, ī	ي	ي	يـ	يـ

Arabic letters are divided into "connector" and "non-connector" letters.

Most letters are connectors. They connect, with small strokes or ligatures, to both the letter that precedes them and the one that follows them, when occurring in the middle of the word.

ي ← ـيـ in سفينة

Non-connectors are ا, د, ذ, ر, ز and و. These letters connect to the letter that precedes them only if that letter is a connector.

و in سوق

They do not connect to any letter if the preceding letter is a non-connector.

و in روضة

2. OTHER ARABIC CHARACTERS AND SYMBOLS

MORE ARABIC CHARACTERS				
Arabic Character	Sound and Transliteration Symbol	Character Name	Arabic Example	Transliteration
ﻯ	ā (final position only)	alif maqSūra	لبنى	lubnā
ة	t (final position only)	Tā' marbūTa	مباراة	mubarat
ﻼ لا	la	lām-alif	اهلا وسهلا	ahlan wa-sahlan
ع	'	hamza	سماء	samā'

A number of diacritic symbols are used in Arabic, in addition to the short vowel diacritics. These symbols are written below or above a letter. Most of them are not used in everyday writing or print, but have to be learned and will be used in this course. The lines used under or above diacritics in the following table are placeholders for consonants.

DIACRITIC SIGNS				
Sign	Transliteration Symbol	Name of the Sign	Arabic Example	Transliteration
´	a	fatHa	رَب	rab
ِ	i	kasra	مِن	min
ُ	u	Damma	دُب	dub
´	an	fatHa tanwin	شَمساً	shamsan
ِ	in	kasra tanwin	كِتابٍ	kitābin
ُ	un	Damma tanwin	ثَوبٌ	thawbun
ء	'	hamza	سَأَل	sa'al
~	'ā or 'a' (always with alif)	madda	قُرآن آذار	qur'ān 'a'thar
°	consonant followed by another consonant	sukūn	بِنْت	bint
ّ	doubled consonant	shadda	فَنّان	fannān

12

LESSON 1
(Modern Standard Arabic)

أَهْلاً وَسَهْلاً!

'ahlan wa sahlan! Hello!

A. Dialogue

Lucy and Samir meet at the American University of Beirut.

سامِر: أَهْلاً وَسَهْلاً!

لوسي: أَهلا بكَ.

سامِر: ما إِسْمُكِ؟

لوسي: إِسْمي لوسي. ما إِسْمُكَ؟

سامِر: إِسْمي سامِر.

sámir: 'áhlan wa sáhlan!
lúsī: 'áhlan bíka!
sámir: má-smuki?
lúsī: ísmī lúsī. má-smuka?
sámir: ísmī sámir.

Samir: Hello!
Lucy: Hello to you, too!
Samir: What is your name?
Lucy: My name is Lucy. What is your name?
Samir: My name is Samir.

B. Writing and Pronunciation

1. BASIC FACTS ABOUT ARABIC WRITING

In the first three lessons of this course you will learn how to use the Arabic script. The most basic fact about Arabic writing is that it is written and read from right to left. For example, the first word of the title of this lesson—أَهْلاً وَسَهْلاً—is أَهْلاً *'ahlan* (hello), the first word from the right, and it is followed by the word وَسَهْلاً *wa sáhlan* (and welcome).

Similarly, the orientation of an Arabic book, magazine, or newspaper is different from that of an English-language reading: The spine is on the right side and the book opens on the left side. In other words, place your Arabic reading material in front of you so that what would be the back cover of an English-language reading faces you and turn the pages from the left to the right.

The Arabic alphabet has twenty-eight letters. Twenty-five letters are consonants and three letters function as both consonants and long vowels. Arabic script is phonetic, meaning that each letter is always pronounced in the same way. At the beginning of the book, easy reference tables, Arabic Sounds and Arabic Script, list all Arabic letters and their sound values in transliteration. Note how letters in the Arabic alphabet are grouped according to shape, so that the letters that share the same basic shape follow each other in the alphabet. For example:

ب	ت	ث
b	t	th

The same is true of the following three letters, among others:

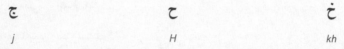

ج	ح	خ
j	H	kh

Looking for such similarities will help you master the Arabic script more quickly. In Lessons 1, 2, 3 and 4, the letters, their shapes, and their sound values will be discussed in detail.

Arabic script is always cursive, whether typewritten or handwritten. While most Arabic letters are connected to the preceding and the following letter with small connecting strokes, six letters, ‍ا, د, ذ, ر, ز and و, connect only to the preceding letter and not to the letter that follows them.

Because letters connect to each other in Arabic, they take different shapes depending on their positions in words: initial, medial, final, and separate. The initial form is used at the beginning of a word or a cluster of letters and has only one connecting stroke on the left side. When a letter is connected both to the preceding letter and the following letter, its form is called medial. All medial forms have connecting strokes on both sides, such as the letter ‍ـهـ hā' in سهلاً sahlan. When the letter ends a word or a group of letters, its form is called final, and it has one stroke on the right side. When the letter is not connected to another letter, its form is called separate. While some letters have four distinct, but related shapes, most letters can be easily reduced to two distinct shapes, initial/medial and final/separate, when the core shape of the letter, without the connecting strokes, is considered.

There is no distinction between capital and lower-case letters in Arabic, but punctuation marks, such as the comma, period, and exclamation mark, are used in Arabic writing.

In everyday usage, newspapers, signs, and books, only consonants and long vowels are written in Arabic. For example, the male name سامر, pronounced sah-meer, is written as s-ā-m-r without the short vowel (ِ) under the m. This is because the diacritics for the short vowels, a, i, and u, are not normally noted in writing, except in very formal (e.g., Qur'an) or pedagogical texts (e.g., children's books). In this course, for your convenience, the short vowels will always be marked (see Arabic Script section at the beginning of the book and section 5.B of this lesson).

2. THE TRANSLITERATION

All Arabic text in this book is transliterated using the Roman alphabet. Check the Arabic Script section at the beginning of the book for a list of transliteration symbols corresponding to each Arabic letter or diacritic symbol. Note that some of the transliteration symbols are capital letters, such as *T* or *D*, which represent specific Arabic sounds, different from those transliterated by *t* or *d*. Therefore, capital letters will not be used in transliteration to start a sentence or to write proper names.

The accute accents (´) on the English words in Lessons 1 and 2 indicate word stress. The position of stress in Arabic is discussed more in section B.3 of Lesson 2.

Transliteration is used in this course to help you start learning the language even before you have completely mastered the Arabic script. As you become more accustomed to Arabic script, you can practice reading without looking at transliterations.

3. PRONOUNCING ARABIC

A large group of Arabic sounds are very similar to those used in English. They are the consonants *b* (as in *bed*), *d* (as in *doll*), *dh* (as in *mother*), *f* (as in *fly*), *h* (as in *hello*), *j* (as in *jelly*), *k* (as in *key*), *l* (as in *lip*), *m* (as in *mother*), *n* (as in *no*), *s* (as in *sit*), *sh* (as in *ship*), *t* (as in *toe*), *th* (as in *thin*), *w* (as in *wind*), *y* (as in *yellow*), and *z* (as in *zebra*).

Other Arabic consonants, which will be discussed in Lessons 1, 2, and 3, don't have English equivalents (see *Arabic Sounds* at the beginning of the book). Most of these are pronounced very far back in the mouth and the throat and give Arabic its distinctive sound. While it may take you some time to master the pronunciation of such sounds, it is possible, even for adult learners, to learn just about any foreign sound well enough to be understood. The best way to learn good pronunciation is to listen over and over to the recordings that come with this course. Once you learn to recognize the novel sounds, you'll have an easier time pronouncing them as well. Do not be afraid to go for an exaggerated imitation of the native speakers' pronunciation; aside from listening to native speakers, this is the best way to master difficult sounds.

4. CONSONANTS AND CONSONANT LETTERS: ك *kāf* , ل *lām*, ب *bā'*, س *sīn*, ر *rā'*, م *mīm*, AND ه *hā'*

You will learn seven consonant letters of the Arabic alphabet in this lesson: ب , م , ك , ل , ر , س and ه. All are used in the dialogue.

A. THE LETTER ك *kāf*; THE SOUND *k*

The letter ك *kāf* has two different shapes. The final and separate forms are the same, as are the initial and medial forms. The only difference between them is in the connecting strokes that are added when the letters are part of a word.

INITIAL	MEDIAL	FINAL	SEPARATE	NAME	SOUND VALUE
ك	ـكـ	ـك	ك	*kāf*	*k*

kāf has a flat bottom and is slightly tilted to the left in its initial and medial forms, which also have a top stroke. The connecting stroke on the final form connects the letter *kāf* to the letter before it, as in لَك *laka* (for you); the absence of such a stroke in the separate form totally separates the letter from the previous cluster of letters, as in أَبوكَ *'abūka* (your father).

kāf is pronounced just like the English *k* in the word *kettle*. In the dialogue, *kāf* was used in its final shape in the following words:

بِكَ *bika* (to you, *m.*)[1]

إِسْمُكَ *ismuka* (your name, *m.*)

Here are additional examples showing *kāf* in other positions:

Initial: كُلّ *kull* (all)

Medial: لِكُلّ *likull* (for all)

Separate: أَبوكَ *'abūka* (your father, *m.*)

B. THE LETTER ل *lām*; THE SOUND *l*

Like *kāf*, ل *lām* has two different shapes. The difference between *lām*'s final and separate forms, and between its medial and initial forms, is in the connecting strokes.

INITIAL	MEDIAL	FINAL	SEPARATE	NAME	SOUND VALUE
ل	ـلـ	ـل	ل	*lām*	*l*

Note that *lām* has a round bottom, hanging below the line, in the separate and final forms.

The sound of *lām* is similar to the clear English *l* in *lip*, but it is pronounced more forward in the mouth, similar to Spanish or Italian *l*. Do not pronounce the Arabic *l* like the dark English *l*-sound found in the word *bulb*, for example.

---

[1] The following abbreviations are used in this book: *m.* = masculine; *f.* = feminine; *sg.* = singular; *pl.* = plural; *du.* = dual; *lit.* = literally; *infml.* = informal; *fml.* = formal; *colloq.* = colloquial.

In the dialogue, *lām* was used in its initial position in:

لوسي *lūsī* (Lucy)

Other examples are:

Medial: كُلُّكُمْ *kullukum* (all of you, *pl.*)

Final: كُلّ *kull* (all)

Separate: كَمَالْ *kamāl* (Kamal)

When *lām* precedes the letter *alif*, the two are connected in a special digraph called *lām-alif*, underlined in the example below:

أَهْلاً وسهلاً *'ahlan wa sahlan* (hello and welcome)

C. THE LETTER ب *bā'*; THE SOUND *b*

The consonant letter ب *bā'*, like *kāf* and *lām*, has two different shapes. Note that *bā'* has one dot underneath. In its final and separate forms, it looks like a flattened bowl.

INITIAL	MEDIAL	FINAL	SEPARATE	NAME	SOUND VALUE
بـ	ـبـ	ـب	ب	*bā'*	*b*

bā' is pronounced just like the English *b* in *bed*.

In the dialogue, *bā'* was used in its initial form in:

بِكَ *bika* (to you, *m.*)

Other examples are:

Medial: كَبِير *kabīr* (big)

Final: كَلْب *kalb* (dog)

Separate: أَبْ *'ab* (father)

D. THE LETTER س *sīn*; THE SOUND *s*

Like the other letters you have learned so far, the letter س *sīn* has two shapes.

INITIAL	MEDIAL	FINAL	SEPARATE	NAME	SOUND VALUE
سـ	ـسـ	ـس	س	*sīn*	*s*

The letter *sīn* is pronounced just like the English *s*. In the dialogue, *sīn* is found in the initial position (either of a word or a letter cluster) in:

17

سامِر *sāmir* (Samir)

لوسي *lūsī* (Lucy)

إِسْمُكَ *ismuka* (your name, *m.*)

Other examples are:

Medial: مِسْمـار *mismār* (nail)

Final: بوليس *būlīs* (police)

Separate: بَأْس *ba's* (courage)

E. THE LETTER ر *rā'*; THE SOUND *r*

The letter ر *rā'* has only one form and, as one of the six non-connector letters, never attaches to the letter that follows it. However, like all other letters, it always attaches to the preceding letter.

INITIAL	MEDIAL	FINAL	SEPARATE	NAME	SOUND VALUE
ر	ـر	ـر	ر	*rā'*	*r*

The consonant *rā'* is different from the English sound *r* in *ray*. It is "rolled" and pronounced using the tip of the tongue just like the Spanish or Italian *r*.[1]

In the dialogue, *rā'* was used in its final shape in:

سامِر *sāmir* (Samir)

Here are examples of *rā'* in other positions:

Initial: رامي *rāmī* (Rami)

Medial: أَسْرار *'asrār* (secrets)

Separate: دار *dār* (house)

F. THE LETTER م *mīm*; THE SOUND *m*

Like *kāf*, *lām*, *ba'*, and *sīn*, م *mīm* has two different shapes.

INITIAL	MEDIAL	FINAL	SEPARATE	NAME	SOUND VALUE
مـ	ـمـ	ـم	م	*mīm*	*m*

---

[1] The "rolled" *r* dominates in everyday speech, but it is avoided in recitation of the Qur'an.

18

mim looks like a little open circle, with a tail in its final and separate forms. When writing *mim* in these positions, start with the circle and then write the tail. The letter *mim* is pronounced just like the English *m* in *more*.

In the dialogue, *mim* was used in the initial position (of a letter cluster) in:

سامِر *sāmir* (Samir)

And in the medial position in:

إِسْمُكَ *ismuka* (your name, *m.*)

إِسْمِي *ismī* (my name)

Other examples are:

Initial: مَهًا *maha* (Maha)

Final: إِسْم *ism* (name)

Separate: أُمّ *umm* (mother)

G. THE LETTER ه *hā'*; THE SOUND *h*

The letter ه *hā'* has four very different forms depending on its position in a word.

INITIAL	MEDIAL	FINAL	SEPARATE	NAME	SOUND VALUE
ـه	ـهـ	ـه	ه	*hā'*	*h*

In its separate form, *hā'* is a circle that you start and finish writing at the top. In its initial form, this circle has a connecting stroke on the left. When you write the letter in this position, start from the top, then move down and back up to make a full loop leading back down into the stroke on the left. In the medial position, start with the stroke on the right, form the upper ellipse, then continue to form the lower ellipse, and end on the left with a connecting stroke. Start writing the final form on the right with a connecting stroke, then go up and form an ellipse coming down.

The consonant *hā'* is pronounced just like the English *h* in *hey*. The *h*-sound in Arabic can also appear in the middle or at the end of the word, as in ماهِر *maher* or مِياه *miyāh*.

In the dialogue, *hā'* was used in its initial form in:

أَهْلاً *'ahlan* (hello)

And in its medial form in:

سَهْلاً *sahlan* (welcome)

Other examples are:

Medial: مَها *mahā* (Maha)

Final: إِسْمُهُ *ismuhu* (his name)

Separate: مياه *miyāh* (water)

5. VOWELS AND VOWEL LETTERS

Arabic has six vowels, three long and three short ones.

A. THE LETTERS ا *alif*, ي *yā'*, AND و *wāw*; THE LONG VOWELS ā, ī, AND ū

The long vowels ā, ī, and ū are represented by the alphabet letters ا, ي, and و respectively. Remember that long vowels, unlike the short ones, are always written in Arabic, as in سامِر *sāmir* or لوسي *lūsī*.

The long vowels ā, ī, and ū are pronounced at twice the length of the short vowels a, i, and u. The line above the vowels in transliteration indicates that the vowel is long. As mentioned earlier, to excel in the pronunciation of Arabic sounds, it is advisable to exaggerate their qualities in the beginning. For example, you may say *saaamir* to pronounce the long ā in the name *sāmir* and *luuusiii* to pronounce the long ū and the long ī in the name *lūsī*.

The letters ا, ي, and و also represent the consonants ('), y, and w, respectively. There is a simple rule that tells you when to pronounce these letters as consonants: when they begin a word, precede or follow another vowel, or stand in between two vowels, pronounce them as consonants. You will find illustrative examples below.

THE LETTER ا *alif*; THE SOUNDS ā AND (')

The long vowel ā is represented by the letter ا *alif*. As a non-connector letter, *alif* does not connect to the following letter. It has two different forms, the initial/separate and the final/medial form.

INITIAL	MEDIAL	FINAL	SEPARATE	NAME	SOUND VALUE
أ	ل, ا	ل, ا	ا	*alif*	ā or (')

alif is a vertical stroke written from top to bottom in the initial/separate form. It is written from bottom to top in the medial/final form, as a continuation of the connecting stroke. *alif* usually represents the long vowel ā.

In the dialogue, *alif* was used in its medial form:

سامِر *sāmir* (Samir)

An example of its use in the final position is:

مَها *mahā* (Maha)

Whenever *alif* appears at the beginning of a word, it is not a long vowel, but the seat for the consonant letter *hamza*. *Hamza* is represented by a supplemental symbol (ٔ) rather than a separate letter of the alphabet; it

appears over or under **ا**, and over the letters **ى** and **و**. *Hamza,* a sound with no equivalent in standard English, resembles the Scottish pronunciation of *t* in *bottle*. Its technical name is "glottal stop," because it is pronounced deep in the throat, by a sudden opening of vocal chords. In transliteration, it is indicated by the apostrophe (**'**). *Hamza* can appear in any position in a word, but at the beginning of a word it is always carried by *alif*. Any of the three short vowels, *a, i,* or *u* can follow *hamza* in that position. They are marked with an appropriate short vowel symbol in writing (that shows short vowels), as in the examples below.

أَهْلاً *'ahlan* (hello)

إِسْمُكَ *'ismuka* (your name, *m.*)

إِسْمِي *'ismī* (my name)

Note that in Arabic writing, *hamza* is often omitted even by native speakers, especially over *alif* at the beginning of words. In the remainder of this book, the word-initial *hamza* will not be transliterated, because its pronunciation there is usually automatic. This is so because no word in Arabic can start with a vowel.

THE LETTER ى *yā'*; THE SOUNDS *ī* AND *y*

The Arabic letter ى *yā'* has two different forms. Note its similarity to *bā'* in the medial/initial form and the distinguishing feature of having two dots underneath. Also notice that *yā',* unlike *bā',* falls under the line in its final/separate form.

INITIAL	MEDIAL	FINAL	SEPARATE	NAME	SOUND VALUE
ـيـ	ـيـ	ـي	ي	*yā'*	*ī* or *y*

Remember that *yā'* can be pronounced either as a vowel or as a consonant depending on what sounds surround it.

In the dialogue, *yā'* was used in the initial position in:

يا *yā* (hey)

Note that it is pronounced as a consonant *y* here because it begins a word.

And in the final position in:

إِسْمِي *ismī* (my name)

لوسي *lūsī* (Lucy)

In these words, it is pronounced as a vowel *ī*, because it follows a consonant.

Other examples of *yā'* are:

Medial: سَميك *samīk* (thick)

Final: مـاي *māy* (May)

Because *yā'* follows a vowel in *māy*, it is pronounced as *y*.

THE LETTER و *wāw*; THE SOUNDS *ū* AND *w*

The letter و *wāw* does not connect to letters that follow it. It has only one shape, with a connecting stroke on the right in the medial/final position.

INITIAL	MEDIAL	FINAL	SEPARATE	NAME	SOUND VALUE
و	ـو	ـو	و	*wāw*	*ū* or *w*

Like *yā'* it is pronounced either as a vowel or as a consonant, depending on the sounds that surround it, according the rule expressed earlier.

In the dialogue, *wāw* is used in the initial form in:

وَسَهْلاً *wa sahlan* (and welcome)

Here it is pronounced as a consonant *w* because it begins a word.

And in the final form in:

لوسي *lūsī* (Lucy)

wāw is pronounced as a vowel *ū* here because it follows a consonant.

Other examples are:

Final: سوريا *sūriyya* (Syria)

Separate: أَوْ *aw* (or)

Because if follows a vowel, *wāw* is pronounced as a consonant here.

B. THE SYMBOLS (◌َ) *fatHa*, (◌ِ) *kasra* AND (◌ُ) *Damma*; THE SHORT VOWELS *a, i,* AND *u*

The Arabic short vowels are *a, i,* and *u*, the counterparts of the long vowels you learned above. They are pronounced like the following English vowels: *a* as in *apple* or *u* as in *cup*, *i* as in *bit*, and *u* as in *put*.

As mentioned earlier, the short vowels in Arabic are not normally represented in Arabic writing, which marks only consonants and long vowels. When short vowels are indicated, it is done by use of small diacritic signs written above or under the consonant letter which the vowel follows.

The orthographic symbol for the vowel *a* is called *fatHa* (pronounced *faht-Hah*) and looks like a short diagonal stroke written above the letter it follows: ـَ. The line under *fatHa* indicates the space where the Arabic letter should be written. The symbol for the vowel *i* is called *kasra* and looks like a diagonal stroke written under the letter: ـِ. The symbol for the sound *u* is called *Damma* and looks like the number nine, slightly rotated to the right, written above the letter ـُ.

Look at the examples of words from the dialogue containing short vowels:

بِكَ *bika* (to you, *m.*)

Notice a *kasra* for the vowel *i* under the letter ب and a *fatHa* for the vowel *a* over the letter ك. Another example is:

إِسْمُكَ *ismuka* (your name, *m.*)

Again, notice the *kasra* for the vowel *i* under the letter ا, the *Damma* for the vowel *u* over the letter م, and the *fatHa* for the vowel *a* over the letter ك.

In this book, the short vowel diacritics will be used on all Arabic text in lessons 1 to 15 and in the Glossaries.

6. THE SYMBOL ـْ *SUKŪN*: MARKING CONSONANT CLUSTERS

When two consonants stand next to each other in Arabic and there is no vowel between them, the lack of the vowel is marked by a special symbol, called *sukūn*, which is a little circle above the first consonant letter in a cluster: ـْ.

Here's an example from the dialogue where a *sukūn* marks the consonant cluster *sm*:

إِسْمُكَ *'ismuka* (your name, *m.*)

Notice that the *sukūn* is over the letter س, the first letter in the consonant cluster *sm*.

sukūn can also be used on the last letter of the word that precedes a period in a sentence and over a final consonant of a word followed by another word. For example:

مِنْ أَيْنَ *min 'ayn?* (from where?)

This final *sukūn* will not be marked in this book.

C. Vocabulary

In this section, you will find a list of new words introduced in the dialogue in the order of their appearance.

أَهْلاً وَسَهْلاً *áhlan wa sáhlan*   hello (*lit.*, hello and welcome)

و *wa*	and
أَهْلاً بِكَ *áhlan bika*	hello to you (a reply, to a male)
بِكَ *bika*	to you, in you (to a male); contains preposition بِ *bi* (to, in), followed by an ending showing person
ما *mā?*	what?
إِسْمُكِ *ísmuki*	your name (to a woman)
ما اسْمُكِ *mā-smukí?*	What is your name? (to a woman)[1]
إِسْمُكَ *ísmuka*	your name (to a man)
إِسْمِي *ísmī*	my name

D. Cultural Note

All Arabic speakers grow up surrounded by two different varieties of their language: the formal variety of Arabic, *fuSHā* (pronounced *fuS-Hā*), and a colloquial variety of Arabic, *'ammiyya*. *fuSHā*, also called Modern Standard Arabic (MSA), is most commonly used in writing as the language of the press, literature, and other formal written settings. MSA is also used in formal situations where spoken language is customary, such as news broadcasts, educational settings, and public speeches. MSA has developed from Classical Arabic, the language of the Qur'an, the Muslim holy book. It is often used by Arabs who speak substantially different native dialects as a kind of *lingua franca* to facilitate communication among them. On the other hand, *'ammiyya,* or a particular colloquial Arabic dialect, is the mother tongue of all Arabs and a language used in everyday communication at home, on the street, in the workplace, and more often than not, in spoken communication in schools and at universities. *'ammiyya* is also used in some informal written communication, such as notes or personal letters. You can also hear *'ammiyya* in movies, plays, most TV and radio programs, and sometimes even in news broadcasts. Unlike *fuSHā*, which does not change significantly from country to country or from region to region, *'ammiyya* has as many different varieties as there are Arabic-speaking countries and regions.

Because everyone grows up learning any language by speaking it first, and because Arab children grow up speaking a specific variety of *'ammiyya* at home, *fuSHā* is the language Arabs acquire as they go through the educational process. Because of this, one's mastery of *fuSHā* varies depending on the person's educational background and hence, a certain amount of prejudice and stereotyping, and not a little disagreement, is associated with its improper use. At the same time, *fuSHā* is a variety of Arabic that varies very little in vocabulary and structure depending on the geographic origin of the speaker. This makes it a convenient mode of communication with foreigners and among Arabs from faraway countries, and Arabic speakers will try to adapt their speech to it as necessary. While

---

[1] Because the word ما *mā* ends in a vowel and the following word starts with a vowel, the *alif* in the word إِسْمُكِ *ísmuki* is not pronounced.

fuSHā and 'ammiyya are mutually intelligible varieties of the same language, there are consistent differences between the two in vocabulary, pronunciation, and grammar. In this course, you will start by first learning fuSHā. This will enable you to acquire the basics of Arabic language, including the sounds, letters, vocabulary, and grammar. Then, depending on your interests and needs, you can build on this base by learning the basics of one or more of the four 'ammiyya dialects taught in the course—Egyptian, Iraqi, Lebanese, and Saudi Arabic. As there is much overlap between the MSA and any particular dialect, you will only need to concentrate on what's different in pronunciation, vocabulary, and grammar. Lessons 1 to 15 teach MSA; Lessons 16 to 20 teach Egyptian Arabic; Lessons 21 to 25 teach Iraqi Arabic; Lessons 26 to 30 teach Lebanese Arabic, and Lessons 31 to 35 teach Saudi Arabic.

E. Exercises

1. Connect the following letters to form words. Use the letters in the order provided, going from right to left.

a. ي و ل أ س ا

b. ب ا ر

c. م م أ ل ا

d. م ي ر ك

e. ك ل ه ا

f. م ا ل س ا

g. م ب ا ر ك

h. س م ا ي

2. Write the following words in Arabic script, marking all the short vowels and using sukūn.

a. *bābā*

b. *amrīkā*

c. *mabrūk*

d. *rasmī*

e. *lībī*

f. *kalām*

g. *muslimūn*

h. *samīr*

3. Transliterate the following words.

a. ميم

b. ليبي

c. بَار
d. مَال
e. سَبَب

4. Say and write the following sentences in Arabic.

a. My name is…
b. Your name is Samir.
c. Your name is Lucy.
d. What is your name? (to a man)
e. What is your name? (to a woman)

5. Translate the following sentences into English.

a. إِسْمِي أَليكْس.
b. إِسْمِي سامي.
c. ما اسْمُكَ؟
d. ما اسْمُكِ؟
e. أَهْلاً وَسَهْلاً، لوسي.

Answer Key

1. a. يسألوا
   b. بار
   c. الأمم
   d. كريم
   e. أهلك
   f. إسلام
   g. مبارك
   h. سامي

2. a. بابا
   b. أَمْريكا
   c. مَبْروك
   d. رَسْمي
   e. ليبي
   f. كَلام
   g. مُسْلِمون
   h. سَمير

3. a. *mīm*
   b. *lībī*
   c. *bār*
   d. *māl*
   e. *sabab*

4. a. إِسْمِي...
   b. إِسْمُكَ سامِر
   c. إِسْمُكِ لوسي
   d. ما اسْمُكَ؟
   e. ما اسْمُكِ؟

5. a. My name is Alex.
   b. My name is Sami.
   c. What is your name? (to a man)
   d. What is your name? (to a woman)
   e. Welcome, Lucy

LESSON 2
(Modern Standard Arabic)

مِنْ أَيْنَ أَنْتَ؟

min ayn ánta? Where Are You From?

A. Dialogue

Lucy and Samir find out more about each other.

لوسي: مِنْ أَيْنَ أَنْتَ يا سامِر؟

سامِر: أَنا مِنْ دِمَشْق.

لوسي: يَعْني أَنْتَ سوري.

سامِر: نَعْم، أَنا مِن سوريا. وَمِنْ أَيْنَ أَنْتِ يا لوسي؟

لوسي: أَنا أَمْريكيَّة. أَسْكُن في مَدينَة واشِنْطُن.

lū́sī: min ayn ánta yā sā́mir?
sā́mir: ánā min dimáshq.
lū́sī: yá'nī ánta sūrī.
sā́mir: na'am, ána min sūriya. wa-min ayn ánti yā lū́sī?
lū́sī: ána amrīkíyya. áskun fī madínat wāshinTun.

Lucy: Where are you from, Samir?
Samir: I am from Damascus.
Lucy: So you are Syrian.
Samir: Yes, I am from Syria. And where are you from, Lucy?
Lucy: I am American. I live in the city of Washington.

B. Writing and Pronunciation

1. CONSONANTS AND CONSONANT LETTERS: ت *tā'*, ن *nūn*, ع *'ayn*, ف *fā'*, ق *qāf*, د *dāl*, ش *shīn*, ط *Tā'*, AND ة *tā' marbūTa*

In this lesson, you will learn how to write and pronounce eight more consonant letters: ط, ش, د, ق, ف, ع, ن, ت, and ة. All of these appear in the dialogue.

A. THE LETTER ت *tā'*; THE SOUND *t*

ت *tā'* has two basic shapes, the initial/medial and the final/separate.

Note that the core form of ت *tā'* is identical to the form of ب *bā'*. The distinctive feature of ت *tā'* is the two dots on top.

INITIAL	MEDIAL	FINAL	SEPARATE	NAME	SOUND VALUE
تـ	ـتـ	ـت	ت	*tā'*	*t*

The sound of ت *tā'* is similar to English *t* in *tip*, except that it is pronounced more forward in the mouth, with the tip of the tongue touching upper teeth, as in Spanish or Italian *t*.

In the dialogue, *tā'* was used in its final form in the following words:

أَنْتِ *ánti* (you, f.)

أَنْتَ *ánta* (you, m.)

Here are additional examples showing *tā'* in other positions:

Initial: تَرَكَ *taraká* (to leave)

Medial: كِتَاب *kitāb* (book)

Separate and initial: تَابوت *tābūt* (coffin)

B. THE LETTER ن *nūn*; THE SOUND *n*

The letter ن *nūn* has two basic forms.

INITIAL	MEDIAL	FINAL	SEPARATE	NAME	SOUND VALUE
نـ	ـنـ	ـن	ن	*nūn*	*n*

nūn resembles a bowl with one dot on top in its final/separate position. Note that it also reaches under the line in this form. In the medial/initial form, ن *nūn* resembles ت *tā'* and ب *bā'*. The only distinguishing features are the number and the position of the dots.

bā'	*tā'*	*nūn*
بـ	تـ	نـ

The Arabic *n* sounds just like English *n* in *no*.

In the dialogue, you encountered *nūn* in its initial position:

أَنْتِ *ánti* (you, f.)

And in its final position in:

مِنْ min (from)

واشِنْطُن wāshinTun (Washington)

أَسْكُن 'askun (I live)

أَيْن؟ 'ayn? (where?)

Other examples are:

Initial and medial: نَنام nanām (we sleep)

Medial and separate: لُبْنان lubnān (Lebanon)

C. THE LETTER ع 'ayn; THE SOUND (')

The consonant letter ع 'ayn has four different shapes.

INITIAL	MEDIAL	FINAL	SEPARATE	NAME	SOUND VALUE
ـعـ	ـعـ	ـع	ع	'ayn	'

In its separate and final forms ع 'ayn has a curved tail hanging below the line.

The sound represented by 'ayn is one of the characteristic sounds of the Arabic language. It resembles gagging and has no equivalent in English. In order to produce it, constrict the throat by tightening its muscles, then let the air flow out freely from your throat producing a lot of friction sound. If you put your fingers on the throat, you should feel the vibration of your vocal cords, as this is a voiced sound. Of course, the best way to master its pronunciation is by repeatedly listening to native speakers pronouncing it. Note that this sound is different from the *hamza* sound, which is also pronounced deep in the throat, but *hamza* is a much softer sound pronounced by the complete closure and then sudden release of the vocal cords. Also note that *hamza* is represented by an apostrophe ('), while an open quote (') stands for 'ayn in transliteration.

In the dialogue, 'ayn was used in its medial form in:

يَعْني yá'nī (so, in other words)

نَعَمْ na'am (yes)

Other examples are:

Initial: عُمان 'umān (Oman)

Final: بَيْع bay' (selling)

Separate: الْبِقاع al-biqā' (the Beqaa, a valley in Lebanon)

D. THE LETTER ف fā'; THE SOUND f

The letter ف fā' has two basic shapes.

INITIAL	MEDIAL	FINAL	SEPARATE	NAME	SOUND VALUE
ﻓ	ﻔ	ﻒ	ف	fā'	f

Note that it looks like a little circle with a dot on top. The letter fā' is pronounced just like the English f in far.

In the dialogue, fā' is found in its initial position in:

في fī (in)

Other examples are:

Medial: سُفُن sufun (ships)

Final: أَنْف anf (nose)

Separate: أُنوف unūf (noses)

E. THE LETTER ق qāf; THE SOUND q

The letter ق qāf resembles fā' in shape. Its distinctive feature is that it has two dots instead of one dot on top. In addition, qāf, unlike fā', has a tail with a deeper scoop that falls under the line in its final/separate form.

INITIAL	MEDIAL	FINAL	SEPARATE	NAME	SOUND VALUE
ﻗ	ﻘ	ﻖ	ق	qāf	q

The consonant qāf is similar to the English k sound in coal, but it is pronounced farther in the back of the mouth.

In the dialogue, qāf was used in its final shape in:

دِمَشْق dimashq (Damascus)

Here are some additional examples showing qāf in other positions:

Medial: تَقْرَأ taqra' (she reads)

Initial: قَرَأ qara' (he read)

Separate: سوق sūq (market)

F. THE LETTER د dāl; THE SOUND d

Like the letters ا alif, ر rā', and و wāw, د dāl has only one basic shape and is a non-connector letter.

INITIAL	MEDIAL	FINAL	SEPARATE	NAME	SOUND VALUE
د	ـد	ـد	د	dāl	d

Note that dāl sits on the line. Start writing it from the upper end. The letter dāl is pronounced just like the English d in duck.

In the dialogue, dāl was used in its initial form in:

دِمَشْق dimashq (Damascus)

Other examples are:

Medial: عَدَد 'adad (number), the first dāl

Separate: عَدَد 'adad (number), the second dāl

G. THE LETTER ش shīn; THE SOUND sh

The letter ش shīn is identical to the letter sīn in shape, but it has three dots on top.

INITIAL	MEDIAL	FINAL	SEPARATE	NAME	SOUND VALUE
شـ	ـشـ	ـش	ش	shīn	sh

The consonant ش shīn is pronounced like the English sh in she.

In the dialogue, shīn was used in its medial form in:

دِمَشْق dimashq (Damascus)

Other examples are:

Initial: شَمْس shams (sun)

Final: مِشْمِش mishmish (apricot)

Separate: أَعْشاش 'a'shāsh (nests)

H. THE LETTER ط Tā'; THE SOUND T

The letter ط Tā' has one basic form, even though it can connect to both the preceding and the following letter.

INITIAL	MEDIAL	FINAL	SEPARATE	NAME	SOUND VALUE
طـ	ـطـ	ـط	ط	Tā'	T

It forms a tilted ellipse which starts at the lower left end and ends there as well. A vertical stroke is written on top of the ellipse from the top down.

The sound *T* is an alternate of the sound *t*. It is one of the four so-called "emphatic" consonants existing in Arabic. *T* and *t* are pronounced in the same position in the mouth; the difference is that when the sound *T* is pronounced, the tongue is depressed in the middle, similar to a small spoon, giving it a "hollow" sound, and the air is released from the lungs very briskly and forcefully. The sound *T*, like other emphatic consonants, strongly affects the sound of the surrounding vowels. The vowel that follows *T* is darker in sound than its counterpart following the sound *t*. For example, the vowel *a* sounds almost like an *o* when preceded by a *T*-sound or other emphatic consonants.

We will transliterate all emphatic sounds with capital letters to distinguish them from their non-emphatic counterparts.

In the dialogue, *Tā'* was used in its medial form in:

واشِنْطُن   *wāshinTun* (Washington)

Other examples are:

Initial: طِفْل *Tifl* (child)

Final (and medial): قِطَط *qiTaT* (cats)

I. THE LETTER ة *tā' marbūTa*

The letter ة *tā' marbūTa* is not a letter of the alphabet. It is a version of the letter ت *tā'*. It has only two forms, the final form and the separate form.

INITIAL	MEDIAL	FINAL	SEPARATE	NAME	SOUND VALUE
-	-	ـة	ة	*tā' marbūTa*	silent or *t*

Many feminine nouns end in the letter ة *tā' marbūTa*, which is most often silent.[1] ة *tā' marbūTa* is always preceded by a *fatHa*.

In the dialogue, it was used in its final form in:

أَمْرِيكِيَّة *amrikíyya* (American, *f.*)

Another example is:

Separate: أُبُوَّة *ubúwwa* (fatherhood)

---

[1] See section C. 3. of this lesson and Lessons 4 and 6 for more discussion of nouns, gender, and the role of *tā' marbūTa*.

2. THE DOUBLED CONSONANTS AND THE USE OF shadda (ّ)

Several different consonant sounds in Arabic, such as *b, d, s, y, w*, etc., can have "doubled" variants. A "doubled" consonant, rendered as *bb, dd, ss, yy, ww*, etc. in transliteration, is longer and pronounced more forcefully than its "non-doubled" counterpart. This distinction is important in Arabic—words can be distinguished solely based on this contrast—so pay attention to the pronounciation of native speakers on the recordings.

كَسَر *kasar* (he broke) vs. كَسَّر *kassar* (he smashed)

عَقَد *'aqad* (he conducted) vs. عَقَّد *'aqqad* (he complicated)

Note that words with "doubled" consonants, such as أَمْريكِيَّة *amrikíyya* and أُبُوَّة *ubúwwa*, have a special sign (ّ) over the "doubled" consonant, called *shadda*. Its function is to show that the consonant above which it is written is "doubled."

Note that short vowels are written on top of or below the *shadda* sign instead of on top of or below the letter itself. For example:

أُبُوَّة *ubúwwa* (fatherhood)

أَمْريكِيِّين *amrikíyyin* (Americans)

3. WORD STRESS

While the rules governing the position of stress in Arabic are complex and are best learned by listening to native speakers, there is one general rule that is very useful. If a word has a long syllable, the stress falls on it. For example:

مَدينَة *madīna* (city)

is pronouced as *mah-DEE-nah*.

Long syllables are syllables that have a) a consonant and a long vowel, e.g., *dī* in the مَدينَة *madīna* (city), or b) a consonant, a short vowel, and another consonant e.g., *kíy* in the word أَمْريكِيَّة *amrīkíyya* (American, f.).

If a word has two long syllables, then the stress falls on the one closer to the end of the word or on the syllable preceding the last one. For example:

أَمْريكِيَّة is *amrikíyya* pronounced as *am-ree-KIY-yah*.

If the second-to-last syllable in the word is short, the stress falls on the preceding syllable. For example:

تَقْرَأ is *taqra'* (she reads) pronounced *TAQ-ra-'*.

C. Grammar and Usage

1. SAYING *IS* AND *ARE* IN ARABIC

While the Arabic sentence ‏مِنْ أَيْنَ أَنْتَ؟‎ *min ayna ántá?* contains three words—*min* (where), *ayna* (from), and *anta* (you, *m.*), its English translation—*Where are you from?*—has four. The extra word in English is the verb *are*, a form of the verb *to be*. Unlike English, Arabic does not use the verb *to be* in present tense sentences of this type.

Below are several other examples of Arabic sentences without the equivalent of *am*, *is*, or *are*. The subject and the predicate of the sentence — an adjective (*American*), a noun (*writer*), an adverb (*here*), or a noun preceded by a preposition (*in my office, in Libya*) — are simply placed next to each other to form a full sentence.

‏أَنا أَمْريكِيَّة.‎

ánā amrikíyya.

I am American. (*lit.*, I American)

‏هُوَ كَاتِب.‎

húwa kátib.

He is a writer. (*lit.*, He writer)

‏كَمَال هُنا.‎

kamál húnā.

Kamāl is here. (*lit.*, Kamal here)

‏أَنَا فِي مكْتَبِي.‎

ánā fī máktabī.

I am in my office. (*lit.*, I in my office)

‏أَنْتَ فِي لِيبْيا.‎

ánta fī líbyā.

You are in Libya. (*lit.*, You in Libya)

2. ASKING YES/NO QUESTIONS

Yes/no questions are questions that have "yes" or "no" for an answer. In spoken Arabic, such questions are often formed simply by raising the intonation at the end of the sentence, which otherwise doesn't differ from a statement. (In writing, a question mark is added.)

‏كَمَال هُنا؟‎

kamál húnā?

Kamal is here?

‏أَنَا فِي مكْتَبِي؟‎

ánā fī máktabī?

Am I in my office?

هُوَ كَاتِب؟

húwa kẩtib?

Is he a writer?

Another way to ask yes/no questions is to add one of the two question particles, أ *a* or هَل *hal,* at the beginning of the sentence. For example:

أَكَمَال هُنا؟

a-kamẩl húnā?

Is Kamāl here?

أَهُوَ كَاتِب؟

a-húwa kẩtib?

Is he a writer?

هَلْ تَسْكُن في أَمْرِيكا؟

hal taskun fi amrïka?

Do you live in America? (*m.*)

هل تَتَكَلَّم الإنجليزية؟

hal tatak·llam al-inglĩzïyya?

Do you speak English? (*m.*)

There is no difference between the two yes/no question markers, but أ *a* is used more often in front of nouns and personal pronouns, and in more formal Arabic.

3. MASCULINE AND FEMININE FORMS OF NOUNS

Arabic nouns come in two different gender forms, masculine and feminine. For example:

رَجُل

rajul

a man (*m.*)

اِمْرَأَة

imra'a

a woman (*f.*)

As in many other languages, all nouns in Arabic, including those that denote objects or abstract ideas, are either feminine or masculine. While one cannot predict whether a noun referring to an object or idea will be feminine or masculine, one can tell whether a noun is masculine or feminine based on its form. For example:

مَكْتَب	مَكْتَبَة
maktab	*maktaba*
office (*m.*)	library (*f.*)

Masculine nouns, with few exceptions, end in consonant sounds. Feminine nouns, with few exceptions, are formed by appending -*a* to the masculine form of the noun, if there is

35

one. Here are more examples:

Masculine Noun	Feminine Noun
والِد	والِدَة
wālid	*wālida*
father	mother
كاتِب	كاتِبَة
kātib	*kātiba*
writer	(female) writer

Notice that in writing, feminine nouns end in the letter ة *tā' marbūTa*, which follows the short -a ending. This letter is either silent, if nothing follows the noun, or pronounced, if another noun follows it. For example:

في مَدينَة

fī madína

in the city

أَسْكُن في مَدينَة واشِنْطُن

áskun fī madínat wāshinTun.

I live in the city of Washington.

4. NATIONALITY AND AFFILIATION ADJECTIVES

Arabic adjectives, which behave very similarly to nouns, also have masculine forms and feminine forms.

Words that indicate nationalities or affiliations, such as American, Syrian, or Lebanese, are adjectives. The masculine form of a nationality adjective (or a *nisba* adjective, in Arabic terminology) is formed by adding ي -ī to the name of the country or another place name. If that name ends in a vowel, the vowel is dropped before the ending is added. If the country name includes an article, the article is dropped before the *nisba* adjective is formed. The feminine form of a nationality adjective is formed by adding يّة -iyya. For example:

أَمْريكا *amrīka* (America)	أَمْريكي *amrīkī* (American, *m.*)
لُبْنان *lubnān* (Lebanon)	لُبْناني *lubnānī* (Lebanese, *m.*)
عَرَب *'arab* (Arabs)	عَرَبِي *'arabī* (Arab, *m.*)

And:

أَمْريكا *amrīka* (America)	أَمْريكِيَّة *amrīkiyya* (American, *f.*)
لُبْنان *lubnān* (Lebanon)	لُبْنانِيَّة *lubnāniyya* (Lebanese, *f.*)
عَرَب *'arab* (Arabs)	عَرَبِيَّة *'arabiyya* (Arab, *f.*)

36

عَرَبِيَّة 'arabiyya is also used to refer to the Arabic language.

Note the slight modification of this pattern in the forms for *Syrian*.

سوريا sūriyya (Syria)

سوري sūrī (Syrian, *m.*)

سوريَّة sūriyya (Syrian, *f.*)

D. Vocabulary

مِنْ	*min*	from
أَيْنَ	*ayna*	where?
أَنْتَ	*ánta*	you, *m.*
يا	*yā!*	hey!, oh!
أَنا	*ana*	I
دِمَشْق	*dimáshq*	Damascus
يَعْني	*yá'nī*	so, in other words
سوري	*sūrī*	Syrian, *m.*
نَعَم	*na'am*	yes
سوريا	*sūriyya*	Syria
أَنْتِ	*ánti*	you, *f.*
أَمْريكيَّة	*amrīkíyya*	American, *f.*
أَسْكُنْ	*áskun*	I live
في	*fī*	in
مَدينَة	*madína*	city
مَدينَة واشِنْطُن	*madínat wáshinTun*	the city of Washington

E. Cultural Note

Currently, twenty-three countries make up what is tentatively called "the Arab world": Algeria, Bahrain, Comoros, Djibouti, Egypt, Eritrea, Iraq, Jordan, Kuwait, Lebanon, Libya, Mauritania, Morocco, Oman, the Palestinian Authority, Qatar, Saudi Arabia, Somalia, Sudan, Syria, Tunisia, United Arab Emirates, and Yemen. These countries are the members of the League of Arab States, based in Cairo, Egypt. The League of Arab States (see www.arableagueonline.org), or in Arabic, *jami'at ad-duwal al-'arabiyya,* was established in

1945 by seven charter members—Egypt, Iraq, Lebanon, Saudi Arabia, Syria, Transjordan (now Jordan), and Yemen—to strenghten and promote economic, cultural, social, and political programs involving its member states and mediate possible disputes. For example, the organization, also called the Arab League for short, coordinates literacy campaigns, sponsors the publication of books, launches youth sports programs, and supports programs advancing the role of women in Arab societies.

Although most Arab League countries have much in common, such as having dominant Muslim, Arab, and Arabic-speaking populations and belonging to the cultural and historical sphere of Arab civilization, there are also important linguistic, cultural, historical, economic, religious, and ethnic differences among them. For example, whereas Bahrain's population consists almost entirely of Muslim Arabs, Lebanon has a large Christian minority and its population is a mixture of Phoenician, Greek, Armenian, and Arab people. Most Saudis are ethnically Arabs and speak a colloquial Arabic dialect as their native language, but the majority of the population of Comoros is not Arab and speaks an East African language, though Arabic is one of the official languages and Islam is a state religion. At the same time, many Arabs from the Middle East and North Africa feel closely connected, in cultural and religious terms, to the Arabs from other countries, so much so that a term "the Arab nation," or *al-umma al-'arabiyya,* is used to refer to this feeling of connectedness. For example, when Nagib Mahfuz (also spelled Naguib Mahfouz), the Egyptian novelist and screenplay writer, was the first Arabic-language writer to receive the Nobel Prize for literature in 1988, many Arabs felt he had won the prize for all Arabs and not only for Egypt.

Much information about Arab countries and on the Arabic language and culture is available on the Web. We encourage you to explore it as a great way to learn about the people, the language they speak, and their culture. Here is one useful Web site to get you started: www.danex-exm.dk/arablink.htm.

F. Exercises

1. Connect the following letters into words.

a. ن أ ك ل

b. ف ل و س

c. م د ر س ة

d. ط م ا ط م

e. د ر و س

f. ت ب ت

g. س ن ة

h. س ن و ا ت

i. ط ا ل ب

j. ق ي ا م

38

2. Write the following words in Arabic script with short vowel diacritics and other necessary signs.

a. *aqlām*

b. *kuntu*

c. *funduq*

d. *laban*

e. *kamāl*

f. *baTāTa*

g. *urduniyya*

h. *sharibtu*

3. Give the English transliteration of the following words.

a. مَشْروب

b. كِتَاب

c. تونِسيَّة

d. كَانَت

e. بِنْت

f. عالِم

g. قافِلَة

4. Translate the following sentences into Arabic.

a. Are you from Syria?

b. No, I am from Lebanon.[1]

c. Is he in Syria?

d. My name is …

e. You are in the city of Damascus.

f. Are you American?

g. No, I am Lebanese.

h. Is Samir here?

5. Make questions in Arabic from the following English statements and say them aloud.

a. You are Tunisian (*tūnisī*, m.).

b. Your name is Samir.

c. You are here.

d. My office is in Lebanon.

e. Lucy is here.

---

[1] The Arabic word for *no* is لا *lā*. Note that *lā* is written using a special combination letter, لا *lām alif*.

Answer Key

1.
a. نَأْكُل
b. فلوس
c. مدرسة
d. طماطم
e. دروس
f. تبت
g. سنة
h. سنوات
i. طالب
j. قيام

2.
a. أَقْلام
b. كُنْتُ
c. فُنْدُق
d. لَبَن
e. كَمال
f. بَطاطَة
g. أُرْدُنِيَّة
h. شَرِبْتُ

3.
a. *mashrūb*
b. *kitāb*
c. *tūnisiyya*
d. *kānat*
e. *bint*
f. *'ālim*
g. *qāfila*

4.
a. أَنْتَ مِنْ سوريا؟
b. لا، أَنا مِنْ لُبْنان.
c. هُوَ في سوريا؟
d. إِسْمي...
e. أَنْتَ في مَدينَة دِمَشْق.
f. أَنْتَ أَمْريكي/ أَمْريكِيَّة؟
g. لا، أَنا لُبْناني/ لُبْنانِيَّة.
h. سَمير هُنا؟

5.
a. *anta tūnisī?*
b. *ismuka samīr?*
c. *anta hunā?*
d. *maktabī fi lubnān?*
e. *lūsī hunā?*

LESSON 3

(Modern Standard Arabic)

ماذا تَعْمَل؟

mādhā ta'mal? What Do You Do?

A. Dialogue

Lucy and Donald are having coffee with Lucy's colleague (زَميل لوسي *zamīl lūsī*) Samir and Donald's friend (صَديق دونالْد *Sadīq dūnald*) in the cafeteria of the American University of Beirut. Samir and Donald's friend meet for the first time and are amazed to find they have a lot in common.

سامِر، زَميل لوسي: صَباح الْخَيْر.

صَديق دونالْد: صَباح النّور. أَهْلاً.

سامِر، زَميل لوسي: أَهْلاً بِك. لُبْناني، أَلَيْسَ كَذَلِك؟

صَديق دونالْد: لا، أَنا مِن الْكَوَيْت. وَحَضْرَتَك ليبي أَمْ مَغْرِبي؟

سامِر، زَميل لوسي: أَنا تونِسي. إسْمي سامِر التّونِسي.

صَديق دونالْد: وَاللَّه؟ وَأَنا أَيْضاً إسْمي سامِر... وَلَكِن سامِر أَبو ثابِت.

سامِر، زَميل لوسي: تَشَرَّفْنا أُسْتاذ سامِر.

صَديق دونالْد: تَشَرَّفْنا بِك.

سامِر، زَميل لوسي: ماذا تَعْمَل حَضْرَتَك؟

صَديق دونالْد: أَنا دُكْتور في مُسْتَشْفَى جامِعَة الْكَوَيْت

سامِر، زَميل لوسي: وَاللَّه؟ وَأَنا أَيْضاً دُكْتور... وَلَكِن دُكْتور في اللُّغَة الْعَرَبِيَّة في الْجامِعَة الأَمْريكِيَّة.

صَديق دونالْد: وَهَلْ تَتَكَلَّم اللَّهْجَة اللُّبْنانِيَّة جَيِّداً جِدّاً؟

سامِر، زَميل لوسي: طَبْعاً، أَتَكَلَّمُها كُلّ يَوْم.

sāmir, zamīl lūsī: SabāH al-khayr.
Sadīq dūnald: SabāH an-nūr. ahlan.
sāmir, zamīl lūsī: ahlan bik. lubnānī, a laysa kadhālik?
Sadīq dūnald: lā. anā min al-kuwayt. wa HaDratak, lībī am maghribī?
sāmir, zamīl lūsī: anā tūnisī. ismī sāmir at-tūnisī.

Sadīq dūnald: wa llāhi? wa anā ayDan ismī sāmir... wa-lākin sāmir abū thābit.

sāmir, zamīl lūsī: tasharrafnā, ustādh sāmir.

Sadīq dūnald: tasharrafnā bik.

sāmir, zamīl lūsī: mādhā ta'mal, HaDratak?

Sadīq dūnald: anā duktōr fī mustashfā jāmi'at al-kuwayt.

sāmir, zamīl lūsī: wa llāhi? wa anā ayDan duktōr, wa lākin duktōr fi l-lugha l-'arabiyya fi l-jāmi'a l-amrīkiyya.

Sadīq dūnald: wa hal tatakallam al-lahja l-lubnāniyya jayyidan jiddan?

sāmir, zamīl lūsī: Tab'an. atakallamuhā kull yawm.

Samir, Lucy's colleague: Good morning.

Donald's friend: Good morning. Hello.

Samir, Lucy's colleague: Hello to you! Lebanese, right?

Donald's friend: No, I am from Kuwait. And you, are you Libyan or Moroccan?

Samir, Lucy's colleague: I am Tunisian. My name is Samir al-Tunisi.

Donald's friend: Really? My name is also Samir, but Samir Abu Thabit.

Samir, Lucy's colleague: Nice to meet you, Mister Samir.

Donald's friend: Nice to meet you, too.

Samir, Lucy's colleague: What do you do, sir?

Donald's friend: I am a doctor at the Kuwait University Hospital.

Samir, Lucy's colleague: Really? I am a doctor, too, but a doctor of Arabic language at the American University.

Donald's friend: And do you speak the Lebanese dialect very well?

Samir, Lucy's colleague: Sure. I speak it every day.

B. Arabic Writing and Pronunciation

1. CONSONANTS AND CONSONANT LETTERS: ص *Sād*, ض *Dād*, ظ *DHā'*, ح *Hā'*, خ *khā'*, ج *jīm*, ز *zāy*, ث *thā'*, ذ *dhāl*, غ *ghayn*, ى *alif maqSūra*

In this lesson you will learn how to write and pronounce ten more consonant letters of the Arabic alphabet: خ, ح, ج, ز, ث, ذ, غ, ض, ص, and ظ. You will also learn about ى *alif maqSūra*, a variant of the letter *alif*.

A. THE LETTER ص *Sād*; THE SOUND *S*

The letter ص *Sād* has two basic shapes, initial/medial and final/separate, just like many other consonants you have learned about so far.

INITIAL	MEDIAL	FINAL	SEPARATE	NAME	SOUND VALUE
ـصـ	ـصـ	ـص	ص	*Sād*	*S*

In the final/separate form, *Sād* is written by drawing a small oblong loop, like a sideways egg, and then dipping down below the line to form a rounded hook. In its medial form, the hook is dropped, leaving a small tooth after the loop.

Like the sound T discussed in Lesson 2, the sound S is an emphatic consonant. It is a counterpart of the sound s (سين sīn), but pronounced further back in the mouth, not at the teeth like sīn. Pronounce it with the tense tongue in a scoop-like shape raised toward the back of the mouth. As with other emphatic consonants, the vowel that precedes and/or follows S sounds much "darker," being pronounced further back in the mouth, than its counterpart. For example, the ā-sound in Sād, the name of the letter, is much closer to the vowel in English fawn than in apple.

In the dialogue, Sād is found in the initial form in:

صَبَاح SabāH (morning)

صَديق Sadīq (friend)

Here are examples showing Sād in other positions:

Medial: قَصير qaSīr (short)

Separate: خاصّ khāSS (special, private)

Final: لِصّ liSS (thief)

B. THE LETTER ض Dād; THE SOUND D

The only difference between the writing of the letter ص Sād and the letter ض Dād is that Dād has a dot over it.

INITIAL	MEDIAL	FINAL	SEPARATE	NAME	SOUND VALUE
ضـ	ـضـ	ـض	ض	Dād	D

Dād is the emphatic counterpart of the sound d. It is produced by raising the tongue, shaped like a scoop, toward the throat and keeping it tense. D is similar to, but "darker" than, the sound d in English dawn.

In the dialogue, you encountered Dād in its medial form in:

أَيْضاً ayDan (also)

Other examples are:

Initial: ضابِط DābiT (officer)

Separate: أَرْض arD (earth, land)

Final: رَكْض rakD (running)

43

C. THE LETTER ظ DHā'; THE SOUND DH

The letter ظ DHā' has only one basic form, to which the connecting strokes are added when necessary.

INITIAL	MEDIAL	FINAL	SEPARATE	NAME	SOUND VALUE
ظ	ظ	ظ	ظ	DHā'	DH

Much like the letter ط Tā', ظ DHā' is a tilted ellipse that you start and end writing on the left side, with a vertical stroke over the left end of the ellipse, and a dot to the right of the stroke.

The consonant sound DH, like other emphatic consonants, has no English equivalent. It is the emphatic counterpart of the consonant ذ dhāl, discussed below, and is pronounced just like English th in that. DH is produced with the root of the tongue tense and raised toward the back of the throat.

None of the words in the dialogue use this sound. DHā' is used in the following words:

Initial: أَبو ظَبي abu DHabī (Abu Dhabi)

Medial: فَظيع faDHī' (detestable)

Final: حَظّ HaDHDH (luck)

Separate: حظوظ HuDHūDH (luck, pl.)

D. THE LETTER ح Hā'; THE SOUND H

The letter ح Hā' has two basic shapes.

INITIAL	MEDIAL	FINAL	SEPARATE	NAME	SOUND VALUE
ح	ح	ح	ح	Hā'	H

In the separate and final forms, ح Hā' looks similar to a letter C dipping below the line, except for a small line on the top of it. The initial/medial form has no tail.

The sound H has no English counterpart. It is important that you distinguish it from the sound h, which exists in both Arabic and English and which you learned in Lesson 1. To pronounce H, force the air out from deep down in the constricted throat with a mouth wide open. Pretending to clear your throat with an ahem would get you close to producing the sound. H is a voiceless counterpart of the sound (') represented by the letter ع 'ayn, which you learned in Lesson 2. Both sounds are among those that give Arabic its typical guttural sound.

In the dialogue, Hā' is found in the initial position in:

حَضْرَتَك HaDratak (you; Sir/Madam)

and in the separate form in:

صَباح *SabāH* (morning)

Other examples are:

Medial: صَحيفة *SaHīfa* (newspaper)

Final: ريح *rīH* (wind)

E. THE LETTER خ *khā'*; THE SOUND *kh*

The consonant letter خ *khā'* has two basic shapes.

INITIAL	MEDIAL	FINAL	SEPARATE	NAME	SOUND VALUE
خـ	ـخـ	ـخ	خ	*khā'*	*kh*

khā' has the same shape as ح *Hā'*, but with a dot above to distinguish it from *Hā'*.

khā' is another Arabic sound that does not exist in the English language. It is an *h*-type sound, pronounced by raising the tongue toward the most posterior part of the mouth and letting the air flow through the narrow passage thus formed. It is similar to the *ch*-sound in the Scottish *loch* or the German *nacht*. Learn to distinguish it from *H* (the letter ح *Hā'*), which is pronounced farther back in the throat. Both sounds are voiceless, i.e., pronounced without the vibration of the vocal cords.

In the dialogue, *khā'* was used in its medial form in:

الْخَيْر *al-khayr* (good)

Other examples are:

Initial: خَبَر *khabar* (news, *sg.*)

Final: تاريخ *tārīkh* (history)

Separate (and initial): خَوْخ *khawkh* (peaches)

F. THE LETTER ج *jīm;* THE SOUND *j*

ج *jīm* has two basic shapes. It looks just like ح *Hā'*, but with a dot inside or underneath.

INITIAL	MEDIAL	FINAL	SEPARATE	NAME	SOUND VALUE
جـ	ـجـ	ـج	ج	*jīm*	*j*

ج *jīm* has the same sound as the letter *j* in the English word *job*.

In the dialogue, *jīm* was used in:

Initial: جامِعَة *jāmi'a* (university)

جَيِّداً جِداً *jayyidan jiddan* (very well)

Medial: اللَّهْجَة *al-lahja* (the dialect)

Here are some additional examples showing *jīm* in other positions:

Separate: دَجاج *dajāj* (chicken)

Separate and initial: خَرَجَ *kharaja* (go out)

G. THE LETTER ز *zāy*; THE SOUND *z*

The letter ز *zāy* has the same shape as the letter ر *rā'*, except for the single dot on top of it.

ز *zāy* has the same sound as the letter *z* in the English word *zebra*.

INITIAL	MEDIAL	FINAL	SEPARATE	NAME	SOUND VALUE
ز	ـز	ـز	ز	*zāy*	*z*

In the dialogue, *zāy* was used in its initial form in:

زَميل *zamīl* (colleague)

Other example of *zāy* are:

Medial: مِزْمار *mizmār* (old Arab flute)

Final: مَركَز *markaz* (center)

Separate: رُزّ *ruzz* (rice)

H. THE LETTER ث *thā'*; THE SOUND *th*

The letter ث *thā'* has two different shapes. ث *thā'* has the basic shape of the letter ت *tā'*, but with three dots on top.

INITIAL	MEDIAL	FINAL	SEPARATE	NAME	SOUND VALUE
ثـ	ـثـ	ـث	ث	*thā'*	*th*

The sound of the letter *thā'* is the same as the sound *th* in the English word *thin*.

In the dialogue, *thā'* was used in:

Initial: أَبو ثابِت *abu thābit*

46

Other examples are:

Medial: باحِثَة bāHitha (female researcher)

Final: بَحْث baHth (search, research)

Separate: تُراث turāth (legacy, heritage)

I. THE LETTER ذ dhāl; THE SOUND dh

The letter ذ dhāl has only one basic form and, as a non-connector letter, doesn't attach to the letter that follows it.

INITIAL	MEDIAL	FINAL	SEPARATE	NAME	SOUND VALUE
ذ	ـذ	ـذ	ذ	dhā'	dh

ذ dhāl looks like the letter د dāl, except that it has one dot above the basic shape.

The sound of the letter dhāl is similar to the sound of th in the English word that. The sound dh is the counterpart of the th sound above. The distinction is that dh is voiced, i.e., pronounced with vibrating vocal cords, while th is voiceless.

In the dialogue, dhāl was used in:

Separate: أُسْتاذ ustādh (professor, mister)

Other examples are:

Initial: ذَكي dhakīy (intelligent)

Medial and final: لَذيذ ladhīdh (delicious)

J. THE LETTER غ ghayn; THE SOUND gh

The letter غ ghayn has four different shapes.

INITIAL	MEDIAL	FINAL	SEPARATE	NAME	SOUND VALUE
غـ	ـغـ	ـغ	غ	ghayn	gh

The shape of غ ghayn is the same as the shape of ع 'ayn, which you learned in Lesson 2. The distinguishing feature is the dot on top of غ ghayn.

The consonant sound gh does not occur in English. It is an r-type sound pronounced with the air flowing through the constricted area in the back of the mouth, like kh. The main difference between gh and kh is that when gh is pronounced the vocal cords vibrate, making the sound voiced, while kh is voiceless. The sound gh is similar to the Parisian French r-sound. Pay attention to the distinction between the pairs of sounds gh (غ) and

' (ع), and *kh* (خ) and *H* (ح). They are similar sounds, but *gh* and *kh* are pronounced at the far end of the mouth, with the raised root of the tongue, while ' and *H* are pronounced farther back, in the throat.

In the dialogue, *ghāyn* was used in its medial form in:

مَغْرِبِي *maghribī* (Moroccan)

Other examples are:

Initial: غَداء *ghadā'* (lunch)

Final: تَبْغ *tabgh* (tobacco)

Separate: فَراغ *farāgh* (space)

K. THE LETTER ى *alif maqSūra*

The letter ى *alif maqSūra* is not a separate letter of the alphabet. It always occurs at the end of the word and has a single shape. The absence of any dots distinguishes it from the final form of the letter ي *yā'*.

INITIAL	MEDIAL	FINAL	SEPARATE	NAME	SOUND VALUE
-	-	ى	-	*alif maqSūra*	*ā*

alif maqSūra is used to represent the long vowel *ā* at the end of words.

In the dialogue, *alif maqSūra* occurs in:

مُسْتَشْفَى *mustashfā* (hospital)

Other examples of *alif maqSūra* are:

ذِكْرَى *dhikrā* (memory)

مُنَى *munā* (Muna)

C. Grammar and Usage

1. THE DEFINITE ARTICLE

In Arabic, as in English, nouns are preceded by articles. For example:

الْبَيْت *al-bayt* (the house)

The Arabic definite article الـ *al* (the) precedes a noun and makes a single unit with it, both in speech and in writing. الـ *al* (the) is used before all nouns, masculine or feminine, singular or plural. For example:

الْبُيوت *al-buyūt* (the houses)

If a word preceding the definite article ends in a vowel, the initial sound *a* of *al* is dropped and the article is pronounced *l*, as in:

في الْبَيْت *fi l-bayt* (in the house)

Arabic doesn't have an equivalent of the English indefinite articles *a* and *an*. A noun that is indefinite, i.e., a noun that does not refer to a specific person, object, or idea, simply has no article. For example:

بَيْت *bayt* (a house)

Less commonly, and in very formal Modern Standard Arabic, indefinite nouns end in the sound *n* or the letter *nūn*, which follows one of the three short vowels.[1] For example:

بَيْتٌ *baytun* (a house)

Here are more examples of indefinite and definite nouns in Arabic.

Indefinite Nouns	Definite Nouns
جامِعَة	الْجامِعَة
jāmi'a (a university)	*al-jāmi'a* (the university)
يَوْم	الْيَوْم
yawm (a day)	*al-yawm* (the day)
مُسْتَشْفَى	الْمُسْتَشْفَى
mustashfā (a hospital)	*al-mustashfā* (the hospital)

When the definite article ال *al* is attached to a noun that starts with one of the "sun" consonants (listed below), the *l* of the article *al* is pronounced just like the sound that begins the noun.

"SUN" CONSONANTS						
n	*l*	*DH*	*T*	*D*	*S*	*sh*
ن	ل	ظ	ط	ض	ص	ش

s	*z*	*r*	*dh*	*d*	*th*	*t*
س	ز	ر	ذ	د	ث	ت

It appears then that the beginning consonant is "doubled." For example:

الصَّديق *aS-Sadīq* (the friend)

الزَّميل *az-zamīl* (the colleague)

الدُّكْتور *ad-duktōr* (the doctor)

---

[1] This phenomenon is often referred to as *nunation*. The short vowels, *-u*, *-a*, and *-i*, to which the *-n* of *nunation* is added, represent case endings (see Lesson 15).

In Arabic script, the *shadda* is used to indicate the "doubling" of the consonant. Notice that the final *l* of the article still figures in the Arabic script, even though it is not pronounced.

If you pronounce the "sun" consonants listed above, you will notice that they are all pronounced with the tip of the tongue approaching or touching the upper teeth or the gums behind them. These consonants are called "sun" consonants simply because the word شمس *shams* (sun) begins in one such sound. The sound of the article remains ال *al* in front of all other consonants.

2. QUESTION WORDS

To ask a specific question, use one of the question words listed below. As in English, a question word is always at the beginning of the sentence in Arabic; no changes in the word order take place.

QUESTION WORDS	
ما *mā*	what, which? (used before a noun)
ماذا *mādhā?*	what?
أَيْن *ayn(a)?*	where?
أَيْن مِنْ *min ayn(a)?*	from where?
مَن *man?*	who?
مَتَى *matā?*	when?
لِمَاذا *limādhā?*	why?
كَيْفَ *kayf(a)?*	how?

ما اسْمُكَ؟
mā-smuká?
What is your name?

ماذا تَعْمَل؟
mādhā ta'mal?
What do you do?

أَيْن الْجامِعَة؟
ayn al-jāmi'a?
Where is the university?

مِنْ أَيْن لوسي؟
min ayn lūsī?
Where is Lucy from?

50

مَنْ لوسي؟

man lūsī?

Who is Lucy?

مَتَى تَتَكَلَّم اللَّهْجَة اللُّبْنانِيَّة؟

matā tatakallam al-lahja l-lubnāniyya?

When do you speak the Lebanese dialect?

لِمَاذا تَتَكَلَّم اللَّهْجَة اللُّبْنانِيَّة؟

limādhā tatakallam al-lahja l-lubnāniyya?

Why do you speak the Lebanese dialect?

3. SUBJECT PRONOUNS

A subject pronoun is a word used to replace a noun that is a subject of a sentence. For instance, in English, the pronoun *he* is a subject pronoun, as in *he runs*. Here is the table with Arabic subject pronouns.

SUBJECT PRONOUNS								
Singular			**Plural**			**Dual**		
أَنا	anā	I	نَحْنُ	naHnu	we			
أَنْتَ	anta	you *(m.)*	أَنْتُمْ	antum	you *(m.)*	أَنْتُمَا	antumā	you two *(m./f.)*
أَنْتِ	anti	you *(f.)*	أَنْتُنَّ	antunna	you *(f.)*			
هُوَ	huwa	he	هُمْ	hum	they *(m.)*	هُمَا	humā	they two *(m./f.)*
هِيَ	hiya	she	هُنَّ	hunna	they *(f.)*			

Arabic subject pronouns are divided into three numbers: singular, for one, plural, for three and more, and dual, for two. Note that English *you* translates into four different forms in Arabic—singular masculine, singular feminine, plural masculine, and plural feminine. There are also masculine and feminine plural equivalents of the English *they*. In the dual, the same forms are used for both masculine and feminine.

Here are some examples:

أَنا مِن الْكَوَيْت

'anā min al-kuwait.

I am from Kuwait.

هُوَ تونِسِي

huwa tūnisī.

He is Tunisian.

أَنْتَ دُكْتُور فِي الْمُسْتَشْفَى.

anta doktōr fi l-mustashfā.

You *(m.)* are a doctor at the hospital.

أَنْتِ دُكْتُورَة فِي الْمُسْتَشْفَى.

anti doktōra fi l-mustashfā.

You *(f.)* are a doctor at the hospital.

The pronouns in the shaded areas of the table are those most commonly used. Dual forms (*antumā, humā*) and the feminine plural forms (*antunna, hunna*) are reserved for the most formal usage. The plural masculine forms often replace them in spoken language.

Subject pronouns are optional if a sentence contains a verb:

تَتَكَلَّم اللَّهْجَة اللُّبْنَانِيَّة.

tatakallam al-lahja l-lubnāniyya.

You speak the Lebanese dialect. (*lit.*, speak the Lebanese dialect)

This is so because the verb form itself clearly indicates the person, gender, and number of the doer of the action in Arabic. We'll start discussing different verb forms in Lesson 4.

D. Vocabulary

صَدِيق	*Sadīq*	friend *(m.)*
زَمِيل	*zamīl*	colleague *(m.)*
صَبَاح الْخَيْر	*SabāH al-khayr*	good morning
صَبَاح النُّور	*SabāH an-nūr*	good morning (a reply)
أَلَيْسَ كَذَلِك	*a laysa kadhālik?*	Right?, Isn't it so?
الْكُوَيْت	*al-kuwayt*	Kuwait
حَضْرَتَك	*HaDratak*	you; Sir/Madam (a respectful form of address)
لِيبِي	*lībī*	Libyan *(m.)*
أَمْ	*am*	or (in questions)
مَغْرِبِي	*maghribī*	Moroccan *(m.)*
تُونِسِي	*tūnisī*	Tunisian *(m.)*
وَاللَّهِ	*wa-llāhí?*	Really?, Is that so?; By God!
أَيْضاً	*ayDan*	also
لَكِن	*lākin*	but

تَشَرَّفْنا tasharrafnā.	Nice to meet you.
أُسْتاذ ustādh	professor, *here:* mister
تَشَرَّفْنا بِك tasharrafnā bik.	Nice to meet you, too.
ماذا mādhā?	what?
تَعْمَل ta'mal	you work
ماذا تَعْمَل؟ mādhā ta'mal?	What do you do?
دُكْتور duktōr[1]	doctor (m.)
مُسْتَشْفَى mustashfā	hospital
جامِعَة jāmi'a	university
اللُّغَة الْعَرَبِيَّة al-lugha l-'arabiyya	Arabic language
تَتَكَلَّم tatakallam	you speak
اللَّهْجَة اللُّبْنانِيَّة al-lahja l-lubnāniyya	Lebanese dialect
جَيِّداً جِدّاً jayyidan jiddan	very well
طَبْعاً Tab'an	sure, of course, certainly
أَتَكَلَّمُها atakallamuhā	I speak it
كُلّ kull	every
يَوْم yawm	day

E. Cultural Note

Customs related to greeting people differ widely from culture to culture. While there are some general tendencies in the Arab world, customs can differ from country to country, group to group, and even person to person. However, it is safe to say that most Arabs shake hands every time they see each other and every time they take their leave. While hand-shaking is not unusual between men and women, more conservative people, especially if they are men, will abstain from it and instead place their hand on their chest as a sign of respect and welcome. While Arabs don't generally hug, in some places, they do greet each other with three kisses on the cheek. Touching and steady eye contact among people, engrossed in a conversation is not unusual or considered inappropriate as it often is in the United States. It is also not unusual to see men kiss each other on the cheeks when they meet or walk hand in hand as a sign of mutual affection.

The greeting ritual takes several turns in Arabic. After the initial greeting and before focusing on the main topic, most Arabs inquire about the health and well-being of their

---

[1] Note the vowel ō, which occurs only in borrowed words such as this one.

interlocutor and his or her family and friends. A Western business person, however, should refrain from asking an Arab man about the well-being of his wife, as it would be considered rude. Some of the appropriate expressions to be used in this situation are:

كَيْف الْحَال؟

kayf al-Ḥāl?

How are you?

كَيْف الصِّحَة؟ إِنْ شاءَ اللَّه تَمام.

kayf aS-SiHa? inshā'allāh tamām.

How is your health? I hope it's fine. (*lit.*, God willing, it's fine)

The answers can be:

الْحَمْدُ لِلَّه.

al-Hamdulillāh.

Thanks, it's fine. (*lit.*, praise to God)

بِخَيْر.

bi-khayr.

Fine.

(كُلّ شَيْء) تَمام.

(kull shay') tamām.

(Everything is) fine.

F. Exercises

1. Connect the following letters into words.

a. ا غ ل ب

b. ا ل م غ ر ب

c. ظ ا ه ر ة

d. خ ل ي ل

e. ث ي ا ب

f. ض ب ا ط

g. ت م س ا ح

h. ص ح ي ح

2. Write the following words in Arabic script, including the signs indicating vowels.

a. *dhanab*

b. *baTTikh*

c. *riyāD*
d. *Habīb*
e. *tujīb*
f. *taSwīr*

3. Match the English transliterations to the Arabic words below.

yazūr / jābir / shubāT / jadhdhāb/ mithāl / DHalla / baHth / khubz

a. شُباط

b. ظَلَّ

c. يَزور

d. جَذّاب

e. بَحْث

f. خُبْز

g. مِثال

h. جابِر

4. Answer the following questions about the dialogue.

a. مِن أَيْن لوسي؟

b. مَن سامِر التّونِسي؟

c. مِن أَيْن سامِر؟

d. أَيْن الْجامِعَة الأَمْريكيَّة؟

e. أَيْن بَيْروت؟

5. Fill in the blanks in the following story with the eight words listed below.

دُكْتور / الْجامِعَة / أَتَكَلَّم / الْمُسْتَشْفَى / في / الْعَرَبيَّة / هُوَ / مَدينَة

أَنا إِسْمي لينا ناصِر. أَنا لُبْنانيَّة. أَسْكُن _____ _____ بَيْروت. أَنا دُكْتورَة. أَعْمَل في _____.

كُلْ يَوْم _____ اللُّغَة _____. صَديقي أَحْمَد ماجِد أَيْضاً _____ وَلَكِن في _____

الأَمْريكيَّة. _____ سوري.

Answer Key

1. a. اغلب
   b. المغرب
   c. ظاهرة
   d. خليل
   e. ثياب
   f. ضباط
   g. تمساح
   h. صحيح

2. a. ذَنَب
   b. بَطِّيخ
   c. رياض
   d. حَبيب
   e. تَجيب
   f. تَصْوير

3. a. شُباط *shubāT*
   b. ظَلَّ *DHalla*
   c. يِزور *yazūr*
   d. جَذّاب *jadhdhāb*
   e. بَحْث *baHth*
   f. خُبْز *khubz*

g. مِثال *mithāl*

h. جابِر *jābir*

4. a. لوسي مِنْ أَمْريكا.
   b. سامِر التّونِسي دُكْتور.
   c. هُوَ تونِسي.
   d. الْجامِعَة الأَمْريكِيَّة في بَيْروت.
   e. بَيْروت في لُبْنان.

5. أنا إِسْمي لينا ناصِر. أنا لُبْنانِيَّة. أَسْكُن في مَدينَة بَيْروت. أنا دُكْتورة. أَعْمَل في الْمُسْتَشْفى. كُلْ يَوْم أَتَكَلَّم اللُّغَة الْعَرَبِيَّة.

My name is Lina Nasser. I am Lebanese. I live in the city of Beirut. I am a doctor. I work in the hospital. Every day I speak the Arabic language.

صَديقي أَحْمَد ماجِد أَيْضاً دُكْتور وَلَكِن في الْجامِعَة الأَمْريكِيَّة. هُوَ سوري.

My friend Ahmad Majid is also a doctor, but at the American University. He is Syrian.

FIRST REVIEW

(Modern Standard Arabic)

---

1. Connect the following letters into words.

a. ا ل م و س ي ق ى

b. ا ل ي م ن

c. د ك ت و ر ة

d. ت ع ب ا ن

e. ف ل س ط ي ن

f. ق ه و ة

g. ع ب د ا ل ل ه

h. ز م ل ا ء

i. ش ا ه د و ا

j. ج و ا م ع

k. ا ب و ظ ب ي

l. ص غ ي ر ة

2. Write the following words in Arabic script marking all the short vowels.

a. *kabīra*

b. *mudun*

c. *Sighār*

d. *Tullāb*

e. *sayyāratukum*

f. *as-sūdānī*

g. *al-Hārr*

h. *al-jaww*

3. Match the following Arabic words with their English translations given below.

أُسْتاذ / التِّلِفون / فَرَنْسا / الْعَرَب / زَميل / مَدينَة

a. the Arabs

b. professor

c. colleague

d. France

e. the telephone

f. city

4. Put the following sentences in the right order to create a meaningful dialogue.

- يَعْني في لُبْنان؟
- نَحْنُ في مَدينَة لوس أَنْجِلوس.
- وَنَحْنُ في مَدينَة بَيْروت.
- نَعَمْ، نَحْنُ في أَمْريكا.
- أَيْنَ أَنْتُم؟
- يَعْني أَنْتُم في أَمْريكا؟
- نَعَمْ، في لُبْنان.

5. Answer the following questions by supplying the appropriate information about yourself.

a. ما اسْمكَ / اسْمكِ؟
b. مِنْ أَيْنَ أَنْتَ / أَنْتِ؟
c. هَلْ أَنْتَ أَمْريكي/ هَلْ أَنْتِ أَمْريكيَّة؟
d. هَلْ أَنْتَ كاتِب؟
e. هَلْ أَنْتَ في المَكْتَب؟

6. Fill in the blanks with an appropriate noun, pronoun, or preposition.

a. سامِر _____
b. _____ كُوَيْتي.
c. يَعْني أَنا _____ الْكُوَيْت.
d. وأَسْكُن _____ مَدينَة الْكُوَيْت.

7. Write the corresponding feminine forms for the following masculine nouns.

a. عِراقي _____
b. كُوَيْتي _____
c. سوري _____
d. ليبي _____
e. كاتِب _____
f. طالِب _____
g. مُعَلِّم _____

8. Translate the following mini-dialogues into Arabic.

- Where are you?
- I am in the office.

58

- Where am I?
- You are here.

- Where are you from?
- I am from America.

- Is she Lebanese?
- Yes, she is.

- Where are they from?
- They are from Damascus.

9. Determine whether the following nouns preceded by definite articles start with "sun" letters or "moon" letters; then add *shadda*s as appropriate, depending on the correct pronunciation of the articles.

Example:

السَلام ← السَّلام

a. الطالِب

b. الأُرْدُن

c. المَدينَة

d. الضـابِط

e. الجامِعَة

f. الرادْيو

g. التليفِزْيون

h. الوالِد

10. Decide whether the words below are definite or indefinite.

a. الوالِدَة

b. لازِق

c. أَصْدِقاء

d. الأُرْدُن

e. طَقْس

f. أَحْمَر

g. الجِمـار

Answer Key

1. a. الموسيقى
   b. اليمن
   c. دكتورة
   d. تعبان
   e. فلسطين
   f. قهوة
   g. عبدالله
   h. زملاء
   i. شاهدوا
   j. جوامع
   k. ابوظبي
   l. صغيرة

2. a. كَبيرَة,
   b. مُدُن,
   c. صِغار,
   d. طُلّاب,
   e. سَيّارَتكم,
   f. السُوداني,
   g. الحارُّ,
   h. الجو

3. a. the Arabs   العَرَب
   b. professor   أُستاذ
   c. colleague   زَميل
   d. France   فَرَنْسا
   e. the telephone   التِّلِفون
   f. city   مَدينة

4. ‑أَيْنَ أَنْتُم؟
   ‑نَحْنُ في مَدينَة لوس أَنْجِلوس.
   ‑يَعْني أَنْتُم في أَمْريكا؟
   ‑نَعَمْ، نَحْنُ في أَمْريكا.
   ‑وَنَحْنُ في مَدينَة بَيْروت.
   ‑يَعْني في لُبْنان؟
   ‑نَعَمْ، في لُبْنان.

5. Answers will vary. Some possible answers are:
   a. إِسْمي . . . .
   b. أَنا مِنْ مَدينَة . . . .
   c. نَعَمُ، أَنا أَمْريكي / أَمْريكيَّة.
   d. نَعَمْ، أَنا كاتِب.
      (لا، أَنا أُستاذ / دُكْتور . . .)
   e. نَعَمْ، أَنا في المَكْتَب.

6. a. إِسْمي سامِر.
   b. أَنا كُوَيتي.
   c. يَعْني أَنا مِنَ الكُوَيت.
   d. وَأَسْكُن في مَدينَة الكُوَيت.

7. a. عِراقي – عِراقيَّة
   b. كُوَيتي – كُوَيتيَّة
   c. سوري – سوريَّة
   d. ليبي – ليبيَّة
   e. كاتِب – كاتِبة
   f. طالِب – طالِبَة
   g. مُعَلِّم – مُعَلِّمَة

8. ‑أَيْنَ أَنْتَ؟
   ‑أَنا في المَكْتَب.

   ‑أَيْنَ أَنا؟
   ‑أَنْتَ هُنا.

   ‑مِنْ أَيْنَ أَنْتَ؟
   ‑أَنا مِنْ أَمْريكا.

   ‑هَلْ هِيَ لُبْنانيَّة؟
   ‑نَعَمْ.

   ‑مِنْ أَيْنَ هُمْ؟
   ‑هُمْ مِنْ دِمَشْق.

9. a. الطّالِب
   b. الأُرْدُن
   c. المَدينَة
   d. الضّابِط
   e. الجامِعَة
   f. الرّادْيو
   g. التِّليفِزْيون
   h. الوالِد

10. a. definite – الوالِدَة
    b. indefinite – لازِق
    c. indefinite – أصْدِقاء
    d. definite – الأُرْدُن
    e. indefinite – طَقْس
    f. indefinite – أحْمَر
    g. definite – الحِمار

61

LESSON 4
(Modern Standard Arabic)

كَيْف كانَت الْحَفْلَة؟

kayf kānat al-Hafla? How Was the Wedding?

A. Dialogue

Lucy went to Muna's wedding last night. The next morning, she chats about it with Nadia, her neigbor, over a cup of coffee.

نادْيَة: صَباح الْخَيْر يا لوسي.

لوسي: صَباح النّور يا نادْيَة. أَهْلاً.

نادْيَة: أَهْلاً بِكِ، أَهْلاً وَسَهْلاً، تَفَضَّلي! كَيْف كانَت الْحَفْلَة أَمْس؟

لوسي: آه، يا نادْيَة، اِنْبَسَطْتُ كَثيراً. تَعَرَّفْتُ عَلَى أَهْل الْعَريس. والِدَة الْعَريس
       دُكْتورَة وَوالِدُهُ صاحِب شَرِكَة.

نادْيَة: يَعْني صَرَفوا فُلوس كَثيرَة عَلَى الْحَفْلَة؟

لوسي: نَعَم، نَعَم، أَكَلْنا أَكَلات كَثيرَة؟وطَيِّبَة جِدّاً مِثل التَّبّولة والْكِبّة والْحَلَويات.

نادْيَة: وماذا شَرِبْتُم؟

لوسي: شَرِبْنا الْبيبْسي والشّاي.

نادْيَة: فَقَطْ؟ ... الْبيبْسي مَشْروب رَخيص والشّاي أَيْضاً والتَّبّولة أَكْلَة عادِيَة مِثْل
       الْكِبّة ... هَلْ كانَتْ هُناك فِرْقَة موسيقِيَّة عَرَبِيَّة عَلَى الأَقَلّ؟

لوسي: لا، ما كانَتْ هُناك فِرْقَة موسيقِيَّة.اِسْتَمَعْنا إِلَى عَمْرو دياب

نادْيَة: عَمْرو ديّاب؟ في الْكاسيت يَعْني؟

لوسي: نَعْم.

نادْيَة: أَتَكَلَّمْتِ باللَّهْجَة اللُّبْنانِيَّة؟

لوسي: طَبْعاً، تَكَلَّمْتُ مَعَ كُلّ الْعالَم، مَعَ ابْن خال مُنَى وَبِنْت عَمَّتِها وجَدَّة
       الْعَريس. صِرْتُ مِثْل الْبُلْبُل؟

nādya: SabāH al-khayr, yā lūsī.

lūsī: SabāH an-nūr, yā nādya. ahlan.

nādya: ahlan biki, ahlan wa sahlan! tafaDDalī, kayfa kānat al-Hafla ams?

lūsī: āh, yā nādya, inbasaTtu kathīran. ta'arraftu 'alā ahl al-'arīs. wālidat al-'arīs duktōra wa wāliduhu SāHib sharika.

nādya: ya'nī Sarafū flūs kathīra 'ala l-Hafla?

lūsī: na'am, na'am. akalnā akalāt kathīra wa Tayyiba jiddan mithl at-tabbuli wa l-kibbi wa l-Halawayāt.

nādya: wa mādhā sharibtum?

lūsī: sharibna l-bebsī wa sh-shāy.

nādya: faqaT?... al-bebsī mashrūb rakhīS wa sh-shāy ayDan wa t-tabbuli akla 'ādiyya mithl al-kibbi... hal kānat hunāk firqa mūsīqiyya 'arabiyya 'ala l-aqall?

lūsī: lā. mā kānat hunāk firqa mūsīqiyya. istama'nā ilā 'amr diyāb.

nādya: 'amr diyāb? fi l-kāsit ya'nī?

lūsī: na'am.

nādya: a takallamti bi l-lahja l-lubnāniyya?

lūsī: Tab'an. takallamtu ma'a kull al-'ālam: ma'a ibn khāl munā, wa bint 'ammatiha wa jaddat al-'arīs. Sirtu mithl al-bilbul.

Nadia: Good morning, Lucy.

Lucy: Good morning, Nadia. Hello.

Nadia: Hello to you. Welcome. Come in. How was the wedding yesterday?

Lucy: Oh, Nadia, I had a lot of fun. I met the groom's family. His mother is a doctor and his father owns a company.

Nadia: So, they must have spent a lot of money on the wedding.

Lucy: Yes, indeed. We ate a lot of tasty foods like tabouli, kibbe, and sweets.

Nadia: And what did you drink?

Lucy: Pepsi and tea.

Nadia: Only? ... Pepsi is a cheap drink, and so is tea (*lit.*, tea also) ... And tabouli is an ordinary dish, like kibbe... Was there at least a band playing Arabic music?

Lucy: No, there was no music band. We listened to Amr Diyab.

Nadia: Amr Diyab? On a cassette, right?

Lucy: Yes.

Nadia: Did you speak the Lebanese dialect?

Lucy: Of course, I spoke to everyone: to Muna's male cousin and her female cousin and to the groom's grandmother. I was like a nightingale.

B. Writing and Pronunciation

1. USING *tanwīn*

As mentioned in Lesson 3, in more formal Arabic, indefinite nouns end in -*n*. The -*n* follows one of the three short vowels, *fatHa, kasra,* or *Damma*: -*an,* -*in* or -*un*. These different endings are indicated in writing by doubling the sign of the short vowel. The resulting symbols are called *tanwīn* in Arabic. Two *fatHas* (˝) stand for the ending -*an*, as in:

كَثِيراً *kathiran* (very much, a lot)

Two *kasras* (ٍ) stand for the ending *-in*, as in:

كَثِيرٍ *kathirin* (numerous, following a preposition)

Two *Dammas* (ٌ) stand for *-un*, as in:

كَثِيرٌ *kathirun* (numerous, when modifying a subject)

tanwin is not normally used in print because the endings *-an, -in,* and *-un* are not usually pronounced in speech, except in fixed and adverbial expressions like *shukran, jiddan,* or *tab'an.* The only exception is the ending *-an,* which is regularly noted in print on nouns that end in a consonant. When such nouns take *-an,* the letter *alif* needs to be added to their end to carry the *fatHa tanwin* (ً). So, while the *tanwin* is not usually marked in print, the "extra" *alif* always is.

In the dialogue, you encountered several nouns that have the additional *alif*:

كَثِيراً *kathiran* (very much, a lot)

أَهْلاً *ahlan* (hello)

أَهْلاً وَسَهْلاً *ahlan wa sahlan* (hello and welcome)

جِدّاً *jiddan* (very)

طَبْعاً *Tab'an* (of course)

كَثِيراً *kathiran* (very much), جِدّاً *jiddan* (very), and طَبْعاً *Tab'an* (of course) are used as adverbs. In fact, one of the main functions of the *fatHa tanwin* in today's language is to form adverbs from nouns. In these adverbs, *-an* is always fully pronounced and the additional *alif* is obligatory even if the *tanwin* is not normally noted.

2. ELISION

In Arabic speech, it is common for certain sounds to be dropped, or elided, when words are tied together in fluent pronunciation.

If a word preceding the definite article ends in a vowel, the initial "hamzated" *'a* of the definite article *'al* is dropped in speech (but not in writing) and the article is pronounced *l,* as in:

في الْبَيْت
fi l-bayt
in the house

Note that *fi* is also usually shortened in connected speech to *fi,* with a short vowel.

The elision of 'a takes place regardless of the actual form of the article, as in:

وَالشَّاي

wa sh-shāy

and tea (lit., and the tea)

The same can happen with other words starting in "hamzated" vowels when they are preceded by words ending in vowels. In the following example, the "hamzated" 'i is dropped in speech (but not in writing).

مَا اسْمُكِ؟

mā-smuki?

What's your name (f.)?

C. Grammar and Usage

1. BASIC SENTENCE STRUCTURE IN ARABIC

As in English, in Arabic sentences normally consist of a subject (an actor about whom information is provided in the sentence) and a predicate (the portion of the sentence providing information about the subject). Predicates can be verbs, nouns, adjectives, or adverbs. If the predicate is a verb, it normally comes first in the sentence. It is followed by the subject, which in turn is followed by any other element of the sentence, such as an object, adverb, etc. For example:

كَانَت الْحَفْلَة أَمْس.

kānat al-Hafla ams.

The party took place yesterday. (lit., was the party yesterday)

كَانَتْ هُنَاك فِرْقَة موسيقيَّة.

kānat hunāk firqa mūsīqiyya.

There was a music band. (lit., was there a music band)

أَكَلَت نادية التَّبُّولة أَمْس

akalat nādya t-tabūla ams.

Nadia ate tabouli yesterday. (lit., ate Nadia tabouli yesterday)

تَكَلَّمَت نادية كَثيراً

takallamat nādya kathīran.

Nadia spoke a lot. (lit., spoke Nadia a lot)

If the predicate is an adjective, a noun, or an adverb, the subject must come first in the sentence, and the predicate follows it. You have encountered many such sentences in the previous three lessons, for example:

أَنا أَمْريكِيَّة.

anā amrīkiyya.

I am American. (lit., I American)

كَمَال هُنَا.

kamāl hunā.

Kamal is here. (*lit.,* Kamal here)

أَنْتَ فِي لِيبِيا.

anta fī lībiyā.

You are in Libya. (*lit.,* you in Libya)

Sentences beginning with a noun or a pronoun are called "nominal sentences," and those beginning with a verb are called "verbal sentences." Both will be discussed further in Lessons 5 and 6.

2. THE POSSESSIVE CONSTRUCTION

In the English phrase *the family of the groom,* the noun *the family* is the possessed, or the property, and *the groom* is the possessor, or the owner. The preposition *of* marks this possessive relationship between the two nouns. English has another, more common way of expressing possession, *the groom's family.* In Arabic, the possessive construction, also called *iDāfa*, is similar to the *of*-construction in English. Look at the examples from the dialogue; the possessor noun is underlined.

أَهْل الْعَرِيس

ahl al-'arīs

the groom's family (*lit.,* family the groom)

والِدَة الْعَرِيس

wālidat al-'arīs

the groom's mother (*lit.,* mother the groom)

جَدَّة الْعَرِيس

jaddat al'arīs

the groom's grandmother (*lit.,* grandmother the groom)

اِبْن خال مُنَى

ibn khāl munā

Muna's maternal cousin (m.) (*lit.,* maternal cousin Muna)

صاحِب شَرِكة

SāHib sharika

a company's owner (*lit.,* owner a company)

As you can see by looking at the examples and the literal translations, the possessive relationship between two nouns is expressed through word order in Arabic: the possessed noun comes first, and the possessor noun comes second (or last in the sequence if the first item consists of more than one word). There are no special prepositions or endings marking this possessive relationship.

Notice a few other important features of the possessive construction:

The first noun in a possessive construction never has an article. Only the possessor noun, underlined in the preceding examples, carries an article. The whole phrase is considered definite or indefinite based on the definiteness of the possessor noun.

While the first noun, the possessed, does not carry an article in a definite possessive phrase, it is still considered definite and never carries the final -n of indefinite nouns.

If the first noun, the possessed, is feminine and ends in ة *tā' marbūTa*, the ة –*t*, being followed by another word, is fully pronounced, as in the second and third examples above (*wālidat, jaddat*).

3. PERFECT TENSE

A. ENDINGS AND VERB FORMS
There are two main tenses in Arabic: the perfect tense and the imperfect tense. We will discuss the imperfect tense in Lesson 6.

The perfect tense describes completed actions and events, usually situated in the past. It can be translated into English with the simple past tense (e.g., *I went*) or the present perfect tense (e.g., *I have gone*).

The perfect tense is formed by adding endings, or suffixes, to the perfect tense stem of the verb. The suffixes, listed in the table below, indicate the person, number, and gender of the doer of the action.

THE PERFECT TENSE SUFFIXES					
Singular		**Plural**		**Dual**	
I	-t(u)	we	-nā		
you *(m.)*	-t(a)	you *(m.)*	-tum	you two *(m.)*	-tumā
you *(f.)*	-ti	you *(f.)*	-tunna	you two *(f.)*	
he	-(a)	they *(m.)*	-ū	they two *(m.)*	-ā
she	-at	they *(f.)*	-na	they two *(f.)*	-atā

Note that a different ending corresponds to every personal pronoun. Only the dual ending -*tumā* is used with both masculine and feminine *you two*. The ending -*ū* has a silent *alif* in Arabic script: او. The parentheses around the vowels in -*t(a)*, -*t(u)*, -*(a)* indicate that these vowels are optional and are usually not pronounced in spoken Modern Standard Arabic.[1] In this course, we will follow this norm, both in writing and in pronunciation of the native speakers on the recordings.

As with personal pronouns, those forms that are most commonly used are in the shaded fields. In less formal usage, the masculine plural forms are often used instead of the feminine plural and dual forms.

---

[1] Note that these vowels are always present when other endings, such as object pronoun suffixes, to be discussed in Lesson 6, are added to the verb.

Here are the perfect tense forms of the verb شَرِب *sharib* (to drink). The perfect tense endings listed above are added to the stem شَرِب *sharib-*.

THE PERFECT TENSE OF THE VERB شَرِب *sharib* (TO DRINK)					
Singular		**Plural**		**Dual**	
أنا I	شَرِبْتُ *sharib-t(u)*	نَحْنُ we	شَرِبْنا *sharib-nā*		
أنْتَ you *(m.)*	شَرِبْتَ *sharib-t(a)*	أنْتُم you *(m.)*	شَرِبْتُم *sharib-tum*	أنْتُما you two *(m.)*	شَرِبْتُما *sharib-tumā*
أنْتِ you *(f.)*	شَرِبْتِ *sharib-ti*	أنْتُنَّ you *(f.)*	شَرِبْتُنَّ *sharib-tunna*	أنْتُما you two *(f.)*	شَرِبْتُما *sharib-tumā*
هُوَ he	شَرِبَ *sharib-(a)*	هُم they *(m.)*	شَرِبوا *sharib-ū*	هُما they two *(m.)*	شَرِبا *sharib-ā*
هِيَ she	شَرِبَت *sharib-at*	هُنَّ they *(f.)*	شَرِبْنَ *sharib-na*	هُما they two *(f.)*	شَرِبَتا *sharib-atā*

The *he* form, شَرِب *sharib-a,* is considered the simplest and most basic form of the Arabic verb, because it is minimally altered. Without the final -*a*, it also serves as a perfect tense stem to which endings for all other persons are added. In an Arabic dictionary, as in the glossary at the end of this book, all verbs are cited in the *he* form. While it is translated there with an English infinitive (e.g., *to drink*), that form does not exist in Arabic.

Note that the *I* and *you* (m.) forms are the same, once the final vowels -*u* and -*a* are dropped.

Here is another verb, أكَل *akal* (to eat), also used in the dialogue, conjugated in the perfect tense.

THE PERFECT TENSE OF THE VERB أَكَل *akal* (TO EAT)

Singular		Plural		Dual	
أنا I	أَكَلْتُ akal-t(u)	نَحْنُ we	أَكَلْنا akal-nā		
أَنْتَ you (m.)	أَكَلَتَ akal-t(a)	أَنْتُم you (m.)	أَكَلْتُم akal-tum	أَنْتُما you two (m.)	أَكَلْتُما akal-tumā
أَنْتِ you (f.)	أَكَلَتِ akal-ti	أَنْتُنَّ you (f.)	أَكَلْتُنَّ akal-tunna	أَنْتُما you two (f.)	أَكَلْتُما akal-tumā
هُوَ he	أَكَلَ akal-(a)	هُم they (m.)	أَكَلُوا akal-ū	هُما they two (m.)	أَكَلا akal-ā
هِيَ she	أَكَلَت akal-at	هُنَّ they (f.)	أَكَلْنَ akal-na	هُما they two (f.)	أَكَلَتا akal-atā

The same perfect tense personal endings are used for all Arabic verbs. However, some verbs may have more than one stem. One of these verbs is the verb كان *kān* (was/were), presented below. The two stems are كُن *kun-*, used with *I, you* singular, *we*, and *you* plural forms, and كان *kān-*, used with *he, she*, and *they* forms.

THE PERFECT TENSE OF THE VERB كَان *kān* (WAS/WERE)

Singular		Plural		Dual	
أنا I	كُنْتُ kunt(u)	نَحْنُ we	كُنَّا kunnā		
أَنْتَ you (m.)	كُنْتَ kunt(a)	أَنْتُم you (m.)	كُنْتُم kuntum	أَنْتُما you two (m.)	كُنْتُما kuntumā
أَنْتِ you (f.)	كُنْتِ kunti	أَنْتُنَّ you (f.)	كُنْتُنَّ kuntunna	أَنْتُما you two (f.)	كُنْتُما kuntumā
هُوَ he	كَانَ kān(a)	هُم they (m.)	كانوا kānū	هُما they two (m.)	كانا kānā
هِيَ she	كَانَتْ kānat	هُنَّ they (f.)	كُنَّ kunna	هُما they two (f.)	كانَتا kānatā

B. AGREEMENT BETWEEN THE SUBJECT AND THE VERB

As mentioned above, the Arabic verb expresses the person, number, and gender of the doer of the action. For instance, we can tell that the subject of the sentence below is the plural and masculine *you*, just by looking at the verb ending.

وَمـاذا شَرِبْتُم؟

wa mādhā sharibtum?

And what did you *(m., pl.)* drink?

In Arabic, a group consisting of both women and men is considered masculine in terms of agreement, so the above sentence could be referring either to men only or, as in this lesson's dialogue, to a group of men and women. Here's another example:

أَكلْنَ أَكَلات كَثيرَة.

akalna akalāt kathīra.

They *(f.)* ate a lot of food. *(lit., they ate many dishes)*

Because the verb expressess the person, gender, and number of the subject, the subject pronoun is optional.

In the following example, the subject is not an implied pronoun but a noun phrase, *Lucy and Muna*. When the verb precedes the subject noun, as it normally does in formal Modern Standard Arabic, it agrees with the subject in gender and person, but not the number. Therefore, the verb below is in the *she*, rather than *they (f.)*, form. Contrast this verb form to the one used in the previous example.

أَكلت لوسي ومنى أَكلات كثيرة.

akalat lūsī wa munā akalāt kathīra.

Lucy and Muna ate a lot of food.

C. NEGATION OF SENTENCES IN THE PERFECT TENSE

Arabic uses different negative particles to form negative statements, depending on the tense of the verb. In the perfect tense, the negative particle مـا *mā* (not) is placed in front of the verb. For example:

مـا كانَت الْحَفْلَة أَمْس.

mā kānat al-Hafla ams.

The party was not yesterday.

مـا تَعَرَّفْتُ عَلَى أَهْل الْعَريس.

mā ta'arraftu 'ala ahl al-'arīs.

I did not meet the groom's family.

مـا صَرَفوا ليرات كَثيرَة.

mā Sarafū lirāt kathīra.

They did not spend a lot of money.

ما شَرِبْنا الْبِيبْسي.

mā sharibnā l-bibsī.

We did not drink Pepsi.

ما كانَتْ هُناك فِرْقَة موسيقيَّة.

mā kānat hunāk firqa mūsīqiyya.

There wasn't a music band.

ما تَكَلَّمْتِ باللَّهْجَة اللُّبْنانِيَّة.

mā takallamti bi l-lahja l-lubnāniyya.

You *(f.)* did not speak in the Lebanese dialect.

لَم *lam* is a more formal way to negate a sentence in the perfect tense. Note that, when *lam* is used, the verb takes the imperfect tense form, while still indicating a past action.

لَمْ أَتَعَرَّفْ على أَهْل العَريس.

lam at'arraf 'ala ahl al-'arīs.

I did not meet the groom's family.

لَمْ نَشْرَب البِيبْسي.

lam nashrab l-bibsi.

We did not drink Pepsi.

4. AGREEMENT BETWEEN NOUNS AND ADJECTIVES

In Arabic, unlike in English, adjectives always follow a noun. For example:

أَكَلات كَثيرَة وطَيِّبَة جِدّاً

akalāt kathīra wa Tayyiba jiddan.

many tasty dishes (*lit.,* dishes many and tasty very)

In addition, an adjective always agrees with a noun in number, gender, definiteness, and case.[1] Note that when the noun is definite, i.e., preceded by the definite article ال *al*, the adjective must also be definite. When the noun is feminine, the adjective carries the feminine ending -*a(t)* as well. All nouns below are singular, as are the adjectives that agree with them.

مَشْروب رَخيص

mashrūb rakhīS

a cheap *(m.)* drink *(m.)*

الْمَشْروب الرَّخيص

al-mashrūb ar-rakhīS

the cheap drink (*lit.,* the drink the cheap)

---

[1] Refer to Lesson 15 to learn more about case in Arabic.

أَكْلَة رَخيصة

akla rakhīSa

a cheap (f.) dish (f.)

اللَّهْجَة اللُّبْنانيَّة

al-lahja l-lubnāniyya

the Lebanese dialect (*lit.,* the dialect the Lebanese)

D. Vocabulary

تَفَضَّلي *tafaDDalī!*	Come in!
كانَت *kānat*	she was
حَفْلَة *Hafla*	party
أَمْس *ams*	yesterday
اِنْبَسَطْتُ *inbasaTtu*	I had fun (Lebanese)
كَثيراً *kathīran*	a lot
تَعَرَّفْتُ عَلَى *ta'arraftu 'alā*	I met (someone)
أَهْل *ahl*	family
عَريس *'arīs*	the groom
والِدَة *wālida*	mother
والِدُهُ *wāliduhu*	his father
صاحِب شَرِكَة *SāHib sharika*	a company owner
صَرَفوا عَلَى *Sarafū 'ala*	they spent on
فُلوس *fulūs* (f.)	money
كَثيرَة *kathīra*	many
أَكَلْنا *akalnā*	we ate
أَكَلات *akalāt*	food(s), dishes
طَيِّبَة *Tayyiba*	delicious, tasty, good
جِدّاً *jiddan*	very
مِثْل *mithl*	like

تَبّولة *tabbūli*	tabouli (a Lebanese salad)
كِبّة *kibbi*	kibbe meatballs (Lebanese)
حَلَوَيّات *Halawayyāt*	sweets
شَرِبْتُم *sharibtum*	you drank *(pl.)*
البِيبْسي *al-bibsī*	Pepsi
شايْ *shāy*	tea
فَقَطْ *faqaT*	only
مَشْروب *mashrūb*	drink
رَخيص *rakhīS*	cheap
أَكْلَة *akla*	dish
عادِيَّة *'ādiyya*	ordinary
هُناك *hunāk*	there; there is/are...
فِرْقَة *firqa*	band
موسيقِيَّة *mūsīqiyya*	musical
عَلَى الأَقَلّ *'ala l-aqall*	at least
اِسْتَمَعْنا إلَى *istama'nā ilā*	we listened to
كاسيت *kāsit*	cassette
تَكَلَّمْتِ *takallamti*	you *(f.)* spoke
مَعَ *ma'a*	with
كُلّ *kull*	all
العالَم *al-'ālam*	the world; *here:* the people (very informal)
ابْن خال *ibn khāl*	cousin (*lit.*, the son of the maternal uncle)
بِنْت عَمَّتِها *bint 'ammatiha*	her cousin (*lit.*, the daughter of her paternal aunt)
جَدَّة *jadda*	grandmother
صِرْتُ *Sirtu*	I became
البُلْبُل *al-bulbul*	the nightingale

E. Cultural Note

The relations among even distant family members of an Arab family are very intimate. Relatives usually visit each other once or twice a week, discuss personal problems, and provide many favors for—and expect many favors from—each other. As a result, the Arabic language is more specific in identifying the different family members. For example, an aunt on the maternal side is خالَة khāla, while an aunt on the paternal side is عمَّة 'amma. The maternal uncle is خال khāl, whereas the paternal uncle is عَمّ 'amm. Cousins are specified as being the sons or the daughters of one of four family members—a paternal uncle, a paternal aunt, a maternal uncle, or a maternal aunt. Because of this, eight different Arabic words translate the English word *cousin*:

PATERNAL		MATERNAL	
Uncle	Aunt	Uncle	Aunt
بِنْت عَمّ bint 'amm	بِنْت عَمَّة bint 'amma	بِنْت خال bint khāl	بِنْت خالَة bint khāla
إِبْن عَمّ ibn 'amm	إِبْن عَمَّة ibn 'amma	إِبْن خال ibn khāl	إِبْن خالَة ibn khāla

F. Exercises

1. Put the verbs in parentheses in the correct perfect tense form.

Example: كَيْف (كان) الْحَفْلَة؟
كَيْف كانَتْ الْحَفْلَة؟

1.. سامِر ما (شَرِب) الْبيبْسي

2.. نادْيَة (شَرِب) الشَّاي / أمْس

3.؟ هَلْ (أَكَلَ + انْتُمْ) التَّبّولة في لُبْنان

4.؟ يا مُنَى، أَ (تَكَلَّمْ) باللَّهْجَة التّونِسيَّة في تونِس

5.؟ أنا وَبِنْت خالَة لوسي (انْبَسَط) كَثيراً في الْحَفْلَة. وأنْتُمْ، هَلْ (انْبَسَط) أَيْضاً

2. Translate the following sentences into Arabic.

a. Samir met the groom's father.

b. Lucy's mother is a doctor at the university hospital.

c. The dish was very tasty and I ate a lot.

d. Did you *(m.)* drink only Pepsi?

e. We listened to a music band.

3. Match the words in the column A with the right words in column B to form meaningful phrases or sentences.

A

وَسَهْلاً
رَخيصَة
عَرَبِيَّة
طَيِّب
الْخَيْر
كَثيراً
عَمّ
السوريَّة

B

أَكْلَة
مَشْروب
بِنْت
حَفْلَة
انْبَسَطوا
أَهْلاً
اللَّهْجَة
صَباح

4. Put the words in the correct order to create sentences. Then translate the sentences into English.

a. ما– هُناك– كانَ– سوري– دُكْتور.

b. أُسْتاذ– مَكْتَب– أَحْمَد– الْجامِعَة– الْعَرَبِيَّة– في– في– بَيْروت.

c. كانَت– بِنْت– ما– عَمّ– أَحْمَد– شَرِكَة– صاحِبَة.

d. الْبيبْسي– طَيِّب– مَشْروب.

e. مَعَ– تَكَلَّمْتِ– أَهْل– الْعَريس– هَلْ؟

Answer Key

1. a. شَرِب sharaba (Samir didn't drink the Pepsi.)

b. شَرِبَت sharibat (Nadya drank the tea yesterday.)

c. أَكَلْتُمْ akaltum (Did you (pl.) eat tabouli in Lebanon?)

d. تَكَلَّمْتِ takallamti (Muna, did you speak Tunisian dialect in Tunisia?)

e. انْبَسَطْنا inbasaTnā; انْبَسَطْتُمْ inbasaTtum (Lucy's and my cousin had a lot of fun at the party. And you, did you also have fun?)

2. a. سامِر تَعَرَّفَ عَلَى والِد الْعَريس.

b. والِدَة لوسي دُكْتورَة في مُسْتَشْفَى الْجامِعَة.

c. كانَتْ الأَكْلَة طَيِّبَة جِداً وأَكَلْتُ كَثيراً.

d. هَلْ شَرِبْتَ الْبيبْسي فَقَط؟

e. اسْتَمَعْنا إِلَى فِرْقَة موسيقيَّة.

3. a. أَكْلَة عَرَبِيَّة (an Arab dish)

b. مَشْروب طَيِّب (a tasty drink)

c. بِنْت عَمّ (a female paternal cousin)

d. حَفْلَة رَخيصَة (a cheap party)

e. انْبَسَطوا كَثيراً (they had a lot of fun)

f. أَهْلاً وَسَهْلاً (hello and welcome)

g. اللَّهْجَة السوريَّة (the Syrian dialect)

h. صَباح الْخَيْر (good morning)

4. a. ما كانَ هُناك دُكْتور سوري.
There was no Syrian doctor.

b. مَكْتَب الأُسْتاذ أَحْمَد في الْجامِعَة الْعَرَبِيَّة في بيروت.

The office of Professor Ahmad is at the Arab University in Beirut.

c. ما كانَت بِنْت عَمّ أَحْمَد صاحِبَة شَرِكَة.

Ahmad's cousin was not a company owner.

d. الْبيبْسي مَشْروب طَيِّب.

Pepsi is a tasty drink.

e. هَلْ تَكَلَّمْتِ مَعَ أَهْل الْعَريس؟

Did you (f.) speak with the groom's family?

LESSON 5

(Modern Standard Arabic)

مُقابَلة شَخْصِية

muqābala shakhSīyya An Interview

A. Dialogue

Donald Harrris, Lucy's husband, is being interviewed for a job with an oil company in Cairo.

المُهَنْدِس مُحَمَّد: المُهَنْدِس دُونالْد، في رَأْيِك، ما أَهَمّ مُؤَهِّلاتك لِلْعَمَل في شَرِكَتِنا؟

المُهَنْدِس دُونالْد: أهمّ مُؤَهِّلاتي هي العَمَل في شَرِكَة أرامكو السَعُودِيَّة.

المُهَنْدِس مُحَمَّد: طَبْعاً شَرِكَة أرامكو مِنْ الشَرِكات المَعْرُوفة، مِنْ المُؤَكَّد أنَّكَ تَعَلَّمْتَ الكَثير في هَذِهِ الشَرِكة.

المُهَنْدِس دُونالْد: نَعَمْ، اكْتَسَبْت الكَثير مِنْ الخِبْرَة، وتعَلَّمتُ اللُغَة العَرَبِيَّة.

المُهَنْدِس مُحَمَّد: ما هِيَ الجامِعَة الَّتي دَرَسْتَ فيها الهَنْدَسة؟

المُهَنْدِس دُونالْد: جامِعَة كولومْبيا.

المُهَنْدِس مُحَمَّد: وماذا فَعَلْتَ بَعْدَ التَخَرُّج؟

المُهَنْدِس دُونالْد: عَمِلتُ بِشَرِكَة بِتْرول في فِنِزويلا، ثُمَّ ذَهَبْتُ للسَعُودِيَّة للعَمَل في شَرِكة أرامْكو.

المُهَنْدِس مُحَمَّد: كَمْ عاماً عَمِلْتَ في فِنِزويلا والسَعُودِيَّة؟

المُهَنْدِس دُونالْد: عَمِلتُ في فِنِزويلا عاماً واحِداً وفي السَعُودِيَّة ثَلاثَة أعْوام اكْتَسَبْت خِلالَها خِبْرَة كَبيرَة.

المُهَنْدِس مُحَمَّد: مِنْ المُؤَكَّد أنَّكَ تَتَحَدَّث العَرَبِيَّة جيِّدًا!

المُهَنْدِس دُونالْد: ليسَت عَرَبيِّتي جيِّدَة جِدًّا، كانَ العَمَل يَأْخُذ مُعْظَم وَقْتِي عِنْدَمَا كُنْتُ في السَعُودِيَّة ولَكِن عِندي المَزيد مِن الوَقْت الآن.

al-muhandis muHammad: al-muhandis dūnald, fi ra'yik mā ahamm muahhilātak li l-'amal fi sharikatinā?

al-muhandis dūnald: ahamm mu'ahhilātī hiya l-'amal fi sharikat arāmku s-sa'ūdiyya.

al-muhandis muHammad: Tab'an sharikat arāmkū min ash-sharikāt al-ma'rūfa, min al-mu'akkad annaka ta'allamt al-kathīr fi hadhihi sh-sharika.

al-muhandis dūnald: na'am, iktasabt al-kathīr min al-khibra wa ta'allamt al-lughat al-'arabiyya.

al-muhandis muHammad: mā hiya al-jāmi'a allatī darast fiha al-handasa?[1]

al-muhandis dūnald: jami'at kulumbiya.

al-muhandis muHammad: wa mādha fa'alt ba'd at-takharruj?

al-muhandis dūnald: 'amilt bi sharikat bitrūl fi finizwīlā, thumma dhahabt li s-sa'ūdiyya li l-'amal fi sharikat arāmkū.

al-muhandis muHammad: kam 'āman 'amilt fi finizwīlā wa s-sa'ūdiyya?

al-muhandis dūnald: 'amilt fi finizwīlā 'ām wāHid wa fi s-sa'ūdiyya thalāthat a'wām. iktasabt khilālahā khibra kabīra.

al-muhandis muHammad: min al-mu'akkad annak tataHaddath al-'arabiyya jayyidan!

al-muhandis dūnald: laysat 'arabiyatī jayyidatan jiddan, kān al-'amal ya'khudh mu'Zam waqtī 'indama kunt fi s-sa'ūdiyya wa-lākin 'indi l-mazīd min al-waqt al-ān.

Engineer Mohamad: Engineer Donald, in your opinion, what is your most important qualification for the work in our company?

Engineer Donald: My most important qualification is the work in Saudi Aramco Company.

Engineer Mohamed: Of course, Aramco is one of the most well-known companies. Certainly, you learned a lot in that company.

Engineer Donald: Yes, I gained much experience, and I learned Arabic.

Engineer Mohamed: At which university did you study engineering?

Engineer Donald: Columbia University.

Engineer Mohamed: And what did you do after graduation?

Engineer Donald: I worked in a petroleum company in Venezuela, then I went to Saudi Arabia to work for Saudi Aramco.

Engineer Mohamed: How many years did you work in Venezuela and Saudi Arabia?

Engineer Donald: I worked for one year in Venezuela and for three years in Saudi Arabia. I gained much experience.

Engineer Mohamed: You certainly speak Arabic well!

Engineer Donald: My Arabic is not very good; work took up most of my time when I was in Saudi Arabia. But I have more time now.

B. Grammar and Usage

1. NOMINAL SENTENCES

It was mentioned in Lesson 4 that there are two main types of sentences in Arabic: nominal sentences, which begin with a noun or another word that is not a verb, and verbal setences, which begin with a verb. The nominal sentence below begins with the underlined noun phrase شَرِكة أرامْكو *sharikat arāmkū* (the Aramco company).

---

[1] *fiha* (at it) stands for *fi* (in) + *hiya* (she).

شَرِكَة أرامكو مِنْ الشَرِكَات المَعْرُوفة.

sharikat arāmkū min ash-sharikāt al-ma'rūfa.

The Aramco Company is among the well-known companies.

The following verbal sentence begins with the verb عَمِلتُ *'amiltu* (I worked).

عَمِلتُ في فِنِزويلا

'amiltu fi finizwilā.

I worked in Venezuela.

In this lesson, we will concentrate on nominal sentences. You will learn more about verbal sentences in Lesson 6.

A. SUBJECT-FIRST NOMINAL SENTENCES

A noun or a pronoun that begins a nominal sentence must always be definite. It is common for nominal sentences to begin with a subject noun or phrase, when it is definite, e.g., المُهَنْدِس *al-muhandis* (the engineer). Pronouns are always definite and often begin a nominal sentence, e.g., أنَا *ana* (I). Other definite elements, often found at the beginning of nominal sentences, are proper names, e.g., دونالد *dūnald* (Donald), possessive phrases, e.g., شَرِكَة أرامكو *sharikat arāmkū* (the Aramco company), and nouns with possessive suffixes, e.g., ابْني *ibnī* (my son).

Many Arabic nominal sentences are so-called equational sentences, where the predicate describes the subject in some way. These sentences have a present tense meaning, as in the following example:

المُهَنْدِس طَويل.

al-muhandis Tawīl.

The engineer is tall. (*lit.*, the engineer tall)

Note that the predicate is an adjective, agreeing with the subject noun in number and gender (masculine singular), but not in definiteness, as no article precedes it. It is important to distinguish a nominal sentence (e.g., *The engineer is tall*) from a definite noun-adjective phrase (e.g., *the tall engineer*). The best way to distinguish the two is to look at definiteness: in a nominal sentence, the subject and the adjective (which is part of the predicate) don't agree in definiteness; in a noun-adjective phrase, they always do. Because the noun and the adjective are both definite in the example below, we know this is a noun-adjective phrase.

المُهَنْدِس الطَويل

al-muhandis aT-Tawīl.

the tall engineer (*lit.*, the-engineer the-tall)

The following example is also a noun-adjective phrase because it has an indefinite noun, which is not allowed in nominal sentences.

مُهَنْدِس طَوِيل

muhandis Tawil

a tall engineer (*lit.*, engineer tall)

When the predicate of a nominal sentence is also a definite noun, and hence, agrees with the subject noun in definiteness, a subject pronoun is inserted before the predicate to distinguish this construction from the definite noun-adjective phrase illustrated above. For example, in the sentence below, the pronoun هُوَ *huwa* (he) is inserted because the predicate noun is definite.

دونالد هُوَ المُدِير

dūnald huwa al-mudīr

Donald is the director. (*lit.*, Donald he the director)

The predicate of a nominal sentence can also be a prepositional phrase or an adverb.

أَنَا في المَكْتَب.

anā fi l-maktab.

I am in the office. (*lit.*, I in the office)

كَمَال هُنَا.

kamāl hunā.

Kamāl is here. (*lit.*, Kamal here)

Finally, the predicate of a nominal sentence can be a verb or a verb followed by its object.

اِبْنِي حَصَل عَلى شِهَادَة البكالوريوس.

Ibnī HaSal 'ala shihadat al-bakaloriūs.

My son <u>received</u> his B.A. (*lit.*, My son, he received the B.A.)

Remember that when the verb follows the subject noun, it agrees with the subject noun in gender, person, <u>and</u> number (see Lessons 4 and 6 for other types of subject-verb agreement).

B. PREDICATE-FIRST NOMINAL SENTENCES

As mentioned earlier, only definite elements can begin a nominal sentence. When the subject of a nominal sentence is indefinite, the word order in the sentence must change, so another definite element begins a sentence. For example:

في المَكْتَب مُدَرِّس.

fi l-maktab mudarris.

There is a teacher in the office. (*lit.*, in the office a teacher)

This is a very common and useful type of sentence structure, which is equivalent to English sentences introduced by *there is…/there are…*. Here's another example:

عَلى المَكْتَب قَلَم.

'ala l-maktab qalam.

There is a pen on the desk. (*lit.*, on the desk a pen)

Another way to construct *there is…/there are…* sentences in Arabic is by starting a sentence with هُنَاكَ *hunāk* (there).

هُنَاكَ مُدَرِّس في المَكْتَب.

hunāk mudarris fi l-maktab.

There is a teacher in the office.

هُنَاكَ قَلَم عَلى المَكْتَب.

hunāk qalam 'ala l-maktab.

There is a pen on the desk.

Notice the order of the words following هُنَاكَ *hunāk*: first the subject, then the predicate. Because it doesn't begin the sentence, the subject here can be indefinite as well as definite.

C. NEGATION OF NOMINAL SENTENCES

Nominal sentences are negated with the verb لَيْسَ *laysa* (am not/is not/are not), which is conjugated to match the subject. *laysa* is usually at the beginning of a sentence.

خالِد طالِب.	لَيسَ خالِد طالِباً.[1]
khālid Tālib.	*laysa khālid Tālib(an).*[1]
Khaled is a student.	Khaled is not a student.
أَصْدِقاؤنا رِجال أَعْمال.	لَيسَ أَصْدِقاؤنا رِجال أَعْمال.
asdiqā'unā rijāl a'māl.	*laysa asdiqā'unā rijāl a'māl.*
Our friends are businesspeople.	Our friends are not businesspeople.
أَنا مُدَرِّس.	لَسْتُ مُدَرِّساً.
ana mudarris.	*lastu mudarris(an).*
I am a teacher.	I am not a teacher.

The following table includes all forms of لَيْسَ *laysa*. Note that while it is conjugated in the perfect tense, لَيْسَ *laysa* refers to a present action or state (see examples above). As before, the more commonly used forms are in shaded boxes.

---

[1] The predicate noun that follows لَيسَ *laysa* ends in -*an*, marked by a *tanwīn* in writing. This case ending, discussed further in Lesson 15, is usually dropped in MSA, but can be pronounced in more formal situations.

CONJUGATION OF لَيْسَ laysa (AM NOT/IS NOT/ARE NOT)					
Singular		Plural		Dual	
أَنا I	لَسْتُ lastu	نَحْنُ we	لَسْنا lasnā		
أَنْتَ you (m.)	لَسْتَ lasta	أَنْتُم you (m.)	لَسْتُم lastum	أَنْتُما you two (m.)	لَسْتُما lastumā
أَنْتِ you (f.)	لَسْتِ lastī	أَنْتُنَّ you (f.)	لَسْتُنَّ lastunna	أَنْتُما you two (f.)	لَسْتُما lastumā
هُوَ he	لَيْسَ laysa	هُم they (m.)	لَيْسوا laysū	هُما they two (m.)	لَيْسا laysā
هِيَ she	لَيْسَت laysat	هُنَّ they (f.)	لَسْنَ lasna	هُما they two (f.)	لَيْسَتا laysatā

لَيْسَ في المَكْتَب مُدَرِّس

laysa fi l-maktab mudarris.

There is no teacher in the office. (*lit.*, not in the office a teacher)

لَيْسَ هُناك قَلَم عَلَى المَكْتَب

laysa hunāk qalam 'ala l-maktab.

There is no pen on the desk. (*lit.*, not there a pen on the desk)

Remember that when an equational sentence in the perfect tense, which always contains the verb كان *kān(a)*, needs to be made negative, the negative particle ما *mā* is used.

ما كُنْتُ مُدَرِّساً.

mā kuntu mudarris(an).

I was not a teacher.

ما كانَ أَصْدِقاؤُنا رِجال أَعْمال.

mā kān(a) asdiqā'unā rijāl a'māl.

Our friends were not businesspeople.

2. COMMON PREPOSITIONS

The following table lists several common prepositions.

COMMON PREPOSITIONS		
فِي	fi	in
عَلى	'ala	on, at
مِنْ	min	from
إلى	'ila	to, toward
عَنْ	'an	about
بِـ	bi	with, by means of
لِـ	li	for
مَعَ	ma'a	with
عِنْد	'ind	at
فَوْق	fawq	above
تَحْت	taHt	under
أمـام	amām	in front of

3. POSSESSIVE SUFFIXES

In English, ownership over an item can be expressed by adding possessive adjectives *my, your, his, her,* etc. in front of the noun, e.g., *my book*. In Arabic, possessive endings or suffixes are attached to the noun instead.

In the following examples, the owner, named in the examples on the left, is replaced by a possessive suffix in the examples on the right:

زَوْجَة دونالد
zawjat dūnald
Donald's wife

زَوْجَتُهُ
zawjatuhu
his wife

صَديق دونالد ولوسي ونادية
Sadiq dūnald wa lūsi wa nādya
Donald's, Lucy's, and Nadia's friend

صَديقُهُم
Sadiquhum
their friend

A complete set of Arabic possessive suffixes is given in the following table. Again, the more commonly used endings are in the shaded boxes.

POSSESSIVE SUFFIXES

Singular		Plural		Dual	
my	-ī	our	-nā		
your (m.)	-ka	your (m.)	-kum	your (m.)	-kumā
your (f.)	-ki	your (f.)	-kunna	your (f.)	
his	-hu	their (m.)	-hum	their (m.)	-humā
her	-hā	their (f.)	-hunna	their (f.)	

Here is the word صَديق *Sadīq* (friend, *m.*), with possessive suffixes attached to it.

صَديقي *Sadīqī* (my friend)	صَديقنا *Sadīqunā* (our friend)	
صَديقكَ *Sadīquka* (your [m.] friend)	صَديقكُم *Sadīqukum* (your [m.] friend)	صَديقكُما *Sadīqukumā* (your friend)
صَديقكِ *Sadīquki* (your [f.] friend)	صَديقكنَّ *Sadīqukunnā* (your [f.] friend)	
صَديقه *Sadīquhu* (his friend)	صَديقهم *Sadīquhum* (their [m.] friend)	صَديقهُم *Sadīquhumā* (their friend)
صَديقها *Sadīquhā* (her friend)	صَديقهنَّ *Sadīquhunna* (their [f.] friend)	

Note that the endings -ka and -ki can be pronounced as -k when a noun ends in a consonant, e.g., مُؤَهِّلاتك *mu'ahhilātak* (your qualifications) used in the dialogue.

When possessive suffixes are added to nouns ending in ة, usually those of the feminine gender, this letter is pronounced and changes to an open ت in writing:

صَديقَة + ي = صَديقتَي
Sadīqa(t) + ī = Sadīqatī
my friend (f.)

Finally, notice that the vowel -u- is added to the masculine noun before the possessive suffix is attached (except in the *my* form). This vowel is a nominative case ending and can change to -a- or -i- depending on the role the noun has in the sentence. The topic of nominal case will be covered in more detail in Lesson 15.

4. SAYING *TO HAVE* IN ARABIC

A. *TO HAVE* IN THE PRESENT: لِ *li*, عِنْدَ *'inda*, AND مَعَ *ma'a*

There is no verb in Arabic that is equivalent to the English verb *to have*. Instead, Arabic uses a construction consisting of a preposition plus the possessive suffix to express the same meaning. In the next example, the preposition لِ *li* (for, to) is combined with the possessive ending ـه *-hu*, yielding the form *lahu*, with the literal meaning of "to him."

دونالد لَه وَظيفَة

dūnald lahu waDHifa.

Donald has a job. (*lit.*, Donald <u>to him</u> a job)

Three different prepositions are used to express possession in this manner: لِ *li* (for, to), عِنْدَ *'inda* (with, at, around), and مَعَ *ma'a* (with).[1] Note how the possessive suffix changes to match the person, number, and gender of the subject.

لَهُ وَلَد.

lahu walad.

He has a son.

لَها وَلَد.

lahā walad.

She has a son.

لَهُمْ وَلَد.

lahum walad.

They *(m.)* have a son.

The following table shows the three prepositions with all the different possessive suffixes.

---

[1] There is also a fourth preposition in this group—لَدَى *ladā*, which is used in more formal writing and speech.

	لِ lī		عِنْدَ 'inda		مَعَ ma'a	
SAYING *TO HAVE*: PREPOSITIONS WITH POSSESSIVE SUFFIXES						
I	لي	lī	عِنْدي	'indī	مَعي	ma'i
we	لنَا	lanā	عِنْدنا	'indanā	مَعَنا	ma'anā
you (m.)	لكَ	laka	عِنْدكَ	'indaka	مَعَكَ	ma'aka
you (f.)	لكِ	laki	عِنْدكِ	'indaki	مَعَكِ	ma'aki
you (m. pl.)	لكُم	lakum	عِنْدكُم	'indakum	مَعَكُم	ma'akum
you (f. pl.)	لكَنَّ	lakunna	عِنْدكُنَّ	'indakunna	مَعَكُنَّ	ma'akunna
you (m. du.)	لكُما	lakumā	عِنْدكُما	'indakumā	مَعَكُما	ma'akumā
he	لَهُ	lahu	عِنْده	'indahu	مَعَه	ma'ahu
she	لَها	lahā	عِنْدها	'indahā	مَعَها	ma'ahā
they (m.)	لَهُم	lahum	عِنْدهُم	'indahum	مَعَهُم	ma'ahum
they (f.)	لَهُنَّ	lahunna	عِنْدهُنَّ	'indahunna	مَعَهُنَّ	ma'ahunna
they (du.)	لَهُما	lahumā	عِنْدهُما	'indahumā	مَعَهُما	ma'ahumā

There are slight differences in how the three prepositions are used to express possession:

لِ *lī* is used when referring to owning abstract things (e.g., dreams, hopes, experience, etc.) or people (e.g., a wife, a son, a friend, etc.).

لي صَديقان.
lī Sadiqān.
I have two friends.

لي خِبْرَة.
lī khibra.
I have experience.

عِنْدَ 'inda is used for people, like لِ lī is, but also expresses ownership over an object (e.g., house, car, etc.), as well as something that is not in the general vicinity of the owner.

عِنْدي خَمْسَة جُنَيْهات في البَنْك.

'indī khamsat junaihāt fi l-bank.

I have five pounds in the bank.

مَعَ ma'a usually refers to having something on your person.

مَعي خَمْسة جُنَيْهات.

ma'ī khamsat junaihāt.

I have five pounds (with me).

Possessive sentences in the imperfect tense are negated with لَيْسَ laysa.

لَيْسَ لي صَديق

laysa lī Sadīq.

I don't have a friend.

B. *TO HAVE* IN THE PAST

To express *to have* in the past, the verb كان kān (was/were) is used in conjunction with the possessive prepositions لِ lī, عِنْدَ 'inda, or مَعَ ma'a.

كانَ مَعي قَلَم.

kān(a) ma'ī qalam.

I had a pen. (*lit.*, was with me a pen)

Notice that كان kān is in the *he* form to agree with قَلَم qalam (pen), which is the subject of the sentence (cf., *A pen was with me*).

As usual, negate كان kān using ما mā.

ما كانَ مَعي قَلَم.

mā kāna ma'ī qalam.

I did not have a pen.

C. Vocabulary

مُهَنْدِس muhandis	engineer
رَأْيَك ra'yak	your opinion
ما mā	what?; that which

أَهَمّ (هامّ) ahamm (hāmm)	most important (important)
مُؤَهِّلاتك (مُؤَهِّل) mu'ahilātak (mu'ahil)	your qualifications (qualification)
أرامكو السَعُودِيَّة arāmkū as-sa'ūdiyya	Saudi Aramco
سَعُودِي sa'ūdī	Saudi Arabian
مِن min	from, among
مَعْرُوف ma'rūf	well-known
مِنْ المُؤَكَّد أنَّ min al-mu'akkad anna...	it is certain that...
تَعَلَّمْت (عَلَّم) ta'allamt ('allam)	you learned
هَذِهِ hādhihi	this (f.)
اكْتَسَبْت iktasabt	I gained
خِبْرَة khibra	experience
الَّتِي allatī	which, that which (f.)
دَرَسْت darast	you studied
هَنْدَسَة handasa	engineering
فَعَلْت fa'alt	you did
بَعْدَ ba'd(a)	after
تَخَرُّج takharruj	graduation
بِتْرُول bitrūl	petroleum
فِنِزويلا finizwīlā	Venezuela
ثُمَّ thumma	then; so
ذَهَبْتُ dhahabtu	I went
السَعُودِيَّة as-sa'udiyya	Saudi Arabia
كَمْ kam	how many
عام (عاماً، أَعْوام) 'ām ('āman, a'wām)	year(s)

88

تَتَحَدَّث (تَحَدَّث)	tataHaddath (taHaddath)	you speak (you spoke)
لَيْسَت	laysat	(she) is not
كانَ	kān(a)	was
يَأخُذَ (أخَذَ)	ya'khudh (akhadh)	he takes (he took)
مُعْظَم	mu'DHam	most, the majority
وَقْت	waqt	time
عِنْدَمَا	'indama	when
عَلِم	'alim	to learn

SUPPLEMENTAL VOCABULARY: OCCUPATIONS		
رَجُل أعْمال	rajul a'māl	businessman
طالِب (طُلَّاب)	Tālib (Tullāb)	student(s)
طَبيب (أطِبَّاء)	Tabīb (aTibbā')	physician
مُدَرِّس	mudarris	teacher
مُدير	mudīr	manager, director
مُمَرِّض	mumarriD	nurse
مُوَظَّف	muwaDHDHaf	employee

Here is Donald's resume.

دونالد هاريس

٢٥ شارِع النَبي دانيال، الأَشْرَفِيَّة، بَيْروت.

التعْليم:

- دُكْتوراه في الهَنْدَسَة الكيمْيائيَّة من جامِعَة كولومْبيا (1999)
- جامعة كولومبيا جامعة مشهورة في الولايات المتحدة الأمريكية.
- ماجِسْتير في الكيمياء مِن جامِعَة أوهايو (1992)
- ليسانْس في التاريخ مِن جامِعَة أوهايو (1990)

الخِبرَة:

- مُهَنْدِس في شَرِكَة أرامْكو السعوديَّة (2004–2001)
- كُنْت مُوَظَّفاً في قِسْم التَنْقيب والإنْتاج.
- مُساعِد مُدير شَرِكَة أناداركو لِلْبِتْرول (2001–2000)
- شَرِكَة أناداركو لِلبِتْرول هِيَ شَرِكَة مَعْروفَة في فِنِزويلا.
- مُدَرِّس مُساعِد في جامِعَة أوهايو (1999–1994)
- كُنْت مُدَرِّساً في قِسْم الهَنْدَسَة.
- نادِل في مَقْهَى ستارْباكس (1990–1998)
- هِيَ شَرِكَة أمْريكِيَّة كَبيرَة تَعَلَّمْت فيها الكْثير عَن العلاقات العامَّة.

Donald Harris
25 Al-Nabbi Daniel St.
Al-Sharafiyya, Beirut

Education
Columbia University, Chemical Engineering, Ph.D. (1999)
Columbia University is a famous university in the U.S.
University of Ohio, Chemistry, MS (1992)
University of Ohio, History, BA (1990)

Experience
Engineer, Saudi Aramco (2001–2004)
I was employed in the department of exploration and production.
Assistant to the General Manager, Anadarko (2000–2001)
Anadarko is a well-known company in Venezuela.
Assistant Professor, University of Ohio (1999–1994)
I was an instructor in the Chemistry Department.
Starbucks Coffee – coffee bartender (1988–1990)
It is a big American company. I learned a lot there about public relations.

D. Cultural Note

The rules of communication are more formal in the Arab world than they are in the United States. For instance, it is still common to use a title in front of a person's name. The title المُهَنْدِس *al-muhandis* (engineer) is used to address engineers in much of the Arab world, similar to the use of the title *doctor* in English, indicating the high prestige that this profession carries.

Note that the person's title is usually followed by the first name, rather than the last name. This is because in many parts of the Arab world, the naming system is genealogical: Most people have only one given name, which is their first name, and take their father's name as a second name and their grandfather's name as a third name, which in turn can be followed by the larger family or tribal name. For example, Lebanon's former prime minister's name is Rafiq Al-Hariri, where Al-Hariri is the family or tribal name. If an individual is named after his father, his first and second names will be the same, as in the case of Boutros Boutros Ghali, the former Egyptian Secretary General of the United Nations.

Often, family names are passed down from a prominent ancestor. For instance, the son of Mohamad Al-Fayad, the Egyptian owner of Harrod's, is known as Imad Al-Fayad and not Imad Mohamad. In many Arab countries, such family names may not be used in official documents, which often ask specifically for the father's and grandfather's first names.

The tradition of genealogical naming is also responsible for the frequent presence of *ibn* or *bin* in Arabic names, especially in the countries of the Arabian Gulf. *bin* is a version of اِبْن *ibn*, meaning "son of." For example, this lesson's author's name, in its full form, may be written as أَحمد اِبْن فِكْري اِبْن مُحَمَّد اِبْن اِبْراهيم *ahmad ibn fikrī ibn muhammad ibn ibrahīm*, meaning "Ahmed son of Fekry son of Mohamed son of Ibrahim." In the Egyptian usage, this can be reduced to Ahmed Fekry Mohamed Ibrahim or more often, simply, Ahmed Fekry. However, this short version of the name is not sufficiently unique for official documents.

E. Exercises

1. Match the subject in column A with the correct predicate in column B to form complete sentences.

A	B
أنا	دَوْلَة¹ عربية
كولومْبيا²	دونالد مُعْظَم وَقته
أرامْكو³	في السَعُودِيَّة.
السعودِيَّة	جامِعَة مَعْروفة
أخَذ عَمِل	شَرِكة سَعودِيَّة كَبيرَة

---

¹ *Dawla* means "country."

² A feminine noun because it refers to a feminine noun *jāmi'a* (university).

³ A feminine noun because it refers to the feminine noun *sharika* (company).

91

2. Turn the sentences you put together in Exercise 1 into the perfect tense using the verb كان *kān*.

3. Turn the following nominal sentences into negative sentences using لَيْسَ *laysa*.

a. أرامْكو شَرِكَة مَعْروفة.

b. أنا مُدير الشَرِكة.

c. هِيَ مِن جامِعَة القاهِرَة.

d. هما طالِبان في الجامِعَة الأمْريكِيّة بالقاهِرَة.

e. هنَّ مُدَرِّسات في جامِعَة دِمَشْق.

4. Look at Donald's résumé, preceding section D, above. Identify each underlined item as either a possessive construction, a complete sentence, or a noun-adjective phrase.

Example: possessive construction – جامِعَة كولومْبيا

5. Fill in the blanks with an appropriate word from the list below.

وَقْت / واحِد / شَرِكَة / المُؤَكَّد - التَخَرُّج

a. أرامْكو _____ سَعودِيَّة مَعْروفة.

b. العَمَل يَأخُذ مُعْظَم _____ دُونالد.

c. _____ عَمِلتُ في فنزويلا عامًا.

d. اِكْتَسَبْت الكَثير مِنْ الخِبْرَة بَعْدَ _____ مِن جامِعَة كولومْبيا.

e. مِنْ _____ أنَّ مُؤَهِّلات دُونالد كَثيرة.

Answer Key

1. السعودية دَوْلَة عَرَبِيَّة.
as-sa'ūdiyya dawla 'arabiyya.
Saudi Arabia is an Arab country.
أخَذَ عَمَل دونالد مُعْظم وَقْتِه.
akhadh 'amal dūnald muDHam waqtihi.
Donald's work took most of his time.
كولومْبيا جامِعَة مَعْروفة.
kulumbia jāmi'a ma'arūfa.
Columbia is a well-known university.
أرامْكو شَرِكَة سعودِيَّة كَبيرَة.
aramku sharika sa'ūdiyya kabira.
Aramco is a large Saudi Arabian company.

أنا في السَعُودِيَّة.
ana fi s-sa'ūdiyya.
I am in Saudi Arabia.

2. كانَت السعودِيَّة دَوْلَة عَرَبِيَّة.
kānat as-sa'udia dawla 'arabiyya.
Saudi Arabia was an Arab country.
كان عمل دونالد يأخُذ معظم وقته.
kān 'amal dūnald ya'khudh muDHam waqtihi.
Donald's work used to take most of his time.
كانَت كولومْبيا جامِعَة مَعْروفة.
kānat kulumbia jāma'a ma'rūfa.
Columbia was a well-known university.

92

كانت أرامكو شَرِكة سعودِيَّة كبيرَة.

kānat arāmku sharika sa'udiyya kabīra.

Aramco was a large Saudi Arabian company.

كُنْت في السَعُودِيَّة.

kunt fī s-sa'ūdiyya.

I was in Saudi Arabia.

3. a. ليست أرامكو شركة معروفة.

laysat aramku sharika ma'rūfa.

Aramco is not a well-known company.

b. لستُ مدير الشركة.

lastu mudīr ash-sharika.

I am not the company director.

c. ليست من جامعة القاهرة.

laysat min jāma'at al-qāhira.

She's not from Cairo University.

d ليسا طالبين في الجامعة الأمريكية بالقاهرة.

laysā Tālibayn fil-jāmi'a al-amrīkīyya bi l-qāhira.

They are not students at the American University in Cairo.

e لسنَ مدرسات في جامعة دمشق.

lasna mudarrisāt fi jāma'at damashq.

They (f. pl.) are not teachers at the University of Damascus.

4. الهندسة الكيميائية

al-handasa al-kimiā'iyya = noun-adjective (chemical engineering)

جامعة كولومبيا جامعة مشهورة.

jāmi'at kulumbia jāmi'a mashhūra. = complete sentence (Columbia University is a famous university.)

قسم التنقيب

qism at-tanquib = possessive construction (Department of Exploration)

مساعد مدير

musā'id mudīr = possessive construction (assistant director)

كنت مدرسا في قسم الهندسة.

kuntu mudarris(an) fi qism al-handasa. = complete sentence (I was a teacher in the Department of Engineering.)

شركة أمريكية كبيرة

sharika amrīkia kabīra (a big American company) = noun-adjective phrase

5. a. أرامكو شَرِكة سَعُودِيَّة مَعْرُوفَة.

arāmku sharika sa'ūdiyya ma'rūfa.

Aramco is a well-known Saudi Arabian company.

b العَمَل يأخُذُ مُعْظَم وَقت دونالد.

al-'amal ya'khudh mu'DHam waqt dūnald.

Work takes up most of Donald's time.

c عَمِلتُ في فنزويلا عاما واحدا.

'amilt fi finizwilā 'ām waHid.

I worked in Venezuela for a year.

d اِكْتَسَبْت الكَثير مِنْ الخِبرَة بَعْدَ التَخَرُّج مِن جامِعَة كولومبيَا.

iktasabt al-kathīr min al-khibra ba'd at-takharruj min jāmi'at kūlumbiā.

I gained a lot of experience after graduation from Columbia University.

e مِنْ المؤكَّد أنَّ مُؤهِّلات دونَالد كَثيرة.

min al-mu'akkad anna mu'ahhilāt dūnald kathīra.

It is certain that Donald's qualifications are many.

LESSON 6

(Modern Standard Arabic)

جوَاز السَفَر مِنْ فَضْلِك.

jawāz as-safar min faDlik. Your Passport, Please.

A. Dialogue

Lucy is taking a trip to Cairo to meet Donald. She is at the Cairo International Airport.

لوسي:‏ مِنْ فَضْلِك، أَيْنَ صالَة الحَقَائِب؟

مُوَظَّف في المَطار:‏ صالَة الحَقَائِب في نِهايَة هَذا المَمَّر إلى اليَمين.

لوسي:‏ هَلْ تَعْرِف مَتى تَصِل الحَقَائِب؟

مُوَظَّف في المَطار:‏ في العادَة، تَصِل الحَقَائِب هُنا بَعْدَ نِصْف ساعَة مِنْ وُصول المُسافِرين.

مُوَظَّف الجوازات:‏ مَرْحَباً بِكِ في القاهِرة، جوَاز السَفَر مِنْ فَضْلِك.

(Looking at her passport). ما سَبَب زِيارَتِك للقاهِرَة؟

لوسي:‏ السِّياحَة.

مُوَظَّف الجوازات:‏ رِحْلَة طَيِّبَة.

لوسي:‏ شُكْراً، مَعَ السَلامَة.

Lucy goes to the information office.

لوسي:‏ مِنْ فَضْلِك، كَيْفَ أَذهَب إلى فُنْدُق هيلْتون؟

مُوَظَّف الاسْتِعْلامات:‏ مِنْ المُمْكِن أَنْ تَأْخُذي التاكْسي أَو الحافِلَة. لا يَسْتَخْدِم المِصريُّون العَدَّاد، سَتَكون الأُجْرَة خَمْسين جُنَيْهاً.

لوسي:‏ وكَمْ ثَمَن الحافِلَة؟

مُوَظَّف الاسْتِعْلامات:‏ الحافِلَة تُكَلِّف جُنَيْهَيْن.

لوسي:‏ شُكْراً جَزيلاً.

lūsī: min faDlik, ayna Sālat al-Haqā'ib?

muwaaf fi l-maTār: Sālat al-Haqā'ib fī nihāyat hādha al-mamarr ilā al-yamīn.

lūsī: hal ta'rif mata taSil al-Haqā'ib?

muwaaf fi l-maTār: fi l-'āda, taSil al-Haqā'ib hunā ba'da niSf sā'a min wuSūl al-musāfirīn.

muwaaf al-jawāzāt: marHaban biki fi l-qāhira. jawāz as-safar min faDlik. (He looks at her passport.) mā sabab ziyāratiki li l-qāhira?

lūsī: as-siyāHa.

muwaDHDHaf al-jawāzāt: riHla Tayyiba.

lūsī: shukran, ma'a as-salāma.

lūsī: min faDlik, kayfa adhhab ila funduq hiltun?

muwaDHDHaf al-isti'lamāt: min al-mumkin an ta'khudhi t-tāksī aw al-Hāfila. lā yastakhdim al-miSriyyūn al-'addād, sa-takūn al-'ujra khamsīn junayhan.

lūsī: wa kam thaman al-Hāfila?

muwaDHDHaf al-isti'lamāt: al-Hāfila tukallif junayhayn.

lūsī: shukran jazīlan.

Lucy: Where is the baggage claim, please?

Airport Worker: The baggage claim is at the end of this corridor on the right.

Lucy: Do you know when the bags are arriving?

Airport Worker: Usually the bags arrive a half-hour after the passengers.

Passport Official: Welcome to Cairo. Your passport, please. (Looks at her passport.) What is the purpose of your visit to Cairo?

Lucy: Tourism.

Passport official: Have a nice trip.

Lucy: Thank you, good-bye.

Lucy: How do I get (*lit.*, go) to the Hilton hotel, please?

Information desk attendant: You can take a taxi or a bus. Egyptians don't use the meter, but the fare won't be more than fifty pounds.

Lucy: And how much is the bus?

Information desk attendant: The bus costs two pounds.

Lucy: Thank you very much.

B. Grammar and Usage

1. THE IMPERFECT TENSE

A. USES OF THE IMPERFECT

In Lesson 4, you learned that the perfect tense is used to express completed actions in the past. The imperfect tense, on the other hand, is used to refer to incomplete actions and actions taking place in the present; it is usually translated with simple present (e.g., *he reads*) or present progressive (e.g., *he is reading*) in English. For example:

أَبْحَث عَن جَوَاز سَفَرَي.

abHath 'an jawāz safirī.

I <u>am searching</u> for my passport.

تَعرف مَتى تَصِل الحَقَائِب.

ta'arif matā taSil al-Haqā'ib.

<u>You know</u> when the bags <u>are arriving</u>.

The imperfect is also used to refer to habitual actions, or actions that happen on a regular basis.

في العَادَة، تَصِل الحَقَائِب هُنا بَعْدَ نِصْف ساعَة.

fi l-'āda, taSil alHaqā'ib hunā ba'da niSf sā'a.

Normally, the bags <u>arrive</u> here after half an hour.

General truths are also expressed using the imperfect.

لا يَسْتَخْدِم المِصْريُون العَدَّاد.

lā yastakhdim al-miSriyyūn al-'addād.

Egyptians don't <u>use</u> the meter.

Similarly, the imperfect is used to ask questions about how something is generally done:

كَيفَ أَذْهَب إلى فُنْدُق هيلتون؟

kayf adhhab ilā funduq hīltun?

How do/can I get to the Hilton Hotel?

An imperfect tense verb can be preceded by the verb كان *kān* (was) to express a habitual action, a general truth, or an incomplete action in the past.

كُنْت أَخُذ تاكْسِيات وحافِلات كُل يوم.

kunt ā'khudh taksiyyāt wa Hāfilāt kull yawm.

I <u>used to take</u> taxis and buses every day.

Or:

I <u>was taking</u> taxis and buses every day.

B. IMPERFECT TENSE ENDINGS

Imperfect tense verbs are formed by adding prefixes and suffixes, listed in the following table, to the imperfect stem.

IMPERFECT TENSE PREFIXES AND SUFFIXES					
Singular		Plural		Dual	
I	a-	we	na-		
you (m.)	ta-	you (m.)	ta- ... -ūn	you two (m.)	ta- ... -ān
you (f.)	ta- ... -in	you (f.)	ta- ... -na	you two (f.)	
he	ya-	they (m.)	ya- ... -ūn	they two (m.)	ya- ... -ān
she	ta-	they (f.)	ya- ... -na	they two (f.)	

C. THE IMPERFECT STEM

Most Arabic verb stems, and indeed Arabic words in general, consist of three root consonants, e.g., k-t-b. These three consonants give the word its basic meaning, in this case the meaning of "writing." The perfect stem has the schematic form CaCaC, where C stands for any root consonant and a for the short vowel fatHa.

The schematic form of the imperfect stem is CCa/i/uC. There is no vowel between the first and the second root consonants, as marked by a sukūn (˚) in writing, and either the vowel i, the vowel i, or the vowel u can stand between the second and the third root consonants, e.g., كْتُب ktub. By adding the he form prefix ya-, we derive the imperfect tense form يَكْتُب yaktub (he writes, he is writing).

Whether the second root consonant will be followed by a, i, or u in the imperfect stem depends on the verb and is therefore best learned on a verb by verb basis. In most Arabic dictionaries, the citation of the three-letter root of the verb is followed by a transliteration of the perfect stem, in turn followed by a single vowel to indicate the short vowel of the imperfect stem. For example:

كَتَب katab (u) to write

In the following table, the verb ذَهَب dhahab (to go) is conjugated in the imperfect tense.[1]

---

[1] Only the most basic verbs, called Form I verbs, are derived in this way. The other verb forms, which behave differently, will be discussed in Lesson 7. You will learn about irregular verbs in Lesson 10.

IMPERFECT TENSE OF THE VERB ذَهَب dhahab (TO GO)

Singular		Plural		Dual	
أنا I	أَذْهَب a-dhhab	نَحْنُ we	نَذْهَب na-dhhab		
أنْتَ you (m.)	تَذْهَب ta-dhhab	أنْتُم you (m.)	تَذْهَبون ta-dhhab-ūn	أنْتُما you (m.)	تذْهَبان ta-dhhab-ān
أنْتِ you (f.)	تذْهَبين ta-dhhab-īn	أنْتُنَّ you (f.)	تذْهَبْنَ ta-dhhab-na	أنْتُما you (f.)	تذْهَبَان ta-dhhab-ān
هُوَ he	يذْهَب ya-dhhab	هُم they (m.)	يذْهَبون ya-dhhab-ūn	هُما they (m.)	يذْهَبَان ya-dhhab-ān
هِيَ she	تذْهَب ta-dhhab	هُنَّ they (f.)	يذْهَبْنَ ya-dhhab-na	هُما they (f.)	تذْهَبَان ta-dhhab-ān

Remember that subject pronouns are not necessary in Arabic, because the doer of the action can be understood from the form of the verb.

يَسْتَخْدِمون العَدَّاد.

yastakhdimūn al-'addād.

They use the meter. (*lit.*, use the meter)

D. NEGATING IMPERFECT VERBS

While a perfect tense verb is made negative by placing the negative word مـا *mā* in front of it, the negative form of an imperfect tense verb is formed by adding the negative word لا *lā* in front of it.

يَسْتَخْدِم المِصْريُّون العَدَّاد.

yastakhdim al-miSriyyūn al-'addād.

Egyptians use the meter.

لا يَسْتَخْدِم المِصْريُّون العَدَّاد.

lā yastakhdim al-miSriyyūn al-'addād.

Egyptians do not use the meter.

2. VERBAL SENTENCES

A verbal sentence is a sentence that starts with a verb. In addition to the verb, it can also include a subject noun, an object noun, and other elements. If a verbal sentence contains a subject noun, such as لوسي *lūsī* in the example below, this noun is placed right after the verb in formal MSA. Hence, the word order in a verbal sentence is *verb-subject-object-other elements.*

تَذهَب لوسي إلى فُنْدُق هيلتون

tadhhab lūsī ilā funduq hīltūn.

Lucy is going to the Hilton Hotel.

3. AGREEMENT BETWEEN THE SUBJECT AND THE VERB

The verb must agree with the subject in Arabic. This means that it takes the form that matches the subject in person, gender, and often, number.

A. NUMBER AGREEMENT

Remember that when the verb precedes the subject noun, it agrees with the noun only in gender and in person, and <u>not</u> in number.

يُسافِر الطُلَّاب إلى سَيْناء كُلّ أُسْبوع.

yusāfir aT-Tulāb ilā sinā' kull usbū'.

The students (travel) to Sinai every week.

The verb يُسافِر *yusāfir* is in the masculine singular form, while the subject noun الطُلَّاب *aT-Tulāb* is masculine and plural.

Compare this sentence with the corresponding nominal sentence below. The verb follows the subject here, and therefore must agree with it in person, gender, <u>and</u> number.

الطُلَّاب يُسافِرون إلى سَيْناء كُلّ أُسْبوع.

aT-Tulāb yusafirūn ilā sinā' kull usbū'.

The students (they) travel to Sinai every week.

Both the subject noun and the verb are in the masculine plural form.

When the subject is not mentioned, the verb agrees in gender, person, <u>and</u> number with the implied subject (here, هُم *hum* "they").

يُسافِرون إلى سَيْناء كُلّ أُسْبوع.

yusāfirūn ilā sina' kull usbū'.

They travel to Sinai every week. (*lit.*, travel to Sinai every week)

A similar rule applies to sentences containing the pronoun نَحْن *naHnu* (we). When the subject is implied, the verb is in the first person plural form.

نأخُذ أمْتِعَتَنا.

na'khudh amti'atnā.

We take our luggage.

If a subject noun follows the verb, such as أنا وجِرْجِس *'ana wa jirjis* (I and Gerges), the verb is in the singular *I* form, agreeing with the pronoun أنا *'anā.*[1]

---

[1] Notice that in Arabic, the pronoun أنا *'anā* can come first in the list.

آخذ أنا وجِرْجِس أُمْتِعَتَنا.

ākhudh anā wa jirjis imti'atnā.

Gerges and I take our luggage.

B. GENDER AGREEMENT

The verb always agrees with the subject noun in gender, whether it follows or precedes the noun. However, when the subject consists of two or more nouns, the verb agrees in gender with the noun closest to it. In the first sentence below, the verb is in the feminine form because it agrees with the female name *Mona*, which directly follows it. In the second sentence, it is masculine because it agrees with the male name *Ahmed*, which directly follows the verb in this case.

تَذَهَب مُنى وأحْمَد وتَامِر إلى أَسْوان بالقِطار.

tadhhab munā wa aHmad wa tāmir ilā aswān bi l-qiTār.

<u>Mona</u>, Ahmed, and Tamir go to Aswan by train.

يَذَهَبَ أَحْمَد وتَامِر ومُنى إلى أَسْوان بالقِطار.

yadhhab aHmad wa tāmir wa muna ilā aswān bi l-qiTār.

<u>Ahmed</u>, Tamir, and Mona go to Aswan by train.

When the subject, whether implied or expressed, refers to a group consisting of both men and women, the verb is in the masculine form.

يَذَهَبون إلى أَسْوان بالقِطار.

yadhhabūn ilā aswān bi l-qiTār

They go to Aswan by train.

C. AGREEMENT WITH NON-HUMAN SUBJECT NOUNS

A plural noun referring to a group of three or more non-human items, e.g., الحافلات *al-Hāfilāt* (buses), is treated as a singular feminine entity from the point of view of agreement. Verbs (and adjectives) that combine with a plural non-human noun take the feminine singular form.

In the following examples, the verbs تُسافِر *tusāfir* (to travel) and تُوجَد *tūjad* (to be found, to be there) are both in the feminine singular form because they agree with plural non-human subjects.

تُسافِر الحافلات المِصْرِيَّة إلى سَيْناء في المَساء.

tusāfir al-Hafilāt al-miSriyya ilā Sina' fi l-masā'.

Egyptian buses travel to Sinai in the evening.

تُوجَد حَقائِب في صالَة الوُصول.

tūjad Haqā'ib fi Sālat al-wuSūl.

There are bags in the arrival hall.

Also note that in the first example, the adjective المِصْرِيَّة *al-miSriyya* (Egyptian) is in the singular feminine form.

100

4. OBJECT PRONOUN SUFFIXES

An object noun is a word in the sentence that receives the action of the verb. For example, العَدَّاد al-'addād (the meter) is the object of the verb لا يَسْتَخْدِم lā yastakhdim (do not use) in the following sentence.

لا يَسْتَخْدِم المِصْرِيُّون العَدَّاد.

lā yastakhdim al-miSriyyūn <u>al-'addād.</u>

Egyptians do not use <u>the meter</u>.

In English, object pronouns, such as *me, him, it,* or *them,* take the place of an object noun, e.g., *Egyptians do not use <u>it</u>.* In Arabic, object pronouns are not independent words, rather, they are attached to the verb as suffixes. العَدَّاد al-'addād (the meter), in the sentence above, is replaced with the suffix ـه *-hu,* attached to the verb, in the following sentence.

لا يَسْتَخْدِمهُ المِصْرِيُّون.

la yastakhdim<u>hu</u> al-miSriūn.

Egyptians do not use <u>it</u>.

Notice that the object pronoun suffix ـه *-hu* (it) has the same form as the possessive suffix, introduced in Lesson 5. Indeed, object pronoun suffixes are the same as the possessive suffixes except in the *I* form: The possessive suffix is ي *-ī* (my), whereas the object pronoun suffix is نِي *-nī* (me).

سَيُكَلِّفُنِي التاكْسِي عِشْرِين جُنَيْهاً.

sayukallif<u>ni</u> t-taksī 'ishrīn junayh(an).[1]

The taxi will cost <u>me</u> twenty pounds.

C. Vocabulary

مِن فَضْلِك *min faDlik*	please
صَالَة الحَقَائِب *Sālat al-Haqā'ib*	baggage claim
حَقَائِب (حَقِيبة) *Haqā'ib (Haqība)*	bags (bag)
مَطَار *maTār*	airport
نِهايَة *nihāya*	end
هَذا *Hādhā*	this *(m.)*
مَمَّر *mamarr*	corridor
إلى *ilā*	to
يَمِين *yamīn*	right (side)

---

[1] The *-an* ending on this word signals that the word جُنَيْها *junayh(an)* (pound) is an object of a verb. Most of the time, this case ending can be ignored, but it is pronounced in more formal situations. You will learn more about case in Arabic in Lesson 15.

مَتَى؟ *matā?*	when?
تَصِل (وَصَل) *taSil (waSal)*	she is arriving (to arrive)
فِي العَادَة *fi l-'āda*	usually
هُنا *hunā*	here
نِصْف *niSf*	half
ساعَة (ات) *sā'a (sā'at)*	hour(s)
وُصول *wuSūl*	arrival
مُسافِرِين *musāfirīn*	travelers
جَوازات السَفَر *jawāzāt as-safar*	passports
مَرْحَباً بِكِ *marHaban biki!*	Welcome to you *(f.)*!
القَاهِرة *al-qāhira*	Cairo
سَبَب *sabab*	reason
زِيَارَة *ziyāra*	visit
سِياحَة *siyāHa*	tourism
رِحْلَة *riHla*	trip
طَيِّب *Tayyib*	good
مَعَ السَلامَة *ma'a s-salāma*	good-bye
اِسْتِعْلامات *isti'lamāt*	information *(pl.)*
مِنْ المُمْكِن أَنْ *min al-mumkin an*	it is possible that
تَأْخُذِين (أخَذ) *ta'khudhīna (akhadh)*	you take (to take)
تاكْسِي *tāksī*	taxi
أو *aw*	or
حَافِلَة *Hāfila*	bus
لا *lā*	no, not
يَسْتَخْدِم (اسْتَخْدَم) *yastakhdim (istakhdam)*	he uses (to use)
عَدَّاد *'addād*	meter
لَنْ *lan*	will not
تَزِيد (زاد) عَن *tazid (zād) 'an*	exceeds (to exceed)

أُجْرَة ujra	fare
جُنَيْه junayh	Egyptian pound
ثَمَن thaman	price
تُكَلِّف (كَلَّف) tukallif (kallaf)	it/she costs (to cost)

D. Cultural Note

Airport customs in the Arab world include restrictions similar to those applied in most of the world's airports, except that more restrictions may apply and infractions may carry higher penalties. In some countries, this is due to a history of economic protectionism: In Egypt, for example, taxes on imported items can be outrageously high, as much as 100% of the value of the product, for items like computer software. In other countries, an item may be taxed when its owner enters the country, but that amount is returned to him or her upon departure with the item in hand. Some restrictions exist as well on currency being carried into or out of the country.

Another area of concern is antiquities. The Middle East is a region rich in ancient sites and treasures. Some precious antiquities or important cultural artifacts may find their way illegally into the open market. You can be arrested for traveling with such items in your possession. A museum export certificate may be required in order for you to travel with some items, but a receipt or certificate verifying that you purchased your antiques from a reputable dealer will keep you out of trouble most of the time.

In some countries, the import of alcohol might be limited or banned completely. Such items, along with any magazines or videotapes considered to be pornographic (even though you might not consider them as such) can be confiscated upon arrival. There is also a high sensitivity to religious materials. Proselytizing is illegal in countries that claim to have Muslim leadership, as conversion from Islam is officially punishable by death. For this reason, on rare occasions, even religious materials may be confiscated. Street drugs are illegal in all countries of the Arab world and strict punishments apply. In some countries drug trafficking is even punishable by death.

E. Exercises

1. **Read this letter from a student living in Jordan to his friend in Beirut about his trip to Petra. Fill in the blanks with the appropriate imperfect forms of the verbs in parentheses.**

عزيزي رامي،

_____ (كتب) لك من البتراء لتي ذهبت إليها مع أصدقائي من الجامعة يوم الخميس.
البتراء مدينة جميلة جداً ولكن من الصعب الوصول إليها فلا _____ (أوجد) الكثير من

وسائل المواصلات العامة، ربما لأن معظم زوارها من السائحين الأجانب فلا _____ (ذهب) إليها الكثير من الأردنيين. معظم السائحين _____ (سافر) إلى بترا في عربات خاصة، أما نحن فقد قررنا أنْ _____ (أخذ) الحافلة لأنها أرخص.

أراك في بيروت الأسبوع القادم إن شاء الله.

المخلص،

مايكل

2. Change nominal sentences into verbal sentences by moving the underlined verb to the beginning of the sentence. Make any necessary changes to the verb.

a. المسافرون يأخذون جوازات السفر.

b. البنات يذهبن إلى فندق هيلتون.

c. المصريون لا يستخدمون العداد.

d. الطلاب يذهبون إلى الجامعة.

e. لوسي ودونالد يأخذان الحافلة كل يوم.

3. Replace the underlined object nouns with appropriate object pronoun suffixes.

a. تأخذ لوسي الحافلة للجامعة كل يوم.

b. لوسي وجدت البنات.

c. المصريون لا يستخدمون العداد.

d. رأيت المسافرين في المطار.

e. تتحدث لوسي اللغة العربية.

4. Complete the following sentences with appropriate vocabulary items from the list below.

جُنَيْهاً / جَوازِ سَفَرٍ/ مَتى/ أيْنَ/ بِكَ / زِيارَة / كَمْ / صالَة / جُنَيْهاً / المُمْكِن

a. _____ يَصِل المُسافِرون؟

b. _____ مكتَب الاسْتِعْلامات؟

c. مِنْ _____ أنْ تَأخُذَ الحافِلَة.

d. مَرْحَباً _____ في القاهِرة.

e. سَبَب _____ لوسي للقاهِرَة السِياحَة.

f. لا تَزيد أُجْرَة التَّاكسي عَنْ خَمْسين _____.

g. _____ ثَمَن الحافِلَة؟

h. _____ .هَذا نِهايَة في الاِستِعْلامات مكتَب

i. الحقائِب؟ _____ إلى أذهَب كَيفَ

j. _____ مَعَه مُسافِر كُلّ

Answer Key

1. أكتب aktub (agrees with أنا)

يوجد tūjad (agrees with الكثير من وسائل المواصلات)

يذهب yadhhab (agrees with الكثير من الأردنيين)

يسافرون yusāfirūn (agrees with السائحين)

نأخذ na'khudh (agrees with نَحن)

aktub lak min al-batrā' allati dhahabt ilayhā ma'a aSdiqā'ī min al-jāmi'a yawm al-khamīs. al-batrā' madīna jamīla jiddan wa lākin min aS-Sa'b al-wuSūl ilayhā falā tūjad al-kathīr min wasā'il al-muwāSalāt al-'āmma, rubbamā li'anna mu'DHam zuwwārhā min as-sā'iHīn al-ajānib falā yadhhab ilayhā al-kathīr min al-urduniyyīn. mu'DHam as-sā'iHīn yusāfirūn ila l-batra' fi 'arabāt khāSSa, ammā naHnu faqad qarrarnā an na'khudh al-Hāfila li'annahā arkhaS.

arāk fi bayrūt al-usbū' al-qādim in shā' allāh.

al-mukhliS,

maykel

I am writing to you from Petra where I traveled with my friends from the university on Friday. Petra is a beautiful town, but it is difficult to get there. There are not many means of public transportation there, perhaps because most of the visitors are foreign tourists, and few Jordanians go there. Most tourists travel to Petra by private car. As for us, we decided to take the bus because it is cheaper.

I will see you in Beirut next week, God willing.

Sincerely,

Michael

2. a. يأخذ المسافرون جوازات السفر.

ya'khudh al-musāfirūn jawāzāt as-safr.

The travelers take passports.

b. تذهب البنات إلى فندق هيلتون.

tadhhab al-banāt ilā funduq hiltun.

The girls go to the Hilton Hotel.

c. لا يستخدم المصريون العداد.

la yastakhdim al-muSriyyūn al-'addād.

Egyptians don't use the meter.

d. يذهب الطلاب إلى الجامعة.

yadhhab aT-Tulāb ila l-jāmi'a.

The students go to the university.

e. تأخذ لوسي ودونالد الحافلة كل يوم.

Ta'khudh lūsi wa dūnald al-Hāfila kull yawm.

Lucy and Donald take the bus every day.

3. a. تأخذها لوسي كل يوم.

ta'khudh-hā lūsi kull yawm.

Lucy takes it every day.

b. لوسي وجدتهن.

lūsi wajadathunna.

Lucy found them (f.).

c. المصريون لا يستخدمونه.

al-miSriyyūn lā yastakhdimūnahu.

Egyptians don't use it.

d. رأيتهم في المطار.

ra'aytuhum fi l-maTār.

I saw them in the airport.

e. تتحدثها لوسي.

tataHadathhā lūsī.

Lucy speaks it.

105

4. a. مَتَى يَصِل المُسَافِرُونَ؟

matā yaSil al-musāfirūn?

When do the travelers arrive?

b. أَيْنَ مكتب الاسْتِعْلامات؟

ayna maktab al-isti'lāmāt?

Where is the information office?

c. مِنْ المُمكِنِ أَنْ تَأخُذ الحافِلة.

min al-mumkin an ta'khudh al-Hāfila.

You can take the bus.

d. مَرْحَبا بِك في القاهِرة.

marHaban bik fi l-qāhira.

Welcome to Cairo.

e. سَبَب زِيارَة لوسي للقاهِرة هو السياحَة.

sabab ziyārat lūsī li l-qāhira huwa s-siyāHa.

The reason for Lucy's trip is tourism.

f. لا تَزِيد أَجْرَة التَّاكسي عَنْ خَمْسين جُنَيْها.

Lā tazid ujrat at-taksī 'an khamsīn junayh(an).

The cab fare isn't more than fifty pounds.

g. كَمْ ثَمَنِ الحافِلَة؟

kam thaman al-Hāfila?

How much is the bus?

h. مكتَب الاسْتِعْلامات في نِهايَة هَذا المَمَّر.

maktab al-isti'lāmāt fi nihāyat hādha l-mumarr.

The information office is at the end of this hall.

i. كَيْفَ أَذهَب إلى صالَة الحقائِب؟

kayf adh-hab ilā Sālat al-Haqā'ib?

How do I go to the baggage claim?

j. كل مُسافِر مَعَه جَواز السَفَر.

kull musāfir ma'ahu jawāz as-safir.

Every traveler has a (*lit.*, the) passport (with him or her).

LESSON 7

(Modern Standard Arabic)

في الفُندُق

fi l-funduq At the Hotel

A. Dialogue

Donald, who has been staying at the Hilton Hotel, and Lucy, who has just arrived in Cairo, are thinking of transferring to a cheaper hotel. They have crossed the Tahrir square to check out the Hotel Cleopatra.

لوسي: مِنْ فَضْلِك، هَلْ عِنْدَكُم غُرْفَة لِشَخْصَيْن؟

مُوَظَّف الاسْتِقْبال: عندنا ثَلاث غُرَف، واحِدَة فَقَط بِها حَمّام خاص.

لوسي: كَمْ سِعْر الغُرْفَة الَّتي بِها حَمّام؟

مُوَظَّف الاسْتِقْبال: مائَة جُنَيْه.

دُونالد: هَلْ مِن المُمْكِن أَنْ نَراها مِنْ فَضْلِك؟

مُوَظَّف الاسْتِقْبال: بِالطَّبْع، تَفَضَّلا مَعي.

لوسي: لِماذا لا نَسْتَخْدِم المِصْعَد؟

مُوَظَّف الاسْتِقْبال: لأَنَّه لا يَعْمَل.

Lucy and Donald are looking at the room.

لوسي: الشُّرْفَة تُطِّل عَلى مَيْدان التَّحْرير، أَسْتَطيع أَنْ أَرى المَتْحَف المِصْريّ!

دونالد: هَلْ بِها قَنَوات فَضائِيَّة؟

مُوَظَّف الاسْتِقْبال: لا، لِلأَسَف لَدَيْنا فَقَط قَنَوات التِليفِزْيون المِصْريّ.

لوسي: ما رَأيك يا دونالد؟

دونالد: الغُرْفَة جَميلَة، ولَكِنّي أَحْتاج لِلقَنَوات الفَضائِيَّة لأُشاهِد كُرَة القَدَم الأَمْريكِيَّة.

لوسي: لا أَعْرِف يَا دونالد. لَسْنا في مِصْر مِنْ أَجْل القَنَوات الفَضائِيَّة، ثُمَّ إِنَّ هَذا الفُنْدُق أَرْخَص كَثيراً مِنْ الهيلْتون.

107

lūsī: min faDlik, hal 'indakum ghurfa li shakhSayn?

muwaDHDHaf al-istiqbāl: 'indanā thalāth ghuraf, wāHida faqaT bihā Hammām khāS.

lūsī: kam si'r al-ghurfa allatī bihā Hammām?

muwaDHDHaf al-istiqbāl: mi'at junayh.

dūnald: hal min al-mumkin an narāha min faDlik?

muwaDHDHaf al-istiqbāl: bi T-Tab', tafaDDalā ma'ī.

lūsī: limādha lā nastakhdim al-miS'ad?

muwaDHDHaf al-istiqbāl: li'annahū lā ya'mal.

lūsī: ash-shurfa tuTill 'ala maydān at-taHrīr, astaTī' an ara l-matHaf al-miSrī!

dūnald: hal bihā qanawāt faDā'iyya?

muwaDHDHaf al-istiqbāl: lā, li l-asaf ladaynā faqaT qanawāt at-tilifizyūn al-miSrī.

lūsī: mā ra'yuk yā dūnald?

dūnald: al-ghurfa jamīla, wa lākinnī aHtāj li l-qanawāt al-faDā'iyya li'ushāhid kurat al-qadam al-amrīkiyya.

lūsī: la a'rif ya dūnald. lasna fī miSr min ajl al-qanawāt al-faDā'iyya, thumma inn hādha l-funduq arkhaS kathīran min al-hilton.

Lucy: Do you have a room for two people, please?

Receptionist: We have three rooms. Only one has a private bathroom.

Lucy: How much is the room with the private bathroom?

Receptionist: One hundred pounds.

Lucy: Can we see it, please?

Receptionist: Of course, please follow me.

Lucy: Why don't we use the elevator?

Receptionist: Because it doesn't work.

Lucy: The balcony looks over Tahrir Square; I can see the Egyptian Museum!

Donald: Do you (*lit.*, Does it) have satellite TV?

Receptionist: No, unfortunately we have only the Egyptian channels.

Lucy: What do you think, Donald?

Donald: The room is nice, but I need satellite TV in order to watch American football.

Lucy: I don't know, Donald. We are not in Egypt for satellite TV, and besides, this hotel is much cheaper than the Hilton.

B. Grammar and Usage

1. FORMING WORDS IN ARABIC: THE ROOT SYSTEM

A. DERIVING WORDS FROM ROOTS

You learned earlier that the different perfect and imperfect forms of an Arabic verb are derived from the root, usually consisting of three consonants, such as ك ت ب *k-t-b* (to write), by changing the vowels between the consonants and adding suffixes and prefixes.

Arabic roots serve as word skeletons from which other new words, such as nouns, adjectives, or adverbs, can be created in uniform ways. The relationship between words created from the same root is similar to the relationship between, for example, the English words *produce, produces, produced, producing, product, production, productive,* and *counterproductive.* All these words are closely related in meaning, being that they share the same root, *prod-,* but suffixes and prefixes modify the basic meaning in different ways.

In Arabic, the process of derivation of different words from the basic root is very productive, and it involves many predictable patterns. Here are some of the words derived from the root ك ت ب *k-t-b* (the act of writing); the root consonants are in boldface.

كَتَبَ *kataba* (he wrote)

تكْتُبُون *taktubūn* (you write, *m. pl.*)

مكْتَب *maktab* (office)

كِتَاب *kitāb* (book)

كاتِب *kātib* (writer)

مكْتوب *maktūb* (something written, letter; destiny)

When vowels between root consonants are changed and prefixes and suffixes are added, new words with new meanings are created. Because this process of word formation is quite systematic in Arabic, you will eventually be able to recognize the different patterns and even guess the meaning of unfamiliar derived words. You will also be able to tell the root apart from the prefixes and suffixes, which you will find helpful when using an Arabic dictionary.

B. DERIVED FORMS OF VERBS

The same principle of deriving words by adding prefixes and suffixes and changing the vowels between the root consonants is used to derive different, but related, verbs. There are ten different verb forms, and their patterns are listed in the table at the end of this section, along with examples. For instance, ذَهَبَ *dhahab* (to go) and أَذْهَب *adhhab* (to remove) are both derived from the root ذ ه ب *d-h-b.* أَذْهَب *adhhab*, which follows pattern IV, is related in a predictable way to the meaning of ذَهَب *dhahab*, following pattern I: verbs belonging to pattern IV usually mean "to cause the action expressed by the pattern I verb to be carried out." In our case, the meaning "to remove" can be understood as "to cause to go away."

While there are ten possible verb forms in theory, few roots use more than three or four of these patterns to derive different verbs, and often, the meanings of the derived verbs are not related in an immediately obvious way. Therefore, it is best that you learn verbs as separate lexical items, the way you would in English or French. However, getting acquainted with the different verbal patterns is important because verbs belonging to different patterns derive their imperfect stems in different ways.

Four commonly used patterns are discussed below.

FORM I – *CaCaC*

CaCaC is the most basic pattern that you have encountered many times so far. It is applied in the formation of the following verbs.

ذَهَب	dhahab	to go
أَخَذَ	akhadh	to take
كَتَب	katab	to write

You learned how to derive the perfect stems of these verbs in Lesson 4, and in Lesson 6, you learned how to derive their imperfect stems.

FORM III – *CāCaC*

Form III verbs always have an ا *ā* after the first root consonant, as in:

سافَرَ	sāfara	to travel
شاهَدَ	shāhada	to see

The imperfect stem of Form III verbs always follows the pattern *yu-CāCiC*.

يُسافِر	yusāfir	he travels
يُشاهِد	yushāhid	he sees

FORM V – *ta-CaCCaC*

You have already learned many verbs belonging to Form V.

تَحَدَّث	taHaddath	to talk
تَخَرَّج	takharraj	to graduate
تَعَرَّف	ta'arraf	to get to know
تَعَلَّم	ta'allam	to learn
تَكَلَّف	takallaf	to incur a cost
تَكَلَّم	takallam	to speak

Each of these verbs has a prefix تَـ *ta-*. In addition, the second root consonant is doubled, which is marked in writing with a (ّ) *shadda*. The imperfect stem vowels are the same as the vowels of the perfect stem; all short vowels are (َ) *fatHa*:

يَتَحَدَّث	yataHaddath	he talks
يَتَخَرَّج	yatakharraj	he graduates
يَتَعَرَّف	yata'arraf	he gets to know
يَتَعَلَّم	yata'allam	he learns

| يَتَكَلَّف | yatakallaf | he incurs a cost |
| يَتَكَلَّم | yatakallam | he speaks |

FORM VIII – i-CtaCaC

Form VIII verbs have a prefix اِ i- before the first letter of the root and an infix تـ -ta-
right after it. The following two verbs, both of which you have encountered in previous
dialogues, follow this pattern.

| اِكْتَسَب | iktasab | to gain |
| اِسْتَمَع | istama' | to listen |

The imperfect stem always has the pattern ya-CtaCiC.

| يَكْتَسِب | yaktasib | he gains |
| يَسْتَمِع | yastami' | he listens |

Here is the table of all ten forms with examples of perfect tense and imperfect tense
stems. Notice how the imperfect tense stem is derived differently for each verb form.

VERB FORMS I TO X					
Form	Pattern	Perfect Tense		Imperfect Tense		Meaning
I	CaCaC	كَتَب	katab	يَكْتُب	yaktub	to write
II	CaCCaC¹	غَيَّر	ghayyar	يُغَيِّر	yughayyir	to change
III	CāCaC	شاهَد	shāhad	يُشاهِد	yushāhid	to see
IV	a-CCaC	أَرْسَل	arsal	يُرْسِل	yursil	to send
V	ta-CaCCaC¹	تَكَلَّم	takallam	يَتَكَلَّم	yatakallam	to speak
VI	ta-CāCaC	تَناوَل	tanāwal	يَتَناوَل	yatanāwal	to discuss
VII	in-CaCaC	اِنْبَسَط	inbasaT	يَنْبَسِط	yanbasiT	to enjoy
VIII	i-C-ta-CaC	اِكْتَسَب	iktasab	يَكْتَسِب	yaktasib	to win
IX	i-C-Ca-CCa	اِبْيَضَّ	ibyaDDa	يَبْيَضّ	yabyaDD	to become white
X	ista-CCaC	اِسْتَخْدَم	istakhdam	يَسْتَخْدِم	yastakhdim	to use

¹ The middle root consonant is doubled in this pattern. This is rendered by a *shadda* in writing.

2. USING AN ARABIC DICTIONARY

In order to use an Arabic dictionary, you must be able to identify the root letters of the word you're looking up.[1] This requires recognizing the prefixes and suffixes added to verbs to form different tenses (see Lessons 4 and 6), the object pronoun suffixes (see Lesson 6), and the letters added to produce verb Forms IV through X.

It will help to know that only ten letters—س, ا, هـ, ي, ن, و, م, ت, ل, and ا—appear in the various prefixes and suffixes added to the roots. While these letters can also be part of the root, they should be the first ones that you suspect when trying to eliminate non-root letters. You can remember these letters if you memorize the word سألتمونيها sa'ltūmnīhā (you [pl.] asked me that), which contains all of them.

A. LOOKING UP VERBS

The citation form of a verb in a dictionary is the perfect singular masculine form of the Form I verb, e.g., كَتَبَ katab(a) (he wrote). This form, being free of prefixes and suffixes (once the final -a is dropped), is considered the simplest and most transparently representative of the root consonants.

The main citation of a verb is followed by the verb form numbers and the meanings of any other verbs derived from the same root. These additional verbs are not written out; instead, their forms need to be figured out based on the verb form numbers provided (see the table in the previous section). For example, the (somewhat simplified) citation for the verbs derived from the root letters ك ت ب k-t-b looks like this.

> كتب kataba u to write; II to make someone write; III to correspond with; IV to dictate; VI to exchange letters; VII to subscribe; VIII to make a copy of something; to be registered; X to ask someone to write something.

As you may see, conjugated forms of a verb, such as يكتُب yaktub (he writes) or تَكتُب taktub (she writes), are not included in a dictionary entry. Therefore, when you encounter a verb form in a text or in speech and want to look up its meaning, e.g., يكتُب yaktub (he writes), you need to identify the initial يَ ya- as a prefix in order to identify the first root letter (in this case ك k), by which the word is alphabetized in the dictionary.

You will also need to identify any letters added to the root to produce new verb forms. For example, if you want to look up اكْتَتَب iktatab (he made a copy), you will need to guess that it is a Form VIII verb in order to eliminate the ا and ت and discover the root letters ك ت ب.

For simplicity's sake, the glossary at the end of this book is not structured like an actual Arabic dictionary. Instead, all verbs, even when they are derived from the same root, are listed individually and ordered alphabetically, in the third person masculine perfect form. For example, look for اكْتَتَب iktatab under the letter "i" and كاتب kātab under the letter "k."

---

[1] Identifying the root letters can be tricky, especially with words in which two of the three root consonants are the same, or when one of the root letters is the vowel و, ا, or ي. We will discuss these types of roots in Lessons 13 and 14.

B. LOOKING UP NOUNS, ADJECTIVES, AND OTHER WORDS

As mentioned above, there are scores of patterns by which nouns and adjectives, with different but related meanings, can be derived from a given root. In an Arabic dictionary, these words are usually given as secondary citations following the list of verb forms. Thus, the words كِتَاب kitāb (book) and مَكْتَب maktab (office) will follow, in the order of the Arabic alphabet, the main verbal entry كتب katab, as secondary citations. Again, this requires that you learn to recognize basic nominal and adjectival patterns so that you can identify the prefixes and suffixes, in order to identify the root consonants. As with verbs, the glossary at the end of this book cites nouns, adjectives, and all other words individually and alphabetically. Thus, in an Arabic dictionary, you would need to look up the noun مَكْتَب maktab (office) under the letter ك k, for the root ك ت ب k-t-b, but you will find it under the letter m in our glossary.

Finally, in an Arabic dictionary, as in our glossary, all words not derived from a root, such as adverbs, prepositions, and borrowed words, are listed alphabetically.

3. NUMBERS ZERO TO TEN

The following table gives Arabic words for numbers zero to ten, as they are used when counting. The rightmost column lists the special numerals used in Arabic-speaking countries.[1]

ARABIC NUMBERS FROM 0 TO 10			
Number	Transliteration	Arabic Script	Arabic Numeral
zero	Sifr	صِفْر	٠
one	wāhid	واحِد	١
two	ithnān (ithnatān)[2] ithnāyn (ithnatayn)	اثْنان (اثْنَتان) اثْنَيْن (اثْنَتَيْن)	٢
three	thalātha	ثَلاثَة	٣
four	arba'a	أَرْبَعَة	٤
five	khamsa	خَمْسَة	٥
six	sitta	سِتَّة	٦
seven	sab'a	سَبْعَة	٧
eight	thamānia	ثَمانية	٨
nine	tis'a	تِسْعَة	٩
ten	'ashara	عَشَرَة	١٠

[1] These numerals are Hindi in origin. Interestingly, the numerals used in English are of Arabic origin.

[2] The number two changes according to case and gender. The forms that include a ت -t (the two forms in parentheses) are feminine. The forms that end in ان -ān are used when referring to the subject of the sentence. The forms ending in ين -ayn are used when referring to an object of a verb or an object of a preposition.

113

All numbers have masculine and feminine forms and have to agree with the noun in gender, just like adjectives. However, in counting, i.e., when used independently, the numbers *zero*, *one*, and *two* are used in their masculine forms, while the numbers *three* to *ten* are used in their feminine forms, which end in *-a* or ـة in writing. The feminine form of the number *two*, which does not follow the regular pattern, is listed in parentheses.

A. THE NUMBER *ONE*
When modifying a noun, the number واحِد *wāhid* is used only for emphasis.

هُناك ضَيْف في بَيْتِنا.

hunāk Dayf fī baytinā.

There is a/one guest at our house.

هُناك ضَيْف واحِد في بَيْتِنا.

hunāk Dayf wāHid fī baytinā

There is only one guest at our house.

B. PAIRS OF THINGS: DUAL SUFFIXES
As you learned in previous lessons, Arabic has a special way of talking about pairs of things. The noun takes on a special form, obtained by adding a dual ending. A dual ending ان *-ān* is attached to a noun that is the subject of the sentence and يَن *-ayn* is attached to a noun that is an object of a verb or a preposition. The suffix ان *-ān* is added to غُرْفة *ghurfa* (room), the subject of the nominal sentence below. When ان *-ān* or يَن *-ayn* is added to a feminine noun ending in ة, this final *t* is pronounced.

الغُرْفَتان جَميلَتان.

al-ghurfatān jamīlatān.

The two rooms are beautiful.

In the following sentence, the ending يَن *-ayn* is used to form the dual of the underlined noun شَخْص *shakhS* (person) because it follows the preposition *li* (for).

هَلْ عِنْدَكُم غُرْفة لِشَخْصَيْن؟

hal 'indakum ghurfa li shakhSayn?

Do you have a room for two people?

Here are two more examples.

عَمِلَ دونالد مع المُديرَين في ارامكو.

'amila dūnald ma'a al-mudirayn fi arāmco.

Donald worked with the two directors *(m.)* in Aramco.

عَمِلَ دونالد مع المُديرَتين في ارامكو.

amila dūnald ma'a al-mudiratayn fi arāmco.

Donald worked with the two directors *(f.)* in Aramco.

114

In spoken MSA, the dual form with يْن -ayn is commonly used regardless of the position of the noun in a sentence.

C. AGREEMENT WITH NUMBERS THREE TO TEN

When numbers three or above are used to modify a noun, a complex construction is used in Arabic, which is usually simplified in speech. There are a few simple rules that you will need to know to get by; they are introduced below. The rest of the rules related to the issue are given in Appendix I as a reference for writing.

For numbers three through ten, the number *disagrees* in gender with the plural noun.

ثَلاثة رِجال	ثَلاث بنات
thalathat (f.) *rijāl* (m. pl.)	*thalath* (m.) *banat* (f. pl.)
three men	three girls

Notice how the masculine form of the numeral is used with the feminine noun, and the feminine form of the numeral is used with the masculine noun.

4. NUMBERS 11 TO 19

The teens are formed simply by putting the ones digit before the tens digit, e.g., *arba'at 'ashara* (*lit.*, four ten). Notice that the Arabic numerals, shown in the table below, are read from left to right, just like English numbers.

ARABIC NUMBERS FROM 11 TO 19			
Number	Transliteration	Arabic Script	Arabic Numeral
eleven	aHad 'ashara	أَحَد عَشَرَ	١١
twelve	ithnān (ithnatā) 'ashara ithnāyn (ithnatay) 'ashara[1]	اثْنا (اثْنَتا) عَشَرَ اثْنَي (اثْنَتَي)	١٢
thirteen	thalāthat 'ashara	ثَلاثَة عَشَرَ	١٣
fourteen	arba'at 'ashara	أَرْبَعَة عَشَرَ	١٤
fifteen	khamsat 'ashara	خَمْسَة عَشَرَ	١٥
sixteen	sittat 'ashara	سِتَّة عَشَرَ	١٦
seventeen	sab'at 'ashara	سَبْعَة عَشَرَ	١٧
eighteen	thamāniat 'ashara	ثَمَانية عَشَرَ	١٨
nineteen	tis'at 'ashara	تِسْعَة عَشَرَ	١٩

[1] Like the number 2, the number 12 changes according to case and gender. The forms that include a ت t (the two forms in parentheses) are feminine. The forms that end in ا ā are used when referring to the subject of the sentence. The forms ending in ي ay are used when referring to an object of a verb or an object of a preposition.

AGREEMENT WITH NUMBERS 11 TO 19

The counted noun that follows numbers 11 to 19 is in the singular form. The gender agreement in the teens is tricky, because the ones digit *disagrees* with the counted noun in gender (the number three is feminine, unlike the noun, which is masculine, in the example below), whereas the tens digit *agrees* (the number ten is masculine, like the noun, in the example below):

ثَلاثَةَ عَشَرَ وَلَداً

thalāthat (f.) *'ashara* (m.) *walad(an)* (m.)[1]

thirteen boys

As in English, 11 and 12 are slightly irregular in form. The و in وَاحِد *wāHid* (one) is dropped when joined to the word عَشَر *'ashara* (ten) to form أَحَدَ عَشَر *aHad 'ashara* (eleven). The number 11 also has a feminine form, إحْدى عَشْرَة *ihdā asharata*.

أَحَدَ عَشَرَ طالِباً

ahad 'ashara Tālib(an)

eleven (male) students

إحْدى عَشْرَةَ طالِبَة

ihdā 'asharata Tāliba

eleven (female) students

Similarly, the ن *-n* is dropped from اثْنان *ithnān* (two) to form the number 12.

اثْنا عَشَرَ جَواز سَفَر

ithna 'ashara jawāz safar[2]

twelve passports

Notice that, unlike the other teen numbers, all elements in the numbers 11 and 12 agree with the counted noun in gender.

5. ASKING ABOUT QUANTITY WITH كَم *kam* AND بِكَم *bikam*

To ask about quantities, use the question word كَم *kam* (how much, how many), as in the following example.

كَمْ غُرْفَة في الفُنْدُق؟

kam ghurfa(tan) fi l-funduq?[3]

How many rooms are in the hotel?

---

[1] The *-an* at the end of the counted noun is a case ending. In spoken language, the ending is optional and rarely pronounced.

[2] The forms اثْنَي *ithnay*, اثْنَتي *ithnatay*, and اثْنَتا *ithnatā* appear in writing, so learn to recognize them. The form *ithna* is the only one you will need in speech.

[3] In formal written and spoken Arabic, the singular noun following كَم carries the accusative case ending *-an*, or in writing, the *tanwin*. This ending is not pronounced in less formal speech. For more information on case endings, see Lesson 15.

Notice that the literal translation of the Arabic sentence above is "How many room?", where the counted noun following كَمْ *kam* is in the singular form, rather than the plural form, as it would be in English. Here are other examples.

كَمْ ضَيْفاً في الفُنْدُق؟

kam Dayf(an) fi l-funduq?

How many guests are in the hotel?

كَمْ لَيْلَةً سَتَبْقَى في الفُنْدُق؟

kam layla(tan) satabqā fi l-funduq?

How many nights will you be staying at the hotel?

كَمْ مَطْعَماً في الفُنْدُق؟

kam maT'am(an) fi l-funduq?

How many restaurants are there in the hotel?

To ask about the price of something, use بِكَمْ *bi kam* (*lit.*, for how much), where the preposition بِ *bi* precedes the question word.

بِكَمْ الغُرْفَة؟

bi kam al-ghurfa?

How much is a room?

The response to *bi kam* بِكَمْ is preceded by the preposition بِ *bi* as well. For example:

بِمئَة دولار

bi mi'at dūlār.

A hundred dollars. (*lit.*, for a hundred dollar)

C. Vocabulary

غُرْفَة	*ghurfa*	room
شَخْصين	*shakhSayn*	two people
اِسْتِقْبال	*istiqbāl*	reception
وَاحِدة	*wāhida*	one (f.)
بِها	*bihā*	in it, in her
حمَّام	*Hammām*	bathroom
خاص	*khāSS*	private
سِعر	*si'r*	price
مائَة	*mi'a*	one hundred
نَراهَا (رأى)	*narāha (ra'ā)*	we see it (to see)

بِالطَبْع bi T-Tab'	of course
تَفَضَّلا tafaDDalā	if you (two) please
مَعِي ma'ī	with me
لِمَاذا limādhā?	why?
مِصْعَد miS'ad	elevator
لأنَّه li'annahu...	because it...
شُرْفَة shurfa	balcony
تُطِل (أَطَلَّ) عَلى tuTill (aTall) 'alā	it overlooks (to overlook)
مِيْدان التحرير maydān at-taHrīr	Tahrir Square (in Cairo)
أَسْتَطِيع أَنْ astatī' an	I can
أَرى (رَأى) ara (ra'ā)	I see (to see)
المُتْحَف المِصْري al-mutHaf al-miSriyy	the Egyptian Museum
قَنَوات (قَناة) فضائِيَّة qanawāt (qanāt) faDā'iyya	satellite channels (channel)
لِلأَسَف li l-'asaf	unfortunately
تِلِيفِزْيون tilifizyūn	television
رَأيك ra'yuk	your opinion (m.)
جَميلة jamīla	beautiful (f.)
أَحْتاج (أَحْتاج) aHtāj (aHtāj)	I need (to need)
أَشَاهِد (شاهَد) ushahid (shahad)	I watch (to watch)
كُرَة القَدَم kurat al-qadam	football
أَعْرِف (عَرَف) a'rif (araf)	I know (to know)
مِصْر miSr	Egypt
مِنْ أجل min 'ajl...	for the sake of...
ثُمَ إنَّ thumma inna	besides
فُنْدُق funduq	hotel
أرْخَص (رَخيص) arkhaS (rakhīS)	cheaper (cheap)

D. Cultural Note

In much of the Arab world, hotels are places where a tourist can find the kind of entertainment that is not traditionally part of local Arab culture. The best bars and nightclubs are often in large hotels, and they may also be the only places where hard liquor is available. Also, while swimming in a bathing suit is a taboo for women in many Arab countries, hotel swimming pools in cities of the same countries can be a good place to take a dip.

At the same time, there may be regulations, applying even to foreign hotel chains located in these countries, on women and men sharing a room. Married couples wishing to share a room may be asked to present a marriage certificate before securing their reservation. As a tourist, however, you will probably not be subjected to this measure.

E. Exercises

1. Look at the following perfect tense verbal forms, identify the root consonants, and determine which of the ten forms (I to X) the verb belongs to.

a. اندْفَعَ (to rush into something)

b. تقاتَل (to fight)

c. انْتَحَرَ (to commit suicide)

d. اسْتَغْرَب (to find something strange)

e. فكّرَ (to think)

f. حاوَلَ (to try)

g. أدْرَكَ (to become aware, to realize)

h. تعلَّم (to learn)

2. Read the following numbers out loud, then write the counted nouns in parentheses in the plural, singular, or dual form, as required.

a. سبعة (جنيه / جنيهات)

b. أحد عشر (قناة / قنوات)

c. اثنان (فندقان / فنادق)

d. ثلاث (غرفة / غرف)

e. اثنا عشر (شخصاً / أشخاص)

3. Fill in the blanks with the correct word.

قنَوات فَضائية / المُمْكِن / تُطِل / غُرْفَة / المِصْعَد

a. لَدَيْنا _____ واحِدَة فَقَطْ بِها حَمَّام خاص.

b. هَلْ مِن _____ أَنْ نَرى مَيْدان التَحْرير مِنْ هُنا؟

c. لِلْأَسَف _____ لا يَعْمَل.

d. الشُرْفَة _____ على مَيْدان التَحْرير.

e. هَلْ لَدَيْكم _____ أَمْ لَدَيْكُم قَنَوات التِليفِزيون المِصْري فَقَطْ؟

4. Form questions by using either كَمْ *kam* or بِكَمْ *bikam*.

a. (كم / بكم) هَذِه الغُرْفَة؟

b. (كم / بكم) يوماً سَتَقْضي في القاهِرة؟

c. (كم / بكم) ضَيْفا في الفُنْدُق ؟

d. (كم / بكم) جُنَيْها مَعَكِ؟

e. (كم / بكم) الغُرْفَة التي بِها حَمَّام خاص؟

5. Choose the correct form of the counted noun (Hint: dual or plural; masculine or feminine) from the choices in parentheses.

a. أَرْبَعَة _____ (سِعْر / أَسْعار)

b. إحْدى عَشْرَةَ _____ (مِصْعَدا / شُرْفَة)

c. تِسْع _____ (حمَّام / قَنَوات)

d. خَمْسَة عَشَرَ _____ (فُنْدُقا / فَنادُق)

e. اثْنا عَشَرَ _____ (ضَيْفا / ضَيوف)

Answer Key

1. a. Form VII, دَفَع
   b. Form VI, قتل
   c. Form VIII, نحر
   d. Form X, غرب
   e. Form II, فكر
   f. Form III, حول
   g. Form IV, درك
   h. Form V, علم

2. a. جَنَيْهات *sab'a junayhāt* seven pounds (plural form)

b. قَناة *aHad 'ashara qanā* eleven channels (singular form)

c. فُنْدُقان *funduqān* two hotels (dual form)

d. غرف *thalāth ghuraf* three rooms (plural form)

e. شَخْصا *ithnā 'ashara shakhS(an)* twelve people (singular form)

3. a. لَدَيْنا غُرْفَة واحِدة فَقط بِها حَمَّام خاص.
   ladaynā ghurfa wāhida faqaT bihā Hamām khāSS.
   We have only one room with a private bath.

b. هلْ مِنِ المُمكِنِ أنْ نَرى مَيدان التحْرير مِنْ هُنا؟

hal min al-mumkin an narā maydān at-taHrīr min hunā?

Can we see Midan al-Tahrir from here? (*lit.*, is it possible that...)

c. لِلأسَف المِصْعَد لا يَعْمَل.

li l-āsaf al-miS'ad lā ya'mal.

Unfortunately, the elevator doesn't work.

d. الشُرْفَة تُطِلّ عَلى مَيْدان التحْرير.

ash-shurfa tuTill 'alā maydān at-taHrīr.

The balcony overlooks Midan al-Tahrir.

e. هَلْ لَدَيْكُم قنَوات فَضائية أمْ لدَيْكُم قنَوات التِليفِزْيون المِصْري فقط؟

hal ladaykum qanawāt faDā'iyya, am ladaykum qanawāt at-tilifizyūn al-miSri faqaT?

Do you have satellite channels, or do you have only Egyptian TV channels?

4. a. بِكم هَذِه الغرفة؟

bi kam hādhihi l-ghurfa?

How much is this room?

b. كمْ يوماً سَتبقى في القاهِرَة؟

kam yawm(an) satabqā fi l-qāhira?

How many days will you stay in Cairo?

c. كم ضَيْفاً في الفُنْدُق؟

kam Dayf(an) fi l-funduq?

How many guests are there in the hotel?

d. كمْ جُنَيْها مَعَكِ؟

kam junayh(an) ma'ak?

How many pounds do you have with you?

e. بِكمْ الغُرْفَة (التي) بها حمّام خاص؟

bi kam al-ghurfa (l-latī) bihā Hammam khāS?

How much is the room with the private bath?

5. a. أرْبَعَة أسْعار *arba'a asa'ār* (four prices)

b. إحْدى عَشْرَة شُرْفَة *ihdā 'ashara shurfa(tan)* (eleven balconies)

c. تِسْع قنَوات *tis' qanawāt* (nine channels)

d. خَمْسَة عَشَرَ فنْدُقا *khamsat 'ashara funduq(an)* (fifteen hotels)

e. اثْنا عَشَرَ ضَيْفا *ithnā 'ashara Dayf(an)* (twelve guests)

121

SECOND REVIEW

(Modern Standard Arabic)

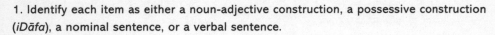

Grammar Exercises

1. Identify each item as either a noun-adjective construction, a possessive construction (*iDāfa*), a nominal sentence, or a verbal sentence.

a. الشركات المعروفة

b. تعلمت اللغة العربية في مصر.

c. جامعة كولومبيا

d. شركة بترول

e. صالة الحقائب

f. أنا أمريكي

g. لهجة لبنانية

h. رحلة طيبة

i. الحافلة تكلف جنيهين

j. لدينا غرفتان

2. Rearrange the following words to make complete sentences.

a. الغرفة / كم / سعر

b. المصري / أستطيع / أن / المتحف / أرى

c. يعمل / شركة / دونالد / أرامكو / في

d. جامعة / كولومبيا / تخرج / دونالد / من

e. من / السفر / فضلك / جواز

3. Fill in the blanks with the correct form of the verb, adjective, or the term in the possessive construction by translating the English word in parentheses.

a. الحقائب _____(arrive) بعد نصف ساعة من وصول المسافرين.

b. علي ودونالد _____(graduated) من جامعة كولومبيا.

c. اللبنانيون _____(use) العدّاد.

d. دونالد ولوسي _____(learned) الكثير عن لبنان.

e. لا _____(travel) الكثير من الأردنيين إلى البتراء.

4. Change the perfect tense verbs into imperfect tense verbs.

a. درسنا اللغة العربية في اليمن.

b. ذهبن إلى الفندق.

c. شربتُ بيبسي.

d. هل عملتما في شركة أرامكو السعودية؟

e. أخذوا الحافلة للمطار.

5. Change the imperfect tense verbs into perfect verbs.

a. يحبُّون التبولة.

b. تتحدثون اللهجة السعودية.

c. هل تدرسن في جامعة كولومبيا؟

d. لا يعمل المصعد.

e. يشاهدان القنوات الفضائية.

Vocabulary Exercises

6. Fill in the blanks with the correct word from the options given below. (Hint: Remember to apply the rules of agreement in gender, number, and person.)

مطار / صالة / الساعة / القنوات / أرخص / الحافلة / غرفة / شركة / أجرة / ألف

a. ــــــــــــــ أرامكو من الشركات المعروفة.

b. سأذهب للقاهرة ــــــــــــــ السابعة والنصف.

c. ــــــــــــــ التاكسي عشرون جنيهاً.

d. وصلت إلى ــــــــــــــ القاهرة الساعة الخامسة والنصف.

e. أخذت ــــــــــــــ إلى المطار.

f. ــــــــــــــ الوصول في نهاية هذا الممر إلى اليمين.

g. يشاهد دونالد ــــــــــــــ الفضائية.

h. هذا الفندق ــــــــــــــ من فندق هيلتون.

i. هل لديكم ــــــــــــــ بحمام؟

j. سعر الغرفة ــــــــــــــ ليرة.

7. Translate the following sentences into English.

a. أسكن في القاهرة مع صديقي.

b. تخرج دونالد من جامعة كولومبيا في عام ١٩٩٥.

c. سافرت لوسي إلى لبنان لتعمل في الجامعة الأمريكية في بيروت.

d. كان دونالد يعمل مهندساً في فنزويلا.

e. مكتب الاستعلامات في نهاية هذا الممر.

123

8. Translate the following sentences into Arabic.

a. Ahmed got his BA from the University of Ohio.

b. Gerges, Hind, and Mohammed have the same teacher.

c. My wife is a physician and my son is a nurse.

d. We traveled to the Sinai Peninsula for (the period of) one week.

e. The guests are eating in the hotel restaurant.

9. Fill in the blank with the correct word by choosing from the options given in parentheses.

a. .أتحدث اللغة العربية ـــــــــــــــــ (بلغة / بأجرة / بلهجة) لبنانية.

b. طلب (to ask for) موظف ـــــــــــــــ (الاستعلامات / الجمارك / الجوازات)
جواز السفر.

c. موظف ـــــــــــــــــــ (الاستعلامات / الجمارك / الجوازات) جواز السفر.

d. كيف أذهب إلى ـــــــــــــــ (صالة / فندق / حافلة) الحقائب؟

e. (ذهبت / وصلت / أخذت) ـــــــــــــــــــ التاكسي لمطار بيروت.

10. Think of three Arabic words belonging to each of the following categories.

a. Family members:

b. Lebanese foods:

c. Professions:

d. Means of transport:

e. Nationalities:

f. Things in a hotel:

Answer Key

1. a. noun-adjective construction
   b. verbal sentence
   c. possessive construction
   d. possessive construction
   e. possessive construction
   f. nominal sentence
   g. noun-adjective construction
   h. noun-adjective construction
   i. nominal sentence
   j. nominal sentence (with a reversed subject)

2. a. كم سعر الغرفة؟
   kam si'r al-ghurfa?
   How much is the room?

b. .أستطيع أن أرى المتحف المصري
   astaTi' an arā al-matHaf al-miSrī.
   I can see the Egyptian museum.

c. .دونالد يعمل في شركة أرامكو
   dūnald ya'mal fī sharikat arāmkū.
   Donald works for Aramco Company.

d. .دونالد تخرج من جامعة كولومبيا
   dūnald takharraj min jāmi'at kulumbiā.
   Donald graduated from Columbia University.

e. .جواز السفر من فضلك
   jawāz as-safar min faDlak.
   Passport, please.

3. a. الحقائب تصل بعد نصف ساعة من وصول المسافرين.

al-Haqā'ib taSil ba'd niSf sā'a min wusūl al-musāfirīn.

The luggage arrives half an hour after the arrival of travelers.

b. علي ودونالد تخرجا من جامعة كولومبيا.

'alī wa dūnald takharrajā min jāmi'at kulumbia.

Ali and Donald graduated from Columbia University.

c. اللبنانيون يستخدمون العداد.

al-libnāniyūn yastakhdimūn al-'addād.

The Lebanese use the meter.

d. دونالد ولوسي تعلما الكثير عن لبنان.

dūnald wa lūsī ta'allamā al-kathīr 'an lubnān.

Donald and Lucy learned a lot about Lebanon.

e. لا يسافر الكثير من الأردنيين إلى البتراء.

lā yusāfir al-kathīr min al-urduniyyīn ila l-batrā'.

Not many Jordanians travel to Petra.

4. a. ندرس اللغة العربية في اليمن.

nadrus al-lugha al-'arabiyya fi l-yaman.

We study Arabic in Yemen.

b. يذهبن إلى الفندق.

yadh-habna ila l-funduq.

They go to the hotel.

c. أشرب بيبسي.

ashrab bibsī.

I drink Pepsi.

d. هل تعملان في شركة أرامكو السعودية؟

hal ta'malān fī sharikat arāmkū s-sa'ūdiyya?

Do you work for Saudi Aramco?

e. يأخذون الحافلة للمطار.

ya'khudhūn al-Hāfila li l-maTār.

They take the bus to the airport.

5. a. أحبُّوا التبولة.

aHabbu t-tabūla.

They liked tabouli.

b. تحدثتُم اللهجة السعودية.

taHaddathtum al-lahja s-sa'ūdiyya.

You spoke the Saudi accent.

c. هل درستُنَّ في جامعة كولومبيا؟

hal darastunna fī jāmi'at kulumbiā?

Did you study at Columbia University?

d. ما عملَ المصعد.

mā 'amil al-miS'ad.

The elevator did not work.

e. شاهدا القنوات الفضائية.

shāhada l-qanawāt al-fadā'iyya.

They watched satellite channels.

6. a. شركة أرامكو من الشركات المعروفة.

sharikat arāmkū min ash-sharikāt al-ma'rūfa.

Aramco is a well-known company.

b. سأذهب للقاهرة الساعة السابعة والنصف.

sa-adh-hab li l-qāhira s-sā'a s-sābi'a wa n-niSf.

I will go to Cairo at 7:30.

c. أجرة التاكسي عشرون جنيها.

ujrat at-tāksī 'ishrūn junayhan.

The taxi fare is twenty pounds.

d. وصلت إلى مطار القاهرة الساعة الخامسة والنصف.

waSalt ilā maTār al-qāhira s-sā'a l-khāmisa wa n-niSf.

I arrived at Cairo Airport at 5:30.

e. أخذت الحافلة إلى المطار.

akhazt al-Hāfila ila l-maTār.

I took the bus to the airport.

f. صالة الوصول في نهاية هذا الممر.

Sālat al-wuSūl fī nihāyat hādha l-mamarr.

The arrival lounge is at the end of this corridor.

g. صالة الوصول في نهاية هذا الممر.

yushāhid dūnald al-qanawāt al-faDā'iyya.

Donald watches satellite channels.

h. هذا الفندق أرخص من فندق هيلتون.

hādhā al-funduq 'arkhaS min funduq hiltun.

This hotel is cheaper than the Hilton.

i. هل لديكم غرفة بحمام؟

hal ladaykum ghurfa bi-Hammām?

Do you have a room with a bath?

j. سعر الغرفة ألف ليرة.

si'r al-ghurfa 'alf lirā.

The price of the room is a thousand lira.

7. a. I live in Cairo with my friend.

b. Donald graduated from Columbia University in 1995.

c. Lucy traveled to Lebanon to work at the American University of Beirut.

d. Donald was working as an engineer in Venezuela.

e. The information desk is at the end of this corridor.

8. a. حصل أحمد على الليسانس من جامعة أوهايو.

b. لجرجس وهند ومحمد نفس المدرس.

c. تعمل زوجتي طبيبة وابني ممرض.

d. سافرنا إلى سيناء لمدة أسبوع.

e. يأكل الضيوف في مطعم الفندق.

9. a. أتحدث اللغة العربية بلهجة لبنانية.

ataHaddath al-lugha l-'arabiyya bi-lahja lubnāniyya.

I speak Arabic with a Lebanese accent.

b. طلب موظف الجوازات جواز السفر.

talab muwaDHDHaf al-jawāzāt jawāz as-safar.

The immigration officer asked for the passport.

c. كم سعر الغرفة ذات الحمام الخاص؟

kam si'r al-ghurfa dhāt al-Hammām al-khāS?

How much is a room with a bath?

d. كيف أذهب إلى صالة الحقائب؟

kayfa adh-hab ilā Sālat al-Haqā'ib?

How can I go to the luggage claim?

e. أخذت التاكسي لمطار بيروت.

akhadht at-tāksī li maTār bayrūt.

I took the taxi to Beirut Airport.

10. a. Family members:

أخ / زوجة / أخت

b. Lebanese foods:

كبة / تبولة / لَبْنة

c. Professions:

مهندس / مدرس / طبيب

d. Means of transport:

الحافلة / التاكسي / الطائرة

e. Nationalities:

مصري / لبناني / سعودي

f. Things in a hotel:

تليفزيون / شرفة / غرفة

READING PASSAGE I
(Modern Standard Arabic)

السفر في اليمن

as-safar fi l-yaman Travel in Yemen

تتوافر رحلات طيران دولية لعدد من المدن اليمنية الكبرى مثل صنعاء
وعدن، ويصل معظم زوار اليمن إلى مطار صنعاء الدولي ثم يستخدمون خطوط
الطيران المحلي للوصول إلى المدن الأخرى، لا توجد حافلات من مطار صنعاء
للمدينة، ويكلف التاكسي ١٢ دولارًا أمريكياً من المطار إلى أي مكان في صنعاء.

يستطيع المسافر أن يتنقل داخل المدن اليمنية في التاكسي والذي يكلف
حوالي دولاراً أمريكياً واحداً للمسافات القصيرة التي لا تزيد عن عشر دقائق ولا
يستخدم اليمنيون العداد. وهناك أيضاً الحافلات الصغيرة التي لا يزيد سعرها عن
١٥ سنتًا أمريكيًا سنت أمريكي للتذكرة، كما يستطيع السائح أن يؤجر سيارة
خاصة بحوالي ٥٠ دولاراً أمريكياً في اليوم الواحد. أما بالنسبة للتنقل بين المدن
الصغيرة في اليمن فيستطيع المسافر أن يستخدم وسائل النقل الجماعي الرخيصة
أو أن يؤجر سيارة خاصة تساعده على حرية الحركة في المناطق البعيدة.

توجد في اليمن سلاسل الفنادق الخمسة نجوم العالمية مثل الشيراتون والتي
يصل سعرها إلى ١٠٠ دولار للغرفة كما توجد فنادق الأربعة نجوم والتي يصل
سعر الغرفة فيها إلى ٥٠ دولاراً، كما توجد بعض الفنادق ذات الثلاثة نجوم
والنجمتين والتي يقل سعرها عن ٢٠ دولاراً.

عملة اليمن هي الريال اليمني ويتكون من ١٠٠ فلس. يستطيع المسافر أن
يغير العملة الأجنبية في أي مكتب صرافة في المدن الكبرى، ولا يوجد سعر رسمي
للدولار أو سوق سوداء، ويصل سعر الدولار إلى حوالي ١٣٠ ريال.

127

International flights are available to a number of major Yemeni cities like San'aa and Aden. Most of Yemen's visitors arrive at San'aa International Airport, then use local airlines to get to other cities. There are no buses from San'aa airport into the city, and taxis from the airport to any part of the city cost twelve U.S. dollars.

The traveler can get around Yemeni cities by taxi, which costs about one American dollar for short distances that take no more than ten minutes. Yemenis do not use a meter. There are also small buses that do not cost more than 15 American cents for a ticket. The tourist can also rent a private car for about 50 U.S. dollars per day. For travel between small cities in Yemen, the traveler can use the inexpensive public means of transportation, or rent a private car, which will allow for more freedom of movement in remote areas.

There are international five-star hotel chains in Yemen, such as the Sheraton, with prices of up to 100 dollars, as well as four-star hotels where rooms can cost as much as 50 dollars. There are also some two- and three-star hotels where prices are less than 20 dollars.

The currency of Yemen is the Yemeni rial. There are 100 fals in a rial. The traveler can exchange foreign currencies at any exchange bureau in the big cities. There is no official rate for the dollar, and no black market. The exchange rate for the U.S. dollar is about 130 Yemeni rial.

Vocabulary

اليَمَن *al-yaman*	Yemen
تَتَوافَر (تَوافَر) *tatawāfar (tawāfar)*	are available (to be available)
رِحَلات الطَّيَرَان *riHalāt aT-Tayarān*	flights
دَوْلية *dawlīya*	international
عَدَد *'adad*	number, a number of
صَنْعاء *San'ā'*	San'aa (the capital of Yemen)
عَدَن *'adan*	Aden (a city in Yemen)
زوَّار (زائر) *zuwwār (zā'ir)*	visitors (visitor)
خُطوط الطَّيران *khuTūT aT-Tayarān*	airlines
مَحَلِّي *maHallī*	local
أخْرَى *ukhrā*	others
الذي *alladhī*	which
أي *ayy*	any

مَكان makān	place
يَستطيع أن yastaTī' 'an	is able to
يَتَنَقَّل (تَنَقَّل) yatanaqqal (tanaqqal)	gets around (to get around)
داخِل dākhil	inside
حَوالي Hawālī	approximately
مَسافات masāfāt	distances
قَصيرة qaSīra	short
دَقائِق (دَقيقة) daqā'iq (daqīqa)	minutes (minute)
سَنْت sant	cent
تَذْكَرَة tadhkara	ticket
كَما kamā	similarly, as, as well
يؤَجِّر (أجَّر) yu'ajjir (ajjar)	rents, hires
أمّا بالنِسْبَة لِ... ammā bin-nisba li...	as for...
بَين bayn	between
وَسائِل (وَسيلة) النقل an-naql wasā'il (wasīla)	means of transportation
تَنَقُّل tanaqqul	transportation
جَماعي jamā'ī	public
تُساعِدُه (سَاعَد) عَلَى... tusā'idhu (sa'ada) 'alā...	helps him to...
حُرِّية Hurrīya	freedom
حَرَكة Haraka	movement
مَناطِق (مِنْطَقة) manāTiq (minTaqa)	regions
نائية nā'iya	remote
سَلاسِل فَنادِق (سِلْسِلة) salāsil fanādiq (silsila)	hotel chains (chain)
نُجوم (نَجْمة) nujūm (najma)	stars (star)
عالمية 'ālamiya	international
بَعْض ba'D	some
ذات dhāt	of, which have
يَقِل (قَل) عن yaqill (qall) 'an	to be less than

عملة 'umla	currency
أَجْنَبِية ajnabiyya	foreign
مكْتَب صِرافة maktab Sirāfa	exchange bureau
رِيال يَمَني riāl yamanī	Yemeni rial
يتكوَّن (تَكوَّن) مِن yatakawwan (takawwan) min	is made up of
فَلْس fals	penny (a unit of a Yemeni rial)
رَسْمي rasmī	official
حَصَل عَلَى HaSal 'alā	to earn, be awarded, get
ليسانْس līsans	B.A.
نَفْس nafs	the same
قَلَم (أَقْلام) qalam (aqlām)	pen(s)
شَهادَة shahāda	degree
طَويل Tawīl	tall
أُخْت (أَخَوات) ukht (akhawāt)	sister(s)
أَحَبّ aHabb	to like, to love
أَسْوان aswān	Aswan (a city in Southern Egypt)
أوجَد (يوجِد) awjad (yūjid)	to bring about
حَمَل Hamal	to carry
المَساء almasā'	evening
قِطار qiTār	train
سَيْناء saynā'	Sinai Peninsula
طائرة Tā'ira	airplane
أُسْبوع usbū'	week
بَيْت (بُيوت) bayt (buyūt)	house(s)
لَيْلة (لَيالي) layla (layāli)	night(s)
مَشَى mashā	he walked
مَطْعَم (مَطاعِم) maT'am (maTā'im)	restaurant(s)
سائحَ (سائحَون) sā'iH (sā'iHūn)	tourist(s)

LESSON 8

(Modern Standard Arabic)

بِكَم تَشْتَري الدولار؟

bikam tashtarī d-dulār? How Much Do You Buy Dollars For?

A. Dialogue

Donald is about to walk into a bank near Khan El-Khalili market in Cairo when he is approached by a black market dealer.

بائِع السُّوق السَّوْداء: هَل تُريد أن تُغَيِّر بَعْض الدُولارات؟

دونالد: نَعَم، ولكِنِّي سَأغَيِّرُها في هَذا البَنْك.

بائِع السُّوق السَّوْداء: سَوْف أدْفَع لَكَ أكْثَر مِن البَنْك.

دونالد: بِكَم تَشْتَري الدولار؟

بائِع السُّوق السَّوْداء: أدْفَع سَبْعَة جُنَيْهات لِلدولار الواحِد.

Donald checks the exchange rates in the bank.

دونالد: وَلكِن الفَرق بَيْن سِعْرِك وسِعْر صَرْف البَنْك لَن يكون كَبيراً.

بائِع السُّوق السَّوْداء: هَذا لَيْس صَحيحاً تَسْتَطيع أن تَشْتَري سِتَّة أرْغِفَة مِن الخُبْز بِهَذا الفَرْق، ما رَأْيُك؟

دونالد: لا أُريد أن أغَيِّر شُكْراً، وَلكِن لِماذا لا تُغَيِّر البُنُوك بنَفْس هَذا السِّعْر؟

بائِع السُّوق السَّوْداء: هَذا هُوَ خَطَأ الحُكُومَة الَّتي تُحاوِل أن تَتَحَكَّم في سِعْر الدُولار. هَل وَجَدْت فُنْدقاً لِتَسْكُن فيه؟

دونالد: نَعَم.

بائِع السوق السَّوْداء: أنَظِّم أيْضاً رَحَلات سَفاري في الصَّحْراء البَيْضاء، تُكَلِّف الرِّحْلَة خَمْسُمائة جُنَيه لِلفَرد. ما رَأيَك؟

دونالد: لَيْس لَدَيَّ الوَقْت الكافي هَذِه الزِّيارة، سَأذْهَب هُناك في الزِّيارَة القادِمَة، إن شاء الله. شُكْراً مَعَ السَّلامَة.

bā'i' as-sūq as-sawdā': hal turīd an tughayyir ba'D ad-dularāt?

dūnald: na'am, wa lākinnī sa'ughayirha fī hādha l-bank.

bā'i' as-sūq as-sawdā': sawfa adfa' laka akthar min al-bank.

dūnald: bikam tashtari d-dulār?

bā'i' as-sūq as-sawdā': adfa' sab'at junayhāt li d-dulār al-wāhid.

dūnald: walākin al-farq bayna si'rak wa si'r Sarf al-bank lan yakun kabīr(an).

bā'i' as-sūq as-sawdā': hādha laysa SaHīH(an), tastaTī' 'an tashtarī sitat 'arghifa min al-khubz bi hādha l-farq. mā ra'yak?

dūnald: lā urīd an ughayyir, shukran, walākin limādha lā tughayyir al-bunūk binafs hādha s-si'r?

bā'i' as-sūq as-sawdā': hādha huwa khaTa' al-Hukūma allatī tuHāwil 'an tataHakkam fī si'r ad-dulār. hal wajadt funduqan li taskun fīh?

dūnald: na'am.

bā'i' as-sūq as-sawdā': unaDHDHim ayDan raHalāt safārī fi S-SaHrā' al-bayDa' tukallif ar-riHla khamsumi'at junayh li l-fard, mā ra'yak?

dūnald: laysa ladayya l-waqt al-kāfi hādhihi z-ziyāra, sa-adhhab hunāk fi z-ziyāra al-qādima, in shā'a l-lāh. shukran, ma'a s-salāma.

Black market dealer: Do you want to change some dollars?

Donald: Yes, but I am going to change them in this bank.

Black market dealer: I will pay you more than the bank.

Donald: How much do you buy dollars for?

Black market dealer: I pay seven pounds for one dollar.

Donald: But the difference between your rate and the bank exchange rate is not a lot.

Black market dealer: That's not true. You can by six loaves of bread for that difference! What do you think?

Donald: I don't want to change any, thank you. But why don't the banks change at the same rate?

Black market dealer: It's the government's fault for trying to control the price of the dollar. Have you found a hotel to stay in?

Donald: Yes.

Black market dealer: I also arrange safaris in the White Desert. The trip costs 500 pounds per person. What do you think?

Donald: I don't have enough time during this visit. I will go along on my next trip, God willing. Thank you, good-bye.

B. Grammar and Usage

1. THE FUTURE TENSE

A. THE FORMATION OF THE FUTURE TENSE

There are two ways of forming the future tense in Arabic: a) the appropriate form of the imperfect verb is preceded by the word سوف *sawfa*, or b) the prefix سـ *sa-* is attached to the appropriate form of the imperfect verb.

سَوْف أَدْفَع لَكَ أَكْثَر مِن البَنْك.

sawfa adfa' laka akthar min al-bank.

I will pay you more than the bank.

سَأُغَيِّرُها في هَذا البَنْك.

sa'ughayirha fī hādha l-bank.

I will change them in this bank.

If the sentence has no verb, the future markers ـس and سَوْف precede an appropriate imperfect form of the verb كَان *kān* (was).

سَيكون سِعْر الجُنَيْه أَرْبَعَة عَشر سنتاً فَقَط.

sayakūn si'r al-junayh arba'at 'ashra santan faqaT.

The value of the pound will only be 14 cents.

سَوْف يكون سِعْر الدولار أَرْبَعَة عَشر سنتاً فَقَط.

sawfa yakūn si'r ad-dulār arba'at 'ashra santan faqaT.

The value of the dollar will only be 14 cents.

The full conjugation of كَان *kān* in the imperfect tense is shown in the following table.

THE IMPERFECT FORM OF THE VERB كَان *kān* (TO BE)					
Singular		Plural		Dual	
أَنا I	أَكون *akūn*	نَحْنُ we	نَكون *nakūn*		
أَنْتَ you (m.)	تَكون *takūn*	أَنْتُم you (m.)	تَكونون *takūnūn*		
أَنْتِ you (f.)	تَكونين *takūnīn*	أَنْتُنَّ you (f.)	تَكُنَّ *takunna*	أَنْتُما you (m./f.)	تَكونان *takunān*
هُوَ he	يكون *takūn*	هُم they (m.)	يكونون *yakūnūn*	هُما they (m.)	يكونان *yakūnān*
هِيَ she	تَكون *takūn*	هُنَّ they (f.)	يكُنَّ *yakunna*	هُما they (f.)	تَكونان *takūnān*

B. NEGATIVE FORM OF THE FUTURE TENSE

لَن *lan* (will not) is used to negate future tense verbs. Because لَن *lan* is both a negative and a future marker, similar to English *won't*, it precedes the imperfect tense verb directly, without ـس *sa-* or سَوْف *sawfa*. For example:

الحُكومَة سَتَتَحكّم في سِعْر الدُولار.

al-Hukūma <u>sa</u>tataHakkam fī si'r ad-dulār.

The government <u>will</u> control the price of the dollar.

الحُكومَة لَن تَتَحكّم في سِعْر الدُولار.

al-Hukūma <u>lan</u> tataHakkam fī si'r ad-dulār.

The government <u>will not</u> control the price of the dollar.

سَأُغَيِّرُها في هَذا البَنْك.

sa'ughayyirha fī hādha l-bank.

I <u>will</u> change them in this bank.

لَن أُغَيِّرُها في هَذا البَنْك.

<u>lan</u> ughayyirha fī hādha l-bank.

I <u>will not</u> change them in this bank.

C. ADVERBS EXPRESSING FUTURE

Here are some common adverbs used in future tense sentences.

COMMON FUTURE TENSE ADVERBS		
غَداً	*ghadan*	tomorrow
الأُسْبوع القادِم	*al-usbū' al-qādim*	next week
الشَّهر القادِم	*ash-shahr al-qādim*	next month
العام القادِم	*al-'ām al-qādim*	next year
فيما بَعْد	*fīma ba'd*	later
في المُسْتَقْبَل	*fi l-mustaqbal*	in the future
هَذا المَساء	*hādha l-masā'*	this evening
بَعْد الظُهْر	*ba'd aDH-DHuhr*	this afternoon

Here are a couple of examples where these adverbs are used in sentences.

سَيَرْتَفِع سِعْر الصَّرْف الأُسْبوع القادِم.

sayartafi' si'r aS-Sarf al-usbū' al-qādim.

The exchange rate will go up next week.

سَأَذْهَب إلى البَنْك غَداً.

sa'adh-hab ila l-bank ghadan.

I will go to the bank tomorrow.

2. RELATIVE PRONOUNS

A noun can be modified by an adjective or by a full sentence, as in the English sentence *This is the bank that John mentioned*. *That John mentioned* is a relative clause and *that* is a relative pronoun that connects the modifying clause to the noun it modifies. English has other relative pronouns, such as *which, whose, whom,* and *who*. In Arabic, the main relative pronoun is الذي *alladhī*.

هُوَ البَنْك الوَحيد الذي يَفْتَح يَوْم الأحَد.

huwa al-bank al-waHid alladhī yaftaH yawm al-aHad.

It is the only bank that opens on Sunday.

هو الرَجُل الذي يَدْفَع سَبْعَة جُنَيْهات لِلدولار.

huwwa r-rajul alladhī yadfaʻ sabʻat junayhāt li d-dulār.

He is the man who pays seven pounds for the dollar.

الذي *alladhī* changes to agree in gender and number with the noun that the relative clause modifies. In the following example, the feminine relative pronoun التي *allatī* is used to refer to the feminine noun الحكومة *al-Hukūma* (the government).

هَذا هُوَ خَطَأ الحكومَة التي تَتَحكَّم في سِعْر الدولار.

hādha huwa khaTa' al-Hukūma llatī tataHakkam fī siʻr ad-dulār.

It's the fault of the government, which controls the price of the dollar.

RELATIVE PRONOUNS		
	Masculine	Feminine
Singular	الَّذي *alladhī*	الَّتي *allatī*
Plural	الَّذينَ *alladhīna*	اللاتي / اللائي / اللَواتي *allwātī/allā'ī/allatī*
Dual	اللَّذَيْن / اللَّذان *alladhni/alladhayni*	اللَّتَيْن / اللَّتان *allatāni/allatayni*

Note that relative clauses always follow a *definite* noun or phrase, e.g., *al-bank, ar-rajul,* and *al-Hukūma* in the sentences above. If extra information is given about an indefinite noun, that information follows it directly, without a relative pronoun.

The following example has a definite noun البائِع *al-bā'iʻ* (the dealer) followed by a relative clause.

رَأَيْت البائِع الَّذي كان يَتَحَدَّث مَع دونالد.

ra'ayt al-bā'iʻ alladhī kān yataHaddath maʻa dūnald.

I saw the dealer who was talking to Donald.

The noun البائع al-bāi' is described by the clause يَتَحَدَّث مَع دونالد yataHaddath ma'a dūnald ([he] was talking to Donald), which is introduced by the relative pronoun الذي alladhī (who). Contrast that with the following example:

رَأَيْت بائعًا يَتَحَدَّث مَع دونالد.

ra'ayt bā'i' yataHaddath ma'a dūnald.

I saw a dealer talking to Donald. (lit., I saw a dealer, [he] was talking to Donald)

In the above example, the clause يَتَحَدَّث مَع دونالد yataHaddath ma'a dūnald ([he] was talking to Donald) follows the indefinite noun without the relative pronoun الذي alladhī.

Here are two more examples illustrating the same contrast.

هَذان هُما الفُنْدُقان اللَذان قَرَأْت عَنْهُما.

hādhān huma l-funduqān alladhān qara't 'anhumā.

Those are the two hotels that I read about.

هَذان فُنْدُقان قَرَأْت عَنْهُما.

hādhān funduqān qara't 'anhumā.

Those are two hotels I read about.

3. NUMBERS FROM 20 TO 1,000

A. THE TENS

Below are the words for numbers 20 through 90. Notice that they do not have separate forms for feminine and masculine.

NUMBERS 20 TO 90			
Number	Transliteration	Arabic Script	Arabic Numeral
twenty	'ishrūn ('ishrīn)	عِشْرون (عِشْرين)	٢٠
thirty	thalāthūn (thalāthīn)	ثلاثون (ثَلاثين)	٣٠
forty	arba'ūn (arba'īn)	أَرْبَعون (أَرْبَعين)	٤٠
fifty	khamsūn (khamsīn)	خَمْسون (خَمْسين)	٥٠
sixty	sittūn (sittīn)	سِتون (سِتين)	٦٠
seventy	sab'ūn (sab'īn)	سَبْعون (سَبْعين)	٧٠
eighty	thamānūn (thamānin)	ثمانون (ثمانين)	٨٠
ninety	tis'ūn (tis'īn)	تِسْعون (تِسْعين)	٩٠

The ones are joined to the tens with و (and). Note that unlike in English, the ones precede the tens for all two-digit numbers above twenty. For example:

سِتٌ وعِشرُون حافِلَة

sitta wa 'ishrūn Hāfila

twenty-six buses (*lit.*, six and twenty buses)

The forms given in parentheses ending in ين -*in* are used almost without exception in spoken Modern Standard Arabic. In writing, the form ending in ون -*ūn* is used when the number is the subject of the sentence, but ين -*in* is used when the number is the object of a verb or a preposition.

B. THE HUNDREDS

The word for *a hundred* in Arabic is مائة *mi'a*, pronounced as if it were spelled مِئَة. مائة *mi'a* must be followed by و *wa* (and) before a number is added to it.

مائة وثَلاث بَنات

mi'a wa thalāth banāt

103 girls

مائة وخَمْس وثلاثون بنتاً

mi'a wa khams wa thalāthūn bint(an)[1]

135 girls

In other words, one says "a hundred <u>and</u> five <u>and</u> thirty" in Arabic. Both the number and the counted noun change according to the rules of agreement discussed in Lesson 7.

To say 200, use the dual suffix (see Lesson 7). 200 is مائتان *mi'atān*, when referring to a subject of the sentence, and مائتين *mi'atayn* otherwise. When followed by a noun, the ن in مائتان *mi'atān* or مائتين *mi'atayn* is dropped. Thus, *200 girls* would be مائتا بنت *mi'atā bināt*.

The numbers 300 through 900 are as follows:

---

[1] The accusative case ending -*an* is added to some counted nouns in more formal usage, but it is usually dropped in spoken MSA. See Lesson 15 for more information about case.

NUMBERS 300 TO 900			
Number	Transliteration	Arabic Script	Arabic Numeral
three hundred	talāthumi'a	ثَلاثَمائة	٣٠٠
four hundred	arba'umi'a	أَرْبَعُمائة	٤٠٠
five hundred	kamsumi'a	خَمْسُمائة	٥٠٠
six hundred	sittumi'a	سِتُّمائة	٦٠٠
seven hundred	sab'umi'a	سَبْعُمائة	٧٠٠
eight hundred	thamānimi'a	ثَمانِمائة	٨٠٠
nine hundred	tis'umi'a	تِسْعُمائة	٩٠٠

C. Vocabulary

سُوق   sūq — market

سَوْداء   sawdā' — black

تُريد (أَراد)   turid (arad) — you want (to want)

سَأُغَيِّرُها (غَيَّر)   sa'ughayyirha (ghayyar) — I will change them (to change)

سَوْفَ   sawfa — will

أكْثَر   akthar (kathīr) — more (a lot)

تَشْتَري (اشْتَرَى)   tashtarī (ishtara) — you buy (to buy)

فَرْق   farq — difference

سِعر صَرْف   si'r Sarf — exchange rate

بَنْك (بُنُوك)   bank (bunūk) — bank(s)

صَحيحاً   SaHīHan — true

تَسْتَطيع (اسْتَطاع)   tastaTī' (istaTā') — you can (to be able to)

أرْغِفَة (رَغيف)   arghifa (raghīf) — loaves

خُبْز   khubz — bread

لَكِن   lākin — but

لِماذا   limādha — why

خَطَأ (أخْطاء) khaTa' (akhTā')	fault; mistake(s)
حكُومَة Hukūma	government
تُحاوِل tuHāwil	it tries
أن an	that
تَتَحكَّم (تَحكَّم) tataHakkam (taHakkam)	it controls (to control)
دولار dulār	dollar
وَجَدْت wajadt	I found
بائِع bā'i'	seller
أُنَظِّم (نَظِّم) unaDHDHim (naDHDHam)	I organize (to organize)
سَفاري safārī	safari
صَحْراء SaHrā'	desert
بَيْضاء bayDa'	white
تُكَلِّف (كَلَّف) tukallif (kallaf)	it costs (to cost)
رِحْلَة riHla	trip
خَمْسُمِائَة khamsuma'a	five hundred
كافي kāfi	enough
قادِمَة qādima	next; coming
إن شاء الله inshā'allah	God willing; hopefully (often appended to a sentence in the future tense)

D. Cultural Note

The black market for currency exchange is only one of many informal economies that exist in Arab countries. It is often blamed on poor government management, as the fictional black market dealer in the dialogue argues, but is also linked to a general lack of resources, making it a common phenomenon in many low-income areas of the world.

For the same reasons, it is common in many Arab countries to find people peddling products from makeshift tables on busy streets of the city or preparing a surprising variety of foods from carts parked on the sidewalk. In Egypt, you can also find sizeable street markets where produce is sold directly from donkey carts, which are used to bring goods into town from the country.

E. Exercises

1. Use سَوفَ sawfa, لَنْ lan, or سَ sa to change the sentences to the future tense.

a. ‏لا أريد أن أغير جنيهات.‏

b. ‏لم أدفع لك أكثر من البنك.‏

c. ‏حاولت الحكومة أن تتحكم في سعر الدولار.‏

d. ‏يشتري دونالد بعض الجنيهات.‏

e. ‏يذهب دونالد إلى البنك كل يوم.‏

2. Use the correct form of the relative pronoun.

a. ‏رأيت موظف البنك _____ كان يتحدث مع دونالد.‏

b. ‏هذه هي الجريدة _____ أحبها.‏

c. ‏أنا مع الحكومات _____ تتحكم في الأسعار.‏

d. ‏الرجل _____ ينظم الرحلات اسمه يحيى.‏

e. ‏هذا هو الرجل _____ حدثتك عنه.‏

3. Put the following words in the right order to make sentences.

a. ‏البنك – يفتح – القادم – الأسبوع – سوفَ.‏

b. ‏إلى – لن – الصحراء – أذهب – غداً.‏

c. ‏في – فرنسا – المستقبل – سأسافر – إلى.‏

d. ‏أخي – هذا – سأزور – المساء.‏

e. ‏كثيرا – فيما – سأشتري – بعد.‏

4. Arrange the following scrambled sentences to make a meaningful paragraph.

‏ثم تحدثا عن مشكلة سُعر صَرْف الدولار في مصر.‏

‏و هناك قابل بائع السوق السوداء.‏

‏عندما كان دونالد في مصر، أراد أن يغير بعض الدولارات.‏

‏ذهب إلى البنك.‏

‏فكّر دونالد، لكنه لم يغيِّر الدولارات.‏

‏قال البائع أنه سيدفع أكثر من البنك.‏

5. There is an error in the underlined portion of each of the following sentences. Find the error and correct it to form a meaningful sentence.

a. ‏لن سأدفع لك الدولارات.‏

b. ‏قابلت بائع الذي يغير الدولارات.‏

c. الحكومة هي الذي تتحكم في سعر الصرف.

d. هذا هو الفندق اللذين ذهبت إليه.

e. رأيت عشرين بنات.

Answer Key

1. a. لن أريد أن أغير جنيهات.

lan urīd an ughayir junayhāt.

I will not want to change any pounds.

b. لن أدفع لك أكثر من البنك.

lan adfa' lak akthar min al-bank.

I will not pay you more than the bank.

c. سوف تحاول الحكومة أن تتحكم في سعر الدولار.

saufa tuhāwil al-Hukuma 'an tataHakim fi si'r ad-dulār.

The government will try to control the price of the dollar.

d. سيشتري دونالد بعض الجنيهات.

Sayashtarī dūnald ba'D al-junayhāt.

Donald will buy some pounds.

e. سوف يذهب دونالد إلى البنك كل يوم.

saufa yadh-hab dūnald ila l-bank kull yawm.

Donald will go to the bank every day.

2. رأيت موظف البنك الذي كان يتحدث مع دونالد.

ra'ayt muwaDHDHaf al-bank alladhī kān yataHaddath ma'a dūnald.

I saw the bank employee who was talking to Donald.

هذه هي الجريدة التي أحبها.

hādhihi hiya l-jarīda allatī uHibbuhā.

This is the newspaper I like.

أنا مع الحكومات التي تتحكم في الأسعار.

ana ma'a al-Hukumāt allatī tataHakkam fi l-'as'ār.

I am supportive of (Lit., with) governments that control prices.

الرجل الذي ينظم الرحلات اسمه يحيى.

ar-rajul alladhī yunaDHDHim ar-riHlāt ismu(hu) yahia.

The man who organizes the trips is named Yehia.

هذا هو الرجل الذي حدثتك عنه.

hādha huwwa ar-rajul alladhī Hadathtak 'anhu.

This is the man that I told you about.

3. سوف يفتح البنك الأسبوع القادم.

saufa yaftaH al-bank al-usbū' al-qādim.

The bank will open next week.

لن أذهب إلى الصحراء غداً.

lan adh-hab ila S-SaHrā' ghadan.

I won't go to the desert tomorrow.

سأسافر إلى فرنسا في المستقبل.

sa'usāfir ilā faransa fi l-mustaqbal.

I will travel to France in the future.

سأزور أخي هذا المساء.

sa'azūr akhī hādha l-masā'.

I will visit my brother tonight.

سأشتري كثيرا فيما بعد.

sa'ashtarī kathīr(an) fīmā ba'd.

I will buy a lot later on.

4. عندما كان دونالد في مصر، أراد أن يغير بعض الدولارات. ذهب إلى البنك. وهناك قابل بائع السوق السوداء. قال البائع أنه سيدفع أكثر من البنك. فكر دونالد، لكنه لم يغير الدولارات. ثم تحدثا عن مشكلة سعر صرْف الدولار في مصر.

'indamā kān dūnald fi miSr, 'arād 'an yughayir ba'D ad-dulārāt. dhahab 'ila l-bank. wa hunāk qābal bāi' as-sūq as-sawdā'. qāl al- bāi' innahu sayadfa' akthar min al-bank. fakkar dūnald, lākin lam yughayyir ad-dulārāt. thumma taHaddathā 'an mushkilat si'r Sarf ad-dulār fī miSr.

When Donald was in Egypt, he wanted to change some dollars. He went to the bank. There he met the black market dealer. The dealer said he would pay more than the bank. Donald thought about it, but he didn't change any dollars. Then they discussed the problem of the dollar exchange rate in Egypt.

5. a. لن أدفع لك الدولارات.

   أدفع 'adfa' (to pay)

b. قابلت البائع الذي يغير الدولارات.

   البائع al-bā'i' (the seller)

c. الحكومة هي التي تتحكم في سعر الصرف.

   التي allatī (who/which)

d. هذا هو الفندق الذي ذهبت إليه.

   الذي alladhī (which/who, sg.)

e. رأيت عشرين بنتاً.

   بنتاً bint(an) (girl, sg.)

LESSON 9
(Modern Standard Arabic)

كَم الإيجار؟

kam al-ījār? How Much Is the Rent?

A. Dialogue

Nadia and Lucy are looking at a furnished apartment in Beirut that Lucy is thinking of renting.

نادية: هَذِه شَقَّة كَبيرَة جِداً، بِها أَرْبَع غُرَف وصالَة وحَمَّامان!

لوسي: هِي شَقَّة جَميلَة جِداً فالشُّرْفَة تُطِل عَلى حَديقَة كَبيرة وهِي قَريبة مِن الجامِعة.

نادية: نَعَم هَذا صَحيح، ولَكِن ما رَأْيَك فِي الأثاث؟

لوسي: لا يُعْجِبُني، ولا تُعْجِبُني أَدَوات المَطْبَخ، فالأطْباق قَديمَة والأوْعِية مَحْروقَة.

صاحِبَ الشَّقَّة: مِن المُمْكِن أَن أَشْتَري أوعِية جَديدَة.

نادية: وَماذا عَن الأثاث؟

صاحِب الشَّقَّة: لا أَسْتَطيع أَن أَشْتَري أثاثاً جَديداً إلا إذا وَقَّعْت عَلى عَقْد إيجار لِمُدَّة سَنَتَيْن عَلى الأقَّل.

لوسي: ولَكِنِّي لا أَعْرِف إذا كُنْت سَأَبْقَى فِي بَيْروت لِمُدَّة سَنَتَيْن. أَريد أَن أُوَقِّع العَقْد لِمُدَة عام.

صاحِب الشَّقَّة: فِي هَذِه الحالَة لَن أستَطيع أَن أُغَيِّر الأثاث.

لوسي: ماذا عَن تَغيير هَذِه الكَراسي وهَذا الدولاب وذَلِك السَّرير فَقَط؟

صاحِب الشَّقَّة: مُوافِق ولَكِن سَأُغَيِّر واحِد فَقط مِن هَذِه الأشْياء كُل شَهْر.

لوسي: كَم إيجار الشَقَّة فِي الشَّهْر؟

صاحِب الشَّقَّة: سَبْعمائة دولار.

لوسي: هَذا أكْثَر مِما كُنْت أتَوَقَّع، سَأَدْفَع خَمْسُمائة دولار فَقَط.

nādya: hādhihī shaqqa kabīra jiddan bihā arba' ghuraf wa Sāla(h) wa Hammāmān!

lūsī: hiya shaqqa jamīla jiddan fa sh-shurfa tuTill 'ala Hadīqa kabīra, wa hiya qarība min al-jāmi'a.

nādya: na'am hādha SaHīH, wa lākin mā ra'yik fi l-athāth?

lūsī: lā yu'jibunī, walā tu'jibunī adawāt al-maTbakh, fa l-aTbāq qadīma wa l-aw'iya maHrūqa.

SāHib ash-shaqqa: min al-mumkin an ashtarī aw'iya jadīda.

nādya: wa mādha 'an al-athāth?

SāHib ash-shaqqa: lā astaTī' an ashtarī athāth(an) jadīd(an) illa idha waqqa't 'ala 'aqd ījār limudat sanatayn 'ala l-aqqal.

lūsī: wa lākinnī lā a'rif idha kunt sa'abqā fī bayrūt limudat sanatayn. urīd an uwaqqi' al-'aqd limudat 'ām.

SāHib ash-shaqqa: fi hādhihi l-Hāla lan astaTī' an ughayyir al-athāth.

lūsī: mādha 'an taghyīr hādhihi l-karāsī wa hādha d-dulāb wa dhalik as-sarīr faqaT?

SāHib ash-shaqqa: muwāfiq wa lākin sa'ughayyir wāHid faqaT min hādhihi l-ashya' kull shahr.

lūsī: kam ījār ash-shaqqa fi sh-shahr?

SāHib ash-shaqqa: sab'umi'at dulār.

lūsī: hādha akthar mimmā kunt atawaqqa', sa'adfa' khamsumi'at dulār faqaT.

Nadia: This apartment is very big; it has four bedrooms and two bathrooms!

Lucy: It is quite beautiful, and the balcony overlooks a big garden. And it's also close to the University.

Nadia: Yes, that's true, but what do you think of the furniture?

Lucy: I don't like it, and I don't like the kitchen utensils. The dishes are old, and the pots are burnt.

Landlord: I can buy you new pots and pans.

Nadia: And what about the furniture?

Landlord: I can't buy you new furniture unless you sign a lease for at least two years.

Lucy: But I don't know if I will be in Beirut for two years. I want to sign a one-year lease.

Landlord: In that case, I won't be able to change the furniture.

Lucy: What about replacing just these chairs, this armoire, and that bed?

Landlord: Agreed, but I will only change one of these things each month.

Lucy: How much is the rent per month?

Landlord: 700 dollars.

Lucy: That's more than I was expecting; I'll only pay 500 dollars.

B. Grammar and Usage

1. DEMONSTRATIVES

Demonstratives are words that are used to point verbally to objects, such as the English *this*, *these*, *that*, and *those*. هٰذِهِ *hādhihī*, the Arabic demonstrative adjective meaning "this," is used in the following sentence.

هَذِه شَقَّة كَبِيرَة.

hādhihī shaqqa kabīra.

<u>This</u> is a big apartment.

In Arabic, demonstratives agree with the noun to which they refer in gender and number. Unlike adjectives, demonstratives always precede the noun in Arabic.

DEMONSTRATIVES			
هَذَا *hādha*	this (m.)	ذَلِكَ *dhalik*	that (m.)
هَذِه *hādhihī*	this (f.)	تِلكَ *tilka*	that (f.)
هَؤُلَاء *hā'ula'i*	these (m.)	أُوْلَئِك *ulā'ik*	those (m.)
هَؤُلَاء *hā'ula'i*	these (f.)	أُوْلَئِك *ulā'ik*	those (f.)
هَذَان (هَذَيْن) *hādhān (hadhayn)*	these two (m.)	ذَانِك (ذينِك) *dhānik (dhaynik)*	those two (m.)
هَاتَان (هَاتَيْن) *hātān (hātayn)*	these two (f.)	تَانِك (تَيْنِك) *tānik (taynik)*	those two (f.)

Remember that plural non-human nouns are treated as feminine singular for purposes of agreement. This is why هَذِه *hādhihī* (this, f. sg.) is used in هَذِه الأَشْياء *hādhihī l-ashyā'* (these things), whereas هَؤُلَاء *hā'ula'i* (these, m. pl.) is used in هَؤُلَاء النَّاس *hā'ulā'i n-nās* (these people).

Note that a noun modified by a demonstrative also has a definite article preceding it:

هَذِه الكَرَاسِي

hādhihī l-karāsī

these chairs (*lit.*, these <u>the</u> chairs)

If a demonstrative is followed by an indefinite noun, the phrase is then interpreted as a full nominal sentence. Contrast the following complete sentence to the previous example:

هَذِه كَرَاسِي

hādhihī karāsī.

These are chairs. (*lit.*, these ones are chairs)

In order to express the meaning *These are <u>the</u> chairs* in Arabic, and to distinguish this sentence from the phrase *these chairs*, one says something like *These ones, <u>they</u> are the* chairs. In other words, a pronoun that agrees with the noun in person, number, and gender is inserted. That pronoun is underlined in the second example below:

هَذِهِ الكَراسي   vs.   هَذِهِ هِيَ الكَراسي.

hādhihī l-karāsī   *hādhihī hiya l-karāsī.*

these chairs   These are the chairs. (*lit.*, these they the chairs)

The same contrast is illustrated in the following three examples:

ذَلِكَ السَرير

dhālik as-sarīr

that bed

ذَلِكَ سَرير.

dhālik sarīr.

That is a bed.

ذَلِكَ هُوَ السَرير.

dhālik huwa s-sarīr.

That is the bed. (*lit.*, that it the bed)

2. MORE NUMBERS: THOUSANDS AND MILLIONS

A. THE THOUSANDS

The word for *thousand* in Arabic is أَلْف *'alf*. The plural form is آلاف *'ālāf* (thousands). To say *2000*, use the dual form أَلْفان *'alfān* (for the subject of the sentence) or أَلْفَيْن *'alfayn* (for the object of a verb or object of a preposition), but note that أَلْفَيْن *'alfayn* is the form usually used in speaking, regardless of the case. To express several (anywhere from 3 to 999) thousands, treat أَلْف *'alf* as any other counted noun, meaning that numbers from 3,000 to 10,000 are expressed using the plural form آلاف *'ālāf*, whereas numbers from 11,000 to 999,000 are expressed using the singular form أَلْف *'alf*.

ثَلاثَة آلاف

thalāthat 'ālāf

three thousand (*lit.*, thousands)

The word آلاف *'ālāf* (thousands) is in the plural form here, because it is a counted noun following the number 3.

Any counted noun that follows whole thousands (1,000, 2,000, 3,000, etc.) should be in the singular form.

ثَلاثَة آلاف ضَيْف

thalāthat 'ālāf Dayf

three thousand guests (*lit.*, three thousands guest)

The word ضَيْف *Dayf* (guest) is in the singular form because it is the counted noun following 3,000.

146

To add other digits, join ألْف *alf* with a و *wa* (and):

أَرْبَعَة آلاف و أَرْبَعَة وأَرْبَعُون ضَيْفاً.

arba'at ālāf wa arba'a wa arba'ūn Dayf(an).[1]

four thousand, forty-four guests (*lit.*, four thousands and four and forty guests)

Note that ضَيْفاً *Dayf(an)* (guest) is in the singular, following the rule for 44.

أَرْبَعَة آلاف وأَرْبَعُمائة وأَرْبَعَة ضِيُوف

arba'at ālāf wa arba'umi'a wa arba'at Diyūf.

four thousand, four hundred four guests (*lit.*, four thousands and four hundred and four guests)

In the last example, the plural form ضُيُوف *Duyūf* (guests) is used. Thus the counted noun—ضَيْف *Dayf(an)* or ضُيُوف *Duyūf* in our examples—is singular or plural depending on the ones and tens digits alone.

Finally, remember that Arabic numerals are written and read from left to right, as in English.

١،٢٣٤

أَلْف ومائَتان وأَرْبَعَة وثَلاثون

alf wa mi'atān wa 'arba'a wa thalāthūn

one thousand, two hundred, thirty-four (*lit.*, one thousand and two hundred and four and thirty)

B. THE MILLIONS

The word *million* works just like ألْف *'alf*. Its plural form is مَلايين *malāyin*, and its dual form is مِلْيونَيْن *milyūnayn* or مِلْيونان *milyūnān*, depending on the function of the noun it modifies.

The rules for numbers will only become natural with practice. You can promote your number reading skills by always reading out loud any numeral that you encounter in a text, especially dates. To get yourself started, memorize these two examples so you will never have to pause when reading them.

عام أَلْف وتِسْعُمائة

'ām alf wa tis'umi'a

the year 1900

عام أَلْفَين

'ām alfayn

the year 2000

---

[1] The counted noun that follows numbers can have the ending *-an*. The pronunciation of this ending is optional in spoken Modern Standard Arabic.

C. Vocabulary

إِيْجار *ijār*	rent
شَقَّة *shaqqa*	apartment
بها *biha*	it has
صالَة *Sāla*	living room
حَمَّامان *Hammāmān*	two bathrooms
حَديقَة *Hadiqa*	garden
قَريبة *qarība*	close
أثاث *athāth*	furnishings
يُعْجِبْني (أَعجَب) *yu'jibunī (a'jab)*	I like (to like)
أَدَوات (اداة) *adawāt (adā)*	utensil(s)
مَطْبَخ *maTbakh*	kitchen
أطْباق (طَبَق) *aTbāq (Tabaq)*	dish(es)
قَديمَة *qadīma*	old
أوْعية (وِعاء) *aw'iya (wi'ā')*	pot(s)
مَحْروقَة *maHrūqa*	burnt
جَديدَة *jadīda*	new
إلا *illa*	except
وَقَّعْت عَلى *waqqa't 'ala*	you signed
عَقْد *'aqd*	contract
سَنَتَيْن *sanatayn*	two years
سَأبْقَى (بَقِيَ) *sa'abqa (baqiya)*	I will stay (to stay)
بَيْروت *bayrūt*	Beirut
في هَذِه الحالَة *fi hādhihi l-Hāla*	in that case
كَراسِي (كُرسي) *karāsi (kursi)*	chair(s)
دولاب *dulāb*	armoire; closet
ذَلِك *dhalik*	that
سَرير *sarīr*	bed

148

مُوافِقة muwāfiqa	agreed
(أَشْياء (شَيْء) 'ashya' (shay')	things (thing)
شَهْر shahr	month
مِمّا mimmā	. . . than what . . .
(أَتَوَقَّع (تَوَقَّع) 'atawaqqa' (tawaqqa')	I expect (to expect)

D. Cultural Note

Most people in Arab cities live in modern high-rises. Before the days of air conditioning, however, those who lived in private houses would often design their homes with an open courtyard or garden in the middle of the house. Its main function was to keep the house cool, but it also allowed the family some privacy. Because most of the windows would overlook the courtyard, the family would have a peaceful garden view shut off from the noises and strangers on the street.

Even in the high-rises of today there are some traces of this architectural style. Many modern apartment buildings built in Arab cities include an open center yard. Kitchens often have windows onto these spaces, which still perform the function of bringing cool air into the house.

E. Exercises

1. Use the correct form of the demonstrative pronoun to complete the following sentences.

a. الدولاب قديم جدا. _____

b. _____ هي البنت التي تسكن معي.

c. ما رأيك في _____ الأثاث؟

d. _____ الشقة تطل على حديقة جميلة.

e. سأبقى في بيروت لكل _____ السنتين.

2. Form complete sentences by matching the demonstrative pronoun in column A with the phrases in column B.

A	B
a. هذا	هم أصدقائي من الجامعة
b. هذه	هو زوج نادية
c. هذه	هي زوجة دونالد
d. هذا	هي بيروت الجميلة
e. هؤلاء	هو صديقي الذي حدثتك عنه

3. Write the following numbers in Arabic.

a. مائة وخمس وثلاثون

b. مائة وأربعون

c. تسعمائة

d. خمسمائة وسبعة

e. ثلاثمائة وأربعون

4. Arrange the following words so that they form complete sentences.

a. حدثتك – هذه – أمس – التي – هي – عنها – الشقة

b. الأطباق – هذه – قديمة – جداً

c. هنا – مدة – جداً – جميلة – فهذه – المدينة – سأبقى – طويلة

d. الدرس – لا – هذا – أفهم

e. الشقة – بها – وصالة – هذه – غرف – وحمامان – خمس

5. Choose the right word to fill in the blanks in the following sentences.

أدوات / تغير / جنيه / حمام / عقد / الإيجار

a. في شقتي خمس غرف ولكن هناك ـــــــــــــــــــــ واحد.

b. سأدفع سبعمائة ـــــــــــــــــــــ فقط لهذه الشقة.

c. أريدك أن ـــــــــــــــــــــ بعض هذا الأثاث.

d. سأوقع ـــــــــــــــــــــ الأسبوع القادم.

e. سوف نشتري ـــــــــــــــــــــ المطبخ غداً.

Answer Key

1. a. هذَا الدولاب قديم جداً.
hādha d-dulāb qadīm jiddan.
<u>This</u> armoire is very old.

b. هذَه هي البنت التي تسكن معي.
hadhihi hiya l-bint allatī taskun ma'ī.
This is the girl who lives with me.

c. ما رأيك في هذا الأثاث؟
mā ra'yak fī hādha l-'athāth?
What do you think of <u>this</u> furnishing?

d. هذَه الشقة تطل على حديقة جميلة.
hādhihi sh-shaqa tuTill 'alā Hadiqa jamīla.
<u>This</u> apartment overlooks a beautiful garden.

e. سأبقى في بيروت لكلتا هاتين السنتين.
s'abqā fī bīrūt likilta hātayn as-sanatayn.
I will stay in Beirut for both of <u>these</u> years.

2. a. هذا هو صديقي <u>الذي</u> حدثتك عنه.

b. هذه زوجة دونالد.

c. هذه هي بيروت الجميلة.

d. هذا هو زوج نادية.

e. هؤلاء هم أصدقائي من الجامعة.

3. ١٣٥ mi'a wa khamas wa thalathūn

   ١٤٠ mi'a wa arba'ūn

   ٩٠٠ tis'umi'a

   ٥٠٧ khamsumi'a wa sab'a

   ٣٤٠ thalathumi'a wa arba'ūn

4. a. هذه هي الشقة التي حدثتك عنها أمس.

   b. هذه الأطباق قديمة جداً.

   c. سأبقى هنا مدة طويلة فهذه المدينة جميلة جداً.

   d. لا أفهم هذا الدرس.

   e. هذه الشقة بها خمس غرف وصالة وحمامان.

5. a. في شقتي خمس غرف ولكن هناك حمام واحد.

   حمام Hammām (bathroom)

   Fi shaqatī khams ghuraf wa lākin hunāk Hammām wāHid.

   In my apartment there are five rooms but there is only one bathroom.

   b. سأدفع سبعمائة جنيه فقط لهذه الشقة.

جنيه junayh (a pound)

sa'adfa' sab'umi'at junayh faqaT li hādhihi sh-shaqqa.

I will only pay seven hundered pounds for this apartment.

c. أريدك أن تغير بعض هذا الأثاث.

تغير tughayyir (to change)

uridak 'an tughayyir ba'D hādha al-'athāth.

I want you to change some of this furniture.

d. سأوقع عقد الإيجار الأسبوع القادم.

عقد الإيجار 'aqd al-ijār (the rental contract)

sauwaqqi' ' aqd al'ijār al-'usbū' alqādim.

I will sign the rental contract next week.

e. سوف نشتري أدوات المطبخ غداً.

أدوات adawāt (utensils)

sawfa nashtari 'adawāt al-maTbakh ghadan.

We will buy the kitchen utensils tomorrow.

LESSON 10

(Modern Standard Arabic)

هَذا كَثير جِدًا.

hādhā kathīr jiddan! That's Too Expensive!

A. Dialogue

Donald wants to buy Lucy a gift for her birthday.

صاحِب مَحَلّ: تَفَضَّل هُنا يا أُستاذ! ما الذي تَبْحَث عَنْه؟

دونالد: أَبْحَث عَنْ هَدِيَّة لِزَوْجَتي.

صاحِب المَحَلّ: اشْتَرِ لَها جَلابِيَّة، سَوف تُعْجِبها.

دونالد: كَم سِعْرُها؟

صاحِب المَحَلّ: سِعْرُها خَمْسون جُنَيهاً فَقَط.

دونالد: هَذا كَثير جِدًا أَرِني شَئ أَرْخَص.

صاحِب المَحَلّ: اُنْظُر إلَى هَذِه العُقود الفِضِّيَّة! سَوف تُعْجِبها أَكْثَر حَتَّى مِنْ الجَلابِيَّة.

دونالد: أَرِني هذا العِقْد مِنْ فَضْلَك.

صاحِب المَحَلّ: هذا أَفْضَل عِقْد عِنْدي، ذَوْقُك جَميل.

دونالد: كَمْ سِعْرُه؟

صاحِب المَحَلّ: ١٠٠ جُنَيه فَقَط.

دونالد: لَكِن هذا العِقْد أَغْلَى بِكَثير مِنْ الجَلابِيَّة.

صاحِب المَحَلّ: هذا أَفْضَل سِعْر سَتَجِده في السُوق.

Donald starts to walk away.

صاحِب المَحَلّ: اِنْتَظِر يا أَستاذ، ماذا تُريد أَنْ تَدْفَع؟

دونالد: أُريد أَنْ أَنْفِق ٥٠ جُنَيهاً أَو ثَمانية دولارات لا أَكْثَر ولا أَقَلّ.

صاحِب المَحَلّ: سَأُعْطيك العِقْد بـ ٧٥ جُنَيهاً لِكَي تُصْبِح زَبوناً دائِماً لي.

دونالد: لَنْ أَدْفَع أَكْثَر مِنْ ٥٠ جُنَيهاً.

Donald turns to leave.

صاحِب المَحَلّ: ما رَأيُك في ٥٥ جُنَيهاً؟

دونالد: اتَّفَقْنا، تَفَضَّل.

SāHib maHall: tafaDDal hunā yā ustādh. ma alladhī tabHath 'anhū?

dūnald: abHath 'an hadiyya li zawjatī.

SāHib al-maHall: ishtari lahā jallābiyya, sawfa tu'jibuhā.

dūnald: kam si'ruhā?

SāHib al-maHall: si'ruhā khamsūn junayhan faqaT.

dūnald: hādhā kathīr jiddan, arinī shay' arkhaS.

SāHib al-maHall: unDHur ilā hādhihi l-'iqūd al-fiDDiyya, sawfa tu'jibhā akthar Hattā min al-jallābiyya.

dūnald: arinī hādhā al-'iqd min faDlak.

SāHib al-maHall: hādhā afDal 'iqd 'indī, dhawquk jamīl.

dūnald: kam si'ruh?

SāHib al-maHall: mi'at junayh faqaT.

dūnald: lākin hādha l-'iqd aghlā bi kathīr min al-jalabiyya.

SāHib al-maHall: hādhā afDal si'r satajiduh fi s-sūq.

SāHib al-maHall: intaDHir yā ustādh, mādhā turīd an tadfa'?

dūnald: urīd an unfiq khamsīn junayh(an) aw thamāniyat dulārāt lā akthar wala aqall.

SāHib al-maHall: sa'u'Tīk al-'iqd bi-khamsa wa sab'īn junayh(an) likay tuSbiH zabūnan dā'iman lī.

dūnald: lan adfa' akthar min khamsīn junayh(an).

SāHib al-maHall: mā ra'yuk fī khamsa wa khamsīn junayh(an)?

dūnald: ittafaqnā, tafaDDal.

Shop Owner: Welcome, sir. What are you looking for?

Donald: I am looking for a present for my wife.

Shop Owner: Buy her a *jalabiyya*.[1] She'll love it.

Donald: How much is it?

Shop Owner: It is only fifty pounds.

Donald: That's too expensive. Show me something cheaper.

Shop Owner: Look at these silver necklaces. She'll like that even more than the *jalabiyya*.

Donald: Show me this necklace, please.

Shop Owner: This is the nicest necklace I have. You have good taste.

Donald: How much is it?

Shop Owner: Only 100 pounds.

Donald: But this necklace is much more expensive than the *jalabiyya*!

Shop Owner: This is the best price you will find in the market.

---

[1] *jalabiyya* is a long loose dress worn by both men and women. It can be as casual as a house shirt or beautifully embroidered for formal occasions.

Shop Owner: Wait, sir, how much do you want to pay?

Donald: I want to spend 50 pounds, or eight dollars. No more and no less.

Shop Owner: I will give the necklace to you for 75 pounds so you will become a regular customer of mine.

Donald: I won't pay more than 50 pounds.

Shop Owner: What do you think of 55 pounds?

Donald: Agreed. Here you are.

B. Grammar and Usage

1. THE IMPERATIVE

The imperative mood is used to issue orders or requests, as in the following examples from the dialogue.

تَفَضَّل.

tafaDDal.

Come in.

اُنْظُر.

unDHur.

Look.

اِنْتَظِر.

intaDHir.

Wait.

The imperative is derived from the imperfect tense (see Lesson 6) of the *you*, singular or plural, form of the verb. Follow these steps to form the imperative:

a. Drop the imperfect tense prefix, e.g., يَتَفَضَّل *yatafaDDal* (he helps himself) -> تَفَضَّل *tafaDDal* (help yourself).

b. Also drop the ن at the end of the imperfect verb in the feminine singular and masculine plural, e.g., يَبْحَثون *yabHathūn* (they look for, *m. pl.*) -> اِبْحَثوا *ibHathū* (look for). But if the verb is in the feminine plural form, the ن is not dropped, as in تَبْحَثْن *tabHathna* -> اِبْحَثْن *ibHathna*.

c. Add an ا after the و of the masculine plural form, as in اِبْحَثوا *ibHathū* (look for).

If the verb is Form II, III or V, there are no more steps. This is how the imperative verb تَفَضَّل *tafaDDal* (come in) is derived.

For Forms I, VII, VIII and X verbs, follow the additional step below:

d. Add an ا to the beginning of the word. The short vowel on the ا will be the same as the short root vowel of the imperfect stem. For example, the short vowel in the

154

imperfect stem of the verb كتب *kataba* (to write) is *u*, as in يكْتُب *yaktub*. Thus the same *u* is the prefix on the imperative form of that verb: اكْتُب *uktub*. For Form IV verbs, add a *hamza*, so the word begins with أ rather than an ا.

	Imperfect		Imperative	
IMPERATIVE OF THE VERB انْظُر ***unDHar*** **(TO LOOK)**				
you (m. sg.)	تَنْظُر	*tanDHur*	اُنْظُر	*unDHur*
you (f. sg.)	تَنْظُرينَ	*tanDHurīna*	اُنْظُري	*unDHurī*
you (m. pl.)	تَنْظُرون	*tanDHurūn*	اُنْظُروا	*unDHurū*
you (f. pl.)	تَنْظُرْن	*tanDHurna*	اُنْظُرن	*unDHurna*
you (m./f. dual)	تَنْظُران	*tanDHurān*	اُنْظُرا	*unDHurā*

Arabic also has a construction similar to the English contraction *let's:* The prefix لِ *li* is added to the beginning of the *we* form of the imperfect verb, as in the following example:

لِنَنْظُر إلَى هَذِه العُقود الفِضيِّة.

linanDHur ilā hadhihi l-'uqūd al-fiDDiyya.

<u>Let's</u> look at these silver necklaces.

Alternatively, the word دَعْنا *da'na* is used, as in the following example from the dialogue:

دَعْنا نَتَحَدَّث عَن السِعر.

da'na nataHaddath 'an as-si'r.

<u>Let's</u> talk about the price.

Both *li* and *da'na* are followed by a full imperfect form of the verb, نَنْظُر *nanDHur* (we look) and نَتَحَدَّث *nataHaddath* (we talk).

2. POLITE REQUESTS

As in English, it is often more polite in Arabic to ask for something indirectly than to use the imperative. The following expressions are often used to replace the imperative.

هَل مِن المُمْكِن أن...؟

hal min al-mumkin an . . . ?

Is it possible to . . . ?/Can you . . . ?

هَل تَسْتَطيع أن...؟

hal tastaTi' an . . . ?
Could you . . . ?

Both expressions end with the word أَنْ *an*, roughly equivalent to English *to* in *to go* or *to be*. أَنْ *an* is always followed by a verb in the imperfect tense, as in the following examples:

هَل مِن المُمْكِن أَن تُرِني هَذا العِقْد؟

hal min al-mumkin an <u>turini</u> hādha l-'iqd?
Can you <u>show</u> me this necklace?

هَل تَسْتَطيع أَن تُعْطِيني هَذا العِقْد بِخَمْسين جُنَيْها؟

hal tastaTi' an <u>tu'Tiani</u> hādha l-'iqd bikhamsīn junayh(an)?
Could you <u>give</u> me this necklace for 50 pounds?

أَنْ *an* requires some slight changes in the form of the imperfect verb that follows it. This special verbal form is called the subjunctive mood and will be discussed in Lesson 15. Although the prefixes of imperfect verbs following أَنْ *an* do not change, the suffixes do, just like in the imperative. Specifically, the نْ *-n* at the end of the feminine singular *you* and the masculine plural *you* and *they* forms is dropped. For example:

هَل مِن المُمْكِن أَن تَنْظُري إِلَى هَذِه العُقود الفِضيِّة؟

hal min al-mumkin an <u>tanDHuri</u> ila hādhihi l-'uqūd al-fiDDiyya?
Can you *(f. sg.)* <u>look</u> at these silver necklaces? (*lit.*, Is it possible for you to . . . ?)

The نْ of the imperfect verb following أَنْ *an* is <u>not</u> dropped in the feminine plural *they* form.

هَل مِن المُمْكِن أَن يَنْظُرْن إِلَى هَذِه العُقود الفِضيِّة؟

hal min al-mumkin an <u>yanDHurna</u> ilā hādhihi l-'uqūd al-fiDDiyya?
Can they *(f. pl.)* <u>look</u> at these silver necklaces? (*lit.*, Is it possible for them to . . . ?)

3. COMPARATIVE AND SUPERLATIVE

A. COMPARATIVE

When adjectives are used to compare two or more things in degree, they take a special comparative form in Arabic, as in English, e.g., *a nice view* vs. *a nicer view*. For example:

عِقْد أَفْضَل

'iqd <u>afDal</u>
a <u>better</u> necklace

العِقْد الأَفْضَل

al-'iqd <u>al-afDal</u>
the <u>better</u> necklace

The word pattern for the comparative is *'a-CCaC*. It is formed by adding the prefix ا *'a-* to the base form of the adjective. If there is a long vowel between the second and third consonants, it changes into a short vowel *fatHa* (ˈ). The same form is used for all genders and numbers. For example:

Base Form	Comparative Form
رَخيص *rakhīS* (cheap)	أَرْخَص *arkhaS* (cheaper)
حَسَن *Hasan* (good)	أَحْسَن *aHsan* (better)
كَثير *kathīr* (many)	أَكْثَر *akthar* (more)
غالي *ghālī* (expensive)	أَغْلَى *aghlā*[1] (more expensive)

The comparative form can also be used to modify a verb, as in the following example:

أَجْري أَسْرَعَ مِن صَديقي.

ajrī asra' min Sadīqī.

I run <u>faster</u> than my friend.

To compare two things, the comparative form is used with the word مِن *min* (than), as in the following examples:

هذا العِقْد أَغْلَى مِنْ الجَلابِيَّة.

hādha l-'iqd aghlā min al-jalābiyya.

This necklace is more expensive <u>than</u> the *jalābiyya*.

هَذا العِقْد أَفْضَل مِن ذَلِك.

hādha l-'iqd afDal min dhālik.

This necklace is better <u>than</u> that one.

B. SUPERLATIVE

The superlative form of an adjective is the form that expresses the highest degree attained in a certain quality under comparison, as in the English *the nicest* person. Arabic doesn't have a special superlative form and uses the comparative form instead.

One way to express the superlative is to use a special construction, comparable to the possessive construction, where the adjective in the comparative form precedes, rather than follows, an indefinite noun.

هذا أَفْضَل عِقْد عِنْدي.

hādhā afDal 'iqd 'indī.

This is <u>the best necklace</u> I have.

---

[1] This comparative is irregular because the last root consonant is the "weak" consonant *y*.

هذا أَفْضَل سِعْر في السُّوق.

hādhā afDal si'r fi s-sūq.

This is <u>the best price</u> in the market.

Another way to form the superlative is by preceding the comparative with the definite article الـ *al.*

هذا العِقْد هو الأغْلَى

hādhā l-'iqd huwa l-aghlā.

This necklace is <u>the most expensive</u>. (*lit.,* This necklace, it is the most expensive)

هذا السِّعْر هو الأفْضَل.

hādhā s-si'r huwa l-afDal.

This price is <u>the best</u>. (*lit.,* This price, it is the best)

4. WORDS FOR COLORS

There are two types of color adjectives in Arabic. The first type consists of adjectives derived from nouns, which have the same form as the adjectives of nationality you learned in Lesson 2. For example:

بُرتُقالِي *burtuqālī* (orange, m.)

بُرتُقالِيَّة *burtuqāliyya* (orange, f.)

Here are some other common adjectives of this type.

COLOR ADJECTIVES ENDING IN *-ī/-iyya*		
Masculine Singular	Feminine Singular	
زَهْري *zahrī*	زَهْرِيَّة *zahriyya*	pink
فِضِّيّ *fiDDī*	فِضِّيَّة *fiDDiyya*	silver
ذَهَبِيّ *dhahabī*	ذَهَبِيَّة *dhahabiyya*	gold
بُنّيّ *bunnī*	بُنِّيَّة *bunniyya*	brown

These adjectives follow the regular patterns of gender and number agreement.

The second type of color words consists of adjectives that have the form *aCCaC* in the masculine singular, e.g., أَحْمَر *aHmar* (red). The feminine form of these adjectives always follows the *CaCCā'* pattern, and the plurals, the *CuCC* pattern.

COLOR ADJECTIVES OF THE *aCCaC FORM*			
Masculine Singular	Feminine Singular	Masculine/ Feminine Plural	
أَحْمَر aHmar	حَمْراء Hamrā'	حُمْر Humr	red
أَصْفَر aSfar	صَفْراء Safrā'	صُفْر Sufr	yellow
أَخْضَر akhDar	خَضْراء KhaDrā'	خُضْر khuDr	green
أَزْرَق azraq	زرقاء zarqā'	زُرْق zurq	blue
أَسْوَد aswad	سوْداء sawdā'	سُوْد sūd	black
أَبْيَض abyaD	بَيْضاء bayDā'	بيض biD	white

Remember that adjectives referring to groups of non-human items must be in the feminine singular form, so the plural forms given above are only used to refer to groups of people.

جَلابيّات بَيْضاء
jalābiyyāt bayDā' (f. sg.)
white jalabiyyas

أَمْريكيّون بيض
amrikiyyūn biD (f. pl.)
white Americans

C. Vocabulary

مَحَّل *maHall* — shop

يَبْحَث (بَحَث) عَن *yabHath (baHath) 'an* — he looks (to look) for

هَدِيّة *hadiyya* — gift

جَلابيّة *jalābiyya* — jalabiyya

أَرِني (أَرى) arini (arā)	show me (to show)
أَرْخَص arkhaS	cheaper
اُنْظُر (نَظَر) unDHur! (naDHar)	Look! (to look)
عُقود (عِقْد) 'uqūd ('iqd)	necklaces
فِضِيّةٌ fiDDiyya	silver (f.)
حَتَّى Hattā	even
ذَوْقُك Dhawquk	your taste
أَغْلَى aghlā	more expensive
أَفْضَل afDal	better, preferable
سَتَجِدُه (وَجد) satajiduh (wajad)	you will find it (to find)
اِنْتَظِر intaDHir!	Wait!
أَنْفِق (نْفَق) unfiq (anfaq)	I spend (to spend)
أَقَلّ aqall	less
سَأُعْطيك (أعطى) sa'u'Tīk (a'Tā)	I will give you (to give)
لِكَي likay	in order to
تُصْبِح tuSbiH	you become
زِبون zabūn	client, customer
دائِماً dā'iman	always
اتَّفَقْنا ittafaqnā!	Agreed! (lit., we are agreed)

D. Cultural Note

In the Arab world, malls and stores similar to those in the West are found side by side with the more traditional commercial institution of the *sūq*, or bazaar. These colorful marketplaces have a large variety of shops, which are usually very specialized. A traditional Arab marketplace is made up of areas specialized by product, for example, areas for gold, textiles, spices and incense, brass, or copper.

Bargaining is traditional and expected in most shops in the Arab world. It is the system by which the savvy salesperson identifies the value of a product to a given individual right on the spot! It is impossible for the customer to tell how far the price of an item is from the wholesale price at which the shopkeeper acquired it. Therefore, it is best to bargain by offering a lower price, or otherwise, simply to walk out of the shop. If you choose the former, think carefully before naming a price, and don't name a price on something you don't actually intend to buy: it is extremely bad form to decide not to buy something after the vendor has agreed to the price you named.

Most people wouldn't bargain in very expensive shops or in places where price tags are marked on items in order not to appear cheap, which is considered to be a terrible quality in the Arab world. Still, if you are not afraid of coming off as a bit stingy, you may find that you can bargain down a hotel room, a rental car, or even products in an up-market shop where items are marked with price tags.

E. Exercises

1. Use the correct imperative form of the verb نَظَر naDHar (to look) to complete the sentences.

a. ـــــــــــــ يا دونالد، يا لوسي، يا نادية.

b. ـــــــــــــ يا سمير، يا دونالد.

c. ـــــــــــــ يا لوسي.

d. ـــــــــــــ يا مريم، يا لوسي، يا نادية.

e. ـــــــــــــ يا دونالد.

2. Change the underlined adjectives into their comparative or superlative form, according to the context.

a. السفر بالطائرة سريع من السفر بالقطار.

b. الطقس في القاهرة فضل من الطقس في سوريا.

c. محمد جميل من لوسي.

d. الطعام في المطعم جيد من الطعام في البيت.

e. دراسة العربية صعب من دراسة الإنجليزية.

3. Put the underlined verbs in the form required after the word أن an.

a. هل من الممكن أن ذهبت معي إلى المكتب؟

b. هل تستطيع أن ستساعدني في هذه المشكلة؟

c. من اللازم أن سوف أعمل واجبي الآن.

d. هل من الممكن أن نظرت إلى هذه العقود الفضية؟

e. هل تستطيع أن سأعطيك العقد بـ ٧٥ جنيها.

4. Put the following words in the right order to make logical sentences.

a. العقد – من – أرخص – هذا – الجلابية

b. العقد – المحل – أغلى – هذا – في

c. هدية – لزوجتي – الجلابية – أفضل – ستكون – هذه

d. اللغة – من – اللغة – أصعب –هذه – العربية

e. أخي – أطول – من – أنا

5. Fill in the blanks by choosing among the words in parentheses.

a. _____ هنا يا أستاذ. (تعجبها / تفضل / أريد)

b. لن _____ أكثر من خمسين جنيهاً في السوق. (أنفق / أنظر/ أرني)

c. _____ مع صاحب المحل على سعر الجلابية. (نظرت / اتفقت / أردت)

d. ما _____ في هذا السعر؟ (تدفع / ذوقك / رأيك)

e. سأعطيك سعراً جيداً _____ تصبح زبوناً دائماً لي. (لكن / لكي / لن)

Answer Key

1. a. يا دونالد، يا لوسي، يا نادية انظروا.
   yā dūnald, yā lūsī, yā nādya unDHurū!
   Donald, Lucy, and Nadia, look!

   b. يا سمير يا دونالد انظرا.
   yā samīr yā dūnald, unDHurā!
   Samir, Donald, look!

   c. يا لوسي انظري.
   yā lūsī, unDHurī!
   Lucy, look!

   d. يا مريم، يا لوسي، يا نادية انظرن.
   yā maryam yā lūsī yā nādya, unDHurna!
   Mariam, Lucy, and Nadia, look!

   e. يا دونالد انظر.
   yā dūnald, unDHur!
   Donald, look!

2. a. أسرع *asra'* (faster)

   b. أفضل *afDal* (better)

   c. أجمل *ajmal* (more beautiful)

   d. أجود *ajwad* (better)

   e. أصعب *aS'ab* (more difficult, harder)

3. a. تذهب *tadh-hab* (you go)

   b. تساعدني *tusā'idnī* (you help me)

   c. أعمل *a'mal* (I work)

   d. تنظر *tanDHur* (she looks)

   e. تعطيَني *tu'Tianī* (you give me)

4. a. هذا العقد أرخص من الجلابية.
   hādha l-'iqd arkhaS min al-jallābiyya.
   This necklace is cheaper than the dress.

   b. العقد أغلى في هذا المحل.
   al-'iqd aghlā fī hādhā l-maHall.
   The necklace is more expensive in this shop.

   c. هذه الجلابية ستكون أفضل هدية لزوجتي.
   hādhihi l-jlalābiyya sa-takūn afDal hadiyya li-zawjatī.
   This dress will be the best present for my wife.

d. هذه اللغة أصعب من اللغة العربية.

hādhihi l-lugha aS'ab min al-lugha l-'arabiyya.

This language is more difficult than Arabic.

e. أنا أطول من أخي.

ana aTwal min akhī.

I am taller than my brother.

5. a. تفضل *tafaDDal* (please come in)

b. أنفق *unfiq* (I spend)

c. اتفقت *ittafaqt* (I agreed)

d. رأيك *ra'yuk* (your opinion)

e. لكي *likay* (in order to)

LESSON 11

(Modern Standard Arabic)

وَجْبَة طَيِّبَة

wajba Tayyiba! Enjoy Your Meal!

A. Dialogue

Donald and Lucy have just been seated for dinner at a nice restaurant and are waiting for Nadia and Samir to arrive.

دونالد: هَلْ أَنْتِ مُتَأَكِّدَة أَنَّ الحَجْزِ السَّاعَة السَّادِسَة؟ السَّاعَة الآن
السَّابِعَة إلا الرُبْع وأنا جَوْعان جِدّاً.

لوسي: يَجِب أن نَنْتَظِر، لا يُمْكِن أَنْ نَطْلُب الطَّعام قَبْل أَن يَصِلا.

دونالد: ولكِنّي سَأموت مِن الجوع، سَأَطْلُب شَطيرَة هامْبورجَر.

Donald finishes ordering just as Samir and Nadia walk in.

نادية: نَأْسَف جِدّاً على هَذا التَّأْخير، فَقد كان المُرور سَيِّئاً جِدّاً.
لِماذا لَمْ تَبْدَءا الأَكْل بِدونِنا؟

لوسي: في الواقِع...

دونالد: بالطَّبْع لا!

They sit down and begin to look over the menu.

سَمير: أُريد حُمُّصاً ووَرَق عِنَب وخِيار وسَلَطَة بالإِضافَة إلى
البَاذِنْجان فَهُو لَذيذ جِدّاً في هَذا المَطْعَم.

دونالد: هَل هُناك لَحْم في وَرَق العِنَب؟

سَمير: نَعَم وبِه أَيْضاً أُرْز وقِرْفَة.

نادية: أُريد أَيْضاً بَعْض الكُبَيْبَة.

دونالد: ما هِي الكُبَيْبَة؟

نادية: هِي عِبارَة عَن كُرات مِن اللَّحْم المَفْروم والبُرْغُل.

لوسي: هَل مِن المُمْكِن أَن نَشْتَرِك في طَلَب مَشْوِيَّات واحِد كَطَبَق
رَئيسي؟ سَيَكون بِه دَجاج وكُفْتَة وكَباب.

The waiter brings Donald his hamburger.

عامِل المَطْعَم: تَفَضَّل الهامْبُرجَر، وَجْبَة طَيِّبَة.

dūnald: hal anti muta'akkida anna al-Hajz as-sā'a as-sādisa? as-sā'a l-ān as-sābi'a illā ar-rub' wa anā jaw'ān jiddan.

lūsī: yajib an nantaDHir, lā yumkin an naTlub aT-Ta'ām qabla an yaSilā.

dūnald: wa lākinnī sa'amūt min al-jū'. sa'aTlub shaTirat hāmburgar.

nādia: na'asaf jiddan 'ala hādha t-ta'khīr faqad kān al-murūr sayyi' jiddan. limādhā lam tabda'ā l-akl bidūninā?

lūsī: fi-l-wāqi' . . .

dūnald: bi T-Tab' lā.

samīr: urīd HummuSan wa waraq 'inab wa khiyār wa salaTa bi l-iDāfa ila l-bādhinjān fahuwa ladhīdh jiddan fī hādha al-maT'am.

dūnald: hal hunāk laHm fī waraq al-'inab?

samīr: na'am, wa bihi ayDan urz wa qirfa.

nadia: urīd ayDan ba'D al-kubayba.

dūnald: mā hiya l-kubayba?

nādya: hiya 'ibāra 'an kurāt min al-laHm al-mafrūm wa l-burghul.

lūsī: hal min al-mumkin an nashtarik fī Talab mashwiyyāt wāHid kaTabaq ra'īsī? sayakūn bihi dajāj wa kufta wa kabāb.

'āmil al-maT'am: tafaDDal al-hāmburgar, wajba Tayyiba!

Donald: Are you sure that the reservation was for 6:00? It is 6:45 now and I am hungry.

Lucy: We have to wait; we cannot order the food before they arrive!

Donald: But I am going to die of hunger. I am going to order a hamburger.

Nadia: Sorry we're late. The traffic was really bad. Why didn't you start without us?

Lucy: Well, actually . . .

Donald: Of course not!

Samir: I would like hummus and grape leaves, cucumber salad, and eggplant dip. It is quite delicious here, too.

Donald: Is there meat in the grape leaves?

Samir: Yes, and rice and cinnamon.

Nadia: I want *kobeba* as well.

Donald: What is *kobeba*?

Nadia: It is made of balls of ground beef and bulgur wheat.

Lucy: Can we share one order of grilled meats for a main dish? It includes chicken, kofta, and kebab.

Waiter: Here is your hamburger. Enjoy your meal!

B. Grammar and Usage

1. THE PLURAL FORM OF NOUNS AND ADJECTIVES

A. THE REGULAR PLURALS

A regular or a "sound" plural form of a noun or an adjective is formed by adding an ending to it, just as in English.

The regular masculine plural ending is ون -*ūn*. For example:

مُدَرِّس
mudarris
teacher

مُدَرِّسون
mudarrisūn
teachers

عامِل
'āmil
worker

عامِلون
'āmilūn
worker

Remember that nouns that refer to objects, rather than humans, take the feminine singular form as their plural form, so the regular plural forms discussed here are only used when nouns refer to groups of people. The plural ending ين -*in* is used when the noun is the object of a sentence or follows a preposition.

مُدَرِّس
mudarris
teacher

مُدَرِّسون
mudarrisūn
teachers (m. pl., subject)

مُدَرِّسين
mudarrisin
teachers (m. pl., object)

In spoken language, the *-in* form is used almost exclusively, whether the noun functions as a subject or an object of a sentence.

The regular feminine plural is formed by adding the suffix ات -*āt*, whether the noun is a subject or an object of a sentence. This plural form is only derived from feminine singular nouns ending in ة -*a(t)*. The singular suffix is dropped before the plural ending is added.

مُدَرِّسة
mudarrisa(t)
teacher (f. pl.)

مُدَرِّسات
mudarrisāt
teachers (f. pl.)

B. THE IRREGULAR PLURALS

Many nouns have irregular plural forms in Arabic, also called "broken" plurals. The vowels of the root are changed, added, or taken out, "breaking" the basic root form of the noun. In some cases, prefixes and/or suffixes are also added. While there are exceptions to this rule, underived nouns, which are short and close to their root forms and have neither prefixes nor suffixes, usually have irregular plurals; longer, derived nouns, those with prefixes and/or suffixes, usually have regular plurals.

There are over forty patterns of "broken" plurals, so it is most practical to memorize the irregular plural form along with the singular form of the noun. Listed below are a few of the more common patterns.

aCCiCā'

صَديق Sadīq (friend)   أَصْدِقاء aSdiqā' (friends)

طَبيب Tabīb (doctor)   أَطِبَّاء aTibbā' (doctors)

aCCāC

سوق sūq (market)   أَسْواق aswāq (markets)

قلَم qalam (pen)   أَقْلام aqlām (pens)

وَلَد walad (boy)   أَوْلاد awlād (boys)

شَخْص shakhS (person)   أَشْخاص ashkhāS (persons)

اِبْن ibn (son)   أَبْناء abnā' (sons)

اِسْم ism (name)   أَسْماء asmā' (names)

maCāCiC

مَطْعَم maT'am (restaurant)   مَطاعِم maTā'im (restaurants)

مكْتَب maktab (desk; office)   مكاتِب makātib (offices)

CuCūC

بَيْت bayt (house)   بُيُوت buyūt (houses)

ضَيْف Dayf (guest)   ضُيُوف Duyūf (guests)

CiCāC

رَجُل rajul (man)   رِجال rijāl (men)

جَمَل jamal (camel)   جِمال jimāl (camels)

In the glossary, the irregular plural forms are included next to the singular forms.

2. ORDINAL NUMBERS

Ordinal numbers indicate the order in which items come, such as "first," "second," or "third" in English. In Arabic, ordinal numbers can be easily distinguished from the numbers used in counting: most of them have an ا-ā- following the first root consonant. The only exception is أَوَّل āwwal (first), which is not derived from واحِد wāHid (one).

The table below includes the numbers *first* to *twelfth*. They are presented together with the definite article because, as you will see below, this is the form used in telling time.

ORDINAL NUMBERS		
الأوّل	al-awwal	the first
الثَّاني	ath-thānī	the second
الثَّالِث	ath-thālith	the third
الرَّابِع	ar-rābi'	the fourth
الخامِس	al-khāmis	the fifth
السَّادِس	as-sādis	the sixth
السَّابِع	as-sābi'	the seventh
الثَّامِن	ath-thāmin	the eighth
التَّاسِع	at-tāsi'	the ninth
العاشِر	al-'āshir	the tenth
الحادي عَشَر	al-Hādī 'ashar	the eleventh
الثَّاني عَشَر	ath-thānī 'ashar	the twelfth

3. TELLING TIME

To tell time, use the word السَّاعَة as-sā'a (the hour) followed by the definite and feminine form of the ordinal number.

كَم السَّاعَة الآن يا لوسي؟

kam as-sā'a l-'ān yā lūsī?

What time is it now, Lucy?

السَّاعَة الآن الرابِعَة مَساءً.

as-sā'a l-'ān ar-rābi'a masā'an.

It is now four o'clock in the evening. (*lit.*, The hour now is the fourth in the evening)

For *one o'clock*, the word واحِدَة *wāHida*, the feminine form of the cardinal number *one*, is used instead of the ordinal number أوّل *awwal* (first).

السَّاعَة الآن الواحِدَة صَباحاً.

as-sā'a l-ān al-wāHida Sabāhan.

It is now one o'clock in the morning.

168

السَّاعَة الحادِيَة عَشْرَة

as-sā'a l-Hādiya 'ashra

eleven o'clock

السَّاعَة الثَّانِيَة عَشْرَة

as-sā'a th-thāniya 'ashra

twelve o'clock

To express a time that is not exactly on the hour, the fractions نِصْف *niSf* (a half), رُبْع *rub'* (a quarter), and ثلث *thulth* (a third) are added following و *wa* (and).

السَّاعَة الرابِعَة والنِصْف

as-sā'a r-rābi'a wa n-niSf

half past four

السَّاعَة الرابِعَة والرُبْع

as-sā'a r-rābi'a wa r-rub'

quarter past four

السَّاعَة الرابِعَة والثُلْث

as-sā'a r-rābi'a wa th-thulth

four twenty (*lit.*, a third past four)

The same fraction words are used with the word إلا *illā* (minus), to express time in the latter part of the hour, as in the following examples:

السَّاعَة الخامِسَة إلا الثُلْث

as-sā'a l-khāmisa illa th-thulth

four forty (*lit.*, five o'clock minus a third)

السَّاعَة الخامِسَة إلا الرُبْع

as-sā'a al-khāmisa illa r-rub'

four forty-five (*lit.*, five o'clock minus a quarter)

Any other interval of time is expressed using the exact number and the words دَقِيقَة *daqīqa* (minute) or دَقائِق *daqā'iq* (minutes) preceded by the word و *wa* (and), as in:

السَّاعَة الثانِية وَخَمس وَعِشرون دَقيقة

as-sā'a th-thāniya wa khams wa 'ishrūn daqīqa

2:25 (*lit.*, eight o'clock and five and twenty minutes)

السَّاعَة الوَاحِدَة وَخَمس دَقائِق

as-sā'a l-wāHida wa khams daqā'iq

1:05 (*lit.*, one o'clock and five minutes)

Numbers three to ten are followed by the plural form of the noun, دَقائِق *daqā'iq* (minutes), while numbers 11 to 59 are followed by the singular form, دَقيقة *daqīqa* (minute), according to the rules you learned in Lesson 7.

C. Vocabulary

مَطْعَم maT'am	restaurant
مُتَأَكِّدَة muta'akkida	sure (f.)
حَجْز Hajz	reservation
جَوْعان jaw'ān	hungry
يَجِب (وَجَب) أن yajib (wajab) an	he must (to have to)
نَطْلُب (طَلَب) naTlub (Talab)	we order (to order)
طَعام Ta'ām	food
قَبْل qabla	before
سَأَموت (مات) sa'amūt (māt)	I will die (to die)
جوع jū'	hunger
شَطيرَة shaTīra	sandwich
هامْبورجَر hāmburgar	hamburger
نَأْسَف (أَسَف) na'saf (a'saf)	we are sorry (to be sorry)
تَأْخير ta'khīr	delay
فَقَد (قَد) faqad (qad)	so, and
مُرور murūr	traffic
سَيِّئ sayyi'	bad
تَبْدَءوا (بَدَأ) tabda'ū (bada')	you (pl.) start (to start)
أَكْل akl	food, eating
بِدونِنا bidūninā	without us
في الواقِع fi l-wāqi'	actually
حُمُّص HummuS	chickpeas; garbanzo beans
وَرَق waraq	leaves
عِنَب 'inab	grape
خيار khiyār	cucumbers
سَلَطَة salaTa	salad
بِالإضافة إلى bi l-iDāfa ila	in addition to

باذِنْجان *bādhinjān*	eggplant
لَذيذ *ladhīdh*	delicious
لَحْم *laHm*	meat
أُرْز *urz*	rice
قِرْفَة *qirfa*	cinnamon
كُبَيْبَة *kubayba*	meatballs
عِبارَة عَن *'ibāra 'an*	equivalent to
كُرات *kurāt*	balls
مَفْروم *mafrūm*	ground
بُرْغُل *burghul*	bulgur wheat
نَشْتَرِك في *nashtarik fī*	we partake in, share
طَلَب *Talab*	order
مَشْويَّات *mashwiyyāt*	grilled meats
رَئيسي *ra'īsi*	principal
دَجاج *dajāj*	chicken
كُفْتَة *kufta*	spiced ground beef grilled on a skewer
كَباب *kabāb*	spiced meat grilled on a skewer
عامِل *'āmil*	worker
وَجْبَة طَيِّبَة *wajba Tayyiba!*	Enjoy your meal!

D. Cultural Note

The diversity of the countries that make up the Arab world has afforded it an equally diverse array of foods. One thing that unites them is the original Bedouin influence. Tracing back to this heritage is the use of staples such as lamb meat, dates, and various forms of yogurt, which are still among the basic components of the Middle Eastern diet.

More recently, Lebanese cuisine has had a broad influence on menus across the region, to such a degree that most foods now generally associated with Arab cuisine are in fact Lebanese in origin. The most typical characteristic of a Lebanese meal is that it begins with *mezza*, a variety of cold and hot finger foods and dips. Also typical of Arab cuisine are the hollow rounds of flat bread called *khubz*. *khubz* often replaces the fork and knife as a utensil for scooping up the delicious dishes, especially in the *mezza* course.

E. Exercises

1. Arrange the following words to form meaningful sentences.

a. النصف – الآن – الثامنة – و – السَّاعَة

b. المطاعم – لأن (because) – ذيذ – أحب – فيها – جداً – اللبنانية – الأكل

c. حُمُّصاً – وسَلَطَة – ورق – بالإضافَة إلى – عنب – أريد

d. ستطلب – اليوم – ماذا – في – المطعم – ؟

e. الثامنة – أتناول الطعام – صباحاً – لم – منذ – الساعة

2. Provide the plural form of the following singular nouns.

a. رجل

b. مطعم

c. مدرس

d. دقيقة

e. مصري

3. Say what time it is in Arabic.

a. 4:15
b. 9 AM
c. 2:30
d. 1:45
e. 3:35

4. Provide the singular forms of the following plural nouns.

a. ضيوف

b. مطاعم

c. أشخاص

d. أسواق

e. رجال

5. Fill in the blank with the appropriate word from the choices in parentheses.

a. من الممكن أن _____ في طلب مشويات واحد. (نضيف / نطلب / نشترك)

b. هل _____ بعض الباذنجان؟ (تريد / تطلب / يكون)

c. هل تحب كرات اللحم _____. (السلطة / المفروم / الشطيرة)

d. هذا هو الطبق _____. (الرئيسي / المشوي / المفروم)

e. سأطلب شطيرة _____. (أرز / سلطة / هامبورجر)

172

Answer Key

1. a. السَّاعَة الآن الثامنة والنصف.
   as-sā'a l-ān ath-thāmina wa n-niSf.
   The time is now 8:30.

   b. أحب المطاعم اللبنانية لأن الأكل
   فيها لذيذ جدا.
   uHibb al-maTā'im al-lubnāniyya li-
   anna l-akl fihā ladhīdh jiddan.
   I like Lebanese restaurants because
   the food there is really delicious.

   c. أريد حُمُّصاً وسَلَطَة بالإضافَة إلى
   ورق عنب.
   urīd hummuSan wa salaTa bi l-iDāfa
   ilā waraq 'inab.
   I would like some chickpeas, salad,
   and stuffed vine leaves.

   d. ماذا ستطلب في المطعم اليوم؟
   mādhā sa-taTlub fi l-maT'am al-
   yawm?
   What will you order at the restaurant
   today?

   e. لم أتناول الطعام منذ الساعة الثامنة
   صباحاً.
   lam atanāwal aT-Ta'ām mundhu s-
   sā'a th-thāmina SabāHan.
   I have not eaten since 8 o'clock in
   the morning.

2. a. رجال rijāl (men)

   b. مطاعم maTā'im (restaurants)

   c. مدرسات mudarrisūn (teachers, m.)

   d. دقائق daqā'q (minutes)

   e. مصريون / مصريات miSriyyūn/
   miSriyyāt (Egyptians, m./Egyptians, f.)

3. a. الساعة الآن الرابعة والربع.
   as-sā'a l-ān ar-rābi'a wa r-rub'.
   It is now 4:15.

   b. الساعة الآن التاسعة صباحاً.
   as-sā'a l-ān at-tāsi'a SabāHan.
   It is now 9 AM.

   c. الساعة الآن الثانية والنصف.
   as-sā'a l-ān ath-thānya wa n-niSf.
   It is now 2:30.

   d. الساعة الآن الثانية إلا الربع.
   as-sā'a l-ān ath-thāniya illa r-rub'.
   It is now a quarter to 2.

   e. الساعة الآن الثالثة وخمس وثلاثون
   دقيقة.
   as-sā'a l-ān ath-thālithā wa khams wa
   thalāthūn daqīqa.
   It is now 3:35.

4. a. ضيف Dayf (a guest)

   b. مطعم maT'am (a restaurant)

   c. شخص shakhS (a person)

   d. سوق sūq (a market)

   e. رجل rajul (a man)

5. a. نشترك nashtarik (we share)

   b. تريد turīd (you want)

   c. المفروم al-mafrūm (ground)

   d. الرئيسي ar-ra'īsī (the main)

   e. هامبورجر hāmburgar (hamburger)

173

THIRD REVIEW

(Modern Standard Arabic)

Grammar Exercises

1. Change the following sentences to the future tense using a future tense word such as غداً.

a. ‫أكلت بعض الحمص في المطعم.‬

b. ‫الجنيه أغلى من الليرة اللبنانية.‬

c. ‫اشترى دونالد أوعية جديدة.‬

d. ‫وقع دونالد العقد لمدة سنة.‬

e. ‫دونالد في الحفلة.‬

2. Put the following sentences in the negative form.

a. ‫سأكون في القاهرة غداً.‬

b. ‫هناك لحم في ورق العنب اللبناني.‬

c. ‫أريد حمصاً وورق عنب.‬

d. ‫سأطلب شطيرة هامبورجر.‬

e. ‫سأدفع سبعة جنيهات للدولار.‬

3. Choose the right relative pronoun to complete the blanks in the following sentences.

‫الذي / التي / اللذان / اللتان / الذين / اللذين / اللتين / اللواتي / اللائي‬

a. ‫رأيت عامل المطعم _____ كنت تتكلم عنه.‬

b. ‫هذه هي الشقة _____ أفضلها.‬

c. ‫هذه هي الأوعية _____ اشتريتها.‬

d. ‫هذان هما الزبونان _____ جاءا إلى المطعم أمس.‬

e. ‫هؤلاء هم أصدقائي _____ قابلتهم في الجامعة.‬

4. Write down the following numbers in Arabic.

a. 25

b. 29

c. 20

d. 200

e. 24

5. Correct the errors in the following sentences.

a. هذا هما الرجلان اللذان كانا يعملان في المطعم.

b. لن سوف أسافر إلى بيروت غداً.

c. هاتان الشقة جميلة.

d. هؤلاء البنك قريب من الفندق.

e. لن سآكل في هذا المطعم.

Vocabulary Exercises

6. Put the following words in the correct order to make complete sentences.

a. يا – إلى – أستاذ – المطعم – تفضل

b. الجلابية – العقد – أريد – أن – التي – أشتريها – من – هذا – أغلى

c. أرى – الممكن - الفضية – من – أن – هذه – العقود – هل – ؟

d. مشويات – في – دونالد – طبق – ستشترك – لوسي – واحد – و

e. واحد – عقد – يوقع – عام – الشقة – دونالد – أن – يريد – لمدة

7. Decide which of the words in the group does not belong.

a. مطبخ / حمام / صالة / إيجار

b. أطباق / أثاث / سرير / بنك

c. رحلة / زيارة / سفاري / الصحراء البيضاء

d. صاحب الشقة / صاحب المطعم / عامل المطعم / دولاب

e. سعر الصرف / الدولار / الجنيه / عقد الإيجار

8. Choose the correct word to fill in the blanks in the following sentences.

العقد / الإيجار / السوداء / جلابية / الأكل

a. سأشتري _____ لزوجتي غداً.

b. كم سعر هذا _____ الفضي؟

c. هل وقعت عقد _____ مع صاحبة الشقة؟

d. ليس الفرق بين سعر البنك والسوق _____ كبيراً.

e. هل تفضل _____ اللبناني أم الأكل المصري؟

9. Place the following sentences in the right order to form a coherent paragraph.

a. دونالد ولوسي يبحثان عن شقة ليسكنا فيها لمدة عام.

b. لوسي تعمل في الجامعة الأمريكية ببيروت.

c. بعد شهر من البحث (looking) وجدا شقة جميلة جداً.

d. ولكن دونالد يبحث (is looking for) عن عمل في شركة بترول.

e. دونالد ولوسي يسكنان في بيروت.

10. Using three to five sentences, summarize the dialogue in Lesson 8.

Answer Key

1. a. سآكل بعض الحمص في المطعم غداً.
   b. سيكون الجنيه أغلى من الليرة اللبنانية الأسبوع القادم.
   c. سوف يشتري دونالد أوعية جديدة في المساء.
   d. سيوقع دونالد العقد لمدة سنة يوم الخميس.
   e. سيكون دونالد في الحفلة يوم الجمعة القادم.

2. a. لن أكون في القاهرة غداً.
   b. ليس هناك لحم في ورق العنب اللبناني.
   c. لا أريد حمصاً وورق عنب.
   d. لن أطلب شطيرة هامبورجر.
   e. لن أدفع سبعة جنيهات للدولار.

3. a. الذي
   b. التي
   c. التي
   d. اللذان
   e. الذين

4. a. خمسة وعشرون
   b. تسعة وعشرون
   c. عشرون
   d. مائتان
   e. أربعة وعشرون

5. a. هذان هما الرجلان اللذان كانا يعملان في المطعم.
   b. لن أسافر إلى بيروت غداً.
   c. هذه الشقة جميلة.
   d. هذا البنك قريب من الفندق.
   e. لن آكل في هذا المطعم.

6. a. تفضل إلى المطعم يا أستاذ.
   b. هذا العقد أغلى من الجلابية التي أريد أن أشتريها.
   c. هل من الممكن أن أرى هذه العقود الفضية؟
   d. ستشترك لوسي ودونالد في طبق مشويات واحد.
   e. يريد دونالد أن يوقع عقد الشقة لمدة عام واحد.

7. a. إيجار
   b. بنك
   c. الصحراء البيضاء
   d. دولاب
   e. عقد الإيجار

8. a. جلابية
   b. العقد
   c. الإيجار
   d. السوداء
   e. الأكل

9. دونالد ولوسي يسكنان في بيروت. لوسي تعمل في الجامعة الأمريكية ببيروت. ولكن دونالد يبحث عن عمل في شركة بترول. دونالد ولوسي يبحثان عن شقة ليسكنا فيها لمدة عام. وبعد شهر من البحث وجدا شقة جميلة جداً.

10. لم يغير دونالد عند بائع السوق السوداء، ثم تحدثا عن مشكلة الدولار في مصر، وبعد ذلك حاول البائع أن يأخذ دونالد في رحلة سفاري.

READING PASSAGE II

(Modern Standard Arabic)

رسالة من مسافر في تونس

risāla min musāfir fi tūnis A Letter from a Traveler in Tunis

عزيزتي سعاد،

بعد التحية والسلام،

أكتب إليك من مدينة تونس. سأحكي لك من البداية، أخذنا القطار القديم من "المرسى" إلى وسط البلد بالعاصمة تونس، ثم مشينا في شارع الحبيب بورقيبة الواسع الأخضر بمبانيه التي بنيت في عهد الاحتلال الفرنسي بجانب المباني السكنية الحديثة والفنادق. وكانت المباني البيضاء تلمع مع سماء البحر المتوسط الزرقاء، وكانت المدينة مليئة بالناس والسيارات، بينما امتلأت المقاهي بالرجال الذين كانوا يتحدثون وهم يشربون القهوة أو الشاي ويدخنون السجائر.

وكان معظم الناس يرتدون الملابس الغربية، باستثناء عدد قليل من النساء اللاتي ارتدين الأحجبة التي تغطي رؤوسهن. لم تكن المدينة أو ساكنوها بنفس درجة المحافظة التي توقعناها من قراءة الدليل السياحي.

وعندما ذهبنا إلى المدينة القديمة لم نصدق أننا أننا في نفس المدينة، دخلنا شوارع ضيقة مزدحمة مليئة بالحياة والحركة والألوان والروائح. يبيع أصحاب المحلات بضائعهم من محلات صغيرة تملأ مساحة لا تزيد عن ميل مربع.

أينما ذهبنا كانت هناك الكثير من المحلات الصغيرة المليئة بالألوان اللامعة والموسيقى والبخور، وامتلأت سوق العطور برائحة العطور الجميلة داخل الزجاجات الملونة. ويجانب سوق العطور، رأينا سوق الطرابيش والتي تصنع فيه الطرابيش كما كانت تصنع منذ قرون، كما رأينا أصحاب المحلات يبيعون الملابس والسجاجيد والهدايا التذكارية والمنتجات الجلدية والسيراميك والجواهر والأثاث والتحف القديمة والكتب والأطعمة والمشروبات، من السهل أن تتوه في المدينة القديمة.

إلى اللقاء.

المخلص،

أحمد

Dear Suad,

Greetings!

I am writing you from Tunis. I will tell you the story from the beginning. We took the old train from La Marsa into the downtown area of the capital, Tunis. Then we walked on the wide, green street of Habib Bourguiba with its buildings built in the French colonial period, alongside the modern residential buildings and hotels. The white buildings glowed in the blue Mediterranean sky. The city was full of people and cars, while the coffee shops were full of men talking and drinking coffee or tea and smoking cigarettes.

Most people were wearing Western clothes except for a small number of women who were wearing veils that covered their heads. The city and its residents were not as conservative as we expected from reading the guidebook.

When we went to the old city, we could not believe we were in the same city. We entered narrow, crowded streets full of life, movement, colors, and scents. The shop owners sell products from small shops filling an area no bigger than one square mile.

Everywhere we went there were lots of tiny shops full of bright colors, music, and incense. The perfumer's market is full of the beautiful scent of perfume in colored bottles. Beside the perfumer's market was the fez-maker's market, where they make fezzes just as they did centuries ago. We also saw the shop owners selling clothes, rugs, souvenirs, leather products, ceramics, jewelry, furniture, antiques, books, food, and drink. It is easy to get lost in the old city.

Until we meet again.

Sincerely,

Ahmed

Vocabulary

عَزيزتي ʿazizatī	my dear
تَحِيَّة taHiyya	greetings
سَأَحْكي لَك (حَكى) saʾaHkī lak (Hakā)	I will tell you (to tell)
بِدايَة bidāya	beginning
وَسَط البَلَد wasaT al-balad	downtown
عاصِمَة ʿāSima	capital city
واسِع wāsiʿ	wide
مَبان (مَبنى) mabān (mabna)	buildings
بُنيَت (بَنى) buniyat (banā)	built

عَهْد 'ahd	era, epoch
اِحْتِلال iHtilāl	occupation
بِجانِب bi-jānib	beside
سَكَنِيَة sakaniyya	residential
حَديثَة Hadītha	modern
تَلْمَع (لَمَع) talma' (lama')	shining
سَماء samā'	sky
البَحْر المُتَوسِّط al-baHr al-mutawassiT	Mediterranean Sea
ناس nās	people
بَيْنَما baynamā	while
اِمْتَلأَت imtala'at	were filled with
مَقاهي (مَقْهى) maqāhī (maqhā)	coffee shops
رِجال (رَجُل) rijāl (rajul)	men
يُدَخِّنون (دَخِّن) yudakhkhinūn (dakhkhan)	they smoke
سَجائِر (سِجارة) sajā'r (sijāra)	cigarettes
يَرْتَدون (اِرْتَدى) yartadūn (irtadā)	they wear
مَلابِس malābis	clothing
غَرْبِيَّة gharbiyya	Western
باسْتِثْناء bistithnā'	with the exception of
قَليل مِن qalīl min	a little of; a few
نِساء (اِمْرأة) nisā' (imrā'a)	women
أحْجِبة (حِجاب) aHjiba (Hijāb)	women's head cover(s)
تُغَطِّي (غَطّى) tughaTTī (ghaTTā)	they cover
ساكِنوها sākinūhā	its residents
دَرَجَة daraja	extent, degree
مُحافَظَة muHāfaDHa	conservativism
قِراءَة qirā'a	reading
دَليل سِياحي dalīl siyāHī	guide book

نُصَدِّق أنَّ nuSaddiq (Saddaq) anna	we believe (to believe) that
دَخَلْنا dakhalnā	we entered
ضَيِّقَة Dayyiqa	narrow
مُزْدَحِمَة muzdaHima	crowded
حَياة Hayā	life

LESSON 12

(Modern Standard Arabic)

عِنْد الطَّبيب

'ind aT-Tabīb At the Doctor's

A. Dialogue

الطَّبيب: ما هِيَ المُشْكِلَة؟

دونالد: أَشْعُر بِأَلَم في صَدْري، وفي ذِراعِي اليُسْرى، أَخاف أن تَكون أَزْمَة قَلْبِيَّة.

الطَّبيب: هَل أُصيب أَحَد أَقارِبك بِأَزَمات قَلْبِيَّة مِن قَبْل؟

دونالد: لا، عَلى حَسَب عِلْمي.

الطَّبيب: هَل تُمارِس التَّمْرينات الرياضيَّة؟

دونالد: أَذْهَب لِصالة التَّمْرينات الرياضيَّة ثَلاث مَرَّات أُسْبوعيّاً لِحَمْل الأَثْقال.

الطَّبيب: هَل تُمارِس أَيَّة تَدْريبات أُخْرى غَيْر حَمْل الأَثْقال؟

دونالد: لا فَأَنا مَشْغول جِدّاً، كَما أُجْريَت لي عَمَليَّة جِراحيَّة في رُكْبَتي العَام الماضي، لِذَلِك كان عَلَيَّ أن أُقَلِّل مِن الجَري والقَفْز لِمُدَة عام.

الطَّبيب: هَل تَأْكُل الكَثير مِن الطَّعام المَليء بالبُهارات؟

دونالد: نَعَم، فَأَنا مِن عاشِقي البوريتو بالبُهارات.

الطَّبيب: لا أَعْتَقِد أن هَذِه أَزْمَة قَلْبِيَّة، ولَكِن سَأَعْطيك رَقَم تِليفون أَخِصَّائي قَلْب لِكَي تَتَأَكَّد مِن ذَلِك.

---

aT-Tabīb: mā hiya l-mushkila?

dūnald: ash'ur bi alam fī Sadrī wa fī dhirā'i l-yusrā akhāf an takūn azma qalbiyya.

aT-Tabīb: hal uSīb aHad aqāribak bi azamāt qalbiyya min qabl?

dūnald: lā 'alā Hasab 'ilmī.

aT-Tabīb: hal tumāris at-tamrīnāt ar-riyāDiyya?

dūnald: adh-hab liSālat at-tamrīnāt ar-riyāDiyya thalāth marrāt usbū'iyyan liHaml al-athqāl.

aT-Tabīb: hal tumāris ayyat tadrībāt ukhrā ghayr Haml al-athqāl?

dūnald: lā fa-anā mashghūl jiddan kamā ujriyat lī 'amaliyya jirāHiyya fī rukbatī al-'ām al-māDī, lidhālik kān yajib 'alayya an uqallil min al-jary wa l-qafz limudat 'ām.

aT-Tabīb: hal ta'kul al-kathīr min aT-Ta'ām al-malī' bi l-buhārāt?

dūnald: na'am, fa-anā min 'āshiqi l-burītū bi l-buhārāt.

aT-Tabīb: lā a'taqid anna hādhihī azma qalbiyya wa lākin sa'u'Tīk raqam tilifūn akhiSSā'i l-qalb likay tata'akkad min dhālik.

Doctor: So, what seems to be the problem?

Donald: I have pain in my chest and in my left arm. I am afraid it might be a heart attack!

Doctor: Has anyone in your family had a heart attack before?

Donald: Not that I know of.

Doctor: Do you exercise?

Donald: I go to the gym three times a week to lift weights.

Doctor: Do you do any exercise besides lifting weights?

Donald: No, because I'm very busy. Also, I had a knee surgery last year, so I have to reduce any running and jumping for a year.

Doctor: Do you eat a lot of spicy foods?

Donald: Yes, I am a big fan of spicy burritos.

Doctor: I don't think it is a heart attack, but I will give you the number of a heart specialist so you can make sure.

B. Grammar and Usage

1. DERIVING NOUNS FROM VERBS

There are four types of commonly used nouns that are derived from verbs: verbal nouns, active participles, passive participles, and nouns of location.

A. THE VERBAL NOUN

Verbal nouns in Arabic are similar in function and meaning to English nouns ending in *-ing*.

يَجِب عَلَيَّ أَن أُقَلِّل مِن ا لجَري والقَفْز لِمُدَة عام.

yajib 'alayya an uqallil min al-jary wa l-qafz limuddat 'ām.

I have to reduce my <u>running</u> and <u>jumping</u> for a year.

The nouns *running* and *jumping* are derived from the verbs *to run* and *to jump*. In Arabic, the verbal nouns derived from Form I verbs, such as يَجْري *yajrī* (run) and يَقْفِز *yaqfiz* (jump), are irregular and must be learned along with the verb. The verbal nouns derived from Forms II through X verbs are formed in a regular manner, presented in Appendix A.

For example, to form the verbal noun from a Form II verb (*CaCCaC*), such as غَيَّر *ghayyāra* (to change), the prefix تَ *ta-* is added to the beginning of the word and a vowel ي *ī* is inserted before the last root consonant. Hence, the verbal noun is تغيير *taghyīr* (changing), and it follows the pattern *ta-CCīC*.

يَجِب عَلى دونالد تَغْيِير عادات أكْله.

yajib 'alā dūnald taghyīr 'ādāt akli.

Donald has to change his eating habits. (*lit.*, necessary for Donald changing his eating habits.)

To form the verbal noun from a Form III verb (*CāCaC*), add مُ *mu-* to the beginning of the stem and a ـة at the end. مُشاهَدَة *mushāhada* (watching) is derived from the verb شاهَد *shahad* (to watch) and has the pattern *mu-CāCaCa*.

يُحِب دونالد مُشاهَدَة التليفِزيون.

yuHibb dūnald mushāhadat at-tilifizion.

Donald likes watching TV.

Notice that not every word ending in *-ing* in English corresponds to an Arabic verbal noun. English *-ing* words are also used to create verbal forms, present or past progressive tenses, such as *I am/was running*.

Compare:

أكْل الطَّعام المَلِيء بالبُهارات يُسَبِّب آلام الصَّدْر.

akl (verbal noun) *aT-Ta'ām al-malī' bi l-buhārāt yusabbib ālām aS-Sadr.*

Eating spicy food causes chest pain.

With the following example:

يَأكُل دونالد طَعاما مَلِيئًا بالبُهارات.

ya'kul (verb in the imperfect tense) *dūnald Ta'ām malī' bi l-buhārāt.*

Donald is eating spicy food.

B. THE ACTIVE PARTICIPLE

The active participle is used to refer to the doer of the action expressed by the verb. It is similar to nouns ending in *-er* or *-ent* in English, e.g., *producer* or *resident*. Here are some examples of Arabic active participles derived from Form I verbs.

كَتَب	كاتِب
katab	*kātib*
to write	writer
صَنَع	صانِع
Sana'	*Sāni'*
to produce	producer
سَكِن	ساكِن
sakan	*sākin*
to reside	resident
عَشِق	عاشِق
'ashiq	*'āshiq*
to love	lover

All active participles derived from Form I verbs follow the pattern *CāCiC*. To derive the active participle from Form II to X verbs, simply add the prefix مُـ *mu-* to the imperfect stem of the verb and replace the vowel between the second and the third root consonants with a *kasra* (ـِ).

يَتَكَلَّم
yatakallam
he speaks

مُتَكَلِّم
mutakallim
speaker

Like other nouns, participles change depending on the gender, number, and case of the subject of the verb to which they refer.

Many nouns referring to professions are active participles. For example:

مُهَنْدِس *muhandis* (engineer)

مُمَرِّض *mumarriD* (nurse)

مُدَرِّس *mudarris* (teacher)

تاجِر *tājir* (trader)

C. THE PASSIVE PARTICIPLE

The passive participle is a noun referring to an object of the action expressed by the verb.

كَتَب
katab
to write

مكتوب
maktūb
written one (*lit.*, something written)

كَسَر
kasar
to break

مكسور
maksūr
broken one (*lit.*, something broken)

شَرِب
shariba
to drink

مَشْروب
mashrūb
a drink (*lit.*, something drunk)

A passive participle can also have an adjectival meaning.

شَغَل
shaghal
to work

أَنا مَشْغول جِدًّا.
ana mashghūl jiddan.
I am very busy. (*cf.* over-worked)

طَبَخ
Tabakh
to cook

الطَّعام مَطْبوخ بِالبُهارات.
al-Ta'ām maTbūkh bi l-buhārāt.
The food is cooked with spices.

عَرَف
araf
to know

هو أخِصّائي قَلْب مَعْرُوف.
huwa akhiSSā'ī qalb ma'rūf.
He is a well-known heart specialist.

184

A passive participle derived from Form I verbs is produced by adding ‑مـ ma- to the beginning of the verb, and و ū between the second and third root consonants. Like the active participle, these nouns change according to gender, number, and case, and can be definite or indefinite.

For Form II to Form X verbs, the only difference between the active participle and the passive participle is the short vowel between the last two root letters. The passive participle has a *fatHa* (ˊ) between the last two root consonants, while the active participle has a *kasra* (ˌ):

مُنْتِج

muntij

producer

مُنْتَج

muntaj

produced, product

Because short vowels are usually not included in written MSA, the active and passive participles for these verb forms are indistinguishable in writing. It is necessary to guess from the context whether the noun is an active participle or a passive participle.

D. NOUNS OF LOCATION

The noun of location refers to the place where the action of the verb occurs. In general, nouns of location are formed by adding ‑مـ ma- to the beginning of the word and a *fatHa* (ˊ) between the last two root consonants. There is no vowel between the first two consonants of the root. You have already learned several nouns from this category:

مَدْرَسَة	مَطار	مَطْعَم	مَكْتَب	مَكْتَبة
madrasa	*maTār*	*maT'am*	*maktab*	*maktaba*
school	airport	restaurant	office	library

Some nouns of location end with the feminine marker ـة, but the appearance of this feature is unpredictable. The plural form of Form I nouns of location is produced by adding a *kasra* (ˌ) after the first root letter and the ا -ā after the second.

مَكْتَب

maktab

office

مَكاتِب

makātib

offices

مَطْعَم

maT'am

restaurant

مَطاعِم

maTā'im

restaurants

Note that the pattern used to derive nouns of location is not used productively in the language to create new words. Still, knowing it will help you guess the meaning of such nouns when you come across them.

2. REFLEXIVE FORMS

A. REFLEXIVE VERBS

As you saw in Lesson 7, some verb forms have a reflexive meaning, such as the Form V verb below, placed next to the non-reflexive equivalent.

غَيَّر

ghayyara

to change (something)

تَغَيَّر

taghayyara

to change oneself

When this reflexive form of the verb is used, the verb does not take an object, because the subject is the same as the intended object of the verb.

لَن يَتَغَيَّر دونالد أبَدا.

lan yataghayyar dūnald abadan.

Donald will never change. (*lit.*, Donald will never change himself)

Contrast this sentence to the example where the non-reflexive Form II verb *ghayyar* (to change) is used.

غَيَّرت لوسي عادات أكْل دونالد.

ghayyarat lūsī 'ādāt akl dūnald.

Lucy changed Donald's eating habits.

The verb is followed by the direct object *Donald's eating habits*.

B. REFLEXIVE CONSTRUCTION

MSA also has a reflexive construction, formed by following a verb with the word نَفْس *nafs* (self), or, less commonly, the word ذات *dhāt* (self), to which the object pronoun suffixes are added.

أجْهَدت نَفْسي.

ajhadt nafsi.

I tired myself out.

أمْرَض نَفْسَه بِكَثْرَة الطَّعام.

amraD nafsahu bikathrat aT-Ta'ām

He made himself sick by overeating (*lit.*, by the large quantity of food).

3. PARTS OF THE BODY

Here are the MSA words for the various parts of the body.

PARTS OF THE BODY		
eye(s)	'ayn ('aynān)	عَيْن (عَيْنان)
arm(s)	dhirā' (dhirā'an)	ذِراع (ذِراعان)
leg(s)	sāq (sāqān)	ساق (ساقان)
hand(s)	yad (yadān)	يَدّ (يَدان)
back	DHahr	ظَهْر
stomach	mi'dda	مِعْدَة
head	ra's	رَأْس
nose	anf	أنْف
throat	zawr	زُور
ear(s)	udhun (udhunān)	أُذُن (أذنان)
heart	qalb	قَلْب
hair	sha'r	شَعْر
nail(s)	DHifr (aDHāfir)	ظِفْر (أظافِر)
neck	raqaba	رَقَبة
mouth	fam	فَم
tooth (teeth)	sin (asnān)	سِن (أسْنان)
elbow(s)	kū' (akwā)	كوع (أكْواع)
knee(s)	rukba (rukab)	رُكْبَة (رُكَب)

C. Vocabulary

طَبيب Tabīb		doctor
مُشْكِلَة mushkila		problem
أشْعُر (شَعَر) 'ash'ur (sha'ar)		I feel
ألَم 'alam		pain
يُسْرى yusrā		left

أخاف (خاف) أن akhāf (khāf) an	I fear that (to fear)
أزْمَة قَلبِيَّة azma qalbiyya	heart attack
أُصيب بِ uSīb bi	was afflicted with
أقاربك (قَريب) aqāribak (qarīb)	your relatives
على حَسَب 'alā Hasab	according to
عِلْمي 'ilmī	my knowledge
تُمارِس (مارَس) tumāris (māras)	you practice
تَمْرينات tamrīnāt	exercises
رياضيَّة riyāDiyya	athletic (f.)
صالة التَّمْرينات الرياضيَّة Sālat at-tamrīnāt ar-riyāDiyya	gym
حَمْل Haml	lifting
أثْقال (ثِقْل) athqāl (thiql)	weights
تَدْريبات tadrībāt	training
مَشْغول mashghūl	busy
أُجْريَت ujriyat	was performed
عَمَليَّة جِراحيَّة 'amaliyya jirāHiyya	surgical operation
رُكْبَتي rukbatī	my knee
مَاضي māDī	past
لِذلك lidhālik	for that reason
يَجِب عَلَيَّ أن yajib 'alayya an	it is necessary for me to
أُقَلِّل مِن uqallil min	I lessen
جَرْي jary	running
قَفْز qafz	jumping
مَليء malī'	full
بُهارات buhārāt	spices
عاشِقين 'āshiqīn	enthusiasts
أعْتَقِد (اِعْتَقَد) أن a'taqid (i'taqad) anna	I think that
رَقَم raqam	number

تِليفون tilifūn	telephone
أخِصَّائي akhiSSā'ī	specialist
تَتَأَكَّد (تَأَكَّد) مِن tata'akkad min	you make sure of

D. Cultural Note

Health and well-being are fundamental topics of casual conversation in the Arab world. For instance, it is common in some Arab countries to ask كيف صِحَّتُك اليَوم؟ kayfa SiHHatuk al-yawm? (How is your health today?) right after greeting the person. At the same time, people will almost never respond negatively to this question, even if their health is not good. Assuming that one's health could always be worse, and that it is always good to be thankful, the typical response to this question is simply الحمْد الله al-Hamdulillāh (Thank God).

There is also a taboo associated with speaking the names of more severe diseases. Sometimes euphemisms are used to refer to them. For example, cancer is consistently referred to as المرَض الوِحِش al-maraD al-wiHish (the bad disease) in Egyptian Arabic.

In most Arab countries, healthcare is provided for free or for a nominal cost, but the service is usually inferior to the much better-equipped, but expensive, private hospitals.

E. Exercices

1. Fill in the blanks with the correct word from the choices in parentheses.

a. ذهب دونالد لطبيب عندما شعر بألم في _____. (أظافره / شعره / معدته)

b. يعمل أحمد كبائع للكتب في _____ (مطعم / مكتب / مكتبة) بالقاهرة.

c. _____ (طباخ / ممرض / مهندس) فندق السلام بدمشق ممتاز.

d. هل تمارس أية _____ (تدريبات / عينان / عمليات) أخرى؟

e. لن أذهب معكم للمطعم فأنا _____ (معروف / متكلم / مشغول) جداً.

2. Fill in the blanks with a verbal noun, an active participle, a passive participle, or a noun of location as required by the context, derived from the verbs in parentheses.

a. أحمد زويل عالم كيمياء _____ (عرف).

b. نجيب محفوظ _____ (كتب) مصري.

c. لم يذهب دونالد إلى الحفلة لأن ساقه _____ (كسر).

d. ذهبت لوسي ودونالد إلى _____ (طعم) ليتناولا طعام الغداء.

e. هذا الطعام _____ (طبخ) بالكثير من البهارات.

3. Derive verbal nouns from the following verbs.

a. كتَب

b. تغيَّر

c. أنتج

d. درَّس

e. أكَل

4. Put the following words in the right order to form meaningful sentences.

a. يومياً – التمرينات – تمارس – لوسي – الرياضية

b. أنّه – بألم – في – دونالد – يشعر

c. مريض – دونالد – عادات – غير – أكله – لأنه

d. مكتبه – يذهب – الصباح – كل – إلى – في – دونالد – يوم

e. العملية – بسبب (because of) – يستطيع – يجري – دونالد – أن – الجراحية – لا

5. Derive the perfect stem of the verb from which the following nouns (verbal noun, active participles, or passive participles) were derived.

a. عاشقي

b. مشغول

c. منتجات

d. مشاهدة

e. تدريبات

Answer Key

1. a. معدته *mi'datuh* (his stomach)

   b. مكتبة *maktaba* (a library)

   c. طبّاخ *tabbākh* (a cook)

   d. تدريبات *tadrībāt* (exercises)

   e. مشغول *mashghūl* (busy)

   b. تغيُّر *taghayyur* (change)

   c. إنْتاج *intāj* (production)

   d. تَدْريس *tadrīs* (teaching)

   e. أكْل *akl* (food; eating)

2. a. معروف *ma'rūf* (famous)

   b. كاتب *kātib* (a writer)

   c. مكسورة *maksūra* (broken)

   d. المطعم *al-maT'am* (the restaurant)

   e. مطبوخ *maTbūkh* (cooked)

3. a. كِتابَة *kitāba* (writing)

4. a. لوسي تمارس التمرينات الرياضيِة يومياً.
   lūsi tumāris at-tamrināt ar-riyāDiyya yawmiyyan.
   Lucy exercises daily.

b. دونالد يشعر بألم في أذنه.

dūnald yash'ur bi-alam fī udhunih.

Donald feels pain in his ear.

c. غيَّر دونالد عادات أكله لأنه مريض.

ghayyar dūnald 'ādāt aklih li-annahu marīD.

Donald changed his eating habits because he is sick.

d. يذهب دونالد إلى مكتبه كل يوم في الصباح.

yadh-hab dūnald ilā maktabuh kull yawm fi S-SabāH.

Donald goes to his office every day in the morning.

e. لا يستطيع دونالد أن يجري بسبب العملية الجراحية.

lā yastaTī' dūnald an yajrī bi-sabab al-'amaliyya al-jirāHiyya.

Donald cannot run because of the surgery.

5. a. عَشِق *'ashiq* (to love)

b. شَغَل *shaghal* (to engage, to occupy)

c. نَتَج *nataj* (to result)

d. شاهَد *shāhad* (to watch)

e. دَرَّب *darrab* (to train)

LESSON 13

(Modern Standard Arabic)

في العَمَل

fi l-'amal At Work

A. Dialogue

Lucy and Nadia are meeting for lunch at Nadia's office.

لوسي: أنا آسِفَة عَلى هَذا التَّأْخِير يا نادِية، المُرور كان سَيِّئاً جداً.

نادية: لَيْسَت هَذِه مُشْكِلَة، هَل ما زال لَدَيْك وَقْت لِتَرَي المَكْتَب قَبْل الغَداء؟

لوسي: نَعَم، أرِيني المَكْتَب.

نادية: تَفَضَّلي مَعي. هَذِه هِيَ صالة الاسْتِقْبال وهَذِه هِيَ حُجْرَة الفاكْس وماكينة التَّصْوير، وتَخْدَم هَذا الطابِق بِالكامِل.

لوسي: كَم مُوَظَّفاً يَعْمَل في هَذا الطابِق؟

نادية: ثَمانِية مُحَرِّرين وتِسْعَة صَحَفيين.

لوسي: واللهِ؟ يا حَرام، في هَذِه المِساحَة الصَّغيرة؟

نادية: فِعْلاً هَذِه المِساحَة صَغيرَة ولكِن كُلّ صَحَفي لَدَيْه كَمْبيوتَر بِشَبَكَة إيثَرنِيت.

لوسي: وأيْن مَكْتَبُك؟

نادية: في الطابِق العُلْوي.

لوسي: آه، هَذا الطابِق لِلْمُحَرِّرين والصَّحَفِيِّين فَقَط، أمّا الطابِق العُلْوي فَلِرَئيسَة التَّحْرير!

نادِية: بِالضَّبْط، سَنَرى إن كُنْت سَوْف تُشْفِقين علَيَّ أيْضاً.

---

lūsī: anā āsifa 'ala hādhā at-ta'khīr yā nādya, al-murūr kān sayyi' jiddan.

nādya: laysat hādhihi mushkila. hal mā zāl ladayki waqt litarai l-maktab qabl al-ghadā'?

lūsī: na'am, arīni l-maktab.

nādya: tafaDDalī ma'ī. hādhihī hiya Salat al-istiqbāl, wa hādhihī hiya Hujrat al-fāks wa mākinat at-taSwīr, wa takhdim hādha T-Tābiq bi l-kāmil.

lūsī: kam muwaDHDHafan ya'mal fī hādha T-Tabiq?

nādya: thamāniat muHarririn wa tis'at SaHāfiyyin.

lūsī: wa l-lāhi? yā Harām fi hādhihi l-misāHa S-Saghira?

nādya: fi'lan hādhihī al-misāHa Saghīra wa lākin kul SaHafi ladayh kumbyūtar bishabakat itharnit.

lūsī: wa ayn maktabuki?

nādya: fi T-Tābiq al-'ulwī.

lūsī: āh, hādha T-Tābiq li l-muHarririn wa S-SaHafiyyin faqaT, amma aT-Tābiq al-'ulwī fa lira'īsat at-taHarīr!

nādya: bi D-DabT, sanarā in kunti sawfa tushfiqin 'alayya ayDan.

Lucy: Sorry I am late. The traffic was horrible.

Nadia: It's ok. Do you still have time to see the office before lunch?

Lucy: I think so. Please show me around.

Nadia: Well, this is the reception lounge, and this is the fax and photocopy room. It serves the whole floor.

Lucy: How many people work on this floor?

Nadia: Eight editors and nine journalists.

Lucy: Really? How terrible! In this little space?

Nadia: Well, there isn't a lot of space, but each desk has a computer on an Ethernet network.

Lucy: Where is your office?

Nadia: Upstairs.

Lucy: Oh, I see. This floor is just for the writers and editors, but the upstairs is for the editor in chief!

Nadia: Exactly. Let's go up and see whether you'll feel bad for me, too!

B. Grammar and Usage

1. IRREGULAR VERBS: VERBS BEGINNING IN A LONG VOWEL IN THE PERFECT TENSE

Verbs that begin with a one of the long vowels, either ـِي, و, or ا, in the perfect tense have slightly irregular behavior. These vowels can either be part of the prefix or the first root letter.

Form IV, VII, VIII, and X verbs, such as اِسْتَقْبَل *istaqbal* (he received), all begin with the letter ا.[1] This letter is replaced with a short vowel in the imperfect tense. In the case of Forms VII to X, the ا changes to *fatHa* (◌َ), following the imperfect prefix *y-*.

اِنْبَسَط

inbasaT

he enjoyed himself

يَنْبَسِط

yanbasiT

he enjoys himself

In the case of Form IV verbs, the ا is replaced with a *damma* (◌ُ) in the imperfect tense,

---

[1] See Lesson 7 for more examples and Appendix A for a summary of different verb patterns.

following the imperfect prefix y-.

أَرْسَل
arsala
he sent

يُرْسِل
yursil
he sends

Other verbs begin with ـ, و, or ا because it is the first letter of their three-letter root. While roots with ـ or ا as their first root consonant are rather rare, you have already encountered several verbs with و as their first root letter.

وَجَب _wajab_ (it was necessary)

وَصَل _wasal_ (he arrived)

Note that the letter و is pronounced as the consonant w, because it precedes a vowel.

In Form I verbs, the letter و turns into a _fatHa_ (´) in the imperfect tense, which follows the imperfect prefix ـ y-.

يَجِب _yajib_ (it is necessary)

يَصِل _yaSi_ (he arrives)

Form VIII verbs, derived from roots having و as the first root letter, have a peculiar form. Look at the formation of the Form VIII verb from the root وَفَق _wafaq_ (to agree to).

1. وَفَق   2. اوتفق   3. اتتفق   4. اتَّفَق

wafaq   _ittafaq_

The Form I verb وَفَق _wafaq_ (to agree to) is first modified according to the pattern used for form VIII verbs, _aCtaCaC_: an ا at the beginning and a ت after the first root consonant are added to create اوتفق. Next, the و is changed to ت, forming اتتفق. Because of the lack of a vowel between the two letters ت, they are compressed into تّ (with a _shadda_) to form the verb اتَّفَق _ittafaq_ (to agree).

2. IRREGULAR VERBS: WEAK VERBS

Weak verbs are those that have a vowel as the last root letter, e.g., ع – ن – ى (mean). These verbs are irregular because the terminal vowel of the perfect stem changes in the imperfect tense. For example:

عَنَى
'anā
it meant

يَعْنِي
_ya'ni_
it means

ع – ن – ى
[root letters]

The last letter of the perfect stem, ى _ā_, changes into ي _i_ in the imperfect. There is a great variety of changes that the terminal vowel of a weak verb can undergo. We will discuss the three most common types below.

• ى _ā_ in the perfect stem changes to ي _i_ in the imperfect stem (see section A, below),

194

- ي *ī* in the perfect stem changes to ى *ā* in the imperfect stem (see section B, below),

- ا *ā* in the perfect stem changes to و *ū* in the imperfect stem (see section C, below).

A. TERMINAL ى *ā* IN THE PERFECT STEM TO TERMINAL ي *ī* IN THE IMPERFECT STEM

The change from the terminal ى *ā* to the terminal ي *ī* is the most common type of change.

جَرَى	يَجْرِي
jara	*yajrī*
he ran (Form I)	he runs

All rules about weak verbs apply equally to any verb form (I through X) derived from the same weak root. For example, the terminal ى *ā* in the perfect form of the Form IV verb أَعْطَى *a'Tā* (to give), derived from the root ع – ط – و, changes to ي *ī* in the imperfect stem, as did the terminal ى *ā* of عَنَى *anā* (to mean).

أَعْطَى	يُعْطِي
a'Tā	*yu'Tī*
he gave (Form IV)	he gives

Notice the same change in the verbs below belonging to Forms VIII and X.

انْتَهَى	يَنْتَهِي	ن – ه – ى
intahā	*yantahī*	
he finished (Form VIII)	he finishes	[root letters]
اشْتَرَى	يَشْتَرِي	ش – ر – ى
ishtarā	*yashtarī*	
he bought (Form X)	he buys	[root letters]

B. TERMINAL ي *ī* IN THE PERFECT STEM TO TERMINAL ى *ā* IN THE IMPERFECT STEM

Verbs with roots that end in ي *ī* in the perfect stem change that vowel into ى *ā* in the imperfect stem.

نَسِي	يَنْسَى	ن – س – ى
nasī	*yansā*	
he forgot	he forgets	[root letters]

C. TERMINAL ا *ā* IN THE PERFECT STEM TO TERMINAL و *ū* IN THE IMPERFECT STEM

Some verbs with roots that end in ا *ā* in the perfect stem change that vowel to و *ū* in the imperfect stem.

دَعا	يَدْعو	د – ع – و
da'ā	yad'ū	
he invited	he invites	[root letters]

بَدا	يَبْدو	ب – د – ا
badā	yabdū	
he seemed	he seems	[root letters]

D. STEM CHANGES BEFORE TENSE SUFFIXES

When tense suffixes are added to weak verbs, there is generally no change in the sound of the stem, only in the way it is written. The long vowel letter simply changes from its final form to its medial form.

يَنْتَهي	تَنْتَهين
yantahī	tantahīn
he finishes	you (f. sg.) finish

However, for stems ending in ى ā, the long vowel changes in sound as well. It becomes ـَيْ ay when a suffix is added, as in:

انْتَهَى	انْتَهَيْتِ
intahā	intahayti
he finished	you (f. sg.) finished

The terminal ى ā of the stem is dropped in the following example when the suffix ـوا is added.

انْتَهَى	انْتَهوا
intahā	intahū
he finished	they finished

Similarly, the terminal ي ī of the stem is dropped when the suffix ـون -ūn is added:

يُعْطي	يُعْطون
yu'Tī	yu'Tūn
he gives	they give

When conjugating weak verbs ending with an ا ā, some forms require that the ا be dropped, while in others it changes to و:

دَعا	دَعَوْتَ	دَعَت
da'ā	da'awta	da'at
he called	you (m. sg.) called	she called

The rules regarding which suffixes force the last letter to change into a short vowel are based on the complex rules of Arabic phonology. You will not need to memorize any of these rules, but you should learn to recognize common weak verbs, even when the last

196

vowel does not appear in writing. For your reference in writing, tables of complete conjugations of the different weak verb types appear in Appendices C through E.

C. Vocabulary

آسِفَة āsifa	sorry
ما زال mā zāl	still (lit., has not stopped)
قَبْل qabl	before
غَداء ghadā'	lunch
حُجْرَة hujra	room
فاكْس fāks	fax
ماكينَة mākina	machine
تَصْوير taSwīr	copying
تَخْدُم (خَدَم) takhdum (khadam)	it serves (to serve)
طابِق Tābiq	story (of a building)
بالكامِل bi l-kāmil	all of it
مُحَرِّرين muHarrirīn	editors
صَحَفيين SaHāfiyyīn	journalists
والله؟ wa l-lāhi?	Really?
يا حَرام! yā Harām!	Oh, what a shame!
مِساحَة misāHa	area
فِعْلاً fi'lan	truly
كُمْبيوتر kumbyūtar	computer
شَبَكَة shabaka	net
إيثَرنيت itharnit	Ethernet
عُلْوي 'ulwī	upper
رَئيسَة التَّحْرير ra'īsat at-taHrīr	editor-in-chief
بالضَّبْط bi D-DabT	exactly
تُشْفِقين (أَشْفَق) على tushfiqīn (ashfaq) 'alayya	you (f. sg.) sympathize with me

SUPPLEMENTAL VOCABULARY: FAXES, COMPUTERS, E-MAIL, INTERNET

مَلَف	malaff	file
إنْتَرنِت	intarnit	Internet
الشاشَة	ash-shāsha	monitor
الفَأَرة	al-fa'ra	mouse
السوفْت وير	aS-Suftwēr	software
الطِباعَة	aT-Tibā'a	printing
مَوقِع عَلى الشَّبَكَة	mawqi' 'ala sh-shabaka	Website
فاكْس	fāks	fax
أرْسَل فاكْسا	arsal fāks(an)	to send a fax
اسْتَلَم فاكسا	istalam fāks(an)	to receive a fax
البَريد الإلِكْتُروني	al-barīd al-iliktrūnī	e-mail
يَفْتَح	yaftaH	to open
مُرْفَق	murfaq	attachment
يَتَصَفَّح الإنْتَرنِت	yataSaffaH al-intarnit	to browse the Internet
فَيْروس كُمْبيوتَر	fayrūs kumbyūtar	computer virus
وَصْلَة الإنْتَرنِت	waSlat al-intarnit	Internet connection
يَتَّصِل بالإنْتَرنِت	yattaSil bi l-intarnit	to connect to the Internet

D. Cultural Note

The workweek in most Arab countries is scheduled based on the weekly holiday of the Muslim majority, which is Friday. Typically, the weekend consists of Friday only or, more rarely, Friday and Saturday.

The demographics of workplaces in Arab countries are as diverse as the peoples that make up the Arab world. Because of the great need for skilled workers in the oil-rich countries of the region, and the lack of employment opportunities in others, many individuals travel abroad looking for work.

In some Arab countries, opportunities for women are severely limited by cultural expectations and taboos. In Saudi Arabia, for instance, women are discouraged from working in professions that require extensive contact with male clients. In other countries, such as Egypt, where workplace culture has been influenced more by the country's socialist history than by its Islamic one, women make up a more significant, if not equal, portion of the working population.

E. Exercises

1. Fill in the blank with the correct word from the choices in parentheses.

a. في مكتب نادية _____. (طابق / حجرة فاكس / ماكينة تصوير)

b. عدد المحررين الذين يعملون في الطابق _____. (عشرة / ثمانية / تسعة)

c. مساحة الطابق _____. (كبيرة / صغيرة / طويلة)

d. مكتب _____ في الطابق العلوي. (الصحفيين / المحررين / رئيسة التحرير)

e. كل صحفي لديه شبكة _____. (إنترنت / إيثرنت / فاكس)

2. Change the following perfect tense verbs into the imperfect tense; use the *huwa* (he) form.

a. وجب

b. استخدم

c. استقبل

d. انبسط

e. أرسل

3. Change the following perfect tense verbs into the imperfect tense; use the *ana* (I) form.

a. وصل

b. اتفق

c. وجد

d. عنى

e. أعطى

4. Change the following perfect tense verbs into the imperfect tense using the person indicated in parentheses.

a. انتهى (هو)

b. اشترى (هو)

c. أعطوا (هم)

d. وصلنا (نحن)

e. رأى (هو)

5. Match the words from column A with the words in column B to form meaningful possessive expressions.

A	B
صالة	إيثرنيت
رئيسة	العلوي
يا	الاستقبال
الطابق	حرام
شبكة	التحرير

Answer Key

1. a. ماكينة تصوير *mākinat taSwir* (copy machine)

   b. ثمانية *thamānya* (eight)

   c. صغيرة *Saghīra* (small, young)

   d. رئيسة التحرير *ra'īsat at-taHrīr* (the editor-in-chief)

   e. إيثرنت *itharnit* (Ethernet)

2. a. يَجب *yajib* (he must)

   b. يَستخدم *yastakhdim* (he uses)

   c. يَستقبل *yastaqbil* (he receives)

   d. يَنبسط *yanbasit* (he is happy)

   e. يُرسل *yursil* (he sends)

3. a. أصل *aSil* (I arrive)

   b. أتَّفق *attafiq* (I agree)

   c. أجد *ajid* (I find)

d. أعني *a'nī* (I mean)

e. أعطي *u'Tī* (I give)

4. a. ينتهي *yantahī* (it ends)

   b. يشتري *yashtarī* (he buys)

   c. يعطون *yu'Tūn* (they give)

   d. نصل *naSil* (we arrive)

   e. يرى *yarā* (he sees)

5. a. صالة الاستقبال *Sālat al-istiqbāl* (reception)

   b. رئيسة التحرير *ra'īsat at-taHrīr* (the editor-in-chief)

   c. يا حرام! *yā Harām!* (How terrible!)

   d. الطابق العلوي *aT-Tabiq al-'ulwī* (upstairs)

   e. شبكة إيثرنت *shabakat itharnit* (Ethernet network)

LESSON 14

(Modern Standard Arabic)

أَلو، أَحْمَد؟

alū, aHmad? Hello, Ahmed?

A. Dialogue

Georgette, Ahmed's girlfriend, calls Ahmed to discuss plans to take a trip to the beach.

أَحْمَد: أَلو؟

جورجات: أَلو، أَحْمَد؟

أَحْمَد: نَعَم، أَنا أَحْمَد، أَهْلا يا جورجات. كَيْف حالِك؟

جورجات: بِخَيْر والحَمْد لله، كَيْف حالُك أَنْت يا أَحْمَد؟

أَحْمَد: بِخَيْر، كَيْف حال أَخيك، هَل يَشْعُر بِتَحَسّْن؟

جورجات: نَعَم، هُو أَفْضَل الآن وعاد اليَوْم لِلْعَمَل.

أَحْمَد: الحَمْد لله.

جورجات: هَل سَتَأْتي مَعَنا صَباح يَوْم السَّبْت إلَى شاطِئ البَحْر لِنَسْبَح؟

أَحْمَد: لَن أَسْتَطيع، يَجِب أَن أَبْقَى في البَيْت لِكَي أَذاكِر.

جورجات: ولَكِن هَذِه هِي الإجازَة الوَحيدَة في فَصْل الرَبيع، وسَيَكون الشاطِئ جَميلاً لأنّ الجَوّ لَيْس حاراً كَما في الصَّيْف.

أَحْمَد: أَنا أَفَضِّل الذَهاب في الصَّيْف لِكَي لا أَفَكِّر في الامْتِحانات طِوال الوَقْت.

جورجات: إذا لَم تَأْتِ مَعَنا فَسَأَحْزَن كَثيراً. عَلى أَيّ حال سَنَذْهَب في السّاعَة العاشِرَة صَباحاً وسَنَعود يَوْم الأَرْبَعاء، أَرْجو أَن تُغَيِّر رَأْيَك.

أَحْمَد: سَأَفَكِّر في هَذا، ولَكِن إذا لَم أَسْتَطِع أَن أَذْهَب مَعَكُم، هَل سَتَذْهَبون في شَهْر يونية؟

جورجات: رُبَّما. لَو كُنْت مكانَك، لَذَهَبْت الآن دُون تَفْكير، مَع السَّلامَة.

أَحْمَد: مَع السَّلامَة.

201

aHmad: alū?

jurjāt: alū, aHmad?

aHmad: na'am, anā aHmad, ahlan yā jurjāt. kayfa Hālik?

jurjāt: bi-khayr wa l-Hamdulillāh, kayfa Hāluk ant yā aHmad?

aHmad: bi-khayr, kayfa hāl akhīk? hal yash'ur bi-taHassun?

jurjāt: na'am, huwa afDal al-ān wa 'ād al-yawm li l-'amal.

aHmad: al-Hamdulillāh.

jurjāt: hal sata'tī ma'anā SabāH yawm as-sabt 'ilā shāTi' al-baHr linasbaH?

aHmad: lan astaTī', yajib an abqā fi l-bayt likay udhākir.

jurjāt: wa lākin hādhihī hiya al-ijāza l-waHīda fī faSl ar-rabī' wa sayakūn ash-shāTi' jamīl li'anna al-jaww laysa Hārr kamā fi S-Sayf.

aHmad: anā ufaDDil adh-dhihāb fi S-Sayf likay lā ufakkir fi l-imtiHānāt Tiwāl al-waqT.

jurjāt: idhā lam ta'ti ma'anā fa-sa'aHzan kathīran. 'ala ayy Hāl sanadhhab fi s-sā'a al-'āshira SabāHan wa sana'ūd yawm al-arbi'ā'. arjū an tughayyir ra'yak.

aHmad: sa'ufakkir fī hādhā, wa lākin idhā lam astaTī' an adhhab ma'akum, hal satadhhabūn fī shahr yunia?

jurjāt: rubbamā. law kunt makānak ladhahabt al-ān dūn tafkīr. ma'a s-salāma!

aHmad: ma'a s-salāma.

Ahmed: Hello?

Georgette: Hello, Ahmed?

Ahmed: Yes, this is Ahmed. Hello Georgette, how are you?

Georgette: Fine, thanks (*lit.*, praise to God). How are you, Ahmed?

Ahmed: Fine. How is your brother? Is he feeling better?

Georgette: He is better now and has gone back to work.

Ahmed: Thank God.

Georgette: Are you coming with us Saturday morning to the beach to go swimming?

Ahmed: I don't think I will make it to the beach. I have to stay at home to study.

Georgette: This is the only vacation this spring. The beaches are so nice now, because the weather is not as hot as in the summer.

Ahmed: I prefer to go in the summer, so I don't have to think about my exams all the time.

Georgette: If you don't come with us, I'll be really sad. In any case, we will be leaving at ten in the morning and returning the following Wednesday. I hope you'll change your mind.

Ahmed: I will think about it, but if I cannot go with you, would you go in June?

Georgette: Maybe, but if I were you, I would go now without thinking twice. Good-bye!

Ahmed: Bye.

B. Grammar and Usage

1. ANSWERING *WHY* QUESTIONS

There are several words in Arabic that are used to answer questions starting with لِماذا *limādha* (why). They include لأنَّ *li'anna* (because), بِسَبَب *bisabab* (because of), لِ *li* (in order to), and لِكَي *likay* (in order to).

A. لِأَنَّ li'anna (BECAUSE)

لِأَنَّ li'anna (because) must be followed by a complete sentence that begins with a noun or a pronoun. In the following example, لِأَنَّ li'anna (because) is followed by a noun.

لَنْ تَذْهَبَ جورجات إلى الشَّاطِئ لِأَنَّ أَحْمَدَ مَشْغُول.

lan tadh-hab jurjāt ila sh-shāTi' li'anna aHmad mashghūl.

Georgette will not go to the beach because Ahmed is busy.

When لِأَنَّ li'anna is followed by a sentence that has a pronominal subject, the pronoun attaches to لِأَنَّ li'anna in the form of a possessive suffix.

لا أَفَكِّر في دِراسَتي لِأَنَّني في إجازَة.

lā ufakkir fī dirāsatī li'anani fī ijāza.

I am not thinking about studies because I am on vacation.

The following table shows لِأَنَّ li'anna with different pronominal suffixes attached to it.

لِأَنَّ li'anna (BECAUSE) WITH PRONOMINAL SUFFIXES		
Singular	Plural	Dual
لَأَنَّني *li'annanī* (because I . . .)	لَأَنَّنا *li'annanā* (because we . . .)	
لَأَنَّكَ *li'annaka* (because you *(m.)* . . .)	لَأَنَّكُم *li'annakum* (because you *(m.)* . . .)	لَأَنَّكُما *li'annakumā* (because you *(m./f.)* . . .)
لَأَنَّكِ *li'annaki* (because you *(f.)* . . .)	لَأَنَّكُنَّ *li'annakunna* (because you *(f.)* . . .)	
لَأَنَّه *li'annahu* (because he . . .)	لَأَنَّهُم *li'annahum* (because they *(m.)* . . .)	لَأَنَّهُمَا *li'annahumā* (because they *(m./f.)* . . .)
لَأَنَّها *li'annahā* (because she . . .)	لَأَنَّهُنَّ *li'annahunna* (because they *(f.)* . . .)	

B. بِسَبَب bisabab (BECAUSE OF)

بِسَبَب bisabab (because of) is always followed by a noun.

لا أُحِبّ الصَّيْف بِسَبَب الحَرارَة المُرتَفِعَة.

lā uHibb aS-Sayyif bisabab al-Harāra al-murtafi'a.

I do not like summer because of the heat.

C. ‍لِ *li* (IN ORDER TO, FOR)

لِ *li* (in order to, for) is followed by an imperfect tense verb or by the corresponding definite verbal noun.

يَجِب أَن أَبْقَى في البَيْت لأذاكِر.

yajib an abqā fi l-bayt li-'udhākir.

I have to stay at home in order to study.

يَجِب أَن أَبْقَى في البَيْت للمُذاكَرَة.

yajib an abqā fi l-bayt li l-mudhākara.

I have to stay at home for studying.

D. لِكَيْ *likay* (IN ORDER TO, SO THAT)

لِكَيْ *likay* (in order to, so that) is followed by an imperfect tense verb.

يَجِب أَن أَبْقَى في البَيْت لِكَيْ أذاكِر.

yajib an abqā fi l-bayt likay udhākir.

I have to stay at home in order to study.

2. CONDITIONAL SENTENCES

Conditional sentences express the idea of *if . . . then*, as in *If I were you, I would go.* Here's a conditional sentence in Arabic from the dialogue.

لَو كُنْت مكانَك لَذَهَبْت دون تَفْكِير.

law kunt makānak ladhahabt dūn tafkīr.

If I were you, I would go without thinking (twice).

A conditional sentence is made up of a clause expressing the condition, *If I were you*, and a clause expressing the result, *I would go without thinking*. There are two words in Arabic that correspond to the English *if*: إذا *idhā* and لَو *law*.

A. إذا *idhā* (IF)

إذا *idhā* is the more common of the two conjunctions. It is always followed by a perfect tense verb, regardless of the tense used in the result clause. The prefix فَ *fa* can optionally be used in the result clause, similar to *then* in English. It attaches to the first word of the result clause. The tenses in MSA result clauses following فَ *fa* match those used in English.

.إذا لَمْ تَأْتِ مَعَنا فَسَأَحْزَن كَثِيراً

idhā lam ta' ti ma'anā fasa'aHzan kathīran.

If you do not come with us, I will be upset.

إذا سافَرْنا في مارِس سَيكون الجَوُّ جَميلاً.

idhā sāfarnā fī māris sayakūn al-jaww jamīla.

If we travel in March, the weather will be nice.

إذا ذَهَبْت إلى الشَّاطِئ سَآتي مَعَك.

idhā dhahabt ila sh-shāTi' sa'ātī ma'ak.

If you go to the beach, I will come too.

The فَ *fa* is never used if the result clause is in the perfect tense, as in the following example:

إذا لَم تُسافِر مَع هالَة حَزِنَت.

idhā lam tusāfir ma'a hāla Hazinat.

If you do not travel with Hala, she will be upset.

B. لَو *law*

The word لَو *law* is used in a conditional sentence where the condition is untrue or impossible, as in this example from the text.

لَو كُنْت مكانَك لَذَهَبْت دون تَفْكير.

law kunt makānak ladhahabt duna tafkīr.

If I were you (*lit.*, in your place), I would go without thinking twice.

The verb following لَو *law* must be in the perfect tense. Note that the verb in the result clause, which is also in the perfect tense, is preceded by the prefix لَ *la*. This prefix has no translation, but simply marks the beginning of the result clause in a conditional sentence beginning with لَو *law*.

3. IRREGULAR VERBS: HOLLOW VERBS

Verbs that have a long vowel as the middle letter of their root are called "hollow verbs." For example:

عاد *'ād* (he returned)	ع – ا – د
كان *kān* (he was)	ك – ا – ن

The middle letter of the perfect stems of these verbs is always ا *ā*, though it changes into a short vowel for some conjugations. In the imperfect tense, it can change to either و *ū* or ـي *ī*, or remain ا *ā*.

زادَ	يَزيد	زِدْتُ
zād	*yazīd*	*zidt*
it increased	it increases	I increased

كَانَ	يكُون	كُنْتُ
kān	*yakūn*	*kunt*
he was	he is	I was

Notice that in the *I* form of the perfect tense, the long vowel in the *he* form of the perfect tense is replaced with the corresponding short vowel. That is, و *ū* is replaced with (ˈ) *u*, and ـِ *ī* is replaced with (ِ) *i*.

You can find a full conjugation of a hollow verb in Appendix F.

4. IRREGULAR VERBS: DOUBLED VERBS

Doubled verbs are those that are derived from roots in which the second consonant and the third consonant are identical. In writing, the repeated root consonant is written only once, if the verb belongs to Form I, with a *shadda* (ّ) on top. For example:

عَدَّ	يَعُدُّ
'adda	*ya'udd*
he counted	he counts (Form I)

Doubled consonants can also be found in Form IV verbs.

أحَبَّ	يُحِبُّ
aHabba	*yuHibb*
he loved	he loves (Form IV)

The addition of some suffixes requires that a short vowel be added between the doubled consonants.

أحْبَبْت *aHbabt* (you loved)

عَدَدت *'adadt* (you counted)

A fully conjugated doubled verb أَحَبَّ *aHabba* (he loved) is included in Appendix G. It is not important that you memorize all of these forms, but that you be able to recognize doubled verbs when the doubled consonant is represented with a *shadda*, as in أَحَبَّ *aHabba* (he loved), as well as when the two letters are separated by a short vowel, as in أحْبَبْت *aHbabt* (you loved).

Remember that Form II verbs always have a doubled second root consonant. For example:

قَدَّم *qaddama* (he presented)

When a Form II verb is derived from a doubled verb root, the derived verb simply has the usual Form II shape: *CaCCaC* is the *he*-form of the perfect tense and *yuCaCCiC* is the *he*-form of the imperfect tense. Hence, حَرَّر *Harrar* (to liberate), a Form II verb derived from the doubled verb root ح — ر — ر, follows the usual pattern. In writing, it has a doubled middle letter, with a *shadda* on top, followed by another instance of the same letter.

حَرَّر

Harrar

he freed

يُحَرِّر

yuHarrir

he liberates

Unlike other forms derived from doubled verbs, perfect and imperfect stems of Form II verbs do not change according to the suffix in any conjugation.

5. SAYING DATES

There are several ways to write dates in Arabic. Like Arabic script, Arabic dates are read from right to left, beginning with the day, then the month, and then the year. The month can either be spelled out or not, depending on how formal the context is.

٢٠٠٥/٤/٢٠

'ishrīn arba'a sanat alfayn wa khamsa

4/20/2005 (informal)

٢٠ إبْريل ٢٠٠٥

al-'ishrūn min ibrīl, sanat alfayn wa khamsa

April 20, 2005 (more formal)

In addition to names of months derived from French, there are also Arabic names for the same months (see next section). These are used in Lebanon, Syria, Jordan, the Palestinian Authority, and Iraq, whereas the Arabized versions of French month names are used in most other parts of the Arab world. Here's the same date with a Levantine month name.

٢٠ أَيَّار ٢٠٠٥

al-'ishrūn min ayyār, sanat alfayn wa khamsa

April 20, 2005

6. MONTHS OF THE YEAR, DAYS OF THE WEEK, SEASONS

The following table includes both Levantine and Arabized versions of the names for months.

MONTHS OF THE YEAR

	Levantine Names		Arabized Names	
January	kānūn ath-thānī	كانون الثاني	yanāyir	يَناير
February	shubāT	شُباط	fibrāyir	فِبْراير
March	ādhār	آذار	māris	مارِس
April	nisān	نيسان	ibrīl	إبْريل
May	ayyār	أيّار	mayū	مايو
June	Huzayrān	حُزيران	yunya	يونية
July	tammūz	تَمّوز	yulya	يولية
August	āb	آب	aghustus	أغسْطُس
September	aylūl	أيْلول	sibtimbir	سِبْتَمْبِر
October	tishrīn al-awwal	تِشْرين الأوّل	uktūbar	أكْتوبِر
November	tishrīn ath-thānī	تِشْرين الثاني	nuvambir	نوفَمْبِر
December	kānūn al-awwal	كانون الأوّل	disambir	ديسَمْبِر

The days of the week are included in the following table.

DAYS OF THE WEEK

Saturday	yawm as-sabt	يَوْم السَّبْت
Sunday	yawm al-aHad	يَوْم الأحَد
Monday	yawm al-'ithnayn	يَوْم الإثْنَيْن
Tuesday	yawm ath-thulāthā'	يَوْم الثُّلاثاء
Wednesday	yawm al-arbi'ā'	يَوْم الأرْبِعاء
Thursday	yawm al-khamīs	يَوْم الخميس
Friday	yawm al-jum'a	يَوْم الجُمْعَة

Here is the table giving the names of the seasons.

SEASONS OF THE YEAR		
summer	faSl aS-Sayf	فَصل الصيْف
fall	faSl al-kharīf	فَصل الخريف
winter	faSl ash-shitā'	فَصل الشِتاء
spring	faSl ar-rabī'	فَصل الرَبيع

C. Vocabulary

أَلو alū	hello
كَيْف حالُك؟ kayfa hāluk?	How are you?
بِخَيْر bi-khayr	well
الحَمْد لله al-Hamdulillāh	thank God
تَحَسُّن taHassun	getting better
أفْضَل afDal	better
عاد 'ād	returned
سَتَأْتي (أتى) sata'ti (atā)	you will come (to come)
شاطِئ البَحْر shāTi' al-baHr	the beach
نَسْبَح nasbaH	we swim
أذاكِر udhākir	I study
إجازة ijāza	vacation
فَصْل faSl	semester; season
جَوّ jaww	weather
حارّ Hārr	hot
أفَضِّل ufaDDil	I prefer
أفَكِّر(فَكَّر) في ufakkir (fakkar) fī	I think (to think) about
امْتَحانات imtiHānāt	exams
طِوال Tiwāl	all along; the length of

إذا 'idhā	if
سَأَحْزَن sa'aHzan	I will be sad
أَيّ 'ayy	any
حال Hāl	situation; condition
أَرْجو (رَجا) أن arjū (rajā) an	I hope (to hope) that
رُبَّما rubbamā	maybe
لَو law	if
دُون Dūn(a)	without
تَفْكير tafkīr	thinking

D. Cultural Note

A variety of calendars are in use in the Arab world. The most commonly used is the Western solar calendar, called the ميلادي milādī calendar. You have learned in the lesson that in some regions of the Arab world, Arabized versions of the French month names are in use. In informal contexts, however, months are referred to by numbers. March, for example would be simply شَهْر ثلاثة shahr thalātha (lit., month three).

Islamic holidays are marked by the Islamic هـجري hijrī calendar, named after Muhammad's migration (هـجْرَة hijra) from Mecca to Medina in 622 AD, which marks its first year. This calendar is lunar, which means that months correspond to moon cycles and fall eleven days earlier on the Western calendar each year. The month of Ramadan, رَمَضـان ramaDān, when Muslims are required to fast during daylight hours, is the most famous of the months in the Islamic calendar. Other Islamic holidays, such as the Feast of Breaking the Fast, عيد الفِطْر 'īd al-fiTr, also called the Small Feast, and the Feast of the Sacrifice, عيد الأَضْحَى 'īd al-aD-Hā, also called the Big Feast, follow the lunar calendar as well.

E. Exercises

1. Answer the following questions using لِـ lī (to; in order to), لِكي likay (in order to), or لأَنّ li'anna (because).

a. ؟لماذا لن يذهب أحمد إلى الشاطئ

b. ؟لماذا يفضل أحمد الذهاب إلى الشاطئ في الصيف

c. ؟أخي هالة (health) لماذا سأل أحمد عن صحة

d. ؟لماذا تدرس اللغة العربية

e. ؟لماذا اتصلت هالة بأحمد

2. Arrange the following words to form complete sentences.

a. مكانك – لو – مع – هالة – لذهبت – كنت

b. ستحزن – إذا – هالة – لم – كثيرا – أحمد – يذهب – مع

c. للعمل – لو – لما – كان – مريضا – ذهب

d. الامتحانات – إذا – أحمد – فكر – فلن – بالرحلة – في – يستمتع

e. سيكون – إبريل – إذا – أفضل – سافرت – الجو – في

3. Change the following affirmative sentences in the perfect tense into negative sentences in the future tense using the particle لَن _lan_.

a. كان أخو هالة مريضا.

b. زاد عدد المسافرين للشاطئ مع هالة.

c. زارت هالة صديقتها في سوريا.

d. قالت هالة لأحمد أنها ستحزن إذا لم يذهب معها.

e. عاد أخو هالة إلى العمل.

4. Write out the following dates in words.

a. ٢٠٠٤/٤/٢٠

b. ١٩٩٩/١١/٦

c. ١٩٨٣/١٢/٢

d. ٢٠٠٢/١/٩

e. ١٩١٨/٨/٢

5. Match the words from column A with words from column B to form meaningful possessive constructions or prepositional phrases.

A	B
a. مع	حالك
b. الحمد	الوقت
c. شاطئ	لله
d. كيف	البحر
e. طوال	السلامة

Answer Key

1. a. لأنه مشغول بالامتحانات.
li-annahu mashghūl bī l-imtiHānāt.
Because he is busy with exams.

b. كي لا يفكر في الدراسة.
kay lā yufakkir fī d-dirāsa.
In order not to think of studying.

c. لأنه كان مريضاً.
li-annahu kān marīd(an).
Because he was sick.

d. لأدرس تاريخ الشرق الأوسط.
li-adrus tārīkh ash-sharq al-awsat.
In order to study the history of the Middle East.

e. كي تطلب منه أن يذهب معها إلى الشاطئ.
kay taTlub minhu an yadh-hab ma'ahā ila sh-shāTi'.
In order to ask him to go with her to the beach.

2. a. لو كنت مكانك لذهبت مع هالة.
law kunt makānak la-dhahabt ma'a hāla.
If I were in your place, I would have gone with Hala.

b. إذا لم يذهب أحمد مع هالة ستحزن كثيرا.
idhā lam yadh-hab aHmad ma'a hāla, sa-taHzan kathīran.
If Ahmed did not go with Hala, she would be very upset.

c. لو كان مريضا لما ذهب للعمل.
law kān marīd(an) lamā dhahab li l-'amal.
If he were sick, he would not have gone to work.

d. إذا فكر أحمد في الامتحانات فلن يستمتع بالرحلة.
idhā fakkar aHmad fī l-imtaHānāt fa-lan yastamti' bi r-riHla.
If Ahmed thought of his exams, he would not enjoy the trip.

e. إذا سافرت في إبريل سيكون الجو أفضل.
idhā sāfart fī ibrīl sa-yakūn al-jaww afDal.
If you travel in April, the weather will be better.

3. a. لن يكون أخو هالة مريضا.
lan yakūn akhū hāla marīd(an).
Hala's brother will not be sick.

b. لن يزيد عدد المسافرين للشاطئ مع هالة.
lan yazīd 'adad al-musāfirīn li sh-shāTi' ma'a hāla.
The number of people going to the beach with Hala will not increase.

c. لن تزور هالة صديقتها في سوريا.
lan tazūr hāla Sadīqat-hā fī sūriya.
Hala will not visit her friend in Syria.

d. لن تقول هالة لأحمد أنها ستحزن إذا لم يذهب معها.
lan taqūl hāla li-aHmad annahā sa-taHzan idhā lam yadh-hab ma'ahā.
Hala will not tell Ahmed that she will be upset if he did not go with her.

e. لن يعود أخو هالة إلى العمل.
lan ya'ūd akhū hāla ila l-'amal.
Hala's brother will not return to work.

4. a. العشرون من إبريل (نيسان) سنة ألفين وأربعة.
al-'ishrūn min ibrīl (nisān) sanat alfayn wa arba'a.
April 20, 2004

b. الحادي عشر من يونية (حزيران) سنة ألف وتسعمائة وتسعة وتسعون.

al-Hādī 'ashr min yunyah (Huzayrān) sanat alf wa tis'umi'a wa tis'a wa tis'ūn.

June 11, 1999

c. الثاني من ديسمبر (كانون الأول) سنة ألف وتسعمائة وثلاثة وثمانون.

ath-thānī min disambir (kānūn al-awwal) sanat alf wa tis'umi'a wa thalātha wa thamānūn.

December 2, 1983

d. التاسع من يناير (كانون الثاني) سنة ألفين واثنان.

at-tāsi' min yanāyir (kānūn ath-thānī) sanat alfayn wa ithnayn.

January 9, 2002

e. الثالث من أغسطس (آب) سنة ألف وتسعمائة وثمانية عشر.

ath-thālith min aghusTus (āb) sanat alf wa tis'umi'a wa thamāniyat 'ashr

August 3, 1918

5. a. مع السلامة

ma'a s-salāma

good-bye

b. الحمد لله

al-Hamdu l-illāh

thank God

c. شاطئ البحر

shāTi' al-baHr

the beach

d. كيف حالك؟

kayfa Hāluk?

How are you?

e. طوال الوقت.

Tiwāl al-waqt

all the time

LESSON 15
(Modern Standard Arabic)

أَخْبار مِن الصَّحافة العَرَبِيَّة

akhbār min aS-SaHāfa al-'arabiyya News from the Arabic Press

A. Text

بِدايَةُ الصِّراعِ بَيْنَ المَشْرِقِ والمَغْرِبِ العَرَبِيَّيْنِ

أَعْلَنَ بَعْضُ المُحَلِّلينَ في الشَّرْقِ الأَوْسَطِ أَنَّ فَشَلَ عَقْدِ القِمَّةِ العَرَبِيَّةِ في تُونِس في شَهْرِ مارِس مِنْ عامِ ٢٠٠٤ قَدْ يُؤَدّي إلى صِراعٍ سِياسِيٍّ بَيْنَ دُوَلِ المَشْرِقِ العَرَبِيّ و دُوَلِ المَغْرِبِ العَرَبِيّ. وكانَ هَذا الصِّراعُ قَدْ بَدَأَ عِنْدَما قَرَّرَتْ تُونِسُ تَأْجيلَ عَقْدِ القِمَّةِ العَرَبِيَّةِ بَعْدَ أَنْ وَصَلَ وُزَراءُ الخارِجِيَّةِ العَرَبُ إلى العاصِمَةِ التُونِسِيَّةِ تُونِس لِمُناقَشَةِ أجِنْدَةِ القِمَّة. وأَعْلَنَتْ مَصادِرُ مَسْؤولَةٌ أَنَّ تُونِسَ قَرَّرَتْ أَنْ تُؤَجِّلَ القِمَّةَ بَعْدَ ظُهورِ خِلافاتٍ حَوْلَ أجِنْدَةِ تُونِس لِلإِصْلاحِ في العالَمِ العَرَبِيّ، وأَنَّها لَمْ تَتَشاوَرْ مَعَ الدُّوَلِ الأَعْضاء.

وقَدْ بَدا أَنَّ هُناكَ تَكَتُّلانِ أَحَدُهُما مَشْرِقيٌّ والآخَر مَغْرِبيٌّ، التَكَتُّلُ المَشْرِقيُّ تَقودُهُ مِصْرُ والسَعوديَّةُ وسوريا والبَحْرَيْنِ ويُحاوِلُ مُعاقَبَةَ تُونِسَ بِنَقْلِ القِمَّةِ لِمَقَرِّ جامِعَةِ الدُوَلِ العَرَبِيَّةِ في القاهِرَةِ، والتَكَتُّلُ الآخَرُ تَقودُهُ تُونِس والمَغْرِبُ والجَزائِرُ ويُطالِبُ بِحَقِّ تُونِس في عَقْدِ القِمَّةِ عَلَى أَراضيها في وَقْتٍ لاحِق.

bidayatu S-Sirā'i bayna l-mashriqi wa l-maghribi l-'arabiyyayn
'a'lana ba'Du l-muHallilīna fī sh-sharqi l-awsaTi 'anna fashala 'aqdi l-qimmati l-'arabiyyati fī
tūnis fī shahri mārisa min 'āmi alfayn wa arba'at qad yu'addī ilā Sirā'in siyāsiyyin bayna
duwali al-mashriqi l-'arabiyyī wa duwali al-maghribi l-'arabiyyī. wa kān hādha S-Sirā'u qad
bada'a 'indamā qarrarat tūnisu ta'jīla 'aqdi l-qimmati l-'arabiyyati ba'da 'an waSal wuzarā'u
l-khārijiyyati l-'arabu ilā l-'āSimati t-tūnisiyyati tūnis limunāqashati ajindati l-qimma. wa
a'lanat maSādiru mas'ūlatun anna tūnisa qarrarat an tu'ajjila l-qimmata ba'd DHuhūri
khilāfātin Hawla ajindati tūnis li l-iSlāHi fi l-'ālami l-'arabiyyī wa annahā lam tatashāwar
ma'a ad-duwali al-a'Dā'.

wa qad badā anna hunāka takattulāni aHaduhuma mashriqiyyun wa l-ākharu maghribiyun,
at-takattulu l-mashriqiyyu taqūduhu miSru wa s-sa'ūdiyyatu wa sūriyā wa l-baHrayn wa
yuHāwilu mu'āqabata tūnis binaqli l-qimmati li-maqarri jāmi'ati d-duwali l-'arabiyyati fī l-

*qāhira, wa t-takattulu al-ākharu taqūduhu tūnisu wa l-maghribu wa l-jazā'iru wa yuTālibu bi-
Haqqi tūnis fī 'aqdi al-qimmati 'alā arāDihā fī waqtin lāHiq.*

THE BEGINNING OF A CONFLICT BETWEEN THE ARAB EAST AND THE ARAB WEST

Some analysts in the Middle East have reported that the failure to hold the Arab Summit
in Tunisia in March of 2004 might lead to a political conflict between the countries of the
Arab East and those of the Arab West. This struggle began when Tunisia decided to
postpone the Arab Summit after the Foreign Ministers from the Arab countries had
already arrived in the Tunisian capital Tunis to discuss the Summit's agenda. Some
responsible sources announced that Tunisia decided to postpone the conference after
some differences arose regarding Tunisia's agenda on reform in the Arab world, and the
fact that it did not consult the other Arab members.

It appeared there were two blocs: one Eastern and the other Western. The Eastern bloc is
led by Egypt, Saudi Arabia, Syria, and Bahrain. This block is trying to punish Tunisia by
moving the Summit to the headquarters of the Arab League in Cairo. The other bloc is led
by Tunisia, Morocco, and Algeria. It calls for Tunisia's right to hold the meeting on its
territory at a later time.

B. Grammar and Usage

1. THE CASE SYSTEM

Depending on the role it plays in a sentence, a noun takes slightly different forms in very
formal MSA. For example, the noun التكتُّل *at-takattul* (the bloc) has three different forms,
as given below.

التكتُّلُ   التكتُّلَ   التكتُّلِ
at-takattulu   *at-takattula*   *at-takattuli*

These different forms are called "cases." MSA has three cases: nominative, accusative,
and genitive. Adjectives also have different case forms. Prepositions and pronouns do not.

A. THE NOMINATIVE CASE

Nouns in the nominative case have the ending (´) *-u* when definite singular, or (˝)
-un when indefinite singular.

المَغْرِبُ *al-maghribu* (Morocco)

البِدايَة *al-bidayatu* (the beginning)

وَزيرٌ *wazīrun* (a minister)

The dual nominative ending is ان *-ān,* and the plural masculine nominative ending is
ون *-ūn,* as in:

أَعْلَنَ المَسْوُولون أَنَّ...

a'lana l-mas'ūlūn anna . . .

The <u>responsible</u> [parties] announced that . . .

A noun must be in the nominative case if it is the subject of the sentence:

تَقودُ المَغْرِبُ التَكَتُّلَ الآخَرَ

taqūdu l-maghribu t-takattula l-'ākhar

<u>Morocco</u> leads the other bloc.

Or a part of the predicate in a nominal sentence.

الآخَرُ تَكَتُّلٌ مَغْرِبِيٌّ.

al-'ākharu <u>takattulun</u> maghribī.

The other is a Western <u>bloc</u>.

As it is a part of the predicate, تَكَتُّل takattulun (bloc) is in the nominative case. The subject of the sentence, الآخَرُ al-ākharu (the other), is also in the nominative case. The adjective مَغْرِبِيٌّ maghribīyyun (Western) is in the nominative case as well, as it has to agree in case with the noun تَكَتُّل takattulun (bloc). Note that the case ending is dropped whenever a noun or an adjective marked by it is at the end of a sentence, so the nominative case (ٌ) -un on the adjective مَغْرِبِيٌّ maghribīyyun is not pronounced in this sentence.

When a nominative, or any other case ending, follows a feminine noun ending in ة -t, this ending, which is often silent, is pronounced.

العَاصِمة

al-'āSima

the capital (no case marker)

العَاصِمةُ

al-'āSimatu

the capital (with a nominative case marker)

B. THE ACCUSATIVE CASE

Accusative nouns end in (َ) -a when definite singular, and in (ً) -an when indefinite singular. As mentioned in Lesson 4, it is a convention of written Arabic to write the tanwīn, representing the ending -an, over an additional letter ا.

صِراعاً

Sirā'an

a conflict

Dual nouns and adjectives carry the ending يَن -ayn in the accusative.

مِصْرِيَّين

miSriyyayn

two Egyptians

The regular plural masculine nouns and adjectives carry the ending ين -in in the accusative case.

سَعوديِّين

sa'ūdiyyīn

Saudi Arabians

The marker of the accusative case for regular feminine plural nouns and adjectives is the short vowel (ِ) -i.

يُناقِشُ المُحَلِّلونَ الخِلافاتِ بين الطَرَفين.

yunāqishu l-muHallilūna l-khilāfāti bayn aT-Tarafayn.

The analysts are discussing the differences between the two parties.

A noun is in the accusative case if it is the object of a verb:

الفَشَلُ سَيُسَبِّبُ صِراعاً.

al-fashalu sayusabbibu Sirā'an.

The failure will cause a conflict.

Or if it follows the particles إِنّ inna (that) or أَنّ anna (that):[1]

أعْلَنَ أَنّ الفَشَلَ سَيُسَبِّبُ صِراعاً.

a'lana anna l-fashala sayusabbibu Sirā'an.

He announced that the failure would cause a conflict.

Or if it functions as an adverb:

بَدَأت القِمةُ أخيراً

bada'at al-qimatu akhīran.

The summit finally began.

C. THE GENITIVE CASE

The genitive case ending is (ِ) -i for definite singular nouns and (ٍ) -in for indefinite singular nouns:

صِراعٍ Sirā'in (conflict)

The genitive case ending for dual nouns is ـَيْن -ayn. For regular masculine plural nouns, it is ـِين -in. Note that these dual endings are the same as the corresponding markers of the accusative case.

مُحَلِّلَين

muHallilayn

two analysts

مُحَلِّلين

muHallilīn

analysts

---

[1] You have seen many examples of the word أَنّ anna (that) in previous chapters. The word إِنّ inna has the same meaning and function, but it is only used with the verb قال qāl (to say) and at the beginning of a sentence.

A noun is in the genitive case if it follows a preposition.

قَد يُوَدِّي إِلَى صِراعٍ طويل.

qad yu'addī 'ilā Sirā'in Tawīl.

It might lead to a long <u>conflict</u>.

The noun صِراع *Sirā'in* (conflict) follows the preposition إِلَى *'ilā* (to) and is in the genitive case.

Or if it follows another noun in a possessive construction.

أَجِنْدَة القِمَّةَ

ajindat al-qimmati

the summit agenda (*lit.*, the agenda [of] the <u>summit</u>)

The word القِمَّةِ *al-qimmati* (the summit) is in the genitive case because it is the second term in a possessive construction.

Here is a table with the different case endings. Note that the gender distinction is made only in the plural, whereas the distinction in definiteness is apparent only in the singular due to the characterictic indefinite ending -n.

THE CASE ENDINGS			
	Nominative (Subject)	Accusative (Object)	Genitive (Object of a preposition)
Singular Indefinite	-un	-an	-in
Singular Definite	-u	-a	-i
Dual	-ān	-ayn	
Plural Masculine	-ūn	-in	
Plural Feminine	-u	-i	

The following table lists the case forms of the noun مَسْؤُول *mas'ūl* (the responsible [one]).

THE CASE FORMS OF مَسْؤُول *mas'ūl* (THE RESPONSIBLE [ONE])

	Nominative	Accusative	Genitive
Singular Indefinite	مَسْؤُولٌ *mas'ūlun*	مَسْؤُولاً *mas'ūlan*	مَسْؤُولٍ *mas'ūlin*
Singular Definite	المَسْؤُولُ *al-mas'ūlu*	المَسْؤُولَ *al-mas'ūla*	المَسْؤُولِ *al-mas'ūli*
Dual	مَسْؤُولان *mas'ūlān*	مَسْؤُولَين *mas'ūlayn*	مَسْؤُولَين *mas'ūlayn*
Plural Masculine	مَسْؤُولون *mas'ūlūn*	مَسْؤُولِين *mas'ūlin*	مَسْؤُولِين *mas'ūlin*
Plural Feminine	مَسْؤُولاتُ *mas'ūlātu*	مَسْؤُولاتٍ *mas'ūlāti*	مَسْؤُولاتٍ *mas'ūlāti*

2. THE MOOD MARKERS

Verbs in the imperfect tense can come in three slightly different forms, called moods: indicative, subjunctive, and jussive. Verbs in the perfect tense do not change according to mood.

A. THE INDICATIVE MOOD

Verbs are normally in the indicative mood, unless they are preceded by a small number of particles, introduced below. For this reason, the indicative is the default representation of verbs in charts and examples. It is the only verbal mood you have encountered so far in this course.

The marker of the indicative mood is the final (ُ) -*u* in the هِيَ *hiya* (she), هُو *huwa* (he), نَحْن *naHnu* (we), أَنا *ana* (I), and أَنْتَ *anta* (you, *m. sg.*) forms.

يُحاوِلُ التكَتُّلُ المَشْرِقيُّ مُعاقَبَةَ تُونِس.
yuHāwilu t-takattulu l-mashriqiyu mu'āqabata tūnis.
The Eastern bloc <u>is trying</u> to punish Tunisia.

The indicative form for all other personal forms is the same as the default form of the verb, listed in the conjugation tables.

يُحاوِلونَ مُعاقَبَةَ تُونِس
yuHāwilūna mu'āqabata tūnis.
They <u>are trying</u> to punish Tunisia.

B. THE SUBJUNCTIVE MOOD

Verbs are in the subjunctive mood when they follow one of the particles listed below:

لَنْ *lan* (will not)[1]

أَنْ *an* (that)[2]

فَـ *fa* (so, therefore)

لِـ *li* (because, in order to)

لِكَي *likay* (in order to)

The following table lists the subjunctive forms of the verb *yaktub* (he writes) next to their indicative counterparts.

THE VERB يَكْتُب *yaktub* (HE WRITES) IN THE INDICATIVE AND THE SUBJUNCTIVE					
Person		Indicative		Subjunctive	
أَنا	ana	أَكْتُبُ	'aktubu	أَكْتُبَ	'aktuba
نَحْنُ	naHnu	نكْتُبُ	naktubu	نكْتُبَ	naktuba
أَنْتَ	anta	تكْتُبُ	taaktubu	تكْتُبَ	taktuba
أَنْتِ	anti	تَكْتُبِينَ	taktubīna	تَكْتُبِي	taktubī
أَنْتُم	antum	تكْتُبُونَ	taktubūna	تكْتُبُوا	taktubū
أَنْتُنَّ	antunna	تَكْتُبْنَ	taktubna	تَكْتُبْنَ	taktubna
أَنْتُمَا	antumā	تَكْتُبَانِ	taktubāni	تَكْتُبَا	taktubā
هُوَ	huwa	يَكْتُبُ	yaktubu	يَكْتُبَ	yaktuba
هِيَ	hiya	تَكْتُبُ	taktubu	تَكْتُبَ	taktuba
هُم	hum	يكْتُبُونَ	yaktubūna	يكْتُبُوا	yaktubū
هُنَّ	hunna	يكْتُبْنَ	yaktubna	يكْتُبْنَ	yaktubna
هُما	humā	يكْتُبَانِ	yaktubāni	يكْتُبَا	yaktubā
هُما	humā	تكْتُبَانِ	taktubāni	تكْتُبَا	taktubā

---

[1] A particle negating a future action using the imperfect

[2] A particle similar to the "to" of the English infinitive form

Notice that the marker of the subjunctive mood is the short vowel ( ) -a at the end of verb forms used with the pronouns هِيَ hiya (she), هُوَ huwa (he), نَحْن naHnu (we), أَنا ana (I), and أَنْتَ anta (you, m.).

بَعْدَ أَنْ يَصِلَ الوَزيرُ...

ba'da an <u>yaSila</u> l-wazir . . .

After the minister <u>arrives</u> . . .

For verb forms that end with -na or -ni in the indicative, the subjunctive is formed by removing this ending. In the following example, the verb يُقَرِّرُونَ yuqarrirūna (they decide) is in the indicative mood.

قد يُقَرِّرُونَ تَأْجيلَ عَقْدِ القِمَّة

qad <u>yuqarrirūna</u> ta'jila 'aqdi al-qimma.

They might <u>decide</u> to postpone holding the summit.

Contrast this to the example below, in which the subjunctive form of the same verb is used.

لَن يُقَرِّرُوا تَأْجيلَ عَقْدِ القِمَّة

lan <u>yuqarrirū</u> t'ajila 'aqdi l-qimma.

They will not <u>decide</u> to postpone holding the summit.

Notice that the letter ا is added to the end of the *they* form of the verb out of convention, but is not pronounced.

C. THE JUSSIVE MOOD

Verbs must be in the jussive mood when they come after one of the following particles:

لَمْ lam (did not)[1]

لِـ li (let's)[2]

In the following table you'll find the verb يَكْتُب yaktub (he writes) conjugated in the indicative and the jussive.

---

[1] A particle used to negate a past action in combination with the imperfect verb
[2] See Lesson 10.

THE VERB يَكْتُب *yaktub* (HE WRITES) IN THE INDICATIVE AND JUSSIVE MOODS

Person		Indicative		Jussive	
أَنا	ana	أَكْتُبُ	aktubu	أَكْتُبْ	aktub
نَحْنُ	naHnu	نَكْتُبُ	naktubu	نَكْتُبْ	naktub
أَنْتَ	anta	تَكْتُبُ	taktubu	تَكْتُبْ	taktub
أَنْتِ	anti	تَكْتُبِينَ	taktubīna	تَكْتُبِي	taktubī
أَنْتُمْ	antum	تَكْتُبُونَ	taktubūna	تَكْتُبُوا	taktubū
أَنْتُنَّ	antunna	تَكْتُبْنَ	taktubna	تَكْتُبْنَ	taktubna
أَنْتُمَا	antumā	تَكْتُبَانِ	taktubāni	تَكْتُبَا	taktubā
هُوَ	huwa	يَكْتُبُ	yaktubu	يَكْتُبْ	yaktub
هِيَ	hiya	تَكْتُبُ	taktubu	تَكْتُبْ	taktub
هُمْ	hum	يَكْتُبُونَ	yaktubūna	يَكْتُبُوا	yaktubū
هُنَّ	hunna	يَكْتُبْنَ	yaktubna	يَكْتُبْنَ	yaktubna
هُمَا (m.)	humā	يَكْتُبَانِ	yaktubāni	يَكْتُبَا	yaktubā
هُمَا (f.)	humā	تَكْتُبَانِ	taktubāni	تَكْتُبَا	taktubā

Notice that the jussive mood is marked by the absence of a final vowel in the verb forms used with pronouns هِيَ *hiya* (she), هُوَ *huwa* (he), نَحْنُ *naHnu* (we), أَنا *anā* (I), and أَنْتَ *anta* (you, m.).

لَمْ تَتَشاوَرْ تُونِس مَعَ الدُّوَلِ الأَعْضاء.

lam tatashāwar tūnis ma'a d-duwali l-a'Dā'.

Tunisia did not <u>consult</u> with the member countries.

تَتَشاوَرْ *tatashāwar* (consult) is in the jussive mood because it follows لَمْ *lam*.

If the verb conjugated with one of these five pronouns is a hollow or weak verb (see Lessons 13 and 14), the vowel is dropped from either the middle or end of the verb, as in the following example:

قَد يُؤَدِّي ذَلِك إِلَى مُعاقَبَةِ تُونِس.

qad yu'addi dhālika ilā mu'āqabati Tunis.

That might <u>lead</u> to punishment of Tunisia.

222

لَم يُؤَدِّ ذَلك إلَى مُعاقَبَةِ تُونِس

lam yu'addi dhālika ilā mu'āqabati Tūnis.

That did not <u>lead</u> to punishment of Tunisia.

The full conjugations of hollow and weak verbs in the jussive are available in Appendices C through F. For the verb forms that end with *-na* or *-ni* in the indicative, the jussive is formed, like the subjunctive, by dropping these endings.

لَمْ يَتَشاوَروا مَعَ الدُّوَلِ الأَعْضاء.

lam yatashāwarū ma'a d-duwal al-a'Dā'

They did not <u>consult</u> with the member countries.

Again, the letter ا is added at the end of the verbs in the *they* form out of convention, but is not pronounced.

C. Vocabulary

أَخْبار (خَبَر) *akhbār (khabar)*	news
صَحافَة *SaHāfa*	journalism, press
بِدايَةُ *bidāyatu*	beginning
صِراع *Sirā'*	struggle
مَشْرِق *mashriq*	East
مَغْرِب *maghrib*	West
أَعْلَن أَنَّ *a'lan anna*	he announced that
مُحَلِّلينَ *muHallilīna*	analysts
الشَّرْق الأَوْسَط *ash-sharq al-awsaT*	the Middle East
فَشَل *fashal*	failure
عَقْد *'aqd*	convening
قِمَّة *qimma*	summit
يُؤَدِّي *yu'addī*	leads to
سِياسي *siyāsī*	political
قَرَّرَت *qarrarat*	she decided
تَأْجيل *ta'jīl*	postponement
وُزَراء (وَزير) الخارِجيَّة *wuzarā' (wazīr) al-khārijiyya*	foreign minister(s)

مُناقَشَة munāqasha	discussion
أَجِنْدَة ajinda	agenda
مَصْدَر (مَصادِر) maSdar (maSādir)	source(s)
مَسْؤُولَة mas'ūla	responsible
تُوَجِّل tu'ajjil	postpone
ظُهور DHuhūr	appearance
خِلافات khilāfāt	differences; divisions
حَوْل Hawl	about; surrounding
إِصْلاح iSlāH	reform
تَتَشاوَر (تَشاوَر) tatashāwar (tashāwar)	she consults (to consult)
أَعْضاء (عُضو) a'Dā' ('uDw)	member(s)
تَكَتُّلان takattulān	two blocs
تَقودُهُ (قاد) taqūduhu (qād)	she leads it (to lead)
سُوريا sūriyā	Syria
البَحْرَيْن al-baHrayn	Bahrain
مُعاقَبَة mu'āqaba	punishing
نَقْل naql	moving
مَقَرّ maqarr	headquarters
جامِعَة الدُوَل العَرَبِيَّة jāmi'at ad-duwal al-'arabiyya	the Arab League (lit., the College of Arab States)
المَغْرِب al-maghrib	Morocco
الجَزائِر al-jazā'ir	Algeria
حَقّ Haqq	right
أراضيها (أرْض) arāDīhā (arD)	her lands (to land)
لاحِق lāHiq	later

D. Cultural Note

The media in most Arab countries have long been subject to government censorship. With the spread of satellite technology to every corner of the Arab world, even remote villages now have access to television programming and news from other Arab countries and beyond. In some cases, this has marginalized the effectiveness of government control of local presses. The most prominent development that has accompanied the spread of satellite technology in the region is the establishment of the Al-Jazeera Network, which broadcasts out of Qatar. This high budget, glossy network is often called the CNN of the Arab world. It offers a more contemporary style of reporting that competes successfully with the local networks and newspapers. You can check it out on the Internet at: www.aljazeera.net.

Some other sites are:

www.akhbarelyom.org.eg
www.ahram.org.eg
www.daralhayat.com

E. Exercises

1. Name the case of the underlined words. Explain why this particular case is used.

a. أعلن المحللون بداية صراع جديد.

b. هناك تكتلان في المنطقة.

c. وصل وزراء الخارجية العرب.

d. وصل وزراء الخارجية العرب.

e. تقود مصر التكتل الأول.

2. The underlined nouns are in the wrong case. Change the case endings to make meaningful sentences.

a. أعلن المسؤولين عن عقد القمة في تونس.

b. أعلنت مصادر مسؤولة أن القمة سوف تعقد في القاهرة.

c. القمة سوف تعقد في تونس.

d. التكتلين أحدهما مشرقي والآخر مغربي.

e. أحب المدرسون الذين يعطون بعض الاستقلال للطلاب.

3. Negate the following sentences using لَنْ *lan* (will not), remembering that this particle must be followed by a verb in the subjunctive mood.

a. تحاول تونس عقد القمة على أراضيها.

b. تقود مصر التكتل المشرقي.

c. سيؤدي هذا الصراع إلى مشاكل سياسية كثيرة.

d. أعلن بعض المحللين عن فشل القمة.

e. الدولتان قررتا تأجيل القمة.

4. Arrange the following words to form sentences.

a. الشهر – سوف – القادم – القمة – العربية – تعقد – على – أراضي – تونس

b. (give up) حقها – لن – القمة – على – عن – في – تونس – عقد – أراضيها – تتخلى

c. و – تكتلان – مغربي - الآخر – هناك – أحدهما – مشرقي– و

d. أعلنت – تونس – مسؤولة – تأجيل – أن – قررت – مصادر – القمة

e. تونس – لم – الدول – مع – تتشاور – الأعضاء

Answer Key

1. a. nominative, subject
   b. nominative, predicate
   c. nominative, subject
   d. genitive, second part of the possessive construction
   e. accusative, object

2. a. المسؤولون
   al-mas'ūlūn
   officials

   b. مصادرُ
   maSādiru
   sources

   c. القمةُ
   al-qimmatu
   the summit

   d. التكتلان
   at-takettulān
   the two blocs

   e. المدرسين
   al-muddarrisīn
   the teachers

3. a. لَن تُحاولَ تُونِس عَقد القمَّة عَلى أراضيها.
   lan tuHāwil tunis 'aqd al-qimma 'ala arādīhā.
   Tunisia will not try to hold the summit on its territory.

   b. لَن تَقودَ مِصر التَكَتُّل المَشرقي.
   lan taqūd miSr at-takattul al-mashriqī.
   Egypt will not lead the Eastern bloc.

   c. لَن يُؤُديَ هذا الصِراع إلى مَشاكِل سِياسِية كثيرة.
   lan yu'addī hādha S-Sirā' ilā mashākil siyāsiyya kathīra.
   This conflict will not lead to many political problems.

   d. لَن يُعلِن بَعْض المُحَلِلِين عَن فَشَل القمَّة.
   lan yu'lin ba'D al-muHallilīn 'an fashal al-qimma.
   Some analysts will not announce the failure of the summit.

   e. الدَوْلَتان لَن تُقَررا تَأجيل القمَّة.
   ad-dawlatān lan tuqarrirā ta'jīl al-qimma.
   The two countries will not decide to postpone the summit.

4. a. سَوف تُعْقَد القمة العربية على أراضي تونس الشهر القادِم.
   Sawfa tu'qad al-qimma l-'arabiyya 'alā 'arāDi tūnis ash-shahr al-qādim.
   The Arab summit will be held on Tunisian territory next month.

   b. لن تتخلى تونس عن حقها في عقد القمة على أراضيها.
   lan tatakhallā tūnis 'an Haqqahā fī 'aqd al-qimma 'alā 'arāDīhā.
   Tunisia will not give up its right to hold the summit on its territory.

هناك تكتلان أحدهما مشرقي والآخر c.
مغربي.

*hunāka takattulān aHaduhumā
mashriqqī wa al-ākhar maghribī.*
There are two blocs, the first of
which is Eastern, and the other is
Western.

أعلنت مصادر مسؤولة أن تونس d.
قررت تأجيل القمة.

*a'lanat maSādir mas'ūla anna tūnis
qarrarat ta'jīl al-qimma.*

High ranking sources have
announced that Tunisia decided to
postpone the summit.

لم تتشاور تونس مع الدول الأعضاء. e.

*lam tatashāwar tūnis ma'a d-duwal al-
a'Dā'.*
Tunisia did not consult with member
states.

FOURTH REVIEW
(Modern Standard Arabic)

Grammar Exercises

1. Define each of the following words either as a verbal noun, an active participle, or a present participle.

a. تغيير

b. كاتب

c. مكتوب

d. مدرّس

e. قَفْز

2. Form verbal nouns from the following verbs.

a. جرى

b. استقبل

c. درّس

d. قفز

e. قدّم

3. Form active participles from the following verbs.

a. عمل

b. شرب

c. ذاكر

d. درّس

e. ذهب

4. Form passive participles from the following verbs.

a. كتب

b. صنع

c. شغل

d. استخدم

e. عقد

5. Rewrite the following sentences in the future tense.

a. استقبل الرئيس التونسي وزير الخارجية المصري.

b. وجد دونالد شقة في بيروت.

c. دعا وزير الخارجية لحل (solving) الصراع بين البلدين.

d. قادت تونس التكتل الغربي.

e. وصلت لوسي من بيروت أمس.

Vocabulary Exercises

6. Rearrange the following words to form complete sentences.

a. السعودية – مصر – التكتل – تقود – المشرقي – و

b. أن – يؤجل – الخارجية – القمة – وزير – قرر

c. المرور – لأن – سيئاً – كان – تأخرت

d. التمرينات – يمارس – الرياضية – هل – دونالد – ؟

e. في – كمدرس – أعمل – القاهرة

7. Decide which word in each group does not belong.

a. صحفي – مكتب – مدرس – محرر

b. وصل – شعر – فكر – غير رأيه

c. حمل الأثقال – القمة – الجري – القفز

d. مشكلة – صراع – خلاف – عملية جراحية

e. ذراع – بهارات – ركبة – قلب

8. Choose the correct word to fill in the blanks.

القمة / قلبية/ رئيسة / الشاطئ/ البهارات

a. قال الطبيب لدونالد "لا تأكل الكثير من _____."

b. دونالد ليست عنده أزمة _____.

c. ذهب أحمد مع هالة إلى _____ في الصيف.

d. لم تعقد _____ في تونس.

e. مكتب _____ التحرير في الطابق العلوي.

9. Match the words in column A with those in column B to create phrases and sentences.

A

a. أَسكن

b. هناك صراع

c. هذه هي

d. سأعطيك رقم

e. سنذهب إلى الشاطئ

B

صالة الاستقبال

لنسبح

في الطابق العلوي

سياسي بين هاتين الدولتين

تليفون أخصائي قلب

10. Reorder the following sentences to form a meaningful paragraph.

لوجود خلافات حول الأجندة.

أدى هذا إلى وجود تكتلين أحدهما مغربي والآخر مشرقي.

ثم أعلنت مصر أن القمة يجب أن تعقد في القاهرة.

أجلت تونس القمة العربية.

Answer Key

1. a. verbal noun
   b. active participle
   c. passive participle
   d. active participle
   e. verbal noun

2. a. جَرْى
   b. استقبال
   c. تدريس
   d. قَفْز
   e. تقديم

3. a. عامل
   b. شارب
   c. مذاكر
   d. مدرّس
   e. ذاهب

4. a. مكتوب
   b. مصنوع
   c. مشغول
   d. مستخدَم
   e. معقود

5. a. سيستقبل الرئيس التونسي وزير الخارجية المصري.
   b. سيجد دونالد شقة في بيروت.
   c. سيدعو وزير الخارجية لحل (solving) الصراع بين البلدين.
   d. ستقود تونس التكتل الغربي.
   e. ستصل لوسي من بيروت غداً.

6. a. تقود مصر والسعودية التكتل المشرقي.
   b. قرر وزير الخارجية أن يؤجّل القمة.
   c. تأخرت لأن المرور كان سيئاً.
   d. هل يمارس دونالد التمرينات الرياضية؟
   e. أعمل كمدرس في القاهرة.

7. a. مكتب

b. وصل

c. القمة

d. عملية جراحية

e. بهارات

8. a. البهارات

b. قلبية

c. الشاطئ

d. القمة

e. رئيسة

9. a. أسكن في الطابق العلوي.

b. هناك صراع سياسي بين هاتين الدولتين.

c. هذه هي صالة الاستقبال.

d. سأعطيك رقم تليفون أخصائي القلب.

e. سنذهب إلى الشاطئ لنسبح.

10. أجلت تونس القمة العربية لوجود خلافات حول الأجندة، ثم أعلنت مصر. أن القمة يجب أن تعقد في القاهرة. أدى هذا إلى وجود تكتلين أحدهما مغربي والآخر مشرقي.

الخاطِبَة.كوم

al-khātiba.com Matchmaker.com

إيْجاد عَروسَ أو عَريسٍ دائِماً يُسَبِّب صُعوبات كَبيرَة في العالَم العَرَبيّ بِسَبَب الفَصْل بَيْن الجِنْسَيْن وأهَمِيَّة الخُصوصِيَّة لِلعائِلَة العَرَبيَّة. في الماضي كان الحُصول عَلى النِصْف الحُلو يَتِم مِن خِلال "الخاطِبَة" وهي امرَأة تَعْرِف الكَثير مِن العائِلات في المِنْطَقة وتَسْتَطيع أنْ تَجِد الشَّخص المُناسِب طِبْقاً لِلمُواصَفات المَطْلوبَة.

ولَكِن في عَصْر التِكْنولوجيا هُناك نَوْع جَديد مِن الخاطِبَة وهُو مَواقِع التَعارُف والزَواج عَلى الإنْتَرْنِت. في عَصْر الإنْتَرْنِت يَسْتَطيع الباحِث عَن زَوْج أو زَوْجَة أن يَخْتار مِن بَيْن عَدَد أكْبَر مِن المُرَشَّحين. الآن لَن تَضْطَر البِنت أن تَقْبَل العَريس الذي لا تُريدُه لأنَّه هُو الاخْتِيار الوَحيد الذي وَجَدَته لَها الخاطِبَة. يَسْتَطيع العُزَّاب العَرَب أن يَبْحَثوا عَن شَريك في مَدينَة أُخْرى بَل في بَلَد أُخْرى أو قارَة أُخْرى.

ولَكِن يَقول بَعْض المُعارِضين لِهَذِه المَواقِع أنَّه مِن السَّهْل إعْطاء مَعْلومات غَيْر صَحيحة مِما قَد يُؤَدي إلى الكَثير مِن المَشاكِل، بِخِلاف الخاطِبَة التَقْليديَّة التي تَعْرِف الكَثير عَن أُسَر المِنْطَقة. عَلى أيَّ حال، يَبْدو أن ظاهِرَة خاطِبَة الإنْتَرْنِت سَتَسْتَمِر لأن آلاف العُزَّاب العَرَب يَزورون مَواقِع الزَواج يَوْمياً.

MATCHMAKER.COM

Finding a bride or groom can cause great difficulties in the Arab world because of the separation of the sexes and the importance of privacy to the Arab family. In the past, finding one's better half was achieved by means of a matchmaker, a woman who knows many families in the area and can find a suitable person based on the qualities requested by the family.

But in the age of technology there is a new type of matchmaker — Internet sites for acquaintance and marriage. In the age of the Internet, those looking for a husband or wife can choose from among a larger number of candidates. A woman will not be forced to accept a partner that she doesn't want because he is the only choice that the matchmaker found for her. Arab singles can look for a partner in another city or even another country or continent.

Still, some opponents of these sites say that it is easy to give false information, leading to many problems, as opposed to the traditional matchmaker, who would know a lot about the families of the neighborhood. In any case, it seems that the phenomenon of Internet matchmaking will continue, because thousands of single Arab persons visit marriage sites every day.

Vocabulary

خاطِبَة *khāTiba*	matchmaker
إيجاد *ijād*	finding
عَروس *'arūs*	bride
فَصْل *faSl*	separation
جِنْسَيْن *jinsayn*	sexes (du.)
أهَمِيَّة *ahamiyya*	importance
خُصوصِيَّة *khuSūSiyya*	privacy
عائِلَة *'ā'ila*	family
حُصول عَلى *HuSūl 'ala*	obtaining
حُلو *Hulw*	sweet, pretty, nice
يَتِمّ (تَمّ) *yatimm (tamm)*	to be achieved
مِن خِلال *min khilāl*	through
مُناسِب *munāsib*	appropriate
طِبْقاً لِـ *Tibqan li*	according to
مُواصَفات *muwāSafāt*	characteristics
مَطْلوبَة *maTlūba*	demanded, required
عَصْر *'aSr*	age, era
تِكْنولوجيا *tiknulujya*	technology
نَوْع *naw'*	kind
تَعارُف *ta'āruf*	acquaintance, getting to know

زَواج zawāj	marriage
باحِث bāHith	one looking for, researcher
يَخْتار (اختار) yakhtār (ikhtār)	he chooses (to chose)
مُرَشَّحين murashshaHīn	candidates
تَضْطَر أن tuDTarr (iDTurr) an	forced to (to force)
تَقْبَل (قَبِل) taqbal (qabil)	he accepts
اِخْتِيار ikhtiyār	choice
وَحيد waHid	only
عُزَّاب (عزَب) 'uzzāb (a'zab)	singles
شَريك sharik	partner
بَل bal	(and) even, rather, however
قارَة qārra	continent
مُعارِضين mu'āriDīn	opponents
سَهْل sahl	easy
إعْطاء i'Tā'	giving
مَعْلومات ma'lūmāt	information
غيْر ghayr	not
بِخِلاف bi khilāf	as opposed to
تَقْليدِيَّة taqlīdiyya	traditional
أُسَر (أُسْرَة) usar (usra)	families
يَبْدو (بَدا) أنَّ yabdū (badā) anna	it seems (to seem) that
ظاهِرَة DHāhira	phenomenon
سَتَسْتَمِر (اسْتَمَر) satastamirr (istamarr)	will continue (to continue)
يَوْمِياً yawmiyyan	daily

LESSON 16

(Egyptian Arabic)

el-ahramāt The Pyramids

A. Dialogue

Donald is taking an afternoon off to visit the Pyramids of Giza. As he is strolling the grounds by the Great Pyramid of Cheops, he sees a sign saying "Camel Rides for $1." He talks to Ahmad, the camel driver.

dūnald: SabāH el-khēr, ya rayyis, 'awiz arkab eg-gamal wi takhudni laffa, iza kān mumkin?

aHmad: SabāH en-nūr. māshi ya bēh, itfaDDal, eg-gamal we g-gammāl taHt amrak.

dūnald: Tayyib, el-yafTa bta'tak bet'ūl dolār wāHid lirkūb eg-gamal ma'a murshid sīyāHi. SaHH ek-kalām dah?

aHmad: aywa ya ustāz, bidolār wāHid barakkibak eg-gamal wi balaffifak Hawalēn el-haram ek-kebīr dah, haram khūfu, wmumkin law Habbēt, bawarrīk fein iS-Sōt wi D-Dō'.

dūnald: māshi kalamak. anā sme't in iS-Sōt wi D-Dō' 'arD gamīl bi-yeHki tarīkh el-ahramāt wabul-hōl. Tayyib, adfa'lak delwa'ti walla ba'd ma nkhallaS?

aHmad: āh, mumkin tedfa'li delwa'ti 'abl mā terkab eg-gamal.

dūnald: Tab, yalla bīna. ādi d-dolār aho. ittikil 'ala-llah.

After going full circle around the pyramid, Donald and Ahmad arrive back where they had started their journey.

dūnald: mutashakkir 'awi, yā rayyis, khalās, nazzilni hena.

aHmad: māshi, yā bēh, khallīk māsik fi 'antar kwayyis.

However, much to Donald's surprise, getting off the camel was not as easy as getting on it. Ahmad did not bring the camel down to its knees, but rather, looked straight up into Donald's eyes and said, in a very serious voice. . .

aHmad: bass 'abl mā'anazzilak min 'a g-gamal, lāzim tedfa'li ba'it el-Hisāb.

dūnald: Hisāb ēh, yā 'amm. anā mish dafa'tilak dolār zayy ma l-yafTa bta'tak bit'ūl?

aHmad: aywa ya ustāz, ed-dolār dah 'alashān rukūb eg-gamal, lākin en-nizūl minnu luh Hisāb tāni.

dūnald: 'aSdak ēh Hisāb tāni?

aHmad: ya'ni mumkin masalan, tis'a w-tis'īn dolār.

dūnald: yanhar iswid, dī sir'a 'alani. iz-zāy te'ūl keda? enta magnūn? anā Haballagh 'annak fi shurtat es-siyāHa. waddīni a'rab maktab sīyaHa au shirkit is-siyāHa.

aHmad: la', la'. d-ana bahazzar ya bēh, ana 'aSdi-l ba'shīsh betā'i.

dūnald: āh, 'ūl keda. Tayyib, 'ashān khaTrak bass, ādi dolār tāni aho ba'shīsh.

Donald: Good morning, boss. I want to ride the camel, and for you to take me around if possible?

Ahmad: Good morning. Okay, sir. Please come. The camel and the camel-driver are at your disposal.

Donald: All right, your sign says one dollar to ride the camel along with a tourist guide. Is that right?

Ahmad: Yes, sir, for a dollar, I'll let you ride the camel and take you around this great pyramid, the Pyramid of Cheops, and perhaps, if you'd like, I can show you where the Sound and Light Show is.

Donald: Sounds good. I heard that the Sound and Light is a beautiful show. It tells the history of the Pyramids and the Sphinx. Okay, should I pay now or when we're finished?

Ahmad: Yes, you can pay me now, before you get on the camel.

Donald: All right, let's go. Here's the one dollar. Trust in God and let's get going.

Donald: Thank you very much, driver. That's enough, let me off here.

Ahmad: Okay, sir. Keep holding on tight to Antar.

Ahmad: But before I let you down off the camel, you have to pay me the rest of the fare.

Donald: What fare are you talking about, man? Didn't I pay you a dollar just like your sign says?

Ahmad: Yes, sir. That dollar is for getting on the camel, but getting off of it is a different fare.

Donald: What do you mean a "different fare"?

Ahmad: I mean, you can say, for instance, ninety-nine dollars.

Donald: Oh my God, that's highway robbery. How can you say that? Are you crazy? I'm going to report you to the Tourist Police. Take me to the nearest tourist office or to a tourist agency.

Ahmad: No, no, sir, I am just kidding. I meant my tip!

Donald: Oh, so that's it. Okay, only for your sake, here's another dollar tip.

B. Pronunciation

1. THE EGYPTIAN DIALECT

Like other Arabic dialects, Egyptian Arabic is primarily a spoken language, rarely used in written communication, where Modern Standard Arabic is the norm. Because the Arabic script was devised to represent the sounds of Classical and Modern Standard Arabic, the additional sounds that exist in Arabic dialects like Egyptian are not represented by it. For these reasons, the transliteration in Latin script is used to represent Egyptian Arabic in Lessons 16 to 20, as in all other dialect lessons.

You may encounter many different varieties of Egyptian Arabic, depending on whether the speakers are from the urban centers or the rural areas, from the North or the South of Egypt. We teach the Cairene variety of Egyptian Arabic in Lessons 16 to 20, as it is the most commonly used Egyptian dialect, spoken in the urban centers of the North but understood throughout Egypt.

2. VOWELS IN EGYPTIAN ARABIC

Like *fuSHā*, Egyptian Arabic has six basic vowels, *ā, ū, ī, a, u,* and *i.* In addition to these, Egyptian Arabic also has the short vowels *o* and *e,* and their long counterparts, *ō* and *ē.* These two vowel sounds often replace the *ū* and *ī* sounds.

arkab (I ride) (short *a*)

'āwiz (I want) (short *i*)

mumkin ([it is] possible, maybe) (short *u*)

SabāH (morning) (long *ā*)

ek-kebīr ([the] large [one]) (long *ī*)

en-nūr (light) (long *ū*)

The short *o*-sound corresponds to the *aw* sound in MSA. For example:

Egyptian Arabic	MSA
Sōt (sound)	صوت *Sawt*
Dō' (light)	ضوء *Daw'*

The short *e* vowel in Egyptian Arabic corresponds to either the short *a* or the short *i* vowel of *fuSHā*. For example:

Egyptian Arabic	MSA
yeHki (to tell a story)	يحكي *yaHkī*
sme't (I heard)	سمعت *sami'tu*

As in many other Arabic dialects, in Egyptian, the definite article has the form *el*, instead of *al*. When *el* precedes "sun" letters, the vowel *e* can change to a short *i* vowel, as in *is-sīyāHa* (travel; tourism) or *iS-Sōt wi D-Dō'* (the sound and light). The pronunciation may vary, so one can hear *en-nūr* (the light) or *in-nūr* and *el-yafTa* (the sign) or *il-yafTa*.

Egyptian Arabic also has two compound vowels, or diphthongs, the *aw* and *ay* sounds, as in:

law (if)

zayy (like).

3. CONSONANTS IN EGYPTIAN ARABIC

Most consonantal sounds in Egyptian Arabic are the same as those used in MSA. We discuss below those consonants where Egyptian Arabic differs from MSA.

A. THE LACK OF THE CONSONANT *q*

Colloquial Egyptian Arabic doesn't have the consonant *q*. This MSA sound is normally reduced in pronunciation to a *hamza* sound.

Egyptian Arabic	MSA
delwa'ti (now)	الوَقْت *el-waqtu*
'abl (before)	قَبْلَ *qabla*
ba'īt (the rest of)	بَقِيَّة *baqiyyah*
'aSdak ēh? (What do you mean?)	قَصْدَك *qaSdak*

Thus, it is not difficult to come up with a *fuSHā* equivalent of an Egyptian Arabic word containing a *hamza*: Simply substitute a *qāf* for the *hamza* and then look up the word in a dictionary to find its meaning. At the same time, a number of words used in Egyptian that belong to the educated and more formal language retain their *qāf*, such as the words *al-iqtiSād* (the economy) and *raqam* (number). Also, you should know that not every *hamza* in Egyptian Arabic corresponds to an MSA *q*-sound; there are also those Egyptian Arabic words with *hamza* where this sounds corresponds to the same sound in MSA.

B. THE CONSONANT *g*

Urban Egyptian Arabic, spoken in Cairo and the northern cities of Egypt, has the consonant *g*, pronounced just like the *g*-sound in the English words *go* and *get*. This sound corresponds to the *j*-sound in *fuSHā* (i.e., the sound found in the English words *jam* and *John*).[1]

Egyptian Arabic	MSA
eg-gamal (the camel)	الجَمَل *aj-jamal*
gamīl (beautiful)	جميل *jamīl*
magnūn (crazy)	مجنون *majnūn*

C. THE LACK OF CONSONANT *dh*

The sound *dh*, represented by the letter ذ *dhāl* in *fuSHā*, is pronounced as a *z*-sound in Egyptian Arabic. Compare the Egyptian Arabic words below to their *fuSHā* equivalents.

Egyptian Arabic	MSA
iza (if)	إذا *idhā*
ustāz (Mr., Sir, Professor)	أستاذ *ustādh*

D. THE LACK OF THE CONSONANT *th*

The *th*-sound of *fuSHā* is pronounced as either a *t*- or an *s*-sound in Egyptian Arabic, and there is no definite rule about this variation.

Egyptian Arabic	MSA
tāni (other, second)	ثاني *thāni*
masalan (for example)	مثلا *mathalan*

C. Grammar and Usage

1. PERSONAL PRONOUNS IN EGYPTIAN ARABIC

The following table lists the subject pronouns used in Egyptian Arabic.

---

[1] In certain rural parts of Egypt, outside of Cairo and other urban centers where Cairene dialect is spoken, the *g*-sound is pronounced in a manner consistent with *fuSHā*, i.e., as a *j*-sound, whereas the *q*-sound is pronounced as a hard *g* instead.

SUBJECT PRONOUNS IN EGYPTIAN ARABIC			
Singular		Plural	
I	*anā*	we	*eHna*
you *(m.)*	*enta*	you *(m./f.)*	*entu(m)*
you *(f.)*	*enti*		
he	*howwa*	they *(m./f.)*	*homma*
she	*heyya*		

Notice that most Egyptian Arabic personal pronouns are very close in form to those in *fuSHā*. The *fuSHā a* corresponds to *e* in Egyptian Arabic forms <u>e</u>nta, <u>e</u>nti, <u>e</u>Hna, and <u>e</u>ntu(m), and *u* corresponds to *o* in Egyptian Arabic forms h<u>o</u>wwa and h<u>o</u>mma. In the plural, *eHna* (we) differs from the *fuSHā naHnu* in that it lacks the initial *n* and ends in *a* instead of *u*. A more important difference is that Egyptian Arabic does not distinguish between masculine and feminine forms in the second and third person plural. The Egyptian Arabic *they* pronoun, *homma,* differs the most from its equivalent in *fuSHā*, *hum*; the two share only the initial *h*-sound.

2. IMPERFECT TENSE IN EGYPTIAN ARABIC

Egyptian Arabic imperfect tense is similar to the one that exists in *fuSHā*. The imperfect verb is formed by adding the appropriate prefixes and/or suffixes to the imperfect tense stem, which follows the pattern *CCVC*. For example, The verb ركب *rakib* (he rode, to ride) is *byerkab* (he rides) in the *he* form of the imperfect tense. Note, however, that the forms of Egyptian Arabic prefixes differ slightly from their forms in MSA; more importantly, the prefix *b-/bi-* precedes the pronominal prefix in all persons.

THE IMPERFECT INDICATIVE OF THE VERB *rakib* (TO RIDE)			
Singular		Plural	
anā	<u>ba</u>rkab	*eHna*	<u>bn</u>erkab
enta	<u>bt</u>erkab	*entu(m)*	<u>bt</u>erkabu
enti	<u>bt</u>erkabi		
howwa	<u>by</u>erkab	*homma*	<u>by</u>erkabu
heyya	<u>bt</u>erkab		

> *dūnald byerkab eg-gamal 'alashan yishūf el-haram.*
> Donald rides the camel to see the pyramid.

When the main verb follows the expressions *lāzim* (should, must), *mumkin* (can, able to; possible, maybe), or *'āwiz* (want), the subjunctive form of the imperfect tense must be used. The subjunctive form in Egyptian Arabic is the same as the indicative form, but without the prefix *b-/bi-*.

A. *lāzim* (SHOULD, MUST)

lāzim is invariant and does not change to match the person or number of the subject. In order to indicate a different subject, the verb that follows *lāzim* has to be used in the right personal form.

> *lāzim tedfa'li ba'it el-Hisāb.*
> You have to pay me the rest of the fare.

> *enta lāzim titkallim ma'āha.*
> You have to speak to her.

> *mish lāzim nikhallaS 'abl ma nimshi?*
> Don't we have to finish before we leave?

B. *'āwiz* (WANT)

'āwiz is the equivalent of the verb *to want* in English. Its counterpart in *fuSHā* is *yurīdu* يريد. *'āwiz* can be followed by an object noun, as in:

> *(howwa) 'āwiz gamal.*
> He wants a camel.

Or it can be combined with a verb, as in:

> *(howwa) 'āwiz yirkab gamal.*
> He wants to ride a camel.

> *(heyya) 'awza tidfa' el-Hisāb.*
> She wants to pay the bill.

'āwiz is a present participle, not a verb (see Lesson 12, explaining the formation and the use of present participles in MSA), that combines with verbs in the imperfect tense. Notice that *'āwiz* changes its form depending on the gender and number of the subject.

THE EXPRESSION *'āwiz arkab* (I WANT TO RIDE)			
Singular		Plural	
anā	*'āwiz arkab*	eHna	*'awzīn nerkab*
enta	*'āwiz terkab*	entu(m)	*'awzīn terkabu*
enti	*'awza terkabi*		
howwa	*'āwiz yerkab*	homma	*'awzīn yerkabu*
heyya	*'awza terkab*		

C. *mumkin* (CAN, ABLE TO; POSSIBLE, MAYBE)

Like *lāzim*, *mumkin* (can, able to; possible, maybe) is an invariant word that can be used as an adverb or as a modal particle, followed by a verb in the imperfect tense. *mumkin* can also be used as a tag question, as in:

> *'āwiz arkab eg-gamal, mumkin?*
> I want to ride the camel; can I?

In the following table, *mumkin* is combined with the imperfect tense verb *yedfa'* (he pays).

THE EXPRESSION *mumkin yedfa'* (HE CAN PAY)			
Singular		Plural	
anā	mumkin adfa'	eHna	mumkin nedfa'
enta	mumkin tedfa'	entu(m)	mumkin tedfa'u
enti	mumkin tedfa'i		
howwa	mumkin yedfa'	homma	mumkin yedfa'u
heyya	mumkin tedfa'		

w-mumkin law Habbēt, bawarrik fēn iS-Sōt wi D-Dō'. (used as an adverb)
And perhaps, if you'd like, I can show you where the Sound and Light Show is.

mumkin tedfa'li delwa'ti 'abl mā terkab eg-gamal. (used as a modal particle)
You can pay me now, before you get on the camel.

D. Vocabulary

SabāH	morning
'āwiz	I want to
el-haram; *el-ahramāt*	the pyramid; the pyramids
gamal; *gimāl*	camel; camels
gammāl	camel-driver
taHt amrak (m.); *amrik* (f.)	at your disposal; all yours
murshid siyāHi	tourist guide
takhudni (m.); *takhdīni* (f.)	take me (e.g., for a ride)
kebīr (m.); *kebīra* (f.)	big; large
eS-Sōt wi D-Dō'	the Sound and Light
gamīl (m.); *gamīla* (f.)	beautiful
laffa	a ride (e.g., around a place or city)
Tayyib	okay, all right
yafTa	sign, poster
beta'tak (m.); *beta'tik* (f.)	yours
wāHid (m.); *waHda* (f.)	one
SaHH?	Right?, Okay?
ek-kalām dah	(that) what you're saying/you said
w(i)	and
aywa	yes, yeah
Hawalēn	around
māshi	okay; will do
da(h) (m.); *di(h)* (f.)	this; that
bass	but, only
walla	or, or else

ba'd	after
'abl	before
yalla bīna	let's go
mutashakkir (m.);	
mutashakkira (f.)	thank you
'awi	very
rayyis	boss, chief (used informally to address a male service provider)
khalās	that's it; right here; no more
nazzilni (m.); *nazzilīni* (f.)	drop me off, let me down
hena	here
khallīk māsik (m.);	
khallīki maska (f.)	keep holding on, don't let go of
Hisāb	account, bill, charge, fare
law	if
tidfa'li (m.); *tifa'īli* (f.)	you pay me (*yidfa* [to pay])
ēh?	what?
zayy	like, as, such as
y'ani . . .	I mean . . .
mumkin	can, able to; maybe, possible
masalan	for example, like
keda	something like, you can say
tis'a w-tis'īn	ninety-nine
yanhar iswid!	Oh, my God! (Lit., Oh, what a black day it is!)
magnūn; *maganin*	crazy
'alani	open, public, flagrant
maktab is-siyāHa	tourist office
shirkit is-siyāHa	tourist company, travel agency
Haballagh 'annak (m.);	
'annik (f.)	I will report you
el-bulīs	the police
shortat is-siyāHa	tourist police
ustāz (m.); *ustāza* (f.)	sir, Mr.; madam, Mrs.; professor
'alashān	because, so that, in order to
'ashān khaTrak (m.); *khaTrik* (f.)	for your sake, for you
kwayyis (m.); *kwayyisa* (f.)	good
lākin	but
bēh (m.)	Sir
sitt hānim (f.)	Madam

E. Cultural Note

Egypt is home to many of the world's most valuable historic monuments, the most notable of which are the Great Pyramids of Giza and the Sphinx. The three pyramids, standing on the Giza Plateau, are the Pyramid of Khufu, the Pyramid of Khafre, and the Pyramid of Menkaure, dating from the time of the Old Kingdom (2650–2134 B.C.). King Khufu, who ruled from 2589–2566 B.C., also known by the Greek name "Cheops," was the father of pyramid building at Giza. He was the son of King Sneferu and Queen Hetpeheres. The Pyramid of Khufu is made up of 2,300,000 individual stones of limestone and granite ranging in weight from 2.5 to 9 tons, and it weighs 6.5 million tons.

Khafre, who was the son of Khufu, was also known as Rakhaef or Chephren. He ruled from 2520–2494 B.C. and is responsible for the second largest pyramid complex at Giza, which includes the Sphinx, a Mortuary Temple, and a Valley Temple. Khafre may be best known for his statues, the most famous among them being, of course, the Sphinx.

Menkaure, also known as Mycerinus, ruled from 2490–2472 B.C. He is believed to be Khufu's grandson.

The pyramids are essentially tombs wherein the kings and their families were buried with their possessions, after being mummified. The belief was that the possessions would be everything the king would need in the afterlife.

F. Exercises

1. Match the words from the A column to those in the B column to form phrases or short sentences.

A	B
a. *SaHH*	*we g-gammāl*
b. *'awiz arkab*	*siyāHi*
c. *ittikil*	*'awi*
d. *mutashakkir*	*wi D-Dō'*
e. *murshid*	*'alani*
f. *eg-gamal*	*is-siyāHa*
g. *lāzim tedfa'li*	*'ala l-lah*
h. *di sir'a*	*eg-gamal*
i. *shurtat*	*ba'it el-Hisāb*
j. *iS-Sōt*	*ek-kalām dah?*

2. Put the words in the correct order to form coherent sentences.

a. *Hisāb / ēh / tāni / 'aSdak / ?*
b. *minnu / tāni / en-nizūl / Hisāb / luh / lākin*
c. *'annak / is-sīyāHa / fi /anā / bulīs / Haballagh*
d. *iS-Sōt / gamīl / sme't / 'arD / anā / wi D-Dō' / inn*
e. *'alashān / dah / eg-gamal / rukūb / ed-dolār*

3. Fill in the blanks with the correct verb in the imperfect tense to form complete sentences.

a. *heyya 'awza _____ eg-gamal.*
b. *eHna _____ nerkab eg-gamal.*
c. *homma _____ eg-gamal fi S-SabāH.*
d. *enti lāzim _____ ba'īt el-Hisāb.*
e. *homma _____ yedfa'ūli delwa'ti 'abl mā yerkabu eg-gamal.*

4. Fill in the blank with the correct personal pronoun.

a. _____ *maganīn?*
b. _____ *'awzīn yedfa'u delwa'ti.*
c. _____ *mutashakkirīn 'awi, yā rayyis.*
d. _____ *mumkin tedfa'i ba'īt el-Hisāb.*
e. _____ *mish lāzim yikhallaS 'abl mā yimshi?*

5. Find and correct the errors in the following sentences. A hint is provided in parentheses.

a. *aywa ya ustāz, bi dolār wāHid arakkibik eg-gamal wa-alaffifkom Hawalein el-haram.* (pronoun-verb agreement)
b. *anā sme't in iS-Sōt wi D-Dō' 'arD gamīla b-yeHku tarīkh el-ahramāt wabul-hōl.* (noun-adjective agreement, pronoun-verb agreement)
c. *āh, mumkin tedfa'ūli delwa'ti 'abl mā yerkab eg-gamal.* (pronoun-verb agreement)
d. *māshi, yā sit, khallīk māsik fi-'antar kwayyis.* (pronoun-verb agreement)
e. *SabāH el-kheir, ya rayyis, 'awzīn arkab eg-gamal w-takhudni laffa, iza kān mumkin?* (pronoun-verb agreement)

Answer Key

1. a. *SaHH ek-kalām dah?*
   b. *'āwiz arkab eg-gamal*
   c. *ittikil 'alallah*
   d. *mutashakkir 'awi*
   e. *murshid siyāHi*
   f. *eg-gamal we g-gammāl*
   g. *lāzim tedfa'li ba'īt el-Hisāb*
   h. *di sir'a a'lani*
   i. *shurtat is-siyāHa*
   j. *iS-Sōt wiD-Dō'*
2. a. *'aSdak ēh Hisāb tāni?*
   b. *lākin en-nizūl minnu luh Hisāb tāni.*
   c. *anā Haballagh 'annak fi bulīs is-siyāHa.*

d. *anā sme't inn iS-Sōt wi D-Dō' 'arD gamīl.*
e. *ed-dolār dah 'alashān rukūb eg-gamal.*

3. a. *heyya 'awza __terkab__ eg-gamal.*
   b. *eHna __'awzīn__ nerkab eg-gamal.*
   c. *homma __beyirkabu__ eg-gamal fi S-SabāH.*
   d. *enti lāzim __tedfa'īli__ ba'īt el-Hisāb.*
   e. *homma __lāzim__ yedfa'ūli delwa'ti 'abl mā yerkabu eg-gamal.*

4. a. __entu(m)__ *maganīn?*
   b. __homma__ *'awzīn yedfa'u delwa'ti.*
   c. __eHna__ *mutashakkirīn 'awi, yā rayyis.*

244

d. _enti_ mumkin tedfa'i ba'it el-Hisāb.

e. _howwa_ mish lāzim yikhallaS 'abl mā yimshi?

5. a. aywa ya ustāz, bi dolār wāHid _arakkibak_ eg-gamal wa-_alaffifak_ Hawalein el-haram.

b. anā sme't in iS-Sōt wi D-Dō' 'arD gamīl bi-_yeHki_ tarikh el-ahramāt w-abu l-hōl.

c. āh, mumkin tedfa'uli delwa'ti 'abl mā _terkabu_ eg-gamal.

d. māshi, yā sitt, _khallīki maska_ f 'antar kwayyis.

e. SabāH el-kheir, ya rayyis, 'awzīn _nerkab_ eg-gamal w-_takhudna_ laffa, iza kān mumkin?

LESSON 17

riHla fi n-nīl A Cruise on the Nile

A. Dialogue

After much walking and sightseeing, Donald and Lucy decided they needed a quiet cruise on the Nile river, the heart and soul of Egypt. They called on their friend Layla to see if she could help them arrange a cruise on a *felucca*.

lūsī: alō, SabāH el-khēr, ya layla, izzayyik? ana lūsī.

layla: ahlan ya lūsī, izzayyik enti? waHashtūna nti w-dūnald. inshallah tkūnu b-khēr.

lūsī: āh eHna kwayyisīn el-Hamdulillāh. isma'i ya layla, anā w-dūnald kunna 'awzīn nirkab felūka 'ala n-nīl w-nitfassaH Hawalēn el-qāhira w-Tab'an 'ashān neshūf ghurūb esh-shams.

layla: aywa ya lūsī, di fikra 'aZīma.

lūsī: hāyil ya layla. eHna min zamān w-nifsina ni'mil keda.

Donald, Lucy, and Layla arrive at the dock where they are met by Karim, Layla's brother, and Mahmud, the *felucca* boatman.

dūnald: ahlan ya karīm, es-salāmu 'alēkum ya rayyis. 'awzīnak ti'millena gawla siyāHeyya Helwa wi t-farragna 'ala l-qāhira wi g-gīza wi g-gezira, w-ba'dein 'awzīn neshūf ghurūb esh-shams. Helw ek-kalām dah?

maHmūd: āh, 'awi ya bēh, itfaDDalu anā taHt amrokum.

dūnald: da kalām gamīl ya rayyis maHmūd. yalla ya lūsī, yalla ya layla, rkabu 'ashān ma n-Dayya'shi wa't.

Everybody gets settled in the *felucca*, while the gentle breeze pulls the sails forward.

layla: ēh ra'yik ya lūsī fi n-nīl wi fi l-manZar?

lūsī: Hāga gamīla 'awi, fō' ma kont atSawwar. mumkin aHoT īdi fi l-mayya?

layla: āh Tab'an, bas khalli bālik el-felūka sa'āt bit-mīl yimīn wi-shmāl, fa-khallīki maska kwayyis fi l-markib. en-nīl dah nahr 'aZīm, ya lūsī, aTwal nahr fi l-'ālam, biykūn 'ariD 'awi f-manāti' w-dayya' fimanāti' tanya.

dūnald: ya salām, dal manZar rā'i'. el-mabāni, wi l-'arabiyyāt, wi t-tamasīl, wi k-kabāri. māsha'allāh.

karim: anā beyit-hayya'li inn ir-rayyis maHmūd el-marakbi biyleff w-byerga' 'ashān nilHa' ghurūb esh-shams.

Lucy: Hello? Good morning, Layla. How are you? This is Lucy.

Layla: Hello, Lucy, how are you? We missed you and Donald. I hope you are both well.

Lucy: Yes, we're fine, thanks. Listen, Layla, Donald and I were thinking of taking a ride on a *felucca* on the Nile. We want to take a tour around Cairo and, of course, see the sunset.

Layla: Yes, Lucy, that's a great idea.

Lucy: That's wonderful, Layla. We have been wanting to do this for so long.

Donald: Hi, Karim. Good-day, boatman. We want you to take us on a nice cruise and show us Cairo, Giza, and Gezira, and after that we want to see the sunset. Sound good?

Mahmud: Yes, sir, no problem at all.

Donald: That sounds beautiful, boatman Mahmud. Lucy, Layla, come on, get on so that we don't lose time.

Layla: So, Lucy, what do you think of the Nile and the view?

Lucy: It is so beautiful, over and above what I had expected. Can I put my hand in the water?

Layla: Yes, of course. But watch out, because the *felucca* sometimes sways to the right and to the left. Be sure that you hold on tight to the boat. Lucy, the Nile is a magnificent river, the longest river in the world. It is very wide in some areas and narrow in others.

Donald: Wow! The view is spectacular. The buildings, cars, statues, bridges—It's amazing!

Karim: I have a feeling that Mahmud the boatman is turning around and back so that we don't miss the sunset.

B. Pronunciation

CONSONANT CLUSTERS IN EGYPTIAN ARABIC

In *fuSHā*, groups of two or more consonants cannot be found at the beginning of a word. In Egyptian Arabic, on the other hand, two-consonant clusters are often found at the beginning of a word. Compare the two alternative pronunciations of the following words in Egyptian Arabic.

ghurūb (sunset)	*ghrūb*
tekūnu (you are, you will be)	*tkūnu*
bekhēr (doing well)	*bkhēr*

C. Grammar and Usage

1. THE PERFECT TENSE: THE VERB *rikib* (TO RIDE)

In Egyptian Arabic, as in MSA, the perfect tense is formed by the addition of suffixes to the perfect tense stem. The following table shows the verb *rikib* (to ride) (*rakiba* in *fuSHā*) in the perfect tense. Notice that the *he* form, *rikib* in the table below, doesn't have a personal ending.

PERFECT TENSE OF THE VERB *rikib* (TO RIDE)			
Singular		Plural	
ana	*rikib-t*	*eHna*	*rikib-na*
enta	*rikib-t*	*entu*	*rikib-tom*
enti	*rikib-ti*		
howwa	*rikib*	*homma*	*rikb-u*
heyya	*rikb-it*		

If you compare the perfect tense endings used in Egyptian Arabic to those in MSA (see Lesson 4), you'll notice that the feminine plural form and the dual form are absent from the colloquial Arabic of Egypt, as from many other dialects of Arabic. Also notice the lack of final vowels on the the *I* and *you* forms in the singular.

2. THE OBJECT PRONOUN SUFFIXES

Object pronouns in Egyptian Arabic can be either independent words or suffixes. The independent pronouns are *iyyay* (me), *iyyak* (you, *m. sg.*), *iyyaki* (you, *f. sg.*), *iyyah* (him), *iyyaha* (her), *iyyana* (us), *iyyakom* (you, *m./f. pl.*), and *iyyahom* (them, *m./f.*). However, they are rarely used in colloquial Egyptian Arabic. The object pronoun suffixes are similar to those in *fuSHā*.

OBJECT PRONOUN SUFFIXES IN EGYPTIAN ARABIC			
Singular		Plural	
me	-ni	us	-na
you *(m.)*	-ak	you *(m./f.)*	-kom/kum
you *(f.)*	-ik		
him	-u	they *(m./f.)*	-hom
her	-ha		

Notice the slight differences in the form of these pronouns as compared to the *fuSHā* forms (see Lesson 6). The following two tables show the object pronoun suffixes attached to the perfect tense verb *shakar* (he thanked) and imperfect tense verb *yoshkor* (he thanks).

PERFECT TENSE OF THE VERB *shakar* (TO THANK) WITH OBJECT PRONOUN SUFFIXES			
Singular		Plural	
ana	shakarni	eHna	shakarna
enta	shakarak	entu	shakarkom
enti	shakarik		
howwa	shakaru	homma	shakarhom
heyya	shakarha		

IMPERFECT TENSE OF THE VERB *shakar* (TO THANK) WITH OBJECT PRONOUN SUFFIXES			
Singular		Plural	
ana	beyoshkorni	eHna	beyoshkorna
enta	beyoshkorak	entu	beyoshkorkom
enti	beyoshkorik		
howwa	beyoshkoru	homma	beyoshkorhom
heyya	beyoshkorha		

ana bashkorak 'ala l-yōm ig-gamīl dah.
I thank you for such a beautiful day.

eHna shakarnāha ba'd ma rgi'na min ir-riHla
We thanked her after we returned from the trip.

howwa beyoshkoru l'innu rāgil Tayyib.
He is thanking him because he is a good man.

3. PREPOSITIONS WITH THE OBJECT PRONOUN SUFFIXES

The following table shows the object pronoun suffixes attached to the preposition *min* (from). Notice the doubling of the last consonant of the preposition when a pronoun is attached to it.

PREPOSITION *min* (FROM) WITH OBJECT PRONOUN SUFFIXES			
Singular		**Plural**	
from me	*minni*	from us	*minnina*
from you *(m.)*	*minnak*	from you *(m./f.)*	*minnokom*
from you *(f.)*	*minnik*		
from him	*minnu*	from them *(m./f.)*	*minnohom*
from her	*minnaha*		

Here is an example from the dialogue of the preposition *l* (to, for) with *eHna* (we) attached to it:

> *anā Hakallimlik karīm akhūya 'alashān yerattib l-ena yōm nrūH fīh kullina ma'a ba'D.*
> I will talk to my brother, Karim, and have him arrange a day <u>when we</u> can all go together.

Note that the *fuSHā li* (to, for) is pronounced as a simple *l* in Egyptian Arabic, and so is the form *ila* (to). Some other Egyptian Arabic prepositions are *'ala* (on), *fi* (in), and *'and* (at).

4. POSSESSIVE SUFFIXES IN EGYPTIAN ARABIC

The possessive suffixes in Egyptian Arabic are very similar in form and function to possessive suffixes in MSA (see Lesson 5). They attach to the end of the noun they modify. Notice that, except for the first person singular, they are also the same as the object pronoun suffixes.

POSSESSIVE SUFFIXES			
Singular		**Plural**	
my	*-ī*	our	*-nā*
your *(m.)*	*-ak*	your *(m./f.)*	*-kom*
your *(f.)*	*-ik*		
his	*-u*	their *(m./f.)*	*-hom*
her	*-ha*		

The table below shows the noun *īd* (hand) with possessive suffixes attached to it. Notice that the initial long *ī* of *īd* is replaced by the short *i* in the *she* form and all the plural forms.

THE NOUN *id* (HAND) WITH POSSESSIVE SUFFIXES			
Singular		Plural	
my hand	*idi*	our hand	*idna*
your hand *(m.)*	*idak*	your hand	*idkum*
your hand *(f.)*	*idik*		
his hand	*idu*	their hand	*idhom*
her hand	*idha*		

Possessive suffixes can be added only to indefinite nouns.

Egyptian Arabic also uses the word *betā'* (*lit.*, thing) to show possession, but only with non-human and definite nouns, which it must follow. The pronominal suffixes are added to *betā'*. Let us use the definite noun *el-kitab* (book) as an example.

ek-kitab betā'i	my book
ek-kitab betā'ak	your book *(m. sg.)*
ek-kitab betā'ik	your book *(f. sg.)*
ek-kitab betā'u	his book
ek-kitab beta'ha	her book
ek-kitab beta'na	our book
ek-kitab beta'kum	your book *(pl.)*
ek-kitab beta'hum	their book

In some instances, particularly when answering a question, an Egyptian Arabic speaker may very well omit the noun and use only *betā'* with suffixes in the response. For example, if the question is:

kitāb mīn dah?
Whose book is this?

The answer can be:

betā'i.
Mine.

5. NUMBERS FROM 1 TO 19 IN EGYPTIAN ARABIC

Egyptian Arabic numbers are similar to their MSA counterparts (Lesson 7). The main difference is in the pronunciation of the MSA *th*, which is pronounced as *t* in Egyptian Arabic. There are also differences in the structure of compound numbers from 11 to 19.

NUMBERS 1 TO 19 IN EGYPTIAN ARABIC	
1	*wāHid*
2	*etnein*
3	*talāta*
4	*Arba'a*
5	*khamsa*
6	*sitta*
7	*sab'a*
8	*tamanya*
9	*tes'a*
10	*'ashra*
11	*Hidāshar*
12	*etnāshar*
13	*talattāshar*
14	*arba'tāshar*
15	*khamastāshar*
16	*sittāshar*
17	*saba'tāshar*
18	*tamantāshar*
19	*tesa'tāshar*

D. Vocabulary

alō?	Hello? (on the phone)
ahlan	hi, hello, welcome
waHashtūna (waHash)	we missed you (to miss)
el-Hamdulillāh	Fine, thanks. (*lit.*, praise to God)
isma' (m.); *isma'i* (f.)	Listen!
felūka	felucca
en-nīl	the Nile
nit-fassaH	we take a tour, go for a ride, go on an outing
el-qāhira	Cairo
eg-gīza	Giza
eg-gezīra	island; Gezira (an island between Cairo and Giza)
el-ma'adi	Maadi (a Cairo suburb)
Tab'an	of course, naturally
ghurūb	sunset
esh-shams	the sun
fikra	idea
'aZīm (m.), *'aZīma* (f.)	great, outstanding
marakbi	boatman
es-salāmu 'alēkum	hello (*lit.*, peace be with you)
gawla	tour

Helw (m.), Helwa (f.)	nice, beautiful, sweet (*m. form*); also: Sounds good!
tifarragna	you show us
ba'dein	later; afterwards
gamīl	beautiful
man Dayya'shi	so that we don't waste
wa't	time
ēh ra'yak? (m.), ēh ra'yik? (f.)	What do you think?
Hāga	thing; something
fō' ma kont atSawwar	beyond what I expected
īd	hand
mayya	water
sā'it	at which time, when
yimīn	right
shemāl	left
markib	boat
nahr	river
aTwal	longer, (the) longest
'ālam	world
'arīD (m.); 'arīDa (f.)	wide
dayya' (m.); dayya'a (f.)	narrow
manTi'a; manāTi'	region(s)
ya salām!	Wow!, Oh my!, Oh dear!
ra'y	opinion
manZar; manāZir	sight(s); spectacles(s)
mabna; mabāni	building(s)
'arabeyya; 'arabiyyāt	car(s)
kobri; kabāri	bridge(s)
timsāl; tamasīl	statue(s)
masha'allāh!	Amazing!, Good!, Bravo!
nilha'	we catch it in time, we make it on time

E. Cultural Note

Egypt stretches vertically along the Nile River, its heart and soul for thousands of years. The Nile is the longest river in the world and runs for 4,187 miles. It has three major tributaries, the White Nile, the Blue Nile, and the Atbara. The source of the Blue Nile is in the highlands of Ethiopia. On each side of the Nile, Egypt stretches into arid desert.

Throughout history, the Nile has provided Egyptians with drinking and irrigation water, fish, and waterfowl. Houses were built with papyrus reeds that grow on its banks. In Ancient Egypt paper was made out of papyrus as well. Until the Aswan dam was built in the 1960s, the Nile flooded the farmlands on a yearly basis, providing natural irrigation and fertilization.

F. EXERCISES

1. Match the words in column A to those in column B to form phrases or short sentences.

A	B
a. *da r-rayyis MaHmūd*	*ya layla*
b. *'awzīn nirkab*	*aS-Sawwar*
c. *ghurūb*	*wi-shmāl*
d. *izzayyik*	*felūka*
e. *gawla*	*fil-ā'lam*
f. *anā taHt*	*el-marakbi*
g. *da kalām*	*esh-shams*
h. *fō' ma kont*	*amrokom*
i. *yimīn*	*gamīl*
j. *aTwal nahr*	*siyāHeyya*

2. Put the words in the correct order to form coherent sentences.

a. *kunna / felūka / 'ala / 'awzīn /n-nīl / nirkab*
b. *'aZīma / di / ya / fikra / lūsī / aywa*
c. *gamīl / ya / da / maHmūd / kalām / rayyis*
d. *fi n-nīl / ra'yik / l-manZar / ya / wi fi / I / ēh / lūsī / ?*
e. *salām / da / rā'i' / ya / l-manZar.*

3. Add the correct possessive suffixes to the following nouns, as instructed in parentheses.

a. *kalām* (our)
b. *manti'a* (his)
c. *nahr* (their)
d. *ra'y* (you, f. sg.)
e. *timsāl* (her)

4. Attach the correct object pronoun suffixes to the conjugated verb in parentheses.

a. *howwa 'awzak (ti'mil) gawla siyāHeyya.*
b. *homma 'awzīnak (takhod) naHyit eg-gezīra.*
c. *heyya 'awza r-rayyis maHmūd (yifarrag) 'al-qāhira.*
d. *ya dūnald, enta w-lūsī, el-falūka sa'āt bit-mīl yimīn w-shemāl, fa (khalli) maskīn kwayyis fi l-markib.*
e. *eHna binleff wi (byerga') a'shān nilha' ghurūb esh-shams.*

5. Correct the errors found in the following sentences. (Hint: The underlined phrases are instances of incorrect pronoun usage, noun-verb agreement, or noun-adjective agreement.)

a. 'ashān teshūfu sh-shams wi <u>homma betoghrob</u> 'ala l-'ahramāt.

b. ēh <u>ra'yikum ya lūsī</u> fi n-nīl wa fi l-manZar?

c. en-nil dah <u>nahr 'aZīma</u>, ya lūsī, aTwal nahr fi l-'ālam, <u>bitkūn 'arīD</u> 'awi f-manāti'.

d. ir-rayyis maHmūd <u>el-marakbi biyleffu w-byerga'u</u> 'ashān nilha' ghurūb esh-shams.

e. ahlan ya <u>lūsī izzayyak enta</u>?

Answer Key

1. a. da r-rayyis maHmūd el-marakbi
   b. 'awzīn nirkab felūka
   c. ghurūb esh-shams
   d. izzayyik ya layla
   e. gawla siyāHeyya
   f. anā taHt amrokom
   g. da kalām gamīl
   h. fō' ma kont aS-Sawwar
   i. yimīn wi shmāl
   j. aTwal nahr fi l-'ālam

2. a. kunna 'awzīn nirkab felūka 'ala n-nīl.
   b. aywa ya lūsī di fikra 'aZīma.
   c. da kalām gamīl ya rayyis maHmūd.
   d. ēh ra'yik ya lūsī fi n-nīl wi fi l-manZar?
   e. ya salam da l-manZar rā'i'.

3. a. kalamna
   b. manti'tu
   c. nahrohom
   d. ra'yik
   e. timsalha

4. a. howwa 'awzak <u>ti'millu</u> gawla siyāHeyya.
   b. homma 'awzīnak <u>takhodhom</u> naHyit eg-gezīra.
   c. heyya 'awza ir-rayyis maHmūd <u>yifarragha</u> 'ala l-qāhira.
   d. ya dūnald, enta w-lūsī, el-falūka sa'āt bit-mīl yimīn wi shmāl, fa <u>khallikom</u> maskīn kwayyis fi l-markib.
   e. eHna binleff wi <u>biy-ragga'na</u> 'ashān nilHa' ghurūb esh-shams.

5. a. 'ashān teshūfu sh-shams wi-<u>heyya</u> btoghrob 'ala l-ahramāt.
   b. ēh <u>ra'yik</u> ya lūsī fi n-nīl wi fi l-manZar?
   c. en-nil dah nahr <u>'aZīm</u>, ya lūsī, aTwal nahr fi l-'ālam, <u>beykūn</u> a'rīD 'awi f-manāti'.
   d. ir-rayyis maHmūd el-marakbi <u>biyleff wi byerga'</u> 'ashān nilHa' ghurūb esh-shams.
   e. ahlan ya lūsī <u>izzayyik enti</u>?

LESSON 18

(Egyptian Arabic)

---

ziyāra li l-matHaf el-maSri A Visit to the Egyptian Museum

A. Dialogue

Layla and Karim decided to take Donald, who has always been fascinated by the ancient Egyptian civilization, to the world-famous Egyptian Museum. Karim hails the taxi which will take them from Heliopolis to downtown Cairo.

karim: es-salamu 'alēkum ya rayyis, el-matHaf el-maSri, law samaHt, el-antik-khāna. bikām el-'ogra min hena l-wisT el-balad?

sawwā' it-taksi: wallāhi illi tshūfu ya sa'att il-bēh. ta'riban keda 'ashara gnēh.

layla: mish kitīr dah ya rayyis?

dūnald: la', kwayyis, ya layla. id-dūlu 'ashara bass 'ala sharT yisū' 'ala mahlu!

karim: āh, enta bitkhāf min Tarī'it es-sewā'a f-maSr.

The taxi arrives at the museum.

karim: khod ya dūnald tazkartak, khodi ya layla. imshu warāya 'ashān Ha-nkhoshsh min el-bāb er-ra'īsi hnāk.

dūnald: ya salām, da l-mabna min barra shaklu 'aZīm, w-biyToll bi-galāla 'ala mdān et-taHrīr.

karim: el-matHaf el-maSri etbana fi 'ahd el-khidēwī 'abbās Helmi et-tāni sanat alf w-tomnomeyya saba'a w-tis'īn. w-iftitāH el-matHaf nafsu kan fi sanat alf w-tos'umeyya w-etnein.

layla: Tab yalla nodkhol, aSl anā ma gitsh el-matHaf dah min sinīn.

Donald, Layla, and Karim enter the museum through the magnificent front door.

dūnald: ommal fēn el-mumyāt?

karim: ma ti'la'sh. mish Ha-nfawwitha!

dūnald: tiftikru Ha-'dar ashūf mumyit ramsīs?

karim: ah Tab'an.

layla: biyit-hayya'li biyiftaHu el-Hogra illi fīha mumyit ramsīs sa'tēn bass kull yōm, 'ashān yeHafZu 'alēha.

karim: Tab yalla niTla' fō' 'abl ma yi'filūha. aheh ya dūnald, Hogrit il-mumya. khoshsh. ma tkhafsh!

dūnald: ana mish misadda' 'enayya! shāyef 'oddāmi mumyit 'insān kan 'āyish min alāf es-sinīn.

karim: w-'abl ma nimshi ya dūnald, Ha-niktiblak 'ismak b il-logha l-hiroghlīfeyya!

Karim: Peace be with you, driver. The Egyptian Museum, please, the Antik-khana. How much is the fare from here to downtown?

Taxi Driver: Well, sir, whatever you think is fair. It will be around ten pounds.

Layla: Isn't that a lot, driver?

Donald: No, that's okay, Layla. Give him ten, but on the condition that he drive slowly.

Karim: Yes, it's scary how (*lit.,* you are scared of the way) they drive in Egypt.

Karim: Here's your ticket, Donald. Here's yours, Layla. Follow me, because we are going to enter at the main entrance over there.

Donald: Oh wow, the building looks magnificent from the outside, so majestic overlooking the Tahrir Square.

Karim: The Egyptian Museum was built during the reign of Khedive Abbas Helmi II in 1897. The opening of the museum itself was in 1902.

Layla: Okay, let's go inside. I have not been to this museum in years.

Donald: Where are the mummies?

Karim: Don't worry! We won't skip that!

Donald: Do you think I will be able to see the mummy of Ramsis?

Karim: Yes, of course.

Layla: I believe they open the chamber with Ramsis' mummy for only two hours every day in order to preserve it.

Karim: Okay, let's go upstairs before they close it. Here it is, Donald, the mummy chamber. Enter. Don't be afraid.

Donald: I can't believe my eyes! I see the mummy of a human being who was alive thousands of years ago.

Karim: And before we leave, Donald, we will write your name in hieroglyphics.

B. Grammar and Usage

1. THE DEFINITE ARTICLE IN EGYPTIAN ARABIC

The definite article in Egyptian Arabic has the same form and follows the same rules as the article in *fuSHā*. The only difference is that in Egyptian Arabic, the article is pronounced *el* or *il*, and not *al*. When preceded by the conjunction *wa* (and), it is usually pronounced *il*.

el-matHaf el-maSri	the Egyptian Museum
es-sewā'a	the driving
et-tāni	the second (one)
er-ra'īsi	the main (one)
el-mumyāt	the mummies

2. THE PERFECT TENSE: THE VERBS *gih* (TO COME) AND *'idir* (TO BE ABLE TO)

Below are the perfect tense forms of the verb *gih* (to come), جاء *ja'a* in MSA, and the verb *'idir* (to be able), قدر *qadira* in MSA.

PERFECT TENSE OF THE VERB *gih* (TO COME)			
Singular		Plural	
ana	*gēt*	*eHna*	*gēna*
enta	*gēt*	*entu*	*gētu*
enti	*gēti*		
howwa	*gīh*	*homma*	*gom*
heyya	*gat*		

PERFECT TENSE OF THE VERB *'idir* (TO BE ABLE TO)			
Singular		Plural	
ana	'idirt	eHna	'idirna
enta	'idirt	entu	'idirtu
enti	'idirti		
howwa	'idir	homma	'idru
heyya	'idrit		

3. THE FUTURE TENSE IN EGYPTIAN ARABIC

In *fuSHā*, the future tense is formed by placing the particle سَوْفَ *sawfa* before the imperfect tense verb or by attaching the suffix *sa-* directly to the beginning of the verb (see Lesson 8). The future tense in colloquial Egyptian Arabic is formed by attaching the prefix *Ha-* (sometimes also reduced to *H-*) to the verb conjugated in the imperfect tense.[1] *Ha-* is followed by a different imperfect prefix depending on the personal form of the verb. For example, in the *howwa* (he) form, *Ha-* is followed by *y-*.

THE FUTURE PREFIX *Ha-* WITH IMPERFECT TENSE PREFIXES			
Singular		Plural	
ana	Ha-	eHna	Ha-n-
enta	Ha-t-	entu	Ha-t-
enti	Ha-t-		
howwa	Ha-y-	homma	Ha-y-
heyya	Ha-t-		

The tables below give the future tense forms of the verbs *yekhoshsh* (he enters) and *ye'dar* (he is able to).

FUTURE TENSE OF THE VERB *yekhoshsh* (HE ENTERS)			
Singular		Plural	
ana	Ha-akhoshsh	eHna	Ha-nkhoshsh
enta	Ha-tkhoshsh	entu	Ha-tkhoshshu
enti	Ha-tkhoshshi		
howwa	Ha-ykhoshsh	homma	Ha-ykhoshshu
heyya	Ha-tkhoshsh		

FUTURE TENSE OF THE VERB *ye'dar* (HE IS ABLE TO)			
Singular		Plural	
ana	Ha-'dar	eHna	Ha-ne'dar
enta	Ha-te'dar	entu	Ha-te'daru
enti	Ha-te'dari		
howwa	Ha-ye'dar	homma	Ha-ye'daru
heyya	Ha-te'dar		

---

[1] *Ha-* is also often pronounced *ha-*.

imshu warāya ‘ashān Han-khoshsh min el-bāb er-ra’isi.
Follow me, because we are going to enter at the main entrance.

tiftikru Ha-’dar ashūf mumyit ramsīs?
Do you think I will be able to see the mummy of Ramsis?

mish Han-fawwit-ha.
We won't skip that.

w-’abl ma nimshi ya dūnald, Han-iktiblak ’ismak . . .
And before we leave, Donald, we will write your name . . .

4. WORD ORDER IN EGYPTIAN ARABIC

As discussed earlier, sentences in *fuSHā* can begin with a verb, a noun, a pronoun, an adjective, an adverb, or a preposition (see Lessons 4, 5, and 6). In colloquial Egyptian Arabic, the preference is to start the sentence with a subject noun or a pronoun, much like in English. So, the most common word order is *Subject - Verb - (Object) - (Other Elements)* in sentences that contain a verb and a subject.

el-matHaf el-maSri etbana fi ‘ahd el-khidēwī ‘abbās Helmi et-tāni.
The Egyptian Museum was built during the reign of Khedive Abbas Helmi II.

enta bitkhāf min Tarī’it es-sewā’a f-maSr.
It is scary how they drive in Egypt.

iftitāH el-matHaf nafsu kan fi sanat alf tos‘umeyya w-etnēin.
The opening of the museum itself was in 1902.

A sentence can also start with an object noun, which, in that case, is emphasized.

el-mumyāt, enta lāzim teshufha aktar min marra.
The mummies, you need to see them more than once.

5. NEGATION IN EGYPTIAN ARABIC

There are two negative particles in Egyptian Arabic, *ma* and *mish*. They are invariable words that precede the word that is negated. *mish* is used with pronouns, nouns, adjectives, and adverbs.

mish ana	not me
mish walad/bint	not a boy/a girl
mish ketīr/a	not much, not many *(m./f.)*
mish delwa’ti	not now
mish bokra	not tomorrow
mish be-sor‘a	not quickly

Just like in *fuSHā*, different particles of negation are used with verbs depending on the tense: *ma* is used with perfect tense, imperative, and imperfect tense verbs; *mish* is used with future tense verbs and sometimes, imperfect tense verbs.

A. THE NEGATIVE PARTICLE *ma*

The negative particle *ma* is used with perfect tense, imperative, and imperfect tense verbs. Below is the verb *kan* (he was) in the negative perfect tense form. Note that the suffix *-sh* is added to the end of all negative verbs regardless of the tense and personal form.

THE NEGATIVE FORM OF THE PERFECT TENSE VERB *kan* (HE WAS)			
Singular		Plural	
anā	*ma kontish*	*eHna*	*ma konnāsh*
enta	*ma kontish*	*entu*	*ma kontūsh*
enti	*ma kontish*		
howwa	*ma kansh*	*homma*	*ma kanūsh*
heyya	*ma kanitsh*		

anā ma kontish fi l-matHaf embārah.
I wasn't at the museum yesterday.

enta ma kontūsh ma'āna 'ala l-felūka.
You were not with us on the felucca.

Here are the negative forms of the perfect tense verb *gih* (he came).

THE NEGATIVE FORM OF THE PERFECT TENSE VERB *gih* (HE CAME)			
Singular		Plural	
anā	*ma gitsh*	*eHna*	*ma gināsh*
enta	*ma gitsh*	*entu*	*ma gitūsh*
enti	*ma gitīsh*		
howwa	*ma gāsh*	*homma*	*ma gūsh*
heyya	*ma gatsh*		

anā ma gitsh el-matHaf dah min sinīn.
I have not been to this museum in years.

howwa ma gāsh ma'āna 'ashān khāf min Hogrit el-mumyāt.
He did not come with us because he was scared of the mummy chamber.

ma is also used with imperfect tense verbs. Here are the negative forms of the imperfect tense verb *yīgi* (he comes). Notice the use of the prefix *bi-/b-* with the imperfect tense verb.

THE NEGATIVE FORM OF THE IMPERFECT TENSE VERB *yīgi* (HE COMES)			
Singular		Plural	
anā	ma bagīsh	eHna	ma bingīsh
enta	ma bitgīsh	entu	ma bitgūsh
enti	ma bitgīsh		
howwa	ma biygīsh	homma	ma biygūsh
heyya	ma bitgīsh		

The common Egyptian Arabic expression *ma fīsh* (there isn't/aren't . . .) makes use of the negative word *ma*.

> *ma fīsh māni'.*
> I have no objection.

> *ma fīsh shakk.*
> There is no doubt.

Without the negative *ma*, we have the expression *fī* (there is/are . . .).

> *fī Hogra li l-mumyāt.*
> There is a chamber for mummies.

fī is the equivalent of the *fuSHā* word هناك *hunāka* (there is/are . . .).

B. THE NEGATIVE PARTICLE *mish*

mish is used with future and sometimes, imperfect tense verbs.

> *ana mish misadda' 'enayya!*
> I don't believe my eyes!

Below, *mish* is used with an imperfect tense verb in a negative question.

> *mish biyToll 'ala mdān et-taHrir?*
> Doesn't it overlook Tahrir Square?

mish is most commonly encountered with future tense verbs.

> *mish Ha-nfawwit-ha!*
> We will not skip it!

> *eHna mish Ha-nrūH el-matHaf bokra.*
> We will not go to the museum tomorrow.

mish is often used with modal expressions, such as *ā'wiz* (want) and *lāzim* (must).

> *howwa mish lāzim yirkab el-felūka.*
> He must not ride the felucca.

> *ana mish 'āwiz adkhol Hogrit el-mumyāt.*
> I do not want to enter the mummy chamber.

mish is also used in verbless, equational sentences.

ana mish Soghayyar.
I am not young.

mish is also used to negate equational sentences in the future tense, which employ the verb *yekūn* (he is), conjugated below in the future tense.

THE NEGATIVE FORM OF THE FUTURE TENSE VERB *Ha-ykūn* (HE WILL BE)			
Singular		Plural	
anā	*mish Ha-kūn*	*eHna*	*mish Ha-nkūn*
enta	*mish Ha-tkūn*	*entu*	*mish Ha-tkūnu*
enti	*mish Ha-tkūni*		
howwa	*mish Ha-ykūn*	*homma*	*mish Ha-ykūnu*
heyya	*mish Ha-tkūn*		

homma mish Ha-ykūnu hnāk fi l-matHaf.
They will not be there at the museum.

ya'ni enti mish Ha-tkūni hena?
You mean you will not be here?

Below are the negative forms of the verb *yīgi* (he comes) in the future tense. Remember that when forming the future tense, the imperfect tense verb loses its initial *bi-/b-* prefix.

THE NEGATIVE FORMS OF THE FUTURE TENSE VERB *Ha-yīgi* (HE WILL COME)			
Singular		Plural	
anā	*mish H-āgi*	*eHna*	*mish Ha-nīgi*
enta	*mish Ha-tīgi*	*entu*	*mish Ha-tīgu*
enti	*mish Ha-tīgi*		
howwa	*mish Ha-yīgi*	*homma*	*mish Ha-yīgu*
heyya	*mish Ha-tīgi*		

anā mish H-āgi ma'ākum li l-matHaf.
I will not come with you to the museum.

homma mish Ha-yīgu min el-bāb el-ra'īsi.
They will not come from the main entrance.

imshu warāya a'shān mish Han-khosh min el-bāb er-ra'īsi henāk.
Follow me, because we are not going to enter from the main entrance over there.

mish Ha-niktiblak 'ismak bi l-logha l-hiroghlīfeyya.
We will not write your name in hieroglyphics.

C. Vocabulary

ziyāra	to visit, a visit
matHaf (matāHif)	museum(s)
maSri (m.); maSreyya (f.)	Egyptian
wisT el-balad	downtown, center of city
law samaHt	please; if you please
antik-khāna	the Egyptian Museum
bikām el-ogra?	How much is the fare?
illi tshūfu	it's up to you, whatever seems right (lit., whatever you see)
sa'att el-bēh	Sir
ta'rīban	approximately; around
kitīr (m.); kitīra (f.)	much, many, a lot
id-dūlu (pl.)	give him
'ala sharT	on condition, provided that
yisū' (m.); tisū' (f.)	he drives; she drives
'ala mehlu (m.); 'ala mehlaha (f.)	slow; slowly, with caution
Tari'it	the way, the method
tazkartak (m.); tazkartik (f.)	your ticket
imshu warāya.	Follow me.
Ha-nkhoshsh	we will enter
el-bab	the door, the entrance
ra'īsi	main, principal
min barra	from the outside, the exterior
shaklu (m.); shaklaha (f.)	(it) looks, (it) appears
biyToll (m.); biTToll (f.)	it overlooks
bigalāla	majestically
midān et-taHrīr	Tahrir Square (famous square in Cairo)
etbana (yibni)	was built (to build)
'ahd	era
el-khidēwī	Khedive
sanat	in the year
iftitāH	the opening
yalla nodkhol!	Let's go inside!
ma gitsh	I have not come, I did not come
sinīn	years
'ommāl	So!, Well, then!, But then!
ma ti'la'sh. (m.); ma ti'la'īsh. (f.)	Don't worry.
mish Hanfawwit-ha.	We will not skip it.
tiftikru? (pl.); tiftikir? (m. sg.); tiftikri? (f. sg.)	Do you think?
Ha-'dar	I will be able
mumya	mummy

ramsīs	Ramses
biyiftaHu	they open, they are open
sa'tēn; *sā'a waHda*	two hours, one hour
yeHafzu	they (can) preserve
ye'fil	he closes
te'fil	she closes
khoshsh (m.); *khoshshi* (f.)	enter; go in
ma-tkhafsh! (m.);	
ma-tkhafish! (f.)	Don't be afraid!
mish misadda'! (m.);	
mish misadda'a! (f.)	I don't/can't believe (it)!
'enayya	my eyes
'insān (m.); *insāna* (f.)	human being; person
kan 'āyish (m.); *kānit 'aysha* (f.)	used to live; once lived; was once living
nimshi	we leave; we depart; we go
Ha-niktiblak (m.); *Ha-niktiblik* (f.)	we will write (for) you
ismak (m.); *ismik* (f.)	your name
el-hīroghlīfeyya	hieroglyphics

D. Cultural Note

The Egyptian Museum is one of the major attractions of Cairo, being world-renowned for its magnificent collection of Ancient Egyptian antiquities. Another area of interest is Old Cairo, where the sights and sounds have hardly changed since its beginnings. There are ancient Coptic Christian churches in Old Cairo near the ruins of the Roman Fortress of Babylon.

Islamic Cairo is a world of ancient mosques, bazaars, or "souks," and medieval forts, such as the Citadel of Saladin (Qal'at al-Jabal) built around 1176 as a defense against the Crusaders. The Citadel, located on the Muqattam (Mu'attam) Hills, has a spectacular view of the city. The Citadel also contains museums, including the Jewel Museum, the Cairo Carriage Museum, and a military museum. It is also home to three historic mosques: the Mohammed Ali Mosque, the Al-Nasir Mohammed Mosque, and the Suleyman Pasha Mosque.

Also worth a visit in Islamic Cairo are the Carpet Market and the Mosque and Mausoleum of Al-Ghouri, where one can see performances of the Whirling Dervishes. There are also Al-Azhar University and Mosque, founded in 969 A.D. and believed to be the oldest university in the world, and the Al-Hussein Square, filled with restaurants and cafes. Next to it is the Bazaar of Khan el-Khalili, which has not only the largest variety of souvenirs, but also the widest selection of household goods, fabrics, and clothes.

In addition to history, Egypt is also famous, especially in the Arab world, for its film industry, which is over a hundred years old. Prolific directors, such as Youssef Chahine, and world-famous stars, like Omar Sharif, have international appeal. Throughout the Arab world, especially during Muslim holidays, TV and film festivals include the older beloved Egyptian films, musicals, dramas, and comedies from the 1950s and newer—some say not as good—contemporary works. A typical retrospective of Egyptian films will include one or more of the following:

1936, *salāma fi kheir* [Salama Is Fine], directed by Niyazi Mustafa, starring Naguib El-Rihani.

1959, *du'aa' el-karawān* [The Nightingale's Prayer], directed by Henri Barakat, starring Fatin Hamama and Ahmed Mazhar.

1969, *el-mumya'* [The Mummy], directed by Shadi Abdel Salam, starring Ahmed Marei and Ahmed Higazi.

1975, *urīdu Hallan* [I Want a Solution], directed by Said Marzouk, starring Fatin Hamama.

1992, *el-irhāb wi l-kabāb* [Terrorism and Kabob], directed by Sharif 'Arafa, starring Adel Emam.

2003, *muwāTin, w-mukhbir, w-Harāmi* [A Citizen, a Detective, and a Thief], directed by Daud Abdel Sayyid, starring Khalid Abu El-Naga and Shaaban Abdel Rahim.

The following are some links to Web sites related to Egyptian cinema.

http://www.sis.gov.eg/movie/html/mov04.htm
http://s3.masrawy.com/masrawy/Top/Regional/Africa/Egypt/Arts_and_Entertainment/
http://www.hejleh.com/countries/egypt.html
http://www.cinematechhaddad.com/Cinematech/LatestNews_3.HTM (in Arabic)
http://cinema.ajeeb.com/ (in Arabic, with videos clips of Egyptian films)

E. Exercises

1. Match the words from column A to those in column B to form phrases or short sentences.

A	B
a. *bikām*	*er-ra'īsi*
b. *yisū'*	*el-maSriyyīn*
c. *el-bāb*	*alf qiT'a*
d. *el-matHaf*	*el-'ogra*
e. *el-qism*	*shakk*
f. *wara'*	*el-maSri*

g. *meyya w-i'shrīn*
h. *ma-fīsh*
i. *Hogrit*
j. *el-qudamā'*

il-mumyāt
el-bardi
'ala mehlu
el-khāmis

2. Put the words in the correct order to form coherent sentences.

a. *min / fimaSr / enta / es-sewā'a / bitkhāf / Tarī'it*
b. *el-bāb / warāya / min / er-ra'īsi / 'ashān / imshu / Han-khoshsh*
c. *mumyit / ashūf / Ha-'dar / ramsīs / tiftikru / ?*
d. *sa'tein / el-Hogra / yōm / bas / koll / biyiftaHu*
e. *mumyit / 'āyish / 'oddāmi / min / shāyef / kan / alāf / es-sinīn / 'insān*

3. Change the tense of the verbs in parentheses as indicated, keeping in mind the rules of agreement.

a. *enti (biykhāf) min Tarī'it es-sewā'a f-maSr.* (imperfect tense)
b. *eHna (yīgi) el-matHaf dah lamma konna Soghayyarīn.* (perfect tense)
c. *'alashān layla Tūl 'omraha ('awiz yodkhol) Hogrit el-mumyāt.* (imperfect tense)
d. *fi Hogrit el-mumyāt homma (yishūf) mumyit ramsīs.* (perfect tense)
e. *fi l-matHaf el-maSri, entu (ye'dar) teshūfu el-Hogra illi fīha el-mumyāt.* (future tense)
f. *ya dūnald, anā (Han-iktib) 'ismak bi l-logha l-hiroghlīfeyya!* (future tense)

4. Use the negative particles *ma* or *mish* to negate the word in parentheses.

a. *en-nās hena (biysū'u) 'ala mehlohom.*
b. *la', (fīh) shakk inn il-matHaf kebīr 'awi.*
c. *dūnald khāyif, ('awiz) yodkhol Hogrit il-mumyāt.*
d. *iftitāH el-matHaf (kan) fi sanat alf tos'umeyya w-talāta.*
e. *eHna bokra (yedkhol) min el-bab er-ra'īsi.*

5. Fill in the blank by selecting the right word from the choices shown in parentheses.

a. *bikām el-'ogra _____ hena l-wisT el-balad?* (*ila - fi - min - a'la - fō'*)
b. *da l-mabna min barra shaklu _____.* (*kitīr - 'aZīma - ra'isi - galāla - 'aZīm*)
c. *tiftikru Ha-'dar _____ mumyit ramsīs?* (*ākhud - adkhol - ashūf - akhoshsh - afawwit*)
d. *el-matHaf el-maSri etbana _____ 'ahd el-khidēwī 'abbās Helmi.* (*min - 'abl - 'ala - ila - fi*)
e. *el-mabna biyTol bi-galāla _____ midān et-taHrīr.* (*fō' - min - fi - a'la - ila*)

Answer Key

1.
   a. *bikām el-'ogra*
   b. *yisū' 'ala mehlu*
   c. *el-bāb er-ra'īsi*
   d. *el-matHaf el-maSri*
   e. *el-qism el-khāmis*
   f. *wara' el-bardi*
   g. *meyya w-'ishrīn 'alf qiT'a*
   h. *ma-fīsh shakk*
   i. *Hogrit il-mumyāt*
   j. *el-maSriyyīn el-qudamā'*

2.
   a. *enta bitkhāf min Tarī'it es-sewā'a f-maSr.*
   b. *imshu warāya 'ashān Hankhoshsh min el-bāb er-ra'īsi.*
   c. *tiftikru Ha-'dar ashūf mumyit ramsīs?*
   d. *biyiftaHu l-Hogra sa'tēn bass koll yōm.*
   e. *shāyef 'oddāmi mumyit 'insān kan 'āyish min alāf es-sinīn.*

3.
   a. *enti <u>bitkhāfi</u> min Tarī'it es-sewā'a f-maSr.*
   b. *eHna <u>gīna</u> el-matHaf dah lamma konna Soghayyarīn.*
   c. *'alashān layla Tūl 'omraha <u>'awza todkhol</u> Hogrit el-mumyāt.*

   d. *fi Hogrit el-mumyāt homma <u>shāfu</u> mumyit ramsīs.*
   e. *fi l-matHaf el-maSri, entu <u>Ha-te'daru</u> tshūfu el-Hogra illi fīha el-mumyāt.*
   f. *ya dūnald, anā <u>Haktib</u> 'ismak bi l-logha l-hiroghlīfeyya!*

4.
   a. *en-nās hena <u>ma biysu'ūsh</u> 'ala mehlohom.*
   b. *la', <u>ma-fīsh</u> shakk inn il-matHaf kebīr 'awi.*
   c. *dūnald khāyif, <u>mish 'awiz</u> yodkhol Hogrit il-mumyāt.*
   d. *iftitāH el-matHaf <u>ma kansh</u> fi sanat alf tos'umeyya w-talāta.*
   e. *eHna bokra <u>mish Hanedkhol</u> min el-bab er-ra'īsi.*

5.
   a. *bikām el-'ogra <u>min</u> hena l-wisT el-balad?*
   b. *da l-mabna min barra shaklu <u>'aZīm</u>.*
   c. *tiftikru Ha-'dar <u>ashūf</u> mumyit ramsīs?*
   d. *el-matHaf el-maSri etbana <u>fi</u> 'ahd el-khidēwī 'abbās Helmi.*
   e. *el-mabna biyToll bi-galāla <u>'ala</u> midān et-taHrīr.*

LESSON 19

(Egyptian Arabic)

azmit es-sakan fi l-qāhera Housing Shortage in Cairo

A. Dialogue

Mohammad and his fiancé, Amira, are planning to get married after Mohammad's graduation and after finding an apartment. Amira has invited her American friend Donald to her home to meet her mother and discuss the housing situation.

amīra: ahlan ya dūnald, itfaDDal, nawwart betna!

dūnald: ahlan ya amīra, izzayyik, wi z-zayyi mHammad? inshallah tkūnu bkhēr. betku gamīl awi.

maHammad: izzayyak ya dūnald, ahlan w-sahlan, itfaDDal, ta'āla hena f-makānak el-mofaDDal fi l-balakōna.

dūnald: enta 'ārif inn il-balakonāt aktar Hāga bte'gebni f-maSr? bizzāt el-balakōna di.

amīra: tishrab ēh ya dūnald? 'andena 'ahwa, w-shai, w-Hagāt sa''a.

dūnald: ākhud 'ahwa maZbūT, min faDlik ya amīra. izzay SiHHit Hadritik, ya ustāza suād?

suād: el-Hamdulillāh ya dūnald, ya ibni, bas wallāhi mashghulīn 'ala mHammad w-'amīra. ba'al-hom aktar min sanatēn biy-dawwaru 'ala sha''a yet-gawwizu fiha.

maHammad: ya dūnald, as'ār esh-sho'a' et-tamlīk ba'it khayaleyya.

dūnald: Tayyib, dawwartu 'ala sha''a igār?

suād: ah, dawwaru f-kull Hitta, bas ma la'ūsh ayy Hāga 'orayyeba. Da Hatta fi l-mudun eg-gedīda, as'ār esh-sho'a' betibda' min metēn alf gnēh w-Tāli'.

amīra: aywa ya māma, w-minhom biyoTlobu khamsīn fiHl-meyya mo'addam, y'ani mīt alf gnēh, we l-bā'i 'ala talat sinīn. minēn nigīb mablagh zay dah? Harām wallāhi, da Zolm.

dūnald: bass anā mistaghrab li'inn ana shāyif 'omarāt ketīra fi l-qāhera w-kullaha sho'a' faDya tamāman. lēh ma-sa'altūsh fiha?

maHammad: aSHab el-o'marāt dol Tamma'īn, ya'ni 'arDinha li l-Taba'āt el-ghaneyya bass.

suād: kull esh-sho'a' di faDya 'ashān qanūn el-'igār eg-gedīd biysmaH li SāHib el-'omāra ye-'aggar esh-sha''a b-se'r es-sū'.

maHammad: eHna Tab'an fakkarna fiha gidiyyan, li'innina mish 'awzīn nitgawwiz wi n'īsh fi byūt ahalina. bass lamma amīra titkharrag w-tishtaghal, mumkin sa'it-ha nit'āsim el-igār.

dūnald: emta Ha-tkhallaSSi g-gam'a ya amīra?

amīra: faDilli sana ya dūnald.

maHammad: ma fish sakan kefāya yestau'ib kull en-nās.

dūnald: ah wallāhi ma'āk ha'. w-bēni w-bēnak, el-Hall el-waHīd līku imma trūHu t'īshu fi l-aryāf, aw tinsu fikrit eg-gawāz!

amīra: ma-t'olsh keda ya dūnald, anā f-'arDak. fal allāh wala fālak! kull 'o'da w-leha Hallal.

Amira: Hello, Donald. Please come in. It's such a pleasure to see you.

Donald: Hello, Amira. How are you, and how is Mohammad? I hope you are well. Your home is very beautiful.

Mohammad: How are you, Donald? Welcome, please come in. Come over here to your favorite place on the balcony.

Donald: Do you know that what I love most in Egypt are the balconies? Especially this balcony.

Amira: Donald, what would you like to drink? We have coffee, tea, and cold drinks.

Donald: I'll have coffee, medium sweet, if you please, Amira. How are you, Ms. Suad?

Suad: Fine, thanks, Donald, my son. But, honestly, we are concerned about Mohammad and Amira. They have been looking for two years for an apartment in which to live once they are married.

Mohammad: Donald, the prices of condominiums have become unreal.

Donald: Okay, have you looked for a rental apartment?

Suad: Yes, they looked everywhere, but they did not find anything close by. Even in the new cities, the prices of apartments start at two hundred thousand pounds and up.

Amira: Yes, Mommy, and some of them ask for a fifty percent down payment, meaning one hundred thousand pounds, and the rest over three years. Where can we come up with an amount like that? By God, shame on them! This is wrong.

Donald: But I'm amazed, because I see many buildings in Cairo and all of them are nothing but empty apartments. Why haven't you asked there?

Mohammad: Those landlords are greedy. In other words, they are offering them exclusively to the wealthy.

Suad: All these apartments are vacant because the New Rent Law allows the landlord to rent the apartment at market price.

Mohammad: Of course, we thought about it seriously, because we do not want to get married and live at our parents' homes. But when Amira graduates and works, we can then share the rent.

Donald: When are you going to finish school, Amira?

Amira: I have one more year left, Donald.

Mohammad: There is not enough housing to accommodate all the people.

Donald: Yes, indeed, you are right. Between you and me, your only solution is either to go live in the countryside or to drop the idea of marriage!

Amira: Don't say that, Donald, I beg you. God forbid! To every problem there is a solution (*lit.*, For every knot, there is someone to untie it).

B. Grammar and Usage

1. QUESTION WORDS IN EGYPTIAN ARABIC

As in MSA, there are two kinds of question words in Egyptian Arabic: The question particle *hal*, used in yes-no questions, and question words such as *min* (who) or *ēh* (what), used in specific questions (see Lesson 3).

QUESTION WORDS IN EGYPTIAN ARABIC	
hal	question particle used in *yes-no* questions
mīn	who
ēh	what
emta	when
fēn	where
min-ēn	from where; where
bi-kām	how much
izzāy	how
ayy	which
mīn illi	who
ēh illi	what
lēh	why
b-ēh	with what . . .
add ēh	how much; how long

In the dialogue, there are several examples of question words used in context:

izzayyak ya dūnald?
How are you, Donald?

lēh ma sa'altūsh fīha?
Why haven't you asked there?

hal dawwartu 'ala sha''a igār?
Have you looked for a rental apartment?

minēn nigīb mablagh zayy dah?
Where can we get such an amount [of money]?

emta Hat-khallaSSi eg-gam'a ya amīra?
When will you finish school, Amira?

Question words normally come at the beginning of the sentence. A question can also be asked using a rising intonation, without placing the question word at the beginning of the sentence, e.g., *tishrab ēh ya dūnald?* (What would like to drink, Donald?, *lit.*, You drink what, Donald?) or *sha'it mīn di?* (Whose apartment is this?, *lit.*, The apartment of who is this?).

2. DEMONSTRATIVE PRONOUNS IN EGYPTIAN ARABIC
Egyptian Arabic demonstrative pronouns and adjectives differ in structure and pronunciation from those in *fuSHā* (see Lesson 9).

DEMONSTRATIVE PRONOUNS IN EGYPTIAN ARABIC				
	Masculine		Feminine	
Singular	*dah/da* (this)	*dah/da, dahowwa* (that)	*dih/di* (this)	*daheyya* (that)
Plural	*dōl* (these)	*dōl, dahomma, dolahomma* (those)	*dōl, dih/di* (these)	*dōl, dahomma, dolahomma* (those)

In Egyptian Arabic, demonstratives always appear after the noun, unlike in MSA, where they can both follow and precede the noun. Also note that there are no dual forms in Egyptian Arabic; plural forms are used instead.

> *el-'omāra di kbīra.*
> This building is large.

> *el-balakōna di*
> this balcony

> *minēn nigīb mablagh zayy dah?*
> Where can we get such an amount?

> *aS-Hab el-'omarāt dōl Tamma'īn.*
> Those landlords are greedy.

> *kull esh-sho'a' di faDya.*
> All these apartments are vacant.

3. NOUN AND ADJECTIVE GENDER IN EGYPTIAN ARABIC

As in *fuSHā*, nouns are either masculine or feminine in Egyptian Arabic. A singular feminine noun in Egyptian Arabic is usually formed by adding the ending -*a*.

ustāz (m.)	*ustāza* (f.)	professor; Mr., Mrs.
SāHib (m.)	*SaHba* (f.)	friend, owner

When a feminine noun is followed by another noun in a possessive construction, its ending changes to -*it*.

ustāzit et-tarikh	history professor
SaHbit karīm	Karim's friend

Adjectives also have a masculine form and a feminine form, as they have to agree with the noun they modify.

gedīd (m.)	*gedīda* (f.)	new
orayyeb (m.)	*orayyeba* (f.)	near
ghani (m.)	*ghaneyya* (f.)	rich; wealthy

When singular masculine nouns have irregular, "broken" plural forms (see next section), the plural noun is actually in the feminine gender. For example:

270

sha''a (m. sg.) (apartment)   *sho'a'* (f. pl.) (apartments)

bēt (m. sg.) (house, home)   *biyūt* (f. pl.) (houses, homes)

4. BROKEN PLURALS IN EGYPTIAN ARABIC

There are two types of plurals in MSA: regular, or "sound," plurals, and irregular, or "broken," plurals. In Egyptian Arabic, the most common form of plural, for both nouns and adjectives, is the irregular, "broken" plural. Below are some broken plurals that appeared in the dialogue.

SOME NOUNS WITH BROKEN PLURALS IN EGYPTIAN ARABIC		
Singular	Plural	
bēt	*biyūt*	house/houses
Hall	*Hulūl*	solution/solutions
sha''a	*sho'a'*	apartment/apartments
'o'da	*'o'ad*	knot/knots
se'r	*as'ār*	price/prices
rīf	*aryāf*	rural area/rural areas
SāHib	*aS-Hāb*	landlord/landlords; friend/friends
ahl	*ahāli*	family/families
'ahwa	*'ahāwi*	coffee/coffees
mablagh	*mabāligh*	amount/amounts
qanūn	*qawanin*	law/laws
gedīda	*gedīda; godād* (pl., animate nouns)	new
ketīra	*ketīra* (sg.); *kotār* (pl., animate nouns)	many
ghani; ghaneyya	*aghneya* (sg.); *ghonāy* (pl., animate nouns)	wealthy

5. MONTHS OF THE YEAR AND DAYS OF THE WEEK

In Egypt, the names of months are derived from the names used in the Gregorian calendar, e.g., January, February, etc.

yanāyer	January
febrāyer	February
māris	March
ebrīl; abrīl	April
māyo	May
yonyo; yonya	June
yolyo; yolya	July
aghostos	August
sebtember	September
oktōbar	October
november	November
disember	December

Here are the names of the days of the week.

el-Hadd	Sunday
el-itnēn	Monday
et-talāt	Tuesday
el-arba'	Wednesday
el-khamīs	Thursday
eg-gom'a	Friday
es-sabt	Saturday

C. Vocabulary

azma	shortage, crisis
sakan	housing
nawwart betna.	It's a pleasure to see you. (lit., you brought light into our home)
sha''a; sho'a'	apartment(s)
ta'āla (ta'āli, ta'ālu) hena	come over here
makān	place, location
mofaDDal	preferred, favorite
bal(a)kōna	balcony
bizzāt	especially
tishrab (tishrabi, tishrabu) ēh?	What would you like to drink?
'andena	(we) have
'ahwa	coffee
shāy	tea
Hagāt (Hāga) sa''a	cold drinks (drink)
maZbūt	medium sweet (coffee)
min faDlak (m.); min faDlik (f.); min faDloku (pl.)	please
ma'āk Ha' (m.); ma'āki Ha' (f.)	you are right, you are correct
ya (i)bni (m.); ya binti (f.)	my son; my daughter
mashghulīn	we are worried
ba'al-hom	they have been
sana; sanatēn (du.), sinīn (pl.)	a/one year, two years, years
dawwar	to look for
yet-gawwiz	he gets married, to get married
as'ār (se'r)	prices (price)
esh-sho'a' et-tamlīk	condominiums
khayāleyya	unreal, unrealistic
kull Hitta	everywhere
orayyeb (m.); orayyeba (f.)	close by, near
el-mudun eg-gedīda	the new cities
tibda' min (yibda' min)	it starts (to start) at
metēn	two hundred

w-Tāli'	and over
bāba	daddy
māma	mommy
minhom . . .	among which are . . .
fi l-meyya	percent
mīt alf	a hundred thousand
minēn?	from where?
mablagh	amount (of money)
Harām!	Have a heart!; Shame on you!
Zolm	unfairness; wrong
ana mistaghrab	I am amazed
shāyif (sg.), *shayfin* (pl.)	I see
'omāra (sg.); *'omarāt* (pl.)	(apartment) building(s)
faDya (f.); *fāDi* (m.)	empty, vacant
tamāman	totally
lēh?	why?
sa'al (m.); *sa'alit* (f.); *sa'alu* (pl.)	he asked; she asked; they asked
aS-Hāb el-'omarāt (pl.), *Sāhib* (sg.)	landlords, landlord
Tamma'īn (pl.); *Tammā'* (sg.)	greedy
'arDinha	they are offering them
el-Taba'āt el-ghaneyya	the wealthy
qanūn	law
el-igār	rent
yismaH (m.); *tismaH* (f.)	it allows
aggar (m.); *aggarit* (f.)	he rented, she rented
sē'r es-sū'	market price
giddiyan	seriously
biyūt; *bēt* (sg.)	houses, homes
ahalīna; *ahl* (sg.)	our parents; family
tishtaghal (f.); *yishtaghal* (m.)	she works, he works
nit'āsim	we share
emta?	when?
faDil-li	I have . . . left, what remains for me . . .
ma fish . . .	there is no . . .
yestaw'ib (m.); *testaw'ib* (f.)	he accommodates, she accommodates
ma'āk Ha'.	You are right.
bēni w-bēnak (w-bēnik)	to tell you the truth, between us
imma . . . aw	either . . . or
aryāf	the countryside
insu (pl.); *ensa, ensi* (f. sg.)	you (can) forget about . . .
fikra	idea
ana f-'arDak (m.); *f-'arDik* (f.)	I beg you

fal allāh wala fālak (m.);	God forbid!
wala fālik (f.)	
kull 'o'da w-leha Hallal.	To every problem there is a solution. (*lit.*, For every knot there is someone to untie it.)

D. Cultural Note

Cairo has had an acute housing shortage since the 1970s. Among the causes are the exploding population (Egypt has one of the highest birth rates in the world), the massive migration from smaller towns and cities to the capital for jobs, the conversion of many apartments to offices and businesses, and the deterioration of existing housing, as there is no housing code. Although a form of rent control is in place, most landlords find clever ways of getting around it to charge large rents. Apartments for sale are either unaffordable or unfit for habitation without expensive renovations. And there are hardly any single-family dwellings in Cairo.

In Egypt, it is considered socially unacceptable for couples to marry unless the groom has secured an apartment. The housing shortage often results in either exceptionally long waits before marriage or the breakup of the couple. Many couples who are determined to marry end up reluctantly living with parents, causing tension in and economic strain on a family.

E. Exercises

1. Fill in the blanks with the correct question word by choosing from the options provided in parentheses and looking at the answer that follows the question.

a. *entu mashghulīn 'ala _____?*
 eHna mashghulīn 'ala mHammad w-amīra.
 (*emta, fein, izzay, mīn, ēh*)

b. *_____ SiHHit HaDritak, ya ustāz aHmad?*
 anā SiHHiti b-kheir el-Hamdullilāh.
 (*emta, fein, ad ēh, lēh, izzayy*)

c. *_____ dawwaru 'ala sha''a?*
 dawwaru f-kull Hitta, bass ma la'ūsh ayy Hāga.
 (*emta, fēn, izzay, min mīn, bikām*)

d. *_____ as'ār esh-sho'a'?*
 as'ār esh-sho'a' betibda' min metēn alf gnēh w-Tāli'.
 (*fein, izzay, bikām, lēh, hal*)

e. *_____ enta mistaghrab ya dūnald?*
 anā mistaghrab li'inn anā shāyif 'omarāt ketīra fi l-qāhera w-kullaha sho'a' faDya tamāman.
 (*fein, izzay, bikām, lēh, hal*)

2. Match the words from column A to those in column B to form phrases or short sentences.

A

a. ta'āla

b. bēni

c. mīt alf

d. el-mudun

e. se'r

f. 'andena

g. ahlan

h. el-Taba'āt

i. SāHib

j. esh-sho'a'

B

el-ghaneyya

es-sū'

et-tamlīk

el-'omāra

hena

w-bēnak

w-sahlan

eg-gedīda

gnēh

'ahwa w-shai

3. Put the words in the correct order to form coherent sentences.

a. min / sha''a / sanatēn / aktar / biy-dawwaru / ba'al-hom / 'ala

b. khayaleyya / esh-sho'a' / ba'it / et-tamlīk / as'ar

c. kefāya / kull / sakan / en-nās / mafīsh / yestaw'ib

d. yet-gawwizu / 'ala / fīha / sha''a / biy-dawwaru

e. el-mofaDDal / hena / fi / ta'āla / fi l-balakōna / makānak

4. Fill in the blanks with the correct demonstrative pronoun.

a. minēn nigīb mablagh zayy _____?

b. el-balakōna _____ bizzāt makānak el-mofaDDal.

c. SāHib el-'omāra _____ biy-'aggar esh-sha''a b-se'r es-sū'.

d. en-nās _____ mish 'awzīn y'īshu ma'a ahalīhom.

e. azmit es-sakan _____ mushkila kbīra.

5. Fill in the blanks with the correct word in parentheses. Pay attention to agreement.

a. el-biyūt di shaklaha Helw, Ha'i'i _____ awi.
   (kebir, ghaneya, gamīla, godad, khayali)

b. fīh f-maSr delwa'ti qawanīn _____ li l-igār.
   (ghaneya, gedīda, gamīla, godād, ketīr)

c. heyya di el-'omāra _____ illi fīha sho'a' faDya.
   (el-gamīl, el-ketīra, el-waHīd, el-khayāleyya, el-waHīda)

d. SāHib el-o'māra Tammā', 'āriD esh-sha'a bi-se'r _____.
   (ghani, gamīl, kobār, khayāli, gamīla)

e. en-nās illi b-yedfa'u metēn alf gnēh fi sha''a, homma nās _____ awi.
   (ghaneya, gamīla, kobār, ghonāy, ketīra)

Answer Key

1. a. *entu mashghulīn 'ala mīn?*
   b. *izzayy SiHHit HaDritak, ya ustāz aHmad?*
   c. *fēn dawwaru 'ala sha''a?*
   d. *bikām as'ār esh-sho'a'?*
   e. *lēh enta mistaghrab ya dūnald?*

2. a. *ta'āla hena*
   b. *bēni w-bēnak*
   c. *mīt alf gnēh*
   d. *el-mudun eg-gedīda*
   e. *se'r es-sū'*
   f. *'andena 'ahwa w-shai*
   g. *ahlan w-sahlan*
   h. *el-Taba'āt el-ghaneya*
   i. *SāHib el-'omāra*
   j. *esh-sho'a' et-tamlīk*

3. a. *ba'al-hom aktar min sanatēn biy-dawwaru 'ala sha''a.*
   b. *as'ar esh-sho'a' et-tamlīk ba'it khayaleyya.*
   c. *mafīsh sakan kefāya yestaw'ib kull en-nās.*
   d. *biy-dawwaru 'ala sha''a yeg-gawwizu fīha.*

4. a. *minēn nigīb mablagh zayy <u>dah</u>?*
   b. *el-balakōna <u>di</u> bizzāt makānak el-mofaDDal.*
   c. *SāHib el-'omāra <u>dah (dahowwa)</u> biy-'aggar esh-sha''a b-se'r es-sū'.*
   d. *en-nās <u>dōl</u> mish 'awzīn y'īshu ma'a ahalīhom.*
   e. *azmit es-sakan <u>di (daheyya)</u> mushkila kbīra.*

5. a. *el-biyūt shaklaha Helw, Ha'i'i <u>gamīla</u> awi.*
   b. *fih fi maSr delwa'ti qawanīn <u>gedīda</u> li l-igār.*
   c. *heyya di el-'omāra <u>el-waHīda</u> illi fiha sho'a' faDya.*
   d. *SāHib el-'omāra Tammā', ā'riD esh-sha''a bi-se'r <u>khayāli</u>.*
   e. *en-nās illi b-yedfa'u metēn alf gnēh f-sha''a, homma nās <u>ghonāy</u> awi.*

LESSON 20
(Egyptian Arabic)

mubarāt el-qimma l-maSreyya The Egyptian Super Bowl

A. Dialogue

It is Friday morning, the day of the soccer match between the traditional archrivals Al-Ahli and Al-Zamalik. Karim, who is a die-hard Zamalik fan, has asked his American friend Lucy to come and watch the game on television with him and his family. And he has invited his friend Samir, a staunch Ahli fan, to join them.

lūsī: el-Hāga illi b-te'gebni yōm match el-ahli we z-zamālik, howwal hudū' we l-rawa'ān fi shawāri' maSr kollaha. ya'ni wa't el-mubarāh biykūn esh-sha'b el-maSri kullu, riggāla w-sittāt, kobār w-'aTfāl, a'dīn 'oddām et-televizyōn b-yit-farragu 'ala l-matsh.

karīm: SaHH. mish bass fi l-qāhera. Hatta fi l-mudun et-tanya, wi l-muHafZāt, illi 'andohom fira' kōra, tela'īhom barDo b-yshagga'u imma l-'ahli aw ez-zamālik.

samīr: boSS ya karīm, boSS! el-ahli ba'ālu khamas sitt da'āyi' b-yhāgim hagamāt khaTīra, w-DāghiT 'ala difā' ez-zamālik. meSayTarīn 'ala noSS el-mal'ab. anā 'albi Hāsis in fī gōn Ha-yīgi.

karīm: ya 'amm da kullu kalām fāDi. khaT el-bakāt beta' ez-zamālik Hadīd we l-golkiper beta'na b-yel'ab fi l-muntakhab, fākir match maSr ma'a l-muntakhab et-tunsi? da bass fi l-bidāya, el-ahli farHān bi nafsu. istanna shwayya lamma z-zamālik yibtidi l-hugūm. es-sanādi farawdit ez-zamālik ra'bīn ed-dawri kullu. enta nesīt eHna 'amalna fik-um ēh fi l-matsh illi fāt? talat tigwān zayy il-'asal. kull wāl·lid aHla mit-tāni. w-kull da b-sabab "sūka" nigm ez-zamālik eg-gedīd fi khaTT en-noSS, Sāni' el-le'b, el-playmaker el-maystro.

samīr: eh, eh, 'o'af 'andak! enta nāsi match el-ittiHād es-sakandari lamma t-hazamtum henāk wāHid Sifr, walla matsh el-ismaī'li illi t'adiltu fih? walla 'āwiz te'olli inn il-ahli ma-fihūsh la''iba dawliyyīn fi l-muntakhab? eHna 'andena aHsan genaHēn fi maSr, "mustafa" w-"shaTTa", el-wing left we l-wing rayt.

karīm: māshi, illi t'ulu. Tayyib homma kānu fēn lamma dakkokom el-olombi etnēn wāHid, walla l-hazīma l-munkara 'oddām et-tirsāna talāta Sifr?

lūsī: entu ya gamā'a 'ammalīn titkallimu ma'a ba'D fi Hagāt tarikheyya wala mihtammīn bi l-matsh 'ala t-televizyōn. ma'a inn el-fir'itēn b-yela'bu mubarāh rā'i'a fiha kull funūn ek-kōra l-Hadīsa. anā shayfa inn ez-zamālik howwa l-farī' el-aHsan, zayy ma b-y'ūlu: le'b, w-fann w-handasa! w-biSarāHa keda, anā bashagga' el-le'ba l-Helwa. ma tiz'alsh minni ya samīr, bass ana zamalkaweya. el-matsh 'arrab 'al hāf tayim, w-lissa mafīsh egwān.

samīr: mat-khafish. fi sh-shōT et-tāni, el-ahli Haygīb gōn.

karīm: da bo'dokom! ez-zamālik Hay-HoTT gonēn gowwa shabakit el-ahli, w Ha-yintihi el-matsh etnēn Sifr.

Lucy: The one thing that I like about the day of the Ahli-Zamalik match is the peace and quiet on the streets of all of Egypt. I mean, during the game, the entire Egyptian population, men and women, adults and children, are sitting in front of their television watching the match.

Karim: That's right. Not only in Cairo, but even in other cities and governorates that have football teams. You will still find them rooting for either Ahli or Zamalik.

Samir: Look, Karim, look! Ahli has been attacking fiercely over the last five, six minutes, and pressuring Zamalik's defense. They have total control over midfield. My heart tells me there's a goal coming.

Karim: That's all good for nothing, man. Zamalik's backfield is made of steel and our goalkeeper plays for the national team. Do you remember the match between Egypt and the Tunisian national team? This is only the beginning and Ahli players are feeling good about themselves. Just wait a bit until Zamalik starts attacking. This year, Zamalik's forwards have instilled fear throughout the league. Did you forget what we did to you in the last match? Three goals [that tasted] like honey. Each one sweeter than the other. And all of that because of Souka, Zamalik's new midfield star, the playmaker, the maestro.

Samir: What, what? Stop right there. Did you forget the match with the Al-Ittihad Al-Sakandri [Alexandria United], when you were defeated there one to nil? Or the Al-Ismaili [Ismailiya team] match, where you ended up in a draw? Or are you trying to tell me that Ahli has no international players on the national team? We have the two best wingers in Egypt, Mustafa and Shatta, the left winger and the right winger.

Karim: Okay, whatever you say. But where were they when Al-Olombi [Olympic] blasted you two to one, or for the humiliating defeat at the hands of Al-Tirsana [Arsenal] three to nil?

Lucy: Guys, you are talking non-stop to each other about past history and are not concerned about the match on TV, even though the two teams are playing a superb match with all the art of modern football. I see that Zamalik is the better team. As they say: It is play, art, and design! And frankly speaking, I am a fan of good games. Don't be upset with me, Samir, but I am a Zamalik fan. The match is close to half time, and still no goals.

Samir: Don't worry. In the second half, Ahli is going to score a goal.

Karim: Don't even think of it! Zamalik is going to score two goals in Ahli's net, and the match will end two to zero.

B. Grammar and Usage

1. GREETINGS IN EGYPTIAN ARABIC

Below are examples of greetings and typical responses to them commonly used in the Egyptian dialect. There are the traditional, formal expressions, used when addressing someone older or higher in rank, and the more common, informal ones used in addressing friends or family members.

Greeting	Typical Response
ahlan; *ahlan w-sahlan*	*ahlan bīk* (m.); *ahlan w-sahlan bīk* (m.)
	ahlan bīki (f.); *ahlan w-sahlan bīki* (f.)
	ahlan bīkom (pl.); *ahlan w-sahlan bīkom* (pl.)
Welcome; Hello; Hi	Hello to you.
izzayyak? (m. sg. infml.);	*izzayyak enta?* (m. sg.); *el-Hamdulillāh, shukran.*
izzay HaDritak? (m. sg. fml.);	*izzayyik enti?* (f. sg.); *el-Hamdulillāh, shukran.*
izzayyik? (f. sg. infml.);	
izzay HaDritik? (f. sg. fml.);	*izzayyokum?*; *izzayyoku?* (pl.);

izzayyokum? (pl. infml.);	*el-Hamdulillāh, shukran.*
izzay HaDaratkum? (pl. fml.)	
How are you?	How are you?; Fine, thanks.
	(*lit.*, Praise to God, thanks)

Still more informal are the following expressions:

izzay SiHHitak? (m. sg. infml.);	*kwayyis, el-Hamdulillāh.*
izzay SiHHitik? (f. sg. infml.);	*kwayyisa, el-Hamdulillāh.*
izzay SiHHitkum? (pl. infml.)	*kwayyisīn, el-Hamdulillāh.*
How's your health?	I'm fine, thanks to God.

ēh akhbārak? (m.)	*wallāhi 'āl; mish baTTāl.*
ēh akhbārik? (f.)	*wallāhi 'āl; mish baTTāla.*
ēh akhbārkom? (pl.)	*wallahi 'āl; mish baTTalīn.*
How's it going?	Well (by God), all right; Not bad.

'āmil ēh? (m.)	*māshi l-Hāl.*
'amla ēh? (f.)	*māshi l-Hāl.*
'amlīn ēh? (pl.)	*māshi l-Hāl.*
How are you doing?	I'm/We're okay.

2. NATIONALITIES

Similar to MSA, in Egyptian Arabic nouns indicating nationality are formed by adding the ending *-i*, for masculine, or *-eyya*, for feminine, to the name of the country.

Name of the Country	Nationality
maSr (Egypt)	*maSri (m.); maSreyya (f.)* (Egyptian)
amrīka (America)	*amrikāni (m.); amrikaneyya (f.)* (American)
tūnis (Tunisia)	*tunsi (m.); tuniseyya (f.)* (Tunisian)
libnān (Lebanon)	*libnāni (m.); libnaneyya (f.)* (Lebanese)
ingiltera (England)	*inglīzi (m.); inglizeyya (f.)* (English)
kanada (Canada)	*kanadi (m.); kanadeyya (f.)* (Canadian)

3. COMMON ADVERBS IN EGYPTIAN ARABIC

Below are lists of common adverbs used in Egyptian Arabic.

ADVERBS OF TIME

imbāraH	yesterday
bokra	tomorrow
delwa'ti	now
en-naharda	today
imbāraH bi l-lēl	last night
Hāleyyan	currently; presently
mo'akharan; min 'orayyib	recently; lately
akhīran	finally; lastly
SabāHan; eS-SobH	in the morning
bokra S-SobH	tomorrow morning
el-lēla; el-lelā di	tonight
'abl	before
ba'd	after
ba'dēn	afterwards; thereafter; then; next

ADVERBS/PREPOSITIONS OF PLACE

hena	here
henāk	there
wara	behind
'oddām	in front of
fō'	above; up
taHt	below; under
Hawalēn	around
Hawāli	about; around; approximately
'ala-mtidād	along
gamb	near; close to; next to
min khilāl; 'an Tarī'	through; by
fi 'ay makān; fi makān tāni	anywhere; elsewhere

ADVERBS OF MANNER

bisor'a; sari'an	quickly; fast
biboT'; bi r-rāHa	slowly; slow
biSōt 'āli	loudly
biSarāHa	frankly; candidly
li Hosn il-HaZZ	fortunately
li sū' il-HaZZ	unfortunately
bifarHa	happily
bighaDab	angrily
bihudū'; bihadāwa	calmly
biz'i'	with shouting/yelling
biquwwa; bi'iwwa	strongly; forcefully
Tabi'i	naturally

ADVERBS OF FREQUENCY	
dayman	always
abadan	never
ketir	frequently
nādir	rarely
aHyānan	sometimes
'ādatan	normally; usually
yawmeyyan; kull yōm	daily; every day
shahreyyan; kull shahr	monthly; every month
sanaweyyan; kull sana	yearly; annually; every year

ADVERBS OF DEGREE	
giddan; awi	very
mish awi	not very; not much
aktar	more
a'all	less
ta'rīban	almost

4. CONNECTING SENTENCES AND IDEAS

The following examples from the dialogue contain speech connectors and conjunctions.

anā shāyef inn ez-zamālik howwa l-fari' el-aHsan, <u>zayy ma b-y'ūlu</u>: le'b, w-fann w-handasa!

I see that Zamalik is the better team, <u>as they say</u>: It is play, art, and design!

<u>biSarāHa keda</u>, anā bashagga' el-le'ba l-Helwa . . .

<u>Frankly speaking</u>, I am a fan of good games . . .

ma-tiz'alsh minni ya samir, <u>bass</u> ana zamalkāwi.

Don't be upset with me, Samir, <u>but</u> I am a Zamalik fan.

Below are examples of other commonly used speech connectors and conjuctions.

SPEECH CONNECTORS AND CONJUNCTIONS	
lākin	however
innama	however
awwalan; sāneyan; sālisan	firstly; secondly; thirdly
ya'ni	meaning . . . ; I mean . . . ; more or less
bisabab	because of; for reasons of
in-natiga innu (innaha)	consequently; as a result
bikhoSūS	with respect to; with regard to; concerning; regarding
kamān	also; moreover; more
bass	but
imma . . . aw . . .	either . . . or
la . . . wala . . .	neither . . . nor
Hatta	even
Hatta law	even if
ma'a inn	even though

5. UNITS OF MEASUREMENT

The metric system is used in Egypt. Below are common units of measurement, including some traditional ones.

WEIGHTS	
kilogrām; kilo	kilogram
noS kilo	half kilo
rob' kilo	quarter kilo
tomn kilo	eighth kilo
grām	gram
noSS grām	half gram
wi''a (old-fashioned)	oka (1.248 kg)
we'iyya; we'iyyāt	ounce; ounces
raTl; arTāl	pound; pounds

VOLUME	
litr	liter
noS litr	half liter
rob' litr	quarter liter
tilt litr	third liter
galōn; galonāt	gallon; gallons

DISTANCE	
kilometr; kilo	kilometer
noSS kilo	half kilometer
sentimetr; santi (santi wāHid)	centimeter
millimetr; milli (milli wāHid)	millimeter
mil; amyāl	mile; miles
yarda; yardāt	yard; yards
'adam; a'dām	foot; feet
būSa; buSāt	inch; inches
faddān; fadadīn	feddan (approx. 4,201 sq. meters)
shibr; ashbār	span(s) of the hand

C. Vocabulary

hudū'	calm; quiet
rawa'a	serenity; peacefulness
esh-sha'b	the people
riggāla	men
sittāt	women
kobār	adults; elderly
aTfāl	children
televizyōn	television
muHafZāt (pl.); muHafza	governorate(s)
fira' kōra (pl.); farī' kōra	soccer team(s)
barDo (barDak)	still (adv.)
hagamāt khaTīra (pl.); hagma	fierce attack(s)
DāghiT (m.); DaghTa (f.)	pressuring
Difā'	defense
miSayTarīn	they are in control of
noSS el-mal'ab	midfield
'albi Hāsis.	I can feel it.
ya 'amm!	Hey, man!; Hey, you!
kalām fāDi	useless
khaTT el-bakāt (khaTT eD-Dahr)	backfield
gōlkīper (Hāris el-marma)	goalkeeper
el-muntakhab	the all-star team, the national team
el-muntakhab et-tunsi	the Tunisian national team
farHān bi nafsu	he is feeling good about himself; vain
istanna! (m.); istanni! (f.)	Wait!
farawda	forwards, attackers

ra'bīn; rā'ib	they are instilling fear
nesīt? (m.); nesīti? (f.)	Have you forgotten?
talat tigwān	three goals
'asal	sweet (lit., honey)
bisabab	because of
nigm	star
khaTT en-noSS	midfield
Sāni' el-le'b	playmaker
'o'af 'andak! (m.); 'o'afi 'andik! (f.)	Hold it! Wait a minute!
wāHid Sifr	one (to) nil
etnēn wāHid	two (to) one
talāta Sifr	three (to) nil
dawliyyīn (pl.); dawli (s.)	international
genaHēn; genāH	winger(s)
māshi, illi t'ūlu.	Okay, whatever you say.
dakkokom (m.); dakkitkom (f.)	he/she demolished you
hazīma munkara	humiliating defeat
funūn ek-kōra l-Hādisa	the art of modern soccer
le'b, w-fann, w-handasa!	It is play, art, and design!
zamalkāwi (m.);	a fan of Zamalik
zamalkaweyya (f.)	
ahlāwi (m.); ahlaweyya (f.)	a fan of El-Ahli
shōT; esh-shōT et-tāni	one half (of a soccer match); the second half
da bo'dokom (pl.);	don't even think of it
da bo'dak (sg.)	
gowwa	in; inside
shabaka	net
Ha-yintihi (m.); Ha-tintihi (f.)	it will end

D. Cultural Note

Egypt's national pastime is soccer. Not only is it the national sport, but it is also something that is an integral part of people's everyday lives. At times, the preoccupation with it gets so extreme that it actually leads to break-ups in families. That is how deep the passion for the sport is in Egypt.

More than 35 teams, from the elite, premier league teams, to the first, second, and third division teams, exist in Egypt. Every major Egyptian city and governorate has a soccer team, and in some of these cities, one can find several teams, either old, established teams or new, privately owned ones. In Cairo alone, there are about five or six teams. For some unexplained reason, Egyptians, regardless of where they are from, have historically been divided into two camps, depending on which of the two major Cairo soccer teams they support, the Zamalik team or the Al-Ahli team. This is a tradition that has been passed on for generations: the Zamalik team, traditionally also called the Nadi Al-Mukhtalat (the Mixed Club), used to represent the upper echelon of society during the monarchy, and its archrival, the Al-Ahli team, the National Team, always represented people from the lower echelons of society.

When these two teams play one another, the entire country is glued to the television sets and radios. Over the years, people have turned this event into a kind of a national holiday. The only unfortunate aspect of this is that on the following day, one half of the country will be happy, while the other half will have to put up with the boastful behavior of the victorious side.

E. Exercises

1. Match the words from column A with those in column B to form phrases or short sentences.

A	B
a. *esh-sha'b*	*khaTira*
b. *hagamāt*	*minni*
c. *al-muntakhab*	*et-tāni*
d. *istanna*	*zamalkāwi*
e. *Sani'*	*'al-maSri*
f. *ma tiz'alsh*	*et-tunsi*
g. *esh-shōt*	*el-le'b*
h. *anā*	*shwayya*

2. Put the words in the correct order to form coherent sentences.

a. *biykūn / kullu / et-televizyōn / el-maSri / wa't / ā'id / el-mubarāh / 'oddām / esh-sha'b*
b. *illi / et-tanya / Hatta / fira' / 'andohom / fi l-mudun / kōra*
c. *'amalna / ēh / fi l-match / illi / eHna / enta / fikum / fāt / nesīt / ?*
d. *fīha / b-yel'abu / funūn / el-fir'itēn / ek-kōra / mubarāh / l-Hadīsa / rā'ia' / kull*
e. *shabakit / gowwa / gonēn / el-ahli / Hay-HoTT / ez-zamālik*

3. Say the following statements or questions in Egyptian Arabic.

a. His heart tells him there's a goal coming.
b. Did you forget what we did to you in the last match?
c. They have the two best wingers in Egypt.
d. Two goals [that tasted] like honey.
e. She is an Ahli fan.

4. Insert the correct word as indicated in parentheses.

a. *lamma ruHna amrika, el-farī' el-maSri kan b-yel'ab ma'a l-farī' _____.*
(nationality)

b. *kunna a'dīn 'oddām et-televizyōn _____ talat sa'āt.*
(pick an adverb of place: *en-naharda, Hawāli, Hāleyan, gamb, henāk*)

c. *_____ inn el-farī' el-aHsan howwa illi Haygīb eg-gōn.*
(pick an adverb of manner: *biboT', li Hosn il-HaZZ, bifarHa, Tabī'i, 'ala mahlak*)

d. *heyya _____ ma rāHit mubarāt kōra.*
(pick an adverb of frequency: *'ādatan, aHyānan, 'omri, yaumeyyan, 'omraha*)

e. *āh wallāhi, anā _____ bashagga' el-le'ba l-Helwa.*
(pick an adverb of degree: *a'all, ta'rīban, mogarrad, Ha'ī'i, aktar*)

5. Fill in the blanks with the appropriate connector phrase.

a. *khaTT el-bakāt beta' ez-zamālik Hadīd, _____ el-golkīper mish kwayyis.*

b. *el-ahli b-yhāgim hagamāt khaTīra, _____ ez-zamālik mesayTar 'ala noSS el-mal'ab.*

c. *eHna 'andena aHsan genaHēn fi maSr, w- _____ aHsan gōlkīper.*

d. *fīh hudū' w-rawa'ān fi shawāri' maSr, w-kull dah _____ match el-ahli we z-zamālik.*

e. *ez-zamālik Haygīb gōn _____ fi sh-shōT el-awwal _____ esh-shōT et-tāni.*

Answer Key

1. a. *esh-sha'b al-maSri*
   b. *hagamāt khaTīra*
   c. *al-muntakhab et-tunsi*
   d. *istanna shwayya*
   e. *Sani' el-le'b*
   f. *ma tiz'alsh minni*
   g. *esh-shōt et-tāni*
   h. *anā zamalkāwi*

2. a. *wa't el-mubarāh biykūn esh-sha'b el-maSri kullu ā'id 'oddām et-televizyōn.*
   b. *Hatta fi l-mudun et-tanya illi 'andohom fira' kōra.*
   c. *enta nsīt eHna 'amalna fīkum ēh fi l-matsh illi fāt?*
   d. *el-fir'itēn b-yel'abu mubarāh rā'i'a fīha kull funūn ek-kōra l-Hadīsa.*
   e. *ez-zamālik Hay-HoTT gonēn gowwa shabakit el-ahli.*

3. a. *howwa 'albu Hāsis in fī gōn Ha-yīgi.*
   b. *enta nesīt eHna a'malna fīkum ēh fi l-matsh illi fāt?*
   c. *homma 'andohom aHsan genaHēn fi maSr.*
   d. *gonēn zayy il-'asal.*
   e. *heyya 'ahlaweyya.*

4. a. *lamma ruHna amrika, el-farī' el-maSri kan b-yel'ab ma'a l-farī' el-amrikāni.*
   b. *kunna a'dīn 'oddām et-televizyōn Hawāli talat sa'āt.*
   c. *Tabī'i inn el-farī' el-aHsan howwo illi Haygīb eg-gōn.*
   d. *heyya 'omraha ma rāHit mubarāt kōra.*
   e. *āh wallāhi, anā Ha'ī'i bashagga' el-le'ba l-Helwa.*

5. a. *khaTT el-bakāt beta' ez-zamālik*
      Hadīd, lakin (bass) el-golkīper mish
      kwayyis.

   b. *el-ahli b-yhāgim hagamāt khaTira,*
      ma'a inn ez-zamālik meSayTar 'ala
      noSS el-mal'ab.

   c. *eHna 'andena aHsan genaHēn fi*
      maSr, w-kamān aHsan gōlkīper.

   d. *fīh hudū' w-rawa'ān fi shawāri' maSr,*
      w-kull dah bisabab match el-ahli we
      z-zamālik.

   e. *ez-zamālik Haygīb gōn imma fish-shōT*
      el-awwal aw esh-shōT et-tāni.

FIFTH REVIEW

(Egyptian Arabic)

---

1. Put the words in the parentheses in the correct form, and then translate the sentences into English.

Example: *lūsi ('āwiz) (yerkab) eg-gamal, lakin eg-gammāl mish hena.*

       lūsi 'awza terkab eg-gamal, lakin eg-gammāl mish hena.

       Lucy wants to ride the camel, but the camel driver is not here.

a. *eHna ('āwiz) (yeTla') fō' eg-gamal delwa'ti.*

b. *entu ('āwiz) (yerkab) felūka, w-(yitfassaH) 'ala n-nīl?*

c. *en-nās (lāzim) (yodkhol) min el-bāb er-ra'īsi beta' el-matHaf.*

d. *esh-sho'a' hena ghalya awi (too expensive), enti (mumkin) (yedawwar) fi Hitta tania.*

e. *anā ('āwiz) (yetfarrag) 'ala t-televizyōn, 'alashān (yeshūf) matsh ek-kōra.*

2. Complete the sentences by forming expressions of possession using the words in parentheses.

a. *ah, mumkin teHoTT (īd + enta) fi l-mayya.*

b. *enti shufti (sha'a + howwa) eg-gedīda?*

c. *eHna f maSr ('and + eHna) aHsan farī' kōra fi afriqya!*

d. *ya rayyis maHmūd, eHna a'wzīn nerkab el-feluka (betā' + enta)!*

e. *anā mish 'āwiz aDayya' (wa't + anā) fi kalām fāDi.*

3. Match the words from column A to those in column B to form phrases or sentences.

A	B
a. *el-yafTa beta'itkom bet'ūl*	*walla ba'd ma n-khallas eg-gawla?*
b. *eHna ma gināsh el-matHaf dah*	*'enēha!*
c. *ya dūnald, as'ār esh-sho'a' en-naharda*	*fi l-balakōna*
d. *farī' ek-kōra bta'na*	*khamsa dolār li rkūb eg-gamal*
e. *nedfa' el-Hisāb delwa'ti*	*min talat sinīn*
f. *heyya mish mesadda'a*	*ba'it khayaleyya!*
g. *itfaDDalu hena*	*b-yel'ab mubarāh rā'i'a*

4. Put the words in the correct order to form coherent sentences.

a. *Ha-yakhodna / el-haram / laffa / ek-kebīr / Hawalēn / howwa*

b. *'abl / yalla / ghurūb / el-felūka / bīna / esh-shams / nerkab / !*

c. *SaHbik / izzayyik, / dūnald / amīra / el-amrikāni / w-izzay / ya / ?*

d. *Ha-nitgawwiz / ma / w-tishtaghal / amīra / eHna / 'abl / mish / titkharrag*

e. *tegibli / min / 'ahwa / karīm / maZbūT / faDlak / ya / mumkin*

5. Read the following passage and translate it into English. Then answer the questions below it.

karīm: alō. Mumkin at-kallim ma'a SāHib el-'omāra, min faDlak?

SāHib el-'omāra: aywa, anā SāHib el-'omāra, ayy khidma?

karīm: ahlan, min faDlak eHna kunna 'awzīn neshūf law 'andak sho'a' faDya.

SāHib el-'omāra: aywa, 'andena sho'a' igār w-tamlīk.

karīm: mumkin as'alak bikām 'igār esh-sho'a' eS-Soghayyara, ya'ni odit nōm [bedroom] waHda?

SāHib el-'omāra: wallāhi esh-sho'a' eS-Soghayyara igarha alf w-metēn ginēh fi sh-shahr.

karīm: ma 'andaksh Hāga arkhaS?

SāHib el-'omāra: la wallāhi, di arkhaS Hāga 'andena delwa'ti.

karīm: Tayyib shukran, anā Ha-dawwar fi makān tāni li'inn el-igār dah ketīr 'alayya.

a. *mīn illi biy-dawwar 'ala sha''a?*

b. *mīn illi 'andu sho'a'?*

c. *esh-sha''a eS-Soghayyara fīha kām ōdit nōm?*

d. *bikām igār esh-sha'a kull shahr?*

e. *ēh illi bi-yfakkaru ye'milūh karīm w-khaTibtu?*

f. *lēh karīm Ha-ydawwar fi makān tāni?*

6. Put the underlined words or phrases in the negative form by using the negative particles *ma* or *mish*.

a. *eHna 'awzīn nerūH el-matHaf en-naharda.*

b. *homma kānu m'āna lamma rkibna l-felūka.*

c. *heyya rāHit esh-sha''a mbāraH.*

d. *dūnald w-lūsi dafa'u Hsāb el-'ahwa we sh-shāy.*

e. *Fi sh-shōT et-tāni, el-farī' beta'kom Ha-ygib gōn.*

f. *ana kont fi l-matHaf lamma shāfu l-mumya?*

7. Pick a word and fill in the blanks. Then, translate the sentences into English.

en-naharda / ma'a innu / li'inn / 'ala mahlak / itnāshar

a. *ana gibt et-tazāker, w-dafa't _____ gnēh.*

b. *ma t-su'sh bisor'a, khallīk māshi _____.*

c. *ma khadnāsh esh-sha'a _____ se'raha kan khayāli.*

d. *dūnald rikib eg-gamal _____ biy-khāf min ig-gimāl.*

e. *kunna 'awzīn nerūH el-matHaf _____, mish bokra.*

8. Choose the right question word to complete the questions below.

lēh / ēh / mīn / izzay / emta / fēn

a. _____ *illi HaTT ek-kōra gowwa eg-gōn?*

b. _____ Ha-nrūH neshūf el-mumya?

c. _____ el-makān illi mumkin negīb minnu tazāker?

d. _____ en-nās fi maSr bi-ysū'u b-Tarī'a magnūna?

e. _____ ek-kalām illi nta bit-'ūlu dah?

f. _____ Ha-n'aggar sha'a w-eHna ma 'andenāsh filūs (money)?

9. Change the gender and/or number of the words in parentheses, as indicated in brackets. Then translate the sentences into English.

a. esh-shāri' illi warāna fīh (beit) (kebīr). [plural + gender]

b. ākhir marra rkibna felūka kānit min khamas (sana). [plural]

c. esh-sha''a bta'itkom (shaklu) gamīl awi. [gender]

d. gowwa l-ōDa, kan fīh (rāgil) w-(sit) a'dīn bi-yitfarragu 'ala t-televizyōn. [plural]

e. lamma kharagna kullina, el-makān ba'a (faDya) tamāman. [gender]

10. Put the verbs in parentheses in the future tense.

a. lamma (ruHna) henāk, (shufna) ghurūb esh-shams.

b. karīm (ye'mil) lina gawla siyāHeyya fi l-qāhera.

c. bokra kull en-nās (yit-farrag) 'ala mubarāt el-qimma.

d. iftitāH el-matHaf (kān) ba'd sanatēn.

e. dūnald w-lūsi (rikbu) felūka 'ala n-nīl, w-ba'dēn anā (khadtohom) fi ziyāra li l-qāhera.

Answer Key

1. a. eHna *'awzin niTla'* fō' eg-gamal delwa'ti.
      We want to get on top of the camel now.

   b. entu *'awzin terkabu* felūka, w-*titfassaHu* 'ala n-nīl?
      Do you want to ride a felucca, and go for a cruise (*lit.*, take a trip) on the Nile?

   c. en-nās *lāzim todkhol* min el-bāb er-ra'īsi beta' el-matHaf.
      People must enter from the museum's main gate.

   d. esh-sho'a' hena ghalya awi, enti *mukin tedawwari* fi Hitta tania.
      Apartments here are very expensive; you can look elsewhere.

   e. ana *'āwiz atfarrag* 'ala t-televizyōn, 'alashān *ashūf* match el-kōra.
      I want to watch television, so that I can see the soccer match.

2. a. ah, mumkin teHoTT *īdak* fi l-mayya.

   b. enti shufti *sha''itu* eg-gedīda?

   c. eHna f maSr *'andena* aHsan farī' kōra fi afriqya!

   d. ya rayyis maHmūd, eHna 'awzīn nerkab el-feluka *bta'tak!*

   e. anā mish 'āwiz aDayya' *wa'ti* fi kalām fāDi.

3. a. el-yafTa beta'itkom bet'ūl khamsa dolār li rkūb eg-gamal.

   b. eHna ma gināsh el-matHaf dah min talat sinīn.

   c. ya dūnald, as'ār esh-sho'a' en-naharda ba'it khayaleyya!

   d. farī' ek-kōra bta'na b-yel'ab mubarāh rā'i'a.

   e. nedfa' el-Hisāb delwa'ti walla ba'd ma nkhallaS eg-gawla?

   f. heyya mish mesadda'a 'enēha!

   g. itfaDDalu hena fi l-balakōna.

4. a. *howwa Ha-yakhodna laffa Hawalēn el-haram ek-kebīr.*

   b. *yalla bīna nerkab el-felūka 'abl ghurūb esh-shams!*

   c. *izzayyik ya amīra, w-izzayy dūnald SaHbik el-amrikāni?*

   d. *eHna mish Ha-nitgawwiz 'abl ma amīra titkharrag w-tishtaghal.*

   e. *min faDlak ya karīm, mumkin tegibli 'ahwa maZbūT.*

5. Karim: Hello. Can I please speak to the landlord?

   Landlord: Yes, I am the landlord; how may I help you?

   Karim: Hi. If you please, we wanted to see if you had any vacant apartments.

   Landlord: Yes, we have rental apartments and condominiums.

   Karim: Can I ask you how much the rental is for the small apartments, I mean, [those with] one bedroom?

   Landlord: Well, the rental for small apartments is one thousand, two hundred pounds a month.

   Karim: Don't you have anything cheaper?

   Landlord: No, I'm sorry, this is the lowest thing we have right now.

   Karim: Okay, thank you. I will look elsewhere, because this rent is too much for me.

   a. *karīm howwa illi biy-dawwar 'ala sha''a.*

   b. *illi a'ndu sho'a' howwa SaHib el-'omāra.*

   c. *esh-sha''a eS-Soghayyara fīha odit nōm waHda.*

   d. *igār esh-sha'a kull shahr alf w-metēn gnēh.*

   e. *karīm w-khaTibtu biy-fakkaru ye'aggaru sha''a.*

6. a. *eHna mish 'awzīn nerūH el-matHaf en-naharda.*

   b. *homma ma kanūsh ma'āna lamma rkibna l-felūka.*

   c. *heyya ma raHitsh esh-sha'a embāraH.*

   d. *dūnald w-lūsi ma dafa'ūsh Hisāb el-'ahwa we sh-shāy.*

   e. *fi sh-shōT et-tāni, el-fari' beta'kom mish Ha-ygīb gōn.*

   f. *ana ma kontish fi l-matHaf lamma shāfu el-mumya?*

7. a. *anā gibt et-tazāker, w-dafa't itnāshar gnēh.*

      I got the tickets and paid twelve pounds.

   b. *ma t-su'sh bisor'a, khallīk māshi 'ala mahlak.*

      Don't drive fast; just keep going slowly.

   c. *ma khadnāsh esh-sha'a li'inn se'raha kan khayāli.*

      We didn't take the apartment because its price was unbelievable.

   d. *dūnald rikib eg-gamal ma'a innu biy-khāf min ig-gimāl.*

      Donald rode the camel, even though he is afraid of camels.

   e. *kunna a'wzīn nerūH el-matHaf en-naharda, mish bokra.*

      We wanted to go to the museum today, not tomorrow.

8. a. *mīn illi HaTT ek-kōra gowwa eg-gōn?*

   b. *emta Ha-nrūH neshūf el-mumya?*

   c. *fēn el-makān illi mumkin negīb minnu tazāker?*

   d. *lēh en-nās fi maSr bi-ysū'u b-Tarī'a magnūna?*

   e. *ēh ek-kalām illi enta bit-'ūlu dah?*

f. *izzay Ha-n'aggar sha'a w-eHna ma 'andenāsh filūs?*

9. a. *esh-shāri' illi warāna fīh biyūt kebīra.*

   b. *ākhir marra rekibna felūka kānit min khamas sinīn.*

   c. *esh-sha''a beta'itkom shaklaha gamīl awi.*

   d. *gowwa el-ōda, kan fīh riggāla w-sittāt a'dīn bi-yitfarragu 'ala t-televizyōn.*

   e. *lamma kharagna kullina, el-makān ba'a fāDi tamāman.*

10. a. *lamma Ha-nrūH henāk, Ha-nshūf ghurūb esh-shams.*

    b. *karīm Ha-ye'mil lina gawla siyāHeyya fi l-qāhera.*

    c. *bokra kull en-nās Ha-titfarrag 'ala mubarāt el-qimma.*

    d. *iftitāH el-matHaf Ha-ykūn ba'd sanatēn.*

    e. *dūnald w-lūsi Ha-yerkabu felūka 'ala n-nīl, w-ba'dēn anā Ha-khod-hom fi ziyāra li l-qāhera.*

LESSON 21

(Iraqi Arabic)

ta'āli niHtifil! Come, Let's Celebrate!

A. Dialogue

Layla receives Lucy in her house. After welcoming her and asking her about her health, Layla sets out to tell Lucy about how her father almost did not bless her marriage to Hassan. But now she can happily show Lucy her wedding dress and chat about her future plans.

lūsi: masā' il-khēr!

layla: masā' in-nūr, lūsi. TfaDHli!

lūsi: shukran!

layla: shlōn iS-SiHHa?

lūsi: zēna l-Hamdilla, inti shlōnich?

layla: l-Hamdilla; tfaDHli starīHi.

lūsi: mabrūk 'al khuTūba!

layla: shukran jazīlan, lūsi.

lūsi: gālaw abūch ma chān mwāfiq 'al-khutūba? lēsh?

layla: abūya lāzāl 'āyish bi l-'uSūr il-wuSTa; chān ygūl mā mumkin azawwij wiHda min banāti l-wāHid kurdi.

lūsi: shlōn akhīran wāfaq?

layla: wāfaq ba'admā 'ammi w-khāli Hichaw wiyyā. l-Hamdilla mishat 'ala khēr. ta'āli niHtifil! tHibbīn sh-shirbīn 'aSir Purtuqāl aw tuffāH?

lūsi: 'aSir Purtuqāl, law samaHti.

layla: shufi badlat iz-zafāf mālti!

lūsi: allah! kullish Hilwa! yamta tizzawjīn?

layla: bi S-Sēf, inshālla.

lūsi: wēn rāH t'īshīn ba'd iz-zawāj?

layla: iHna lāzim nrūH li l-baSra.

lūsi: tHibbīn il-baSra?

layla: amūt 'al baSra! l-baSrah kullish Hilwa!

lūsi: inshālla azūrich hnāk.

layla: akīd!

Lucy: Good afternoon!

Layla: Good afternoon, Lucy. Come in!

Lucy: Thanks!

Layla: How are you?

Lucy: I'm fine, thanks. And you?

Layla: Fine. Please sit down.

Lucy: Congratulations on the engagement!

Layla: Thanks a lot!

Lucy: They said your father did not agree to the engagement? Why?

Layla: My father still lives in the Middle Ages! He was saying that he would never marry any one of his daughters to a Kurdish man.

Lucy: How did he eventually agree?

Layla: He consented after my uncles (*lit.*, maternal uncle and paternal uncle) had talked to him. Thank God, it went all right! Come, let's celebrate! Would you like orange juice or apple juice?

Lucy: Orange juice, please.

Layla: Look at my wedding dress!

Lucy: Wow! It is so pretty. When is the wedding?

Layla: In the summer, hopefully.

Lucy: Where are you going to live after after the wedding?

Layla: We have to live in Basrah.

Lucy: Do you like Basrah?

Layla: I love Basrah (*lit.*, I'm dying for Basrah)! Basrah is very beautiful!

Lucy: I hope to visit you there.

Layla: Of course!

B. Pronunciation

1. WRITING THE IRAQI DIALECT

Like other Arabic dialects, Iraqi Arabic is primarily a spoken language, rarely used in written communication, where Modern Standard Arabic is the norm. Because the Arabic script was devised to represent the sounds of Classical and Modern Standard Arabic, the additional sounds that exist in Arabic dialects like Iraqi are not represented by it. For these reasons, the transliteration in Latin script is used to represent Iraqi Arabic in Lessons 21 to 25, as in all other dialect lessons.

Many widely different dialects are spoken in Iraq, but we have chosen to present here the dialect spoken in Baghdad, the capital of Iraq, while avoiding any too strongly marked features of the dialect.

2. VOWELS IN IRAQI ARABIC

In addition to the six vowels found in MSA (*ā, ū, ī, a, u,* and *i*), Iraqi Arabic has two more vowels: the long vowel *ō*, found in *shlōnich?* (How are you?) and *ē*, corresponding the MSA *ay*, as in *zēn* (good)—MSA *zayn*. The long vowel *ō* often corresponds to the vowel combination *aw* in the MSA, as in *yawm* (day) or *nawm* (sleep), pronounced in Iraqi as *yōm* and *nōm*.

3. CONSONANTS IN IRAQI ARABIC

Iraqi Arabic has all the consonants found in *fuSHā* except for the emphatic consonant *D* (ض), which is always replaced by the emphatic *DH* sound. A *fuSHā* word like *tafaDDali*

(Sit down; Come in; Have some, please) is *tfaDHli* in Iraqi Arabic, and *ayDan* (also, too) is pronounced *ayDHan*. However, Iraqi Arabic also has three consonants not found in *fuSHā*: *g*, *ch*, and *p*.

A. THE CONSONANT *g*
In Iraqi Arabic, the hard *g*-sound (found in the English words *go* and *give*) replaces the MSA consonant *q* (ق).

Iraqi Arabic	MSA
gal	*qāla* (said)
gam	*qāma* (stood up)

However, not all *q*'s are pronounced as *g*'s in Iraqi Arabic. The word *mwāfiq* (agreeing) in the dialogue (MSA *muwafiq*) retains its *q*. So do the words *qalam* (pen), *qamīS* (shirt), *qadīm* (old), and many others. There are no set rules regarding this transformation, and sometimes a certain word can be pronounced either way: *qarīb* or *girīb* (nearby), *qalb* or *galib* (heart), and *quwwa* or *guwwa* (strength, force). *fuSHā* pronunciation with *q* is often used in the spoken Iraqi dialect in more formal situations and by highly educated individuals. Remember, however, that all the *g*'s in Iraqi Arabic are MSA *q*'s, except when the word is borrowed from foreign sources, such as *gallan* (gallon) and *glāS* (drinking glass).

B. THE CONSONANT *ch*
The consonant *ch*, found in the expression *shlōnich?* (How are you?), is similar to the *ch* in the English word *chess*, and replaces the MSA sound *k*.

Iraqi Arabic	MSA
chān	*kān* (was)
simach	*samak* (fish)

Again, not every *k* turns into *ch* in Iraqi Arabic; the words *kalām* (speech), *kāmil* (perfect), and *kursi* (chair) are among the many *fuSHā* words that have the same pronunciation in Iraqi Arabic. On the other hand, some words are pronounced with either *k* or *ch*: *kam* or *cham* (how many), and *kīs* or *chīs* (paper/plastic bag). This transformation of *k* into *ch* also occurs in the feminine possessive/object suffixes—but not in their masculine equivalents: *shlōnich* (f.) vs. *shlōnak* (m.). While most occurrences of *ch* correspond to MSA *k*, some words with *ch* have come to Iraqi Arabic from foreign languages, such as Turkish and Persian: *tarāchi* (earrings), *chaTal* (fork), and *chādar* (blanket).

C. THE CONSONANT *p*
This sound, found in the word *purtuqāl* in the dialogue, is identical to the English *p* sound in *pen*. It is mostly found in words borrowed from other languages. Iraqis say *pācha* for a lamb's cooked head; *pāsha*, as in the Ottoman title; and *chorpāya* for *bed*—all words not

found in *fuSHā*. However, people in the south of Iraq tend not to use the *p* sound, and the above words are pronounced *bācha*, *bāsha*, and *chorbāya*.

C. Grammar and Usage

1. THE FEMININE ENDING IN IRAQI ARABIC

As in MSA, the feminine endings of Iraqi nouns and adjectives are represented by the suffix *-a(t)*. For instance, the word *Hilwa* (nice) is the equivalent of the *fuSHā* word *Hulwa*. (The only difference is that, in very formal MSA, *Hulwa* can have the form *Hulwatun*, *Hulwatan*, or *Hulwatin*, depending on its grammatical case. Grammatical case does not exist in Iraqi Arabic or in any other colloquial dialect of Arabic.)

Note how a word like *badla* (dress) in the dialogue becomes *badlaṯ* when it is followed by another word in a possessive construction, as in *badlaṯ iz-zafāf* (wedding dress) or *badlaṯ layla* (Layla's dress). Compare this to *badlạ Hilwa* (nice dress) and *Hadīqạ jamīla* (a beautiful garden).

2. GREETINGS AND GOOD-BYES IN IRAQI ARABIC

There are many greeting expressions in Iraqi Arabic, one being the *fuSHā as-salāmu 'alaykum* (peace be upon you), which is known all around the Arab and the Islamic worlds. Other common Iraqi greetings and good-byes are listed in the following table.

GREETING	RESPONSE
SabāH il-khēr (good morning)	*SabāH in-nūr* (good morning)
masā' il-khēr (good afternoon)	*masā' in-nūr* (good afternoon)
halaw, hala (hello)	*halaw, hala, halaw bīk/bīch* (Hello to you!, *m./f.*)
shlōnak?/shlōnich? (How are you?, *m./f.*)	*zēn/zēnạ l-Hamdilla* (Good, thank God, *m./f.*)
shlōn iS-SiHHa? (How are you?)	*zēn/zēnạ l-Hamdilla* (Good, thank God)
marHaba (hello; welcome)	*marHaba*
tiSbaH (m.) 'ala khēr (good night); *tiSbaHīn (f.) 'ala khēr*; *tiSbaHūn (pl.) 'ala khēr*	*ajma'īn* (you, too)
ma'a s-salāma (good-bye)	*ma'a s-salāma*

Iraqis tend to prolong their greetings by saying the above phrases more than once and by asking about the health of the person (*shlōn iS-SiHa?*) and of his or her family.

3. PERSONAL PRONOUNS IN IRAQI ARABIC

The subject personal pronouns in Iraqi Arabic are similar to those in MSA, but fewer in number, as dual and feminine plural forms are not used.

Note that the initial *a* sound in all pronouns but *ana* changes to *i*, and that *huwa* and *hiya* double the middle consonants *w* and *y* into *huwwa* and *hiyya*. Also, a single plural *you* pronoun, *intu*, and a single *they* pronoun, *humma*, are used for both masculine and feminine.

PERSONAL PRONOUNS IN IRAQI ARABIC			
Singular		Plural	
I	*āni*	we	*iHna*
you (m.)	*inta*	you (m./f.)	*intu*
you (f.)	*inti*		
he	*huwwa*	she	*humma*
they (m./f.)	*hiyya*		

4. IMPERFECT TENSE IN IRAQI ARABIC

As a general rule, Iraqi Arabic verb forms are simpler and more regular than *fuSHā* verb forms. For example, in the imperfect tense, no distinction is made in Iraqi Arabic between the indicative mood and the subjunctive mood; instead, the indicative forms are used in all contexts. Compare the Iraqi Arabic imperfect forms of the verb *gāl* (to say) with their *fuSHā* equivalents in the following table, where the verbs are used with personal pronouns.

IMPERFECT TENSE OF THE IRAQI ARABIC VERB *gāl* (TO SAY) AND ITS EQUIVALENT IN MSA			
Singular		Plural	
Iraqi Arabic	*fuSHā*	Iraqi Arabic	*fuSHā*
āni agūl	*ana aqūlu*	*iHna ngūl*	*naHnu naqūlu*
inta tgūl	*anta taqūlu*	*intu tgūlūn* (m.)	*antum taqūlūna*
inti tgūlin	*anti taqūlina*	*intu tgūlūn* (f.)	*antunna taqulna*
huwwa ygūl	*huwa yaqūlu*	*humma ygūlūn* (m.)	*hum yaqūlūna*
hiyya tgūl	*hiya taqūlu*	*humma ygūlūn* (f.)	*hunna yaqulna*

Again, the *fuSHā* dual (*antuma taqūlāni*) is not found in Iraqi Arabic, which uses the plural for this purpose.

5. FUTURE TENSE AND MODAL PARTICLES IN IRAQI ARABIC

Imperfect verbs can be coupled with different invariant modal words, such as *rāH* (going to), used to express near future, *yimkin* (may, may be), *lāzim* (must, should), and *mumkin* (maybe, possible, can). These words, in an unchanged form, combine with any imperfect conjugated form to express different modalities of verbal meaning. Below is the particle *rāH* with the conjugated forms of the verb *zzawaj* (to marry).

rāH azzawaj	I am going to get married.
rāH tizzawaj	You (m.) are going to get married.
rāH tizzawjin	You (f.) are going to get married.
rāH yizzawaj	He is going to get married.
rāH tizzawaj	She is going to get married.

rāH nizzawaj	We are going to get married.
rāH tizzawjūn	You (m./f. pl.) are going to get married.
rāH yizzawjūn	They are going to get married (m./f. and du.).

You need, however, to differentiate between *rāH*, the invariant modal particle, and *rāH*, the verb (to go) (*rāHa* in *fuSHā*), a full verb conjugated in section 6, below. So *rāH arūH* means "I'm going to go."

To negate *rāH*, *lāzim*, and *mumkin*, use *ma* or *mā*; to negate *yimkin* (which is more regularly used in the affirmative), use *la* or *lā*.

āni mā mumkin arūH li l-Hafla.
I cannot go to the party.

layla ma lāzim trūH li l-mūSil.
Layla should not go to Mosul.

hummala yimkin yrūHūn li l-madrasa.
They may not go to school.

6. VERB CONJUGATION IN IRAQI ARABIC

The following table shows the conjugation of five Iraqi Arabic verbs, all found in the dialogue of this lesson.

VERB CONJUGATION: THE IMPERFECT IN IRAQI ARABIC					
	'āsh (to live)	rāH (to go)	Habb (to love)	zār (to visit)	wāfaq (to agree)
āni	a'īsh	arūH	aHibb	azūr	awāfiq
inta	t'īsh	trūH	tHibb	tzūr	twāfiq
inti	t'īshīn	trūHīn	tHibbīn	tzūrīn	twāfqīn
huwwa	y'īsh	yrūH	yHibb	yzūr	ywāfiq
hiyya	t'īsh	trūH	tHibb	tzūr	twāfiq
iHna	n'īsh	nrūH	nHibb	nzūr	nwāfiq
intu	t'īshūn	trūHūn (tirHūn)	tHibbūn	tzūrūn	twāfqūn
humma	y'īshūn	yrūHūn (yirHūn)	yHibbūn	yzūrūn	ywāfqūn

The pattern is quite similar to that of *fuSHā*: all forms for the same person start with the same sounds. One difference is that the *fatHā* or *Damma* following the first consonant sound is omitted in Iraqi Arabic, creating consonant clusters at the beginning of the word. Note how the *fuSHā* form *tazūru* (she visits) becomes *tzūr*, *tarūHu* (she goes), *trūH*, and *nuHibbu* (we love), *nHibb*. The same applies to the other verb forms. In Iraqi Arabic, *fuSHā* verb forms are often shortened and pronounced without their final vowels.

D. Vocabulary

tfaDHli.	Please; Please, come in.
shukran	thanks
shukran jazīlan	thanks a lot
shlōn iS-SiHHa?	How are you? (*lit.,* How is the health?)
zēna l-Hamdilla (f.).	Fine, thanks. (*lit.,* Fine, praise to God)
tfaDHli starīHi.	Please, sit down.
mabrūk	congratulations
gālaw	they said
abūch	your father
lāzāl 'āyish	still living
bi l-'uSūr il-wuSTa	in the Middle Ages
kurdi	Kurdish
khāli	my maternal uncle
'ammi	my paternal uncle
zēn (m.)	good
ta'āli! (f.)	Come!
'aSīr purtuqāl	orange juice
'aSīr tuffāH	apple juice
law samaHti	if you please
kullish Hilwa	very nice
wēn rāH t'ishīn?	Where will you live?
ba'd iz-zawāj	after marriage
inshālla	I hope; hopefully (*lit.,* God willing)
azūrich (f.)	visit
hnāk	there

E. Cultural Note

Iraq is a country with many ethnic groups and religious sects. There are the Arabs, who constitute about 75 percent of the population, the Kurds, between 15 and 20 percent, and several other minority groups such as the Turkmens, Armenians, and Assyrians. Of all these groups, most are Muslims, and the rest are mostly Christians of different denominations. The Muslims are divided into Shiites (about 60 percent) and Sunnis (about 40 percent). On an individual and communal level, Arabs and Kurds, Shiites and Sunnis, and other ethnic and religious groups have always been able to interact and intermarry and generally coexist peacefully (even when the political situation helped to enhance the separateness of these groups). However, a small percentage of the population still believe that they should keep to themselves and preserve the "purity" of their origin, thus resisting the crossing of ethnic, religious, and, to a lesser extent, sectarian barriers. However, biases of this kind are gradually wearing out in Iraq.

At the same time, the majority of Muslims in Iraq would still be adamantly opposed to marrying their daughters to Christian men, because in Islam a Muslim woman's marriage to a Christian man is not a valid one. On the other hand, a marital union between a Muslim man and a Christian woman is legal, and, therefore, interreligious marriages of this kind are performed in Iraq.

Although arranged marriages still take place in Iraq, especially in rural areas, a woman can generally choose her future husband. Her parents or guardians, however, must also be approached before the engagement can take place. They normally consent after inquiring about the man's religion, family name, reputation, credentials, and economic standing. If these are satisfactory, parents normally give their approval; if not, a woman may encounter mild or severe opposition, and may need to enlist the help of relatives and/or neighbors, whose role is to intercede on her behalf. Whatever the case, the family's "blessing" gives the marriage its needed "legality."

F. Exercises

1. Put the imperfect verbs in parentheses in the correct form. Then translate the sentences into English.

Example: *Hassan (tHibb) nādya, bas nādya (yHibb) khālid.*
        Hassan yHibb nādya, bas nādya tHibb khālid.
        Hassan loves Nadia, but Nadia loves Khalid.

a. *āni lāzim (nrūH) li l-baSra ba'd iz-zawāj.*
b. *huwwa yimkin (tzūr) baghdād.*
c. *hiyya rāH (t'īshīn) bi l-mūSil.*
d. *abūya mā mumkin (tizzawwaj) wiHda 'arabbiyya.*
e. *layla (yishrab) 'aSīr tuffāH.*

2. Fill in the blanks with the following words.

    zēna / in-nūr / zēn / zēna (or zēn) l-Hamdilla / SabāH in-nūr / il-khēr

a. *lūsi tgūl masā'_____, w- layla tgūl masā' _____.*
b. *shlōnich? _____ l- Hamdilla.*
c. *shlōnak? _____ l-Hamdilla.*
d. *SabāH l-khēr? _____.*
e. *shlōn iS-SiHHa? _____.*

3. Match the words in column A with those in the column B to form correct phrases or sentences.

A
a. *iHna*
b. *lūsi*
c. *inti*
d. *layla w lūsi*

B
rāH yrūH lil-Hafla (to the party)
tzūrīn karīma
jamīla
yshirbūn (drink) 'aSīr

e. *āni*

f. *huwwa*

g. *'aSīr*

h. *Hadīqa*

tHibb dūnald

nwāfiq 'al khuTūba

lāzim azūr zaynab

laymūn (lemon)

4. Say the following sentences in Iraqi Arabic.

a. How are you *(f.)*?

b. I'm going to drink orange juice.

c. Apple juice, please.

d. How are you, Dūnald?

e. She is going to get married.

5. Put the words in the correct order to form coherent sentences.

a. *āni / w- / lūsi / tuffāH / 'aSīr / nishrab*

b. *ywāfiq / abūya / mā / mumkin*

c. *t'īshīn / wēn / rāH / ?*

d. *kurdi / āni*

e. *starīHi / tfaDHli*

Answer Key

1. a. *āni lāzim (arūH) li l-baSra ba'd iz-zawāj.*
      I must go to Basrah after I get married.
   b. *huwwa yimkin (yzūr) baghdād.*
      He may visit Baghdad.
   c. *hiyya rāH (t'īsh) bi l-mūSil.*
      She is going to live in Mosul.
   d. *abūya mā mumkin (yizzawwaj) wiHda 'arabbiyya.*
      My father cannot marry an Arab woman.
   e. *layla (tishrab) 'aSīr tuffāH.*
      Layla drinks apple juice.

2. a. *lūsi tgūl masā' il-khēr, w-layla tgūl masā' in-nūr.*
   b. *shlōnich? zēna l-Hamdilla.*
   c. *shlōnak? zēn l-Hamdilla.*
   d. *SabāH il-khēr? SabāH in-nūr.*
   e. *shlōn iS-SiHHa? zēna (or zēn) l-Hamdilla.*

3. a. *iHna nwāfiq 'al khuTūba.*
   b. *lūsi tHibb dūnald.*
   c. *inti tzūrīn karīma.*
   d. *layla w-lūsi yshirbūn* (drink) *'aSīr.*
   e. *āni lāzim azūr zaynab.*
   f. *huwwa rāH yrūH li l-Hafla* (to the party).
   g. *'aSīr laymūn.*
   h. *Hadīqa jamīla.*

4. a. *shlōnich?*
   b. *āni rāH ashrab 'aSīr purtuqāl.*
   c. *'aSīr tuffāH, law samaHti.*
   d. *shlōnak dūnald?*
   e. *hiyya rāH tizzawwaj.*

5. a. *āni w-lūsi nishrab 'aSīr tuffāH.*
   b. *mā mumkin abūya ywāfiq.*
   c. *wēn rāH t'īshīn?*
   d. *āni kurdi.*
   e. *tfaDHli starīHi.*

LESSON 22
(Iraqi Arabic)

li s-sīnama To the Movies

A. Dialogue

Nadia wants Lamis to go with her to the movies, but Lamis can only go to the afternoon show, as she has other arrangements in the evening. What kind of film will they see? Will they be going by bus or by taxi? Or should they ask Lucy to take them in her car?

nādya: ta'āli nrūH li s-sīnama yōm il-khamīs ij-jāy.

lamīs: khosh fikra! bas yā dōr nrūH?

nādya: dōr is-sā'a sab'a, lēsh?

lamīs: āni mā agdar arūH wiyyāch, li'an lāzim ashūf Sadīqti fātin sā'a sitta.

nādya: ma-yhim, nrūH dōr il-'aSir, aw nrūH yōm ij-jum'a.

lamīs: shinu rāH nshūf? filim 'arabi lō filim ajnabi?

nādya: hassa māku filim 'arabi zēn, bas aku filim hindi kullish Hilu.

lamīs: idhan nshūf il-film il-Hindi. bas shlōn nrūH li s-sīnama?

nādya: nākhudh taksi aw nrūH bi l-bāS.

lamīs: lēsh idha ma-nshūf lūsi tigdar tākhkudhna b sayyāratha?

nādya: āni rāH akhābirha bāchir.

lamīs: aHsan fikra! bēsh is-sā'a niTla' mn il-bēt?

nādya: niTla' sā'a thintēn w-rubu' aw thintēn w-nuS.

lamīs: kullish zēn! l-filim yibdi tlātha w-rubu' w-yintihi khamsa w-thilith. Bas minu yrāfiqna li s-sīnama?

nādya: 'ummi rāH tiji wiyyāna.

lamīs: 'aDHīm! ttifaqna?

nādya: ttifaqna. ashūfich bāchir.

lamīs: ·inshālla.

Nadia: Let's go to the movies this Thursday.

Lamis: A good idea! But which show should we go to?

Nadia: The seven o'clock show; why?

Lamis: I can't go with you, because I have to see my friend Fatin at six.

Nadia: No problem; we can go to the afternoon show, or go on Friday.

Lamis: What are we going to see, an Arabic or a foreign film?

Nadia: Right now there is no good Arabic film showing, but there's a very good Indian film.

Lamis: Let's see the Indian film, then. But how are we going to go to the movies?

Nadia: We will take a taxi or go by bus.

Lamis: Why don't we see if Lucy could take us in her car?

Nadia: I will call her tomorrow.

Lamis: Great! (*lit.*, the best idea) What time shall we leave (the house)?

Nadia: We'll leave at 2:15 or 2:30.

Lamis: Very good! The movie starts at 3:15 and ends at 5:20. But who will accompany us to the movies?

Nadia: My mother will come with us.

Lamis: Great! Agreed? *(lit., Did we agree?)*

Nadia: Agreed. I'll see you tomorrow.

Lamis: Okay! *(lit., God willing!)*

B. Pronunciation

The negative particle *mā*, used in *fuSHā* to negate verbs and other words, is often pronounced as *ma*, with a shorter vowel, in Iraqi Arabic. Exceptions are reserved for contexts where the particle is followed by an imperfect verb in the *I* form, as in *āni mā agdar arūH wiyyāch* (I can't go with you). *mā* is also used before the possession-denoting prepositions *'ind* and *I*, as in *mā'indi* and *māli* (I don't have). *māli* (I don't have), which should not be confused with the possessive *māli* (mine) discussed below, is used in idiomatic contexts, as in *māli khulug* (I don't feel well) or *māli shughul* (I have no business; i.e., doing something or being somewhere). Unlike *mā*, *ma* is generally merged with the word it negates, as in Nadia's *ma-yhim* (It doesn't matter) and Lamis's *ma-nshūf* above.

> *āni ma-riHit.*
> I didn't go.

> *mā 'indi sayyāra.*
> I don't have a car.

> *l-filim ma-Hilu.*
> The film is not good.

Note that in the last sentence, *ma* is followed by an adjective, something that *fuSHā* does not permit.

C. Grammar and Usage

1. THE DEFINITE ARTICLE IN IRAQI ARABIC

The definite article in Iraqi Arabic has two distinct forms: *il* and *I*. *il* is used when the previous word ends in a consonant, and *I* is used when it ends in a vowel or when the article starts the phrase or the sentence.

> *yōm il-khamīs*
> Thursday

> *dōr il-'aSir*
> the afternoon show

> *nshūf il-filim il-hindi.*
> We'll see the Indian film.

mn il-bēt
from the house

nrūH bi l-bāS.
We'll take the bus (*lit.,* We go by bus).

l-filim yibdi tlātha w-rubu'.
The film starts at 3:15 (*lit.,* at three and a quarter).

When the definite article precedes a "sun" consonant, it takes the sound of that consonant, as it does in MSA.

li s̲-s̲īnama
to the cinema

bēsh is̲-s̲ā'a?
What time is it?

In Iraqi Arabic, however, the consonant *j* is treated as a "sun" letter, too.

yōm il-khamīs ij̲-j̲āy
the coming Thursday

yōm ij̲-jum'a
Friday

Remember that when a noun with the definite article is modified by an adjective, the adjective, too, is preceded by a definite article, as in *il-film il-Hindi* (the Indian film).

2. QUESTION WORDS IN IRAQI ARABIC

Iraqi Arabic has a number of question words, which are quite different from those in MSA. The most common among these are *minu* (who?), *shinu* (what?), *shaku* (what's up?), *yemta* (when?), *wēn* (where?), *shlōn* (how?), *bēsh* (how much?), *lēsh* (why?), *yā* (which?), and *mnēn* (where from?). They all have a fixed form and are used with all genders and numbers.

minu (who?) is the equivalent of the MSA *man* (who?).

minu yrāfiqna?
Who is going to accompany us?

minu baTal il-filim?
Who is the main actor (*lit.,* hero) of the film?

Note that the MSA *man huwa?* (Who is he?), *man hiya?* (Who is she?), and *man hum?* (Who are they?) have Iraqi Arabic equivalents in *minhuwwa?*, *minhiyya?*, and *minhumma?* In Iraqi Arabic, however, the two words are (or seem to be) merged into one.

shinu (what?) is the equivalent of the MSA *mādha*.

> *shinu rāH nshūf?*
> What are we going to see?

> *shinu yrīd?*
> What does he want?

shaku? (What's up?/What's happening?) is the equivalent of the MSA *mādha HaSal?* or *mādha yaHSil? shaku* is sometimes coupled with the word *māku—shaku māku?—*to convey the same meaning.

Like the MSA *mata*, *yemta* (when?) is used to inquire about when something is, was, or will be done.

> *yemta nākul?*
> When shall we eat?

> *yemta akaltu?*
> When did you eat?

wēn (where?) is used, like the MSA *ayna*, to inquire about where something is found or taking place.

> *wēn il-maT'am?*
> Where is the restaurant?

> *wēn riHtu?*
> Where did you go?

In the previous lesson, you learned how to use *shlōn* in greetings, as in *shlōn iS-SiHa?* (How are you?). *shlōn* (how?), the equivalent of the MSA *kayfa*, is also used to ask about how things are, were, or will be done.

> *shlōn nrūH li s-sinama?*
> How do we go to the cinema?

> *shlōn sawwētī?*
> How did you *(f. sg.)* do it *(m.)*?

bēsh (how much?) precedes both nouns and verbs, functioning as the equivalent of the MSA *bikam*, as in:

> *bēsh il-baTTikh?*
> How much are the melons?

> *bēsh ishtirēti l-badla?*
> How much did you *(f. sg.)* pay for the dress?

Used with different structures (such as nouns, verbs, and participles) or on its own, *lēsh* (why?) is the equivalent of the MSA *limādha*.

lēsh nākul bi l-bēt?
Why do we eat at home?

In this lesson's dialogue, *lēsh* is used at the end of the sentence.

dōr is-sā'a sab'a, lēsh?
The seven o'clock show; why?

Followed by nouns only, *yā* (which?) is the equivalent of the MSA *ayyu* or *ayya*, as in:

yā dōr rāH trūHūn?
Which showing will you be going to?

Note that Iraqi Arabic also uses the word *ay* to express the same meaning.

ay filim nshūf?
Which film shall we see?

ay maT'am nrūH?
Which restaurant shall we go to?

mnēn-mmēn (where from?) is a short form of *min wēn* (from where), which is also used, but less frequently, in Iraqi Arabic.

mnēn jibti t-tuffāH?
Where did you *(f. sg.)* get the apples from?

mnēn inta/inti/intu?
Where are you *(m./f./pl.)* from?

Note that in more formal contexts (and also to sound more courteous), Iraqis say *min ay balad jāy* (m. sg.)/*jāyya* (f. sg.)/*jāyyin* (pl.)? (*lit.*, Which country or town do you come from?)

Finally, yes-no questions in Iraqi Arabic, as in *fuSHā*, are asked by simply using a rising intonation at the end of the sentence. No other changes are necessary.

nākhudh taksi?
Do we/shall we take a taxi?

akaltu?
Did you *(pl.)* eat?

trūHūn lō ma-trūHūn?
Do you *(pl.)* want to go or not?

'indak waqit?
Do you *(m.)* have time?

3. TELLING TIME IN IRAQI ARABIC

To ask the time, say:

> *bēsh is-sā'a?*
> or *is-sā'a bēsh?*
> What time is it?

To tell the time, start with the hour and then add or deduct the minutes and/or the seconds. For instance, Iraqis say *sitta w-khamsa* (five minutes after six) and *sitta illa 'ashra* (ten minutes to six), phrases which literally mean "six and five" and "six minus ten," respectively. Let's go around the clock to learn the basics about telling the time in Iraqi Arabic.

s-sā'a wiHda (or *bi l-wiHda*)	one o'clock
s-sā'a wiHda w-khamsa	five minutes after one (*lit.*, one and five)
s-sā'a wiHda w-'ashra	ten minutes after one
s-sā'a wiHda w-rubu'	one fifteen (*lit.*, one and a quarter)
s-sā'a wiHda w-thilith	one twenty (*lit.*, one and a third)
s-sā'a wiHda w-nuS illa khamsa	one twenty-five (*lit.*, one and a half minus five)
s-sā'a wiHda w-nuS	one thirty (*lit.*, one and a half)
s-sā'a wiHda w-nuS w-khamsa	one thirty-five (*lit.*, one and a half and five)
s-sā'a thintēn illa thilith	one forty (*lit.*, two minus one third)
s-sā'a thintēn illa rubu'	quarter to two (*lit.*, two minus a quarter)
s-sā'a thintēn illa 'ashra	ten to two
s-sā'a thintēn illa khamsa	five to two
s-sā'a thintēn	two o'clock
s-sā'a tlātha	three o'clock
s-sā'a arba'a	four o'clock

Note that the hours are equivalent to the Iraqi Arabic cardinal numbers (e.g., one, two, ...), unlike MSA, which uses ordinal numbers (e.g., first, second, ...). The feminine forms *wiHda* (one) and *thintēn* (two) are used instead of *wāHid* and *thnēn*.

Here are the Iraqi Arabic numbers from 5 to 12.

> *khamsa* (five)
> *sitta* (six)
> *sab'a* (seven)
> *thmānya* (eight)
> *tis'a* (nine)
> *'ashra* (ten)
> *(H)da'ash* (eleven)
> *thna'ash* (twelve)

Like MSA, Iraqi Arabic also uses smaller divisions of time, such as *daqīqa* (minute) and *thāniya* (second) to specify the exact time.

wiHda w-daqīqa (one minute after one)

wiHda w-daqīqtēn (two minutes after one)

wiHda w-tlath daqāyiq w-thāniya (three minutes and one second after one)

wiHda w-arba' daqāyiq w-tlath thawāni (four minutes and three seconds after one)

Although telling the time in Iraqi Arabic is based on the same method used in MSA, Iraqis drop the definite article from the words expressing time, reserving it sometimes for the initial word, *sā'a*, only: *sā'a sab'a* or *is-sā'a sab'a* and *sā'a khamsa w-rubu'* are the equivalents of the MSA <u>as</u>-sā'a <u>s</u>-sābi'a and <u>as</u>-sā'a <u>l</u>-khāmisa wa-<u>r</u>-rub'.

4. SAYING "YES" OR "NO" IN IRAQI ARABIC

A. *na'am, bali*, AND *ī*: YES

In conversation, these words are used as short answers or as a part of longer ones. Although they are used interchangeably, *na'am* is the most formal term, *bali* is less formal, and *ī* is very colloquial:

riHtu li s-sīnama?
Did you go to the movies?

na'am/bali/ī.
Yes.
or
na'am/bali/ī, riHna.
Yes, we went.

B. *lā*: NO

Like *na'am*, *lā* is used as a short answer or as a part of a longer one.

riHti li l-maT'am?
Did you go to the restaurant?

lā./lā, ma-riHit.
No./No, I didn't go.

One needs, however, to differentiate between *lā* (no) and *la* (don't). *la* is the equivalent of the MSA *lā*, which, in combination with an imperfect tense verb, forms a negative request or a command, as in the following sentences:

<u>la</u> tākhudh taksi!
Don't take a taxi!

<u>la</u> trūH bi l-bāS!
Don't go by bus!

5. POSSESSIVE SUFFIXES AND POSSESSIVE EXPRESSIONS IN IRAQI ARABIC

Iraqi Arabic possessive endings approximate those found in MSA.

POSSESSIVE ENDINGS IN IRAQI ARABIC			
Singular		Plural	
my	-i	our	-na
your (m.)	-ak	your (m./f.)	-kum
your (f.)	-ich		
his	-a	her	-ha
their (m./f.)	-hum		

The -i (my) form and all of the plural forms are the same as those found in MSA, as in *Sadīqti* (my friend), *Sadīqatkum* (your friend), or *Sadīqathum* (their friend).

For the other forms, the difference may or may not be slight: Compare *Sadīqtak* to the MSA *Sadīqatuka*, *Sadīqtich* to *Sadīqatuki*, *Sadīqta* to *Sadīqatuhu*, and *Sadiqatha* to *Sadīqatuhā*.

The words *māl* (lit., property) and *'ind* (with) are also used to express possession: The possessive endings are attached to these words rather than to the possessed noun itself. In the structure *l-filim māli* (my film), for instance, the word *filim* (film) remains the same, while the word *māl*, which follows it, undergoes the changes in person and number: *māli*, *mālak*, *mālich*, *māla*, *mālha*, *mālna*, *mālkum*, *mālhum*. Coupled with a feminine noun, such as *sā'a* (watch), the word *māl* becomes *mālt* or *mālat*: *s-sā'a mālti*, *māltak*, *māltich*, *mālta*, *mālat-ha*, *mālatna*, *mālatkum*, *mālat-hum*.

'ind, on the other hand, precedes the item being possessed, as in *'indi/'indak/'indich /'inda/'indha/'idna/'idkum sayyāra* (I/you, m./you, f./he/she/we/they have/has a car). Note that the *n* sound in *'idha, 'idna,* and *'idkum* is omitted to avoid a three-consonant cluster.

6. OBJECT PRONOUN SUFFIXES IN IRAQI ARABIC

An object pronoun replaces a noun that functions as the grammatical object of a sentence. Like those in *fuSHā*, Iraqi Arabic object pronouns take the form of suffixes attached to verbs. The attached pronoun may vary slightly according to the ending of the verb to which it is attached. The following table shows the verb *nTa* (to give) with object pronouns attached to its imperfect form.

nTa (TO GIVE) WITH OBJECT PRONOUN SUFFIXES IN IRAQI ARABIC		
	Singular	Plural
huwwa	*yinTini* (he gives me)	*yinTina* (he gives us)
	yinTik (he gives you, m.)	*yinTikum* (he gives you, f./m.)
	yinTich (he gives you, f.)	
	yinTi (he gives him/it)	*yinTihum* (he gives them)
	yinTiha (he gives her/it)	

Note that the final vowel in the imperfect verb *yinTi* (he gives) is lengthened when the object pronoun is attached to it. Compare:

> *huwwa rāH yinTi lūsi sā'a.*
> He'll give Lucy a watch.

with

> *huwwa rāH yinTīha sā'a.*
> He'll give her a watch.

Some of these pronouns, however, have slightly different forms when attached to a verb that ends with a consonant, such as the verb *shāf* (to see).

THE VERB *shāf* (TO SEE) WITH SUBJECT PRONOUN SUFFIXES		
	Singular	Plural
huwwa	*yshūfni* (he sees <u>me</u>)	*yshūfna* (he sees <u>us</u>)
	yshūfak (he sees <u>you</u>, m.)	*yshūfkum* (he sees <u>you</u>, f./m.)
	yshūfich (he sees <u>you</u>, f.)	
	yshūfa (he sees <u>him</u>/<u>it</u>)	*yshūfhum* (<u>he</u> sees <u>them</u>)
	yshūfha (he sees <u>her</u>/<u>it</u>)	

As you can see, the differences occur when the *you* and *him* suffixes are attached to the verbs.

7. PERFECT TENSE IN IRAQI ARABIC

Iraqi Arabic has a perfect tense form that is very similar to the MSA form. When conjugated, however, the Iraqi Arabic perfect verb, like the imperfect verb, has fewer forms. The difference in pronunciation can be easily noted in the chart below, which presents the verb *shirab* (to drink) in combination with personal pronouns.

PERFECT TENSE OF THE IRAQI ARABIC VERB *shirab* (TO DRINK) AND ITS EQUIVALENT IN MSA			
Singular		Plural	
Iraqi Arabic	*fuSHā*	Iraqi Arabic	*fuSHā*
āni shirabit	*ana sharibtu*	*iHna shirabna*	*naHnu sharibna*
inta shirabit	*anta sharibta*	*intu shirabtu* (m.)	*antum sharibtum*
inti shirabti	*anti sharibti*	*intu shirabtu* (f.)	*antunna sharibtunna*
huwwa shirab	*huwa shariba*	*humma shirbaw* (m.)	*hum sharibu*
hiyya shirbat	*hiya sharibat*	*humma shirbaw* (f.)	*hunna sharibna*

Apart from dispensing with the final *fatHa* and *damma* (compare *shirabit* to the MSA *sharibtu*), Iraqi Arabic verbs change the initial and sometimes the middle vowels of perfect verbs that are not hamzated (starting with $\mathbf{\hat{I}}$, as in *akala* [he ate], or hollowed, like *shāf* [he saw]). A verb like *Sana'a* (he made) becomes *Sina'*, with the first *fatHa* changing into *kasrah*. Furthermore, Iraqi Arabic does not always accommodate consonant clusters, especially at the ends of words. For instance, the MSA verb *nimtu* (I slept) is pronounced *nimit* in Iraqi Arabic, a pattern that repeats itself in most verbs of the same category: the MSA *qumtu*, *waqaftu*, and *Halimtu* have *gimit*, *wigafit*, and *Hilamit* (got up, stood up, and dreamed) as their equivalents.

8. VERB CONJUGATION IN IRAQI ARABIC

The table below shows the conjugation of five Iraqi Arabic verbs in the perfect tense.

VERB CONJUGATION: THE PERFECT TENSE IN IRAQI ARABIC					
	rāH (to go)	*shāf* (to see)	*akhadh* (to take)	*rād* (to want)	*Tila'* (to go out)
āni	*riHit*	*shifit*	*akhadhit*	*ridit*	*Tila'it (or Tla'it)*
inta	*riHit*	*shifit*	*akhadhit*	*ridit*	*Tila'it (or Tla'it)*
inti	*riHti*	*shifti*	*akhadhti*	*ridti*	*Tila'ti*
huwwa	*rāH*	*shāf*	*akhadh*	*rād*	*Tila'*
hiyya	*rāHat*	*shāfat*	*akhdhat*	*rādat*	*Til'at*
iHna	*riHna*	*shifna*	*akhadhna*	*ridna*	*Tila'na*
intu	*riHtu*	*shiftu*	*akhadhtu*	*ridtu*	*Tila'tu*
humma	*rāHaw*	*shāfaw*	*akhdhaw*	*rādaw*	*Til'aw*

Some of the marked differences between Iraqi Arabic and MSA can be seen in the *you* plural forms of the verbs *rāH* (to go) and *akhadh* (to take), *riHtu* and *akhadhtu*, where the final *m* found in the MSA, *ruHtum* and *akhadhtum,* is dropped. Compare also the *-aw* ending of the *they* verb form, as in *rāHaw* and *Til'aw*, with its MSA equivalent in *rāHū* and *Tala'ū*.

D. Vocabulary

yōm	day
yōm il-khamīs	Thursday
khōsh fikra	a good idea
yā dōr rāyHīn?	To which showing are you going?
dōr is-sā'a sab'a	the seven o'clock show (*lit.*, session)
lēsh?	Why?
mā agdar arūH	I can't go
wiyyāch (f. sg.)	with you
li'an	because
lāzim ashūf	I must see
Sadīqti (f.)	my friend
ma-yhim	no problem (*lit.*, it doesn't matter)
dōr il-'aSir	the afternoon show
kullish Hilu	very good (*lit.*, sweet)
hassa	now

māku	there isn't
ajnabi	foreign
l-film il-hindi	the Indian film
nrūH bi l-bāS	we'll take the bus
idha	if
tākhudhna	she takes us
b-sayyāratha	in her car
akhābirha	I call her
bāchir	tomorrow
mn il-bēt	from here (*lit.*, from the house)
yibdi	it starts
yintihi	it ends
minu yrāfiqna?	Who will accompany us?
'ummi	my mother
'aDHīm	great
ttifaqna?	Agreed? (*lit.*, Did we agree?)
ashūfich. (f. sg.)	I'll see you.

E. Cultural Note

The official workweek in Iraq, as in most of the Arab world, includes six days, from Saturday through Thursday. Friday, the Muslim holy day, is the weekend break during which people catch up on their household duties, visit each other, or entertain themselves and their families by having a picnic, walking along the river, eating at a restaurant, or going to the movies. War conditions have undoubtedly affected these activities. Not many people like to wander out in the streets, especially after dark, and few can afford eating out nowadays. However, Iraqi restaurants still prepare their inimitable dishes: *tikkah* (grilled meat or liver pieces) and *kebab* (grilled minced meat) are sold at hundreds of small stands in Iraqi cities. The movies, too, are still drawing varied customers, who insist on going to see their favorite films.

Egyptian films are popular in Iraq; so are Indian ones, whose sentimental plots and singing and dancing Iraqis find very appealing. "Foreign" movies, including any film (other than Indian) with Arabic subtitles, also have their fans; action-filled American and British movies are especially attractive to young Iraqi males. For many young Iraqi women, however, going to see a film may not be an easy thing. Parents often decide what their daughters can or cannot watch; they may also insist on having their daughters accompanied by a brother or an older female relative.

When going out, Iraqis depend heavily on buses and taxis, both being relatively inexpensive forms of transportation. Although there are many bridges built on main rivers (such as the Tigris, the Euphrates, and Shat Al-Arab), people still use ferries and small boats to move from one side to the other. The destruction of many bridges during war times has somewhat increased the popularity of river transportation.

312

F. Exercises

1. Fill in the blanks in the sentences below with the following perfect verbs.

shifit / akhadhti / rādat / shirabtu / riHna / Til'aw

a. *inti* _____ *taksi.*

b. *intu* _____ *may* (water).

c. *āni* _____ *filim 'irāqi.*

d. *iHna* _____ *li s-sīnama.*

e. *lūsi* _____ *qalam* (pen).

f. *nādya w-lamīs* _____ *qabil sā'a.*

2. Answer the following questions with the appropriate time of day for the following activities.

a. *yemta tug'ud/tgu'dīn* (wake up) *min in-nōm?*

b. *yemta tiTla'/TTil'īn lish-shughul* (work) *aw li l-madrasa* (school)?

c. *bēsh is-sā'a titghadda/titghaddīn* (take your lunch)?

d. *bēsh is-sā'a tirja'/trij'īn* (return) *lil-bēt?*

e. *bēsh is-sā'a tnām/tnāmīn?*

3. Choose the correct question word to form a question.

a. *(yā; shinu) badla rāH tishtirīn?*

b. *(lēsh; shaku) ma-trūH li l-matHaf?*

c. *(minu; bēsh) yrīd akil* (food)?

d. *(yemta; minu) tzūrūn lūsi?*

e. *(shinu; wēn) rāyiH?*

f. *(mnēn; shinu) jibti l-'aSīr* (juice)?

4. Match the questions in column A with the correct answers in column B.

A	B
a. *minu yiji wiyyāna?*	*ī, arūH wiyyākum.*
b. *bēsh is-sā'a tiji l-bētna?*	*bētna lōna aHmar.*
c. *trūH wiyyāna li l-madrasa?*	*'ukhti* (my sister) *tiji wiyyāna.*
d. *s-sā'a bi t-tis'a lo bi l'ashra?*	*aji bi l-arba'a.*
e. *aku maT'am* (restaurant) *amrīki?*	*lā, māku maT'am amrīki.*
f. *shifit layla lo ma-shifit ha?*	*is-sā'a bi l-'ashra.*
g. *shlōn lōn* (color) *bētkum?*	*shifit-ha.*

5. Say the following in Iraqi Arabic.

a. Where did you *(m. sg.)* go?

b. Did Lucy see the Indian film?

c. You *(f. sg.)* wanted to go by car.

d. When did you *(pl.)* leave the house?

e. Why did you *(f. sg.)* take the pen?

Answer Key

1. a. *inti akhadhti taksi.*

   b. *intu shirabtu may.*

   c. *āni shifit filim 'irāqi.*

   d. *iHna riHna li s-sīnama.*

   e. *lūsi rādat qalam.*

   f. *nādya w-lamīs Til'aw qabil sā'a.*

2. Answers will vary, but here are some possibilities:

   a. *s-sā'a thmānya.*

   b. *s-sā'a tis'a illa rubu'.*

   c. *s-sā'a thna'ash.*

   d. *s-sā'a khamsa w-nuS.*

   e. *s-sā'a 'ashra ('ashra w-nuS or Hda'ash or thna'ash illa rubu').*

3. a. *yā badla rāH tishtirīn?*

   b. *lēsh ma trūH li l-matHaf?*

   c. *minu yrīd akil?*

   d. *yemta tzūrūn lūsi.*

   e. *wēn rāyiH?*

   f. *mnēn jibti l-'aSir?*

4. a. *minu yiji wiyyāna? 'ukhti tiji wiyyāna.*

   b. *bēsh is-sā'a tiji l-bētna? aji bi l-arba'a.*

   c. *trūH wiyyāna li l-madrasa? ī, arūH wiyyākum.*

   d. *s-sā'a bi t-tis'a lo bi l'ashra? s-sā'a bi l-'ashra.*

   e. *aku maT'am amriki? lā, māku maT'am amrīki.*

   f. *shifit layla lo ma-shifit ha? shifit ha.*

   g. *shlōn lōn (color) bētkum? bētna lōna aHmar.*

5. a. *wēn riHit?*

   b. *shāfat lūsi l-film il-hindi?*

   c. *inti ridti trūHīn bi s-sayyāra.*

   d. *yemta Tila'tu?*

   e. *lēsh akhadhti l-qalam?*

LESSON 23

sh-rāH tishtirīn? What Are You Going to Buy?

A. Dialogue

Fatima and Lucy go shopping. They like the sūg, but have to bargain in a marketplace where the prices of food and other goods have been on the rise.

fāTma: hādha s-sūg isma l-kaDHmiyya, jiddan qadīm.

lūsi: allah! āni aHibb il-aswāq il-qadīma. ma-shift ha-s-sūg min qabil.

fāTma: shūfi l-fākiha shgad Hilwa!

lūsi: ī, wi-l-khuDHra ayDHan!

fāTma: sh-rāH tishtirīn? hnāna ybi'ūn malābis nisā'yya w-rijālliyya, w-kulshi.

lūsi: SaHīH? āni miHtāja qamīS wi-blūza, w-Hidhā', w-janTa w-malābis dākhiliyya. ha-l-isbū' rāH asāfir il-bayrūt.

fāTma: awwal nishtiri fākiha w-khuDHra w-ba'dēn nishtiri l-ashyā' il-'ukhrah.

lūsi: ta'āli nishtiri min hādha l-bayyā'.

fāTma: bēsh iT-Tamāta?

bayyā': l-kīlū b-khamsīn dīnār.

fāTma: kullish ghālya! tbī'ha b-khamsa wi-tlāthīn?

bayyā': lā-walla ma-ySīr.

fāTma: b-arba'īn?

bayyā': yalla ikhdhu. shgad tirdūn?

fāTma: kīlu w-nuS.

lūsi: qabil sana chānat iT-TamāTa rikhīSa.

fāTma: hal-ayyām kulshi ghāli. sh-tishtirīn ba'ad?

lūsi: arīd min hādha t-tuffāH w-dhāka l-'inab.

fāTma: w-āni rāH ashtiri hāy il-baTTikha.

lūsi: ybi'ūn laHam hnāna?

fāTma: bali, min dhāka l-gaSSāb, hnāka.

lūsi: w-arīd ayDHan buSal w-khas wi-khyār w-Halib w-miliH.

fāTma: nishtiri qisim minhum min dhich il-mara, khuDHrat-ha zēna.

lūsi: shūfi hadhōla l-awlād! ybi'ūn 'ilich w-Habb w-fistiq. tijīn nishtiri?

fāTma: yella, lēsh lā!

Fatima: This market is called Al-KaDHimiyya. Very old.

Lucy: I love old shopping places. I haven't seen this one before.

Fatima: See how good the fruits are?

Lucy: And the vegetables, too!

Fatima: What are you going to buy? Here they (also) sell women's and men's clothes and everything.

Lucy: Really? I need a shirt, a blouse, a pair of shoes, a bag, and (some) underwear. This week I am traveling to Beirut.

Fatima: Let's first buy the fruits and vegetables and then (we can) buy the other things.

Lucy: Let's buy from this vendor.

Fatima: How much are the tomatoes?

Vendor: Fifty dinars a kilos.

Fatima: Very expensive! Can you sell it for thirty-five?

Vendor: No (by God), it's not possible.

Fatima: For forty?

Vendor: You can take it (for this price). How much do you want?

Fatima: One and a half kilos.

Lucy: A year ago the tomatoes were cheap.

Fatima: These days everything is expensive. What else do you want?

Lucy: I want some of these apples and those grapes.

Fatima: And I will buy this melon.

Lucy: Do they sell meat here?

Fatima: Yes, see that butcher there?

Lucy: And I also want onions, lettuce, cucumbers, milk, and salt.

Fatima: We'll buy some of them from that woman. Her vegetables are fresh.

Lucy: See these boys? They're selling gum, (pumpkin) seeds, and pistachio (nuts). Shall we have some?

Fatima: Let's, why not!

B. Pronunciation

CONSONANT CLUSTERS IN IRAQI ARABIC

Consonant clusters mostly occur at the beginning and in the middle of an Iraqi Arabic word, often following patterns that contrast with those found in MSA. Namely, Iraqi Arabic tends to use consonant clusters where MSA separates them with a vowel, and vice-versa. Compare the following Iraqi Arabic words, all containing initial clusters, with their equivalents in MSA.

IA	*hnāna* (here)	*hnāka* (there)	*khyār* (cucumbers)	*trīd* (she wants)	*ybī'* (he sells)	*ySīr* (it's possible)	*ygūl* (he said)
MSA	*huna*	*hunāka*	*khiyār*	*turīd*	*yabī'*	*yaSīr*	*yaqūl*

However, Iraqi Arabic is also known for adding a vowel where there is a consonant cluster in *fuSHā*, especially at the end of a word. In the previous lesson you saw this in the perfect tense of hollow verbs, such as *nimit* (I slept), *riHit* (I went), and *shifit* (I saw), verbs whose *fuSHā* equivalents have a consonant cluster at the end. The table below contains other Iraqi words, all taken from this lesson's dialogue.

IA	qabil (before)	laHam (meat)	'ilich (chewing gum)	miliH (salt)	qisim (a part)	ba'ad (after)
MSA	qabl	laHm	'ilk	milH	qism	ba'd

Relevantly, too, the short vowels found in the MSA prepositions *li* (to, for) and *bi* (for, in) are generally dropped from their Iraqi Arabic equivalents:

IA	l-bayrūt (to Beirut)	l-lūsi (for Lucy)	b-sittīn dīnār (for sixty dinars)	b-khamsa w arba'īn (for forty-five)	b-baghdād (in Baghdad)
MSA	li bayrūt	li lūsi	bi sittīn	bi khamsatin wa arba'īn	bi baghdād

When the above prepositions are followed by a word starting with the definite article, the form produced has the same pronunciation as the MSA form.

> *layla bi l-madrasa.*
> Layla is in school.

> *layla rāHat li l-madrasa.*
> Layla went to school.

> *lūsi bi l-mūSil.*
> Lucy is in Mosul.

Similarly, clustering is occasioned when the Iraqi Arabic coordinating conjunction *w* (and) is followed by a word not introduced by the definite article.

> *hnāna ybī'ūn malābis nisā'yya w-rijālliyya, w-kulshi.*
> Here they sell women's and men's clothes and everything.

However, the clustering disappears when *w* is followed by a word made definite by *il* or *l*.

> *wi l-khuDHra ayDHan!*
> And the vegetables, too!

> *wi t-tuffāH bēsh?*
> And how much are the apples?

In the last example, note that the definite article mirrors the "sun" consonant that follows it.

C. Grammar and Usage

1. DEMONSTRATIVES IN IRAQI ARABIC

Like MSA, Iraqi Arabic has demonstrative words expressing nearness and distance, used either alone or with a noun.

317

Two of these forms, *hādha* and *dhāka*, are identical to their counterparts in MSA, and *hādhi* is similar to *hādhihi*; the rest, however, are quite different, and for beginning learners of Iraqi Arabic, it is sufficient to remember the first of each set of variations.

DEMONSTRATIVES IN IRAQI ARABIC				
	Masculine		Feminine	
Singular	*hādha* (this)	*hadhāka/dhāka* (that)	*hādhi/hāya* (this)	*hadhicha/ dhicha* (that)
Plural	*hadhōla/dhōla* (these)	*dhakōla/hadhōlāk* or *dhōlāk* (those)	*hadhōla/dhōla/ hadhanni* (these)	*dhakōla/dhōlāk/ hadhōlāk* (those)

Iraqi Arabic also has the demonstrative *ha*, always used with a noun, which can be used in place of any demonstrative expressing nearness. In the dialogue, Lucy says: <u>*ha*</u>*-l-isbū' rāH asāfir il-bayrūt* (This week, I'll be traveling to Beirut) and *ma-shifit <u>ha</u>-s-sūg min qabil* (I haven't seen this market before). *ha* can be prefixed to nouns of all genders and numbers.

2. *hnāna/hnā* AND *hnāka/hnāk* (HERE AND THERE)

hnāna/hnā (here) and *hnāka/hnāk* (there), like their counterparts in *fuSHā*, *huna* (here) and *hunāk* (there), are used to indicate the nearness or distance of things. Note the consonant clusters in the Iraqi Arabic expressions and the addition of *na* to *hnā*, especially in the Baghdadi dialect.

> *sh-rāH ySīr hnāna?*
> What's going to happen here?

> *ta'āli hnāna!*
> Come here!

> *nrūH hnāka?*
> Shall we go there?

> *āni mā-rūH hnāka.*
> I don't go there.

3. THE VERB *chān* (TO BE) IN IRAQI ARABIC

chān is the equivalent of the MSA *kān* (to be).

> *chān il Halīb Ghāli.*
> Milk was expensive.

> *chānat iT-TamāTa rikhīSa.*
> The tomatoes were cheap.

When *chān* is used with a verb in the imperfect tense, it expresses a progressive action in the past.

> *chānat tissawwag.*
> She was shopping.

> *chān yishtighil.*
> He was working.

The conjugation of *chān* is in the table below.

THE VERB *chān* (TO BE) IN THE PERFECT TENSE AND THE IMPERFECT TENSE		
	Perfect	Imperfect
āni	chinit	akūn
inta	chinit	tkūn
inti	chinti	tkūnīn
huwwa	chān	ykūn
hiyya	chānat	tkūn
iHna	chinna	nkūn
intu	chintu	tkūnūn
humma	chānaw	ykūnūn

4. VERB CONJUGATION IN IRAQI ARABIC

Three new verbs from this lesson's dialogue are conjugated in the perfect tense and the imperfect tense below.

THE PERFECT TENSE OF THE VERBS *shtira* (TO BUY), *bā‘* (TO SELL), AND *sāfar* (TO TRAVEL)		
	shtira (to buy)	*bā‘* (to sell)	*sāfar* (to travel)
āni	shtirēt	bi'it	sāfarit
inta	shtirēt	bi'it	sāfarit
inti	shtirēti	bi'ti	sāfarti
hiyya	shtirat	bā‘at	sāfrat
huwwa	shtira	bā‘	sāfar
iHna	shtirēna	bi'na	sāfarna
intu	shtirētu	bi'tu	sāfartu
humma	shtiraw	bā‘aw	sāfraw

THE IMPERFECT TENSE OF THE VERBS *shtira* (TO BUY), *bā'* (TO SELL), AND *sāfar* (TO TRAVEL)			
	shtira (to buy)	*bā'* (to sell)	*sāfar* (to travel)
āni	ashtiri	abī'	asāfir
inta	tishtiri	tbī'	tsāfir
inti	tishtirīn	tbī'īn	tsāfrin
hiyya	tishtiri	tbī'	tsāfir
huwwa	yishtiri	ybī'	ysāfir
iHna	nishtiri	nbī'	nsāfir
intu	tishtirūn	tbī'ūn	tsāfrūn
humma	yishtirūn	ybī'ūn	ysāfrūn

D. Vocabulary

hādha s-sūg	this market
isma . . .	its name
jiddan qadīm	very old
aHibb	I like/love
il-aswāq il-qadīma	old markets
min qabil	before (*lit.*, from before)
shūfi l-fākiha!	Look at the fruit(s)!
shgad Hilwa	very beautiful
wi-l-khuDHra ayDHan	and the vegetables too
shinu rāH tishtirīn?	What are you going to buy?
hnāna ybī'ūn	they sell here
malābis nisā'yya w-rijālliyya	women's and men's clothes
kulshi	everything
SaHiH?	Really?
miHtāja (f.)	I need (*lit.*, I'm in need of)
qamiS w-blūza	a shirt and a blouse
Hidhā' w-janTa	a pair of shoes and a bag
malābis dākhiliyya	underwear
hal-isbū'	this week
awwal	first
nishtiri	we buy
ba'dēn	then
l-ashyā' il-'ukhra	the other things
min hādha l-bayyā'	from this vendor
hādhi T-TamāTa	these (*lit.*, this) tomatoes
ghālya (f.)	expensive
qabil sana	a year before
iT-TamāTa	the tomatoes
rikhīSa (f.)	cheap

320

kīlū w-nuS	a kilo and a half
ba'ad shinu tirdīn?	What else do you want?
hādha t-tuffāH	these apples
dhāka l-'inab	those (*lit.,* that) grapes
hāy il-baTTīkha	this melon
ybi'ūn laHam hnāna?	Do they sell meat here?
il-gaSSab	the butcher
buSal	onions
khas	lettuce
khyār	cucumbers
Halīb	milk
miliH	salt
qisim minhum	some (*lit.,* a part) of them
dhīch il-mara	that woman
hadhōla l-awlād	these boys
'ilich	gum
Habb	pumpkin (or watermelon) seeds
fistiq	pistachio nuts
yella, lēsh lā!	Let's, why not!

E. Cultural Note

The big cities of Iraq, such as Bagdhad, Mosul, and Basrah, are full of old, even ancient, marketplaces (*sūg*s) where items of daily living, together with luxury goods, are sold. There are meat markets, fish markets, vegetable and fruit markets, and various other markets where clothes, footwear, and all kinds of accessories are put out for sale. And there are gold and silver markets where jewelry, decorative objects, and silverware can be found. There are also those markets where the shop owners spend a good portion of their days making the products they want to sell. For those interested in copper, bronze, and pottery, Iraqi cities pride themselves on having some exquisite markets where household articles and souvenirs, all hand-crafted, are sold at reasonable prices.

To find the best values, however, one must learn how to bargain. There are those buyers who would slash the cost by half, and gradually, following the seller's response, raise the offer to something that is acceptable to both parties.

Nowadays, traders and business owners unanimously favor the American dollar over the Iraqi dinar, which has so considerably lost its value that those who go shopping often carry their Iraqi money in sacks—reserving their wallets for dollars, if they have them. There were times when the *dirham* (equal to 1/20 of a dinar) bought a whole meal or two and when the *fils* (1/1,000 of a dinar) bought one or two rock candies. They have survived only in history books and in proverbs such as *l-fils il-aHmar yinfa'ak bi l-yōm il-aswad* (*lit.,* a red fils will be useful to you on a black day).

F. Exercises

1. Fill in the blanks below with the correct form of the following imperfect verbs.

  trūH / tishtirūn / tsāfrīn/ tbī' / ysāfrūn / nishtiri

a. *dūnald w lūsi rāH* _____ *il baghdād.*
b. *samīra trīd* _____ *li s-sūg.*
c. *l-mara* _____ *Halib.*
d. *intu* _____ *'inab.*
e. *tHibbin* _____ *li l-baSrah?*
f. *iHna* _____ *laHam.*

2. Fill in the blanks below with the correct form of the following perfect verbs.

  shtirēti / sāfarit / sāfar / shtirat / riHit / bi'tu

a. *lūsi* _____ *janTa w Hidhā'.*
b. *dūnald* _____ *il 'ammān.*
c. *inta* _____ *li s-sīnama.*
d. *āni* _____ *li l-khārij (abroad).*
e. *inti* _____ *miliH w-filfil (salt and pepper).*
f. *intu* _____ *dhaHab w-fiDHa (gold and silver).*

3. Translate the following dialogue into English.

dūnald: bēsh il-mishmish (apricots)?
bayyā': l-kilu b-khamsa w-arba'īn dīnār.
dūnald: wir-rummān (pomegranates)?
bayyā': b-sittīn.
dūnald: tinTī b-khamsīn?
bayyā': shgad trīd?
dūnald: nuS kīlu.

4. Use the correct perfect form of the verb *chān* (to be) to fill in the blanks.

a. *l-laHam* _____ *rihkīS.*
b. *lūsi* _____ *farHāna* (happy).
c. *āni* _____ *bi s-sūg.*
d. *layla w lūsi* _____ *bi l-mūSil.*
e. *iHna* _____ *bi l-baS* (in the bus).
f. *intu* _____ *hnāna lō hnāk?*
g. *dūnald* _____ *bi sh-shughul* (at work).

5. Match the words in column A with those in column B to form grammatically correct phrases or sentences.

A

a. *hnāna ybī'ūn*

b. *āni w-lūsi*

c. *dhakōla l-awlād*

d. *wēn il qalam?*

e. *dhāk iddukkān* (store)

f. *tishtirīn chāy* (tea)*?*

g. *hādhi l-binit* (girl)

h. *trūHīn li l-madrasa* (school)*?*

B

l-qalam hna

ybī' khas w khyār

laHam w-khubuz (bread)

nishtiri fākiha w-khuDHra

bali, ashtiri

yishtirūn 'ilich

bali arūH

chānat farHāna

Answer Key

1. a. *dūnald w lūsi rāH ysāfrūn il baghdād.*
   b. *samīra trīd trūH li s-sūg.*
   c. *l-mara tbi' Halib.*
   d. *intu tishtirūn 'inab.*
   e. *tHibbin tsāfrīn li l-baSrah?*
   f. *iHna nishtiri laHam.*

2. a. *lūsi shtirat janTa w Hidhā'.*
   b. *dūnald sāfar il 'ammān.*
   c. *inta riHit li s-sīnama.*
   d. *āni sāfarit li l-khārij.*
   e. *inti shtirēti miliH w-filfil.*
   f. *intu bi'tu dhaHab w-fiDHa.*

3. Donald: How much are the apricots?
   Vendor: Forty-five dinars a kilo.
   Donald: And the pomegranates?
   Vendor: Sixty.
   Donald: Can you give them (*lit.*, it) for fifty?

Vendor: How much do you want?
Donald: Half a kilo.

4. a. *l-laHam chān rihkīS.*
   b. *lūsi chānat farHāna.*
   c. *āni chinit bis-sūg.*
   d. *layla w lūsi chānaw bi l-mūSil.*
   e. *iHna chinna bi l-baS.*
   f. *intu chintu hnāna lō hnāk?*
   g. *dūnald chān bi sh-shughul.*

5. a. *hnāna ybī'ūn laHam w-khubuz.*
   b. *āni w-lūsi nishtiri fākiha w-khuDHra.*
   c. *dhakōla l-awlād yishtirūn 'ilich.*
   d. *wēn il-qalam? l-qalam hna.*
   e. *dhāk iddukkān ybī' khas w-khyār.*
   f. *tishtirīn chāy? bali, ashtiri.*
   g. *hādhi l binit chānat farHāna.*
   h. *truHīn li l-madrasa? bali arūH.*

LESSON 24

(Iraqi Arabic)

taHDHīrāt il-'īd Eid Preparations

A. Dialogue

It is the last week of Ramadan, but Maha is not quite ready for Eid. She has to shop, bake, and finish some sewing jobs. She and Lucy discuss what they have to do and offer to help each other.

maha: bāqi isbū' al-'īd w-āni liHad il-ān ma-khallaSit ashghāli.

lūsi: w-ala āni! 'indi ashyā' hwāya lāzim asawwiha.

maha: sh-bāqīlich issawwīn?

lūsi: lāzim ajīb Hājāt iT-Tabikh w-abdi asawwi l-kēk wili-klēcha w-arattib il-bēt.

maha: āni nafs ish-shī; SSawri li l-ān ma-waddēt badilti li l-khayyāT.

lūsi: āni bāchir rāyHa li s-sūg, ajīblich shī wayāya?

maha: law samaHti jibīli TaHīn w-bēDH w-zibid li l-kēk; w-jibīli bakirtēn, wiHda Hamra w-wiHda bēDHa.

lūsi: inshālla. bas sh-rāH tkhayTīn bi l-bakrāt?

maha: akhayyiT bīhum badlat binti nūr w-qamīS ibni aHmed. w-'indi pardāt ithnēn lāzim akhayyiThum.

lūsi: inTīni l-malābis āni akhayyiThum.

maha: lā, mustaHīl!

lūsi: lēsh mustaHīl? 'ūd sā'dīni bi l-kēk.

maha: fikra 'aDHīma. khalli nkhalliS shughulna bsur'a Hatta nirtāH nafsiyyan.

lūsi: rāyHīn makān bi l-'uTla?

maha: zawji rāyiH li l-mūSil Hatta yshūf abū w-'umma. w-intu?

lūsi: iHna bāqīn hnā li'an ahal dūnald rāH yijūn il-baghdād.

maha: jībīhum yemna, w-kulna nrūH il-madīnat il-al'āb.

lūsi: khōsh fikrah! nākhudh ij-jahāl w il-'ā'ila kulha.

maha: akūn jiddan sa'īda.

Maha: One week is left (to prepare) for Eid, and I haven't finished my work or chores yet.

Lucy: Neither have I. I have many things to do.

Maha: What else do you have to do?

Lucy: I have to get the baking ingredients and start making the cake and the *klēcha*[1] and tidying up the house.

Maha: Same with me; imagine, I still haven't taken the fabric for my dress to the tailor.

Lucy: I am going to the market tomorrow; can I bring you anything?

Maha: Please bring me flour and eggs and butter for the cake, and bring me two cotton reels, one red and one white.

---

[1] *klēcha* is a kind of pastry stuffed with either nuts or dates.

Lucy: Okay (*lit.*, God willing). But what do you want to sew with the reels?

Maha: I'll sew my daughter Noor's dress and my son Ahmed's shirt. I also have two curtains that I have to sew.

Lucy: Give me the clothes and I'll sew them (for you).

Maha: No! Impossible!

Lucy: Why impossible? You could help me with preparing the cake.

Maha: A great idea! Let's finish our work quickly so that we can relax.

Lucy: Are you going anywhere during the holiday?

Maha: My husband is going to Mosul to see his mother and father. And you?

Lucy: We're staying here because Donald's family is coming to Baghdad.

Maha: Bring them over (*lit.*, near us), and we'll all go to the play-land.

Lucy: A good idea! We'll take the kids and the whole family.

Maha: I'll be very pleased!

B. Pronunciation

1. SHORT FORMS OF *'ala* (ON, FOR) AND *shinu* (WHAT?)

'ala (on, for) is often shortened to *'a* when it precedes a noun beginning with the definite article.

> *bāqi isbū' 'a l-'īd.*
> One week is left (to prepare) for Eid.

> *l-kēk 'a l-mēz.*
> The cake is on the table.

But:

> *shinu 'ala qamīSich?*
> What is on your *(f. sg.)* shirt?

> *'ala qamīSi warda Hamra.*
> On my shirt is a red flower.

shinu (what?) is shortened to *sh-* and merged with the word following it.

> *sh-bāqīlich issawwin?*
> What else do you have to do?

> *sh-rāH issawwin bāchir?*
> What are you going to do tomorrow?

2. DOUBLE CONSONANTS *ss* AND *SS*

In this lesson's dialogue, the words *ssawwin* and *SSawri* start with double consonants. The first *s* sound is in fact a transformation of the consonant *t*, which should mark the beginning of both verbs. Because the *t* sound precedes a "sun" consonant, it often mirrors that consonant in pronunciation, hence the words *tizzawjin* (you get married), not *titzawjin*; *shshūfīn* (you see), not *tshūfīn*; and *ssibHīn* (you swim), not *tsibHīn*—all have the *t* sound reflecting the consonant that follows it. The *t*, however, retains its pronunciation when it is followed by a "moon" consonant (or a vowel) as in *trūHīn* (you go), *trij'īn* (you come back), *tkhayTīn* (you sew), and *tāklīn* (you eat).

C. Grammar and Usage

1. IMPERATIVE VERBS IN IRAQI ARABIC

Iraqi Arabic has only three forms for the imperative: masculine, feminine, and plural, unlike MSA, which also has dual and feminine plural forms. Imperative verbs are formed in the same way their equivalents in MSA are; the difference lies mostly in pronunciation. Compare the imperative verbs in this lesson's dialogue with their counterparts in *fuSHā*:

IRAQI ARABIC IMPERATIVE VERBS	*fuSHā* EQUIVALENTS
SSawri (imagine, f. sg.)	*taSawwari*
sā'dīni (help me, f. sg.)	*sā'idīni*
jībīli (bring me, f. sg.)	*ijlibīli*
jibīhum (bring them, m./f. pl.)	*ijlibīhum*
nTīni (give me, f. sg.)	*'a'Tīni*
khalli (let/let's)	*khalli* (or *da'i*)

Iraqi Arabic imperative verbs are generally more like their MSA equivalents than is apparent in the above table. The one below shows a number of commonly used imperative verbs with their *fuSHā* equivalents.

IRAQI ARABIC IMPERATIVE VERBS IN MASCULINE SINGULAR	*fuSHā* EQUIVALENTS
ishrab (drink)	*ishrab*
irbaH (win)	*irbaH*
imna' (prevent)	*imna'*
isma' (listen, hear)	*isma'*
itruk (leave something or someone alone)	*utruk*
irja' (come back)	*irji'*
nāqish (discuss)	*nāqish*
Hārib (fight)	*Hārib*
dāwim (continue)	*dāwim*
jurr (pull)	*jurra*
rūH (go)	*rūH* or *idhhab*
shtīri (buy)	*ishtari*
bī' (sell)	*bī'*

When used to address females or a group, the Iraqi Arabic imperative verb acquires, as in *fuSHā*, final *i* and *u* vowel sounds respectively: *SSawwar* (imagine) becomes *SSawri*, and *SSawru* and *sā'id* (help) become *sā'di* and *sā'du*. But unlike their counterparts in *fuSHā*, many of these verbs may undergo further changes, such as losing their initial *i* sound and adding or dropping middle vowels: *irja'* becomes *rij'i*; *ishrab, shirbi; irbaH, rubHi; imna', min'i; isma'; sim'i; nāqish, nāqshi; Hārib, Hārbi;* and *dāwim, dāwmi*. The plural forms of all these verbs are like the feminine, except of course for the final vowel sound *u*. Some imperative verbs, however, remain the same (except for the addition of the final vowel sounds *i* and *u*) when they are used to address a female or a group. See, for example, some of the verbs listed in the above table: *jurr, jurri, jurru; rūH, rūHi, rūHu;* and *bī', bī'i, bī'u*.

Negative orders, requests, or commands are formed in Iraqi Arabic by using the particle *la* in front of the imperfect verb, as in *la tsā'dīni* (don't help me), *la jjībīli* (don't bring me), and *la tinTīni* (don't give me).

The expressions *min faDHlak, min faDHlich,* and *min faDHilkum* or *law samaHt, law samaHti,* and *law samaHtu*—all meaning "please/if you please"—often precede the request or command, as in the following sentences:

> *min faDHlak, inTīni chāy.*
> Please *(m. sg.)*, give me tea.

> *law samaHti, jībīli Halīb.*
> Please *(f. sg.)*, get/bring *(f. sg.)* me milk.

2. THE DUAL IN IRAQI ARABIC

In Iraqi Arabic the dual is formed by adding the suffix -*ēn* to singular nouns. Note some singular nouns, all of them masculine, and their dual counterparts from this lesson's dialogue below.

DUAL NOUNS	
Singular	**Dual**
isbū' (a week)	*isbū'ēn* (two weeks)
bēt (a house)	*bētēn* (two houses)
sūg (a mall or market)	*sūgēn* (two malls or markets)
makān (a place)	*makānēn* (two places)
'id (Eid)	*'idēn* (two Eids)

The dual of feminine nouns, ending in -*a(t)*, is also formed also by adding -*ēn*, but the *t* that precedes it is pronounced.

DUAL NOUNS	
Singular	Dual
kēka (one cake)	*kēktēn* (two cakes)
badla (one dress)	*badiltēn* (two dresses)
bakra (a spool/cotton reel)	*bakirtēn* (two spools/cotton reels)
bēDHa (one egg)	*bēDHtēn* (two eggs)
fikra (idea)	*fikirtēn* (two ideas)

Note the insertion of the vowel *i* in *badiltēn*, *bakirtēn*, and *fikirtēn* to avoid the clustering of three consonants.

Generally speaking, the dual in Iraqi Arabic takes much simpler forms than it does in MSA. Because there is no grammatical case in Iraqi Arabic, the dual ending is always *-ēn*. In addition, the adjective following the Iraqi Arabic dual is usually in the plural, not dual, form.

> *l-bēDHtēn* (f. du.) *zurug* (m. pl.)
> The two eggs are blue.

> *shtireyt bēDHtēn* (f. du.) *zurug* (m. pl.)
> I bought two blue eggs.

The plural form of nouns is often used instead of the dual form, even with the number *thnēn* (two), as in:

> *bēDHāt ithnēn*
> two eggs

> *pardāt ithnēn*
> two curtains

Note that the word *thnēn* in all the examples above acquires an initial *i* to avoid a hard-to-pronounce clustering of three consonants, *pardāt ithnēn*.

3. FAMILY MEMBERS
The following are the Arabic Iraqi words used to refer to family members.

FAMILY MEMBERS

Family Member	Example
'umm/māma (mother)	'ummi (my mother)
'abu/'ab/bāba (father)	'abūya (my father)
zawja/mara (wife)	zawijti/marti (my wife)
zawj/rajil (husband)	zawji/rajli (my husband)
bint/binit (daughter)	binti (my daughter)
'ibin (son)	'ibni (my son)
'ukhut (sister)	'ukhti (my sister)
'akhu/'akh (brother)	'akhūya (my brother)
jidda/bībi (grandmother)	jiddīti/bībiti (my grandmother)
jiddu (grandfather)	jiddi (my grandfather)
'amm/'ammu (paternal uncle; also used as a term of respect for older men)	'ammi (my paternal uncle)
khāl/khālu (maternal uncle)	khāli (my maternal uncle)
khāla (maternal aunt)	khālti (my maternal aunt)
'amma (paternal aunt)	'amti (my paternal aunt)
binit khāl (maternal cousin, f.)	bit khāli (my maternal cousin)
'ibin khāl (maternal cousin, m.)	'ibin khāli (my maternal cousin)
binit 'amm (paternal cousin, f.)	bit 'ammi (my paternal cousin)
'ibin 'amm (paternal cousin, m.)	'ibin 'ammi (my paternal cousin)
Hafida/bint il 'ibin/bint il-binit (granddaughter)	Hafidti/bit ibni/bit binti (my granddaughter)
Hafid/'ibn il-ibin/'ibn il-binit (grandson)	Hafidi/'ibn ibni/'ibn binti (my grandson)
bint il-'ukhut/bint il-'akh (niece; lit., sister's daughter and brother's daughter, respectively)	bitt ukhti/bitt akhūya (my niece)

In general, these and other terms used for family members resemble their equivalents in MSA. For instance, the word *channa* (daughter-in-law) has *kanna* for its *fuSHā* counterpart, the word *nisīb* (a male in-law) has *nasīb*, the word *ahal* (kin, family) has *ahl*, and the words *'ā'ila* (family) and *qarīb* (relative) are usually pronounced as they are in MSA.

4. VERB CONJUGATION IN IRAQI ARABIC

In the following tables, four new verbs, all taken from this lesson's dialogue, are conjugated in the perfect, the imperfect, and the imperative, respectively.

THE PERFECT TENSE OF *sawwa* (TO DO), *khallaS* (TO FINISH), *khayyaT* (TO SEW), AND *jāb* (TO BRING)				
āni	*sawwēt*	*khallaSit*	*khayyaTit*	*jibit*
inta	*sawwēt*	*khallaSit*	*khayyaTit*	*jibit*
inti	*sawwēti*	*khallaSti*	*khayyaTti*	*jibti*
huwwa	*sawwa*	*khallaS*	*khayyaT*	*jāb*
hiyya	*sawwat*	*khalaSat*	*khayTat*	*jābat*
iHna	*sawwēna*	*khallaSna*	*khayyaTna*	*jibna*
intu	*sawwētu*	*khallaStu*	*khayyaTtu*	*jibtu*
humma	*sawwaw*	*khalSaw*	*khayTaw*	*jābaw*

THE IMPERFECT TENSE OF *sawwa* (TO DO), *khallaS* (TO FINISH), *khayyaT* (TO SEW), AND *jāb* (TO BRING)				
āni	*asawwi*	*akhalliS*	*akhayyiT*	*ajīb*
inta	*ssawwi*	*tkhalliS*	*tkhayyiT*	*jjīb*
inti	*ssawwin*	*tkhalSin*	*tkhayTin*	*jjībin*
huwwa	*ysawwi*	*ykhalliS*	*ykhayyiT*	*yjīb*
hiyya	*ssawwi*	*tkhalliS*	*tkhayyiT*	*jjīb*
iHna	*nsawwi*	*nkhalliS*	*nkhayyiT*	*njīb*
intu	*ssawwūn*	*tkhalSūn*	*tkhayTūn*	*jjībūn*
humma	*ysawwūn*	*ykhalSūn*	*ykhayTūn*	*yjībūn*

Note the doubling of the consonants *s* and *j* in imperfect tense forms verbs *sawwa* (to do) and *jāb* (to bring), requiring an initial *t,* as discussed earlier.

THE IMPERATIVE FORM OF *sawwa* (TO DO), *khallaS* (TO FINISH), *khayyaT* (TO SEW), AND *jāb* (TO BRING)				
inta	*sawwi*	*khalliS*	*khayyiT*	*jīb*
inti	*sawwi*	*khalSi*	*khayTi*	*jībi*
intu	*sawwu*	*khalSu*	*khayTu*	*jībū*

D. Vocabulary

bāqi	there remain(s)
'al-'īd	for Eid
liHad il-ān	until now
ma khallaSit	I have not finished
ashghāli	my work/chores
'indi ashyā' hwāya.	I have many things.
sh-bāqilich issawwīn?	What else do you have to do?
ajīb	I bring
Hājāt iT-Tabikh	cooking ingredients
abdi	I start
asawwi	I make/do

arattib il-bēt.	I tidy up the house.
nafs ish-shī	the same thing
ssawri! (sg.)	Imagine!
li l-ān	until now (not to be confused with *li'an* [because])
ma waddēt	I didn't take
li l-khayyāT	to the tailor
ajīblich	I'll bring/get you
TaHīn	flour
bēDH	eggs
zibid	butter
bakirtēn	two spools
wiHda Hamra	a red one
wiHda bēDHa	a white one
sh-rāH tkhayTīn?	What are you going to sew?
bakrāt	spools
'ibni	my son
pardāt ithnēn	two curtains
'ūd sā'dīni	(you could) help me
khalli nkhalliS	let's finish
shughulna	our work
Hatta nirtāH	so that we can rest
makān	place
bi l-'uTla	during the holiday
zawji	my husband
'abū w-'umma	his father and mother
'ahal dūnald	Donald's family
jībīhum yemna!	Bring them over (*lit.*, near us)!
kulna	all of us
madīnat il-al' āb	play-land
nākhudh	we take
ij-jahāl	the children
il-'ā'ila kulha	the whole family
akūn jiddan sa'īda.	I'll be very pleased.

E. Cultural Note

Like other Arabic and Islamic nations, Iraq celebrates *'īd ul-fiTr*, a three-day holiday that follows Ramadan, the fasting month, and *'īd ul-aD-Ha*, a four-day holiday that commemorates Abraham's sacrifice of his son. For both *'īd*s, or feasts, people start to prepare well in advance the food they will serve, the clothes they will wear, and the trips to relatives and friends they will undertake. The Eid is also a time when people tend to show almost unbridled generosity toward the less fortunate among relatives and friends, but also toward children, theirs in particular, whom they shower with gifts (mostly of money) and take along to fairs or amusement parks. Children learn early in life to say *ayyāmkum sa'īda!* (Happy are your days!) or *'īdkum mbārak!* (Blessed be your Eid!)—

magic words that will make the most firmly established Scrooge among relatives open his or her purse.

Iraqis, however, are generally well-known for their generosity and strong sense of obligation toward family and friends. They like to help each other, and just before Eid, the whole family gets together to make one of the most popular Eid pastries, *klēcha*—a turnover-like dessert, stuffed with dates or nuts, called *kaHk* or *ka'k* elsewhere in the Arab world.

The two Eids are the only holy days during which Iraqis also enjoy a break from official work. Other holidays are mainly limited to the mid-year and summer vacations for teachers and students—everyone else is allowed a much shorter yearly vacation, which most people tend to enjoy during the summer.

F. Exercises

1. Use one of the following imperative verbs to fill in the blanks in the sentences below.

   rūH (go) / *shtirīli* (buy me) / *jībi* (bring) / *inTīni* (give me) / *sawwinna* (make for us)

a. *lūsi, _____ 'ibnich w-ta'āli l-bētna.*

b. *aHmad, _____ li l-madrasa.*

c. *māma, _____ kēk.*

d. *bāba, _____ badla.*

e. *'ammu, _____ l-kitāb* (the book) *min faDHlak.*

2. Match the words in column A with those in column B to form grammatically correct sentences.

A	B
a. *khallaSit*	*rāH il-arbīl*
b. *law samaHti*	*l-bēt aHmad*
c. *nTīni*	*sā'idni*
d. *'abūya*	*jībīli kēk*
e. *'ummi*	*ashghāli kulha*
f. *la trūHūn*	*ssawwi baqlawa*
g. *min faDHlak*	*'aSīr* (juice) *min faDHlak*

3. Change the following requests/commands into the negative form.

a. *rūH l-madīnat il-al'āb.*

b. *sawwi klēcha.*

c. *khalliS ish-shughul kulla* (finish all the work).

d. *jīb bēDH w-TaHīn.*

4. Change the underlined singular nouns into dual ones.

a. *arīd qalam* (pen).

b. *abūya jāb tuffāHa* (brought an apple).

c. *'ummi shtirat badla.*

d. *'ukhti jābat* (gave birth to) *walad.*

e. *khāli 'inda* (has) *bēt.*

f. *layla khayTat qamīS.*

5. Change the imperative verbs in the following sentences into the plural form.

a. *rūH li s-sīnama.*

b. *khallis b-sur'a* (finish quickly).

c. *khayyiT il-malābis.*

d. *jīb il-ahal yemna.*

Answer Key

1. a. *lūsi, jībi ibnich w-ta'āli l-bētna.*
   b. *aHmad, rūH li l-madrasa*
   c. *māma, sawwīnna kēk.*
   d. *bāba, shtirīli badla.*
   e. *'ammu, nTīni l-kitāb* (the book) *min faDHlak.*

2. a. *khallaSit ashghāli kulha*
   b. *law samaHti jibili kēk*
   c. *nTīni 'aSīr* (juice) *min faDHlak*
   d. *abūya rāH il-arbīl*
   e. *'ummi ssawwi baqlāwa*
   f. *la trūHūn l-bēt aHmad*
   g. *min faDHlak sā'idni*

3. a. *la trūH l-madīnat il-al'āb.*
   b. *la ssawwi klēcha.*
   c. *la tkhalliS ish-shughul kulla.*
   d. *la jjīb bēDH w-TaHīn.*

4. a. *arīd qalamēn.*
   b. *abūya jāb tuffāHtēn.*
   c. *'ummi shtirat badiltēn.*
   d. *'ukhti jābat* (gave birth) *waladēn.*
   e. *khāli 'inda* (has) *bētēn.*
   f. *layla khayTat qamīSēn.*

5. a. *ruHu li s-sīnama.*
   b. *khalSu b-sur'a.*
   c. *khayTu il-malābis.*
   d. *jību il-ahal yemna.*

LESSON 25

isbū' malyān! A Full Week!

A. Dialogue

It's Thursday, and Yasmin, a university teacher, is telling Donald about the highlights of her week. Yasmin has taken the children to the zoo, given an evening lecture on the poet Nazik al-Malaika, gone to Habbaniyya Lake for a swim, and dined out with some friends. Next week, however, she will have to stay at home to correct exams.

yāsmīn: hal-isbū' khallaS bsur'a!

dūnald: ī, SaHīH; SSawri hal-yōm khamīs! 'indi alif shaghla w-mā adri yemta asawwīha. māku wakit!

yāsmīn: kulna hīchi; bas tidri, āni sawwēt hwāya ashyā' hal-isbū'.

dūnald: kullish zēn; shinu sawwayti?

yāsmīn: nibdi min yōm is-sabit: ba'd id-dawām akhadht ij-jahāl l-Hadīqat il-Haywānāt. chān yōm jamīl. shifna Haywānāt ma-shāyfīha min zamān.

dūnald: mathalan?

yāsmīn: chān aku asad w-nimir w-dubba wiyya awlād-ha, w Hayya Tūlha akthar min khamis amtār, w-aku Tyūr gharība: zurug, w-khuDHur, w-Humur, w-Sufur. twannasna dhāk il-yōm. bas yōm il-aHHad, ma-gidarit aTla'; chān 'indi taSlīH.

dūnald: w-yōm ith-thinēn?

yāsmīn: yōm ith-thinēn inTēt muHāDHara b-jāmi'at baghdād.

dūnald: muHāDHara? b-'ay mawDHū'?

yāsmīn: tkallamit 'an nāzik il-malā'ika.

dūnald: 'aDHīm!

yāsmīn: w-yōm ith-thalāthā' riHna li l-Habbānniya. l-awlād rādaw ysibHūn. wi l-bārHa, l-arbi'ā' akalna barra wiyya ba'DH il-aSdiqā'.

dūnald: khōsh sawwayti! l-wāHid lāzim yiTla' ba'd id-dawām.

yāsmīn: bas tidri, sbū' ij-jāy lāzim abqa bi l-bēt aSalliH imtiHānāti.

Yasmin: This week went by (*lit.*, finished) very quickly.

Donald: Yes, indeed! Imagine, today is Thursday! I have a thousand tasks, and I don't know when to do them. There's no time.

Yasmin: We're all like that. But you know what? I did a lot of things this week.

Donald: Very good! What did you do?

Yasmin: Starting from Saturday, after work, I took the children to the zoo. It was a beautiful day. We saw animals we hadn't seen in a long time.

Donald: Like what?

Yasmin: There was a lion, a tiger, a bear with her cubs, a snake more than five meters long, and some unusual birds: blue, green, red, and yellow. We enjoyed ourselves that day, but on Sunday, I could not go out; I had to do some correcting.

Donald: And on Monday?

Yasmin: On Monday, I gave a lecture at Baghdad University.

Donald: A lecture? On what subject?

Yasmin: I talked about Nazik al-Malaika.

Donald: Great!

Yasmin: And on Tuesday, we went to Habbaniyya. The boys wanted to swim. And yesterday, Wednesday, we ate out with some friends.

Donald: You did well! One needs to go out after work!

Yasmin: But you know what? Next week I'll have to stay home to correct my exams.

B. Pronunciation

In Iraqi Arabic, a word's last consonant cluster is often separated by a vowel when the word is followed by a word starting with a consonant to avoid having a three-consonant cluster, but the cluster remains intact when it is followed by a vowel or sometimes, the coordinating conjunction *w*.

riHit amis.	*riHt il-yōm.*
I went yesterday.	I went today.
ba'ad wēn riHti?	*ba'd id-dawām riHit li s-sūg.*
Where else did you go?	After work I went to the market.
shifit-ha qabil yōm ij-jum'a.	*shifit-ha qabl il-bārHa.*
I saw her before Friday.	I saw her before last night.
mā 'indi wakit.	*rāH shūfak wakt id-dawām.*
I don't have time.	I'll see you *(m. sg.)* during working hours.
'inda alif dīnār.	*'inda alf w-miyyat (mīt) dīnār.*
He has one thousand dinars.	He has one thousand, one hundred dinars.

The preposition *min* (from) becomes *mn* (a cluster) when it precedes a vowel, but it remains as it is before a consonant.

yemta Tila'tu min Hadīqat il-Haywānāt?
When did you leave the zoo?

yemta Tila'tu mn il-bēt?
When did you leave the house?

C. Grammar and Usage

1. COMPARATIVE AND SUPERLATIVE IN IRAQI ARABIC

In Iraqi Arabic, the comparative and the superlative forms of adjectives are formed, as in MSA, by changing the vowel pattern in the word to *a-CC-a-C*. For example, *jamīl* (beautiful) becomes *ajmal* (more beautiful); *Tawīl* (long), *aTwal* (longer); and *chibīr* (big/old), *akbar* (bigger). The comparative form of the adjective is used with the particle *min* (than), as in:

layla aqwa min salwa.
Layla is stronger than Salwa.

aHmad aTwal min akhū.
Ahmed is taller than his brother.

For the superlative form, Iraqi Arabic uses the comparative form preceded by the definite article *il/l*:

lamīs il-akbar.
Lamis is the oldest.

maha l-azghar.
Maha is the youngest.

The comparative form without *min* and without an article can also be used, as in:

lamīs akbar khawāt-ha.
Lamis is the oldest among her sisters.

The comparative and superlative forms of adjectives do not change for number or gender. The following table contains a number of commonly used comparatives and superlatives, some of which appear in this lesson's dialogue.

IRAQI ARABIC ADJECTIVES	COMPARATIVE	SUPERLATIVE
zēn (good/nice)	aHsan (better/nicer)	l-aHsan (the best)
sayyi', mū zēn (bad)	aswa' (worse)	l-aswa' (the worst)
'aDHīm (great)	a'DHam (greater)	l-a'DHam (the greatest)
gharib (strange/unusual)	aghrab (more unusual)	l-ghrab (the most unusual)
jamīl (beautiful)	ajmal (more beautiful)	l-ajmal (the most beautiful)
dhaki (clever)	adhka (cleverer)	l-adhka (the cleverest)
Hilu (sweet)	aHla (sweeter)	l-aHla (the sweetest)
wāsi' (wide/spacious)	awsa' (wider)	l-awsa' (the widest)
bārid (cold)	abrad (colder)	l-abrad (the coldest)
Hār (hot)	aHHar (hotter)	l-aHHar (the hottest)
qalīl (little)	aqall (less/fewer)	l-aqall (the least/fewest)

2. THE VERB *gidar* (CAN)

The verb *gidar* (can) is widely used in combination with other verbs to denote the ability to do or to be. It comes in the perfect tense and the imperfect tense, but not in the imperative, and the verb following it is always imperfect. Compare the following sets of sentences with *gidar* coupled with verbs from this lesson's dialogue.

THE VERB *gidar* (CAN)	
Imperfect	Perfect
āni agdar asbaH. I can swim.	*āni gidarit asbaH.* I could swim.
inta tigdar tibdi. You can start.	*inta gidarit tibdi.* You could start.
inti tgidrīn titkallimīn. You can speak.	*inti gidarti titkallimīn.* You could speak.
huwwa yigdar yibqa. He can stay.	*huwwa gidar yibqa.* He could stay.
hiyya tigdar tākul. She can eat.	*hiyya gidrat tākul.* She could eat.
iHna nigdar nākhudh il-imtiHān. We can take the exam.	*iHna gidarna nākhud il-imtiHān.* We could take the exam.
intu tgidrūn tSalHūn imtiHānātkum. You can mark your own exams.	*intu gidartu tSalHūn imtiHānātkum.* You could mark your own exams.
Humma ygidrūn ykhalsūn bsur'a. They can finish quickly.	*humma gidraw ykhalsūn bsur'a.* They were able to finish quickly.

To negate this verb, the particle *mā* or *ma* is used.

mā agdar asbaH.
I can't swim.

ma yigdar yākul.
He can't eat.

3. NUMBERS FROM 1 TO 20 IN IRAQI ARABIC

Except for differences in pronunciation and grammatical form, Iraqi Arabic numbers are the same as those in MSA (see Lessons 7 and 8).

NUMBERS FROM 1 TO 20			
1	*wāHid*	11	*Hda'ash*
2	*thnēn*	12	*thna'ash*
3	*tlātha*	13	*tlaTa'ash*
4	*arba'a*	14	*arba'Ta'ash*
5	*khamsa*	15	*khumuSTa'ash*
6	*sitta*	16	*siTTa'ash*
7	*sab'a*	17	*sabi'Ta'ash*
8	*thmānya*	18	*thminTa'ash*
9	*tis'a*	19	*tsi'Ta'ash*
10	*'ashra*	20	*'ishrīn*

When used in sentences, Iraqi Arabic numbers assume the same form regardless of their function in the sentence (i.e., they do not have different case forms), and, with the exception of *wāHid* (one), regardless of the gender of the noun they modify: Iraqis say *asad* (m.) *wāHid* (one lion) and *Hayya* (f.) *wiHda* (one snake), but they say *asadēn ithnēn* (two lions) and *Haytēn ithnēn* (two snakes), *tlath isūd* (three lions) and *tlath Hayyāt* (three snakes), *arba'* *isūd* and *arba'* *Hayyāt*, and so on: *khamis/sitt/sabi'/thman/tisi'/'ashir isūd/Hayyāt*. From 11 upward, however, the numbers usually modify singular nouns, as in MSA: *Hda'ash nimir* (eleven tigers), *thna'ash dubba* (twelve she-bears), and *'ishrin ghazāla* (twenty deer).

Compound numbers from 20 to 99 are formed, as in MSA, by adding any one of the single numbers from 1 to 9 to *'ishrin* (twenty), *tlāthin* (thirty), *arba'in* (forty), etc., as in: *wāHid w-'ishrin* (twenty-one), *thnēn w-'ishrin* (twenty-two), *tlātha w-'ishrin* (twenty-three), *arba'a w-'ishrin* (twenty-four), etc. The remaining numbers in Iraqi Arabic follow the pattern found in MSA but differ, often slightly, in pronunciation: *miyya* (hundred), *mītēn* (two hundred), *tlathmiyya* (three hundred), *arba'miyya* (four hundred), *khamismiyya* (five hundred) and so on, with the word *miyya* (hundred) being added to the number. The same can be done with *alf* or *alif* (thousand) and its plural *ālāf*, and with *milyōn* (million) and its plural *malāyin*: *alf*, *alfēn* (two thousand), *tlattālāf* (three thousand), *arba'tālāf* (four thousand), *khamistālāf* (five thousand), etc.; and *milyōn*, *milyōnēn* (two million), *tlath malāyin* (three million), *arba'* *malāyin* (four million), *khamis malāyin* (five million), etc.

4. COLORS IN IRAQI ARABIC
Most of the words used for colors in MSA are also found in Iraqi Arabic, with small differences in pronunciation that characterize the dialect. Iraqi Arabic colors are pluralized when used to modify plural and dual nouns.

> *Tērēn khuDHur*
> two *(du.)* green birds *(pl.)*

> *Tyūr khuDHur*
> green *(pl.)* birds *(pl.)*

The feminine forms of color apply when they follow singular nouns, as in *Tēra Safra* (a yellow female bird), but also in *mīt baTTa Safra* (a hundred yellow ducks), and *alif ghazāla Safra* (a thousand yellow deer). The following table contains the most common Iraqi Arabic words for colors, used in phrases.

COLOR WORDS IN IRAQI ARABIC

Masculine Singular	Feminine Singular	Plural
bēt abyaDH (a white house)	*badla bēDHa* (a white dress)	*badlāt biDH* (white dresses)
dubb aswad (a black bear)	*dubba soda* (a black she-bear)	*dubbab/dubbāt sūd* (black bears) (m./f.)
Tēr aHmar (a red bird)	*Tēra Hamra* (a red bird) (f.)	*Tyūr Humur* (red birds)
Hidhā' akhDHar (a pair of green shoes)	*janTa khaDHra* (a green bag)	*aHdhiya khuDHur* (green shoes)
bāb aSfar (a yellow door)	*sayyāra Safra* (a yellow car)	*sayyārāt Sufur* (yellow cars)
qalam azraq (a blue pen)	*waraqa zarga* (a blue paper)	*aqlām zurug* (blue pens)
dukkān qahwā'i (a brown store/shop)	*qanafa qahwā'iyya* (a brown couch)	*qanafāt qahwā'iyyāt* (brown couches)
DHuwa banafsaji (a purple light)	*warda banafsajiyya* (a purple flower)	*aDHwiya banafsajiyya* (purple lights)
qamiS wardi (a pink shirt)	*tannūra wardiyya* (a pink skirt)	*tannūrat wardiyyāt* (pink skirts)
nimir purtiqāli (an orange tiger)	*dijāja purtiqāliyya* (an orange hen)	*dijājāt purtuqāliyyāt* (orange hens)
ribāT riSāSi (a grey tie)	*blūza riSāSiyya* (a grey blouse)	*blūzāt riSāSiyyāt* (grey blouses)
kūb fiDHDHi (a silver cup)	*khāshūga fiDHDHiyya* (a silver spoon)	*kwāba fiDHDHiyya* (silver cups)
Hzam dhahabi (a golden belt)	*sā'a dhahabiyya* (a golden watch)	*sā'āt dhahabiyya* (golden watches)

However, the above rules are often broken. For instance, the colors that end with the vowel sound *i* (m. sg.) in the first column are used to refer to plural, both feminine and masculine, entities. One may say *blūzāt* (f. pl.) *riSāSi* (grey shirts) instead of *blūzāt riSāSiyyāt*. One may also say *blūza riSāSi* instead *blūza riSāSiyya*, treating just as loosely all the other words in this category: *lōn Hashīshi* (grass-green color) and *alwān hashishi/hashīshiyya* (grass-green colors).

5. DAYS OF THE WEEK IN IRAQI ARABIC

The Iraqi week starts on Saturday and ends on Friday. The words denoting the days of the week are:

sabit (Saturday)
aHHad (Sunday)
thinēn (Monday)
thalāthā' (Tuesday)
arbi'ā' (Wednesday)
khamīs (Thursday)
jum'a (Friday)

These words are preceded by the definite article when used in phrases or sentences, except when they are intended to be indefinite.

yōm il-khamis akhalliS imtiHānāti.
On Thursday, I('ll) finish my exams.

yōm is-sabit ʻidna mtiHān.
On Saturday, we have an exam.

But:

chān yōm thalāthā', mū arbi'ā'.
It was a Tuesday, not a Wednesday.

6. *aku* (THERE IS) AND *māku* (THERE ISN'T)

aku (there is) and *māku* (there isn't) are common Iraqi Arabic expressions, used in questions or statements, depending on the context and intonation. Note their use in the following sentences:

aku arba' jāmi'āt b-baghdād.
There are four universities in Baghdad.

aku dawām yōm is-sabit?
Is there work on Saturday?

lā, māku.
No, there isn't.

māku 'indi filis aHmar.
I'm broke. (*lit.* I don't have one red "cent.")

akīd māku fīl b-Hadīqat il-Haywānāt?
Are you sure there is no elephant in the zoo?

7. VERB CONJUGATION IN IRAQI ARABIC

The following tables show the conjugation of five new Iraqi verbs in the perfect, imperfect, and imperative forms. Note that the verb *dira* (to know) does not have an imperative form. Note also that the verb *tkallam* (to talk) can be used interchangeably with another Iraqi Arabic verb, *Hicha* (to talk), which is the counterpart of the MSA *Haka*, and conjugates in exactly the same way as *bida* (to start) and *biqa* (to stay), below.

VERB CONJUGATION: THE PERFECT TENSE					
	bida (to start)	*dira* (to know)	*biqa* (to stay)	*sibaH* (to swim)	*tkallam* (to speak)
āni	*bidēt*	*dirēt*	*biqēt*	*sibaHit*	*tkallamit*
inta	*bidēt*	*dirēt*	*biqēt*	*sibaHit*	*tkallamit*
inti	*bidēti*	*dirēti*	*biqēti*	*sibaHti*	*tkallamti*
huwwa	*bida*	*dira*	*biqa*	*sibaH*	*tkallam*
hiyya	*bidat*	*dirat*	*biqat*	*sibHat*	*tkallimat*
ihna	*bidēna*	*dirēna*	*biqēna*	*sibaHna*	*tkallamna*
intu	*bidētu*	*dirētu*	*biqētu*	*sibaHtu*	*tkallamtu*
humma	*bidaw*	*diraw*	*biqaw*	*sibHaw*	*tkallimaw*

VERB CONJUGATION: THE IMPERFECT TENSE

	bida (to start)	dira (to know)	biqa (to saty)	sibaH (to swim)	tkallam (to speak)
āni	abdi	adri	abqa	asbaH	atkallam
inta	tibdi	tidri	tibqa	tisbaH	titkallam
inti	tibdīn	tidrīn	tibqin	tsibHīn	titkalmīn
huwwa	yibdi	yidri	yibqa	yisbaH	yitkallam
hiyya	tibdi	tidri	tibqa	tisbaH	titkallam
ihna	nibdi	nidri	nibqa	nisbaH	nitkallam
intu	tibdūn	tidrūn	tibqūn	tsibHūn	titkalmūn
humma	yibdūn	yidrūn	yibqūn	ysibHūn	yitkalmūn

VERB CONJUGATION: THE IMPERATIVE

	bida (to start)	biqa (to stay)	sibaH (to swim)	tkallam (to speak)
inta	ibdi	ibqa	isbaH	tkallam
inti	ibdi	ibqi	sibHi	tkallimi/tkalmi
intu	ibdu	ibqu	sibHu	tkallimu/tkalmu

D. Vocabulary

khallaS bsur'a	finished quickly
hal-yōm khamīs.	Today is Thursday.
'indi	I have
alif shaghla	a thousand tasks
mā adri.	I don't know.
māku wakit.	There's no time.
kulna hīchi.	We're all like that.
bas tidri?	You know what? (lit., But do you know?)
nibdi min	we start from
ba'd id-dawām	after work
akhadht ij-jahāl.	I took the children.
Hadīqat il-Haywānāt	the zoo
chān yōm jamīl.	It was a beautiful day.
shifna Haywānāt	we saw animals
ma-shāyfiha min zamān.	We haven't seen (them) in a long time.
mathalan?	like what?, for example
chān aku	there was
asad	lion
nimir	tiger
dubba	she-bear
Hayya	snake
Tūlha	its length
akthar min	more than
khamis amtār	five meters

aku Tyūr gharība.	There were unusual birds.
zurug	blue
khuDHur	green
Humur	red
Sufur	yellow
twannasna.	We enjoyed ourselves.
ma-gidarit aTla'.	I could not go out.
taSlīH	grading
inTēt muHāDHara	I gave a lecture
b-jāmi'at baghdād	at the university of Baghdad
b-'ay mawDHū'?	On what subject?
tkallamit	I talked
yōm ith-thalāthā'	Tuesday
rādaw ysibHūn.	They wanted to swim.
l-arbi'ā'	Wednesday
akalna barra.	We ate outside.
ba'DH il-aSdiqā'	some friends
abqa bi l-bēt.	I am staying home.
aSalliH imtiHānāti.	I grade my exams.

E. Cultural Notes

Once known as Mesopotamia, Iraq is a country where the most ancient civilization known to the world took root and flourished and produced leaders like Assurbanipal and Hammurabi, men whose monuments still exist in museums today. And though wars and invasions have heedlessly ravaged the precious relics of this civilization, Iraq has been known to bounce back, to rebuild, and to reassert its love for learning in both the arts and the sciences.

Modern Iraq is one of the few Arab countries where women, too, have left their mark on the nation's heritage and culture. Women have found a space of their own outside the house and have sought some worthy vocations for themselves since the early decades of this century. At first, teaching in segregated schools was the favored occupation for women, who, due to Islamic habits, preferred to work in environments dominated by their sex. Gradually, however, more women found their way to professions previously controlled by men, and worked side by side with them, not just as nurses, but as doctors and university professors. Iraq has also produced some fine female poets, famous among whom is Nazik al-Malaika, whose poetry and nonfiction works have been widely anthologized and translated into many languages.

Iraqis, however, are also fun-loving and highly sociable people. If they are not spending time with friends and relatives, they may be engaging in other recreational pursuits, such as strolling by the river, going to the zoo, or swimming in a lake on weekends or after work, the late afternoon sun furnishing a much cooler climate for such activities. Iraqis can be truly devout Muslims, but they also acknowledge the claim this world has on them.

F. Exercises

1. Choose one of the verbs in parentheses to make a correct sentence.

a. *dūnald, b-'ay mawDHū' (tkallamiti, tkallamit)?*
b. *yāsmīn (biqa, biqat) bi j-jāmi'a li s-sā'a sitta.*
c. *layla (khalSat, khallaS) shughulha bsur'a.*
d. *bāsil (sibaH, sibHat) bi l-Habbāniyya amis.*
e. *lūsi rāH (yibdi, tibdi) tSalliH imtiHānāt-ha.*
f. *l-awlād bidaw (yimshūn, timshūn).*

2. Say the following sentences in Iraqi Arabic:

a. I can't swim.
b. Shall we go on Thursday or on Sunday?
c. I gave a lecture.
d. Rania is stronger than Jumana.
e. Lucy went to the university.

3. Fill in the blanks with the following comparative and superlative adjectives:

l-akbar / asra' / akthar / l-aHsan / aqua / aTwal

a. *Hādhi il-Hayya _____ min dhīch il-Hayya.*
b. *ma-shifit _____ min hadha l-asad.*
c. *minu _____, lamīs lo Sadīqat-ha?*
d. *minu _____, hādhi l-badla lo badlat ummi?*
e. *dūnald yākul _____ min lūsi.*
f. *lūsi tisbaH _____ min dūnald.*

4. Which of the two colors in the parentheses below better matches each noun?

a. *l-Hashīsh (aswad; akhDHar)*
b. *s-sima (sky) (zarga; Hashīshi)*
c. *l-walad (riSāSi; asmar)*
d. *t-tuffāHa (sōda; Hamra)*
e. *l-warda (banafsajiyya; fiDHiyya)*
f. *n-nimir (abyaDH; purtuqāli)*
g. *Sadīqti (shagra; dhahabiyya)*

5. Match the words in column A with those in column B to create complete sentences.

A	B
a. *chān yōm*	*bīha asad w-nimir*
b. *amis Tila'it*	*rāHaw li j-jāmi'a*

343

c. *hal-yōm thalāthā',*

d. *Hadīqat il-Haywānāt*

e. *yōm ij-jum'a*

f. *dūnald w-yāsmīn*

g. *yāsmīn khalSat*

h. *tkallamit 'an*

māku dawām

jamīl

mū arbi'ā'

ba'd id-dawām

nāzik il-malā'ika

shighilha

Answer Key

1. a. *dūnald, b-'ay mawDHū' tkallamit?*

   b. *yāsmīn biqat bi j-jāmi'a li s-sā'a sitta.*

   c. *layla khalSat shughulha bsur'a.*

   d. *bāsil sibaH bi l-Habbāniyya amis.*

   e. *lūsi rāH tibdi tSalliH imtiHānāt-ha.*

   f. *l-awlād bidaw yimshūn.*

2. a. *āni mā agdar asbaH.*

   b. *nruH yōm il-khamīs lo yōm il-aHHad?*

   c. *nTēt muHāDHara.*

   d. *rānya aqwa min jumāna.*

   e. *lūsi rāHat li j-jāmi'a.*

3. a. *Hādhi il-Hayya aTwal min dhīch il-Hayya.*

   b. *ma-shifit aqwa min hādha l-asad.*

   c. *minu l-akbar, lamīs lo Sadīqāt-ha?*

   d. *minu l-aHsan, hādhi l-badla lo badlat 'ummi?*

   e. *dūnald yākul akthar min lūsi.*

   f. *lūsi tisbaH asra' min dūnald.*

4. a. *l-Hashīsh akhDHar*

   b. *s-sima zarga*

   c. *l-walad asmar*

   d. *t-tuffāHa Hamra*

   e. *l-warda banafsajiyya*

   f. *n-nimir purtuqāli*

   g. *Sadīqti shagra*

5. a. *chān yōm jamīl.*

   b. *amis Tila'it ba'd id-dawām.*

   c. *hal-yōm thalāthā', mū arbi'ā'.*

   d. *Hadīqat il-Haywānāt bīha asad w-nimir.*

   e. *yōm ij-jum'a māku dawām.*

   f. *dūnald w-yāsmīn rāHaw li j-jāmi'a.*

   g. *yāsmīn khalSat shighilha.*

   h. *tkallamit 'an nāzik il-malā'ika.*

SIXTH REVIEW

(Iraqi Arabic)

---

1. Fill in the blanks with the following verbs.

yzūrūn / nwāfiq / Tila'it / yrūH / ashrab / tāklūn / t'īsh

a. l-awlād rāH _____ 'amhum.

b. iHna _____ 'ala kulshi tgūla.

c. lamīs _____ bi l-baSrah.

d. intu rāH _____ bi l-maT'am hal-yom?

e. āni _____ amis w-awwal amis.

f. dūnald ma-yrīd _____ li l-mūSil.

g. arīd _____ 'aSir.

2. Fill in the blanks with the following nouns.

banāt / iS-SiHa / sā'a / Halīb / bēDHtēn / dawām / 'uTla

a. shlon _____?

b. aHtāj _____ w-khubuz (bread).

c. bēsh _____?

d. yom is-sabit 'idna _____.

e. bil-'īd 'idna _____.

f. tiHtājīn _____ lo tlath bēDHāt?

g. l-madrasa bīha _____ w-awlād.

3. Choose the correct adjective from the options given in the parentheses.

a. zawji (karīm; karīma)

b. ukhti (qawi; qawiyya)

c. l-Hadīqa (wās'a; wāsi')

d. yāsmīn insāna (laTīfa; laTīf)

e. dūnald ishtira l-lūsi badla (jamīl; jamīla)

f. abūya jāb baTīkha (chibira; chibīr)

g. l-Hayya (Tawīl; Tawīla)

4. Replace the words in parentheses below with the following possessive suffixes.

-hum / -ha / -i / -a / -na / -kum / -ak

a. hādha galam (lūsi).

b. shifit kitāb (dūnald)?

c. dhāka bēt (ani).

d. *rāH nākhudh akil (iHna) wiyyāna.*

e. *rāH ashtiri min dukkān (mājid w-khālid).*

f. *hādhi malābis (intu).*

g. *yemta tsāfir il-balad (inta)?*

5. Replace the words in parentheses below with the following attached object pronouns.

-ha / -a / -ni / -hum / -kum / -ich / -na

a. *nTēt (lūsi w-dūnald) kitābēn.*

b. *aHmad rāH yshūf (saffāna).*

c. *zūru (āni) sbū' ij-jāy.*

d. *wēn shift (intu) 'ammi w-'amti?*

e. *rāH anTi (inti) il-miftāH (key) bāchir.*

f. *ta'ālu sā'du (iHna) isbū' i-jāy.*

g. *noor tHibb (aHmad).*

6. Use the correct form of the verb *chān* in each of the following sentences.

a. *l-walad (chān; chānat) zēn.*

b. *inti (chān; chinti) bi l-baSrah.*

c. *ukhti (chānaw; chānat) bi j-jāmi'a.*

d. *khāli w-khālti (chinna; chānaw) ysibHūn.*

e. *āni w-zawijti (chinna; chintu) bi s-sūg amis.*

f. *inta w-akhūk (chānaw, chintu) b-Hadīqat il-Haywānāt.*

g. *āni (chānat, chinit) anTi muHāDHara.*

7. The verbs *Hicha* (to talk), *misha* (to walk), *bicha* (to cry), and *nisa* (to forget) conjugate in the same way as the verb *bida* (to begin) (see Lesson 30). Fill in the spaces in the following table with the correct <u>perfect</u> forms of these verbs.

	Hicha	misha	bicha	nisa
ani	Hichēt			
inta		mishēt		
inti			bichēti	
huwwa			bicha	
hiyya				nisat
iHna				nisēna
intu		mishētu		
humma	Hicha			

8. Match the words in column A with those in column B to make grammatically correct sentences.

A	B
iHna mā 'idna	yrīd ysāfir bi l-'īd
lamīs w-lūsi	w-moz w-'inab
dūnald	sayyāra
āni w-awlādi	w-nuS illa khamsa
inta w-zawijtak	bil-isbū'
SabāH	b-almānya
jib wiyyāk tuffāH	sāfraw qabil yomēn
s-sā'a thmānya	n'īsh b-baghdād
ummi w-abūya chānaw	il-khēr
halyom shinu	ta'ālu l-bētna

9. Say the following sentences in Iraqi Arabic.

a. I love animals.

b. I'll see you after work.

c. I went to the movies.

d. What do you have in the bag?

e. Which apple do you want?

f. I have a thousand dinars.

10. Provide the appropriate responses to the following Iraqi Arabic greetings.

a. masā' il-khēr.

b. ma'a s-salāma.

c. shlonak?

d. shlonich?

e. marHaba?

f. s-salāmu 'alaykum.

g. tiSbaHūn 'ala khēr.

Answer Key

1. a. l-awlād rāH _yzūrūn_ 'amhum.

   b. iHna _nwāfiq_ 'ala kulshi tgūla.

   c. lamīs _t'īsh_ bi l-baSrah.

   d. intu rāH _tāklūn_ bi l-maT'am hal-yom?

   e. āni _Tila'it_ amis w-awwal amis.

   f. dūnald ma-yrīd _yrūH_ li l-mūSil.

   g. arīd _ashrab_'aSīr.

2. a. shlon _iS-SiHa_?

   b. aHtāj _Halib_ w-khubuz (bread).

   c. bēsh _is-sā'a_?

   d. yom is-sabit 'idna _dawām_.

   e. bil-'īd 'idna _'uTla_.

   f. tiHtājīn bēDHtēn lo tlath bēDHāt?

   g. l-madrasa bīha banāt w-awlād.

3. a. zawji _karīm_

   b. ukhti _qawiyya_

   c. l-Hadīqa _wās'a_

   d. Yāsmīn insāna _laTīfa_

   e. dūnald ishtira l-lūsi badla _jamīla_

   f. abūya jāb baTīkha _chibīra_

   g. l-Hayya _Tawīla_

4. a. hādha galamha.

   b. shifit kitāba?

c. *dhāka bētị.*

d. *rāH nākhudh akilna wiyyāna.*

e. *rāH ashtiri min dukkānhum.*

f. *hādhi malābiskum.*

g. *yemta tsāfir il-baladak?*

5. a. *nTēt-hum kitābēn.*

b. *aHmad rāH yshūfha.*

c. *zūrūni sbū' ij-jāy.*

d. *wēn shiftu 'ammi w-'amti?*

e. *rāH anTīch il-miftāH (key) bāchir.*

f. *ta'ālu sā'dūna isbū' ij-jāy.*

g. *noor tHibba.*

6. a. *l-walad chān zēn.*

b. *inti chinti bi l-baSrah.*

c. *ukhti chānat bi j-jāmi'a.*

d. *khāli w-khālti chānaw ysibHūn.*

e. *āni w-zawijti chinna bi s-sūg amis.*

f. *inta w-akhūk chintu b-Hadīqat il-Haywānāt.*

g. *āni chinit anTi muHāDHara.*

7.

	Hicha	misha	bicha	nisa
ani	*Hichēt*	*mishēt*	*bichēt*	*nisēt*
Inta	*Hichēt*	*mishēt*	*bichēt*	*nisēt*
Inti	*Hichēti*	*mishēti*	*bichēti*	*nisēti*
Huwwa	*Hicha*	*misha*	*bicha*	*nisa*
Hiyya	*Hichat*	*mishat*	*bichat*	*nisat*
iHna	*Hichēna*	*mishēna*	*bichēna*	*nisēna*
Intu	*Hichētu*	*mishētu*	*bichētu*	*nisētu*
Humma	*Hichaw*	*mishaw*	*bichaw*	*nisaw*

8. *iHna mā 'idna sayyāra*

lamīs w-lūsi sāfraw qabil yomēn

dūnald yrīd ysāfir bi l-'īd

āni w-awlādi n'īsh b-baghdād

inta w-zawijtak ta'ālu l-bētna

SabāH il-khēr

jīb wiyyāk tuffāH w-moz w-'inab

s-sā'a thmānya w-nuS illa khamsa

ummi w-abūya chānaw b-almānya

halyom shinu bil-isbū'

9. a. *āni aHibb il-Haywānat.*

b. *ashūfak ba'd id-dawām.*

c. *riHit li s-sīnama.*

d. *shaku 'indich bi j-janTa?*

e. *yā TuffāHa trīdīn?*

f. *'indi alif dīnār.*

10. a. *masā' in-nūr.*

b. *ma'a s-salāma.*

c. *zēn il-Hamdilla.*

d. *zēna l-Hamdilla.*

e. *marHaba/ahlan.*

f. *'alaykum is-salām.*

g. *ajma'īn.*

LESSON 26

(Lebanese Arabic)

shū l-mishkle? What's the Problem?

A. Dialogue

Nadia's son Ahmad and his girlfriend Georgette want to get married. Ahmad's family is opposed to the marriage because Georgette is Christian and Ahmad is Muslim. In the following conversation they are talking to Lucy about their troubles.

aHmad: mā ba'rif kīf baddi ZabbiTa ma' ahlī. anā bHebba la-jorjet bas ahlī mā byismaHūli itjawwaza.

lūsī: lē yā aHmad? shū l-mishkle? lē mā bysmaHūlak ahlak titjawwaza la-jorjet?

aHmad: ma bta'rfī . . . anā shī'i w-lēzim itjawwaz waHdi shī'iyye mitlī w-hiyye mārūniyye 'a shēn heyk lēzim titjawwaz wāHad mārūni mitla. shū baddnā na'mul? ba'd khamsta'shar sine Harb ahliyye libnēn ba'du Tāyfi.

lūsī: shū 'indak ikhtiyarēt lēkin?

aHmad: fīyī itrika la jorjet w-itjawwaz bint tēniye ta'jibun la-ahlī. bas anā mā baddi.

lūsī: mish bayyak kēn baddu yēk titjawwaza la-bint 'amtak, shū kēn isma?

aHmad: zeineb.

lūsī: aywā, zeineb.

aHmad: bala. bas anā baddi jorjet w-bas.

lūsī: mishkle kbīre. Tab, shū raH ta'mul ya'ni?

aHmad: walla, fīyī ēkhida la-jorjet w-nrūH 'a 'ubruS - izā badda - w-ntjawwaz jawēz madani.

jorjet: lā, yā aHmad, kīf baddnā nrūH 'a 'ubruS la-Hālnā? shū raH yi'ūlu ahlī w-ij-jīrān? mish ma''ūl kīf 'am bitfakkir.

aHmad: bas hayda mish kil shī, yā lūsī. anā ba'dnī mā 'indi shi''a w-ba'dnī 'am-bfattish 'a shighel w-mā blē'i Sarlī sine.

jorjet: aSdu yā lūsī, izā tjawwaznā, shū baddnā nēkul w-nishrab? w-weyn baddnā n'īsh?

lūsī: ya'ni l-waD' l-iqtiSādi kamēn Diddak yā aHmad, mish heyke?

Ahmad: I don't know how I will work things out with my family. I love Georgette, but my family wouldn't let me marry her.

Lucy: Why, Ahmad? What's the problem? Why wouldn't your family let you marry Georgette?

Ahmad: You know . . . I am a Shiite and I should marry a Shiite girl (*lit.*, like myself). Georgette is Maronite. So she has to marry a Maronite (*lit.*, like herself). What can we do? After 15 years of civil war, Lebanon is still sectarian.

Lucy: But what alternatives do you have?

Ahmad: I could leave Georgette and marry a girl (*lit.*, another girl) that my family likes. But I don't want to.

Lucy: Didn't your father want you to marry your cousin? What was her name?

Ahmad: Zeineb.

Lucy: Exactly, Zeineb.

Ahmad: Yes, he did. But I want Georgette only.

Lucy: This is a big problem. Okay, so what are you going to do?

Ahmad: Well, I can take Georgette to Cyprus—if she wants—and we can have a civil marriage [there].

Georgette: No, Ahmad, how can we go to Cyprus alone? What are my family and the neighbors going to say? I can't believe you think like this! (*lit.*, it's unbelievable how you think)

Ahmad: But that's not all, Lucy. I still don't have an apartment, and I'm still looking for a job and haven't been able to find anything for a year now.

Georgette: In other words, Lucy (*lit.*, he means, Lucy): If we get married, what are we going to eat and drink? And where are we going to live?

Lucy: So, the economic situation is also against you, Ahmad, isn't it?

B. Pronunciation

1. WRITING THE LEBANESE DIALECT

Like other Arabic dialects, Lebanese Arabic is primarily a spoken language, rarely used in written communication, where Modern Standard Arabic is the norm. Because Arabic script was devised to represent the sounds of Classical and Modern Standard Arabic, the additional sounds that exist in Arabic dialects like Lebanese are not represented by it. For these reasons, the transliteration in Latin script is used to represent Lebanese Arabic in Lessons 26 to 30, as in all other dialect lessons.

While there are differences in pronunciation among different Lebanese speakers, depending on the region they come from, the Lebanese Arabic you will learn in the following five lessons is the most commonly used variant of modern Lebanese Arabic which doesn't reflect regional specificities in pronunciation.

2. VOWELS IN LEBANESE ARABIC

In addition to the six vowels in *fuSHā*, *ā, ū, ī, a, u,* and *i*, Lebanese Arabic has four more vowels: two long vowels, *ē* and *ō*, and two short vowels, *e* and *o*. The Lebanese Arabic words *lē* (why), *mishkle* (problem), and *jorjet* (Georgette), all from the dialogue, contain these vowels.

3. CONSONANTS IN LEBANESE ARABIC

A. THE CONSONANT *q*

The MSA consonant *q* is normally replaced with a *hamza* sound (') in Lebanese Arabic, as in:

'ubruS (Cyprus)   قُبْرُص

yi'ūlu (they say)   يَقولوا

'aSdu (he means)   قَصْدُه

ma''ūl (understandable, reasonable) مَعْقول

At the same time, the many *fuSHā* words that contain a *hamza* almost always lose it in Lebanese Arabic. This is why it is reasonable to suspect that whenever a *hamza* is found in Lebanese Arabic, it corresponds to the consonant *q* in *fuSHā*. A number of words in Lebanese Arabic that belong to the educated and more formal language retain their *qāf*, such as *iqtiSādi* (economics).

B. THE CONSONANT *j*

The consonant *j* is pronounced as the sound *zh* in the English word *pleasure*. Take a look at the following examples and compare them to their *fuSHā* equivalents.

jorjet Georgette	جورْجيت
itjawwaza. I am marrying her.	أَتزَوَّجُها
ta'jibun. They like her.	تُعْجِبُهُم

C. THE CONSONANT *dh*

The *fuSHā* sound *dh* is pronounced as a *z* sound in Lebanese Arabic. Compare the Lebanese Arabic words below to their *fuSHā* equivalents.

izan (so)	إذاً
izā (if)	إذا

D. THE CONSONANT *th*

The *fuSHā* sound *th* is pronounced as either *s* or *t* in Lebanese Arabic, without a specific rule governing this variation. Notice how the following two words, written and pronounced identically in *fuSHā*, differ in their pronunciation of the *th*.

sēniye (second, measure of time)	ثانِيَة
tēniye (second, ordinal number; another)	ثانِيَة

4. THE FEMININE ENDING

In *fuSHā*, the feminine form of nouns and adjectives is indicated by the ending -*a*.

In Lebanese Arabic, the feminine ending is pronounced in two ways. Compare the following examples with their *fuSHā* equivalents.

- After *q*, *'*, *t*, *z*, *d*, *s*, and in most cases after *r*, the feminine ending is *-a*.

  shī'a (Shi'a)   شِيعَة

  shi''a (apartment)   شَقَّة

- After all other sounds, the feminine ending is *-e*, and frequently also *-i*, without any distinction between the two.

  mishkle (problem)   مُشْكِلَة

  sine (year)   سَنَة

  Tāifiye (sectarianism)   طَائِفِيَة

  mārūniyye (Maronite)   مَارونِيَّة

  ahliyye (civil)   أَهْلِيَّة

  tēniye (another)   ثَانِيَة

  waHdi (one, f.)   واحِدَة

C. Grammar and Usage

1. THE PERSONAL PRONOUNS

The following table lists the personal pronouns used in Lebanese Arabic.

PERSONAL PRONOUNS			
Singular		**Plural**	
I	anā	we	naHna
you *(m.)*	enta/ente	you *(m./f.)*	entu
you *(f.)*	enti		
he	huwwi	they *(m./f.)*	hinni
she	hiyyi		

Notice that most Lebanese Arabic personal pronouns are very close in form to those in *fuSHā*. The main difference consists in the fact that the *fuSHā a* sound is pronounced as either *e* (*enta/ente* and *enti*) or *i* (*huwwi*, *hiyyi* and *enti*) in Lebanese Arabic. In the plural, *naHna* (we) differs from the *fuSHā naHnu* only in the last vowel. The plural *you* pronoun, *entu*, starts with the Lebanese Arabic *e* and lacks the final consonant *m*, unlike its *fuSHā* counterpart, *antum*. The Lebanese Arabic *they* pronoun, *hinni*, differs the most from its equivalent in *fuSHā*, *hum*; the two share only the initial sound *h*. A more important difference between Lebanese Arabic and *fuSHā* is that Lebanese Arabic does not distinguish between masculine and feminine forms in the plural and has no dual pronouns.

2. THE POSSESSIVE SUFFIXES

The possessive endings in Lebanese Arabic are presented in the following table.

POSSESSIVE SUFFIXES			
Singular		**Plural**	
my	-ī	our	-nā
your (m.)	-ak	your (m./f.)	-kun
your (f.)	-ik		
his	-u	their (m./f.)	-un
her	-a		

The Lebanese Arabic possessive endings for the *we* and *you* plural forms are identical to those in *fuSHā*. For all other persons they differ slightly and need to be learned. In contrast to *fuSHā*, possessive endings in Lebanese Arabic are attached directly to the end of the noun without an intervening vowel. The following table shows the noun *ahl* (family) with the possessive endings attached to it.

THE NOUN *ahl* (FAMILY) WITH POSSESSIVE SUFFIXES			
Singular		**Plural**	
my family	*ahlī*	our family	*ahlnā*
your (m.) family	*ahlak*	your (m./f.) family	*ahlkun*
your (f.) family	*ahlik*		
his family	*ahlu*	their (m./f.) family	*ahlun*
her	*ahla*		

3. THE IMPERFECT TENSE

Lebanese imperfect tense has two forms, the imperfect indicative and the imperfect subjunctive.

THE IMPERFECT INDICATIVE OF THE VERB *'eref* (TO KNOW)			
Singular		**Plural**	
anā	*ba'rif*	*naHna*	*mna'rif*
enta	*bta'rif*	*entu*	*bta'rifu/bta'rfu*
enti	*bta'rifi/bta'rfi*		
huwwi	*bya'rif*	*hinni*	*bya'rifu/bya'rfu*
hiyyi	*bta'rif*		

> *mā ba'rif kīf baddi ZabbiTa ma' ahlī.*
> I don't know how I will work things out with my family.

> *bta'rfi anā shī'i.*
> You know I am Shiite.

The imperfect subjunctive form is used after modal words, such as *lēzim* (should, must), *baddi* (I want to), and *fiyī* (I can). This form of the imperfect tense lacks the prefixes *b-* and *m-*, but is otherwise indistinguishable from the indicative form.

• *lēzim* (should, must)

lēzim (should, must), a participle, is invariant, i.e., its form doesn't change depending on the person and number of the subject. Instead, the verb that follows *lēzim* is conjugated in the imperfect tense and indicates the person, gender, and number of the subject.

> *lēzim rūH 'a beirūt.*
> I need to go to Beirut.

> *shū lēzim ta'mal bukra?*
> What do you have to do tomorrow?

> *mish lēzim tZabbTu l-ūDa?*
> Don't you need to tidy the room?

• *baddi* (I want to)

baddi (I want to) is a noun with a possessive pronoun attached to its end to indicate the subject of the action expressed. When the subject changes, the pronominal suffix attached to *baddi* changes as well. The following table shows the different forms of *baddi* (I want to) followed by the imperfect verb *'eref* (to know).

THE EXPRESSION *baddi* (I WANT TO)			
Singular		**Plural**	
anā	baddi a'rif	naHna	baddnā na'rif
enta	baddak ta'rif	entu	baddkun ta'rifu/ta'rfu
enti	baddik ta'rifi/ta'rfi		
huwwi	baddu ya'rif	Hinni	baddun ya'rifu/ya'rfu
hiyyi	badda ta'rif		

> *kīf baddā trūH 'a 'ubruS la-Hālā?*
> Why does she want to go to Cyprus alone?

> *shū baddak tēkul w-tishrab?*
> What do you want to eat and drink?

Another function of *baddi* (I want to) is to indicate the future tense.[1] Its equivalent in English is either the future with *going to* or with *will*. Which translation of *baddi* is the correct one, *want to*, *going to*, or *will*, depends on the context. Take a look at some examples.

> *shū baddnā nēkul w-nishrab?*
> What are we going to eat and drink?

> *shū baddnā na'mul?*
> What are we going to do?

> *mā ba'rif kīf baddi ZabbiTa ma' ahlī.*
> I have no idea how I will work things out with my family.

---

[1] For a more detailed discussion of the future tense, see Lesson 27.

• *fīyī* (I can)

fīyī (I can) consists of the preposition *fī* (in) followed by an object pronoun suffix. The object pronoun suffix expresses the subject and therefore, has to change accordingly, e.g., *fīy* (he can), *fīyā* (she can), etc. *Fīyī* is followed by the imperfect subjunctive form of the verb, without the prefix *b-/m-*. In the following table, the verbal phrase *fīyī ikhtār* (I can/could choose) is fully conjugated.

THE EXPRESSION *fīyī ikhtār* (I CAN/COULD CHOOSE)			
Singular		Plural	
I can choose	*fīyī ikhtār*	we can choose	*fīnā nikhtār*
you *(m.)* can choose	*fīk tikhtār*	you *(m./f.)* can choose	*fīkun tikhtāru*
you *(f.)* can choose	*fīki tikhtārī*		
he can choose	*fīy ikhtār*	they *(m./f.)* can choose	*fīyun yikhtāru*
she can choose	*fīyā tikhtār*		

For a negative form, add the negative particle *mā* in front of *fīyī*.

> *mā fīyī ikhtār.*
> I can't choose.

4. VERB CONJUGATION

The conjugational patterns of Lebanese Arabic verbs are generally similar to those in *fuSHā*. However, *fuSHā* and Lebanese Arabic verbs differ in their internal vowels; e.g., *samaHa* (he allowed) in *fuSHā* is *semeH* in Lebanese.

In the table below, you will find five verbs from the dialogue, conjugated in the imperfect indicative. The first three columns have verbs in Form I: sound, hamzated, and hollow (see Lessons 13 and 14). The last two columns present a verb in Form II and a verb in Form V. Because the differences in the internal voweling between Lebanese Arabic verbs and their *fuSHā* counterparts are too elaborate to explain here, simply study the conjugation patterns of these five commonly used verbs.

THE IMPERFECT INDICATIVE IN LEBANESE ARABIC					
	semeH (to allow)	*akhad* (to take)	*rāH* (to go)	*ZabbiT* (to fix)	*tjawwaz* (to marry)
Verb Form	I (sound)	I (hamzated)	I (hollow)	II	V
anā	*bismaH*	*bēkhud*	*brūH*	*bZabbiT*	*bitjawwaz*
enta	*btismaH*	*btēkhud*	*btrūH*	*bitZabbiT*	*btitjawwaz*
enti	*btismaHi*	*btēkhdi*	*btrūHi*	*bitZabTi*	*btitjawwazi*
huwwi	*byismaH*	*byēkhud*	*byrūH*	*byiZabbiT*	*byitjawwaz*
hiyyi	*btismaH*	*btēkhud*	*btrūH*	*bitZabbiT*	*btitjawwaz*
naHna	*mnismaH*	*mnēkhud*	*mnrūH*	*minZabbiT*	*mnitjawwaz*
entu	*btismaHu*	*btēkhdu*	*btrūHu*	*bitZabTu*	*btitjawwazu*

D. Vocabulary

baddi	I want
ZabbiTa	I fix it
bas	but; only
byismaHūli	they allow me
tjawwaza	I marry her
lē	why
shū	what
mishkle	problem
shī'i (shī'iyye, f.)	Shiite
lēzim	should, must
w	and
mārūniyye	Maronite
'a shēn heyk	that's why
ba'd	yet, still
Harb ahliyye	civil war
Tāyfi	sectarian
ikhtiyarēt (ikhtiyār, sg.)	choices
fiyi	I can
itrika	I leave her
mish	not
bayyak	your father *(m.)*
yēk	you (independent object pronoun)
bala	yes
kbīre (kbīr, m.)	big
Tab	okay, well
raH	will, shall
walla	well, *adv.* (*lit.* by God)
ēkhida	I take her
nrūH	we go
'a	to
'ubruS	Cyprus
izā	if
jawēz madani	civil marriage
la-Hālnā	(we) alone
yi'ūlu	they say
jīrān (jār, sg.)	neighbors
ma''ūl	understandable, believable
bitfakkir	(you) think (conjugate like *Zabbit*)
hayda	this
shi''a	apartment
bfattish 'a shighel	I look for a job (conjugate like *Zabbit*)
blē'i	I find

l-waD' l-iqtiSādi	the economic situation
kamēn	also
Diddak	against you
mish heyke?	Isn't it so?, Right?

E. Cultural Note

Lebanon is a multi-religious society with eighteen officially recognized religious sects, twelve Christian and six Muslim. Different sects do not have equal power; their share of the legislative, executive, political, and administrative power depends on the number of their adherents and historical role. One of the key functions of each sect is the execution of the personal status law, which primarily regulates marriage and divorce, by its religious echelon.

As in neighboring Israel, inter-religious marriage ceremonies cannot be officially performed in Lebanon. Therefore, many Lebanese favor the introduction of civil marriage in Lebanon. They believe that civil marriage in Lebanon would be cheaper, as there would be no need to travel to Cyprus to be married in a civil court, and it would allow them to preserve their religious identity while marrying a person of another religion. Proponents of civil marriage also believe it will gradually help eliminate sectarianism in Lebanon. In an attempt to present the Lebanese with such an alternative, President Elias Hrawi submitted a draft law to institute civil marriage in 1998. This law was not ratified by the Parliament, although it was endorsed by the Council of Ministers. While the younger generation embraced Hrawi's proposal, the powerful Muslim and Christian clergy condemned civil marriage as a threat to public morals and the traditional Lebanese family.

F. Exercises

1. Put the words in the parentheses in the correct form, then translate the sentences into English.

Example: *anā (baddi) (bēkul) tabbule bas bint 'amti (baddi) (bēkul) salaTa tēniye.*
   anā baddi ēkul tabbule bas bint 'amti badda tēkul salaTa tēniye.
   I want to eat tabouli but my cousin wants to eat a different salad.

a. *mariam (lēzim) (bZabbit) kill il-mashēkil ma' ahla.*
b. *yā mona, (lēzim) (bitjawwaz) wāHad libnēni.*
c. *khāltī rimā (baddi) (itrik) libnēn w-('īsh) b-amerika.*
d. *bayyi (bifakkir) ba'dni 'ind ij-jīrān.*
e. *naHna mā (ba'rif) izā sāmir w-aHmad (bifattish) 'a shighel bi beirūt.*

2. Say the following statements or questions in Lebanese Arabic.

a. What's this?
b. Where is Ahmad's apartment?
c. Do you (f.) want to know our neighbors?
d. I am Maronite (m.) also.
e. We have to go to Beirut.

3. Match the words from column A to those in column B to form phrases or short sentences.

A

a. *lēzim*
b. *baddkun*
c. *shū*
d. *raH tēkhdi*
e. *'a shēn*
f. *jawēz*
g. *mish*

B

shāy yā betīna?
madani
heyk
trūHī 'a sh-shighel
ma''ūl
tishrabu shī?
baddak ta'mul bi-'ubruS?

4. Put the words in the correct order to form coherent sentences.

a. *yfattish / maHmūd / khāli / baddu / 'a / shi''a / akbar*
b. *ma / btismaHli / zeineb / 'a / l-baHr / la-Hāli / rūH*
c. *kill / hayda / shī*
d. *sine / Sarlī / b-libnēn*
e. *ma / bya'jibnī / l-iqtSādi / l-waD'*

5. Read the following passage and answer the questions that follow it.

ahlan. anā ismi zeineb. anā bint 'amtu la aHmad. bayyu la aHmad byismaHlu yitjawwaz bas bint shī'iyye mitli. anā bHebbu la aHmad bas huwwi ma baddu yitjawwazni. baddu bas haydi . . . shu isma . . . l-mārūniyye . . . jorjēt. hiyye lēzim titjawwaz wāHad mārūni w-titrik aHmad.

a. *mīn (who) byaHki?*
b. *shu isma?*
c. *hiyye bitHebbu la aHmad?*
d. *aHmad byiHebba?*
e. *hiyye bitHebba la jorjēt?*

Answer Key

1. a. *mariam lēzim tZabbit kill il-mashēkil ma' ahla.* Mariam should fix all problems with her family.

   b. *yā mona, lēzim titjawwazi wāHad libnēnī.* Mona, you should marry a Lebanese [guy].

   c. *khāltī rīmā badda titrik libnēn w-t'īsh b-amerika.* My aunt Rima wants to leave Lebanon and live in America.

   d. *bayyi byifakkir ba'dnī 'ind ij-jīrān.* My father thinks I'm still at the neighbors'.

   e. *naHna mā mna'rif izā sāmir w-aHmad byifattishu 'a shighel bi-beirūt.* We don't know if Samir and Ahmad are looking for a job in Beirut.

2. a. *shū hayda?*
   b. *weyn shi''at aHmad?*

c. *baddik ta'rfi jirānnā?*

d. *anā mārūni kamēn.*

e. *lēzim nrūH 'a beirūt.*

3. *lēzim trūHi 'a sh-shighel.* You *(f.)* have to go to work.
baddkun tishrabu shī? Do you *(pl.)* want to drink something?
shū baddak ta'mul bi-'ubruS? What do you *(m.)* want to do in Cyprus?
raH tēkhdi shāy yā betīna? Are you *(f.)* going to get tea, Betina?
'a shēn heyk because of that
jawēz madani civil marriage
mish ma''ūl unbelievable

4. a. *khālī maHmūd baddu yfattish 'a shi''a akbar.* My uncle Mahmud wants to look for a bigger apartment.

b. *ma btismaHli zeineb rūH 'a l-baHr la-Hāli.* Zeineb doesn't let me go to the sea alone.

c. *hayda kill shī.* This is all.

d. *Sarlī sine b-libnēn.* I've been in Lebanon for a year.

e. *ma bya'jibnī l-waD' l-iqtSādi.* I don't like the economic situation.

5. Hi. My name is Zeineb. I am Ahmad's cousin. His father allows him to marry only a Shiite girl, like myself. I love Ahmad but he doesn't want to marry me. He wants only this . . . what's her name . . . the Maronite . . . Georgette. She should marry a Maronite and leave Ahmad.

a. *bint 'amtu la aHmad btaHki.*

b. *isma zeineb.*

c. *hiyye bitHebbu la aHmad.*

d. *aHmad ma byiHebba.*

e. *hiyye ma bitHebba la jorjēt.*

LESSON 27

(Lebanese Arabic)

feyrūz Feiruz

A. Dialogue

Nadia's husband Ali is a huge fan of the famous Lebanese singer Feiruz, and he doesn't tolerate any criticism of his idol. He has just attended her concert in the city of Ba'lbek and is sharing his impressions with Lucy and Donald.

dūnald: kīf kēnet il-Hafli bi-ba'lbek yā 'alī?

'alī: bitjannin!

lūsī: mbayyen nbasaTet ktīr, mā heike?

'alī: nbasaTet w-noSS! mīn mā byinbusiT? feyrūz haydi, mish Hada tēnī . . . bta'rfu uSSata?

lūsī: ba'rif shwayye 'annā. kēnet min 'ile fa'ira . . .

'alī: bi-ZZabeT. mā kēn 'indun shī''a, kēnu sēknīn b-ūDa. bas bayyā kēn insēn ktīr Tayyib.

lūsī: kīf kēn Tayyib w-mā byismaHlā trūH 'ā rrādio Hatta tghannī?

'alī: bala, kēn 'am byitrikā trūH bas b-sharT, bta'rfi shū huwwe?

lūsī: mā ba'rif.

dūnald: anā kamēn ma ba'rif. shū huwwe?

'alī: mā tkun la-Hālā. trūH bas iza kēnu immā aw khayyā ma'ā. bta'rfu fi l-awwal bas kēnet zghīre, kēnet bitghannī la-jjirān?

dūnald: akīd Habbu Sawtā ktīr.

'alī: mā fi shakhS mā byHebb Sawtā la-feirūz.

nādya: shu ha l-Haki yā 'alī? kīf mā fī? ma ibnu li-zghīr la-abu yūsef mā byHebbā la-feyrūz.

'alī: enti kamēn! hayda mā byifham shī bi l-musī'a l-'arabiyye . . . shū baddik fīh!

lūsī: bta'rfu shū ismā l-Ha'ī'i?

dūnald: kīf, mish ismā feyrūz?

lūsī: lā, ismā nuhād Haddād.

'alī: brāvo 'aleyki, yā lūsī! Sirti bta'rfi ktīr 'an libnēn.

dūnald: akhadet isem shuhra, ya'nī?

'alī: bala, bas Sāret mashhūra. mā ba'rif le bas kēn fiyya tekhtār ismēn: shahrazēd aw feyrūz. w-hiyye Habbet it-tēni.

Donald: How was the concert in Ba'lbek, Ali?

Ali: Incredible!

Lucy: Looks like you had a lot of fun, didn't you?

Ali: I sure did! Who wouldn't have fun? This is Feiruz we're talking about—the one and only . . . Do you know her story?

Lucy: I know a little about her. She comes from a poor family . . .

Ali: Exactly. They didn't own an apartment; instead, they lived in a single room. Her father was a very good man, though.

Lucy: How was he a good man if he wouldn't (*lit.*, didn't) let her go to the radio station to sing live?

Ali: But he did let her go to the radio station on one condition; do you know what it was?

Lucy: I don't.

Donald: I don't either. What was it?

Ali: That she not go by herself. (*lit.*, that she is not alone) That she might go only if her mother or brother were to accompany her (*lit.*, were with her). Did you know, at first, when she was little, she used to sing for the neighbors?

Donald: They must have loved her voice.

Ali: There isn't anyone who doesn't love the voice of Feiruz.

Nadia: What are you talking about, Ali? What do you mean there isn't anyone? (*lit.*, how isn't there) Abu Yusef's younger son doesn't like her.

Ali: What are you talking about! (*lit.*, you too) That guy doesn't know anything about Arabic music . . . Don't even mention him!

Lucy: Do you know her real name?

Donald: What do you mean; isn't it Feiruz?

Lucy: No, her name is Nuhad Haddad.

Ali: Bravo, Lucy! You have learned a lot about Lebanon lately.

Donald: So, she took a stage name?

Ali: Yes, on the way to getting famous. I don't know why, but she could choose between two names—Shahrazad or Feiruz. And she loved the latter one.

B. Pronunciation

THE DEFINITE ARTICLE

In Lebanese Arabic, the definite article has two forms: *il* and *l*. *il* is used when the previous word ends in a consonant, and *l*, when it ends in a vowel. For example:

> *kīf kēnet il-Hafli?*
> How was the concert?

> *fi l-awwal*
> in the beginning

> *shu ha l-Haki?*
> What are you talking about? (*lit.* What is this talk?)

As in fuSHā, when the definite article precedes a "sun" consonant (*t, th, j, d, dh, r, z, s, sh, S, D, T, Z, l, n*), it mirrors the sound of that consonant.

> *Habbet it-tēni.*
> She loved the second one.

> *trūH 'ā r-rādio.*
> She goes to the radio.

Note that the letter *j*, pronounced like the sound *zh* in English *measure*, is a "sun" consonant in Lebanese Arabic.

> *kēnet bitghannī la j-jirān.*
> She used to sing for the neighbors.

When the definite article precedes words starting with two consonants and the first one is a "sun" consonant, the article takes the form *li,* as in:

> *ibnu li-zghīr la abu yūsef*
> Abu Yusef's younger son

Be careful not to confuse the definite article *li* with the preposition *la* (for).

Finally, in Lebanese Arabic, as in MSA, when a definite noun is modified by an adjective, the adjective is also definite and must be preceded by an article, as in:

> *ismā l-Ha'i'i*
> her real name

The noun *ismā* (her name) is definite because the possessive pronoun *-ā* (her) is attached to it.

C. Grammar and Usage

1. OBJECT PRONOUN SUFFIXES

Lebanese Arabic object pronouns, like those in the MSA, take the form of pronominal endings attached to verbs.

OBJECT PRONOUN SUFFIXES			
Singular		Plural	
me	-nī	us	-nā
you *(m.)*	-ak	you *(f./m.)*	-kun
you *(f.)*	-ik		
him/it	-u	them *(f./m.)*	-un
her/it	-a		

Object pronoun suffixes are identical to the possessive endings, presented in Lesson 26, except for *-nī* (me).

The following table shows the verb *byitrik* (he lets/leaves) in the imperfect tense with object pronouns attached to it.

THE VERB *byitrik* (HE LETS/LEAVES) IN THE IMPERFECT TENSE WITH OBJECT PRONOUN SUFFIXES			
Singular		Plural	
he lets me	*byitrik<u>ni</u>*	he lets us	*byitrik<u>nā</u>*
he lets you *(m.)*	*byitrik<u>ak</u>*	he lets you *(m./f.)*	*byitrik<u>un</u>*
he lets you *(f.)*	*byitrik<u>ik</u>*		
he lets him/it	*byitrik<u>u</u>*	he lets them *(m./f.)*	*byitrik<u>un</u>*
he lets her/it	*byitrik<u>ā</u>*		

2. THE PERFECT TENSE

Lebanese Arabic has a single perfect tense form, which is very similar to the corresponding MSA form.

In the following table, the verb *akhad* (to take) is conjugated in the perfect tense. Note that the stress in the *I* and *you* forms, singular and plural, falls on the second syllable, while in the *he, she,* and *they* forms, it is on the first syllable (the stressed syllables are underlined).

THE VERB *akhad* (TO TAKE) IN THE PERFECT TENSE			
Singular		Plural	
I took	a*khad(e)t*	we took	*akhadnā*
you *(m.)* took	a*khad(e)t*	you *(m./f.)* took	*akhadtu*
you *(f.)* took	*akhadti*		
he took	*akhad*	they *(m./f.)* took	*akhadu*
she took	*akhad(e)t*		

Note the lack of the final *-m* in the Lebanese Arabic form *akhadu* (they took), contrasting with the MSA form *akhadtum* (you took, *pl.*). The *I*, *you* (m.), and *he* forms are identical to the MSA so-called pausal forms, in which the final short vowels are not pronounced.

MSA: *akhadtu* (full form); *akhadt* (pausal form)

vs.

Lebanese Arabic: *akhadt/akhad(e)t* (I took)

The optional *-e-* in *akhad(e)t* is dropped when the verb is followed by a pronominal suffix and sometimes, when followed by another word.

Here is the verb *akhad* (he took) in the perfect tense with object pronouns attached to it.

THE PERFECT TENSE OF THE VERB *akhad* (TO TAKE) WITH OBJECT PRONOUN SUFFIXES			
Singular		Plural	
he took me	*akhadni*	he took us	*akhadnā*
he took you *(m.)*	*akhadak*	he took you *(m./f.)*	*akhadkun*
he took you *(f.)*	*akhadik*		
he took him/it	*akhadu*	he took them *(m./f.)*	*akhadun*
he took her/it	*akhada*		

When an object pronoun suffix follows the verb in the perfect tense, as in the examples below, the final vowel *-u* of the *you* (pl.) and *they* forms becomes long and the stress moves to it. The ending *-nā* changes to *-nē* when any object pronoun is added to the verb, and the stress moves there as well.

akhadtu + -u ⟶ *akhadtū*
you *(pl.)* took + him ⟶ You *(pl.)* took him/it.

akhadtu + *-a* → *akhadtūa*

you *(pl.)* took + her/it → You *(pl.)* took her/it.

akhadu + *-u* → *akhadū*

they took + him → They took him.

akhadnā + *-u* → *akhadnē*

we took + him → We took him/it.

akhadnā + *-ak* → *akhadnēk*

we took + you *(m.)* → We took you *(m.)*.

The perfect tense verb is negated by placing the particle *mā* in front of it.

mā akhadnē.
We didn't take him.

mā akhadtū.
You didn't take him.

mā akhadū.
They didn't take him.

3. VERB CONJUGATION

Below are the conjugations of five verbs in the perfect tense.

VERB CONJUGATION: THE PERFECT TENSE					
	semaH (to allow)	*akal* (to eat)	*rāH* (to go)	*ZabbaT* (to fix)	*tjawwaz* (to marry)
Verb Form	I (sound)	I (hamzated)	I (hollow)	II	V
I	*samaH(e)t*	*akal(e)t*	*reH(e)t*	*ZabbaT(e)t*	*tjawwaz(e)t*
you *(m.)*	*samaH(e)t*	*akal(e)t*	*reH(e)t*	*ZabbaT(e)t*	*tjawwaz(e)t*
you *(f.)*	*samaHti*	*akalti*	*reHti*	*ZabbaTti*	*tjawwazti*
he	*semaH*	*akal*	*rāH*	*ZabbaT*	*tjawwaz*
she	*semHet*	*akalet*	*rāHet*	*ZabbaTet*	*tjawwazet*
we	*samaHnā*	*akalnā*	*reHnā*	*ZabbaTnā*	*tjawwaznā*
you *(pl.)*	*samaHtu*	*akaltu*	*reHtu*	*ZabbaTtu*	*tjawwaztu*
they	*semHu*	*akalu*	*rāHu*	*ZabbaTu*	*tjawwazu*

Below are two verbs from the dialogue conjugated first in the perfect and then in the imperfect indicative tense. The verb *fehim* (to understand) is a sound Form I verb and the verb *ikhtār* (to choose) a hollow Form VIII verb.

364

THE SOUND VERB *fehim* (TO UNDERSTAND)		
	Perfect Tense	Imperfect Tense
I	*fhim(e)t*	*bifham*
you *(m.)*	*fhim(e)t*	*btifham*
you *(f.)*	*fhimti*	*btifhami*
he	*fehim*	*byifham*
she	*fehmet*	*btifham*
we	*fhimnā*	*mnifham*
you *(pl.)*	*fhimtu*	*btifhamu*
they	*fehmu*	*byifhamu*

4. THE VERB *kēn* (WAS, WERE) IN THE PERFECT TENSE

THE VERB *ikhtār* (TO CHOOSE)		
	Perfect Tense	Imperfect Tense
I	*khtar(e)t*	*bikhtār*
you *(m.)*	*khtar(e)t*	*btikhtār*
you *(f.)*	*khtarti*	*btikhtāri*
he	*khtār*	*byikhtār*
she	*khtāret*	*btikhtār*
we	*khtarnā*	*mnikhtār*
you *(pl.)*	*khtartu*	*btikhtāru*
they	*khtaru*	*byikhtāru*

The hollow verb *kēn* (was/were) is a verb with a weak middle radical.[1] *kēn* has three uses, similar to its *fuSHā* counterpart *kān* (was/were): a. it expresses the past of the verb *to be*, b. it expresses a habitual past and incomplete action, similar to English *used to*, and c. it expresses the past progressive action, similar to English *was/were doing*. When used in a habitual or past progressive context, *kēn* precedes a verb in the imperfect indicative tense. In the following sentence *kēn*, in the form of *kēnet*, means first "was," and then "used to."

   bas kēnet zghīre kēnet bitghannī la j-jirān.
   When she was little she used to sing for the neighbors.

kēn has two stems in the perfect tense, *kēn-* and *kin-*. Here is its complete conjugation.

THE PERFECT TENSE OF THE VERB *kēn* (WAS/WERE)			
Singular		Plural	
I was	*kinet/kint*	we were	*kinnā*
you *(m.)* were	*kinet/kint*	you were	*kintu*
you *(f.)* were	*kintī*		
he was	*kēn*	they were	*kēnu*
she was	*kēnet*		

---
[1] See Lesson 14 for a discussion of hollow verbs.

D. Vocabulary

bitjannin	incredible (*lit.*, it makes you crazy)
mbayyen	obvious
w-noSS	indeed, surely (an emphatic expression that follows the emphasized word—verb, noun, or adjective, *lit.*, and a half)
haydi	this *(f.)*
Hada	one, someone
uSSata	her story
shwayye	a little
'annā	about her
'īle	family
fa'īra	poor
'indun	they have
kēnu sēknīn	they used to live
ūDa	room
insēn	man, person
Tayyib	good-hearted
Hatta	in order to
tghannī	she sings
b-sharT	on a condition
immā	her mother
khayyā	her brother
awwal	beginning
zghīre (zghīr, m.)	little
akīd	sure
Sawtā	her voice
shu ha l-Haki?	What are you talking about? (*lit.*, What is this talk?)
mā fī	there isn't
byifham	he understands
musī'a	music
Ha'ī'i	real
isem shuhra	stage name (*lit.*, fame name)
mashhūra (mashhūr, m.)	famous
tekhtār	she chooses
ismēn	two names

E. Cultural Note

Feiruz is not only the most famous Lebanese singer but also a legend of contemporary Arabic music (visit www.fairouz.com for more information and music samples). Born Nuhad Haddad on November 21, 1935, in a little Lebanese village, Feiruz soon moved with her family to a poor neighborhood of Beirut where her father worked in typesetting.

Her voice was discovered by a teacher from the National Conservatory, who was looking for new talents. He helped her join the national radio choir and two months later, after her conservative father was assured that Feiruz would sing only patriotic songs, she recorded her first solo songs. She became a huge success overnight.

At the radio, Feiruz met Aasi Rahbani, a budding composer who was working as a police officer at the time. Aasi became her husband in 1954 and the composer with whom Feiruz recorded most of her songs. Their musical style is famous and combines the exclusive beauty of her passionate, Eastern voice with Western musical nuances.

Her first live concert was in the summer of 1957 in the temple of Jupiter in the city of Ba'lbek, in front of the largest audience that ever gathered there. Since then, until the beginning of the civil war, Feiruz sang on that stage almost yearly. She returned to Ba'lbek in 1998 and her concerts were a smashing success. In the late 1970's, Feiruz started singing the jazz-influenced songs of her son Ziad (see www.ziad-rahbani.net). In May of 1999, Feiruz performed at the MGM Grand Hotel in Las Vegas in front of 10,000 fans.

F. Exercises

1. Read the dialogue in Lesson 26 and find all nouns with a definite article. How many different forms of the definite article did you find? Explain the differences.

2. Supply the correct form of *kēn* (was/were), then translate the sentences into English.

Example: *bintu (kēn) ktīr Tayyibe.*
  bintu kēnet ktīr Tayyibe.
  His daughter was very nice.
a. *bayyi mā (kēn) yismaHli rūH 'ā j-jām'a la-Hāli.*
b. *jīrānnā mā (kēn) bi beytun.*
c. *anā w-khālti rimā (kēn) jīrān b-amerika.*
d. *yā, zeineb, shu (kēn) ta'mlu enti w-khayyik bas (kēn) sāknin b-libnēn?*
e. *anā mā (kēn) a'rif izā sāmir w-aHmad fattashu 'a shighel bi beirūt.*

3. Translate the following sentences into Lebanese Arabic.

a. I don't know (*lit.*, understand) anything at work.
b. Isn't his name Kamal?—No, his name is Ahmad.
c. He can go to the concert with his father and mother.
d. I don't like Enrique Iglesias's voice. He doesn't sing well.
e. Our father leaves us alone.
f. Did you (*f.*) take him to the hospital?—No, I didn't take him yet.

4. Match the questions from column A to their answers in column B to create a dialogue.

A

nbasaTTi bi-l-Hafli?

nbasaTet w-noSS. lē mā nbasaTTi enti?

shu ha l-Haki? kīf mā bta'rfi?

kēn Tayyib il-akel, kif mā 'ajabik?

anā mā bifham bi-l-akel? it-tabbūle bitjannin w-l-kibbe kamēn . . .

shwayye? bas akīd Habbu l-musī'a?

B

mā 'ajabni l-akel.

mā ba'rif.

bala, Habbūā.

lā, it-tabbūle mā kēnet Tayyibe, bas immi w-bayyi Habbu l-kibbe shwayye . . .

mā kēn Tayyib. enti mā btifhami bi-l-akel.

mish ktīr. w-enti?

5. Answer the following questions.

a. *shu bta'rif lūsī 'an feirūz?*

b. *kīf kēnet t'īsh 'īlet feirūz (or 'īletā la feirūz)?*

c. *'alī byiHebb feirūz? lē?*

d. *w-enta/enti bta'rif/bta'rfi feirūz? bitHebb/bitHebbi Sawtā?*

e. *bta'rif/bta'rfi shakhS mashhūr mitl feirūz b-amerika?*

f. *bitHebb/bitHebbi l-musī'a l-'arabiyye?*

Answer Key

1. *l-mishkle, l-waD'* — The form of the definite article is *l* because the preceding words *shū* and *ya'ni* end in vowels.

   ij-jīrān — The form of the definite article is *ij* because it precedes the word *jīrān,* beginning in a sun consonant, and follows a word, *w-,* ending in a consonant.

2. a. *bayyi mā kēn yismaHli rūH 'ā j-jām'a la-Hāli.* My dad didn't let me go to the university alone.

   b. *jīrānnā mā kēnu bi-beytun.* Our neighbors were not at [their] home.

   c. *anā w-khālti rīmā kinnā jīrān b-amerika.* My aunt and I were neighbors in America.

   d. *yā, zeineb, shu kintu ta'mlu enti w-khayyik bas kintu sāknīn b-libnēn?* Zeineb, what were you and your brother doing when you were living in Lebanon?

   e. *anā mā kint a'rif izā sāmir w-aHmad fattashu 'a shighel bi beirūt.* I didn't know if Samir and Ahmad had searched for work in Beirut.

3. a. *mā bifham shī bi sh-shighel.*

   b. *mish ismu kamāl? lā, ismu aHmad.*

   c. *fiy yrūH 'ā l-Hafli ma' bayyu w- immu.*

   d. *mā bHebb Sawtu la Enrique Iglesias. mā byighanni mnēH.*

   e. *bayynā byitriknā la-Hālnā.*

   f. *akhadtī 'ā l-mustashfa? lā, mā akhadtu ba'd.*

4. *nbasaTTi bi-l-Hafli?*
   mish ktīr. w-enti?
   Did you have fun at the party?
   Not much. And you?
   nbasaTet w-noSS. lē mā nbasaTTi enti?
   mā ba'rif.

I had a lot of fun. You didn't you have fun?
I don't know.
shu ha l-Haki? kif mā bta'rfi?
mā 'ajabni l-akel.
What kind of an answer (*lit.* talk) is that? How come you don't know?
I didn't like the food.
kēn Tayyib il-akel, kif mā 'ajabik?
mā kēn Tayyib. enti mā btifhami bi-l-akel.
The food was tasty; how come you didn't like it?
It wasn't tasty. You don't know what good food is (*lit.*, you don't understand food).
anā mā bifham bi-l-akel? it-tabbūle bitjannin w-l-kibbe kamēn . . .
lā, it-tabbūle mā kēnet Tayyibe, bas immi w-bayyi Habbu l-kibbe shwayye . . .
I don't know what good food is? The tabouli was fantastic, and the kibbe too . . .
No, the tabouli wasn't tasty, but my mom and dad liked the kibbe a little . . .
shwayye? bas akīd Habbu l-musī'a?
bala, Habbūā.
A little? But they surely [must have] liked the music?
Yes, they liked it.

5. a. *shu bta'rif lūsī 'an feirūz? – bta'rif isma l-Ha'ī'i w-kamēn shwayye 'an 'īletā.*
   What does Lucy know about Feiruz?

– She knows her real name and also a little about her family.

b. *kif kēnet t'īsh 'ilet feirūz ['īletā la-feirūz]? – kēnet 'ilet feirūz fa'īra, kēnu sēknīn b-ūDa, mish b-shi''a.*
   How did Feiruz's family use to live?
   – Feiruz's family was poor; they lived in a [single] room, not in an apartment.

c. *'alī byiHebb feirūz? lē? – bala, 'alī byiHebb feirūz ktīr 'a shēn Sawtā byijannin.*
   Does Ali like Feiruz? Why? – Yes, Ali likes Feiruz a lot because her voice is fantastic.

d. Answers may vary.
   w-enta/enti bta'rif/bta'rfi feirūz? bitHebb/bitHebbi Sawtā?
   And you, do you know Feiruz? Do you like her voice?
   bala, a'rifa w-bHebb Sawta ktīr.
   Yes, I know her, and I like her voice a lot.

e. Answers may vary. *bta'rif/bta'rfi shakhS mashhūr mitl feirūz b-amerika?*
   Do you know a famous person like Feiruz in America?
   ba'rif / mā ba'rif . . .
   I know / don't know . . .

f. Answers may vary.
   bitHebb/bitHebbi l-musī'a l-'arabiyye?
   Do you like Arabic music?
   shwayye/ktīr . . .
   A little/a lot . . .

LESSON 28

(Lebanese Arabic)

shū 'am ta'mli? What's Up?

A. Dialogue

Lucy, a visiting professor at the American University in Beirut, advises her undergraduate student Amal about her future job options and graduate study. Amal, who is majoring in English literature, feels ambivalent about teaching English in Lebanese schools because of the low salary and discipline issues, and is considering other options.

lūsī: ahlan amal, kīfik? kīf iS-SaHa?

amal: mēshi l-Hāl, kīfik enti?

lūsī: mnēHa, tfaDDali!

amal: mersi.

lūsī: shū 'am ta'mli?

amal: walla, mitl ma bta'rfi ha s-sine raH khalliS ij-jēm'a.

lūsī: shū ha ta'mli ba'deyn?

amal: ma 'ashēn heyk baddi iHke ma'ik. b-SarāHa baddi a'rif shū 'indi ikhtiyārēt.

lūsī: awwal shī iza mā baddik tidrisi ba'd, fiki trūHi tishtighli. ikhtiSāSik ktīr mēshi b-libnēn. fiki tlē'i shighel b-sur'a. kill il-madēris halla baddun asētze bi'allmu inglīze.

amal: bas mā raH a'baD ktīr.

lūsī: ma'ik Ha'.

amal: w-kamēn mā fiyi 'allim wlēd Zghār. mā byisma'u l-kalēm. ta'rfi shū alla ibna la-jārti haydik il-yōm? bas reji' min il-madrase alla "yā māmā, il-yōm ta'allamna l-ktēbe". allatlu "w-shū katabtu, yā māmā?". alla "mā ba'rif, ba'd mā ta'allamna l-irēye."

lūsī: mahDūm, walla.

amal: mish ma''ūl!

lūsī: Tab, izan fiki tfattshi 'a shighel tēni aw tkaffi dirāstik.

amal: aSdik 'addim 'a mājistēr?

lūsī: ē, fiki trūhi tidrisi b-amerika. lē mā t'addmi 'a jjēm'a tē'i?

amal: yu si el ey?

lūsī: ē.

amal: shū l-"web sait" tabā'a?

lūsī: ma'ik alam?

amal: lā, mā ma'i.

lūsī: tilmīze bala alam? hayda alam, tfaDDali, ktibi l-'inwēn. ilik Hada b-amerika?

amal: bala, khālti sēkni b-los angeles.

Lucy: Hi, Amal, how are you? How are you doing?

Amal: Well, things are fine, how are you?

Lucy: Good, come on in!

Amal: Thanks.

Lucy: What's up? (*lit.*, What are you doing?)

Amal: Well, as you know, this year I'm graduating.

Lucy: And what are you going to do after that?

Amal: Well, that's why I want to talk to you. To tell you the truth, I want to know what options I have.

Lucy: First, if you don't want to study anymore, you could find a job (*lit.*, you could go to work). Your major is very popular in Lebanon. You can find a job quickly. All schools now are looking for English teachers.

Amal: But I wouldn't get paid very much.

Lucy: You're right.

Amal: And also I can't teach little kids. They don't listen. Do you know what my neighbor's son told her the other day? When he got back from school he said to her: "Mom, today we learned how to write". She told him: "What did you write, sweetie?" He said to her: "I don't know, we still haven't learned how to read".

Lucy: That's cute.

Amal: Unbelievable!

Lucy: Well then, you can look for another job or continue your education.

Amal: You mean apply for an M.A.?

Lucy: Yeah, you can go study in the United States. Why don't you apply to my university?

Amal: UCLA?

Lucy: Right.

Amal: What's its Web site?

Lucy: Do you have a pen?

Amal: No, I don't.

Lucy: A student without a pen? Here's a pen; here you go, write the URL. Do you have any family (*lit.*, anyone) in the United States?

Amal: Yes, my aunt lives in LA.

B. Pronunciation

CONSONANT CLUSTERS

While in *fuSHā* no more than two consonants can appear together, in Lebanese Arabic, as in other Arabic dialects, even three-consonant clusters can be found in many words. In the examples below, the short vowel, which exists in corresponding MSA words, is dropped in Lebanese Arabic, creating a two-consonant cluster.

LA	*sēkni* (living)	*jārti* (my neighbor)	*Zghār* (little)	*asētze* (teachers)	*bta'rfi* (you know)	*ta'mli* (you do)	*tfaDDali* (come on in)
MSA	*sākina*	*jārati*	*Sighār*	*asātidha*	*ta'rifi*	*ta'mali*	*tafaDDali*

The short vowel *i* is dropped from the preposition *bi* (in) in the following examples.

LA	*b-sur'a* (quickly)	*b-libnēn* (in Lebanon)	*b-SarāHa* (honestly)
MSA	*bi-sur'a*	*bi-lubnān*	*bi-SarāHa*

In Lebanese Arabic, as in other dialects, words can also contain clusters of three consonants. This usually happens in the imperfect tense of Form II verbs, specifically the singular *you* or *they* form.

LA	t'addmi (you apply, f.)	tfattshi (you search, f.)	b'allmu (they teach)	inglize (English)
MSA	tuqaddimi	tufattishi	yu'allimūn	ingiliziyya

Lebanese Arabic is well-known for the opposite phenomenon as well. Where *fuSHā* has a *sukūn*, signaling a consonant cluster, Lebanese Arabic adds an extra vowel.

LA	shighel (work)	isem shuhra (stage name)	bi Z-ZabeT (exactly)
MSA	shughl	ism shuhra	bi D-DabT

C. Grammar and Usage

1. THE FUTURE TENSE

In Lebanese Arabic the future tense is formed by placing the particles *raH* or *ha* (used interchangeably) before the imperfect tense form of the verb without *b-/m-* prefix. This tense corresponds to either the future tense (using *will* or *going to*) or to the present progressive tense (*to be doing*) in English.

> ha ssine raH khalliS ij-jēm'a.
> I'm graduating (*lit.*, finishing university) this year.

> shū ha ta'mli ba'deyn?
> What are you going to do afterwards?

> raH a'baD ktīr.
> I'll get paid a lot.

To negate the future simply add the negative particle *mā* in front of *raH* or *ha*.

> ha ssine mā raH khalliS ij-jēm'a.
> I'm not graduating this year.

> shū mā ha ta'mli ba'deyn?
> What aren't you going to do afterwards?

> mā raH a'baD ktīr.
> I'm not going to get paid much.

2. DEMONSTRATIVES

Lebanese Arabic demonstrative pronouns are fewer and simpler than their counterparts in *fuSHā*.

DEMONSTRATIVES IN LEBANESE ARABIC			
	Masculine		Feminine	
Singular	hayda (this)	haydēk (that)	haydi (this)	haydēki (that)
Plural	haydōl (these)	haydolēk (those)	haydōl (these)	haydolīki (those)

Note that the *dh* sound in MSA demonstratives (e.g., *hādha* [this, *m.*]) is replaced by the *d* sound in Lebanese Arabic. Lebanese Arabic also adds a *y* in the middle of the word.

hayda alam.
This is a pen.

hayda mish kill shī.
That's not all.

hayda mā byifham shī.
This [guy] doesn't understand anything.

feyrūz haydi.
This is Feiruz.

The Lebanese Arabic demonstratives for nearness (*this, these*) given in the above table always function as pronouns, i.e., they cannot modify a noun. A single demonstrative adjective, *ha* (this), is used with nouns of any gender or number.

ha ssine raH khalliS ij-jēm'a.
This year I'm graduating.

shu ha l-Haki?
What are you talking about? (*lit.*, What's this talk?)

Note that a demonstrative is used in the expression *haydēk il-yōm* (that day), meaning "the other day," as in:

ta'rfi shū alla ibna la-jārti haydēk il-yōm?
Do you know what my neighbor's son told her the other day?

3. EXPRESSING POSSESSION

Three different constructions involving the prepositions *la* (for), *ma'* (with), and *'ind* (at, on) are used in Lebanese Arabic to express the concept of possession. Possessive suffixes are added to these prepositions to express different persons and number. The preposition *la* is usually used in combination with *il*, its variant form, which carries the possessive endings.

POSSESSIVE CONSTRUCTIONS			
	la (for)	*ma'* (with)	*'ind* (at, on)
I have	(la) ili	ma'i	'indi
you have	(la) ilak	ma'ak	'indak
you (f.) have	(la) ilik	ma'ik	'indik
he has	(la) ilu	ma'u	'indu
she has	(la) ila	ma'a	'inda
we have	(la) ilnā	ma'nā	'innā
you have	(la) ilkun	ma'kun	'inkun
they have	(la) ilun	ma'un	'indun

The three possessive constructions are used in different contexts with slightly varying meanings.

A. *la* (FOR)

The possessive construction with *la* (for) expresses different forms of possession, as described below. Depending on its function, it takes different forms.

- *il-*

In this construction, *la*, taking the form of *il*, indicates relationships between people, such as those within a family. Depending on the grammatical person of the owner, *il-* combines with different possessive suffixes. For example:

> *ilik Hada b-amerika?*
> Do you have someone (i.e., family) in America?

> *ila ikht b-amerika.*
> She has a sister in America.

- *la il-*

The possessive construction with *la* is also used to express ownership over an object, and corresponds to the English possessive pronouns *mine, yours, hers,* etc. It can be also translated with the construction "X belong(s) to Y." When used with this meaning, it always appears as *la il-* . For example:

> *ha l-bēt la ilkun?*
> Is this house yours *(pl.)*?/Does this house belong to you? (*lit.,* Is this house for you?)

> *hayda la ilik?*
> Is this yours?/Does this belong to you? (*lit.,* Is this for you?)

In short, whenever you want to say "X is mine" or "X belong(s) to me" use *la il-* in "X *la ili*", and when you want to say "I have X," where X is a person, use *ili* alone in "*ili X.*"

- *la*

la can also be used in a possessive construction, or an *iDāfa*, as an alternative way of marking the possessive relationship between two nouns.[1] For example:

> *ibna la-jārti*
> my neighbor's son (*lit.,* her son for my neighbor)

> *Sawta la-feyrūz*
> Feiruz's voice (*lit.,* her voice for Feiruz)

---

[1] See Lesson 4 for a discussion of the possessive construction in MSA.

Note that *la* is also frequently used in its original prepositional meaning, which should not be confused with the expression of possession, as in:

> *kēnet bitghanni la-jjirān.*
> She used to sing for the neighbors.

B. *ma'* (WITH)

The possessive construction with the preposition *ma'* (with) expresses the meaning of having something on oneself, at the particular moment. Its literal meaning is "X is with someone." Negate it with *mā*.

> *ma'ik alam?*
> Do you have a pen on you? (*lit.*, Is a pen with you?)

> *mā ma'i.*
> No, I don't. (*lit.*, No [pen] with me.)

> *ma'ik Ha'.*
> You are right. (*lit.*, The right is with you.)

C. *'ind* (AT, ON)

The possessive construction with *'ind* (at, on) denotes a general sense of being in possession of something. It is also used in statements such as *I have a class, I have school,* or *I have a choice.* It is negated with *mā*. Note that in the *we* and *you* plural forms (*'innā* and *'inkun*), the *d* in *'ind* is dropped. The preposition *fi* can be added in front of *'ind* with no change in meaning.

> *mā kēn (fi) 'indun shi''a.*
> They didn't have an apartment.

> *baddi a'rif shū (fi) 'indi ikhtiyārēt.*
> I want to know what options I have.

> *kam siyyāra 'inkun?*
> How many cars do you own?

> *fi 'indik madrase bukra?*
> Do you have school tomorrow?

4. EXPRESSING POSSESSION WITH *tē'* AND *tabā'*

The expressions *tē'* and *tabā'*, meaning "belonging to," resemble possessive pronouns and adjectives in function. *tē'* and *tabā'* are followed by possessive suffixes and represent another way to express belonging and ownership in Lebanese Arabic. Sometimes, they indicate not so much ownership as association, for example, with an institution.

POSSESSIVE EXPRESSIONS *tē'* AND *tabā'* WITH POSSESSIVE SUFFIXES		
my/mine	*tē'i*	*tabā'i*
your/yours *(m.)*	*tē'ak*	*tabā'ak*
your/yours *(f.)*	*tē'ik*	*tabā'ik*
his, its	*tē'u*	*tabā'u*
her/hers, its	*tē'a*	*tabā'a*
our/ours	*tē'nā*	*tabā'nā*
your/yours	*tē'kun*	*tabā'kun*
their/theirs	*tē'un*	*tabā'un*

When used as possessive pronouns, *tē'* and *tabā'* are interchangeable with *la il-*; when they are used as possessive adjectives, they may be replaced with the possessive endings (*-ī, -ak, -ik,* etc.) or the possessive *la,* an alternative to the *iDāfa.*

Like adjectives in Arabic, the possessive words *tē'* and *tabā'* follow the noun they modify.

> *lē mā t'addmi 'a j-jēm'a tē'i?*
> Why don't you apply to my university? (*lit.,* . . . to the university to which I belong/with which I am associated?)

Compare this with *lē mā t'addmi 'a jēm'ati?* (Why don't you apply to my university?), where a possessive suffix *-ī* is used instead.

If *tabā'* is followed by a noun, it contracts to *taba',* as in:

> *l-"web sait" taba' l-istēz*
> the professor's Web site/the Web site belonging to the professor

Compare this with *"web-sait"-u la l-istēz* (the professor's Web site/the Web site belonging to the professor), where *la* is used.

> *hayda tabā'ik?*
> Is this yours?/Does this belong to you?

Compare this with *hayda la ilik?* (Is this yours?/Does this belong to you?).

5. VERB CONJUGATION

Below you will find three verbs, *āl* (to say, to tell), *Hiki* (to speak, talk), and *abaD* (to get paid, earn), conjugated in the perfect and imperfect indicative. If *āl* (to say, to tell) is followed by a pronominal object, as in *I told him,* the verb has to combine with the preposition *la* (for), to which an object pronoun suffix is added. Below is the conjugation of *āl* (to say, to tell) with and without the preposition. After a perfect tense verb ending in a vowel, the preposition *la* becomes *l*; after a perfect tense verb ending in a consonant, it becomes *ill* (except for the *she* form, where it is *l*). In the imperfect tense, the preposition is *l* for all forms.

THE VERB āl (TO SAY, TO TELL)

	Perfect	With la (to) and -u (him)	Imperfect	With la (to) and -u (him)
I	il(e)t	iltillu (I said to him)	b'ūl	b'illu (I say to him)
you (m.)	il(e)t	iltillu	bit'ūl	bit'illu
you (f.)	ilti	iltīlu	bit'ūli	bit'ilīlu
he	āl	āllu	by'ūl	by'illu
she	ālet	aletlu	bit'ūl	bit'illu
we	ilnā	alnēlu	min'ūl	min'illu
you (pl.)	iltu	iltūlu	bit'ūlu	bit'ilūlu
they	ālu	ālūlu	byi'ūlu	byi'ilūlu

THE VERB Hiki (TO SPEAK, TALK)

	Perfect	Imperfect
I	Hkēt	beHki
you (m.)	Hkēt	bteHki
you (f.)	Hkīti	bteHki
he	Hiki	byeHki
she	Hikyet	bteHki
we	Hkīnā	mnel lki
you (pl.)	Hkitu	bteHku
they	Hikyu	byeHku

THE VERB abaD (TO GET PAID, TO EARN)

	Perfect	Imperfect
I	abaD(e)t	ba'baD
you (m.)	abaD(e)t	bta'baD
you (f.)	abaDti	bta'baDi
he	abaD	bya'baD
she	abaDet	bta'baD
we	abaDnā	mna'baD
you (pl.)	abaDtu	bta'baDu
they	abaDu	bya'baDu

D. Vocabulary

mēshi l-Hāl.	Things are going fine.
mnēHa	good (f.)
sine	year
khalliS	I finish (conjugate like Zabbat)
jēm'a	university
ba'deyn	afterwards
iHke	I speak, I talk

tidrisi	you *(f.)* study
ikhtiSāSik	your *(f.)* major, specialty
mēshi	popular (*lit.,* going)
b-sur'a	fast (*lit.,* with speed)
halla	now
asētze (*istēz,* sg.)	teachers
byi'allmu	they teach (conjugate like *Zabbat*)
a'baD	I get paid, I earn
inglīze	English
ma'ik Ha'.	You are right.
wlēd	children
Zghār (*Zghīr,* sg.)	little
mā byisma'u l-kalēm.	They don't listen.
alla	he told her
haydik il-yōm	the other day
reji'	he came back, he returned
māmā	mommy
ktēbe	writing (verbal noun)
irēye	reading (verbal noun)
mahDūm	cute
izan	then, in that case
tkaffi	you *(f.)* continue
dirāstik	your *(f.)* education
'addim	I apply (conjugate like *Zabbat*)
mājistēr	master's degree
tē'i	my
tabā'a	its, her
ē	yeah
bala	without
alam	pen
'inwēn	address
ilik	you *(f.)* have

E. Cultural Note

Studying languages is an essential part of Lebanese education. Most elementary, junior high, and high schools use two languages as their official languages of instruction: Arabic for the subjects of history, Arabic literature, and Arabic language, and either French or English for all the science subjects. In junior high or high school a third language is usually added, so by the time students graduate from high school, it is assumed that they have mastered two languages and have a strong background in a third one. However, many people whose language of instruction at school was French feel they need to study English in specialized language schools. Most of these are members of the younger generation who have realized that English is a huge asset when you look for a job.

To teach in language schools, called *madēris ir-rāshidīn* (adult schools), or in any school in Lebanon, you don't need any teaching credentials. A Bachelor's is often enough for schoolteachers and a relative mastery of English for language school instructors. Many Americans who go to Lebanon to study Arabic find their first employment in such language schools. A lot of Lebanese prefer them to working at regular schools as well, since the wages are a little higher, the working hours are more flexible, and there are no discipline issues.

F. Exercises

1. Give the *fuSHā* equivalents for the following Lebanese Arabic words. (Tip: Supply the short vowels.)

mishkle, waHdi (one, f.), *b-sharT, zghīre, tghanni*

2. Transform the following statements from the imperfect or the perfect tense to the future tense. In your sentences, include the information provided in the parentheses.

a. *bitHebba la-feyrūz. (bas btisma' Sawta)*
b. *l-asētze mā by'allmu l-faransi, bas il-inglīze. (bi-l-madēris il-inglīziye)*
c. *jārti amal mā kēnet bi-beyta. (ba'd yōm)*
d. *yā, Hasan, shu kintu ta'mlu enta w-khayyak? (bas riHtu 'a libnēn)*
e. *akhadti 'a l-mustashfa? (bukra)*

3. Translate the following statements into Lebanese Arabic.

a. This is a school.
b. These are schools.
c. This is a Lebanese girl.
d. They teach Arabic in this school.
e. I don't like this job.
f. These little kids know how to write and read well (*lit.*, know writing and reading).

4. Answer the following questions.

a. *lē mā kēn ya'rif ibna la-jjāra shu ketib bi-l-madrase?*
b. *lē mā badda amal tishtighl bi-l-madēris?*
c. *w-enta/enti bta'rif/bta'rfi asētze by'allmu inglīze? byiHebbu shighlun?*
d. *shu aHsan shighel b-amerika?*

5. Put the words in the parentheses in the correct form to make expressions of possession.

a. *ha l-alam (tē' + enti)?*
b. *(ma' + entu) sayyāra?*
c. *bint ij-jīrān ('ind + hiyyi) shi''a bitjannin.*

d. *il-ktēbe w-il-irēye mish la (la + anā). anā bHebb ishtighel bas ma bHebb id-dirēse.*

e. *'am bfakkir Sarli sē'a. ma ba'rif shū baddi a'mul—il-ikhtiSaSāt (tabā') ha jjēm'a mā by'ajbūni. raH addim 'a jēm'a tēniye.*

Answer Key

1. *mushkila, wāHida, bi-sharT, Saghīra, tughannī*

2. a. *raH/ha tHebba la-feyrūz bas btisma' Sawta.*
   You'll like Feiruz when you hear her voice.

   b. *bi-l-madēris il-inglīziye l-asētze mā raH/ha y'allmu l-faransi, bas il-inglīze.*
   In the English schools, teachers won't teach French, just English.

   c. *jārti amal mā raH/ha tkūn bi-beyta ba'd yōm.*
   My neighbor Amal isn't going to be at [her] home in a day.

   d. *yā, Hasan, shu raH/ha ta'mlu enta w-khayyak bas btrūHu 'a libnēn?*
   Hasan, what are you and your brother going to do when you go to Lebanon?

   e. *raH/ha tēkhdī 'a l-mustashfa bukra?*
   Are you (f.) going to take him to the hospital tomorrow?

3. a. *haydi madrase.*
   b. *haydōl madēris.*
   c. *haydi binet libnēniye.*
   d. *b-ha l-madrase by'allmu 'arabe.*
   e. *mā by'jibni ha shshighel.*
   f. *ha l-wlēd li-Zghār bya'rfu l-ktēbe w-il irēye mnēH.*

4. a. *lē mā kēn ya'rif ibna la-jjāra shu ketib bi-l-madrase?*
   Why didn't the neighbor's son know what he wrote at school?
   huwwi mā bya'rif il-irēye.
   He doesn't know how to read.

   b. *lē mā badda amal tishtighl bi-l-madēris?*
   Why doesn't Amal want to work in schools?
   mā raH ta'baD ktīr wi-l-wlēd mā byisma'u l-kalēm.
   She's not going to get paid much and kids don't listen.

   c.–d. Answers may vary.
   Model answers:

   c. *w-enta/enti bta'rif/bta'rfi asētze by'allmu inglīze? byiHebbu shighlun?*
   Do you know teachers of English? Do they like their job?
   khayyī by'allim inglīze b-madrase Zghire b-"Santa Monica" w-mā byiHebb shighlu ktīr.
   My brother teaches English at a small school in Santa Monica, and he doesn't like his job very much.

   d. *shu aHsan shighel b-amerika?*
   What's the best job in the United States?
   la ilī, aHsan shighel b-amerika istēz jēm'a/duktūr/tishtighil bi-lkompiūtar.
   For me, the best job in the United States is a university professor/a physician/to work in computer[s].

5. a. *ha l-alam tē'ik?*
   Is this pen yours (f.)?

   b. *ma'kun sayyāra?*
   Do you (pl.) have a car with you?

   c. *bint ij-jīrān 'inda shi''a bitjannin.*
   The neighbor's daughter has a fantastic apartment.

   d. *il-ktēbe w-il-irēye mish la ilī. anā bHebb ishtighel bas ma bHebb id-dirēse.*

Writing and reading are not for me. I like working but I don't like studying.

e. 'am bfakkir Sarli sē'a. ma ba'rif shū baddi a'mul—il-ikhtiSaSāt taba' ha j-jēm'a mā by'ajbūni. raH addim 'a jēm'a tēniye.

I've been thinking for an hour. I don't know what to do—I don't like the majors at this university. I'll apply to another university.

LESSON 29

(Lebanese Arabic)

'an jad bta'rfi tiTbukhi! You Really Know How to Cook!

A. Dialogue

Nadia is teaching Lucy how to cook a traditional Lebanese rice garnish.

lūsī: ktīr 'ajabni l-ghada mbēriH! 'an jad bta'rfi tiTbukhi!

nādya: shū 'ajabik aktar—ttabbūle walla llūbya b-rizz?

lūsī: ttabbūle ktīr 'ajabetni bas ir-rizz byijannin. fīki t'allmīni kīf biTbukhu?

nādya: tikram 'aynik! 'a fikra, halla ken baddi iTbukhu. ta'i 'a l-maTbakh Hatta farjīki.

lūsī: emtīn, halla?

nādya: ē, iza ma fī 'indik shī.

lūsī: lā.

nādya: Tab. awwal shī, lēzim yikun fī 'indik rizz, w-sha'riyye w-zēt. tēkhdi kibbeyyet rizz w . . .

lūsī: kibbeyyet rizz? mish alīle? la-kam wāHad 'am niTbukh?

nādya: shakhSēn aw tlēte. Tayyib. tghaSSlī ktīr mnēH . . .

lūsī: kām marra bghayyir il-māy?

nādya: shi tlet marrāt, ba'dēn btHoTTī 'a janab w-btēkhdi shwayyet sha'riyye . . .

lūsī: mish abel ma nēkhud ish-sha'riyye lēzim nHoTT iz-zēt 'a l-ghāz?

nādya: mennik alīle yā binet, mennik alīle! bta'rfi tiTbukhi aHsan minni! ya'ni btēkhdi nuS kibbeyyet zēt w-bitHoTTi 'a l-ghāz. bas byighli tēkhdi shwayyet sha'riyye shī nuS kibbeyye w-bti'liya bi z-zēt Hatta tSīr lawna dahabi. ba'dēn, bitHoTTi r-rizz li ghaSSaltī min abel w-kamēn bitHoTTi kibbeyytēn w-nuS māy w-btitrikī la-stawi.

lūsī: mā aTyab rizzik yā nādya!

nādya: yalla, bukra enti ha ta'llmīni Tabkha amerikaniyye.

lūsī: tikrami. bas ana mā ba'rif iza fiyi iTbukh mitlik. akīd mā raH iZbaT ma'i.

nādya: raH iZbaT w-nuS, mā tkhāfi! w-iza mā ZabaT ktīr ha tēklī. shū raH tkibbī ya'ni?

lūsī: lā, ha a'mal mitl juHa. kēn 'indu tlet tiffeHēt. kēn baddu yēkul weHdi bas abel ma akala shēfa shwayye kharbēni. ām kibba w-akhad it-tēniye. Tuli'et kharbēni kamēn, am kibba tēni.

nādya: shū, mā yikūn kibbun killun?

lūsī: lā, Taffa DDaw w-akal it-tēlte.

Lucy: I liked the lunch a lot yesterday! You really know how to cook!

Nadia: Which did you like more—the tabouli or the green beans and rice?

Lucy: I liked the tabouli, but the rice was incredible. Can you teach me how to cook it?

Nadia: Sure, with pleasure! By the way, I wanted to cook it just now. Come along to the kitchen and I'll show you (*lit.*, in order to show you).

Lucy: When, now?

Nadia: Yeah, unless you have something to do.

Lucy: No, I don't.

Nadia: Great. First of all, you need [to have] rice, vermicelli, and oil. You take a cup of rice and then you . . .

Lucy: One cup? Isn't that too little? How many people are we cooking for?

Nadia: Two or three. Okay. You wash the rice thoroughly . . .

Lucy: How many times do I run the water through it (*lit.*, change the water)?

Nadia: Well, about three times; then put it aside. So, take a little vermicelli . . .

Lucy: Before we do the vermicelli, don't we need to put the oil on the stove?

Nadia: You really are something, girl. You know how to cook better than me! So, you take a half a cup of oil and put it on the stove. When it just begins to bubble, you take a bit of the vermicelli, about half a cup, and fry it in the oil until it (*lit.*, its color) gets to be sort of golden. Then, add the rice, which you've already washed, and add two and a half cups of water and let it cook till it's done.

Lucy: Your rice is really great, Nadia!

Nadia: Well, some day you'll teach me an American dish.

Lucy: Sure, with pleasure. But I don't know if I can cook as well as you (*lit.*, like you). For sure, it's not going to work out so well with me.

Nadia: Oh, it will! Don't worry! And if you don't get it right, you'll still eat it. What, are you going to throw it away?

Lucy: No, I'll do like Juha. He had three apples and wanted to eat one, but before he did, he saw that it had gone a little bad. So, he threw it away and got another one. But that one also turned out to be a little bad, so he threw it away as well.

Nadia: What, he didn't throw them all out?

Lucy: No, he switched off the light and ate the third one.

B. Grammar and Usage

1. QUESTION WORDS

Lebanese Arabic question words are presented in the following table, followed by example sentences.

QUESTION WORDS	
mīn	who
shū	what
weyn	where
la weyn	where to
min weyn	from where
emtin	when
lē	why
kīf	how
addē	how much
kam	how many

mīn Tabakh il-ghada mbēriH?
Who cooked lunch yesterday?

shū 'am biySīr?
What's going on?

weyn rāH bayyak?
Where did your father go?

la weyn rāyiH?
Where are you going (to)?

min weyn akhadti ha zzēt?
From where did you get this oil?

emtīn rāyiHa 'a ssū'?
When are you going to the market?

lē ma baddik trūHi ma'i?
Why don't you want to go with me?

kīf baddak ir-rizz?
How would you like the rice?

addē ha''u la l-khebez?
How much is the bread?

kam walad 'inkun?
How many kids do you *(pl.)* have?

2. NEGATIVE FORM OF NOUNS, ADJECTIVES, ADVERBS, AND PARTICIPLES

A. *mish* (NO, NOT)
The negative particle *mish* is used to negate nouns, adjectives, adverbs, numbers, and participles. Its equivalent in English is either *no* or *not*.[1]

- Nouns

  min weyn akhadti ha r-rādio?
  From where did you get this radio?

  hayda mish rādio. haydi msajjle.
  This is not a radio. (*lit.,* This is no radio.) This is a tape recorder.

- Numbers

  kam walad 'inkun? tlēte?
  How many kids do you *(pl.)* have? Three?

  lā, mish tlēte. tnēn bas.
  No, not three. Just two.

---

[1] Note that verbs are negated using the negative particle *mā*. See Lessons 26 and 27.

- Adjectives

  shū 'am biySīr?
  What's going on?

  mish mhimm.
  [It's] not important.

- Adverbs

  emtin baddak trūH 'a ssū'?
  When do you go to the market?

  mish halla.
  Not now.

  bas akid il-yōm?
  But today for sure?

  lā, mish il-yōm.
  No, not today.

  lē, mā bitHebbu la ha ssū'?
  Why, don't you like this market?

  mish ktīr.
  Not much.

- Participles

  bitHebb feirūz?
  Do you like Feiruz?

  mā ba'rif. mish sēm'a Sawta.
  I don't know. I have not heard her [voice].

B. *menn-* (NO, NOT)

menn- is another particle used to negate nouns, adjectives, adverbs, and participles. Like *mish*, *menn-* does not negate verbs. This particle is followed by possessive suffixes, as shown in the table below. Note that the suffix indicates the gender, number, and person of the grammatical subject of the sentence in which *menn-* occurs. Bear in mind that in Arabic what is negated is actually a noun, an adjective, an adverb, or a participle. In almost all cases, *menn-* can be used instead of *mish*. If *mish* negates the subject, a separate subject pronoun is necessary, but because *menn-* carries possessive suffixes indicating the subject, it is not necessary to add a separate subject pronoun, e.g., *menni hōn* vs. *anā mish hōn* (I am not here).

THE NEGATIVE PARTICLE *menn-* WITH POSSESSIVE SUFFIXES			
I'm not	*menni*	we're not	*mennā*
you're not *(m.)*	*mennak*	you're not *(pl.)*	*menkun*
you're not *(f.)*	*mennik*		
he/it's not	*mennu*	they're not	*mennun*
she/it's not	*menna*		

- Nouns

  shū hayda? bēt?
  What is this? A house?

  la, mennu bēt (= mish bēt). haydi binēye.
  No, it's not a house. This is a building.

- Adjectives

  lē ma baddik trūHi ma'i?
  Why don't you want to go with me?

  li-ennū mennak sarī' (= li-ennū enta mish sarī'). w-siyyārtak menna mnēHa (= mish mnēHa).
  Because you're not fast. And your car is not good.

  addē ha''u la l-khebez?
  How much is the bread?

  mennu ghāli (= mish ghāli).
  It's not expensive.

- Adverbs

  emtīn il-Hafle? bukra?
  When is the party? Tomorrow?

  la, menna bukra (= mish bukra).
  No, it's not tomorrow.

- Participles

  la weyn rāyiH?
  Where is he going (to)?

  mennu rāyiH (= mish rāyiH) 'a maTraH.
  He's not going anywhere. (*lit.,* He is not going to a place.)

  emtīn rāyiHa 'a ssū'?
  When are you going to the market?

  menni rāyiHa (= mish rāyiHa) 'a ssū' il-yōm.
  I'm not going to the market today.

3. USING *fī* (THERE IS/ARE . . .)

To express *there is* . . . and *there isn't* . . ., use *fī* . . . and *mā fī* . . . respectively.

> *fī shī il-yōm?*
> Is there anything today?

> *lā, mā fī shī.*
> No, there's nothing./There isn't anything.

> *mā fī Hafle?*
> Isn't there a party?

> *bala, fī. 'ind yūsef. baddak trūH?*
> Oh, yes, there is. At Yusef's. Do you want to go?

4. PLURAL NOUNS

Lebanese Arabic plural nouns are formed in a similar way to plural nouns in MSA (see Lesson 11). Like *fuSHā*, Lebanese Arabic has three grammatical numbers: singular, dual, and plural. To express the singular, Lebanese uses the singular noun without any qualifiers, e.g., *binet* (a/one girl), *walad* (a/one boy). The dual has only one ending, *-ēn* (occasionally pronounced as *-eyn*), used with both the masculine and feminine nouns, e.g., *bintēn*[1] (two girls), *waladēn* (two boys). When a dual noun ends in *tā' marbūTā*, the *t*-sound becomes audible before the dual suffix, e.g., *sayyara* (a car), *sayyartēn* (two cars). The plural is indicated by the use of a plural noun, e.g., *banēt* (girls), *awlēd* (boys).

5. NUMBERS

Much like in *fuSHā*, in Lebanese Arabic an unmodified singular noun implies the number "one," e.g., *binet* (one girl), *walad* (one boy). The word for "one" is *wāHad* (m.)/*weHdi* (f.) and can be added after the noun for emphasis, e.g., *bin(e)t weHdi* (one girl), *walad wāHad* (one boy). To say two, Lebanese uses the dual noun, *e.g., bintēn* (two girls), *waladēn* (two boys). Again, the number is not obligatory, but can be used for emphasis, as when ordering something in a restaurant, e.g., *tnēn ahwi* (two coffees). The feminine form of *two*, *tintēn*, is used in telling the time, e.g., *tintēn w-nuS* (half past two). Like in *fuSHā*, when the cardinal numbers from 3 to 10 are followed by a noun, the noun must be in the plural form, e.g., in *fuSHā* we say *thalāthat ashkhāS* (three people), *khams sa'āt* (five hours).

However, Lebanese Arabic differs from *fuSHā* in one fundamental way. In MSA we find opposite gender agreement between the number and the noun, meaning that a masculine noun is modified by a feminine number, and vice versa (see Lesson 7). Lebanese Arabic, on the other hand, always uses the masculine form of the number to modify both masculine and feminine nouns. However, when numbers between 3 and 10 are not

---

[1] The short vowel *e* in the singular form *binet* (a/one girl), typically added in Lebanese Arabic, is dropped in other forms, as in the dual form *bintēn* (two girls/daughters) or the possessive form *bintī* (my daughter).

followed by a noun in Lebanese Arabic, they appear in their feminine form, ending in
-a/e. Furthermore, if the noun modified by a number starts with a vowel, the feminine
form of the number is used, e.g., *arba't iyēm* (four days), *'ashrat ālēf* (ten thousand). The
table below gives examples of both of these usages—when the number is used alone
and when it is followed by a noun. Two examples are given for the latter case—one with
a masculine noun and the other with a feminine noun.

NUMBERS 1 TO 10			
	Independent	Followed by a Noun	
one	*wāHad/weHdi*	*ktēb (wāHad)/walad*	*siyyāra (weHdi)/binet*
two	*tnēn (tintēn)*	*ktēbēn/waladēn*	*siyyārtēn/bintēn*
three	*tlēte*	*tlet kutub/awlēd*	*tlet siyyārāt/banēt*
four	*arba'a*	*arba' kutub*	*arba' siyyārāt*
five	*khamse*	*khams kutub*	*khams siyyārāt*
six	*sitte*	*sitt kutub*	*sitt siyyārāt*
seven	*saba'a*	*saba' kutub*	*saba' siyyārāt*
eight	*tmēne*	*tmen kutub*	*tmen siyyārāt*
nine	*tisa'a*	*tisa' kutub*	*tisa' siyyārāt*
ten	*'ashra*	*'ashr kutub*	*'ashr siyyārāt*

When numbers between 11 and 19 are not followed by a noun, they lose their final *r*.
Like in *fuSHā,* the noun following the number is in the singular form in Lebanese Arabic.

NUMBERS 11 TO 19		
	Independent	Followed by a Noun	
eleven	*Hdāsh*	*Hdāshar ktēb*	*Hdāsh siyyāra*
twelve	*tnāsh*	*tnāshar ktēb*	*tnāshar siyyāra*
thirteen	*tlettāsh*	*tlettāshar ktēb*	*tlettāshar siyyāra*
fourteen	*arba'atāsh*	*arba'atāshar ktēb*	*arba'atāshar siyyāra*
fifteen	*khamstāsh*	*khamstāshar ktēb*	*khamstāshar siyyāra*
sixteen	*sittāsh*	*sittāshar ktēb*	*sittāshar siyyāra*
seventeen	*saba'atāsh*	*saba'atāshar ktēb*	*saba'atāshar siyyāra*
eighteen	*tmantāsh*	*tmantāshar ktēb*	*tmantāshar siyyāra*
nineteen	*tisa'atāsh*	*tisa'atāshar ktēb*	*tisa'atāshar siyyāra*

A single form, ending in *-in,* is used for the tens, whether the number is used
independently or is followed by a singular noun.

NUMBERS 20 TO 90	
twenty	*'ashrin*
thirty	*tletin*
forty	*arba'in*
fifty	*khamsin*
sixty	*sittin*
seventy	*sab(a)'in*
eighty	*tmenin*
ninety	*tis(a)'in*

The noun following the hundreds and the thousands is also in the singular form.

NUMBERS 100 TO 9,000			
one hundred	*miyye*	one thousand	*al(e)f*
two hundred	*mitēn*	two thousand	*alfēn*
three hundred	*tletmiyye*	three thousand	*tlet ālēf*
four hundred	*arba'miyye*	four thousand	*arba't ālēf*
five hundred	*khamsmiyye*	five thousand	*khamst ālēf*
six hundred	*sittmiyye*	six thousand	*sitt ālēf*
seven hundred	*saba'miyye*	seven thousand	*saba't ālēf*
eight hundred	*tmenmiyye*	eight thousand	*tment ālēf*
nine hundred	*tisa'miyye*	nine thousand	*tisa't ālēf*

6. DAYS OF THE WEEK

Days of the week in Lebanese Arabic differ from their MSA counterparts only in pronunciation. Notice how all rules of the distinctive Lebanese Arabic pronunciation apply here, e.g., the pronunciation of the definite article, the change of the sound *th* into a *t*-sound, the omission of the *hamza*, etc. To say *on Tuesday*, just use the word for the day of the week by itself, e.g., *ttalēta* (Tuesday/on Tuesday).

DAYS OF THE WEEK						
s-sabet	*l-aḥad*	*t-tanēn*	*t-talēta*	*l-arba'a*	*l-khamīs*	*j-jima'a*
Saturday	Sunday	Monday	Tuesday	Wednesday	Thursday	Friday

shu ra'yak nrūH 'a s-sinema j-jima'a?
Do you want to go to the movies on Friday?

khallīnā nrūH as-sabet.
Let's go on Saturday.

ma Sirnā rāyHin kill sabet. khallīnā nghayyir il-yōm.
We've been going every Saturday. Let's change the day.

C. Vocabulary

ghada	lunch
mbēriH	yesterday
'an jad	really
tiTbukhi	you cook (*f.*)
walla	or
rizz	rice
tikram 'aynik!	You are welcome!/With pleasure!
'a fikra	by the way
halla	now
ta'i!	Come! (*f.*)

maTbakh	kitchen
farjiki	I am showing you (f.)
emtīn	when
sha'riyye	vermicelli
zēt	cooking oil
kibbeyye	cup
alīle	little
tlēte	three
tghaSSlī	you wash it (f.)
bghayyir	I change
māy	water
tHoTTī	you put (f.)
'a janab	aside
shwayye	a little
abel	before
ghāz	cooker
mennik	you are not (f.)
byighli	it boils
bti'liya	you (f.) fry it (f.)
lawna	its color
dahabi	golden
li	which
stawi	it is ready/it is cooked
Tabkha	dish
tikrami!	You are welcome!, With pleasure!
akīd	sure
tkhāfi	you are afraid (f.)
tkibbī	you throw it (f.)
tiffeHēt	apples
shēfa	he saw it
Tuli'et	it turned out to be
Taffa	he switched off
Daw	light
tēlte	third (f.)

D. Cultural Note

Preparing food and eating together is an important part of family life in Lebanon. Many families not only eat dinner together but lunch as well. Employees return home during their lunch hour to eat with their families and relax for an hour. Women usually prepare more than one main course daily with many side dishes. Female relatives and neighbors often exchange recipes and cook meals together. Showing hospitality is very important, so when relatives and friends visit a family, they are served food and beverages. Coffee or tea is followed or preceded by a helping of fresh fruit and then, sweets and cookies.

Even if the guest is not hungry, it is polite to try the served food. Expect also that the hosts will urge you insistently.

Many stores serve coffee and tea to their customers even on their first visit to the store. When clients of a shop are also neighbors, they frequently come down and sit with the owner to drink a hot or cold beverage and chat about family affairs, politics, or culture.

E. Exercises

1. Translate the English sections of the following dialogue into Lebanese Arabic.

Muna: Who went to the concert with you?
Grace: *binet min ij-jēm'a.*
Muna: *libnēniyye?*
Grace: No, she's not Lebanese. She's Syrian.
Muna: *sēkne hōn, b-libnēn?*
Grace: *ē, ma' wlēda.*
Muna: *shu isma?*
Grace: *Su'ād.*
Muna: *anā ba'rifa.* How many kids does she have? Four?
Grace: No, not four. Actually, she has five.
Muna: *ā, mā ba'rifa.*
Grace: She'll teach me how to make tabouli.
Muna: *emtīn? bukra?*
Grace: No, not tomorrow.

2. Answer the following questions.

a. *weyn sēkin/sēkni?*
b. *kam yōm bi-j-jima'a (a week) tishtighel/i?*
c. *abel kam sine tjawwazu immak w-bayyak/immik w-bayyik?*
d. *lē 'am tidrus/tidrsi libnēni?*
e. *addē Ha'' siyyartak/ik?*
f. *shū 'amalt embēriH?*

3. Fill in the blanks by choosing the correct word—a number, a question word, or a noun.

khamst'ashar / tlēt / khams / marra / weyn / (i)j-jima'a / arba' / emtīn / (i)t-tanēn / ma'ī / 'ashrīn / ma'i

a. *mbēriH bas rja'et min as-sū' akalet _____ tiffeHēt.*
b. *kam _____ iltillak: mā fīk trūH 'a ssinema abel ma khallaset min il-irēye.*
c. *_____ raH t'addim 'a jjēm'a? l-khamīs aw _____?*

d. *lē ma baddak tishrab ahwi ma'nā?*

_____ *bas dolar wāHad.*

mā tkhāf, anā ma'i _____ *dolar. bkaffūnā.*

e. *min* _____ *akhadtu kill ha l-kutub?*

4. Put the following sentences in the negative form. Make any additional changes as necessary.

a. *fī 'inna akel bi l-bēt bas iza baddak finā nrūH 'a maT'am.*

b. *aHmad bi l-bēt?*

c. *min baddu tiffēHa?*

d. *ha l-alam la ilik?*

e. *'indun bēt kbīr bi beyrūt.*

f. *shū, ma'ak alam?*

5. Say the following numbers followed by each of the three nouns.

1 / 2 / 3 / 11 / 12 / 13 / 20
apples / girls / kids

Answer Key

1. Muna: *mīn rāH 'a l-Hafli ma'ik?*
   Grace: *binet min ij-jēm'a.*
   Muna: *libnēniyye?*
   Grace: *menna/mish libnēniyye. sūriyye.*
   Muna: *sēkne hōn, b-libnēn?*
   Grace: *ē, ma' wlēda.*
   Muna: *shu isma?*
   Grace: *Su'ād.*
   Muna: *anā ba'rifa. kam walad 'inda? arba'a?*
   Grace: *lā, mish arba'a. b-SarāHa 'inda khamse.*
   Muna: *ā, mā ba'rifa.*
   Grace: *raH t'allimnī kīf ba'mul tabbūle.*
   Muna: *emtīn? bukra?*
   Grace: *lā, mish bukra.*

2. Model answers:
   a. Where do you live?
      (anā) sēkni b-los anjelos/bi-beirūt. I live *(f.)* in Los Angeles/Beirut.
   b. How many days a week do you work?
      bishtighel khamst/arba't/tlet iyēm bi-jjima'a. I work five/four/three days a week.
   c. How many years ago did your Mom and Dad get married?
      immi w-bayyi tjawwazu abel 'ashrīn/khams w-'ashrīn/tletīn sine. My Mom and Dad got married twenty/twenty-five/thirty years ago.
   d. Why are you studying Lebanese?
      baddi rūH 'a libnēn./baddi ishtighel b-libnēn./khayyi jawwaz binet libnēniyye. I want to go to Lebanon. /I want to work in Lebanon./My brother married a Lebanese woman.
   e. How much is your car?
      siyyartī Ha''a khamsmit dolar/alfēn dolar/'ashrat ālēf dolar/'ashrīn alf dolar. My car costs $500/$2,000/$10,000/$20,000.
   f. What did you do yesterday?
      mish ktīr./mā 'amalet shī./reHet 'a shshighel./kint bi jjēm'a. Not much./I didn't do anything./I went to work./I was at the university.

3. a. *mbēriH bas rja'et min as-sū' akalet tlēt/arba'/khams tiffeHēt.*
   Yesterday, when I got back from the market, I ate three/four/five apples.

   b. *kam marra iltillak: mā fik trūH 'a ssinema abel ma khallaset min il-irēye.*
   How many times did I tell you? You can't go to the movies until you finish reading.

   c. *emtin raH t'addim 'a jjēm'a? l-khamīs aw ij-jima'a/it-tanēn?*
   When are you going to apply to the university? On Thursday or on Friday/Monday?

   d. *lē ma baddak tishrab ahwi ma'nā?*
   Why don't you want to drink coffee with us?
   ma'i bas dolar wāHad.
   I have only one dollar.
   mā tkhāf, anā ma'i khamst'ashar/'ashrin dolar. bkaffūnā.
   Don't worry, I have fifteen/twenty dollars. That'll be enough.

   e. *min weyn akhadtu kill ha l-kutub?*
   Where did you get all these books from?

4. a. *mā fī 'inna akel bi l-bēt w-iza baddak fīnā nrūH 'a maT'am.*
   We don't have food at home, and if you want, we can go to a restaurant.

   b. *aHmad mish/mennu bi l-bēt?*
   Isn't Ahmad at home?

   c. *mīn mā baddu tiffēHa?*
   Who doesn't want an apple?

   d. *ha l-alam mish/mennu la ilik?*
   Isn't this pen yours?

   e. *mā 'indun bēt kbīr bi beyrūt.*
   They don't have a big house in Beirut.

   f. *shū, mā ma'ak alam?*
   What, don't you have a pen on you?

5. *tiffēHa, tiffēHtēn, tlēt tiffēHēt, Hdashar tiffēHa, tnashar tiffēHa, tlettashar tiffēHa, 'ashrin tiffēHa*
   binet, bintēn, tlēt banēt, Hdashar binet, tnashar binet, tlettashar binet, 'ashrin binet
   walad, waladēn, tlēt awlēd, Hdashar walad, tnashar walad, tlettashar walad, 'ashrin walad

LESSON 30

(Lebanese Arabic)

weyn rāyHa? Where Are You Going?

A. Dialogue

Donald needs to go to the American Embassy, located in the Antelias neighborhood of East Beirut, on the other side of town. He is talking to Ahmad's father Ali about the best way to get there.

dūnald: yā aHmad, bta'rif weyn is-safāra l-amerikaniyye?

aHmad: anā mish ktīr ba'rif 'a l-maZbūt. khalli bayyi y'illak.

dūnald: yā abu aHmad, baddi rūH 'a ssafāra l-amerikaniyye. ta'rif kīf baddi rūH?

'ali: ē, Tab'an ba'rif. is-safāra l-amerikaniyye b-onToliēs.

dūnald: ā, na'am, b-shar'īye. Tab, shū btanSaHni—bēkhud taksi walla servīs?

'ali: khud servīs, arkhaSlak bas il-mishwār baddu yēkhud wa'et ktīr.

dūnald: ma'lē, 'indi wa'et ktīr.

'ali: awwal shī btēkhud servīs min vardān 'a d-dawra w-Tab'an byēkhud minnak is-suwwā ijrat servisēn.

dūnald: lē servisēn?

'ali: liennu byimurr awwal shī bi l-ashrafiyye—min vardān 'a l-ashrafiyye servīs wāHad w-min il-ashrafiyye 'a ddawra kamēn servīs wāHad, 'arift kīf.

dūnald: ē, na'm.

'ali: halla, btinzil bi d-dawra w-btisal "min wēn baddi ēkhud servīs 'a onToliēs" w-n-nēs byidillūk hawnīki. intibih mā yilTush 'aleyk is-suwwā liennu suwwāin beyrūt ktīr fannasīn.

dūnald: ma'rūf.

'ali: halla l-iHtimēl it-tēni, iza Habbēt tēkhud taksi fāSlu 'a l-ijra.

Donald signals to a "service" car.

dūnald: dawra?

is-suwwā: servisēn.

dūnald: mēshi.

is-suwwā: tfaDDal, rkab.

On the way, the driver of the "service" car picks up another passenger.

is-suwwā: weyn rāyHa yā demwazēl?

il-binet: ashrafiyye.

is-suwwā: tfaDDali, rkabi. weyn baddik tinzili bi-l-ashrafiyye?

il-binet: Hadd il-MTV.

is-suwwā: tikrami. bwaSSlik.

The driver of the "service" speaks to Donald over his shoulder.

is-suwwā: yā istēz, mbayyen mennak libnēni?

dūnald: ma'ak Ha'. anā min amerika.

is-suwwā: walla? bta'rif haydek il-yōm rikib ma'i min il-maTār wāHad libnēni rēji' min amerika.

dūnald: sēkin hawnīki?

is-suwwā: la, rāH a'ad 'ind ikhtu shi shaher. il-mhimm, saaltu "min shu staghrabet b-amerika aktar shī?" ta'rif shu alli?

dūnald: shū?

is-suwwā: alli ma staghrabet aktar min ennu kill il-wlēd byaHku inglīzi.

Donald: Ahmad, do you know where the American Embassy is?

Ahmad: I don't know exactly. Let my dad tell you.

Donald: Abu Ahmad, I want to go to the American Embassy. Do you know how I can get there? (*lit.*, Do you know how I should go?)

Ali: Yeah, of course I know. It's in Antelias.

Donald: Oh, yes, in East Beirut. Okay, what would you advise me to take, a "service" car or a taxi?

Ali: Take the "service"; it's cheaper but the trip will take longer.

Donald: Well, that's fine. I have a lot of time.

Ali: First, you take a "service" from Verdun to Dawra. The driver will take two fares (*lit.*, two "services") from you, of course.

Donald: Why two fares?

Ali: Because he'll pass through Ashrafiye; from Verdun to Ashrafiye it's one fare, and from Ashrafiye to Dawra it's another one, you understand.

Donald: Sure.

Ali: Then, you get off at Dawra and ask 'From where exactly do I take a "service" to Atelias?,' and people will give you directions there. You have to make sure that the driver doesn't cheat you; the drivers in Beirut are cheats.

Donald: That's pretty well-known.

Ali: Now, here's another possibility; if you want to take a regular taxi, be sure to bargain with the driver over the fee.

Donald: Dawra?

Taxi driver: Two fares.

Donald: Fine.

Taxi driver: Get in, please.

Taxi driver: Where are you going, Miss?

Girl: Ashrafiye.

Taxi driver: Please, get in. Where do you want to get off in Ashrafiye?

Girl: Near the MTV.

Taxi driver: All right. I'll take you there.

Taxi driver: Sir, it seems like you're not Lebanese.

Donald: You're right. I'm from the States.

Taxi driver: Really? You know, the other day at the airport, I picked up a Lebanese guy, coming from the United States.

Donald: He lives there?

Taxi driver: No, he went to stay with his sister for about a month. So, I asked him, "What surprised you in America?" You know what he told me?

Donald: What?

Taxi driver: He told me, "Nothing surprised me more [than the fact] that all kids [there] speak English."

B. Grammar and Usage

1. IMPERATIVE

Commands are expressed using a special verbal form, called the imperative. The imperative in Lebanese Arabic has three forms: *you* (m.), *you* (f.) and *you* (m./f. pl.). The *you* singular masculine imperative is formed by removing the prefix *bti-/bta-/bte-/bit-* from the corresponding imperfect tense form. For example:

bitrūH (you go) *rūH* (Go!)

Sometimes, when the stem of the verb starts in a consonant cluster, the prefix *bti-/bta-/bte-/bit-* is replaced by the imperative prefix *i-*, e.g., *bas imshi!* (Just walk!) The *you* singular feminine and the *you* plural forms are formed by adding the endings *-i* and *-u*, respectively, to the masculine singular imperative, just like in *fuSHā*.[1] The table below shows the imperative forms of six verbs. The first row shows the corresponding imperfect tense form.

	IMPERATIVE				
	mishi (walk)	*riji'* (go back)	*rāH* (go)	*nizil* (go, come down)	*semi'* (listen)
you, *m. sg.*	*btimshi*	*btirja'*	*bitrūH*	*btinzil*	*btisma'*
you, *m. sg.*	*(i)mshi*	*(i)rja'*	*rūH*	*(i)nzil*	*(i)sma'*
you, *f. sg.*	*(i)mshi*	*(i)rja'i*	*rūHi*	*(i)nzili*	*(i)sma'i*
you, *pl.*	*(i)mshu*	*(i)rja'u*	*rūHu*	*(i)nzilu*	*(i)sma'u*

Here are examples from the dialogue.

tfaDDal, rkab!
Please, get in! *(m. sg.)*

tfaDDali, rkabi!
Please, get in! *(f. sg.)*

Here are more examples:

yalla, rja'u 'a l-bēt b-sur'a!
Come on, go back home quickly! *(f./m. pl.)*

---

[1] If the verb ends in *-i*, the masculine and feminine imperatives are identical, e.g., the form *mshi* (walk!) is used when addressing either a woman or a man.

nzili min is-servīs, ba'dēn mshi shi mi't metr w-rkabi servīs tēni!

Get off the "service," then walk about 100 meters and get on another "service"!

(f. sg.)

Lebanese verbs (e.g., *akhad* [take]) whose equivalents in *fuSHā* have an initial *hamza* (e.g., *'akhadha*), never add the optional *i-* prefix in their imperative form. For some verbs, such as the verbs *btēkul* (eat) and *btēkhud* (take), shown in the table below, the stem vowel changes in the feminine singular and plural forms.

A similar change takes place in the masculine form when a pronoun is attached to it (see example in the table).

THE VERBS *btēkul* (TO EAT) AND *btēkhud* (TO TAKE) IN THE IMPERATIVE		
you, *m. sg.*	*btēkul* (you eat)	*btēkhud* (you take)
you, *m. sg.*	*kul*	*khud*
you, *m. sg.* (with a pronoun)	*kila* (eat it)	*khida* (take her/it)
you, *f. sg.*	*kili*	*khidi*
you, *pl.*	*kilu*	*khidu*

yā, zeyneb, kili ha ttiffēHa!

Zeyneb, eat this apple!

yā, wlēd, khidu shokolāTa!

Kids, take some chocolate!

The imperative form of the verb *ija* (to come) has a different stem altogether.

THE VERB *ija* (TO COME) IN THE IMPERATIVE	
you, *m. sg.*	*btiji*
you, *m. sg.*	*ta'*
you, *f. sg.*	*ta'i*
you, *pl.*	*ta'u*

ta'i la hōn! baddi illik shi.

Come here! *(f. sg.)* I want to tell you something.

ta'u bukra! raH farjīkun.

Come tomorrow! *(pl.)* I'll show you.

The negative imperative is formed by placing the negative particle *mā* in front of the verb, which is in the imperfect tense, but without the prefix *b-/bi-*. For example, the negative imperative of the verb *btēkul* (you eat) is *mā tēkul* (Don't eat!). For the feminine form, add the suffix *-i,* and for the plural form, add the suffix *-u* to this form of the verb.

THE NEGATIVE IMPERATIVE

	don't eat	don't take	don't go	don't come	don't listen	don't get in/ride
you, m. sg.	mā tēkul	mā tēkhud	mā trūH	mā tiji	mā tisma'	mā tirkab
you, f. sg.	mā tēkli	mā tēkhdi	mā trūHi	mā tiji	mā tisma'i	mā tirkabi

yā muna, bas btrūHi 'ind khāltik, mā tēkhdi ikhtik ma'ik!
Muna, when you go to your aunt, don't take your sister with you!

yā wlēd, mā tēklu shokolāTa abl il-ghada!
Kids, don't eat chocolate before lunch!

2. RELATIVE CLAUSES

A relative clause is a dependent clause that provides additional information about a noun. It is a clause that modifies the noun and hence, functions a little bit like an adjective. For example, the sentence *I don't know the woman who helped me find my dog* has one relative clause: *who helped me find my dog*. This clause can be replaced with a single adjective such as *helpful*: *I don't know the helpful woman*.

When the relative clause modifies a definite noun, the relative pronoun *li* is used to introduced it, for all persons and genders, and both animate and inanimate nouns. An alternative form of *li* is *yilli*.

bitHoTTi rriz li ghaSSalti min abel.
You're adding the rice, which you have previously washed.

As in *fuSHā*, when a relative clause modifies an indefinite noun, no relative pronoun is used to introduce this clause in Lebanese Arabic. There is no equivalent to the English *who* in the underlined Lebanese Arabic relative clause in the following example.

rikib ma'i wāHad rēji' min amerika.
A guy who had just returned from America rode with me. (*lit.*, Rode with me someone [who] had returned from America.)

3. DERIVING NOUNS FROM VERBS: PARTICIPLES

Participles in MSA were discussed in Lesson 12. In Arabic dialects, participles, especially active participles, are used more frequently than in *fuSHā*. The participial form of the verb is commonly used in Lebanese Arabic in places where *fuSHā*, like English, uses a verb in the imperfect or perfect tense. For example, the English question *Where do you live?*, containing the present tense verb *live*, would only rarely be expressed using the imperfect tense verb *btiskun* (live) in Lebanese Arabic, as in *weyn btiskun?* In most cases, the participle *sēkin* (living) is used to form this question, e.g., *weyn sēkin?* (*lit.*, where living).

There are two types of participles in Lebanese Arabic, just like in *fuSHā*: The active participle, e.g., *sēkin* (living, having lived), *sēm'* (hearing, having heard), and the passive participle, e.g., *maktūb* (written), *maftūH* (opened). In the next section we will examine the forms and the usage of the active participle.

A. THE ACTIVE PARTICIPLE

In Lebanese Arabic, the active participle does not carry any marks for person or tense, but it has different forms expressing the grammatical categories of gender and number. Therefore, similar to an adjective, the Lebanese Arabic active participle must match the gender and number of the subject.

> *līna* (f. sg.) *rāyHa* (f. sg.) *'a j-jēm'a.*
> Lina is going to the university.

For the Form I verbs, the active participle has the pattern *CēCiC* for the masculine, *CēCCi* for the feminine, and *CēCCin* for the plural. If its first root consonant is D, Z, S, H, ', T, or occasionally, r, the the first vowel is *ā*, e.g., *rāyiH* (going). Because the final letter of the feminine participle in *fuSHā* is *tā' marbūTa*, all the rules for its pronunciation apply (see Lesson 21).

ACTIVE PARTICIPLES OF FORM I VERBS					
	returning/ having returned	going/ having gone	hearing/ having heard	riding/ having ridden	living/ having lived
Masculine Singular	*rēji'/rēj'*	*rāyiH*	*sēmi'/sēm'*	*rēkib*	*sēkin*
Feminine Singular	*rēj'a*	*rāyiHa*	*sēm'a*	*rēkbi*	*sēkni*
Masculine/ Feminine Plural	*rēj'in*	*rāyiHīn*	*sēm'in*	*rēkbīn*	*sēknīn*

The participle does not bear any reference to tense and therefore, it can refer to past, present, and future actions. The tense of the action is understood from the context.

> *sēm'īn 'an feyrūz?*
> Have you *(pl.)* heard about Feiruz?

> *ba'dni rēj' min il-maTār.*
> I've just returned from the airport.

> *la-weyn rāyiHa bukra?*
> Where are you going tomorrow?

Object pronoun suffixes can be attached to active participles just as they are attached to other verbal forms.

> *katabt il-maktūb? ē, mbēriH kētibu.*
> Did you *(m. sg.)* write the letter? Yeah, I wrote it yesterday.

katabtu l-maktūb? ē, mbēriH kētbīnu.

Did you *(m./f. pl.)* write the letter? Yes, we wrote it yesterday.

Because the participle does not refer to a specific grammatical person, the doer of the action is understood from the context in which the interaction takes place. Think of the English question *Going home?* It can be asked of one, two, or more people depending on the context.

The negative form of the active participle is formed by placing the negative particle *mish* in front of it.

mish kētbīnu mbēriH.

We (or you *(pl.)* or they) didn't write it yesterday. (*lit.*, Not having written *(pl.)* it yesterday.)

mish sēm'īn 'an feyrūz.

We (or you *(pl.)* or they) haven't heard about Feyruz.

mish rāyiHa bukra.

I *(f.)* (or you *(f.)* or she) am (are/is) not going tomorrow.

C. Vocabulary

safāra	embassy
'a l-maZbūt	exactly
khalli!	Leave!, Let! *(f. sg.)*
shar'īye	East Beirut
btanSaHni	you advise me *(m. sg.)*
servīs	taxi service (in Beirut)
khud!	Take! *(m. sg.)*
arkhaSlak	it's cheaper for you
mishwār	trip, going out
wa'et	time
ma'lē.	It's fine., It's nothing.
suwwā	driver
ijra	fee
liennu	because
byimurr	he passes
btinzil	you get off *(m. sg.)*
btisal	you ask *(m. sg.)*
nēs	people
byidillūk	they give you directions
Intibih!	Watch out! *(m. sg.)*

yilTush	he cheats
fannasin	crooks, cheats
ma'rūf	well-known
iHtimēl	possibility
fāSlu	bargain with him (*m. sg.*)
rkab	get on (*m. sg.*)
demwazēl	Miss
Hadd	next to, near
bwaSSlik	I'll take you
istēz	Sir
rikib	he got on
maTār	airport
rēji'	returning (*participle*)
a'ad	he stayed
shaher	month
il-mhimm	What's important is . . . (*lit.,* The important thing [is] . . .)
staghrabet	I was/He was astonished, surprised
aktar shī	most of all
ennu	that

D. Cultural Note

A lot of socializing in Lebanon takes place in transportation. Most people rely on the "service" ride to go to work or visit relatives and friends. The "service" is a taxi, in most cases an old Mercedes, with a fixed low fare. Its direction is determined by the first passenger, but other passengers can be picked up on the way if they're going in the same direction. If you are going to a faraway area, the "service" driver might ask you for a double fare or drop you off at a certain location from which you have to take another "service" ride.

Drivers often engage passengers in a conversation or tell stories of things that happened to them or their acquaintances. They might play the radio and sing along with their favorite Arab singers while occasionally shouting at other drivers or pedestrians, much in the fashion of cab drivers in other big cities. One or more passengers in the "service" car might be smoking and might offer you a cigarette as well. If you are a non-smoker, you will have the biggest chance of success in persuading other passangers to abstain from smoking if you give a medical reason.

If you need directions, ask your taxi driver. If the driver doesn't know the particular place, he or she will often stop the car and talk to store owners in the area. Fellow riders will also try to help. Because addresses in Lebanon do not include street numbers or zip codes, but rather only the names of the building owners, frequently, the only way to get somewhere is to ask.

E. Exercises

1. Say the following sentences in Arabic as if you were addressing a male person.

a. When you take a "service," get in and out of the car quickly.
b. Don't go to the market tomorrow. We have to go to the American Embassy.
c. What would you advise me, doctor? —Drink water a lot, walk a lot, and don't eat a lot!
d. Take a taxi from Dawra!
e. Watch out! There's a car!

2. Now say the sentences from the previous exercise as if you are addressing a woman.

3. Transform the following statements into commands.

Example: *juHa byēkul it-tiffēHa.*
        kul it-tiffēHa yā juHa!

a. *yalla, bukra enti ha taʻllmīni shi Tabkha amerikaniyye yā lūsī.*
b. *tēkhdi kibbeyyet rizz.*
c. *tghaSSli ktīr mnēH.*
d. *bitghayyri l-māy shi tlet marrāt.*
e. *baʻdēn btHoTTi ʻa janab w-btēkhdi shwayyet shaʻriyye.*
f. *abel ma btēkhdi shshaʻriyye lēzim tHoTTi zzēt ʻa l-ghāz.*

4. Combine two sentences into one using relative clauses. (You might find that there is more than one way to connect the two sentences.) Then translate the sentences you created.

Example: *ha l-binet kenet hōn. hyyi btaʻrif weyn sēkin aHmad.*
        ha l-binet li kenet hōn btaʻrif weyn sēkin aHmad.
        The girl who was here knows where Ahmad lives.
        ha l-binet li btaʻrif weyn sēkin aHmad kenet hōn.
        The girl who knows where Ahmad lives was here.

a. *il-istēze rāHet ʻa maSar. ken baddi iHke maʻa.*
b. *kill il-madēris halla baddun asētze. il-asētze biʻallmu inglīze.*
c. *mā fīyi ʻallim il-wlēd iZ-Zghār. il-wlēd iZ-Zghār mā byismaʻu l-kalēm.*
d. *fīki tʻīshi ʻind khāltik. khāltik sēkni b-los anjelos.*
e. *ʻindik alam? il-alam byiktub mnēH.*
f. *maʻik il-alam? il-alam byiktub mnēH.*

5. Rephrase the following sentences, containing verbs in the imperfect tense, using participles.

a. *bukra ha irja' min faransa.*
b. *bta'rfu uSSata?*
c. *ba'rif* (f.) *shwayye 'annā.*
d. *byisknu b-ūDa.*
e. *bayya byitrikā trūH 'a rrādio b-sharT wāHad.*
f. *anā* (m.) *kamēn ma ba'rif shū huwwe shsharT.*
g. *hayda mā byifham shī bi-l-musī'a l-'arabiyye.*

6. Now, transform the positive statements in the previous exercise into negative statements, and vice versa.

Answer Key

1. a. *bas btēkhud servīs inzil w-rkab is-siyyāra b-sur'a!*
   b. *mā trūH 'a ssū' bukra! lēzim nrūH 'a s-safāra l-amerikaniyye.*
   c. *shū btanSaHnī yā doktōr? shrab māy ktīr, imshi ktir, w-mā tēkul ktīr!*
   d. *khud servīs min id-dawra!*
   e. *intibih! fī siyyāra!*

2. a. *bas btēkhdi servīs inzili w-rkabi s-siyyāra b-sur'a!*
   b. *mā trūHi 'a ssū' bukra! lēzim nrūH 'a s-safāra l-amerikaniyye.*
   c. *shū btanSaHīnī yā doktōra? shrabi māy ktīr, imshi ktīr, w-mā tēkli ktīr!*
   d. *khidi servīs min id-dawra!*
   e. *intibihi! fī siyyāra!*

3. a. *yalla, bukra 'allmīni shi Tabkha amerikaniyye yā lūsī.*
   b. *khidi kibbeyyet rizz.*
   c. *ghaSSlī ktīr mnēH.*
   d. *ghayyri il-māy shi tlet marrāt.*
   e. *ba'dēn HoTTi 'a janab w-khidi shwayyet sha'riyye.*
   f. *abel ma btēkhdi sh-sha'riyye HoTTi z-zēt 'a l-ghāz.*

4. a. *il-istēze li rāHet 'a maSar ken baddi iHke ma'a.*
   I wanted to talk to the professor who went to Egypt.
   il-istēze li ken baddi iHke ma'a rāHet 'a maSar.
   The professor to whom I wanted to talk went to Egypt.
   b. *kill il-madēris halla baddun asētze bi'allmu inglīze.*
   All the schools now want teachers who teach English.
   c. *mā fīyi 'allim il-wlēd iZ-Zghār li mā byisma'u l-kalēm.*
   I can't teach the little kids who don't listen.
   d. *fīki t'īshi 'ind khāltik li sēkni b-los anjelos.*
   You can live with your aunt who lives in LA.
   e. *'indik alam byiktub mnēH?*
   Do you have a pen that writes well?
   f. *ma'ik il-alam li byiktub mnēH?*
   Do you have on you the pen that writes well?

5. a. *bukra rēji'/rēj'a min faransa.*
   b. *'ārfīn uSSata?*
   c. *'ārfi shwayye 'annā.*
   d. *sēknīn b-ūDa.*
   e. *bayya tērikā trūH 'a r-rādio b-sharT wāHad.*
   f. *anā kamēn mish 'ārif shū huwwe sh-sharT.*
   g. *hayda mish fēhim shī bi-l-musī'a l-'arabiyye.*

6. a. *bukra mish rēji'/rēj'a min faransa.*
   b. *mish 'ārfīn uSSata?*
   c. *mish 'ārfi shwayye 'annā.*
   d. *mish sēknīn b-ūDa.*
   e. *bayya mish tērikā trūH 'a rrādio b-sharT wāHad.*
   f. *anā kamēn 'ārif shū huwwe sh-sharT.*
   g. *hayda fēhim shī bi-l-musī'a l-'arabiyye.*

Seventh Review

(Lebanese Arabic)

---

1. Put the words in the parentheses in the correct form, then, translate the sentences into English.

Example: *bayyi (baddu) (byirūH) 'a madrīd bas immi (badda) (bitrūH) 'a Tokyo.*

bayyi baddu yirūH 'a madrīd bas immi badda trūH 'a Tokyo.

My dad wants to go to Madrid, but my mom wants to go to Tokyo.

a. *betina (lēzim) (bitjawwaz) wāHad milionēr.*

b. *shu ya khālti, mish (lēzim) (btiTbukhili) shi Tabkha bitjannin il-yōm?*

c. *bint khāli nadīn (badda) (btitrik) libnēn w-(bit'īsh) b-amerika.*

d. *immi (bitfakkir) ba'dnī walad Zghīr.*

e. *baddak walla ma baddak (lēzim) (btiji) ma'i.*

2. Put the words in the parentheses in the correct form to produce expressions of possession.

a. *(ibn + entl) biyjannin!*

b. *(ma' + huwwi) kibbeyet māy?*

c. *kam walad ('ind + hiyyi)?*

d. *ya, aHmad, weyn id-diplōm (tabā' + enta).*

e. *ha ssiyyara mish (tē' + huwwi)? la, siyyartu kharbēni (broken).*

3. Match the words from column A to those in column B to form phrases or short sentences.

A	B
a. *'indi milyōn dolar*	*ya doktōr?*
b. *shu mahDūm*	*arkhaSlik!*
c. *ma 'indi wa'et ktīr*	*mishwār Tawil.*
d. *shū btanSaHni ēkul*	*ibna la-jārti!*
e. *khidi bas ktēb wāhad—*	*bi l-bank.*
f. *min hōn 'a lībiya*	*marti (my wife) mish Tābkha shi.*
g. *lēzim nrūH 'a maT'am il-yōm—*	*'a shēn heyk, illi halla!*

4. Put the words in the correct order to form coherent sentences.

a. *il-ktēbe / emtīn / ta'allamt / ?*

b. *khālid / ya, / D-Daw / bas / btrūH / Taffi / !*

c. *baddik /tēkli / ya /shu / Habibti / ?*

d. *'indik / ya / wlēd / madām / ?*

e. *iltillak / milyōn / marra / : / baddi / ma / shāy / ishrab*

5. Read the following passage and answer the questions.

abel (before, ago)
ba'd (yet, still)

ahlan. anā ismi rōz. halla sēkni bi beyrūt bas abel sintēn kint sēkni b-amerika ma' immi w-bayyi w-khayyi ziyād. bayyi ma by'ajibu kīf il-banēt b-amerika w-'ashēn heyk rja'na 'a libnēn bas Sirt khamstāshar sine. hōn b-libnēn ma byismaHli bayyi rūH 'a Haflēt mitl kint 'am ba'mul b-amerika. ha s-sine raH addim 'a l-AUB bas ba'd ma ba'rif shu baddi idrus. bas khalliS il-AUB - alli bayyi - fiyī addim 'a majistēr b-amerika.

a. *mīn byaHki?*
b. *weyn sēkni halla?*
c. *abel kam sine kēnet sēkni b-amerika?*
d. *lē rēj'u 'a libnēn?*
e. *fiya tirja' 'a amerika? emtīn?*
f. *shu badda tidrus bi l-AUB?*

6. Put the following sentences into the negative form. Make any additional changes as necessary.

a. *iza timshi min hōn, raH tūSal 'a bētu.*
b. *zeyneb bi l-bēt?*
c. *siyyartu kharbēne Sarla sine.*
d. *ha l-kibbeye la ilik?*
e. *khayyu la-ziyād 'allam wlēdi 'arabi.*
f. *lē baddak taHke ma'i?*

7. Fill in the blanks using the correct word—a number, a verb, or a possessive expression. Choose from the words given below. Then, translate the sentences into English.

tinzli / tkhalliS / tiskun / 'ashrīn / 'indu

a. *binti ha s-sine raH _____ ij-jēm'a.*
b. *_____ dolar mish ktīr. kill shi halla Sar ghāli.*
c. *weyn baddik _____ ya madām?*
d. *khayyak _____ shighel?*
e. *ma' min raH _____ bi beyrūt?*

8. Translate the English sentences in the following dialogue into Lebanese Arabic.

Muna: When did you come back from America?
Grace: *haydik il-yōm. lē?*
Muna: *ken baddi iji la 'indik.*
Grace: You can come today, if you want.
Muna: I can't today.

Grace: *lē, weyn rāyHa?*

Muna: It's Friday. *kill jim'a b'allim inglīze b-madraset "il-Hikme."*

Grace: And tomorrow?

Muna: *bukra ma 'indi shighel.*

Grace: *Tayyib, tfaDDali.*

Muna: *bas b-sharT.*

Grace: What is it?

Muna: We'll cook *tabbule.*

Grace: You're welcome.

9. Combine the two sentences provided in each example into a single sentence using a relative pronoun. Then translate the sentences you created.

Example: *is-siyāra kenet hōn. hyyi ktīr 'ajabetni.*

is-siyāra li kenet hōn ktīr 'ajabetni.

I liked the car that was here very much.

a. *'jabetnī T-Tabkha. Tabakhta mbēriH.*
b. *baddi inzil 'a j-jēm'a. hiyye b-ashrafiyye.*
c. *mā fīyi tjawwaz binet. ma ba'rif il-binet.*
d. *fīki t'īshi 'ind khayyik. khayyik sēkin bi beyrūt.*
e. *bHebb bas il-wlēd. il-wlēd byisma'ū l-kalēm.*

10. Circle the following words in Lebanese Arabic, horizontally or vertically:

a. afterwards
b. kitchen
c. children
d. writing
e. without
f. Take! *(m.)*
g. time
h. It's fine.
i. now
j. sure

s	r	j	a	u	S	ā	'	m
H		m	k	t	ē	b	e	a
r	h	a	ī	D	'	T	q	T
b	a	'	d	e	y	n	y	b
n	l	l	ā	i	b	a	l	a
w	l	ē	d	k	h	u	d	k
w	a	'	e	t	ō	S	w	h

407

Answer Key

1. a. *betina lēzim tjawwaz wāHad milionēr.*
   Bettina has to marry a millionaire.

   b. *shu ya khālti, mish lēzim tiTbukhili shi Tabkha bitjannin il-yōm?*
   So, auntie, don't you [think you] have to cook me some terrific dish today?

   c. *bint khāli nadīn badda titrik libnēn w-t'īsh b-amerika.*
   My cousin Nadine wants to leave Lebanon and live in America.

   d. *immi bitfakkir ba'dnī walad Zghīr.*
   My mom thinks I am still a little child.

   e. *baddak walla ma baddak lēzim tiji ma'i.*
   Whether you want to or not, you have to come with me.

2. a. *ibnik biyjannin!*
   b. *ma'u kibbeyet māy?*
   c. *kam walad 'inda?*
   d. *ya, aHmad, weyn id-diplōm tabā'ak.*
   e. *ha ssiyyara mish tē'u? la, siyyartu kharbēni.*

3. a. *'indi milyōn dolar bi l-bank.*
   b. *shu mahDūm ibna la-jārti!*
   c. *ma 'indi wa'et ktīr 'a shēn heyk, illi halla!*
   d. *shū btanSaHni ēkul ya doktōr?*
   e. *khidi bas ktēb wāhad—arkhaSlik!*
   f. *min hōn 'a lībiya mishwār Tawīl.*
   g. *lēzim nrūH 'a maT'am il-yōm—marti* (my wife) *mish Tābkha shi.*

4. a. *emtīn ta'allamt il-ktēbe?*
   b. *ya khālid, bas btrūH—Taffi D-Daw!*
   c. *shu baddik tēkli ya Habibti?*
   d. *'indik wlēd ya madām?*
   e. *iltillak milyōn marra: ma baddi ishrab shāy.*

5. Hello. My name is Rose. Now, I live in Beirut, but two years ago, I lived in America with my dad, my mom, and my brother Ziyad. My dad doesn't like how girls in America are and that's why we returned to Lebanon when I turned 15. Here in Lebanon, dad doesn't allow me to go out, as I used to do in America. This year I will apply to AUB but I still don't know what I want to study. Dad told me that when I finish AUB, I can apply for a Master's in America.

   a. *rōz btaHki.*
   b. *halla sēkni bi beyrūt.*
   c. *kēnet sēkni b-amerika abel sintēn.*
   d. *rēj'u 'a libnēn 'a shēn bayya ma by'ajibu kīf il-banēt b-amerika.*
   e. *ē, fiya tirja' 'a amerika bas tkhalliS il-AUB.*
   f. *ba'd ma bta'rif shu badda tidrus bi l-AUB.*

6. a. *iza ma timshi min hōn, ma raH tūSal 'a bētu.*
   If you don't walk from here, you won't get to his house.

   b. *zeyneb mish (menna) bi l-bēt?*
   Isn't Zeyneb at home?

   c. *siyyartu mish (menna) kharbēne Sarla sine.*
   His car has not been out of order for a year.

   d. *ha l-kibbeye mish la ilik?*
   Isn't this glass yours?

   e. *khayyu la-ziyād ma 'allam wlēdi 'arabi.*
   Zyad's brother didn't teach my kids Arabic.

   f. *lē ma baddak taHke ma'i?*
   Why don't you want to talk with me?

7. a. *binti ha s-sine raH tkhalliS ij-jēm'a.*
   My daughter will finish school this year.

b. 'ashrīn dolar mish ktīr. kill shi halla
   Sar ghāli.
   $20 is not much. Everything now has
   become expensive.

c. weyn baddik tinzli ya madām?
   Where do you want to get off,
   Madam?

d. khayyak 'indu shighel?
   Does your brother have a job?

e. ma' min raH tiskun bi beyrūt?
   With who are you going to live in
   Beirut?

8. Muna: emtīn rja'ti min amerika?
   Grace: haydik il-yōm. lē?
   Muna: ken baddi iji la-'indik.
   Grace: fīkī tiji l-yōm, iza baddik.
   Muna: ma fīyi l-yōm.
   Grace: lē, weyn rāyHa?
   Muna: il-yōm jjim'a. kill jim'a b'allim
         inglīze b-madraset "il-Hikme".
   Grace: w-bukra?
   Muna: bukra ma 'indi shighel.
   Grace: Tayyib, tfaDDali.
   Muna: bas b-sharT.
   Grace: shu huwwe?
   Muna: raH niTbukh tabbule.
   Grace: tikrami.

9. a. 'jabetnī T-Tabkha li Tabakhta mbēriH.
   I liked the dish (that) I cooked
   yesterday.

b. baddi inzil 'a j-jēm'a li hiyye b-
   ashrafiyye.
   I want to get off at the university,
   which is in Ashrafiyye.

c. mā fīyi tjawwaz binet ma ba'rifa.
   I can't marry a girl (whom) I don't
   know.

d. fīki t'īshi 'ind khayyik li sēkin bi
   beyrūt.
   You can stay with your brother who
   lives in Beirut.

e. bHebb bas il-wlēd li byisma'ū l-kalēm.
   I like only children who listen.

10. a. afterwards – ba'deyn
    b. kitchen – maTbakh
    c. children – wlēd
    d. writing – ktēbe
    e. without – bala
    f. Take! (m.) – khud!
    g. time – wa'et
    h. It's fine. – ma'lē.
    i. now – halla
    j. sure – akīd

			a					m
	m	k	t	ē	b	e	a
	h	a	ī					T
b	a	'	d	e	y	n		b
	l	l			b	a	l	a
w	l	ē	d	k	h	u	d	k
w	a	'	e	t				h

409

LESSON 31

(Saudi Arabic)

aHub a'arrefek bi nefsi! I'd Like to Introduce Myself!

A. Dialogue

Mr. David Jones is on the plane traveling to Jeddah. He strikes up a conversation with Mr. Ra'ad Al-Darwish, his wife, and their sixteen year-old son. Mr. Al-Darwish teaches in an Islamic school in Washington, D.C. He is going to Saudi Arabia with his family for a summer vacation. Mr. Jones is a consultant, visiting Saudi Arabia to conduct research on schools in Saudi Arabia.

mister jōnz: marHabā, aHub a'arrafak bi nafsī. anā ismī deyvid jōnz, wa aHub at'arraf bīk.

as-sayyid ra'ad: ahlan bik, ana ismī ra'ad wu hādi al-madām, wu hadā Ìbni, wu huwwa ya sīdi amrikāni.

mister jōnz: wani'm ya sayyid ra'ad, itsharraft bi ma'rifatak.

as-sayyid ra'ad: iHnā illi itsharrafnā bi ma'rifatak, ish lōnek?

mister jōnz: Tayyib al-Hamdulillāh, wa inta kēf Hālak?

as-sayyid ra'ad: zen al-Hamdulillāh.

mister jōnz: bes ya sayyid ra'ad, mumkin as'alak su'āl?

as-sayyid ra'ad: itfaDDal.

mister jōnz: bes kēf yukūn ibnek amrikāni?

as-sayyid ra'ad: li'innu itkhalag fi amrīka.

mister jōnz: ēsh ismū ibnek?

as-sayyid ra'ad: ismū aHmad, 'indu sitta'shar sanah.

mister jōnz: mashā'allāh, allāh yiHfaZu.

as-sayyid ra'ad: allah yiHfaZak inta. bes inta titkallam 'arabi Tayyib, kēf yiSīr?

mister jōnz: ana darast al-'arabi, khaSSatan al-lahje al-hijāziyye, fi jāme'at jorjtawin limuddet sanatēn. we daHīn misāfir li jiddah asawwi baHth 'an al-madāris wa al-tedrīs fi al-mamlakah.

as-sayyid ra'ad: be s-sanatēn, muma'gūl, inta titkallam 'arabi bilmarra Tayyib. insha'allah muwaffag fi muhimmetek.

mister jōnz: shukran, we inta ya seyyid ra'ad ēsh tishtaghil?

as-sayyid ra'ad: ana ya mister jōnz mudarris fi madrasat al-huda fi washintun, wa badarris 'arabi.

mister jōnz: subHānallāh ya akhī, ya'ni inta we ana tagrīben fi nafs al-muhime.

as-sayyid ra'ad: hada SaHiH. we bi'idhnillāh miTawwil ma'ana fi jiddah?

mister jōnz: Hawāli sitet shuhūr.

as-sayyid ra'ad: gadīsh, sitet shuhūr bes? hada galīl, bes lāzim tuzūreni fi jiddah.

mister jōnz: Tab'an, akīd. yekūnli 'ash-sharaf bizyartak.

as-sayyid ra'ad: fēn tuskun fi jiddah?

mister jōnz: la-lHīn ma 'adri, bes insha'allah yukūn garīb minnek.

as-sayyid ra'ad: insha'allah, hada huwwa 'inwān maktabi, lāzim tutzūreni.

mister jōnz: akīd, itsharraft bi ma'refetek ya 'akh ra'ad.

el sayyed Ra'ad: we ana kamān ya siyyid jōnz. fi amānillāh.

mister jōnz: ma'a s-salāma.

Mr. Jones: Hello, I'd like to introduce myself. My name is David Jones, and I would like to make your acquaintance (*lit.*, to know you).

Mr. Ra'ad: Hello, my name is Ra'ad. This is my wife, and this is my son; he is American.

Mr. Jones: It's an honor, Mr. Ra'ad. I am honored to make your acquaintance.

Mr. Ra'ad: We are the ones who are honored to make your acquaintance. How are you?

Mr. Jones: Fine, thank God, and you how are you?

Mr. Ra'ad: Good, thank God.

Mr. Jones: But, Mr. Ra'ad, can I ask you a question?

Mr. Ra'ad: Please, go ahead.

Mr. Jones: How come your son is American?

Mr. Ra'ad: Because he was born in America.

Mr. Jones: What's his name?

Mr. Ra'ad: His name is Ahmad, and he is sixteen years old.

Mr. Jones: Praise God. May God protect him.

Mr. Ra'ad: May God protect you. But you speak Arabic well; how come?

Mr. Jones: I studied Arabic, especially the Hijazi dialect, at Georgetown University for two years. And now I am going to Jeddah to do some research on schools and education in the kingdom.

Mr. Ra'ad: Only two years, this is not possible. You speak Arabic very well. Hopefully (*lit.*, God willing), you will be successful in your mission.

Mr. Jones: Thank you. And you, Mr. Ra'ad, what do you do?

Mr. Ra'ad: I, Mr. Jones, work as a teacher in Al-Huda School in Washington, and I teach Arabic.

Mr. Jones: What a coincidence (*lit.*, Glory to God), brother. You and I are (*lit.*, work) almost in the same profession.

Mr. Ra'ad: This is true. Hopefully, you will be staying long in Jeddah. (*lit.*, With God's permission, are you staying long in Jeddah?)

Mr. Jones: Nearly six months.

Mr. Ra'ad: What, only six months! This is little. You must visit me in Jeddah.

Mr. Jones: Of course, definitely. It will be my honor to visit you.

Mr. Ra'ad: Where are you staying in Jeddah?

Mr. Jones: I don't know yet, but I hope it will be close to you.

Mr. Ra'ad: Let's hope (*lit.*, God willing). This is the address of my office. You must visit me.

Mr. Jones: Certainly. I am honored to have made your acquaintance, brother Ra'ad.

Mr. Ra'ad: Me, too, Mr. Jones. Good-bye (*lit.*, in God's security).

Mr. Jones: Good-bye.

B. Pronunciation

1. WRITING SAUDI ARABIC

Like other Arabic dialects, Saudi Arabic is primarily a spoken language, rarely used in written communication, for which Modern Standard Arabic is the norm. Because Arabic script was devised to represent the sounds of Classical and Modern Standard Arabic, the additional sounds that exist in Arabic dialects like Saudi are not represented by it. For this reason, the transliteration in Latin script is used in Lessons 31 to 35 to represent Saudi Arabic.

There are three main Arabic dialects spoken in Saudi Arabia: Hijazi, spoken in the western regions of Saudi Arabia and in the cities of Jeddah, Medina, Mecca, and Tayyef; Najdi, spoken by the royal family and in the city of Riyadh; and Shargi, spoken in the eastern regions of Saudi Arabia. Hijazi is the most widely spoken variety and also the language used in the government, by the media, and in business transactions. In Lessons 30 to 35 you will learn the basics of this dialect, also referred to as the Urban Hijazi Arabic.

2. CONSONANTS

Most Urban Hijazi Arabic (UHA) consonants and vowels are the same as those in MSA. We discuss below several consonants that are different.

A. THE LACK OF *dh* AND *th*

The MSA consonant *dh* is pronounced as either *d* or *z*, and the consonant *th* is pronounced as *t* or *s*. Compare the UHA and MSA pronunciations of the following words:

UHA	MSA
hadā (this)	هذا *hādha*
asta'zan (ask for permission)	استأذن *ista'dhan*
talāta (three)	ثلاثة *thalātha*
masalan (for example)	مثلا *mathalan*

B. THE LACK OF *q*

The MSA *q*, as in *Haqīqa* (truth), is pronounced as *g* in UHA. All *g*-sounds in the examples below correspond to MSA *q*-sounds.

UHA	MSA
itkhalag (was born)	خُـلِـق *khuliq*
muwaffag (successful)	مُوَّفق *muwaffaq*
tagrīban (nearly)	تقريبا *taqrīban*
al-Hagīga (the truth)	الحقيقة *al-Haqīqa*
galīl (little)	قليل *qalīl*

3. VOWELS

In addition to the vowels *a, i, u, ā, ī,* and *ū,* which are the same as those in MSA, UHA also has the long vowels *ē* and *ō.* The long vowels *ē* and *ō* correspond to the *fusHā* sounds *ay* and *aw,* respectively. For example, the MSA word *bayn* (between) is *bēn* in UHA, and *rawH* (spirit) is *rōH* in UHA. Here are examples of words containing the different UHA vowels:

a — *hada* (this)   *ā* — *al-madāris* (schools)
i — *ma 'adri* (I don't know)   *ī* — *daHīn* (now)
u — *shukran* (thank you)   *ū* — *shuhūr* (months)
     ē — *kēf* (how)
     ō — *hadōl* (these)

C. Grammar and Usage

1. GREETINGS AND SOCIAL PHRASES

Greetings are very important in Saudi Arabia. Neither casual conversations nor business interactions can start without a fairly long greeting procedure, which includes inquiring about health. Many greetings and other social phrases make reference to *allah* (God). For example, *mashā 'allah* (it is what God wills) is a common phrase used to compliment or praise someone. Through everyday usage, many of these phrases have lost their religious connotations and are used by speakers regardless of their faith, similar to the colloquial English phrase *Thank God!*

GREETINGS AND SOCIAL PHRASES WITH RESPONSES			
Greeting		Response	
marHaba.	Hello.	*shukran.* or *allah yiHfaZak.*	Thank you. *or* May God protect you.
yā halā.	Hello.	*shukran.* or *allah yiHfaZak.* or *yā halā bīk.*	Thank you. *or* May God protect you. *or* Welcome to you.
ahlan.	Welcome.	*shukran.* or *allah yiHfaZak yā.* or *halā bīk.*	Thank you. *or* May God protect you. *or* Welcome to you.
ahlan bīk.	Welcome to you.	*shukran.* or *allah yiHfaZak.* or *yā halā bīk.*	Thank you. *or* May God protect you. *or* Welcome to you.
'itsharrafnā.	We are honored.	*shukran, allah yiHfaZak.*	Thank you. May God protect you.
ēshlōnak?	How are you? *(m.)*	*zen, al-Hamdulilah.* or *Tayyib, al-Hamdulillah.*	Fine, thanks. (*lit.*, praise to God)
ēshlōnik?	How are you? *(f.)*	*zen, al-Hamdulilah.* or *Tayyiba, al-Hamdulillah.*	Fine, thanks. (*lit.*, praise to God)
kēf Hālak?	How are you? *(m.)*	*zen, al-Hamdulilah.* or *Tayyib, al-Hamdulillah.*	Fine, thanks. (*lit.*, praise to God)
kēf Hālik?	How are you? *(f.)*	*zen, al-Hamdulilah.* or *Tayyiba, al-Hamdulillah.*	Fine, thanks. (*lit.*, praise to God)
fi'amānillah.	Good-bye. (*lit.*, go in God's safety)	*ma'a s-salāma.*	Good-bye. (*lit.*, go with peace)

2. PERSONAL PRONOUNS

The following table lists the full set of subject personal pronouns in UHA and their equivalents in MSA. Notice the differences between the UHA and MSA pronouns in vowels and some consonants. As in other dialects, there are no dual pronouns, and the masculine plural pronouns are used for both the masculine plural and the feminine plural.

UHA	MSA	
anā	أَنا *anā*	I
inta	أنتَ *anta*	you *(m.)*
inti	أنتِ *anti*	you *(f.)*
huwwa	هُوَ *huwa*	he
hiyya	هِيَ *hiya*	she
niHna/iHna	نَحْنُ *naHnu*	we
intu *(m./f. pl.)*	أنتُم *antum*	you
humma *(m./f. pl.)*	هُمْ *hum*	they

3. POSSESSIVE SUFFIXES

In UHA, as in MSA, possessive pronouns are suffixes attached to nouns. Possessive pronouns can be attached to nouns, as in *ismi* (my name), or to prepositions, as in *'indu* (he has, *lit.*, at him) or *minnak* (from you).

ism- (NAME) WITH POSSESSIVE SUFFIXES		
UHA	**MSA**	
sm*i*	اسمي *ismi*	my name
ism*ak*	اسمك *ismuk*	your *(m.)* name
ism*ik*	اسمكِ *ismuki*	your *(f.)* name
ism*ū*	اسمه *ismū*	his name
ism*aha*	اسمها *ismuha*	her name
ism*ina*	اسمنا *ismuna*	our name
ism*akum*	اسمكم *ismukum*	your *(pl.)* name
ism*ahum*	اسمهم *ismuhum*	their name

'ind (AT) WITH POSSESSIVE SUFFIXES		
UHA	MSA	
'ind<u>i</u>	عندي 'ind<u>i</u>	I have
'and<u>ak</u>	عندك 'ind<u>ak</u>	you (m.) have
'ind<u>ik</u>	عندكِ 'ind<u>aki</u>	you (f.) have
'ind<u>ū</u>	عنده 'ind<u>ū</u>	he has
'ind<u>aha</u>	عندها 'ind<u>aha</u>	she has
'ind<u>ana</u>	عندنا 'ind<u>ana</u>	we have
'ind<u>akum</u>	عندكم 'ind<u>akum</u>	you (pl.) have
'ind<u>ahum</u>	عندهم 'ind<u>ahum</u>	they have

4. VERB CONJUGATION

In UHA, as in fuSHā, verbal inflections are represented by prefixes or suffixes added to the verb stem. There are two main verb tenses in UHA: perfect, formed with suffixes, and imperfect, formed with prefixes and suffixes. The future tense is used as well.

The perfect tense refers to past or completed actions, and the imperfect tense refers to past and incomplete actions. Note that UHA verbs inflect for number, singular and plural, but not for dual. UHA is also different from MSA in that it does not have the subjunctive and jussive moods, but it does have the imperative.

In the tables that follow, three common verbs in UHA and in MSA are conjugated in the imperfect tense. Note the lack of final vowels in most UHA forms.

IMPERFECT TENSE OF THE VERB *daras* (TO STUDY)

UHA		MSA		
anā	adrus	anā	ادرسُ adrusu	I study
inta	tudrus	anta	تدرسُ tadrusu	you (m.) study
inti	tudrusī	anti	تدرسين tadrusīna	you (f.) study
huwwa	yudrus	huwa	يدرسُ yadrusu	he studies
hiyya	tudrus	hiya	تدرسُ tadrusu	she studies
iHna/niHna	nudrus	naHnu	ندرسُ nadrusu	we study
intu	tudrusū	antum	تدرسون tadrusūna	you (pl.) study
humma	yudrusū	humm	يدرسون yadrusūna	they study

IMPERFECT TENSE OF THE VERB *Hab* (TO LIKE, TO LOVE)

UHA		MSA		
anā	āHub	anā	أحِبُ uHibbu	I like/love
inta	tuHub	anta	تحِبُ tuHibbu	you (m.) like/love
inti	tuHubi	anti	تحِبين tuHibbīna	you (f.) like/love
huwwa	yuHub	huwa	يحِبُ yuHibbu	he likes/loves
hiyya	tuHub	hiya	تحِبُ tuHibbu	she likes/loves
iHna/niHna	nuHub	naHnu	نحِبُ nuHibbu	we love
intu	tuHubu	antum	تحِبون tuHibbūna	you (pl.) love
humma	yuHubu	humm	يحِبون yuHibbūna	they love

IMPERFECT TENSE OF THE VERB *ishtaghal* (TO WORK)				
UHA		MSA		
anā	*ashtaghil*	*anā*	أَشتغلُ *ashtaghilu*	I work[1]
inta	*tishtaghil*	*anta*	تشتغلُ *tashtaghilu*	you *(m.)* work
huwwa	*yishtaghil*	*huwa*	يشتغلُ *yashtaghilu*	he works
Hiyya	*tishtaghil*	*hiya*	تشتغلُ *tashtaghilu*	she works
iHna	*nishtaghil*	*naHnu*	نشتغلُ *nashtaghilu*	we work
intu	*tishtaghilu*	*antum*	تشتغلون *tashtaghiluna*	you *(pl.)* work
humma	*yishtaghilu*	*humm*	يشتغلون *yashtaghiluna*	they work

5. NEGATIVE PARTICLES

As in MSA, negative particles *mā* (not) and *mū* (not) are placed in front of the word to make its meaning negative. *mā* is used before verbs and the expressions *fī* (there is) and *'indi* (I have); *mū* is used elsewhere. Consider the following examples:

mā fī madrasa bukra.
There is no school tomorrow.

mā 'indi māni'.
I have no objection.

anā mā āHub shughli.
I don't like my work.

mū kabīr
not big *(m.)*

ana mū Tayyib.
I am not well.

6. QUESTION WORDS

The following are commonly used question words in UHA.

kēf (how)
ēsh (what)
lēsh (why)
fēn (where)
mīn (who)
mita (when)

---

[1] Note that the verb *ishtaghal* means "to be busy with" in *fuSHā*.

Here are some examples. Note that the question words come at the beginning of the sentences.

> *kēf tuHub tishtaghil?*
> How do you like to work?

> *ēsh tuHub tishtaghil?*
> What do you like to do?

> *lēsh tuHub tishtaghil?*
> Why do you like to work?

> *fēn tuHub tishtaghil?*
> Where do you like to work?

> *mīn yuHub yishtaghil?*
> Who likes to work?

> *mita tuHub tishtaghil?*
> When do you like to work?

D. Vocabulary

marHaba.	Hello.
āHub ā'arrafak bi nefsi.	I would like to introduce myself.
āHub . . .	I would like . . .
āt'arref bik	to know you
āhlan bīk.	Welcome to you.
kēf Hālak?	How are you?
Tayyib, āl-Hamdulillah.	Fine, thanks (*lit.*, praise to God).
zen, āl-Hamdulillah.	Fine, thanks (*lit.*, praise to God).
hādi	this
al-madām	my wife
ibni	my son
ya sidi!	My friend!, My man!
āmrikāni	American
yā halā	welcome
itsharrafnā.	I am honored to make your acquaintance.
mumkin as'alak su'āl?	Can I ask you a question?
bes	but
kēf yukūn?	How come?
ibnek	your son
li'innu . . .	because he . . .
itkhalag	was born
fi amrīka	in America
mashā 'allah	Great! (*lit.*, it is what God wills)

esh ismu?	What is his name?
'andu sita'shar sana.	He is sixteen years old (*lit.*, he has sixteen years).
allah yiHfaZu.	God bless him (*lit.*, God keep him).
kēf yiSīr?	How come? (*lit.*, how it becomes)
daHīn	and now
asawwi	I am conducting
baHth	research
il-madāris we il-tadrīs	schools and teaching
fi l-mamlakah	in the kingdom
insha 'allah muwaffag!	Good luck! *(lit.* If God wills, you will be successful!)
ēsh tishtaghil?	What do you do?
subHanallah.	Glory be to God.
tagrīben	almost
fi nefs il-mihne	in the same profession
hada SaHiiH	this is true
we bi'idhnillāh.	With God's permission.
miTawwil	you are staying
ma'ana	with us
al-hagiga	actually
sittat shuhūr	six months
gadīsh?	How long?
hada galīl.	This is little.
Tab'an	of course
akīd	for sure
yekūnli sh-sharaf bi zyartak.	I will be honored to visit you. (*lit.*, by visiting you)
mumkin as'al su'āl?	Can I ask you a question?
itfaDDal!	Go ahead!
li l-Hīn	till now
ma'adri	I don't know
'inwān maktabi	my office address
lāzim tzūreni.	You should visit me.
itsharraft.	I am honored.
bi ma'reftek	to get to know you
ya 'akh ra'ad	brother Ra'ad
we ana kamān.	Me, too.

E. Cultural Note

NAMES AND TITLES

Saudi names consist of the person's first name, the middle or father's name, and the family name. The middle name may be preceded by *ibn* (son) or *bint* (daughter). Thus, a person's name may be *sa'd ibn yousif ibn ibrahim al-kheriji*, or *fatma bint 'aqil ibn mohammed al-gazzaz*. The family name is often preceded by the definite article, but there are names without it, for example, *hamza ibn safi shaker*.

First names are used when addressing people. Therefore, Mr. Ra'ad Al-Darwish is addressed as *as-sayyid ra'ad*. Various titles, such as "Dr.," are also used with first names, for example, *Dr. ra'ad*. When people feel especially friendly toward each other, even on their first encounter, they may use the term *akh* (brother) or *ukht* (sister) followed by the first name, as in *akh ra'ad* (brother Ra'ad) and *ukht haya* (sister Haya).

As mentioned earlier, greetings are extremely important in Saudi Arabia. Mastering an assortment of greeting exchanges is essential in coming across as well-mannered. People also ask about each other's health and the health of the members of their families, immediate and extended. In Saudi Arabia, people can spend a few minutes repeatedly greeting each other and asking about their families and relatives. Even if you see someone you know across the room and nod to the person, the greeting ritual will take place regardless of whether you can hear or make out the words.

Expressions refering to God are part of people's everyday speech in Saudi Arabia. God is mentioned in a variety of contexts: when engaging in an important task or giving a presentation or a speech, you say *bism ilāh ar-raHman ar-raHīm* (In the name of God, the Merciful, the Compassionate); when someone is announcing good news to you, similar to English *Guess what!*, you say *khēr insh'allah* (Let it be good, if God wills); when expressing uncertainty, you say *allahu a'lam* (Only God knows for sure); when speaking of future plans, you say *rabbana yisahhil* (May our Lord make it easy); and when offering praise or to cast the evil eye away, you say *mashā' allah* (It is what God wills), *tabārak allah* (May God be blessed), or *subHan allah* (Glory to God).

F. Exercises

1. Match the phrases in column A with the right responses in column B.

A	B
a. *shlōnek?*	*akīd.*
b. *mumkin as'al su'āl.*	*ismu 'ali.*
c. *ana ismi mesh'al.*	*zen, al-Hamdulillah.*
d. *insha 'allah muwaffag.*	*yā halā.*
e. *ēsh ismu?*	*itfaddal.*
f. *lāzim tzūreni.*	*itsharrafnā.*
g. *marHaba.*	*allah yiHfaZak.*

2. Put the verbs in parentheses in the singular *you* form of the imperfect tense to make complete sentences.

a. *lāzim (shūrani).*
b. *fēn (skun)?*
c. *kēf (rūH)?*
d. *ēsh (Hub)?*
e. *mumkin (drus).*

3. Fill in the blanks by choosing among the following prefixes, suffixes, and particles.

-ū / -i / mā- / -kum / -ē / -hum / -ak / n- / a- / mū-

a. *ana ta'bān bi l-marra, lāzim ___rūH albēt.*

b. *kēf Hala___ 'asakum bekhēr?*

c. *intu ēsh tuHub___.*

d. *aHub a'arrefek bi nefs___.*

e. *ana ___ a'raf fēn huwwa.*

f. *huwwa ___mawjūd.*

g. *yisawwu baHth___ fi tadrīs.*

h. *shukran, Hāl___ Tayyib.*

i. *'afsh___ katīr.*

j. *iHna ___ishtaghil galīl.*

4. Translate the following English utterances into UHA.

a. How do you like to do your research?

b. Where do you like to work?

c. How long do you work?

d. Can I ask you a question?

5. Complete your part of the following dialogue.

'aHmad: marHaba.
You: _____
'aHmad: 'inta min fēn?
You: _____
'aHmad: kēf Halak?
You: _____
'aHmad: fēn tishtaghil?
You: _____
'aHmad: ēsh tsawwi fi shughul?
You: _____
'aHmad: fēn tiskun?
You: _____
'aHmad: tuHub tzūreni garīb.
You: _____
'aHmad: fi 'amānillah.
You: _____

Answer Key

1. a. *shlōnek?—zen, al-Hamdulillah.*
   b. *mumkin as'al su'āl.—itfaddal.*
   c. *ana ismi mesh'al.—itsharrafnā.*
   d. *insha' allah muwaffag.—allah yiHfazak.*
   e. *ēsh ismu?—ismu 'ali.*
   f. *lāzim tzūreni.—'akīd.*
   g. *marHaba.—yā halā.*

2. a. *lāzim tshūreni.*
   b. *fēn tuskun?*
   c. *kēf trūH?*
   d. *ēsh tHub?*
   e. *mumkin tudrus.*

3. a. *ana ta'bān bi l-marra, lāzim arūH al-bēt.*
   b. *kēf Halakum 'asakum bekhēr?*
   c. *intu ēsh tuHubū.*
   d. *aHub a'arrefek bi nefsi.*
   e. *ana ma a'raf fēn huwwa.*
   f. *huwwa mūmawjūd.*
   g. *yisawwu baHthēn fi tadrīs.*
   h. *shukran, Hālhum Tayyib.*

   i. *'afshak katīr.*
   j. *iHna nishtaghil galīl.*

4. a. *kēf tuHub tisawil baHth?*
   b. *fēn tuHub tishtaghil?*
   c. *li-mita tishtaghil?*
   d. *mumkin 'as'alak su'āl?*

5. *aHmad: marHaba.*
   You: yāhalā.
   aHmad: inta min fēn?
   You: amrikāni.
   aHmad: kēf Halak?
   You: Tayyib, al-Hamdulillah.
   aHmad: fēn tishtaghil?
   You: ashtaghil fi al-tadrīs.
   aHmad: ēsh tsawwi fi shughul?
   You: asawwi baHth.
   aHmad: fēn tiskun?
   You: garīb min hina.
   aHmad: tuHub tzūreni garīb.
   You: akīd.
   aHmad: fi amānillah.
   You: ma'a s-salāma.

LESSON 32

(Saudi Arabic)

'andi mashawīr. I Have Errands to Run.

A. Dialogue

Mr. Jones has some errands to run. He needs to go to the post office to send letters and postcards to his family and friends in the United States. Then, he needs to stop at the bank. The hotel doorman gives him directions.

jōnz: salām 'alaykum.

al-bawāb: wa 'alaykum is-salām.

jōnz: ismaHli, kēf arūH agrab maktab barīd?

al-bawāb: luff yamin fi akhir ash-shari', wu ba'den, rūh li l-ishara, wu igTa' ish-shari' ba'ad kida, imshi shwayya tagriben khamsīn metir, tilagi madrasa, al-barid mugabil al-madrasa.

jōnz: Tayyib, hal fi bank garīb?

al-bawāb: al-bank al-āwaTani, fi l-taHliya senter, bes lazim takhud taksi.

jōnz: ya tara ta'rif ēsh hiyya awgātal-dawām bi l-bank?

al-bawāb: kul al-'ayām ma'ada al-khamīs wa al-jum'a min as-sa'a tamanya aS-SubuH ilā talata wa nuS fi l-misa.

jōnz: jazak allah kulli khēr.

al-bawāb: ahlan bīk.

At the post office.

jōnz: abgha arsil jawāb li amrika barīd jawwi musajjal.

muwazzaf al-barīd: hada waznu tag il, min-faDDlak HuTT bi khamsa riyaal Tawābi' 'ala Z-Zarf.

jōnz: abgha arsil Tard kamān, mita yiwSal?

muwazzaf al-barīd: law sari' fi talatat iyam.

jōnz: mashkūr.

muwazzaf al-barīd: la shukur 'ala wājib.

Jones hails a taxi and goes to the National Bank at the Tahliya Center.

jōnz: abgha arūH al-TaHliya senter, kam takhud?

sawwāg al-taksi: 'ashara riyāl.

jōnz: 'ashara riyāl, hada katīr.

sawwāg al-taksi: abadan mu katir, hadi hiyya al-ta'rifa.

jōnz: Tayyib. yala nimshi li l-TaHliya senter, abgha arūH al-bank al-waTani.

sawwāg al-taksi: abshir.

jōnz: kam yahkhud wagt?

sawwāg al-taksi: 'ashara dagīga.

jōnz: mumtāz. ismaHli, ēsh hadōla l-'amāyir?

sawwāg al-taksi: hadōla 'imarāt sakan li l-ta'jīr.

jōnz: sūg shwaya shwaya, min-faDlak.

sawwāg al-taksi: lēsh, ana basūg bisur'a, inta manak mabsūT min siwāgati?

jōnz: illa, bi l-'aks, inta tsūg bi l-mara Tayyib, wa lākin abgha ashūf al-'amāyir.

sawwāg al-taksi: abshir, daHin akhlīk tshūf el-makan min garīb.

jōnz: shukran.

sawwāg al-taksi: wara al-'imara hādi al-bank haggak.

jōnz: Tayyib. itfaDDal al-'ashara riyāl. ma'a s-salāma.

Jones: Hello.

Doorman: Hello.

Jones: Excuse me, how can I get to the nearest post office?

Doorman: Turn right at the end of this street, and then walk down the street to the traffic light. Cross the street at the traffic light and walk another 50 meters or so. You will see a large school building. The post office is just opposite the school.

Jones: Okay, is there a bank nearby?

Doorman: The National Bank, in Tahliya Center, but you will need to take a taxi.

Jones: Do you know the working hours at the bank?

Doorman: Every day except Thursday and Friday, from eight in the morning to 3:30 in the afternoon.

Jones: Thank you (*lit.*, May God give you all good).

Doorman: You're welcome.

Jones: I want to send an airmail registered letter to America.

Post Office Employee: It weighs a lot, so put five riyals' worth of postage on the envelope, please.

Jones: I would like to send a package, too. When will it get there?

Post Office Employee: If it is express, it will take three days.

Jones: Thanks.

Post Office Employee: You're welcome (*lit.*, no thanks for a duty).

Jones: I would like to go to Al-Tahliya Center; how much do you charge?

Taxi Driver: Ten riyals.

Jones: Ten riyals? Isn't that a lot?

Taxi Driver: Not at all. That's the usual fare.

Jones: Okay. Then let's go to Tahliya Center; I want to go to Al-Watani Bank.

Taxi Driver: Sure.

Jones: How long will it take to get there?

Taxi Driver: Ten minutes.

Jones: Great. Excuse me, what are those buildings?

Taxi Driver: These buildings are condominiums for rent.

Jones: Drive slowly, please.

Taxi Driver: Why, do I drive fast? Aren't you happy with my driving?

Jones: No, on the contrary, you drive very well, but I want to look at the buildings.

Taxi Driver: Sure, now I will let you see the place from near.

Jones: Thanks.

Taxi Driver: Your bank is behind this building.

Jones: Okay. Here are the ten riyals. Good-bye.

B. Pronunciation

CONNECTING WORDS INTO PHRASES

As in MSA, the article *al* changes its form to *l* when it is preceded by a word that ends in a vowel.

> *ēsh hadōla al-'amāyir* ⟶ *ēsh hadōla l-'amāyir*
> these buildings

Elision of the vowel in the article *al* often happens when an article follows a preposition ending in a vowel.

> *ma'a al-'ēlā* ⟶ *ma'a l-'ēlā* (with the family)
> *fī al-bēt* ⟶ *fī l-bēt* (in the house)
> *li il-ishāra* ⟶ *li l-ishāra* (to the traffic signal)

C. Grammar and Usage

1. SAYING *I WOULD LIKE TO*

Use *abgha* to express English *I would like to*:

> *abgha asruf hada ash-shēk.*
> I would like to cash this check.

While *abgha* literally means "I want," it is an appropriate equivalent of *I would like to* in UHA. Here are some more examples:

> *abgha arūH al-bank.*
> I would like to go to the bank.

> *abgha aftaH Hisāb fi l-bank.*
> I would like to open an account at the bank.

2. NUMBERS FROM 1 TO 12

The numbers in UHA are very similar to those in *fuSHā*.

wāHid	one
itnēn	two
talāta	three
arba'a	four
khamsa	five
sitta	six
sab'a	seven
tamanya	eight
tis'a	nine
'ashara	ten

| iHda'sh | eleven |
| itna'sh | twelve |

3. DAYS OF THE WEEK

Here are the names for the days of the week. They differ slightly from those used in MSA.

as-sabt	Saturday
al-aHad	Sunday
al-itnēn	Monday
at-talūt	Tuesday
ar-rabū'	Wednesday
al-khamīs	Thursday
al-jum'a	Friday

4. VERB CONJUGATION

Below are the imperfect tense forms of the verb *rāH* (to go). Note that the consonant *w* changes into a long vowel *ū*.

Here is the imperfect tense conjugation of *laff* (to turn, to fold).

THE IMPERFECT TENSE OF THE VERB *rāH* (TO GO)			
ana	*arūH*	iHna/niHna	*nurūH*
inta	*turūH*	intum	*turūHu*
inti	*turūHi*		
huwwa	*yurūH*	humma	*yurūHu*
hiyya	*turūH*		

5. THE IMPERATIVE

The imperative is the command form of the verb. UHA has only three forms for the

THE IMPERFECT TENSE OF THE VERB *laff* (TO TURN, TO FOLD)			
ana	*aluff*	iHna/niHna	*nuluff*
inta	*tuluff*	intum	*tuluffu*
inti	*tuluffi*		
huwwa	*yuluff*	humma	*yuluffu*
hiyya	*tuluff*		

imperative: masculine, feminine, and plural. The imperative is formed in the same way as in MSA (see Lesson 10), from the imperfect verb, with minor differences in pronunciation.

THE IMPERATIVE

	to walk, to go	to cut	to cash, to spend	to eat	to drive
inta	*imshi*	*igTa'*	*iSruf*	*kull*	*sūg*
inti	*imshi*	*igTa'i*	*iSrufi*	*kulli*	*sūgi*
intum	*imshu*	*igTa'u*	*iSrufu*	*kullu*	*sūgu*

6. ADJECTIVES: AGREEMENT AND COMPARISON

A. AGREEMENT

As in MSA, adjectives must agree in gender and number with the noun they modify. For example:

> *shāri'* (m. sg.) *Tawīl* (m. sg.)
> long street

> *'imāra* (f. sg.) *Tawīla* (f. sg.)
> tall building

Because *shāri'* (street) is masculine and singular, the adjective *Tawīl* must be in the masculine singular form. Because *'imāra* (building) is feminine and singular, the adjective *Tawīla* must be in the feminine singular form as well. Here are two more examples.

> *bēt Saghīr* (m. sg.)
> a small house

> *biyūt Sughār* (m. pl.)
> small houses

B. COMPARATIVE AND SUPERLATIVE

The same form of an adjective is used for both the comparative (e.g., English *bigger*) and the superlative (e.g., English *the biggest*) in UHA. Here are some common adjectives with their comparative/superlative forms.

Base Form	Comparative/Superlative Form
kabīr (big; old)	*akbar* (bigger, older; biggest, oldest)
Saghīr (small; young)	*aSghar* (smaller, younger; smallest, youngest)
katīr (much)	*aktar* (more; most)
ba'īd (far)	*ab'ad* (farther; farthest)
garīb (near)	*agrab* (nearer; nearest)

As in MSA, the pattern used to derive the comparative/superlative from the root form is *aCCaC*.

> *k-b-r* ⟶ *akbar* (bigger; the biggest)

> *j-m-l* ⟶ *ajmal* (more beautiful; the most beautiful)

428

s-r-' ⟶ *asra'* (quicker; the quickest)

T-w-l ⟶ *aTwal* (longer/taller; the longest/the tallest)

Like any other adjective, the comparative/superlative adjective is preceded by the definite article if the noun it modifies is definite.

al-bint al-kabīrah
the elder daughter

7. OBJECT PRONOUN SUFFIXES

In Lesson 31 you learned that possessive pronoun suffixes are attached to nouns in order to express possession. As in MSA, object pronoun suffixes are added to verbs and prepositions to denote the object. Their forms, given in the table below, are virtually the same as those in MSA (see Lesson 6).

OBJECT PRONOUN SUFFIXES			
anā	*-ni*	*tarakni* (he left me)	*li* (to me)
inta	*-ak*	*tarakak* (he left you, *m.*)	*lak* (to you, *m.*)
inti	*-ik*	*tarakik* (he left you, *f.*)	*liki* (to you, *f.*)
huwwa	*-u*	*taraku* (he left him)	*lu* (to him)
hiyya	*-aha*	*tarakha* (he left her)	*laha* (to her)
iHna/niHna	*-ana*	*tarakna* (he left us)	*lana* (to us)
intu	*-akum*	*tarakkum* (he left you, *pl.*)	*lakum* (to you, *pl.*)
humma	*-ahum*	*tarahum* (he left them)	*lahum* (to them)

gidāmana
in front of us

akhadu.
He took him.

al-sawwāg akhadu li l-bank.
The driver took him to the bank.

Here's the verb *ismaH* (to permit, to give permission) with object pronoun suffixes attached.

asmaHlak	permit you *(m.)*
asmaHlik	permit you *(f.)*
asmaHlu	permit him
asmaHlaha	permit her
asmaHlana	permit us
asmaHlakum	permit you *(pl.)*
asmHlahum	permit them

8. DEMONSTRATIVES

Demonstrative adjectives, like other adjectives, must agree with the nouns they modify in gender and number.

DEMONSTRATIVES					
Masculine Singular		Feminine Singular		Plural	
hadā	this	*hādi*	this	*hadōla*	these
hadāk	that	*hadīk*	that	*hadolāk*	those

hada sh-shēk (m. sg.)
this check

hādi s-siyāra (f. sg.)
this car

hadōla al-beyūt (m. pl.)
these houses

hadōla al-'amāyer (f. pl.)
these buildings

hadāk ar-rijjaal (m. sg.)
that man

hadīk as-sitt (f. sg.)
that woman

hadolāk an-naas (m. pl.)
those people

hadolāk as-sittāt (f. pl.)
those women

9. ADVERBS

Here are some essential adverbs of place and manner.

hina (here)
hināk (there)
shiwaya shiwaya (slowly)
bi shwēsh (slowly)
bi sur'a (quickly)

Note that many adverbs have the same form as masculine adjectives.

titkallam 'arabi Tayyib.
You speak Arabic well.

zahamtalu katīr.
I called for him many times.

D. Vocabulary

'andi mashawīr.	I have errands [to run].
ismaHli.	Excuse me. (*lit.*, give me permission)
agrab	nearest
maktab barīd	post office
fi akhir	at the end of
ash-shari'	the street
ba'dēn	then
tagrīban	nearly
mugabil	across from, opposite
al-madrasa	the school
jazak allah kulli khēr	Thank you. (*lit.*, May God grant you all his blessings.)
jawāb	letter
barīd jawwi musajjal	registered airmail
waznu	its weight
tagīl	heavy
khamsa riyāl	five riyals
Tard	package
mita yiwSal?	When will it arrive?
abgha arsil	I would like to send
talata	three
iyām	days
la shukur 'ala wajib.	You're welcome. (*lit.*, No thanks for a duty.)
al-taHliya senter	Tahliya Center
kam takhud?	How much do you charge (*lit.*, take)?
'ashara	ten
mū katīr	not a lot
abshir	sure (*lit.*, be happy)
wagt	time
mumtāz	great, wonderful
hadōla l-'amāyir	those buildings
'imarāt sakan	apartment buildings
sh(i)waya	little
manak?	Aren't you?
mabsūT	happy
siwāgati	my driving
tshūf	you see
al-makan	the place
garīb	near
al-bank	the bank
haggak	yours
awgāt al-dawām	working hours
as-sa'a tamanya	eight o'clock

| aS-SubuH | the morning |
| Tābi' (Tawābi') | stamp(s) |

E. Cultural Note

People in Saudi Arabia are very friendly and will happily provide you with directions on the street. You can draw their attention by using phrases such as *ismaHli!* (Excuse me!) or *mumkin dagīga!* (Just a minute!). Terms such as north, south, west, or east are not normally used when street directions are given. Instead, listen for *yemīn* (right), *shumāl/yasār* (left), *dughri* (straight ahead) or other related words, such as *guddām* (in front), *wara* (behind), *jamb* (beside), *fōg* (up, above), *taHat* (down, below) *barra* (outside), and *juwwa* (inside).

Because taxis do not have meters, it is advisable that you ask about the fare before deciding on a ride. While it is acceptable to bargain over the fare, it is always preferable to find out about the fare ranges before taking a cab. It is also appropriate to ask the taxi driver to drive slowly if you think he or she is driving fast.

Numbers are normally given out to the customers waiting in lines at banks and post offices in Saudi Arabia. This prevents problems arising from cutting, because standing in lines is not a custom that is firmly observed in the Arab world.

F. Exercises

1. Match the nouns in column A with the corresponding adjectives in column B.

A	B
a. *'imāra*	*kabīr*
b. *sayyāra*	*Saghīr*
c. *shāri'*	*Tawīl*
d. *bēt*	*Saghīra*
e. *maktab*	*kabīra*

2. Put the verbs in parentheses in the *I* form of the imperfect tense to make complete sentences.

    a. *ana ma aHub (luff) katīr.*
    b. *aHub (mshi) katīr.*
    c. *madri fēn (rūH).*
    d. *ma a'raf aT-Tarīga (gTa') fiha al-HabHab.*
    e. *ana aHub (shtaghil) katīr.*

3. Fill in the blanks by choosing the right verb and putting it in the appropriate conjugated form.

   Sāg / Habb / rāH / gaTa' / mishi

a. _____ *bishwēsh, ana ma aHub as-suwaga bi sur'a.*

b. _____ *ash-shari' min hina.*

c. _____ *min hina, hada al-makān mu Tayyib.*

d. *intu* _____ *bi shwēsh bi l-mara.*

e. *niHna ma* _____ *as-sur'ah.*

4. Choose the correct word to agree with the demonstrative.

a. *hada (as-sayyara / al-beyūt / sh-shekēn / al-HabHab) mu Tayyib.*

b. *hādi (aT-Tarīga / ash-shari' / al-bank / maktab al-barīd) mumtāza.*

c. *hadōla (ash-shari' / aj-jawāb / aT-Tard / as-sayyarāt) timshi bi sur'a.*

d. *hadak (as-sit / as-sittāt / ar-rijjāl / aT-Tarīga) yuluf bi shwēsh.*

e. *hadīka (al-masāfa / al-baTīkh / awSāl / ash-shēk) tawīla.*

5. Translate the following sentences into UHA.

a. Do you have any stamps?

b. I want to go to the post office.

c. Turn right at the traffic light.

d. Cross this street quickly.

e. Don't drive quickly.

6. Imagine you're asking someone for the directions to a hotel. Complete your part of the following dialogue.

You: _____

Bystander: *itfaDDal.*

You: _____

Bystander: *hada sh-shari' fi akhru al-bank.*

You: _____

Bystander: *imshi shwayya 'ala al-yamīn wa ba'dēn luff shumāl.*

You: _____

Bystander: *la mu ba'īd, garīb. kamān isharatēn.*

You: _____

Bystander: *la shukr 'ala wajib.*

Answer Key

1. a. *imāra kabīra*
   b. *sayyāra Saghīra*
   c. *shāri' Tawwīl*
   d. *bēt kabīr*
   e. *maktab Saghīr*

2. a. *ana ma aHub aluff katīr.*
   b. *aHub amshi katīr.*
   c. *madri fēn arūH.*
   d. *ma a'raf aT-Tariga agTa' fiha al-HabHab.*
   e. *ana aHub ashtaghil katīr.*

3. a. *sūg bi shwēsh, ana ma aHub as-suwaga bi sur'a.*
   b. *igTa' ash-shari' min hina.*
   c. *rūH min hina, hada al-makān mu Tayyib.*
   d. *intu timshu bi shwēsh bi l-mara.*
   e. *niHna ma nuHub as-sur'ah.*

4. a. *hada al-HabHab mu Tayyib.*
   b. *hādi aT-Tariga mumtāza.*
   c. *hadōla as-sayyarāt timshi bi sur'a.*
   d. *hadak ar-rijjāl yuluf bi shwēsh.*
   e. *hadīka al-masāfa tawīla.*

5. a. *'andak Tawābi'?*
   b. *abgha arūH maktab al-barīd.*
   c. *luff yamīn 'ind al-ishara.*
   d. *igTa' aT-Tarīg/as-shari' bi sur'a.*
   e. *la tusūg bi sur'a.*

6. You: *ismaHli.*
   Bystander: *itfaDDal.*
   You: *fēn al-bank?*
   Bystander: *hada sh-shari' fi akhru al-bank.*
   You: *kēf arūH?*
   Bystander: *imshi shwayya 'ala al-yamīn wa ba'dēn luff shumāl.*
   You: *al-bank ba'īd?*
   Bystander: *la mu ba'īd, garib. kamān isharatēn.*
   You: *mashkūr.*
   Bystander: *la shukr 'ala wajib.*

LESSON 33

miHtaj shigga li l-ijār. I Need to Rent an Apartment.

A. Dialogue

David Jones wants to rent an apartment in Jeddah. The realtor, Mr. Sa'id, does not have any apartments available and suggests a house.

muwazzef al-istigbāl: maktab al-makkawi li l-iskān, ay khidma?

jōnz: min faDlak, as-sayyid sa'īd mawjūd?

muwazzef al-istigbāl: tawwu kharaj.

jōnz: mita yiji tāni?

muwazzef al-istigbāl: rāji' ba'd shiwayya.

jōnz: mumkin atruk risāla?

muwazzef al-istigbāl: itfaDDal.

jōnz: ana ismi dēvid jōnz wa badawwir 'ala shigga li l-ijār. gullu innī jay li l-maktab.

muwazzef al-istigbāl: marHaba bak, maHallak wa maktabak.

In the realtor's office.

as-sayyid sa'īd: 'ahlan wa sahlan, Mr. jōnz, itfaDDal, galuli inka kalamtani Hawāli gabl nuS-Sa'a. ēsh tishrab, sukhun walla barid?

jōnz: lā shukran shārib.

as-sayyid sa'īd: mū mumkin, lāzim tishrab Haja, tishrab gahwa.

jōnz: la shukran, shiribt gahwiti min shiwayya.

as-sayyid sa'īd: illa, billāhi 'alēk, lāzim tishrab Haja.

jōnz: Tayyib, ākhud shāy.

as-sayyid sa'īd: mā tiDDāyag law shiribtu fi kūb guzāz.

jōnz: la bi l-mara.

as-sayyid sa'īd: Tayyib, daHīn nigdar nushūf al-biyūt al-mutāHa hadōla humma. shagatēn jamb al-taHliya senter wa talāta biyūt fi l-bughdadiyya.

jōnz: ana ma abgha bēt, ana afaDDil shigga wasT al-balad.

as-sayyid sa'īd: al-'ilā jet ma'ak?

jōnz: dubaha mā jat. insha'allah kamān shahrēn.

as-sayyid sa'īd: Tayyib, fi l-Hāla hādi aHsanlak tuskun fi bēt. li'annu al-'awāyyil fi l-mamlaka la tuHub sakan al-shugag. al-'uzāb bes humma illi yuskunu fi shugag.

jōnz: tayyib al-bēt aghla mū kida?

as-sayyid sa'īd: mū sharT, nigdar nurūH daHīn nushūfahum. 'asa tilagi wāHid yināsbak.

Receptionist: Al-Makkawi real estate office, can I help you?

Jones: Is Mr. Sa'īd in, please?

Receptionist: He just stepped out.

Jones: When is he coming back?

Receptionist: He will be back in a short while.

Jones: Can I leave a message?

Receptionist: Sure, go ahead.

Jones: My name is David Jones, and I am looking for an apartment for rent. Tell him that I am coming to the office.

Receptionist: You are most welcome. (*lit.,* Welcome to you, consider it your office.)

Mr. Sa'id: Welcome, please come in. They told me you called me half an hour ago. Would you like something to drink, something hot or cold?

Jones: No, thank you, I am fine.

Mr. Sa'id: Impossible, you must drink something; would you like to have coffee?

Jones: No, thank you, I had my coffee a little while ago.

Mr. Sa'id: No, for God's sake, you must drink something.

Jones: Okay, I will take tea.

Mr. Sa'id: Would it bother you if you drink it in a glass?

Jones: No, not at all.

Mr. Sa'id: Okay. Now we can look at the available houses. Here they are. Two apartments near Al-TaHliya Center and three houses in Al-Bughdadiyya.

Jones: I don't wish to rent a house. I prefer an apartment downtown.

Mr. Sa'id: Is your family with you?

Jones: They have not arrived yet; hopefully, they will arrive in two months.

Mr. Sa'id: Okay, then in this case, it is better for you to live in a house. Families in the Kingdom do not like to live in apartments. Single men are the only people who live in them.

Jones: Okay, but the house is more expensive, right?

Mr. Sa'id: Not necessarily; we can go now and see a few of them. I hope you will find one that is suitable for you.

B. Pronunciation

THE DEFINITE ARTICLE

As in MSA, the form of the definite article *al* in UHA changes if the noun that follows it begins with a "sun" consonant (see Lesson 3).

> *as-salām 'alaykum* (peace be on you)
> *aT-Tard* (the package)
> *aZ-Zarf* (the envelope)

C. Grammar and Usage

1. POLITE EXPRESSIONS

As mentioned in earlier lessons, *itfaDDal* is a very polite expression, used to mean "sure; please come in; here you are; go ahead," depending on the situation or question preceding it. Consider the following exchanges.

Question	Response
mumkin atruk risāla?	*itfaDDal.*
(Can I leave a message?)	(Sure, go ahead.)
ahlan wa sahlan, itfaDDal.	*shukran.*
(Welcome, please come in.)	(Thanks.)
mumkin al-Hisāb?	*itfaDDal.*
(Can I have the check?)	(Here you are.)

The expression *wa ni'm,* shown in the example below, is similar to *itsharafna* (*lit.,* we are honored), but expresses more praise and acknowledgement of the origin or the family of the person being addressed. It is an extremely polite response to the mention of a name or origin.

> *ana min bēt al-sindi.*
> I am from the Al-Sindi family.

> *wa ni'm.*
> My pleasure.

2. PREPOSITIONS

Most prepositions in UHA are very similar to those used in *fuSHā.* Occasionally, there are differences in how prepositions are used with verbs. For example, the verb *yittaSil* (to contact) combines with the preposition *fi* (in) in UHA, whereas in MSA, it combines with *bi* (with).

The following table lists common prepositions and their meanings in isolation. Note how their meanings can change when they accompany verbs in the examples that follow the table.

PREPOSITIONS							
li (for, to)	*fi* (in)	*'ala* (on, for)	*bi* (by)	*ma'a* (with)	*gabl* (before)	*ba'd* (after)	
fōg (over)	*taHt* (below, under)	*guddām* (in front of)	*wara* (behind)	*min* (from)	*'an* (about)	*zay* (as)	

> *fi l-bēt*
> at home

> *fōg/'ala al-maktab*
> over/on the desk

> *aHub a'raf 'annak.*
> I would like to know more about you.

> *maktab al-makkawi li l-iskān*
> Al-Makkawi real estate office

a'Ti ar-risāla hādi li as-sayyid sa'īd.
Give this message to Mr. Sa'īd.

kalam li as-sayyid sa'īd.
Call Mr. Sa'īd for me.

HuTT bi khamsa riyāl Tawābi' 'ala az-zarf.
Put five riyals' worth of postage on the envelope.

badawwir 'ala shugag.
I am looking for apartments.

bi s-salāma
with safety

bi l-muftāH
with the key

3. NOUNS

Nouns in UHA inflect for gender and number. Feminine nouns usually end in *-a(t)*, e.g., *risāla* (letter). Many nouns have irregular plurals, which need to be memorized. The table below gives the singular and plural forms of some common nouns.

SINGULAR AND PLURAL FORMS OF NOUNS			
Singular		Plural	
ar-risāla	the letter	*ar-rasā'il*	the letters
ash-shigga	the apartment	*ash-shugag*	the apartments
ar-ragam	the number	*al-argām*	the numbers
al-fundug	the hotel	*al-fandādig*	the hotels
al-bēt	the house	*al-biyūt*	the houses
al-'ilā	the family	*al-'awāyyil*	the families
al-'āzib	the single man	*al-'uzāb*	the single men/people

4. EXPRESSING DURATION

To express a progressive or durative action in the present tense, the *ba-/bi-* prefix is added to the imperfect tense verb form. Look at the following table with examples.

IMPERFECT TENSE WITH THE PREFIX *ba-/bi-*		
ana	<u>ba</u>dawwir 'ala shigga	I am looking for an apartment
inta	<u>bi</u>tdawwir 'ala shigga	you *(m.)* are looking for an apartment
inti	<u>bi</u>tdawwir<u>i</u> 'ala shigga	you *(f.)* are looking for an apartment
huwwa	<u>bi</u>ydawwir 'ala shigga	he is looking for an apartment
hiyya	<u>bi</u>tdawwir 'ala shigga	she is looking for an apartment
inHna/niHna	<u>bi</u>ndawwir 'ala shigga	we are looking for an apartment
intum	<u>bi</u>tdawwir<u>ū</u> 'ala shigga	you are *(pl.)* looking for an apartment
humma	<u>bi</u>ydawwir<u>ū</u> 'ala shigga	they are looking for an apartment

5. THE PERFECT TENSE

The perfect tense in UHA is very similar to the perfect tense in MSA. It indicates an action that was completed in the past. Here are the perfect tense forms of the verbs *kharaj* (to go), *gāl* (to say), and *kān* (was).

THE PERFECT TENSE OF THE VERB *kharaj* (TO GO)			
	UHA	MSA	
ana	kharaj<u>t</u>	خَرَجْتُ *kharajtu*	I went
inta	kharaj<u>t</u>	خَرَجْتَ *kharajta*	you *(m.)* went
inti	kharaj<u>ti</u>	خَرَجْتِ *kharajti*	you *(f.)* went
huwwa	kharaj	خَرَجَ *kharaja*	he went
hiyya	kharaj<u>at</u>	خَرَجَتْ *kharajat*	she went
iHna/niHna	kharaj<u>na</u>	خَرَجْنا *kharajna*	we went
intum	kharaj<u>tu</u>	خرجتُم *kharajtum*	you *(pl.)* went
humma	kharaj<u>u</u>	خَرَجوا *kharajū*	they went

THE PERFECT TENSE OF THE VERB *gāl* (TO SAY)

	UHA	MSA	
ana	*gult*	قلتُ *qultu*	I said
inta	*gult*	قلتَ *qulta*	you (m.) said
inti	*gulti*	قلتِ *qulti*	you (f.) said
huwwa	*gāl*	قال *qāla*	he said
hiyya	*gālat*	قالت *qālat*	she said
iHna/niHna	*gulna*	قُلنا *qulna*	we said
intum	*gultu/gultum*	قُلتم *qultum*	you (pl.) said
humma	*gālu*	قالوا *qālu*	they said

THE PERFECT TENSE OF THE VERB *kān* (WAS)

	UHA	MSA	
ana	*kunt*	كنتُ *kuntu*	I was
inta	*kunt*	كنتَ *kunta*	you (m.) were
inti	*kunti*	كنتِ *kunti*	you (f.) were
huwwa	*kān*	كان *kāna*	he was
hiyya	*kānit*	كانت *kānat*	she was
iHna/niHna	*kunna*	كُنا *kunna*	we were
intum	*kuntu/kuntum*	كُنتم *kuntum*	you (pl.) were
humma	*kānu*	كانوا *kānu*	they were

6. PARTICLES OF TIME: *tawwu* (JUST), *dūbu* (JUST), AND *gidi* (ALREADY)

tawwu (just), *dūbu* (just), and *gidi* (already) are particles of time used to modify verbs. Note that these particles carry different object pronoun suffixes depending on the person expressed by the subject of the verb. They precede the verb in the perfect tense.

    tawwu kharaj.
    He has just gone out.

440

dūbi shiribt.
I have just drunk.

gīdi hina min shahrēn.
I have already been here for two months.

As in MSA, the independent subject pronouns in these sentences are optional, because the agent is expressed by the verbal form and the suffix on the particle.

PARTICLES OF TIME WITH OBJECT SUFFIXES			
	taww (just)	*dūb* (just)	*gīd* (already)
ana	tawwi	dūbi	gidi
inta	tawwak	dūbak	gidak
inti	tawwik	dūbik	gidik
huwwa	tawwu	dūbu	gidu
hiyya	tawwuha	dūbaha	gidaha
iHna/niHna	tawwuna	dūbana	gidana
intu	tawwukum	dūbukum	gidakum
humma	tawwuhum	dūbuhum	gidahum

7. THE PARTICLE *'asa* (IT IS HOPED)

'asa is a particle that expresses the meaning of the English verb *to hope*. It precedes the main verb and can carry object pronoun suffixes expressing the person of the subject of the verb.

THE PARTICLE *'asa* (IT IS HOPED) WITH OBJECT PRONOUN SUFFIXES	
'asāni	it is hoped that I
'asāk	it is hoped that you *(m.)*
'asāki	it is hoped that you *(f.)*
'asāh	it is hoped that he
'asāha	it is hoped that she
'asāna	it is hoped that we
'asākum	it is hoped that you *(pl.)*
'asāhum	it is hoped that they

'asa tilāgi wāHid yinasibak.
You hope you will find the one you will like. (It is hoped that...)

'asāni anjaH.
I hope I will pass the test. (It is hoped that...)

'asā yinjaHū / 'asāhum yinjaHū.
They hope they will pass the test. (It is hoped that...)

D. Vocabulary

shigga	an apartment
li l-ijār	for rent
maktab	office
li l-iskān	for housing
muwazzef	employee
al-istigbāl	the reception
ay	any
khidma	service
mawjūd	present
tawwu	just
kharaj	he went out
mita	when
yiji	he comes
tāni	again
ba'd	after
atruk	I leave
risāla	message
badawwir 'ala	I am looking for
gullu	tell him
innu	that
kalamak	he phoned you
yibgha	he wants
inni jay	I am coming
al-mutāH	the available (ones)
marHabā bak.	You are most welcome.
maHalak	your place
as-simsār	the realtor
galuli inka . . .	they told me that you . . .
kalamtani	you called me
Hawāli	around, nearly, almost
gabl	before
nuS-sa'a	half an hour
wasT	middle
ēsh tishrab?	What would you like to drink? (*lit.*, What do you drink?)
sukhun	hot
walla	or
barid	cold
mū mumkin	impossible
lāzim tishrab Haja.	You must drink something.
gahwa	coffee
min shiwayya	a while ago (*lit.*, from little)
illa, billāhi 'alēk!	No way!, For God's sake! (*lit.*, with God on you)

Tayyib	okay
ākhud shāy.	I'll take tea.
mā tiDDāyag	you will not be bothered
law	if
kūb guzāz	a glass cup
shiribtu	you drank it
la bi l-mara	no, not at all; completely, very
nigdar	we can
nushūf	we see
nurūH	we go
daHīn	now
al-biyūt	the houses
kam bēt	a few houses
shagatēn (shigga, shugag)	two apartments (apartment, apartments)
jamb	near
wasT al-balad	downtown (*lit.*, middle of the town)
al-bēt aghla, mū kida?	The house is more expensive, isn't it?
al-'ilā	the family
ma'ak	with you
jat	she came
dubaha	yet
mā jat	she did not come
fi l-Hala hādi	in this case
a'ajir	to rent
li'annu	because
al-'awāyy'il	the families
fi l-mamlaka	in the Kingdom
'āzib	bachelor, single man
mū sharT	not necessarily
'asa	it is hoped
tilagi	you find
yināsbak	suitable for you
yalla nimshi.	Let's go.

E. Cultural Note

Hospitality is extremely important in Suadi Arabia. Therefore, even during a short visit to an office, expect to be served something to drink, and if you want to look polite and respectful, try not to refuse the offer. It is quite appropriate for the host to keep insisting until the guest accepts the offer. In fact, not doing so may be interpreted as stinginess on his or her part. This is the Saudi way to show how welcomed you are.

The attitude toward time is rather relaxed in Saudi Arabia. Although people make appointments and attempt to keep them, they are usually made for an approximate time. Coming late is generally considered inappropriate, but it is tolerated and even expected, much more than in the United States. You can anticipate that the other person will arrive as much as an hour late.

F. Exercises

1. The following two columns include parts of an exchange. Please match the sentences in column A with the appropriate responses in column B.

A

a. *huwwa as-sayyid maHmūd mawjūd?*

b. *mumkin atruk risāla?*

c. *abgha ajīk al-maktab.*

d. *mita al-'ilā tiji?*

e. *mātiDDāyag law ruHna daHīn?*

B

marHaba bak, maHallak wa maktabak.

la bi l-mara.

la' tawwu mishi.

itfaDDal.

kamān shahrēn.

2. Change the imperfect tense verbs in parentheses into the perfect tense.

a. *ma (ashrab) gahwa.*

b. *ana (akhruj) kul yōm.*

c. *huwwa (yugūl) la' mu mumkin innu yirūH.*

d. *hiyya (tikūn) fi l-bēt min shiwayya.*

e. *humma (yishrabū) shāy katīr.*

f. *inti (tigulī) al-Hagīga mūkida?*

g. *niHna dūbna (ma nikhruj).*

h. *ana (agūl) al-Hagīga.*

i. *inta (tishūr) hadā al-muwazzaf?*

j. *inti (tizuri) maSir?*

3. Fill in the blanks by choosing among the prepositions below. Notice that some prepositions combine with nouns, and others, with verbs.

   fi / li / 'ala / bi

a. *huwwa bi ydawwir _____ bēt.*

b. *arsil hāda aT-Tard _____ maSir.*

c. *aftaH _____ al-bāb min faDlak.*

d. *massākum allah _____ khēr.*

e. *mumkin tittaSil _____ aHmad kamān yomēn.*

f. *shūfi _____ kam bēt, min faDlak.*

g. *mish _____ l-bēt, mū kida.*

4. Use the appropriate form of the particles *taww*, *dūb*, and *gīd* to match the subject of the verb.

a. *humma (gīd) raHū al-bēt.*
b. *iHna (dūb) shiribna shay.*
c. *inti (taww) kalamtīni fi l-telefōn, lēsh titkallami tāni.*
d. *al-'anūd (dūb) mishiyit, ma 'adri fēn.*
e. *ana (gīd) waSilt min sa'a.*

5. Fill in the blanks with an appropriate nationality adjective based on the information given in parentheses.

a. *inta _____? (min amerika)*
b. *intum _____? (min holandā)*
c. *ana _____. (min makka)*
d. *humma _____. (min najd)*
e. *ibni _____. (min maSr)*
f. *ommi _____. (min turkiya)*
g. *hadā ar-rijjāl _____. (min HaDramūt)*
h. *Hādi as-sit _____. (min al-madīna)*

6. The verbs in the parentheses are in the *he* form of the imperfect tense. Provide the appropriate prefix to make the verbs express duration.

a. *fatama (yiDawwir) 'ala bēt akbar min bēta'ha.*
b. *huwwa (yimshi) bi l-mara katīr.*
c. *hiyya ma tigdar tiji la'innaha (yudrus) daHīn.*
d. *humma (yurūH) makka katīr.*
e. *lēsh (yiqTa') al-HabHab kida?*
f. *kēf (yuSruf) il-fulūs hādi kulaha.*
g. *inta (yusūg) bi l-mara Tayyib.*
h. *intum lēsh (yukhruj) galīl?*
i. *mīn (yigūl) ana mū mawjūd?*
j. *hiyya (yiluff) waraq al-'inab bi l-mara Saghīr.*

Answer Key

1. a. *huwwa as-sayyid maHmoud mawjūd? la' tawwu mishi.*
   b. *mumkin atruk risāla? itfaDDal.*
   c. *abgha ajīk al-maktab. marHaba bak, maHallak wa maktabak.*
   d. *mita al-'ilā tiji? kamān shahrēn.*
   e. *mātiDDāyag law ruHna daHīn? la bi l-mara.*

2. a. *ma shiribt gahwa.*
   b. *ana kharajt kul yōm.*
   c. *huwwa gāl la' mu mumkin innu yirūH.*
   d. *hiyya kānat fi l-bēt min shiwayya.*
   e. *humma shirabū shāy katīr.*
   f. *inti gultī al-Hagīga, mū kida?*
   g. *niHna dūbna ma kharajna.*
   h. *ana gult al-Hagīga.*
   i. *inta shurt hadā al-muwazzaf?*
   j. *inti zurti maSir?*

3. a. *huwwa biydawwir 'ala bēt.*
   b. *arsil hāda aT-Tard li maSir.*
   c. *aftaH li al-bāb min faDlak.*
   d. *massākum allah bi l-khēr.*
   e. *mumkin titaSil fiyya kamān yomēn.*
   f. *shūfi lihum kam bēt, min faDlak.*
   g. *mish 'al fi l-bēt, mū kida.*

4. a. *humma gīdahum raHū al-bēt.*
   b. *iHna dūbana shiribna shay.*

c. *inti tawwik kalamtīni fi l-telefōn, lēsh titkallami tāni.*
d. *al-'anūd dūbaha mishiyit, ma 'adri fēn.*
e. *ana gīdani waSilt min sa'a.*

5. a. *inta amrikani.*
   b. *intum holandiyyīn.*
   c. *ana makāwi.*
   d. *humma najdiyyīn.*
   e. *ibni maSri.*
   f. *ommi turkiyya.*
   g. *hadā ar-rijjāl HaDramūti.*
   h. *hādi as-sit madīniyya.*

6. a. *fatama bitDawwir 'ala bēt akbar min bēta'ha.*
   b. *huwwa biyimshi bi l-mara katīr.*
   c. *hiyya ma tigdar tiji la'innaha bitudrus daHīn.*
   d. *humma biyurūHū makka katīr.*
   e. *lēsh inta bitiqTa' al-HabHab kida?*
   f. *kēf biyuSruf fulūs hādi kulaha.*
   g. *inta bitsūg bi l-mara Tayyib.*
   h. *intum lēsh bitukhrujū galīl?*
   i. *mīn biygūl ana mū mawjūd?*
   j. *hiyya bitluff waraq al-'inab bi l-mara Saghīr.*

LESSON 34

(Saudi Arabic)

ēsh ismaha hādi al aklah? What Is the Name of This Dish?

A. Dialogue

Mr. Jones has been invited to dinner at *as-sayyid ra'ad*'s home. At dinner, Mr. Jones meets his other male friends. Their wives are with the hostess in her quarters. During dinner the conversation is about Islamic festivities.

ra'ad: itfaDDalū, al-'akil jāhiz 'a as-sufra.

jōnz: shukran.

ra'ad: itfaDDal ya mister jōnz khud min hadā.

jōnz: ēsh ismaha hādi al-aklah?

ra'ad: hadā ismu "salīg", min aklātnā ash-sha'biyya. wa huwwa 'ibāra 'an waSlāt laHam wa ruz. bi l-mara Ti'im, itfaDDal bi l-'afiyya. ta'rif Tab'an innu ramaDān ba'ad bukrah.

jōnz: iywa adrī, ēsh hiyya al-'adāt fi ramaDān? ēsh yisawwū an-nās? samHūni li l-su'āl bes mā'indi fikra bi l-marra.

ra'ad: ahlan fik-māfi mushkilah. ya sīdī al-muslimīn kullahum haySumu Tūl ash-shahr wa ma hayakulū min al-fajr ilā al-maghrib. wa ma raH yishrabū aww yidakhanū kamān min Tulū' ash-shams ilēn ghurubaha. wa lākln ylgdarū yākulū ba'ad al-ghurūb Hatta al-fajr. Sōm ramaDān min arkān al-islām.

jōnz: na'am, wa al-Hajj kamān, mūkida? 'ala fikra huwwa mitā al-Hajj?

ra'ad: al-Hajj fi shahr zul Hijjah. al-muslimīn min kul al-'ālam hayiju yi'addū fariDat al-Hajj. simi't innu, as-sana hādi al-Hujj'āj hayukunū aktar min al'ām al-māDī.

jōnz: mumtāz, Tayyib ēsh yigulū an-nās li ba'aD fi hadōla al-munāsabāt?

ra'ad: fi ramaDān al-'awādim tibārik ba'aD bi-gōlahum "ramaDān mubārak", wa fi l-Hajj, yugulu "Hajj mabrūr."

jōnz: Tayyib, wa fi l-munasabāt at-tānya zayy al-afrāH masalan?

ra'ad: fi l-'urs, al-'awādim tugūl li l-'arūsa wa li l-'arīs "allah yis'idhum" aww, "bi l-afrāH wa al-banīn."

jōnz: Tayyib, fi ziyarat al-mariD, ēsh rah agūl?

ra'ad: bara wa ba'īd ya shīkh, bes 'indak Hag lāzim ta'rif ēsh tugūl fi kul al-mawāgif al-ijtimā'iyya. lizālik law zurt mariD tugūllu "gidāmak al-'afiyya," aww "la ba's 'alēk." wu kamān tigdar tugūli salāmtak min kul sharr." ēshbak ya mister jōnz! inta mā btākul. lāzim tākhud laHam kamān.

jōnz: shukran, ana akalt bi kifāya.

ra'ad: lā māyiSīr, lāzim tākhud tāni, a'Tini saHnak.

jōnz: la 'an jadd, ma agdar ākul aktar.

ra'ad: la lāzim tākhud tāni, billāhi 'alēk tākhud kamān.

Ra'ad: Please go ahead, the food is (ready) on the table.

Jones: Thank you.

Ra'ad: Please go ahead, have some of this.

Jones: What is the name of this dish?

Ra'ad: This is called *salīg*, one of our popular dishes. It is made with pieces of meat and rice. It is very delicious, have some (to your health). You know of course that Ramadan is the day after tomorrow.

Jones: Yes, I know. What are the customs during Ramadan? Excuse my question, but I don't have any idea at all.

Ra'ad: You are welcome to ask, no problem. All Muslims will fast all through the month of Ramadan; they will not eat from dawn to sunset. And they will also not drink or smoke from sunrise to sunset. Everyone says the sunset prayers collectively. Fasting during Ramadan is one of the main pillars of Islam.

Jones: Yes, and so is pilgrimage, isn't it? By the way, when is the pilgrimage?

Ra'ad: It is in *zul Hijjah* month. Muslims from all over the world will come to do their pilgrimage. I heard that this year there will be more pilgrims than last year.

Jones: Great. Okay, what do you say to each other on such occasions?

Ra'ad: During Ramadan people bless each other by saying "Blessed Ramadan," and in pilgrimage they say "Blessed pilgrimage."

Jones: Okay, and on other occasions, like weddings for example?

Ra'ad: At a wedding, people say to the bride and the groom, "May God make them happy," or, "With more happiness and sons."

Jones: Okay, when visiting a sick person, what should I say?

Ra'ad: May it be outside and distant, brother. If you visit a sick person, you say, "you'll find strength ahead." And you can also say, "Your safety from all evil." What's wrong with you, Mr. Jones! You are not eating. You must take more meat.

Jones: Thanks, I ate enough.

Ra'ad: Impossible, you must help yourself again, give me your plate.

Jones: No, really, I cannot eat more.

Ra'ad: No, you should help yourself again. For God's sake, take more.

B. Grammar and Usage

1. MORE SOCIAL EXPRESSIONS

In Saudi Arabia, different social or religious occasions require unique social expressions. The following examples illustrate these expressions and appropriate responses to them.

SOCIAL EXPRESSIONS			
Occasion/Expression		Response	
During Ramadan			
ramaDān karim. *ramaDān mubārak.* *kul ramaDān wa intum bi kheir.*	Ramadan is generous. Blessings for Ramadan. Every Ramadan and you are in good health.	*allahu akram.* *ramaDān mubārak 'ala j-jami'.* *wa inta bikheir wa 'afiyya.*	God is more generous. Blessings for all for Ramadan. And you are in good health and strength.
On the Occasion of the Pilgrimage			
Hajj mabrūr.	Blessed pilgrimage.	*'ōgbālak.*	May you also have it.
During Religious Festivities			
kul 'ām wa intum bi kheir.	May you be in good health every year.	*allah yi 'ūdu 'alēkum wa 'alēna bi l-yomn w al-barakāt.*	May God return it to you and to us with his blessings and prosperity.

For Work Being Completed			
allah yi'Tīk al-'afiyya.	May God give you strength.	*allah yi'āfik.*	May God strengthen you.

Facing a Difficult Situation			
a'ūzu billāh.	I take refuge in God.	*allah yikūn fi 'ōnak.*	May God give you aid.

Giving Condolences			
'aZZam allah ajrak.	May God greaten your reward.	*ajrak wa ajrina.* *wu fi Hayātak.* *meytākum wa meytana.*	Yours and ours. And your life. Yours and our deceased ones.
al-bagiyya f Hayātak.	May the remainder be added to your life.		
askan allah meytākum al janah. *allah yirHamu.*	May God home your deceased in paradise. May God have mercy on him (speaking of the deceased).		
al-marHūm (+ name)	The late (+ name)		

After Someone Drinks			
hanī'an.	(May you be) healthy.	*hanāk allah.*	May God give you happiness.

Before a Trip			
bis-salāma inshā 'allah tisāfir wu tirja' bis-salāma.	May you travel and return with safety.	*allah yisallimak.*	May God make you safe.

Apologizing			
la mu'akhza.	No offense.	*ma'lēsh.*	Never mind.

Speaking of Something Bad			
la samaH allah. *barra wa ba'īd.*	May God not permit it. May it be outside and distant.		

When Something Is Broken			
ankasar as-shar.	The evil is broken.		

Upon Hearing News			
kheir inshā 'allah.	Let it be good.		

Upon Engaging in a Serious or Dangerous Task			
bism ilāh ar-raHmān ar-raHīm.	In the name of God, the Merciful, the Compassionate.		

Expressing Uncertainty			
allahu a'alam.	Only God knows for sure.		

2. MONTHS OF THE YEAR

Saudis do not use the western or Gregorian calendar. Instead, the *hijri* calendar is used. Here are the names of the *hijri* months in UHA.

	MONTHS OF THE YEAR	
1	*muHarram*	محرم
2	*Safar*	صفر
3	*rabi' al-awwal*	ربيع الأول
4	*rabi' al-tāni*	ربيع الثاني
5	*jumād al-awwal*	جماد الأول
6	*jumād al-tāni*	جماد الثاني
7	*rajab*	رجب
8	*sha'bān*	شعبان
9	*ramaDān*	رمضان
10	*shawwāl*	شوال
11	*zu l-qi'da*	ذو القعدة
12	*zu l-Hijja*	ذو الحجة

3. THE FUTURE TENSE

There are two ways to express the future tense in UHA. Either the prefix *ha-* can be attached to the verb in the imperfect tense or the word *rāH* (go) can be placed in front of the verb. Notice that this is different from *fuSHā*, where the future tense is formed with *sa-* or *sawfa*.

haySumu ramaDān.
They will fast during Ramadan.

hatakul daHīn.
You *(m.)* will eat now.

hatakul daHīn.
She will eat now.

rāH yishrabū ash-shay.
They are going to drink the tea.

hāji l-Haflah.
I will come to the party.

450

In the following tables, the future tense forms of the verbs *yukun* (he is) and *yaSūm* (he fasts) are given. Notice the deletion of the vowel from the imperfect prefix when *ha-* is added, e.g., *haykūn*, not *hayakūn*.

FUTURE TENSE OF THE VERB *yukūn* (HE IS)			
ana	<u>h</u>akūn	<u>rāH</u> akūn	I will be, I am going to be
inta	<u>h</u>atkūn	<u>rāH</u> t<u>u</u>kūn	you *(m.)* will be, you're going to be
inti	<u>h</u>atkūni	<u>rāH</u> t<u>u</u>kūni	you *(f.)* will be, you're going to be
huwwa	<u>h</u>aykūn	<u>rāH</u> y<u>u</u>kūn	he will be, he is going to be
hiyya	<u>h</u>atkūn	<u>rāH</u> t<u>u</u>kūn	she will be, she is going to be
iHna/niHna	<u>h</u>ankūn	<u>rāH</u> n<u>u</u>kūn	we will be, we are going to be
intum	<u>h</u>atkūnū	<u>rāH</u> t<u>u</u>kūnū	you *(pl.)* will be, you are going to be
humma	<u>h</u>aykūnū	<u>rāH</u> y<u>u</u>kūnū	they will be, they are going to be

FUTURE TENSE OF THE VERB *yaSūm* (HE FASTS)			
ana	<u>h</u>aSūm	<u>rāH</u> <u>a</u>Sūm	I will fast, I am going to fast.
inta	<u>h</u>atSūm	<u>rāH</u> t<u>u</u>Sūm	you *(m. sg.)* will fast, you *(m. sg.)* are going to fast
inti	<u>h</u>atSūm<u>i</u>	<u>rāH</u> t<u>u</u>Sūmi	you *(f. sg.)* will fast, you *(f. sg.)* are going to fast
huwwa	<u>h</u>aySūm	<u>rāH</u> y<u>u</u>Sūm	he will fast, he is going to fast
hiyya	<u>h</u>atSūm	<u>rāH</u> t<u>u</u>Sūm	she will fast, she is going to fast
iHna/niHna	<u>h</u>anSūm	<u>rāH</u> n<u>u</u>Sūm	we will fast, we are going to fast
intum	<u>h</u>atSūmū	<u>rāH</u> t<u>u</u>Sūmū	you *(pl.)* will fast, you *(pl.)* are going to fast
humma	<u>h</u>aySūmū	<u>rāH</u> y<u>u</u>Sūmū	they will fast, they are going to fast

A future tense verb is made negative by placing the negative particle *ma* (not) in front of it.

ana ma harūH al-maktab daHīn.
I won't go to the office now.

huwwa ma hayrūH al-bēt illa fi l-masā.
He won't go to the house except in the evening.

inta ma raH tuSruf ash-shēk?
Aren't you going to cash the check?

C. Vocabulary

as-sufra	the table
al-akil	the food
jāhiz	ready
khud	to take
al-aklah	the dish
aklātnā	our dishes
ash-sha'biyya	popular
'ibāra 'an	tantamount to
waSlāt	pieces
laHam	meat
ruz	rice
bi l-mara Ti'im	very delicious
itfaDDal bi l-'afiyya.	Please, have some.
ta'rif	you know
Tab'an	of course
ba'ad bukrah	after tomorrow
iywa	yes
adrī	I know
al-'adāt	the customs
an-nās	the people
ēsh yisawwū?	What do they do?
samHūni li l-su'āl.	Excuse me for asking.
bass	but
mā'indi fikra bi l-marra.	I have no idea.
ahlan fik.	You're welcome to ask.
māfi mushkilah.	No problem.
ya sīdī!	Oh master! Oh brother! (showing surprise or wonder)
al-muslimīn	the Muslims
kullahum	every one of them
haySumu	they will fast
Tūl ash-shahr	all along the month
ma hayakulū	they will not eat
yakulū	they eat
min al-fajr	from dawn
ilēn al-maghrib	to dusk
ma raH yishrabū	they will not drink

452

aww	or
yidakhanū	they smoke
kamān	also, again
min Tulū' ash-shams	from sunrise (*lit.*, from the rise of the sun)
ilā ghurūbaha	to the sunset (*lit.*, to its setting)
yigdarū	they can
ba'ad	after
al-ghurūb	the sunset
Hatta	until; even
hall	whether
yiSallū	they pray
Salāt al-maghrib	sunset prayers
jama'a	collectively, in congregation
Sōm ramaDān	fasting during Ramadan
arkān al-islām	from the pillars of Islam
al-Hajj	pilgrimage
shahr	month
min kull al-'ālam	from around the world (*lit.*, all the world)
hayiju	they will come
yi'addū farīDat al-Hajj	they will perform the duty
simi't	I heard
as-sana hādi	this year
al-Hujāj	the pilgrims
al-'ām al-māDī	the previous year
li ba'aD	to each other
hadōla	those
al-'awādim	people
tibārik ba'aD	bless each other, congratulate each other
bigōlahum	by their saying
ramaDān mubārak!	Blessed Ramadan!
Hajj mabrūr!	Blessed pilgrimage!
al-munasabāt at-tānya	other occasions
zayy	like, as
al-afrāH	the weddings
masalan	for example
fi l-'urs	in a wedding
tugūl	you say
'arūsa	bride
'arīs	groom
allah yis'idhum!	May God make them happy!
bi l-afrāH wa al-banīn!	With happiness and sons!
al-mariD	the sick (person)
ziyara	visit

rah agūl	I am going to say
bara wa ba'īd!	Outside and distant! (when talking about something bad)
ya shīkh!	Oh, sheikh! (showing wonder and disbelief)
indak Hag!	You are right! (*lit.*, you have right)
al-mawāgif	the situations
ijtimā'iyya	social
laww	if
zurt	you visited
gidāmak al'-afiyya!	May you recover quickly! (*lit.*, in front of you the strength)
la ba's 'alēk!	No trouble on you! (wishing a sick person health)
tigdar	you can
ēshbak?	What's wrong with you?
bikifāya	enough
lā māyiSīr	it can't be
a'Tini	give me
saHnak	your plate
'an jadd	honestly
ma agdar	I can't
ākul	to eat
bi l-lāhi 'alēk!	For God's sake!

D. Cultural Note

hijri months, or months of the Islamic calendar, follow the lunar calendar. Each lunar month begins with the new moon, i.e., the moon in the crescent form, hence, the Islamic symbol of the crescent. The first year of the *hijri* calendar is year 622 A.D., in memory of the year when the prophet Muhammad emigrated from Mecca to Medina. This emigration is called *al-hijra* in Arabic. The *hijri* year has twelve months, but it is shorter than the Gregorian calendar year by eleven days. The Gregorian calendar is referred to in Arabic as the *mīlādi* calendar.

Saudi Arabians put great emphasis on socializing, especially within the family. Relatives visit with each other regularly, especially during religious holidays. During the Eid festivities, children get *'idayyah*, money gifts, from their parents and grandparents. The two main feasts are *'īd al-fiTr*, the feast of breaking the fast after Ramadan, and *'id al-'aDHa*, the feast of the sacrifice. It is during *'īd al-'aDHa*, the feast of the sacrifice, that devout Muslims come from all over the world to Mecca to perform their pilgrimage, or *farīDat al-Hajj* (the duty of performing the pilgrimage). During Ramadan, people fast from dawn until sunset. If they work, their workload is usually smaller to allow time for prayers and devotions. After breaking their fast each evening, followers go to the mosque to perform *al-tarāwiH*, prayers consisting of forty *sajdah* during which they read verses from the Qur'an with the goal of having completed the whole Qur'an by the end of month of Ramadan.

There are some important rules to remember during visits to people's homes. During dinner parties, as a rule, men eat separately from women. Couples will be separated, too, and women will eat in the hostess's quarters. A woman's section of the house usually has its own entrance and pathway. Before eating, Saudis often say *bism illah ar-raHmān ar-raHīm* (In the name of God, the Merciful, and Compassionate). During dinner, the host and the hostess will constantly offer to serve more food to their guests. This is their way of showing their hospitality and their pleasure at having you over. You may need to thank them and say that you have had enough more than once, because they will not hesitate to serve you again and again. After the meal, it is customary to say *al-Hamdulillāh* (thanks to God) or *'āmer*, an expression meaning "May your house be always prosperous."

E. Exercises

1. Please match the phrases in column A with the appropriate responses in column B.

A	B
a. *ramaDān karīm.*	*allah yisallimak.*
b. *allah yi'Tik al-'afiyya.*	*hanāk allah.*
c. *'aZZam allah ajrak.*	*allahu akram.*
d. *hanī 'an.*	*allah yi'āfīk.*
e. *bis-salāma inshā' allah.*	*ajrak wa ajrīna.*

2. Change the imperfect tense verbs in the brackets into the future tense.

a. *ana (arūH) makka bukra.*

b. *fahad (yi'zim) Duyufu al-asbū' al-jayy.*

c. *inta (tudrus), mūkida?*

d. *fēn (nimshi) al-yōm.*

e. *jawahir (tuSruf) al-fulūs kullaha.*

f. *humma (yirja'ū) min al-madina fi l-masa.*

g. *inti (tākhdi) ibnik ma'āki li l-doktōr?*

h. *mita (yiwSalū) al-jamā'ah?*

i. *min (yugūl) li'omī al-Hagīga?*

j. *ana (azūr) bēt al-fitiHi garīb.*

3. Group the social expressions below by applicable social situation (funeral, visiting a sick person, wedding, pilgrimage, wishing good luck). Phrases may be repeated in more than one situation.

a. *a'ūzu billāh.*

b. *allah yi'Tik al-'afiyya.*

c. *kul 'ām wa intum bi kheir.*

d. *'aZZam allah ajrak.*

e. *allah yis'idhum.*

f. *gidāmak al-'afiyya.*

g. *bi l-afrāH wa al-banīn.*

h. *la ba's 'alēk.*

i. *ramaDān karīm.*

j. *Hajj mabrūr.*

k. *salāmtak min kul sharr.*

l. *bism illāh ar-raHmān ar-raHīm.*

4. Put the following verb roots in the appropriate form of the imperfect tense. Then fill in the blanks and form future sentences by placing the future markers *ha-* or *rāH* in front of them.

> *s-w-m* (to fast) / *sh-r-b* (to drink) / *kh-d-d* (to take) / *g-d-r* (to be able) / *'-r-f* (to know) / *s-m-'* (to hear) / *q-w-l* (to say) / *z-r-t* (to visit) / *r-j-'* (to return) / *kh-r-j* (to go out)

a. *kull al-muslimīn _____ ramaDān al-jay.*

b. *arwa _____ _____'ilat-hā kamān yōmēn.*

c. *Sa'ab wa ghiyath ma _____al-lēla.*

d. *fēn _____bi l-sayyāra.*

e. *inta _____ fēn al-bank, mūkida?*

f. *mita hatirja'u _____ min makka?*

g. *ana billāhi _____ li 'aHad.*

h. *al-marīDa _____ ba'ad kida.*

i. *_____ shay aww haja tānya?*

j. *mafi mushkila, bukra _____ al-akhbār.*

5. Fill in your part in the following conversation with Sakhr.

sakhr: Tayyib kēf hatrūHū li bēt ad-darwīsh.

inta: _____.

sakhr: 'ārif, bass, ta'rifū laww al-makān garīb aww ba'īd?

inta: _____.

sakhr: mumtāz, kida agdar agūl innu māfi mushkilah. bass min rāH yisūg?

inta: _____.

sakhr: inta rāH tusūg, akīd ta'rif al-shawāri' tayyib.

inta: _____.

sakhr: Tayyib bi s-salāma.

Answer Key

1. a. *ramaDān karīm. allahu akram.*
   b. *allah yi'Tik al-'afiyya. allah yi'āfīk.*
   c. *'aZZam allah ajrak. ajrak wa ajrina.*
   d. *hani'an. hanāk allah.*
   e. *bi s-salāma inshā' allah. allah yisallimak.*

2. a. *ana harūH makka bukra.*
   b. *fahad hayi'zim Duyufu al-asbū' al-jayy.*
   c. *inta hatudrus, mūkida?*
   d. *fēn hanimshi al-yōm.*
   e. *jawahir hatuSruf al-fulūs kullaha.*
   f. *humma hayirja'ū min al-madina fi l-masa.*
   g. *inti hatākhdi ibnik ma'āki li l-doktōr?*
   h. *mita hayiwSalū al-jamā'ah?*
   i. *mīn hayugūl li 'omī al-Hagīga?*
   j. *ana hazūr bēt al-fitīHi garīb.*

3. Funeral:
   'aZZam allah ajrak.
   Visiting a sick person:
   gidāmak al-'afiyya.
   la ba's 'alēk.
   salāmtak min kul sharr.
   Wedding:
   allah yis'idhum.
   bi l-afrāH wa al-banīn.
   Pilgrimage:
   Hajj mabrūr.
   Good luck:
   a 'ūzu billāh.
   bism ilāh ar-raHmān ar-raHīm.

4. a. *kull al-muslimīn haySūmū/rāH yuSūmū ramaDān al-jay.*
   b. *arwa hatuzūr (rāH tuzūr) 'ilat-hā kamān yōmēn.*
   c. *Sa'ab wa ghiyath ma hayukhrūjū (rāH yukhrūjū) al-lēla.*
   d. *fēn hatākhudni (rāH tākhudni) bi l-sayyāra.*
   e. *inta hata'rif (rāH ta'rif) fēn al-bank, mūkida?*
   f. *mita hatirja'u (rāH tirja'ū) min makka?*
   g. *ana billāhi ma hagūl (rāH agūl) li 'aHad.*
   h. *al-marīDa ma hatigdar (rāH timishi) ba'ad kida.*
   i. *hatishrabi (rāH tishrabi) shay aww Haja tānya?*
   j. *mafi mushkila, bukra hanisma' (rāH nisma') al-akhbār.*

5. *sakhr: Tayyib kēf hatrūHū li bēt ad-darwīsh.*
   inta: hanrūH bi s-sayyāra.
   sakhr: 'ārif, bass, ta'rifū laww al-makān garīb aww ba'īd?
   inta: la' garīb.
   sakhr: mumtāz, kida agdar agūl innu māfi mushkilah. bass min rāH yisūg?
   inta: ana hasūg.
   sakhr: inta rāH tusūg, akīd ta'rif al-shawāri' Tayyib.
   inta: īwa a'rifha tayyib.
   sakhr: Tayyib bi s-salāma.

LESSON 35

(Saudi Arabic)

jōnz yurūH as-sūg Jones Goes to the Market

A. Dialogue

Mr. Jones goes shopping. He first passes by the fish market.

jōnz: ēsh ismu hāda as-samak?

al-bayya': hāda as-samak ismu samak mūsa.

jōnz: TāZa walla metallij?

al-bayya': la' TāZa, alyōm iSTadnah.

jōnz: a'Tini huwwa min faDDlak ashūf.

al-bayya': itfaDDal.

jōnz: Tayyib, kām sa'ru?

al-bayya': al-kīlō bi 'ashara riyāl.

jōnz: mumtāz, min faDDlak, abgha minu itnēn kīlō.

al-bayya': ibshir.

jōnz: fēn anaDDif as-samak?

al-bayya': anā anaDDif lak huwwa.

jōnz: mashkūr. Tayyib, abgha agDi magāDi tānniya.

al-bayya': ēsh humma?

jōnz: khuDār wu fakiha.

al-bayya': lāzim turūH al-Halaga.

jōnz: fēn al-Halaga?

al-bayya': garīb min hina, hagūl li S-Sabi yiwarrik aT-Tarīg.

jōnz: Tayyib, abgha kafiyya kamān, fēn alagīha?

al-bayya': fi s-sūg jamb al-Halaga. ya walad, khud hadal rijjāl li l-Halaga wu kamān warrih fēn as-sūg.

jōnz: shukran.

After shopping for food, Jones looks for a *kafiyya* (men's headscarf).

jōnz: ēsh shakil il-kafiyya illi 'indak?

al-bayya': 'indi talāta ashkāl.

jōnz: abgha ashufahum kullahum.

al-bayya': ibshir.

jōnz: Tayyib, hadōla mū Tayyibīn, abgha shakil aHsan.

al-bayya': itfaDDal.

jōnz: hādi l-kafiyya bi kām?

al-bayya': bi khamasta'sh riyāl.

jōnz: hādi ghalliya jiddan, ākhir kalām kam?

al-bayya': lā, ma abaddil kalāmi abadan, kalām wāHid, khamasta'sh riyāl.

jōnz: lā tigdar ta'Tini l-kafiyya bi tna'sh riyāl.

al-bayya': lā, abadan. inta mannak fāhim al-maSna'iyya fi l-kafiyya.

jōnz: 'ala kēfak, ma abgha, ana harūH hadāk ad-dukkān.

al-bayya': ta'āl, ya sayyid, ta'āl ta'āl. raH abī'lak hiyya bi tna'sh riyāl.

Jones: What is the name of this fish?

The seller: This is a sole. (*lit.*, the fish of Moses)

Jones: Is it fresh or frozen?

The seller: No, (it is) fresh; we caught it today.

Jones: Give it to me, please, so I can have a look.

The seller: Here you are.

Jones: Okay, how much is it?

The seller: One kilo is ten riyals.

Jones: Great, I would like two kilos, please.

The seller: Sure.

Jones: Where can I have the fish cleaned?

The seller: I can clean it for you.

Jones: Thanks. Okay, I would like to buy other groceries.

The seller: What are they?

Jones: Vegetables and fruits.

The seller: You must go to the produce market.

Jones: Where is the produce market?

The seller: Nearby (*lit.*, close to here); I will tell the boy to show you the way.

Jones: Okay, I would like to buy a *kafiyya*, too; where can I find it?

The seller: At the *souk* next to the produce market. Hey boy, take this gentleman to the produce market and also show him where the *souk* is.

Jones: Thank you.

Jones: What kind of *kafiyyas* do you have?

The seller: I have three kinds.

Jones: I want to see them all.

The seller: Sure.

Jones: These are not good. I would like something nicer.

The seller: Here you are.

Jones: How much is this *kafiyya*?

The seller: Fifteen riyals.

Jones: This is very expensive; what is your last word?

The seller: No, I don't change my word. I have one word and that is fifteen riyals.

Jones: No, you can give me the *kafiyya* for twelve riyals.

The seller: No, never. You don't understand the craftsmanship of the *kafiyya*.

Jones: As you wish. I don't want it anymore. I will go to that other shop.

The seller: Come, hey, mister, come, come. I am going to sell it to you for twelve riyals.

B. Grammar and Usage

1. THE VOCATIVE PARTICLE *yā*

The vocative particle *yā* (oh, hey) is frequently used in both UHA and MSA. It can be followed by a noun, an adjective, or a relative clause. Depending on the tone, the intonation, and the word following the particle, *yā* can be used for calling attention, complimenting, calling someone's name, exclamation, and warning.

THE USES OF THE VOCATIVE PARTICLE *yā*			
Structure	Example	Situation	
yā + proper noun	*yā 'ali*	calling attention	Hey, Ali!
yā + indef. noun	*yā bint*	complimenting	Wow, miss!
yā + noun phrase	*yā bayyā' al-hāwa; ya sidi*	calling someone's name; showing wonder; agreeing	You, candy-seller!; Wow, sir!; Indeed, sir!
yā + adjective	*yā fannān; yā sātir*	complimenting; exclamation	A true maestro!; Oh my God!
yā + rel. clause	*ya ill fōg*	warning	You who are upstairs!

ya walad, khud hadal rijjāl li l-Halaga.
Hey boy, take this gentleman to the produce market.

ta'āl, ya sayyid, ta'āl, ta'āl.
Come, hey mister, come, come.

2. INDEPENDENT PRONOUNS

In UHA, independent pronouns are sometimes used emphatically to replace an object noun. When an independent pronoun is used, the object is indicated both by the object pronoun suffix on the verb and by the independent pronoun. First, consider the following sentences in which the verb is suffixed with *-ni/-li* and followed by the direct object noun.

a'Tini as-samk.
Give me the fish.

warrini ash-shugag.
Show me the apartments.

jibli as-sayyāra.
Bring me the car.

In the examples below, the object nouns are replaced by corresponding independent pronouns, *huwwa*, *hiyya*, or *humma*.

a'Tini huwwa.
Give it to me.

jibli hiyya.
Bring it to me.

warrini humma.
Show them to me.

Here are more examples:

anā anaDDif lak huwwa.
I will clean it for you.

warrētlaha huwwa.
I showed it to her.

sallamni hiyya.
Hand it to me.

jābli humma.
He brought them to me.

3. EXPRESSIONS OF QUANTITY

Expressions of quantity such as *kull* (all) and *ba'D* (a few) can occur either before or after the noun. When they come after the noun, an object pronoun suffix must be added to the expression of quantity. Consider the following examples.

kull an-nās
all the people

an-nās kullahum
all the people

ba'D an-nās
some of the people

an-nās ba'Dahum
some of the people

4. MODAL PARTICLES

UHA does not have modal verbs similar to the English *can, must, would*, or *should*. Instead, like MSA, it uses particles to express notions of obligation, necessity, probability, or possibility. The following examples illustrate the relevant particles.

• *yimkin* (perhaps; may, might)

yimkin asāfar bukra.
Perhaps I will travel tomorrow./I may travel tomorrow.

yimkin yijū bukra.
Perhaps they will come tomorrow./They may come tomorrow.

• *mumkin* (it is possible; could)

huwwa mumkin yimshi aHsan ba'd al-'amaliyya.
It is possible that he will walk better after the operation./He could walk better after the operation.

- *lāzim* (it is necessary; must)

lāzim tuzurani fi l-maktab.
It is necessary that you visit me in the office./You must visit me in the office.

lāzim turūH al-Halaga.
It is necessary that you go to the produce market./You must go to the produce market.

5. NEGATION

In MSA, nominal sentences are negated with the verb *laysa*. In UHA, the particle *man*, followed by object pronoun suffix, is used to negate both nominal and verbal sentences.

inta mannak fāhim al-maSna'iyya fi l-kafiyya.
You are not considering the craftsmanship of the scarf.

intum mannakum fahmanīn.
You *(pl.)* don't understand.

huwwa mannu kaslān.
He is not lazy.

hiyya mannaha/mahi 'arfa.
She does not know.

niHna mannana/maHna jayyīn li l-'asha.
We are not coming to the dinner.

humma mannahum/mahum mabsuTīn.
They are not happy.

The following table gives *man* with the different object pronoun suffixes in examples.

THE NEGATIVE PARTICLE *man* WITH OBJECT PRONOUN SUFFIXES		
Person	UHA	
anā	*man<u>ni</u> mabsūT.*	I am not happy.
inta	*man<u>nak</u> nājiH.*	You *(m.)* are not passing the test.
inti	*man<u>nik</u> mabsūTa.*	You *(f.)* are not happy.
huwwa	*man<u>nu</u> jay.*	He is not coming.
hiyya	*man<u>naha</u>/ma<u>hi</u> hina.*	She is not here.
iHna/niHna	*man<u>nana</u>/maH<u>na</u> rayHīn.*	We are not going.
intu	*man<u>nakum</u> nājiHīn.*	You *(pl.)* are not passing the test.
humma	*man<u>nahum</u>/ma<u>hum</u> kazabīn.*	They are not liars.

C. Vocabulary

as-samak	the fish
TāZa	fresh
walla	or
metallij	frozen
al-yōm	today
iSTadnah	we caught (*lit.*, fished) it
kām?	How much?
a'Tini	give me
ashūf	I see
sa'ru	its price
al-kīlō	the kilo
bi 'ashara riyāl	for ten riyals
mumtāz	great
min faDDlak	please
abgha	I would like
itnēn kīlō	two kilos
ibshir	sure
fēn?	Where?
anaDDif lak huwwa	I can clean it for you
mashkūr	thanks
agDi magāDi tānniya	I go shopping
khuDār wu fakiha	vegetables and fruits
al-Halaga	the produce market
garīb	near
hina	here
hagūl	I will say
li S-Sabi	to the boy, to the messenger, to the apprentice
yiwarrik	he shows you
alagīha	you find it
aT-Tarīg	the way
khud	take
hadal rijjāl	this man
kamān	also
warrīh	show him
ēsh shakil?	What type?
il-kafiyya	the men's headscarf
illi 'indak	that you have
'indi	I have
ashkāl	types
kullahum	all of them
shakil aHsan	a better quality
hādi l-kafiyya bi kām?	How much is this headscarf?

bi khamsta'sh riyāl	fifteen riyals
ghalliya jiddan	very expensive
ākhir kalām kam	your last word
ma abaddil	I don't change
kalāmi	my words
abadan	never
fāhim	understanding
'ala kēfak	as you wish
ma abgha	I don't want
harūH	I will go
ad-dukkān	the store
ta'āl	come
raH abī hiyya	I am going to sell it
al-bayyā'	the seller
ba'D	some
ba'Dahum	some of them
jāb	he brought
sallam	he delivered
warrēt	I showed
fannān	artist
sātir	a protector, a protector screen
al-hāwa	the air
yuDrub	he hits
ishtara	he bought
al-'amaliyya	the operation
al-maSna'iyya	the craftsmanship

D. Cultural Note

Most shopping in Saudi Arabia requires some fiSāl (bargaining). You are expected to bargain in the Halaga (the produce market), the bangala (the fish market), and in the sūk (market, bazaar), where you can find items such as kaffiyyas (men's headscarves), mishlaH (cloaks for men), 'abayyas (cloaks for women), and TarHa (women's head covers). In big department stores, pharmacies, and supermarkets, bargaining is not appropriate.

Politeness and respect are very important to Saudis, and they are especially expected in interactions with elders. To show respect, one should use the plural pronoun intum (you) when addressing them, together with the corresponding plural form of the verb, as in inshā 'allah 'ajabatkum al-hidiyya (I hope you (pl.) liked (pl.) the present). This form is also used when addressing superiors.

Saudis, like other Arab peoples, have many unique gestures with special meanings. Here are some examples:

• Placing the right hand to the heart shows affection, respect, or gratitude.

• Among women, to make an offer of food or drink with utmost sincerity, place the right hand to the heart after you make the offer.

• To show utmost respect, Saudis, especially those from the Eastern region or from the royal family, kiss their elders on the forehead, nose, right shoulder, or right hand.

• To show that you have had enough of food and to offer thanks, place the right hand on the heart and pat the heart a few times.

• To express that something is excellent, touch the outer edges of your eyes with your fingertips.

• When making a promise, touch your nose with the tip of your right index finger.

• To express full admiration for the beauty of someone or something, put your right index finger on top of your right cheekbone and go downward diagonally toward the corner of your mouth.

• To show that you are broke, flick your right thumbnail on your front teeth.

• To drive someone away, hold your right hand up and shake it.

E. Exercises

1. Match the phrases in column A with the appropriate response in column B.

A	B
a. *kam si'r hadā al-HabHab?*	*la' mitallij.*
b. *'indak farawla?*	*'indi Tawīl, wu gaSīr.*
c. *hadā as-samak TāZa?*	*kalām wāHid.*
d. *ēsh shakil il-kafiyya illi 'indak?*	*na'am 'indi.*
e. *hādi as-sayyara ghalliya jiddan,* *ākhir kalām kam?*	*bi 'ishrīn riyāl.*

2. Fill in the blanks by choosing the right word from the two provided in parentheses.

a. *humma (mabsuTīn, mabsuTa) fi l-'urs.*

b. *al-bayyā' (jāb, ad-dukkān) il-kafiyya.*

c. *(min faDDlak, ibshir) abgha ashūf kafiyya.*

d. *('indi, illi) talāta shakil.*

e. *intu (mannkum, mannahum) fi s-sūg, mū kida?*

3. Translate the following English utterances into UHA using the negative particle *man*. Pay attention to the object pronoun suffixes.

a. You *(m.)* are not lazy.

b. I am not coming.

c. She is not happy.

d. We don't know.

e. They do not understand.

4. Insert the right modal particle *(lazim, mumkin, or yimkin)* and put the verbs in parentheses in the appropriate form to match the subject.

a. *inta* _____ *(rāH) li l-bank li Sarf ash-shēk hadā.*

b. *hiyya* _____ *(mishi) Tayyib ba'd al-'amaliyya.*

c. *intum* _____ *(sāfar) bukra bas mū akīd.*

d. *anā* _____ *(daras) al-yōm.*

e. *niHna* _____ *(mishi) li l-taHliyya senter, bas aHsan lana nudrus.*

5. Imagine you are shopping at the market. Fill in your part in the following conversation with the vendor.

You: _____

al-bayyā': iwā Taza.

You: _____

al-bayyā': al-kīlō bi 'ashara riyāl.

You: _____

al-bayyā': kīlō wāHid bass, hadā bi l-mara Tayyib, khud aktar.

You: _____

al-bayyā': Tayyib abshir, hadā huwwa al-kīlō, itfaDDal.

You: _____

Answer Key

1. a. *kam si'r hadā al-HabHab? bi 'ishrīn riyāl.*
   b. *'indak farawla? na'am 'indi.*
   c. *hadā as-samak TāZa? la' mitallij.*
   d. *ēsh shakil il kafiyya illi 'indak? 'indi Tawīl, wu gaSīr.*
   e. *hādi as-sayyara ghalliya jiddan, ākhir kalām kam? kalām wāHid.*

2. a. *humma <u>mabsuTīn</u> fi l-'urs.*
   b. *al-bayyā' <u>jāb</u> il-kafiyya.*
   c. *<u>min faDDlak</u> abgha ashūf kafiyya.*
   d. *<u>'indi</u> talāta shakil.*
   e. *intu <u>mannkum</u> fi s-sūg, mū kida?*

3. a. *inta mannak kaslān.*
   b. *anā manni jāy.*
   c. *hiyya mannaha mabsūTa.*
   d. *niHna mannā 'arfīn.*
   e. *humma mannahum fahmīn.*

4. a. *inta lāzim turūH li l-bank li Sarf ash-shēk hadā.*
   b. *hiyya mumkin timshi Tayyib ba'd al-'amaliyya.*
   c. *intum yimkin tusāfarū bukra bas mū akīd.*
   d. *anā lāzim adrus al-yōm.*
   e. *niHna mumkin nimshī li l-taHliyya senter, bas aHsan lana nudrus.*

5. You: *hadā as-samak Taza?*
   al-bayyā': iwā Taza.
   You: *kām si'ru?*
   al-bayyā': al-kīlō bi'ashara riyāl.
   You: *Tayyib a'Tini minnu kīlō wāHid,
   minfaDDlak.*

   *al-bayyā': kīlō wāHid bas, hadā bi l-mara
   Tayyib, khud aktar.*
   You: *lā shukran abgha kīlō wāHid bass.*
   *al-bayyā': Tayyib abshir, hadā huwwa al-
   kīlō, itfaDDal.*
   You: *shukran.*

EIGHTH REVIEW

(Saudi Arabic)

---

1. Match the phrases in column A with the appropriate response in column B.

A	B
a. *ēsh lōnak?*	*ma'a s-salāma.*
b. *fi 'amānillah.*	*hanāk allah.*
c. *ēsh hāda?*	*allah yi'āfīk.*
d. *fēn tuHub tishtaghil?*	*mūba'īd min hina.*
e. *ismaHli.*	*la shukr 'ala wājib.*
f. *mashkūr.*	*fi madrasa.*
g. *fēn maktab al-barīd?*	*itfaDDal.*
h. *allah yi'Tik al-'afiyya.*	*manni 'ārif.*
i. *hanī' an.*	*zen al-Hamdulillah.*

2. Fill in the blanks by choosing an appropriate verb and putting it in the imperfect tense form.

    shirib / daras / Hab / ishtaghal / timshi / tigTa' / takul / iSruf / kharajt / gult

a. *'umar _____ shay kulli yōm fi S-SubuH.*

b. *ibni _____ katīr.*

c. *anā _____ al-masa aktar min al-SubuH.*

d. *fēn hiyya _____ 'ala il kornīsh?*

e. *ta'rifū kēf _____ al-HabHab?*

f. *ēsh _____ kul yōm fi SubuH?*

g. *iHna lāzim _____ ash-shēk hāda bukra.*

h. *humma _____ min aS-SubuH ilēn al-masa.*

i. *ana _____ innu mannu jay.*

j. *ēsh _____ ibnik?*

3. Choose from among the prepositions below to complete the following sentences.

    fi / 'ala / fōg / taHt / 'an / bi / li

a. *mumkin tirsil aT-Tard hadā _____ amerika.*

b. *fēn al-jawwāb? ma lagītu _____ al-tawla.*

c. *'asa tittaSil _____ muwazzaf al-bank.*

d. *badawwir _____ shigga li l-ijār.*

e. *mumkin as'al _____ si'r hādi as-sayyāra?*

4. Put the verbs in parentheses in the future tense.

a. *ana (rāH) ash-shirka ba'd yōmēn.*

b. *samāhir (daras) Tibb fi aj-jami'a.*

c. *intum (Sām) as-sanna hādi mū kida?*

d. *fēn (rāH) aS-Sēf al-jay?*

e. *mita (riji') min aS-Safar?*

f. *inta (kharaj) tāni?*

g. *humma (Salla) fi j-jāmi' jamā'a.*

h. *sa'ad ma (sāfar) hādi as-sana.*

5. Group the following expressions into their appropriate categories: religious festivities, visiting the sick, funeral, wedding, before a trip.

gidāmak al-'afiyya.

ramaDān karim.

'aZZam allah ajrak.

bi s-salāma inshā'allah.

al-bagiyya fi Hayātak.

allah yis'idhum.

Hajj mabrūr.

tisāfir wu tirja' bi s-salāma.

kul 'ām wa intum bi kheir.

askan allah meytākum al-janah.

la ba's 'alēk.

bi l-afrāH wa al-banīn.

kul ramaDān wa intum bi kheir.

6. Put the verbs in parentheses in the perfect tense.

a. *as-sana al-maDiyya (adrus) fi jorjtawin.*

b. *min yōmēn (arūH) atmashi fi al-TaHliya senter.*

c. *mīn (yugūl) innu ramaDān bukra?*

d. *ams inti (tishtiri) awā'i katīra.*

e. *anā ta'bān bi l-marra, li'anni gīdi ma (ashrab) ash-shay.*

f. *al-yōm (nimshi) li l-sūg bas ma (nilāgi) shāy tayyib.*

g. *ya tara (tuSrūfū) ash-shēk illi (a'Titikum) huwwa?*

h. *hal jawāhir (tirsil) al-jawāb walla lissa'.*

7. One word in each of the following expressions is wrong; find the mistake and make a correction, making the expression suitable for its social situation.

To express uncertainty you say:
allah ma'āk.
Upon hearing any news:
bisalāma inshā'allah.

When something is broken:

ba'd as-shar.

Speaking of something bad:

subHān allah.

Facing a difficult situation:

bi'izn illāh.

8. Put the verbs in parentheses in the imperative form.

a. *min faDlak (yigTa') aTTarī' min hina.*

b. *(yudrus) aHsanlak ya ibni.*

c. *(tukhruj) min al-ghurfa anā 'indi shughul katīr.*

d. *(tikalimūna) bukra min faDDlikum.*

e. *(turūH) gūl li 'ommak yalla nimshi.*

9. Match the questions in column A with their short answers in column B.

A	B
a. *kēf nurūH li TaHliyya senter?*	*mugābil al-madrasa.*
b. *mita misāfir?*	*marīD bi l-marra.*
c. *ēsh tuHub tākul?*	*bi l-taksi.*
d. *lēsh mannak mabSūT?*	*al-yōm inshallāh.*
e. *fēn al-bank?*	*salīg min faDDlak.*

10. Make the following sentences negative by inserting an appropriate negative particle.

a. *anā _____ a'rif fēn al-maktab haggu.*

b. *inta 'indak 'ila _____ 'āzib.*

c. *hiyya _____ hina, kharajat min shiwayya.*

d. *hadā _____ SaHīH, anā a'rif al-Hagīga.*

e. *_____ yiSir, lāzim tākul kamān.*

f. *iHna _____ fahmīn illi biySīr.*

g. *an-nās illi fōg _____ mawjūdīn.*

h. *inta _____ bitudrus Tayyib, anā za'lān minnak.*

Answer Key

1. a. *ēsh lōnak? zen al-Hamdulilah.*
   b. *fi 'amānillah. ma'a s-salāma.*
   c. *ēsh hāda? manni 'ārif.*
   d. *fēn tuHub tishtaghil? fi madrasa.*
   e. *ismaHli. itfaDDal.*
   f. *mashkūr. la shukr 'ala wājib.*
   g. *fēn maktab al-barīd. mūba'īd min hina.*
   h. *allah yi'Tik al-'afiyya. allah yi'āfīk.*
   i. *hani' an. hanāk allah.*

2. a. *'umar yishrab shay kulli yōm fi S-SubuH.*
   b. *ibni yudrus katīr.*
   c. *anā aHub al-masa aktar min al-SubuH.*
   d. *fēn hiyya timshi 'ala il-kornīsh.*

e. *ta'rifū kēf tigTaū' al-HabHab?*

f. *ēsh takul kul yōm fi SubuH?*

g. *iHna lāzim nuSruf ash-shēk hāda bukra.*

h. *humma yukhrujū min aS-SubuH ilēn al-masa.*

i. *ana agūl innu mannu jay.*

j. *ēsh yishtaghil ibnik?*

3. a. *mumkin tirsil aT-Tard hadā li amerika.*

   b. *fēn al-jawwāb? ma lagītu 'ala/fōg al-tawla.*

   c. *'asa tittaSil fi/bi muwazzaf al-bank.*

   d. *badawwir 'ala shigga li l-ijār.*

   e. *mumkin as'al 'an il si'r hādi as-sayyāra?*

4. a. *ana harūH ash-shirka ba'd yōmēn.*

   b. *samāhir hatudrus Tibb fi aj-jami'a.*

   c. *intum hatSumu as-sanna hādi mū kida?*

   d. *fēn hanrūH aS-Sēf al-jay?*

   e. *mita hatirja'i min aS-Safar?*

   f. *inta hatukhruj tāni?*

   g. *humma haySallū fi j-jāmi' jamā'a.*

   h. *sa'ad ma haysafar hādi as-sana.*

5. Religious festivities:
   ramaDān karīm.
   Hajj mabrūr.
   kul 'ām wa intum bi kheir.
   kul ramaDān wa intum bi kheir.
   At funerals:
   'aZZam allah ajrak.
   al-bagiyya fi Hayātak.
   askan allah meytākum al janah.
   Visiting the sick:
   la ba's 'alēk.
   gidāmak al-'afiyya.
   At weddings:
   bi l-afrāH wa al-banīn.
   allah yis 'idhum.
   Before a trip:

bi s-salāma inshā'allah.
tisāfir wu tirja' bi s-salāma.

6. a. *as-sana al-maDiyya darast fi jorjtawin.*

   b. *min yōmēn ruHt atmashi fi al-TaHliya senter.*

   c. *mīn gal innu ramaDān bukra?*

   d. *ams inti ishtarīti awā'i katīra.*

   e. *anā ta'bān bi l-marra, li'anni gīdi ma shiribt ash-shay.*

   f. *al-yōm mishīna li l-sūg bas ma lagīna shāy tayyib.*

   g. *ya tara Saraftū ash-shēk illi a'Titakum huwwa?*

   h. *hal jawāhir rasalit al-jawāb walla lissa'.*

7. To express uncertainty:
   allah ma'āk.
   allahu a'alam.
   Upon hearing any news:
   bi s-salāma inshā'allah.
   kheir inshā'allah.
   When something is broken:
   ba'd as-shar.
   ankasar as-shar.
   Speaking of something bad:
   SubHān allah.
   la samaH allah.
   Facing a difficult situation:
   bi 'izn illāh.
   a'ūzu billāh.

8. a. *min faDlak igTa' aTTarī' min hina.*

   b. *idrus aHsanlak ya ibni.*

   c. *ukhruj min al-ghurfa anā 'indi shughul katīr.*

   d. *kalimūna bukra min faDDlikum.*

   e. *rūH gūl li 'ommak yalla nimshi.*

9. a. *kēf nurūH li TaHliyya senter? bi l-taksi.*

   b. *mita misāfir? al-yōm inshallāh.*

   c. *ēsh tuHub tākul? salīg min faDDlak.*

d. *lēsh mannak mabSūT? mariD bi l-marra*

e. *fēn al-bank? mugābil al-madrasa.*

10. a. *anā ma a'rif fēn al-maktab haggu.*

b. *inta 'indak 'ila mannak 'āzib.*

c. *hiyya mannaha hina, kharajat min shiwayya.*

d. *hadā mū SaHīH, anā a'rif al-Hagīga.*

e. *ma yiSir, lāzim tākul kamān.*

f. *iHna mannana fahmīn illi biySīr.*

g. *an-nās illi fōg mannahum mawjūdīn.*

h. *inta ma bitudrus Tayyib, anā za'lān minnak.*

APPENDICES

APPENDIX A: VERB FORMS

VERB FORMS

	Perfect		Imperfect		Verbal Noun	
						(irregular)
I	كَتَبَ	kataba	يَكْتُب	yaktub		
II	غَيَّرَ	ghayyira	يُغَيِّر	yughayyir	التَّغْيير	at-taghayyir
III	شاهَدَ	shāhada	يُشاهِد	yushāhid	المُشاهَدَة	al-mushāhada
IV	أَرْسَلَ	arsala	يُرْسِل	yursil	الإِرْسال	al-irsāl
V	تَكَلَّمَ	takallama	يَتَكَلَّم	yatakallam	التَّكَلُّم	at-takallum
VI	تَناوَلَ	tanāwala	يَتَناوَل	yatanāwal	التَّناوُل	at-tanāwul
VII	اِنْبَسَطَ	inbasaTa	يَنْبَسِط	yanbasiT	الاِنْبِساط	al-inbisāT
VIII	اِكْتَسَبَ	Iktasaba	يَكْتَسِب	yaktasib	الاِكْتِساب	al-iktisāb
IX	اِبْيَضَّ	ibyaDDa	يَبْيَضّ	yabyaDD	البَياض	al-bayāD
X	اِسْتَخْدَمَ	istakhdama	يَسْتَخْدِم	yastakhdim	الاِسْتِخْدام	al-istikhdām

APPENDIX B: ACTIVE AND PASSIVE PARTICIPLES

ACTIVE AND PASSIVE PARTICIPLES

Form	Perfect		Active Participle		Passive Participle	
I	كَتَبَ	kataba	كَاتِب	katib	مَكْتُوب	maktūb
II	غَيَّرَ	ghayyara	مُغَيِّر	mughayyir	مُغَيَّر	mughayyar
III	سَافَرَ	sāfara	مُسَافِر	musāfir	مُسَافَر	musāfar
IV	أَرْسَلَ	arsila	مُرْسِل	mursil	مُرْسَل	mursal
V	تَكَلَّمَ	takallama	مُتَكَلِّم	mutakallim	مُتَكَلَّم	mutakallam
VI	تَنَاوَلَ	tanāwala	مُتَنَاوِل	mutanāwil	مُتَنَاوَل	mutanāwal
VII	اِنْبَسَطَ	InbasaTa	مُنْبَسِط	munbasiT	مُنْبَسَط	munbasaT
VIII	اِكْتَسَبَ	Iktasaba	مُكْتَسِب	muktasib	مُكْتَسَب	muktasab
IX	اِبْيَضَّ	ibyaDDa	مُبْيَضّ	mubayiDD	مُبْيَضّ	mubayyaDD
X	اِسْتَخْدَمَ	istakhdama	مُسْتَخْدِم	mustakhdim	مُسْتَخْدَم	mustakhdam

APPENDIX C: FIRST CONJUGATION OF WEAK VERBS

FIRST CONJUGATION OF WEAK VERBS

mashā مَشَى – yamshi يَمْشِي

Pronoun		Perfect	Imperfect Indicative	Imperfect Subjunctive	Imperfect Jussive
1st	أنَا	mashaytu	amshi	amshia	amshi
	نَحْنُ	mashaynā	namshi	namshia	namshi
2nd	أنْتَ	mashayta	tamshi	tamshia	tamshi
	أنْتِ	mashayti	tamshina	tamshi	tamshi
	أنْتُمْ	mashaytum	tamshūna	tamshūna	tamshū
	أنْتُنَّ	mashaytunna	tamshina	tamshina	tamshina
	أنْتُمَا	mashaytumā	tamshiāni	tamshiāni	tamshiā
3rd	هُوَ	mashā	yamshi	yamshia	yamshi
	هِيَ	mashat	tamshi	tamshia	tamshi
	هُمْ	mashū	yamshūna	yamshū	yamshū
	هُنَّ	mashayna	yamshina	yamshina	yamshina
	هُمَا (m)	mashayā	yamshiāni	yamshiā	yamshiā
	هُمَا (f)	mashatā	tamshiāni	tamshiā	yamshiā

APPENDIX D: SECOND CONJUGATION OF WEAK VERBS

SECOND CONJUGATION OF WEAK VERBS

nasiya نَسِيَ – yarsā يَنْسَى

	Pronoun	Perfect	Imperfect Indicative	Imperfect Subjunctive	Imperfect Jussive
1st	أَنَا	nasītu	ansā	ansā	ansa
	نَحْنُ	nasinā	nansā	nansā	nansa
2nd	أَنْتَ	nasīta	tansā	tansā	tansa
	أَنْتِ	nasīti	tansayna	tansay	tansay
	أَنْتُمَا	nasītumā	tansawna	tansaw	tansaw
	أَنْتُمْ	nasītunna	tansayna	tansayna	tansayna
	أَنْتُنَّ	nasītuma	tansayāni	tansayā	tansayā
3rd	هُوَ	nasiya	yansā	yansā	yansa
	هِيَ	nasiyat	tansā	tansā	tansa
	هُمَا	nasū	yansawna	yansaw	yansaw
	هُمَا	nasina	yansayna	yansayna	yansayna
	هُمَا (m)	nasiyā	yansayāni	yansayā	yansayā
	هُمَا (f)	nasiyatā	yansayāni	yansayā	yansayā

APPENDIX E: THIRD CONJUGATION OF WEAK VERBS

THIRD CONJUGATION OF WEAK VERBS

yad'u – da'a   يدعو – دعا

دعا

	Pronoun	Perfect	Imperfect Indicative	Imperfect Subjunctive	Imperfect Jussive
1st	أنا	da'awtu	ad'ū	ad'ua	ad'u
	نحن	da'awnā	nad'ū	nad'ua	nad'u
2nd	أنتَ	da'awta	tad'ū	tad'ua	tad'u
	أنتِ	da'awti	tad'īna	tad'ī	tad'ī
	أنتُم	da'awtum	tad'ūna	tad'ū	tad'ū
	أنتُنّ	da'awtunna	tad'ūna	tad'ūna	tad'ūna
	أنتُما	da'awtumā	tad'uāni	tad'uā	tad'uā
3rd	هو	da'ā	yad'ū	yad'ua	yad'u
	هي	da'at	tad'ū	tad'ua	tad'u
	هم	da'aw	yad'ūna	yad'ū	yad'ū
	هنّ	da'awna	yad'ūna	yad'ūna	yad'ūna
	هما (m)	da'auā	yad'uāni	yad'uā	yad'uā
	هما (f)	da'atā	tad'uāni	tad'uā	tad'uā

APPENDIX F: FIRST CONJUGATION OF HOLLOW VERBS

FIRST CONJUGATION OF HOLLOW VERBS

zāra زَارَ – yazūr يَزُور

	Pronoun	Perfect	Imperfect Indicative	Imperfect Subjunctive	Imperfect Jussive
1st	أنا	زُرْتُ zurtu	أَزُورُ azūru	أَزُورَ azūra	أَزُرْ azur
	نحن	زُرْنَا zurnā	نَزُورُ nazūru	نَزُورَ nazūra	نَزُرْ nazur
2nd	أنتَ	زُرْتَ zurta	تَزُورُ tazūru	تَزُورَ tazūra	تَزُرْ tazur
	أنتِ	زُرْتِ zurti	تَزُورِينَ tazūrīna	تَزُورِي tazūrī	تَزُورِي tazūrī
	أنتم	زُرْتُمْ zurtum	تَزُورُونَ tazūrūna	تَزُورُوا tazūrū	تَزُورُوا tazūrū
	أنتنَّ	زُرْتُنَّ zurtunna	تَزُرْنَ tazurna	تَزُرْنَ tazurna	تَزُرْنَ tazurna
	أنتما	زُرْتُمَا zurtumā	تَزُورَانِ tazūrāni	تَزُورَا tazūrā	تَزُورَا tazūrā
3rd	هو	زَارَ zāra	يَزُورُ yazūru	يَزُورَ yazūra	يَزُرْ yazur
	هي	زَارَتْ zārat	تَزُورُ tazūru	تَزُورَ tazūra	تَزُرْ tazur
	هم	زَارُوا zārū	يَزُورُونَ yazūrūna	يَزُورُوا yazūrū	يَزُورُوا yazūrū
	هنَّ	زُرْنَ zurna	يَزُرْنَ yazurna	يَزُرْنَ yazurna	يَزُرْنَ yazurna
	هما (m)	زَارَا zārā	يَزُورَانِ yazūrāni	يَزُورَا yazūrā	يَزُورَا yazūrā
	هما (f)	زَارَتَا zāratā	تَزُورَانِ tazūrāni	تَزُورَا tazūrā	تَزُورَا tazūrā

479

APPENDIX G: CONJUGATION OF DOUBLED VERBS

CONJUGATION OF DOUBLED VERBS

aHabba أَحَبَّ – yuHibbu يُحِبُّ

	Pronoun	Perfect		Imperfect	
1st	أَنَا	أَحْبَبْتُ	aHbabtu	أُحِبُّ	uHibbu
	نَحْنُ	أَحْبَبْنَا	aHbabnā	نُحِبُّ	nuHibbu
2nd	أَنْتَ	أَحْبَبْتَ	aHbabta	تُحِبُّ	tuHibbu
	أَنْتِ	أَحْبَبْتِ	aHbabti	تُحِبِّينَ	tuHibbina
	أَنْتُمْ	أَحْبَبْتُمْ	aHbabtum	تُحِبُّونَ	uHibbūna
	أَنْتُنَّ	أَحْبَبْتُنَّ	aHbabtunna	تُحْبِبْنَ	tuHbibna
	أَنْتُمَا	أَحْبَبْتُمَا	aHbabtuma	تُحِبَّانِ	tuHibbāni
3rd	هُوَ	أَحَبَّ	aHabba	يُحِبُّ	yuHibbu
	هِيَ	أَحَبَّتْ	aHabbat	تُحِبُّ	tuHibbu
	هُمْ	أَحَبُّوا	aHabbū	يُحِبُّونَ	yuHibbūna
	هُنَّ	أَحْبَبْنَ	aHbabna	يُحْبِبْنَ	yuHbibna
	هُمَا (m)	أَحَبَّا	aHabbā	يُحِبَّانِ	yuHibbāni
	هُمَا (f)	أَحَبَّتَا	aHabbatā	تُحِبَّانِ	tuHibbāni

APPENDIX H: DEMONSTRATIVE PRONOUNS/ADJECTIVES

DEMONSTRATIVE PRONOUNS/ADJECTIVES

	"Close"		"Removed"	
	Singular	Plural	Singular	Plural
Masculine	هٰذَا *hādha*	هٰؤُلَاءِ *hā'ulā'i*	ذٰلِكَ *dhālika*	أُولٰئِكَ *ula'ika*
Feminine	هٰذِه *hadhihi*	هٰؤُلَاءِ *h'ulā'i*	تِلْكَ *tilka*	أُولٰئِكَ *ula'ika*
	this	these	that	those

APPENDIX I: SUMMARY OF NUMBERS

	GENDER	CASE	THE COUNTED NOUN
Numbers 3 to 9	The number disagrees in gender with the counted noun.	The case of these numbers changes depending on their function in the sentence and is marked with short vowels. For example: ثَلَاثَةُ *thalāthatu*, ثَلَاثَةِ *thalāthati*, ثَلَاثَةَ *thalāthata* (three)	Use the *plural genitive form* of the counted noun.
Numbers 20 to 90	These numbers do not change in gender.	The case of these numbers changes depending on their function in the sentence. For example: ثَلَاثُونَ *thalāthūn*, ثَلَاثِينَ *thalāthīn* (thirty)	Use the *singular accusative form* of the counted noun. For example: ثَلَاثُونَ بِنْتًا *thalāthūn bintan* (thirty girls)
Hundreds	These numbers do not change in gender.	The case of these numbers changes depending on their function in the sentence and is marked with short vowels. The dual has two forms— اَنِ and يَنِ	Use the *singular accusative form* of the counted noun if there are zeros in the tens and ones places. Otherwise, follow the rule for the last two digits. For example: مِائَةٌ وَخَمْسٌ وَثَلَاثُونَ بِنْتًا *mi'a wa khams wa thalāthūna bintan* (135 girls), مِائَةٌ وَخَمْسٌ بَنَاتٍ *mi'a wa khams banātin* (105 girls), مِائَةُ بِنْتٍ *mi'at bintin* (100 girls)

	GENDER	CASE MARKER	THE COUNTED NOUN
Thousands and above	These numbers do not change in gender.	The case of these numbers changes depending on their function in the sentence and is marked with short vowels. The dual has two forms— ـَيْن and ان.	Follow the rule for the last two digits for case and gender. For example: ألف وخمس وثلاثون بنتاً (1,035 girls), *alf wa khams wa thalāthūna bintan* ألف وخمس بنات (1,005 girls) *alf wa khams banātin* (1,005 girls)
Numbers with strange behavior: The teens The numbers from 11 to 19 are not separated by و as are the other numbers. Compare: ثمانية وخمسون ولد *thamāniya wa khamsūna waladan* (58 boys) with: ثمانية عشر ولد *thamāniyata 'ashara waladan* (18 boys)	عشرة *'ashara* (ten) disagrees in gender with the counted noun. When it is joined to form a number from 13 to 19, it agrees with the counted noun. Compare: عشر بنات *'ashru banatin* (ten girls) with: خمس عشرة بنتاً *khamsa asharata bintan* (15 girls)	These numbers do not change in case. They always have a *fatHa* at the end, with the exception of 12, which changes in case like a normal dual. For example: سبعة عشر ولد *sab'ata 'ashara waladan* (17 boys), سبع عشرة بنتاً *sab'a 'asharata bintan* (17 girls)	The counted noun that follows the number 10 behaves exactly as the counted noun following numbers 3 through 9. It is *plural* and *genitive*. For example: عشر بنات *'ashru banatin* (ten girls) The counted noun that follows numbers 11 to 19 behaves exactly as the counted noun following the numbers 20 through 90. It is *singular* and *accusative*. For example: خمسة عشر ولد *khamsata 'ashara waladan* (15 boys)

These details are not necessary in speech. You should follow the common dialectical simplifications explained in the main text, and only learn to recognize the forms discussed here. You may also use this table as a reference for writing.

APPENDIX J: 250 BASIC PHRASES IN EGYPTIAN, IRAQI, LEBANESE, AND SAUDI ARABIC

Appendix J contains more than 250 basic phrases in Egyptian, Iraqi, Lebanese, and Saudi Arabic. You can listen to the recording of the phrases in each dialect on Recording Set B: Disc 1 (Egyptian), Disc 2 (Iraqi), Disc 3 (Lebanese), and Disc 4 (Saudi).

Greetings and Introductions

	EGYPTIAN	IRAQI	LEBANESE	SAUDI
Hello.	ahlan, iz-zayyak/iz-zayyik/iz-zayyokom.	Halaw, marHaba, s-salāmu 'alaykum.	ahlēn, marHaba.	marHaba.
Bye.	ma'a s-salama, salam.	ma'a s-salāma, baybāy.	yalla, bai bai.	fi 'amān illāh.
Good morning.	SabaH el-khēr.	SabāH il-khēr.	sabāH l-khēr.	SabāH al-khēr.
Good evening.	misa' el-khēr.	masā il-khēr.	masa l-khēr.	masā' al-khēr.
Good-bye.	ma'a s-salama.	ma'a s-salāma.	ma' s-salēmi, b-khāTrak/b-khāTrik, yi'aTik il-'āfiye.	ma'a s-salāma.
Title for a married woman/an older unmarried woman	madame, ustaza	sayyida, sitt	madām, sitt	sitt, sayyida
Title for a young/unmarried woman	ānisa	ānisa, sitt	demuazel, mis	ānesa
Title for a man	ustaz	sayyid	mosyu, istēz	sayyid
I am . . .	ana . .	āni	ana...	āna...
My name is	(ana) ismi . . .	'ismi	ismi...	ismi...
What is your name?	ismak/ismik eh?	shismak/shismich?, l-ism il-karim?	shu ismak/ismik?, (shu) ism, HaDrtak/HaDrtik?, ism il-karim?	ēsh ismak?
Nice to meet you.	itsharrafna.	tsharrafna, ahlan wa sahlan.	tsharrafna, ilna sh-sharaf.	itsharrafna.
You, too.	itshar-rafna bik, esh-sharaf lina.	wiHna ayDHan.	b-HaDrtak/b-HaDrtik.	bilmugābil.
I'd like you to meet . . .	ahibb a'adimlak/a'adimlik . . .	nHib nshūfak/nshūfich/nshūfkum	b-Hebb 'arrfak/'arrfik 'a . . .	aHub inak tigābil . . .
I'd like to introduce . . . to you.	ahibb a'adimlak/a'adimlik . . .	(aHib) a'arrifak 'ala . . .	b-Hebb 'arrfak/'arrfik 'a . . .	aHub agaddim lak . . .

	EGYPTIAN	IRAQI	LEBANESE	SAUDI
What is your nationality?	ginsey-yitak/-yitik êh?	shinu jinsitak/jinsitich?	shu hawiytak/hawiytik?	êsh/mahiyya jinsiyatak?
Where are you from?	enta/enti min ay balad?	min ay balad?	min weyn enta/enti?; enta/enti min weyn?	inta min fên?
I am an American.	ana amriki/amrikiyya.	āni amriki/amrikiyya.	ana amerikêni/amerikaniyye.	anā amerikāni.
I am an Egyptian/Iraqi/Lebanese/Saudi.	ana maSri/maSriyya.	āni 'irāqi/'irāqiyya.	ana libnêni/libneniyye.	anā sa'ūdi.
How are you?	iz-zayyak/iz-zayyik? 'amil/'amla êh?	shlonak/shlonich/shlonkum?	kifak/kifik?	kêf Hālak?
Fine, thanks. And you?	be khêr, al-Hamdulillah. w-enta/ wenti z-zayyak/z-zayyik?	l-Hamdilla. inta/inti/intu shlonak/shlonich/shlonkum?	mnêH/mnēHa, w-enta/enti?; mêshi l-Hāl, w-enta/enti?; tamêm, w-enta/enti?	Tayyib al-Hamdulillāh. wu inta?
I'll see you later.	il al-liqa'.	khallūna nshūfkum.	yalla, bshūfak/bshūfik ba'dên.	ashufak ba'dên.

Polite Expressions

	EGYPTIAN	IRAQI	LEBANESE	SAUDI
Please.	min faDlak/min faDlik.	min faDHlak/min faDHlich, rajā'an.	iza bitrid/bitridi; iaw samaHet/samaHti.	min faDlak.
Thank you.	shukran.	shukran.	shukran; mersi; yislamu.	shukran.
Thank you very much.	shukran gazilan.	shukran jazilan. alif shukur.	shukran ktir; mersi ktir.	shukran jazilan.
You're welcome.	el-'afwu.	l-'afu, hādha wājib.	tikram/tikrami; tikram 'aynak/'aynik.	ahlan fik/ahlan bik.
It's my pleasure.	ay khidma.	hādha wājibi; ta'abkum rāHa.	'a rāsi w 'aini.	mamnūn.

	EGYPTIAN	IRAQI	LEBANESE	SAUDI
Yes, thank you.	aywa, shukran.	na'am, shukran.	ē, shukran.	na'am, shukran.
No, thank you.	la, shukran.	lā, shukran.	la, mersi; la, shukran.	la', shukran.
I beg your pardon?	'afwan?	l-'afu, sh-gilit/sh-gulti?	'afwan?	la mu'akhza.
I'm sorry.	(ana) asif/asfa.	l-'afu, āni āsif/āsfa.	sori; (ana) ēsif/ēsfi.	āsif.
Excuse me.	'afwan.	l-'afu, 'dhurni/'dhurini; l-'afu, sāmiHni/sāmHini.	bi l-izn; 'afwan.	ismaHli.
Pardon me.	lau tismaH/tismaHi.	l-'afu, 'dhurni/'dhurini; l-'afu, sāmiHni/sāmHini.	'afwan.	'afwan/faDlan.
That's okay.	m'ālesh.	zeyn, māshi, khosh.	ma'ale.	ma'lish.
It doesn't matter.	may-himmish.	mayhim, maykhālif.	mish mhimm.	la yihmak/la yihimik.
No problem.	mish mushkila.	māku mushkila.	mish mishkle.	mafi mushkila.

Deciding on the Language

	EGYPTIAN	IRAQI	LEBANESE	SAUDI
Do you speak Arabic/English?	bitit-kallim/kallimi 'arabi/inglizi?	tiHchi 'arabi/ngilizi?	taHki (m./f.) 'arabi/inglizi?	titkalam 'arabi/inglizi?
Yes./No.	aywa/la'(a).	na'am/lā; i/lā; bali/lā	ē, (na'm)/la.	na'am/iwa; lā/la'a.
I can speak a little.	bat-kallim shuwayya basiTa.	aHchi shwayya.	baHki shwayye.	atkalam galil.
I understand a lot, but I don't speak very well.	bafham el-kalam, bas ma-batkallimsh kuwayyis.	afham hwāya, bas ma aHchi kullish zēn.	bifham mnēH, bas ma baHki ktir mnēH; bifham mnēH, bas ma ba'rif aHki ktir mnēH.	afham shiwayya/galli bas ma atkalam tayyib.
I don't understand.	mish fahim.	mā afham.	ma bifham; mish fēhim/fēhme.	manni fāhim.
Could you repeat that, please?	mumkin te'ūlha/te'ūlha tani; min faDlak?	mumkin tgūlha/tgūliha marra thānya, min faDHlak/faDHlich?	fik tirja' tkarrir ma ilet, law samaHet (m.)?; fiki tirja'i tkarriri ma ilti, law samaHti (f.)?	tu'ud ēsh gult, min faDalk.
Sure.	awi.	akid.	akid; tikram/tikrami.	akid/ibshir.

	EGYPTIAN	IRAQI	LEBANESE	SAUDI
What does this mean?	di ma'naha eh?	hādha shinu ma'nā?	shu ya'ni hayda?	hadā ēsh ma'nāh?
What does that mean?	dah m'anah eh?	dhhāka shinu ma'nā?	shu ma'nēta?	hadāka ēsh ma'nāh?
How do you say... in Egyptian/Iraqi/Lebanese/Saudi?	iz-zay te'oul/te'ouli... bi l-maSri?	shlon tgūl/tilfiDH... bi l-'irāqi?	shu ya'ni... bi libnēni?; kif baddi ūl... bi libnēni?; kif minūl... bi libnēni?	kēf tugul... bi l-sa'udi?
I don't know.	ma-'rafsh, mish 'āref.	mā adri.	ma ba'rif, mish 'ārif/'āfri; shu ba'rifni. (very informal)	manni 'ārif.

Needs and Question Words

	EGYPTIAN	IRAQI	LEBANESE	SAUDI
I'd like...	'āwiz/'āwza...	arīd...	bHebb...; baddi...	abgha.
I need...	miHtag/miHtaga...	aHtāj...	meHtēj/meHtēji...	miHtāj.
I am looking for...	ba-dawwar 'ala...	adawwir 'ala...; arīd...	'am bfattish 'ā...	badawwir 'ala.
I'm hungry.	(ana) ga-'ān/ga-'āna.	(āni) jo'ān.	ana jū'ān/jū'āni.	anā ju'ān.
I'm thirsty.	(ana) 'aTshān/'aTshāna.	(āni) 'aTshān.	ana 'aTshān/'aTshāi.	anā 'aTshān.
It's important.	dah muhimm.	muhimm.	mhimm; hayda mhimm.	hadā mūhim.
It's urgent.	dah mist'agil.	musta'jil; muliHH; Dharūry.	'ājil.	hadā 'ājil.
I need a restroom.	miHtag/miHtaga li l-Hammam.	arīd arūH li l-marāfiq.	meHtēj/meHtēji Hamr:ēm; baddi rūH 'a l-Hammēm.	miHtāj arūH al-Hammām.
Where is the bathroom (toilet)?	fēn el-Hammam?	wēn il-marāfi?	weyn il-Hammēm?	fēn al-Hammām?
How?	iz-zāy?	shlon?	kif?; adde?	kēf?
How much?	be-kam?	shgad?	adde Ha'a...?; b-adde...?	kām?, bikām?
How many?	kam wāHid?, kam waHda?	kam wāHid/wiHda?	kam?; kam wāHad/waHde?	kām?

	EGYPTIAN	IRAQI	LEBANESE	SAUDI
Which?	ayy wāHid?, ayy waHda?	ay wāHid/wiHda?, minu?	ay?; ay wāHad/waHdi?	ayyat?
What?	eh?	shinu?	shu?	ēsh?
What kind of?	eh nō'?	eh nō'?	ay no'?	ēsh shakil?
Who?	min?	minu?	min?	min?
Where?	fēn?	wēn?	weyn?	fēn?
When?	emta?	yemta?, ay waqit?	emtīn? emta?	mita?

At the Airport

	EGYPTIAN	IRAQI	LEBANESE	SAUDI
Where is...	fēn...	weyn...	weyn...	fēn...
customs?	eg-gomrok?	l-gamārig?	il-jamārik?	al-jamārik?
passport control?	eg-gawazat?	j-jawazāt?	taftīsh pasporāt?	al-jawazāt?
the information booth?	maktab (koshk) el-Ist'i'lamāt?	l-isti'āmāt?	keshk il-isti'lamāt?	al-isti'lamāt?
the ticketing counter?	et-tazākir?, nerouH 'ashan nishtiri tazāker?	maHall/makān biTāqāt is-safar?	maktab it-tazkarāt?	maktab al-tazākir?
baggage claim?	makān istilām esh-shonaT?	il-muTālaba bi l-junat?	istirdād il-amti'a?	istilām al-'afsh?
the ground transportation?	nilā'i muwaSlāt?, nerūH 'ashan nila'i muwaSalāt?	bāSāt in-naqil?	it-tanaqqulēt (il-arDiyye)?	al-muwaSalāt?
the taxi stand?	maw'af et-taksiyyāt?	mawqif it-taksiyyāt?	maw'if it-taksiyēt?	mawgif al-taksi?
the car rental?	maktab/makān ta'gir el-'arabiyyāt?, maktab/makān ta'gir es-sayyarāt?	maHal ta'jir is-sayyārāt?	(maktab) ta'jir is-siyarāt?	maktab ta'jir is-sayyarāt?
the subway?	maHaTit el-metro? metro l-'anfā?	in-nafaq?	l-metro?	al-metro?

	EGYPTIAN	IRAQI	LEBANESE	SAUDI
the bus stop?	maHaTit el-otobis?, maw'af el-otobisat?	mawqif il-baSat?	maw'if al-otobis?	mawgif al-otobis/al-Hafila?
the lost and found service?	maktab el-mafqudat?	khidmat' il-mafqudat?	l-mafqudet?	maktab al-mafqudat?
the post office?	maktab el-barid?, el-bosta?	da'irat il-barid?	(maktab) l-barid?	maktab al-barid?
the public telephone?	et-telefon el-'omumi?	i-tilifon il-'umumi?	telefon 'am/'umum?	al-hatif al-'umumi?
How far is the center of the city?	wisT el-balad yib'id add eh min hina?	shgad tib'id il-madina?	'ala bu'd adde l-balad?	kam yib'ad waSta l-balad min hina?
How do I get to...?	iz-zay aruH...?	shlon aruH l...?	kif buSal 'a...?	kef arHl li...?
Where are...	fen...	wen...	weyn...	fen...
the international departures?	Salit mughadrit er-rihlat ed-dawliya?	Salat il-mughadara id-dawliyya?	mughadara bi l-maTar id-dawli?	Salat al-mughadara?
the international arrivals?	Salit woSul er-rihlat ed-dawliyya?	Salat il-wuSul id-dawliyya?	wuSul bi l-maTar id-dawli?	Salat al-wuSul?
Where can I exchange money?	fen mumkin aHawwil felus?, fen mumkin aSrif felus?, fen maktab es-Sirafa?	wen maHal tabdil il-'umla?	fi maktab Sarf?; fi Sarrof?	fen abaddil fulus?

At the Hotel

	EGYPTIAN	IRAQI	LEBANESE	SAUDI
I have a reservation under the name...	'andi Hagz bi-ism...	'indi Hajiz bi -isim...	'indi Hajiz b-ism...	'indi hajiz bi ism...
I would like a room...	'awiz/'awza oda...	arid ghurfa...	baddi uDa...	abgha ghurfa...
for one person.	li shakhS waHid.	l- shakhiS waHid.	la shakhS waHid.	li shakhiS waHid.

	EGYPTIAN	IRAQI	LEBANESE	SAUDI
for two people.	li shakSēn.	l-shakhSēn.	la shakhSēn.	li shakhSēn.
for tonight.	lēla waHda.	l-hal-lēla; l-hal-yom.	la l-leyli.	li l-lēla.
for two nights.	li lēltēn.	l-leyltēn; l-yomēn.	la leytēn.	li lilitēn.
for a week.	li osbū' wāHid.	l-isbū' wāHid.	la jim'a.	li isbū'.
Do you have a different room?	'andak/'andik ōDa tanya?	'indak ghurfa gheyrha?	'inkun ūDa tēni?	'indak ghurfa tanniya?
with a bath	bi Hammam	biha bānyo	fiya Hammēm	bi Hammām
with a shower	bi dosh	biha dūsh	fiya dūsh	bi dush
with a toilet	bi twalet	biha mirHāDH	fiya twalēt	bi mirHaD
with air-conditioning	bi takyif	biha ērkondishin; mubarrida	fiya takyīf hawa	bi takyif
How much is it?	kam si'raha?	shkad is-si'ir?, bēsh?	adde Ha'a?	kām il Hisāb?
I'd like to have my bill, please.	mumkin tid-dīni faturti, min faDlak/min faDlik?	l-fātūra min- faDHlak/ min faDHlich.	i''Tini l-Hisēb, law samaHt.	abgha l-fatūra min faDlak?

At the Restaurant

	EGYPTIAN	IRAQI	LEBANESE	SAUDI
Where can I find a good restaurant?	fēn mumkin ala'i maT'am kuwayyis?	wēn aku maT'am zēn?	weyn blē'i maT'am mnēH?	fēn alāgi maT'am Tayyib?
I'd like a (n)...restaurant.	'āwiz/'āwza maT'am...	arid maT'am...	baddi maT'am...	abgha maT'am...
casual	kajual, mish rasmi awi	'ādi	mish rasmi	mū rasmi
elegant	fākhir	rāqi	fakhem	murattab
fast-food	wagabāt/aklāt sari'a	wajbāt sari'a	wajbēt sari'a	akil sari'
inexpensive	rekhiS	rikhiS; mū ghāli	rkhiS	rakhis
seafood	asmāk	aklāt baHriyya; asmāk	asmēk	akil baHar

	EGYPTIAN	IRAQI	LEBANESE	SAUDI
vegetarian	nabāti	nabāti	nabēti	nabāti
with good local food	akl sh'abi kuwayyis	bi aklāt sha'biyya	fih akel maHalli mnēH	yigaddim akil sha'bi
Where can I find a café?	fēn mumkin alā'i 'ahwa?	wēn aku gahwa/gazino?	weyn blē'i café/maqha?	fēn alāgi gahwa?
A table for two, please.	tarabēza letnēn, min faDlak.	mēz l-nafareyn min faDHlak/min faDHlich.	Tāwile la shakhSēn, law samaHet.	Tāwla li itnēn min faDlak.
Waiter, a menu, please.	garsōn, el-kart el-menyil, min faDlak.	qā'imat iT-Ta'ām min faDHlak/min faDHlich.	garson, (i'Tini) il-menu, law samaHet.	law samaHt listat il-akil.
I'd like the wine list, please.	mumkin ashūf listit en-nebit, min faDlak.	qā'imat il-khumūr min faDHlak/min faDHlich.	baddi lista nnabit, law samaHet.	(Does not apply.)
appetizers	el-muqabbilāt, el-mushahhiyāt	muqabbilāt, mezzāt	mēza; mqabbalēt	al-mugabbilāt
main course	et-taba' er-ra'isi	l-wajba ir-ra'isiyya	wajbe l-asasiyye	al-Tabag al-ra 'isi
dessert	el-helw	Halawiyyāt	Halawayēt	al-Hlw
What would you like?	tiHib takhud ēh? (m.), tiHibb toTlob ēh? (m.), tiHibbi takhdi ēh? (f.), tiHibbi toTlobi ēh? (f.)	shi 'ijbak/shi 'ijbich?	shu bitHebb/bitHebbi?	ēsh tuHub?
What would you like to drink?	tiHib/tiHibbi tishrab/tishrabi ēh?	shi 'ijbak tishrab/shi 'ijbich ish-shirbin?	shu bitHebb tishrab/bitHebbi tishrabi?	ēsh tuHub tishrab?
Can you recommend a good wine?	mumkin teqtiriH nibit kuwayyis?	shinu tiqtiriH nishrab?; shinu bra'yak khamir zēn?	shu aHsan nabit 'inkon?	(Does not apply.)
I didn't order this.	(ana) ma-Talabtish dah.	ma Tilabit hādha.	ma Talabet hayda.	anā maTalabt hadā.
That's all, thanks.	bass keda, shukran.	kāfi, shukran.	hayda kil shi, mersi.	shukran hadā kullu.
I'd like the check, please.	(mumkin) el-hisāb, min faDlak.	l-Hisāb min faDHlak.	'amul ma'rūf, jibilna l-Hisēb.	al-Hisāb, min faDDlak.
Cheers!	fi SiHHitak!, fi SiHHitkl, fi SiHHitkom!	fi SiHHitak!	kēsak!	bi l-'afiyya!

Out on the Town

	EGYPTIAN	IRAQI	LEBANESE	SAUDI
Where can I find...	fēn mumkin ala'i...	wēn il...	weyn blē'i...	fēn alāgi...
an art museum?	matHaf fenūn?	matHaf finūn?	matHaf funūn?	matHaf fanni?
a museum of natural history?	matHaf tarīkh Tabi'i?	matHaf tārīkh Tabi'i?	matHaf tarīkh Tabi'i?	matHaf at-tarikh aT-Tabi'i?
a history museum?	matHaf tarīkh?	matHaf tārīkhi?	matHaf tarīkh?	matHaf tarikhi?
an archaeology museum?	matHaf asār?	matHaf āthār?	matHaf asār?	matHaf jiyolōji?
interesting architecture?	m'imar gamil?	āthār muhimma?	'imarāt Hilwe?	'imāra mutamiyyiza/ mi'mār mutmiyyiz?
a church/mosque?	kenisa/gāmi'?	kanisa/jāmi'?	knise/jēmi'?	kanisa/masjid?
the zoo?	genēinat el-Hayawanāt?	Hadiqat il-Hayawānāt?	jneynet l-Haywanēt?	Hadigat al-Hayawanāt?
the old city?	el-madina el-'adima?	l-amākin il-qadīma bi l-madina	l-madine l-adime'?	al-madina al-gadima?
I'd like...	'āwiz/'āwza...	arīd...	bHebb...	abgha/aHub/ashtahi...
to see a play.	ashūfaruH masraHiyya.	ashūf masraHiyya.	shūf/uHDur masraHiyye.	ashūf masraHiyya.
to see a movie.	ashūf el-film, arūH es-sinema.	ashūf filim.	shūf filim.	ashūf filim.
to see a concert.	arūH Hafla musiqiya.	ashūf Hafla mūsiqiyya.	uHDur Hafle musi'iyye.	asma' Hafla mūsigiyya.
to see the opera.	arūH el-opera.	ashūf opra.	shūf opera.	ashūf al-ōbira.
to go sightseeing.	arūH fi gawla siyaHeyya.	ashūf il-amākin il-muhimma.	itfarraj 'al-amēkin siyaHiyye.	atfassaH.
to go on a bike ride.	arkab 'agala/biskilett.	aj-jawwal 'al bāysikil.	irkab il-bisikle.	arkab biskilitta.

Shopping

	EGYPTIAN	IRAQI	LEBANESE	SAUDI
Where is the best place to go shopping for...	fēn aHsan makan arūHu 'ashan ashtiri...	wēn aHsan makān ashtiri bi...	weyn aHsan maHall la-jib...	fēn aHsan maHall li taswig...
clothes?	hudūm/malābis?	malābis?	tiyēb?	awā'i?

	EGYPTIAN	IRAQI	LEBANESE	SAUDI
food?	akl?	akl?	akel?	akil?
souvenirs?	hadāya tizkareyya?	hadāya tidhkāriyya?	hadēya tazkariyye?	hajat li l-zikra/sufinir?
furniture?	'afsh?	athāth?	mafrushēt?	'afsh?
fabric?	omashāt?	qmāshāt?	imēsh?	gumāsh?
antiques?	toHaf asareyya?	'antikāt?	tuHfiyēt?	hajat gadima/antigs?
books?	kotob?	kutub?	kutub?	kutub?
sporting goods?	adawat riyaDeyya?	adawāt riyāDHiYYa; 'idat riyāDHa?	mu'addēt riyāDa; mu'addēt il-al'āb ir-riyāDiyye?	awā'i riyadah?
electronics?	ag-hiza elektroneyya?	kahrabā'iyyāt?	elektroniyētjajhiza elektroniyye?	elektroniyyāt?

Directions

	EGYPTIAN	IRAQI	LEBANESE	SAUDI
Excuse me. Where is…	lau samaHt/samaHti. fēn…	min faDHlak. weyn…	bi l-izn, weyn…	ismaHli, fēn…
the bus stop?	maHattit el-otōbis?	mawqif il-bāS?	maw'if il-bāS?	mawqif al-otōbis/al-Hafila?
the subway station?	maHattit el-metro?	muHaTTat in-nafaq?	maw'if il-metro?	maHaTTat al-metro?
the rest room?	el-Hammam?	l-marāfiq?	il-Hammēm?	al-Hammam?
the taxi stand?	maw'af et-taksi/et-taksiyyāt?	mawqif it-taksiyyāt?	maw'if it-taksiyyēt?	mawgif at-taksi?
the nearest bank?	a'rab bank?	aqrab bank?	a'rab bank?	agrab bank?
the…hotel?	fundu'…?, lokandit…?	findiq,…?	otēl…/fundu'…?	fundug…?
to the right	'ala l-yemin	li l-yamin;? al-yamin	'a l-yamin	yimin al
to the left	'ala sh-shimāl	li l-yasār; 'al-yasār	'a sh-shmēl	yisār al
straight ahead	'ala Tūl	gubal	daghri	dughri

	EGYPTIAN	IRAQI	LEBANESE	SAUDI
next to...	gamb...	yam...	Hadd...	janb al...
across the street from	en-neHya at-tania min esh-shar'i oSād...	'ibr ish-shāri...	b-wijh...	migābil ash-shāri'...
around this corner	ba'd ma tiHwid naSyit esh-shar'i dah. (m.) ba'd ma tiHwidi naSyit esh-shar'i dah. (f.)	Hawl iz-zāwiya	'a z-zēwiye	'ala rukn ash-shāri'
It's near here.	(howwa) orayyib min hena.	qarib; qarib min hal-makān.	arib la hōn.	garib min hina.
It's far from here.	(howwa) be'id min hena.	ba'id; ba'id min hal-makān.	ba'id min hōn.	ba'id min hina.
Go back.	irga'.	irga'.	rja'/rija'i.	rūH wara.
I'm lost.	ana tāyih.	(āni) tayyaht iT-Tariq; āni tāyih/DHāyi'.	dayya'et.	ana tāyih.

Numbers

	EGYPTIAN	IRAQI	LEBANESE	SAUDI
0	Sifr	Sifr	Sifir	Sifir
1	wāHid	wāHid	wāHad	wāHid
2	itnēn	thnēn	tnēn	itnēn
3	talata	tlātha	tlēte	talāta
4	arba'a	arb'a	arb'a	arba'a
5	khamsa	khamsa	khamse	khamsa
6	sitta	sitta	sitte	sitta
7	sab'a	sab'a	sab'a	sab'a
8	tamania	thmānya	tmēne	tamanya
9	tis'a	tis'a	tis'a	tis'a

	EGYPTIAN	IRAQI	LEBANESE	SAUDI
10	'ashara	'ashra	'ashra	'ashara
11	Hidashar	hda'ash	Hda'sh	Hida'sh
12	itnashar	thna'ash	tna'sh	itna'sh
13	talattāshar	tlaTa'ash	tletta'sh	talata'sh
14	arba'tāshar	arba'Ta'ash	arba'ta'sh	arba'tash
15	khamastāshar	khumusTa'ash	khamsta'sh	khamasta'sh
16	sittāshar	siTTa'ash	sitta'sh	sitta'sh
17	saba'tāshar	sabia'Ta'ash	saba'ta'sh	saba 'ta'sh
18	tamantāshar	thminTa'asn	tmanta'sh	tamanta'sh
19	tisa'tāshar	tisi'Ta'ash	tisi'ta'sh	tisa 'ta'sh
20	'ishrin	'ishrin	'ashrin	'ishrin
21	wāHid wi-'ishrin	wāHid w-'ishrin	wāHad w-'ashrin	wāHid wu-'ishrin
22	itnēn wi-'ishrin	thnēn w-'ishrin	tnēn w-'ashrin	itnēn wu 'ishrin
23	talata w-'ishrin	tlātha w-'ishrin	tlete w-'ashrin	talāta wu 'ishrin
30	talatin	tlāthin	tletin	talātin
40	arb'in	arba'in	arba'in	arba'in
50	khamsin	khamsin	khamsin	khamsin
60	sittin	sittin	sittin	sittin
70	sab'in	sab'in	saba'in	sab'in
80	tamanin	thmānin	tmenin	tamānin
90	tis'in	tis'in	tisa'in	tis'in
100	meyya	miyya	miyye	miyya
1,000	alf	alif	alf	alf
1,100	alf wi meyya	alf w miyya	alf w miyye	alf wu miyya

	EGYPTIAN	IRAQI	LEBANESE	SAUDI
2,000	alfēn	alfēn	alfēn	alfēn
10,000	'ashart alāf	'ashittālāf	'ashrt ālēf	'asharat alāf
100,000	mit alf	mit alif	mit alf	mit alf
1,000,000	milyōn	milyon	miliōn	milyōn
first	el-awwil	awwal	awwal	al-awwal
second	et-tāni	thāni	tēni	alt-tāni
third	et-tālit	thālith	tēlit	alt-tālit
fourth	er-rābi'	rābi'	rābi'	alt-rābi'
fifth	el-khāmis	khāmis	khāmis	alt-khāmis
sixth	es-sādis	sādis	sēdis	als-sādis
seventh	es-sābi'	sābi'	sēbi'	als-sābi'
eighth	et-tāmin	thāmin	tēmin	alt-tāmin
ninth	et-tāsi'	tāsi'	tēsi'	alt-tāsi'
tenth	el-'āshir	'āshir	'āshir	al-'āshir
eleventh	el-Hidāshar	Hdá'ash	Hda'ash	al-Hida'sh
twelfth	l-itnāshar	thna'ash	tna'ash	al-'itna'sh
thirteenth	et-talattāshar	tlaTa'ash	tletta'ash	alt-talatTa'sh
fourteenth	l-arba'tashar	arba'Ta'ash	arba'ash	alarba'Ta'sh
fifteenth	el-khamastāshar	khumusTa'ash	khamst'ash	al-khamasTa'sh
sixteenth	es-sittāshar	siTTa'ash	sitta'ash	als-sitTa'sh
seventeenth	es-saba'tāshar	sabi'Ta'ash	saba't'ash	als-saba'ta'sh
eighteenth	et-tamantashar	thminTa'ash	tmant'ash	alt-tamanta'sh
nineteenth	et-tisa'tāshar	tisi'Ta'ash	tis'at'ash	alt-tisa'ta'sh
twentieth	el-'ishrin	'ishrin	'ashrin	al-'ishrin
twenty-first	el-waHid wi 'ishrin	wāHid w-'ishrin	wāHad w-'ashrin	al-wāHid wu 'ishrin
twenty-second	el-itnēn wi 'ishrin	thneyn w-'ishrin	tēni w-'ashrin	al-itnēn wu 'ishrin

|---|---|---|---|---|
thirtieth	et-talatin	tlātīn	tlētīn	tit-talātīn
fortieth	el-arb'in	arba'in	arba'in	al-arba'in
fiftieth	el-khamsin	khamsin	khamsin	al-khamsin
sixtieth	es-sittin	sittin	sittin	as-sittin
seventieth	es-sab'in	sab'in	saba'in	as-sab'in
eightieth	et-tamanin	thmānin	tmenin	at-tamānin
ninetieth	et-tis'in	tis'in	tisa'in	at-tis'in
hundredth	el-meyya	miyya	miyye	al-miyya
thousandth	el-alf	alf	alf	al-alf

Time

	EGYPTIAN	IRAQI	LEBANESE	SAUDI
What time is it?	es-sa'a kām?	bēsh is-sā'a?	addēsh is-sē'a?	kām as-sā'a?
It is noon.	es-sa'a tinashar eD-Dohr.	thn'aash iDH-DHuhur.	Duhr.	as-sā'a itna'sha al-Duhur.
It is midnight.	es-sa'a itnashar bi l-lēl.	nuS il-lēl.	noSS il-lēl.	as-sā'a itna'sha nuS-Salēl.
It is 9:00 AM.	es-sa'a tis'a SabāHan.	tis'a iS-SubuH.	tis'a S-SubuH.	as-sā'a tis'a aS-SubuH.
It is 1:00 PM.	es-sa'a waHda ba'd eD-Dohr.	wiHda iDH-DHuhur.	waHdi ba'd iD-Duhr.	as-sā'a waHda aD-Duhur.
It is 3 o'clock.	es-sa'a talāta.	is-sā'a tlātha.	(sē'a) tlēti.	as-sā'a talāta.
5:15	khamsa w- rob'	khamsa w rubu	khamsi w rub'	khamsa wu rubu'
7:30	sab'a w noSS	sab'a w-nuS	sab'a w-noS	sab'a wu nuSS
9:45	'ashra l-la rob'	'ashra illa rubu	'ashara illa rub'	'ashara illa rubu'
now	delwa'ti	hassa; l-ān	halla	daHin

	EGYPTIAN	IRAQI	LEBANESE	SAUDI
later	ba'dēn	ba'dēn	ba'dēn	ba'din
immediately	'ala Ṭūl	Ḥālan	daghri/fi l-Ḥāl (formal)	fi l-Ḥāl
soon	orayyib	qariban; ba'd shwayya	ba'd shwayye; arīb bukra	'ala Ṭūl

Days of the Week/Months of the Year

	EGYPTIAN	IRAQI	LEBANESE	SAUDI
Monday	(yom) el-itnēn	th-thinēn	t-tanēn	al-itnēn
Tuesday	(yom) el-talāt	th-thalāthā'	t-talēta	at-talūt
Wednesday	(yom) el-arba'	l-arbi'ā'	l-arba'a	ar-rabū'
Thursday	(yom) el-khamīs	l-khamīs	l-khamīs	al-khamīs
Friday	(yom) el-gom'a	j-jum'a	j-jim'a	al-jum'a
Saturday	(yom) el-sabt	s-sabit	s-sabet	as-sabt
Sunday	(yom) el-Hadd	l-aHHad	l-aHad	al-aHad
What day is today?	(howwa) en-naharda ēh fi l-iyyām?, (howwa) en-naharda yom ēh?	halyom shinu (bi l-isbū')?	shu l-yōm?	al-yōm ēsh?
January	yanāyer	kānūn ith-thāni	kānūn it-tēni	yanayir
February	febrāyer	shubāT	shbāT	fubrāyir
March	māris	āthār	azār	māris
April	ebril	nisān	nisēn	abril
May	māyo	māys	ayyār	māyo

498

	EGYPTIAN	IRAQI	LEBANESE	SAUDI
June	yonyo/yonya	Huzayrān	Hzayrān	yunya
July	yolyo/yolya	tammūz	tammūz	yulya
August	aghostos	āb	āb	aghustus
September	september	aylūl	aylūl	sibtambir
October	oktobar	tishrin il-awwal	tishrin il-awwal	oktōbir
November	november	tishrin ith-thāni	tishrin it-tēni	nōvambir
December	desember	kānūn il-awwal	kānūn il-awwal	disambir
What is the date today?	(howwa) tarikh en-naharda kam/eh?	shinu tārikh il-yom?	shu t-tārikh il-yōm?	tārikh al-yōm kām?
Today is Thursday, September 22.	en-naharda l-khamis, itnēn wi-'ishrin september.	l-yom khamis, thnyen w-'ishrin aylūl.	il-yōm il-khamis thēn w-'ashrin aylūl.	al-yōm al-khamis itnēn wu 'ishrin sibtambir.
Yesterday was Wednesday, September 21.	em-bariH kan l-arba', wāHid wi-'ishrin september.	amis arbi'ā', wāhid w-'ishrin aylūl.	mbēriH kēn il-arba'a vāHad w-'ashrin aylūl.	al-ams ar-rabū' wāHid wu 'ishrin sibtambir.
Tomorrow is Friday, September 23.	bokra g-gom'a, talāta w 'ishrin september.	bāchir jum'a, tlātha w 'ishrin aylūl.	bukra j-jim'a tlete w-'ashrin aylūl.	bukra al-jum'a talāta wu 'ishrin sibtambir.

Modern Connections

	EGYPTIAN	IRAQI	LEBANESE	SAUDI
Where can I find...	fēn mumkin alā'i...	wēn agdar aHHaSSil...	weyn fiyyi lē'i...	fēn alāgi...
a telephone?	telefon?	tilifōn?	telefōn?	tilifōn/al-hātif?
a fax machine?	gihaz faks?	faks?	fāks (ālit fāks)?	fāks?
an Internet connection?	waSla li l-internet?	internet?	internēt (internēt café)?	khaT 'ala al-intirnat?

	EGYPTIAN	IRAQI	LEBANESE	SAUDI
How do I call the United States?	iz zay attaSil bi amrika?	shlon akhābir il-wilāyāt il-muttaHida?	kīf baddi iTTiSil b amerika?	kēf agdar attaSil bi l-wilayāt al-muttaHida?
I need...	(ana) miHtāgi/'āwiz... (ana) miHtāga/'āwza...	aHtāj...; arīd...	lēzim; baddi; ana b Hāji la/beHtēj...	miHtāj...
a fax sent.	ab'at faks.	adizz faks.	ib'at fāks.	arsil fāks.
a hook-up to the Internet.	tawSila li l-internet.	tawSilat internet.	iTTiSil bi l-intirnat.	attiSil bi l-intirnat.
a computer.	kombyuter.	kompyūtar.	la compyutar.	Hasūb āli/kōmbiyutar.
a package sent overnight.	ab'at Tard mista'gil l il-woSul bokra.	ruzma tiTla' bi l-leyl.	ib'at ha-T-Tard barid sari'.	arsil aT-Tard fi l-barid as-sari'.
some copies made.	a'mil Sowar li ba'D el-mustanadat, aSawwar ba'D el-mustanadāt.	assawwi nisakh.	kam nuskha.	nusakh min hāda.
a VCR and monitor.	gihaz video wa televizyon.	VCR w shāsha/tilfizyon.	jihāz video w-shēshi.	fidiyo wu shashat 'arD.
an overhead projector and markers.	projektor gihaz li-'arD Sowar 'ala sh-shasha wi shuwayyit i'lam molawwana.	jihāz'ariDh slāydāt w-aqlām ta'shir.	makanat 'arD 'slaidz' w-ālēm la takhTiT.	ālit 'arD wa aglām khāSa li ālit al-'arD .

Emergencies and Safety

	EGYPTIAN	IRAQI	LEBANESE	SAUDI
Help!	ilHa'ūni!	sā'dūni!; arīd musā'ada!	ilHa'ūni n-najda!	al-Hagūni!
Fire!	Hari'a!	Hariga!	Hari'!	Hariga!
I need a doctor.	(ana) miHtāg/miHtāga doktōr.	aHtāj Tabib.	ana miHtēj/miHtēji Tabib.	miHtāj dōktōr/Tabib.
Call an ambulance!	oTlobuli l-is'āf!	khabru il-as'āf!	(u)Tlub/(u)Tlubi (siyyaret) is'āf!	ittaSil bi-l-is'āf!
What happened?	ēh illi HaSal?	shil-qiSSa?, shinu Sār?, shaku?	shu Sār?	ēsh HaSal?

	EGYPTIAN	IRAQI	LEBANESE	SAUDI
I/My wife/My husband/My friend/Someone…	ana/mrāti/gōzi/SaHbi (SaHbiti, f.)/fi wāHid (waHda, f.)…	āni/zawijti/zawji/Sadiqi/wāHid…	ana/marti/jōzi/rifi'i/shakhS…	anā/zōjti/zōji/sāHbi/zimili/shakhiS…
am/is very sick.	'ayyān/'ayyāna awi.	kullish mariDH/mariDHa.	mariD/mariDa ktir.	mariD bilmarra.
am/is having a heart attack.	gatli/gatlu (m.)/ gatlaha (f.) azma fi l-alb.	'indi/'idha/'inda nawba qalbiyya.	ijit li/lu/la azmi albiyye; ijit li/lu/la kriza bi l-alb.	'indi sakta galbiyya.
am/is choking.	'andi/'andaha (f.)/ 'andu (m.) 'ikhtinā'	da-akhtinig/da-tikhtinig/da-yikhtinig.	bghoSS/byighoSS/bitghoSS.	batkhinig.
am/is losing consciousness.	beyoghma 'alayya/beyoghma 'alēha (f.)/beyoghma 'aleih (m.).	dā-afqid/da-tifqid/da-yifqid il-wa'i.	faqadt/faqad il-wē'i.	hayughma 'alayya.
am/is about to vomit.	Hasis inni Hastafragh (m.)/ Hassa inni Hastafragh (f.), Hasis innu Hayestafragh (m.)/ Hassa innaha Hatistafragh (f.)	rāH astafrigh/tistafrigh/yistafrigh.	raH istafrigh/irēj'.	hastafragh.
am/is having a seizure.	gatli/gatlaha (f.)/gatlu (m.) sakta (nōba)	'indi/'idha/inda nawbat Sara'.	ijit li/lu/la nawbe maraDiyye.	'indi nōba dimaghiyya.
am/is stuck.	itzana'it w-mish 'ārif akhrog/'ārfa tokhrog (f.)/ 'ārif yokhrog (m.).	maHshūr/maHshūra.	'al'ān/'al'āni.	maHbūs.
I can't breathe.	mish ādir atnaffis.	mā agdar atnaffas.	mish ēdir/ēdri itnaffas.	manni gādir atnaffis.
I tripped and fell.	itka'abilt wi-w'e't.	'itharit w-TiHt.	zallēt ijri w-wa'et.	TiHt.
I broke my bone.	'andi 'aDma in-kasarit.	ksarit 'aDHmi.	kassart 'aDmi.	'indi 'aDma maksūra.
I cut myself.	garaHt nafsi.	jraHit rūHi; injiraHit.	jaraHt/a'Ta'et Hāli.	jaraHt nafsi.
I have a food poisoning.	gali tasammum min el-akl.	'indi tasammum bi l-akil.	'indi tasmim ghizē.	'indi tasammum.
I don't know.	ma'rafsh, mish 'ārif.	mā adri.	ma b'ārif.	ma adri/manni 'ārif.

	EGYPTIAN	IRAQI	LEBANESE	SAUDI
I've injured my...	'awwart...	'indi iSāba bi...	jaraHet, rawwaHet...	sa'alt'an...
head	rāsi	rāsi	rāsi	rāsi
neck	ra-'abti	rugubti	ra'bti	ragabati
back	Dahri	DHahri	Dahri	Dahri
arm	dirā'i	dhrā'i	idi	Sā'idi
leg	regli	rijli	fakhdi	rijli
foot	adami	rijli; qadami	ijri	gadami
eye(s)	'ēni/'enayya	'ēni/'yūni	'ayni	'ēni/'iyūni
I've been robbed.	it-sara't.	nsiraqit.	sara'ūni.	itsaraqt.

502

GLOSSARY

1. Words in the Arabic–English Glossary are alphabetized according to the English alphabet, by the first letter of the transliterated word. Arabic words appearing in Lessons 1 to 15 are included.

2. Arabic words beginning with an upper-case letter in transliteration follow the words beginning with a lower-case letter. For example, words beginning with *D* follow those beginning with *d*.

3. Arabic letters represented by digraphs in transliteration are alphabetized in their own category. For example, words beginning with *dh* follow words beginning with *d*.

4. Verbs are cited in the third person masculine singular form (the *he* form) of the perfect tense. The Form I verbs are followed by a single italicized vowel—*a*, *u*, or *i*—in parentheses. This vowel is the second vowel of the imperfect stem. Verbs with an irregular perfect stem are followed by the third person masculine singular form (the *he* form) of the imperfect tense in parentheses.

5. The citation form for nouns and adjectives is the masculine singular form. Irregular or "broken" plural forms follow the citation form in parentheses, as do irregular feminine forms.

6. The following abbreviations are used in the Glossary: *adj.* (adjective), *adv.* (adverb), *coll.* (colloquial), *comp.* (comparative), *du.* (dual), *f.* (feminine), *m.* (masculine), *n.* (noun), *pl.* (plural), *prep.* (preposition), *sg.* (singular), *sub. conj.* (subordinating conjunction), *sup.* (superlative), *v.* (verb).

ARABIC–ENGLISH GLOSSARY

‘

‘ā’ila	عائِلَة	family
‘ād (ya‘ūd)	عاد (يَعود)	to return
‘āda	عادَة	usual
fi l-‘āda	في العادَة	usually
‘ādiyya	عادِيَة	ordinary
‘ālam	عالَم	world
‘ālamī	عالَمي	international
‘ām (a‘wām)	عام (أَعْوام)	year(s)
‘āmil	عامِل	worker
‘āshiq	عاشِق	enthusiast, lover of
‘āshir	عاشِر	tenth
‘āSima (awāSim)	عاصِمَة (عَواصِم)	capital city
‘adad	عَدَد	number, a number of
‘adan	عَدَن	Aden (a city in Yemen)
‘addād	عَدَّاد	meter; counter
‘ahd	عَهْد	era
‘ala	عَلى	on; toward; in the manner of
‘alā Hasab	عَلى حَسَب	according to
‘alim (a)	عَلِم	to learn
‘amil (a)	عَمِل	to work
‘amaliyya jirāHiyya	عَمَلِيَّة جِراحِيَّة	surgical operation
‘an	عَنْ	from; about
‘anā (ya‘ni)	عَنى (يَعْني)	to mean
‘aqd	عَقْد	convening
‘aqd (‘uqūd)	عَقْد (عُقود)	contract(s)
‘arūs	عَروس	bride
‘aris	عَريس	groom
‘arabiyya	عَرَبِيَّة	Arabic

‘araf (i)	عَرَف	to know
‘ashara	عَشَرَة	ten
‘aSr	عَصْر	age, era
‘ayn (‘aynān)	عَيْن (عَيْنان)	eye(s)
‘azīz	عَزيز	dear
‘ibāra ‘an	عِبارَة عَن	meaning, equivalent to
‘ilm	عِلْم	knowledge
‘inab	عِنَب	grapes
‘inda	عِنْدَ	at; around; have (with pronoun)
‘indama	عِنْدَمَا	when
‘iqd (‘uqūd)	عِقْد (عُقود)	necklace(s)
‘uDw (a‘Dā’)	عُضْو (أَعْضاء)	member(s)
‘ulwī	عُلْوي	upper
‘umla	عُمْلَة	currency
‘ulā’ika	أوْلَئِكَ	those

a

āb	آبْ	August
ādhār	آذار	March
alaysa kadhālik?	أَلَيْسَ كَذَلِك	Right?, Isn't it so?
a‘jab	أَعْجَب	to please, to like
a‘lan anna	أَعْلَن أَنَّ	to announce
a‘Tā (yu‘Ti)	أَعْطى (يُعْطي)	to give
a‘zab (‘uzzāb)	أَعْزَب (عُزّاب)	single(s)
abū DHabi	أَبو ظَبْي	Abu Dhabi
abyaD	أَبْيَض	white
adā (adawāt)	أداة (أَدَوات)	utensil(s); tool(s)

addā (yu'addī) ilā	أَدَّى (يُوَدِّي) إلى	to lead to; to result in		alū?	ألو	Hello? (on the phone)
aDHāfir	أظافِر	nails		alam	ألَم	pain
afDal	أفْضَل	better, preferable		alf (alāf)	ألْف (آلاف)	thousand(s)
aHabb	أحَبّ	to like, to love		alladhī	الَّذي	which
aHad 'ashara	أحَدَ عَشَرَ	eleven		allāh	الله	God
ahamiyya	أهمِيَّة	importance		wa-llāhi?	واللهِ	By God!, Really?, Is that so?
ahhala (yu'ahhil)	أهَّلَ (يُؤهِّل)	to qualify (someone)		in shā' allāh	إن شاء الله	God willing!
ahl	أهْل	family		al-Hamdulillāh	الحَمْدُ لله	Praise (be) to God.
ahlan!	أهْلاً	Welcome!; Hello!		allatī	الَّتي	which, that which (f.)
ahlan! wa-sahlan	أهْلاً وَسَهْلاً	Welcome!; Hello!		am	أمْ	or (in questions)
aHmar	أحْمَر	red		amkan (yumkin)	أمْكَنَ (يُمكِن)	to be able
ajjal (yu'ajjil)	أجَّل (يُؤجِّل)	to postpone		ammā bin-nisba li	أمّا بالنِسْبَة لِ	as for
ajjar (yu'ajjir)	أجَّر (يؤجِّر)	to rent		amrīkī	أمْريكي	American
ajinda	أجِنْدَة	agenda		ams	أمْس	yesterday
ajnabī	أجْنَبي	foreign		amti'a	أمْتِعَة	luggage
akal (u)	أكَل	to eat		an	أنْ	to (as in I want to go)
akhadh (u)	أخَذ	to take		ana	أنا	I
akhDar	أخْضَر	green		anf	أنْف	nose
akhiSSā'ī	أخِصائي	specialist		anna	أنَّ	that (sub. conj.)
akl	أكْل	food		anta	أنْتَ	you (m.)
akthar	أكْثَر	more		anti	أنْتِ	you (f.)
al-ān	الآن	now		arā (yurī)	أرى (يُري)	to show
al-baHar al-mutawassiT	البَحْر المتَوَسِّط	Mediterranean Sea		arād (yurīd)	أراد (يُريد)	to want
al-baHrayn	البَحْرَيْن	Bahrain		arāmkū asa'ūdiyya	أرامكو السَعُودِيَّة	Saudi Aramco
al-jazā'ir	الجَزائِر	Algeria		arba'a	أرْبَعَة	four
al-kuwayt	الكُوَيْت	Kuwait		arba'at 'ashara	أرْبَعَة عَشَرَ	fourteen
al-maghrib	المَغْرب	Morocco		arba'umi'a	أرْبَعُمائة	four hundred
as-sa'udiyya	السَعُودِيَّة	Saudi Arabia				
ash-sharq al-awsaT	الشَرْق الأوْسَط	the Middle East				

arD (arāD)	أَرْض (أَراض)	land(s)
aSbaH (yuSbiH)	أَصْبَح (يُصْبِح)	to become
aSfar	أَصْفَر	yellow
ashfaq 'alā	أَشْفَق على	to sympathize with
'asif (a)	أَسِف	to be sorry
āsif	آسِف	to be sorry, to be regretful
aSl	أَصْل	origin
aswad	أَسْوَد	black
aswān	أَسْوان	Aswan (a city in Southern Egypt)
ata (ya'ti)	أَتَى (يَأْتي)	to come
aTall 'ala	أَطَلَّ عَلَى	to overlook
athāth	أَثاث	furnishings
aw	أَو	or
awjad (yūjid)	أَوْجَد (يوجِد)	to be found (there are)
awwal	أَوَّل	first
ayDan	أَيْضاً	also
aylūl	أَيْلول	September
ayna	أَيْنَ	where
ayy	أَيّ	any
ayyār	أَيّار	May
azma qalbiyya	أَزْمَة قَلْبِيَّة	heart attack
azraq	أَزْرَق	blue

b

bādhinjān	باذِنْجان	eggplant
bāHith	باحِث	researcher
bāi'	بائِع	seller
ba'īd	بعيد	far away
ba'D	بَعْض	some
ba'd	بَعْد	after
badā (yabdū)	بَدا (يَبْدو)	to seem, to appear

bada' (a)	بَدَأ	to begin
baHath' an (a)	بَحَث عَن	to search for
bal	بَلْ	(and) even, rather, however
bana (yabni)	بَنى (يَبْني)	to build
bank (bunūk)	بَنْك (بُنُوك)	bank(s)
bins	بِنس	cent
baqiya (yabqā)	بَقِيَ (يَبْقى)	to stay
bayDā'	بَيْضاء	white
bayna	بَينَ	between
baynamā	بَيْنَما	while
bayrūt	بَيْروت	Beirut
bayt (buyūt)	بَيْت (بُيوت)	house(s)
bi	بِ	by means of; at, in, with
bi jānib	بِجانِب	beside
bi D-DabT	بالضَّبْط	exactly
bi dūn	بِدون	without
bi dāya	بِدايَة	beginning
bi kam	بِكَم	how much?, for how much?
bi khilāf	بِخِلاف	as opposed to
bi l-kāmil	بالكامِل	all of it
bi T-Tab'	بالطَّبْع	of course
bulbul	بُلْبُل	nightingale
bint	بِنت	girl; daughter
bitrūl	بِتْرول	petroleum
buhār	بُهار	spice
bunn	بُنّ	coffee grounds
bunni	بُنّيّ	brown
burghul	بُرْغُل	bulgur wheat
burtuqāli	بُرْتُقالي	orange (color)
burtuqāla	بُرْتُقالَة	orange (fruit)

506

d

dā'iman	دائماً	always
dākhil	داخِل	inside
dūna	دُونَ	without
dafa'a (a)	دَفَع	to pay
dajāj	دَجاج	chicken
dakhal (u)	دَخَل	to enter
dakhkhan	دَخّن	to smoke
dalīl siyāHī	دَليل سِياحي	guidebook
daqīqa (daqā'iq)	دَقيقة (دَقائِق)	minute(s)
daraja	دَرَجَة	extent, degree
daras (u)	دَرَس	to study
dawlī	دَوْلي	international
dimashq	دِمَشْق	Damascus
disambir	ديسَمْبِر	December
duktōr	دُكْتور	doctor
dulāb	دولاب	armoire; closet
dulār	دولار	dollar

D

Dayf (Duyūf)	ضَيْف (ضُيوف)	guest(s)
Dayyiqa	ضَيِّقَة	narrow

dh

dhākar	ذاكر	to study
dhū (dhāt)	ذو (ذات)	having, endowed with
dhahab (a)	ذَهَب	to go
dhahab	ذَهَب	gold (metal)
dhahabī	ذَهَبيّ	golden (adj.)
dhalik	ذَلِك	that (m. sg.)
dhawq	ذَوْقُ	taste, politeness
dhirā' (dhirā'an, du.)	ذِراع (ذِراعان)	arm(s)

DH

DHāhira	ظاهِرَة	phenomenon
DHahr	ظَهْر	back
DHuhr	ظُهْر	midday
DHuhūr	ظُهور	appearance

f

fāks	فاكْس	fax
fa'al (a)	فَعَل	to do
fa'ra	فَأْرَة	mouse
faDā'iya	فَضائِيَّة	satellite channel
faDDal	فَضَّل	to prefer
min faDlik	مِن فَضْلِك	please
fakkar fī	فَكَّر في	to think about
fals (fulūs)	فَلْس (فُلوس)	penny
faqaT	فَقَط	only
farq (furūq)	فَرْق (فُروق)	difference(s)
fashal	فَشَل	failure
faSl	فَصْل	separation
faSl	فَصْل	semester; season
fī	في	in
fi'lan	فِعْلاً	truly
fibrāyir	فِبْراير	February
fiDDī	فِضيّ	silver (adj.)
fiDDa	فِضَّة	silver (metal)
finizwīlā	فِنِزويلا	Venezuela
firqa	فِرْقَة	band
funduq (fanādiq)	فُنْدُق (فَنادِق)	hotel(s)

gh

ghālī (aghlā)	غالي (أغْلَى)	expensive (more expensive)
ghadā'	غَداء	lunch
ghadan	غَدَاً	tomorrow

gharbī	غَرْبِي	Western
ghaTTā (yughaTTi)	غَطَّى (يُغَطِّي)	to cover
ghayr	غَيْر	not
ghayyar	غَيَّر	to change (something)
ghurfa (ghuraf)	غُرْفَة (غُرَف)	room(s)

h

hādha	هَذَا	this (m.)
hām	هَامّ	important
hāmburgar	هَامْبُورجَر	hamburger
ha'ula'i	هَؤُلَاء	these
hadiyya	هَدِيَّة	gift
hādha	هَذَا	this (m.)
hādhihi	هَذِهِ	this (f.)
hal	هَلْ	question particle (in yes-no questions)
handasa	هَنْدَسَة	engineering
huna	هُنَا	here
hunāk	هُنَاك	there

H

Hādī 'ashar	حَادِي عَشَر	eleventh
Hadīqa	حَدِيقَة	garden
Hadīth	حَدِيث	modern
Huzn	حُزْن	sadness
HaDratak	حَضْرَتَك	your excellence
Hāfila	حَافِلَة	bus
Hafla	حَفْلَة	party
Hajz	حَجْز	reservation
Hakā (yaHki)	حَكَى (يَحْكِي)	to tell
Hāl	حَال	situation; condition
Hāla	حَالَة	condition; situation; case

fi hādhihī l-Hāla	فِي هَذِه الحَالَة	in that case
Halawayāt	حَلَوَيات	desserts; sweets
Hamal (i)	حَمَل	to carry; to lift
Haml	حَمْل	carrying, lifting; pregnancy
Hammām	حمَّام	bathroom
Haqība (Haqā'ib)	حقِيبة (حَقَائِب)	bag(s)
Haqq (Huqūq)	حَقّ (حُقُوق)	right(s)
Harām	حَرَام	forbidden; shame
yā Harām!	يا حَرَام!	Oh, what a shame! (coll.)
Haraka	حَرَكَة	movement
Hārr	حَارّ	hot
HaSal 'alā(u)	حَصَل عَلَى	to earn, to be awarded, to get
Hattā	حَتَّى	even
Hawālī	حَوَالِي	approximately
Hāwal	حَاوَل	to try
Hawla	حَوْلَ	about; surrounding
Hayā	حَيَاة	life
Hazīrān	حَزِيران	June
Hijāb (aHjiba)	حِجَاب (أَحْجِيَة)	veil(s)
Hujra	حُجْرَة	room
Hukūma	حكُومَة	government
Hulw	حلُو	sweet, pretty, nice
HummuS	حمُّص	chickpeas, garbanzo beans
Hurrīya	حُرِّية	freedom
HuSūl 'ala	حُصُول عَلَى	obtaining

i

i'Tā'	إعْطَاء	giving
i'taqad anna	اعْتَقَد أَنَّ	to think; to believe that

ibn	اِبْن	son
ibrīl	إِبْريل	April
iDāfa	إِضافَة	addition
bi l-iDāfa ila	بِالإِضافَة إِلى	in addition to
idhā	إِذا	if
iDTurr an	اِضْطُرّ أَن	to be forced to
iHtāj	اِحْتاج	to need
iHtilāl	اِحْتِلال	occupation
ijād	إِيْجاد	finding
ījār	إِيْجار	rent
ijāza	إِجازة	vacation
ikhtār	اِختار	to choose
ikhtiyār	اِختِيار	choice
iktasab	اِكْتَسَب	to gain
iktatab	اِكْتَتَب	to make a copy
ilā	إِلى	to
illa	إِلّا	except
imrā'a (nisā')	اِمْرأة (نِساء)	woman (women)
imtiHān	اِمْتِحان	exam
imtala'	اِمْتَلأ	to be filled
inbasaT	اِنْبَسَطَ	to have fun
intarnit	إِنْتَرنت	Internet
intaDHar	اِنْتَظِر	to wait
irtada	اِرْتَدي	to wear
irtafa'	اِرْتَفَع	to increase
ishatara (yashtarī)	اِشْتَرى (يَشْتَري)	to buy
ishtarak fi	اِشْتَرَك في	to partake in, to share, to participate in
iSlāH	إِصْلاح	reform
ism (asmā')	اِسْم (أَسْماء)	name(s)
istakhdam	اِسْتَخْدَم	to use
istama' ilā	اِسْتَمِعْ إِلى	to listen to
istamarr	اِسْتَمَرّ	to continue

istaTā' (yastaTī')	اِسْتَطاع (يَسْتَطيع)	to be able
isteqbāl	اِسْتِقْبال	reception; welcome
isti'lāmāt	اِسْتِعْلامات	information
istithnā'	اِسْتِثْناء	exception
itharnit	إِيثَرنيت	Ethernet
ithnān (ithnatn)	اِثْنان (اِثْنَتان)	two
ittafaq	اِتَّفَق	to agree

j

jū'	جوع	hunger
jāmi'a	جامِعة	university
jāmi'at ad-duwal al-'arabiyya	جامِعَة الدُوَل العَرَبِيَّة	the Arab League
jadīd (judud)	جَديد (جُدُد)	new
jadda	جَدَّة	grandmother
jalābiyya	جَلابِيَّة	a traditional robe, nightshirt
jamā'ī	جَماعي	collective
jamīl	جَميل	beautiful
jary	جَرْي	running
jawāz as-safar	جَواز السَفَر	passport
jaw'ān	جَوْعان	hungry
jaww	جَوّ	weather
jayyid	جَيِّد	good, well
jiddan	جِداً	very
jins	جِنْس	sex, gender
junayh	جُنَيْه	pound (currency)

k

kayfa	كَيْفَ	how
kāfi	كافي	enough
kān (yakūn)	كان (يكون)	to be

kānūn al-awwal	كانون الأوَّل	December		khadam (i)	خَدَم	to serve
				khamsa	خَمْسة	five
kānūn ath-thānī	كانون الثاني	January		khamsat 'ashara	خَمْسة عَشَر	fifteen
kāsīt	كاسيت	cassette		khamsumi'a	خَمْسُمائة	five hundred
kātab	كاتَب	to correspond with		kharif	خَريف	fall (season)
kabāb	كَباب	kebabs, spiced meat grilled on a skewer		khāSS	خاصّ	private; specific; special
kabīr (kibār) (kubrā)	كَبير (كِبار) (كُبْرى)	big (big, pl.) (big, f.)		khaTa' (akhTā')	خَطَأ (أَخْطَاء)	fault; mistake(s)
kallaf (i)	كَلَّف	to cost		khayr	خَيْر	well-being
kam	كَم	how many		khibra	خِبْرة	experience; expertise
kamā	كَما	similarly, as; as well		khilāf	خِلاف	difference; division
kathīr (akthar)	كَثير (أَكْثَر)	many (more)		khilāl	خِلال	through
				khiyār	خيار	cucumbers
kibbi	كِبّة	Lebanese dish consisting of meat and bulgur wheat		khubz	خُبْز	bread
				khuSūSiyya	خُصوصِيَّة	privacy
kubayba	كُبَيْبَة	meatballs		khuTūT aT-Tayarān	خُطوط الطيران	airline
kufta	كُفْتة	spiced ground beef grilled on a skewer				
kull	كُلّ	every		**l**		
kumbiyūtar	كُمْبيوتر	computer		lāHiq	لاحِق	later
kura	كُرَة	ball		lākin	لَكِن	but
kurat al-qadam	كُرَة القَدَم	football		la	لا	no, not
kursī (karāsī)	كُرْسي (كَراسي)	chair(s)		lada	لَدَى	at, by, with; have (with pronoun)
				ladhīdh	لَذيذ	delicious, good
kh				lahja	لَهْجَة	dialect
khāf (yakhāf) an	خاف (يَخاف) أن	to fear		laHm	لَحْم	meat
khāl	خال	maternal uncle		lama' (yalma')	لَمَع (يَلْمَع)	to shine
khāmis	خامِس	fifth		lan	لَنْ	not (future negation particle)
khārijī	خارِجي	foreign				
khāTiba	خاطِبَة	matchmaker		law	لَوْ	if
khabar (akhbār)	خَبَر (أَخْبار)	news		layla (layālī)	لَيْلَة (لَيالي)	night(s)
				laysa	لَيْسَ	to not be

510

lī	لِ	for, to, in order; to have (with pronoun)	maghrib	مَغْرِب	West, sunset
			maghribī	مَغْرِبي	Moroccan
lībī	ليبي	Libyan	maHall	مَحَلّ	shop
līrā	ليرة	pound	maHallī	مَحَلّي	local
līsans	ليسانْس	B.A. (college degree)	maHrūq	مَحْروق	burnt
li'anna	لأنّ	because	makān (amākin)	مكان (أَماكِن)	place(s)
lidhālik	لِذَلِك	for that reason	maktab (makātib)	مَكْتَب (مَكاتِب)	office(s)
likayy	لِكَيْ	in order to	min al-mumkin an	مِنْ المُمْكِن أن	it is possible that
li l-'āsaf	للأَسَف	unfortunately			
li mādhā	لِمَاذا	why	malī'	مَلِيء	full
limuddat	لِمُدَّة	for a period of	malābis	مَلابِس	clothing
lubnānī	لُبْناني	Lebanese	malaff	مَلَفّ	file
lugha	لُغة	language	mamarr	مَمَرّ	corridor
			maqarr (maqārr)	مَقَرّ (مَقَارّ)	headquarter(s)

m

mā	ما	that which; what	maqhā (maqāhi)	مَقْهى (مَقاهي)	coffee shop(s)
mā zāl	ما زال	still *(adv.)*			
māDī	مَاضي	past	marHaban bik	مَرْحَباً بك	welcome
mādhā	ماذا	what	masā' (umsiya)	مَسَاء (أُمْسِية)	evening(s)
mākina	ماكينَة	machine			
māras	مارَس	to practice	masāfa	مَسافة	distance
māris	مارِس	March	mas'ūla	مَسْؤُولَة	responsible
mūsīqi	موسيقيّ	musical	maSdar (maSādir)	مَصْدَر (مَصادِر)	source(s)
māt (yamūt)	مات (يَموت)	to die			
ma'a	مَعَ	with	mashā (yamshī)	مَشَى (يَمْشي)	to walk
ma'a s-salāma	مَعَ السَلامَة	good-bye			
			mashghūl	مَشْغول	busy
ma'lūmāt	مَعْلومات	information	mashrūbāt	مَشْروبات	drinks
ma'rūf	مَعْرُوف	well-known	mashriq	مَشْرِق	East
mabnā (mabān)	مَبْنى (مَبان)	building(s)	mashwiyyāt	مَشْوِيَّات	grilled meats
madīna (mudun)	مَدينة (مُدُن)	city (cities)	matā	مَتَى	when (in questions)
madrasa (madāris)	مَدْرَسَة (مَدارِس)	school(s)	mathaf	مَتْحَف	museum
			maTār	مَطَار	airport
mafrūm	مَفْروم	ground	maT'am (maTā'im)	مَطْعَم (مَطاعِم)	restaurant(s)

maTbakh (maTābikh)	مَطْبَخ (مَطابِخ)	kitchen(s)
maTlūb	مَطْلوب	demanded, required, requested
mawqi' 'ala ash-shabaka	مَوْقِع عَلى الشَّبَكة	Web site
mayū	مايو	May
maydān at-taHrīr	مَيْدان التَّحْرير	Tahrir Square (in downtown Cairo)
mi'dda	مِعْدَة	stomach
mi'a	مائَة	one hundred
mi'a bil-mi'a	مائَة بِالمائة	one hundred percent
min	مِنْ	from
min ajl	مِنْ أَجْل	for the sake of
minTaqa (manāTiq)	مِنْطقة (مَناطِق)	region(s)
misāHa	مِساحَة	area
miS'ad	مِصْعَد	elevator
misr	مِصْر	Egypt
mismār	مِسْمار	nail
mithl	مِثْل	like
mizmār	مِزْمار	flute
mu'āqaba	مُعاقَبَة	punishment
mu'āriD	مُعارِض	opponent
mu'DHam	مُعْظَم	most, the majority
mu'ahhil	مُؤَهِّل	qualification
mu'akkad	مُؤَكَّد	certain
min al-mu'akkad anna	مِنْ المُؤَكَّد أَنّ	it is certain that
mudīr	مُدير	director
mudarris	مُدَرِّس	teacher
mudda	مُدَّة	a period of time
muHāfaDHa	مُحافَظَة	conservatism, county
muHallil	مُحَلِّل	analyst
muhandis	مُهَنْدِس	engineer

muHarrir	مُحَرِّر	editor
mumarriD	مُمَرِّض	nurse
munāqasha	مُناقَشة	discussion
munāsib	مُناسِب	appropriate
murūr	مُرور	traffic
murashshaH	مُرَشَّح	candidate
musāfir	مُسافِر	traveler
mushkila (mashākil)	مُشْكِلَة (مَشاكِل)	problem(s)
mustaqbal	مُسْتَقْبَل	future
mustashfa	مُسْتَشْفى	hospital
muta'akkid	مُتَأَكِّد	sure
muwāfiq	مُوافِق	agreed
muwāSafāt	مُواصَفات	characteristics
muwaDHDHaf	مُوَظَّف	bureaucrat; employee
muzdaHima	مُزْدَحِمَة	crowded

n

nās	ناس	people
na'am	نَعَمْ	yes
anfaq (yunfiq)	أَنْفَق (يُنْفِق)	to spend
nafs	نَفْس	the same
najma (nujūm)	نَجْمة (نُجوم)	star(s)
naql	نَقْل	moving
naw'	نَوْع	kind
naDHar (u) ilā	نَظَر إِلى	to look at
naDHDHam	نَظَّم	to organize
nihāya	نِهايَة	end
nisān	نيسان	April
niSf	نِصْف	half
nuvambir	نوفَمْبِر	November

q

qād (yaqūd)	قاد (يَقود)	to lead
qādima	قادِمَة	next; coming
al-qāhira	القاهِرة	Cairo
qārra	قارّة	continent
qabil (a)	قَبِل	to accept
qabl	قَبْل	before
qad	قَدْ	already (with perfect); maybe (with imperfect)
qadīm	قَديم	old
qafz	قَفْز	jumping
qalam (aqlām)	قَلَم (أَقْلام)	pen
qalb	قَلْب	heart
qalīl (aqall)	قَليل (أَقَلّ)	little (less)
'alal-aqall	عَلَى الأَقَلّ	at least
qalīl min	قَليل مِن	a little of
qall (yaqill)	قَلَّ عَنْ	to be less than
qallal min	قَلَّل مِن	to lessen
qanā (qanawāt)	قَناة (قَنَوات)	channel(s)
qarīb	قَريب	close
qarīb (aqārib)	قَريب (أَقارِب)	relative(s)
qarrar	قَرَّر	to decide
qaSīr	قَصير	short
qimma	قِمَّة	summit
qirā'a	قِراءَة	reading
qirfa	قِرْفَة	cinnamon
qiTār	قِطار	train

r

rābi'	الرّابِع	fourth
ra'ā	رأى (يَرَى)	to see
ra'y	رَأْي	opinion

ra'īsī	رَئيسي	principal, main
ra'īsat at-taHarīr	رَئيسَة التَّحْرير	editor-in-chief (f.)
ra's	رَأْس	head
rabī'	رَبيع	spring (season)
raghīf (arghifa)	رَغيف (أَرْغِفَة)	loaf (loaves)
rajā (yarjū) an	رَجا (يَرْجو) أن	to hope that
rajul (rijāl)	رَجُل (رِجال)	man (men)
rajul a'māl	رَجُل أَعْمال	businessperson
rakhīS (arkhaS)	رَخيص (أَرْخَص)	cheap (cheaper)
raqam (arqām)	رَقَم (أَرْقام)	number(s)
rasmī	رَسْمي	official
riHla	رِحْلَة	trip
riyāDī	رِياضي	athletic
riyāl	رِيال	riyal (unit of currency)
rubbamā	رُبَّما	maybe
rukba (rukab)	رُكْبَة (رُكَب)	knee(s)

s

sā'a	ساعَة	hour
sā'd 'alā	ساعِد عَلَى	to help
sā'iH	سائِحَ	tourist
sābi'	سابِعئ	seventh
sādis	سادِس	sixth
sāfar	سافَر	to travel
sākin (sukkān)	ساكِن (سُكّان)	resident(s)
sūq (aswāq)	سوق (أَسْواق)	market(s)
sāq (sāqān, du.)	ساق (ساقان)	leg(s)
sūrī	سوري	Syrian

sūriyā	سُوريا	Syria
sa'ūdi	سَعُودِي	Saudi Arabian
sab'a	سَبْعَة	seven
sab'at 'ashara	سَبْعَة عَشَر	seventeen
saba'umi'a	سَبْعُمائة	seven hundred
sabab (asbāb)	سَبَب (أَسْباب)	reason(s)
sabaH (a)	سَبَح	to swim
safārī	سَفاري	safari
safar	سَفَر	traveling; trip, journey
sahl	سَهْل	easy
sakan (u)	سكَن	to live, to reside
sakani	سكَنِي	residential
salaTa	سَلَطَة	salad
samā'	سَماء	sky
sana (sinīn)	سَنَة (سِنِين)	year(s)
sarīr (asirra)	سَرِير (أَسِرَّة)	bed(s)
sawfa	سَوْفَ	(it) will
saynā'	سَيْناء	Sinai Peninsula
sayyi'	سَيِّئ	bad
si'r (as'ār)	سِعْر (أَسْعار)	price(s); rate(s)
si'r Sarf	سِعْر صَرْف	exchange rate
sibtambir	سِبْتَمْبِر	September
sijāra (sajā'ir)	سيجارة (سَجائِر)	cigarette(s)
silsila (salāsil)	سِلْسِلة (سَلاسِل)	chain(s)
sitta	سِتَّة	six
sittat 'ashara	سِتَّة عَشَر	sixteen
sittumi'a	سِتُّمائة	six hundred
siyāHa	سِياحَة	tourism
siyāsī	سِياسي	political
suftwir	سوفْتوير	software

S

SāHib	صاحِب	owner
Sāla	صالَة	living room
Sālat al-Haqā'ib	صالَة الحَقائِب	baggage claim
Sālat at-tamrīnāt ar-riyāDiyya	صالَة التَّمْرينات الرياضيَّة	gym
Sāra (yaSīr)	صار (يَصير)	to become
SabāH al-khayr.	صَباح الْخَيْر	Good morning.
SabāH an-nūr.	صَباح النّور	Good morning. (response)
Sadīq (aSdiqā')	صَديق (أَصْدِقاء)	friend(s)
Saddaq anna	صَدَّق أنَّ	to believe that
SaHāfa	صَحافَة	journalism, press
SaHafī	صَحَفي	journalist
SaHīH	صَحيح	true
SaHarā'	صَحْراء	desert
San'ā'	صَنْعاء	San'a, (the capital of Yemen)
Sirāfa	صِرافة	currency exchange
Saraf (i)	صَرَف	to spend, to exchange currency
Sarf	صَرْف	exchange (currency)
Sayf	صَيْف	summer
Sifr	صِفْر	zero
Sirā'	صِراع	struggle

sh

shay' (ashyā')	شَيْء (أَشْياء)	thing(s)
shāsha	شاشة	monitor
shāTi' al-baHr	شاطِئ البَحْر	the beach
shāy	شّاي	tea

sha'ar (yash'ur)	شَعَر (يَشْعُر)	to feel		taghayyar	تَغَيَّر	to change (oneself)
sha'r	شَعْر	hair		taHaddath	تَحَدَّث	to speak
shabaka	شَبَكَة	net		taHakkam	تَحَكَّم	to control
shāhad	شاهَد	to watch		taHassun	تَحَسُّن	getting better
shahr (shuhūr)	شَهْر (شُهور)	month(s)		taHiyya	تَحِيَّة	greetings
shakhS (ashkhāS)	شَخْص (أَشْخَاص)	person (people)		takallam	تَكَلَّم	to speak
				takattul	تَكَتُّل	bloc
shaqqa (shuqaq)	شَقَّة (شُقَق)	apartment(s)		takawwan min	تَكَوَّن مِن	to be made up of
				takharruj	تَخَرُّج	to graduate; graduation
sharik	شَريك	partner				
sharib (a)	شَرِب	to drink		tamm (i)	تَمّ	to be achieved
shaTira	شَطيرَة	sandwich		tammūz	تَمّوز	July
shahāda	شَهادَة	degree, testimony		tamrin	تَمْرين	exercise
shitā'	شِتاء	winter		tanaqqal	تَنَقَّل	to move; to get around
shubāT	شُباط	February				
shukran	شُكْراً	thank you		tanaqqul	تَنَقُّل	transportation
shurfa	شُرْفَة	balcony		tanāwal	تَناوَل	to eat, partake of food

t

taksī	تاكْسِي	taxi		taqlīdī	تَقْليدي	traditional
tūnisi	تونِسي	Tunisian		tashāwar	تَشاوَر	to consult
tāsi'	تاسِع	ninth		tasharraf	تَشَرَّف	to be honored
ta'āruf	تَعارُف	acquaintance, getting to know		taSwir	تَصْوير	copying
				tawāfar	تَوافَر	to be available
ta'allam	تَعَلَّم	to learn		tawaqqa'	تَوَقَّع	to expect
ta'arraf 'alā	تَعَرَّف عَلَى	to meet; get to know		tiknulūjya	تِكْنولوجيا	technology
ta'akkad min	تَأَكَّد مِن	to make sure of		tilifūn	تِليفون	telephone
ta'jil	تَأْجيل	postponement		tilifizyūn	تِليفِزْيون	television
ta'khir	تَأْخير	delay		tilka	تِلْكَ	that (f. sg.)
tabbūli	تَبُّولة	tabouli (salad)		tis'a	تِسْعَة	nine
tadhkara (tadhakir)	تَذْكَرَة (تَذاكِر)	ticket(s)		tis'at 'ashara	تِسْعَة عَشَرَ	nineteen
				tis'umi'a	تِسْعُمائة	nine hundred
tadrīb	تَدْريب	training		tishrīn al-awwal	تِشْرين الأَوَّل	October
tafaDDal	تَفَضَّل	if you please		tishrīn ath-thāni	تِشْرين الثَّاني	November
tafkīr	تَفْكير	thinking				

T

Tā'ira	طائرة	airplane
Tābiq (Tawābiq)	طابِق (طَوابِق)	story (of a building)
Tālib (Tulāb)	طالِب (طُلاَّب)	student(s)
Ta'ām	طَعام	food
Tabīb (aTibbā')	طَبيب (أطِبَّاء)	doctor(s), physician(s)
Tab'an	طَبْعاً	of course, certainly
Tabaq (aTbāq)	طَبَق (أطْباق)	dish(es); plate(s)
Talab	طَلَب	an order
Talab (u)	طَلَب	to order
Tawīl	طَويل	tall
Tayarān	طَيَران	flying
Tayyib	طَيِّب	delicious, good
Tibā'a	طِياعة	typing
Tibqan li	طِيْقاً لِـ	according to
Tawāl	طَوال	all along; the length of

th

thālith	ثالِث	third
thāmin	ثامِن	eighth
thānī	ثاني	second
thānī 'ashar	ثاني عَشَر	twelfth
thalātha	ثلاثة	three
thalāthat 'ashara	ثلاثة عَشَر	thirteen
thalāthumi'a	ثَلاثُمائة	three hundred
thamānia	ثَمانية	eight
thamāniat 'ashara	ثَمانية عَشَر	eighteen
thamānimi'a	ثَمانِمائة	eight hundred
thaman	ثَمَن	price
thiql (athqāl)	ثِقْل (أثْقال)	weight(s)

thumma	ثُمَّ	then; so
thumma inna	ثُمَ إنّ	besides

u

udhun (udhunān, du.)	أُذُن (أذنان)	ear(s)
ughustus	أغُسْطُس	August
ujriya	أُجْرِيَ	to be performed
ujra	أُجْرَة	fare
ākhar (ūkhrā)	آخَر (أخْرَى)	other (f.)
ukht (akhawāt)	أُخْت (أخَوات)	sister(s)
uktūbar	أكْتوبِر	October
urz	أُرْز	rice
uSīb bi	أُصيب بِـ	to be afflicted with
usbū' (asābī')	أُسْبوع (أسابِيع)	week(s)
usra (usar)	أُسْرة (أُسَر)	family (families)
ustādh (asātidha)	أُسْتاذ (أساتِذة)	professor, sir

w

wāhid	واحِد	one
wālid	والِد	father
wālida	والِدَة	mother
wāqi'	واقِع	actual, real; event, fact
fi l-wāqi'	في الواقِع	actually
wāsi'	واسِع	wide
wa	وَ	and
wāshinTun	واشِنْطُن	Washington
wi'ā' (aw'iya)	وِعاء (أوْعِية)	pots
waHīd	وَحيد	only
wajab (yajib)	وَجَب (يَجِب)	to be necessary
(yajib) an	أنْ	to . . .

wajad	وَجَد	to find
wajba Tayyiba!	وَجْبَة طَيِّبَة	enjoy your meal!
walākin	وَلَكِن	but
walad (awlād)	وَلَد (أَوْلاد)	boy(s)
waqqa' 'ala	وَقَّع عَلَى	to agree to, signed
waqt (awqāt)	وَقْت (أَوْقات)	time(s)
waraq (awrāq)	وَرَق (أَوْراق)	leaf (leaves); sheet(s) of paper
wasā'il an-naql	وَسائِل النَقْل	means of transport
wasīla (wasā'il)	وَسيلة (وَسائِل)	means
waSal (yaSil)	وَصَل (يَصِل)	to arrive
wasaT al-balad	وَسَط البَلَد	downtown
wazīr (wuzarā')	وَزير (وُزَراء)	minister(s)
wuSūl	وُصول	arrival

y

ya	يا	hey, oh (vocative particle)
yāsār	يَسار	left (side)
yad (yadān)	يَد (يَدان)	hand(s)
yamīn	يَمين	right (side)
yanāyir	يَناير	January
yawm	يَوْم	day
yawum al-'ithnayn	يَوْم الاثْنَيْن	Monday
yawum al-aHad	يَوْم الأحَد	Sunday
yawum al-arba'ā'	يَوْم الأرْبَعاء	Wednesday
yawum al-jum'a	يَوْم الجُمْعَة	Friday
yawum al-khamīs	يَوْم الخَميس	Thursday
yawum as-sabt	يَوْم السَّبْت	Saturday
yawum ath-thulāthā'	يَوْم الثُلاثاء	Tuesday
yawmiyyan	يَوْمياً	daily
yulyah	يولْية	July
yunyah	يونْية	June
yusrā	يُسْرَى	left (side)

z

zawāj	زَواج	marriage
zā'ir (zuwwār)	زائِر (زوَّار)	visitor(s)
zād (yazīd) 'an	زاد (يَزيد) عَن	to go over; exceed
zabūn (zabā'in)	زَبون (زَبائِن)	customer(s), client(s)
zahrī	زَهْري	pink
zahra	زَهْرة	blossom (n.)
zamīl	زَميل	colleague
zawja (zawj)	زَوْجَة (زَوْج)	wife (husband)
zawr	زَوْر	throat
ziyāra	زِيارَة	visit

517

ENGLISH–ARABIC GLOSSARY

A

about	'an; Hawl	عَنْ، حَوْل
Abu Dhabi	abū DHabī	أَبو ظَبْيْ
accept	qabil (a)	قَبِل
according to	'alā Hasab; Tibqan li	عَلىٰ حَسَب، طِبْقاً لِـ
achieve (be achieved)	tamm (i)	تَمَّ
actual	wāqi'	واقِع
actually	fi l-wāqi'	في الواقِع
Adan	'adan	عَدَن
addition	iDāfa	إِضافَة
in addition to	bi l-iDāfa ila	بِالإِضافَة إِلى
after	ba'd	بَعْدَ
age	'aSr	عَصْر
agenda	ajinda	أَجِنْدَة
agree (on)	ittafaq	اتَّفَق
agree (to)	ittafaq' 'ala	اتَّفَق عَلى
agreed	muwāfiq	مُوافِق
airline	khuTūT aT-Tayarān	خُطوط الطَّيران
airplane	Tā'ira	طائِرَة
airport	maTār	مَطار
Algeria	al-jazā'ir	الجَزائِر
all of it	bi l-kāmil	بِالكامِل
along (adv. of place)	Tawāl	طَوال
also	ayDan	أَيْضاً
always	dā'iman	دائِماً
American	amrīkī	أَمْريكي
amuse oneself	inbasaT	إِنْبَسَطَ
analyst	muHallil	مُحَلِّل
and	wa	وَ
announce (that)	a'lan anna	أَعْلَن أَنَّ
any	ayy	أَيّ
apartment	shaqqa (shuqaq)	شَقَّة (شُقَق)
appearance	DHuhūr	ظُهور
appropriate	munāsib	مُناسِب
approximately	Hawālī	حَوالي
April	ibrīl; nisān	إِبْريل، نيسان
Arab League	jāmi'at ad-duwal al-'arabiyya	جامِعَة الدُّوَل العَرَبِيَّة
Arabic (f.)	'arabiyya	عَرَبِيَّة
area	misāHa	مِساحَة
arm(s)	dhirā' (dhirā'an)	ذِراع (ذِراعان)
armoire	dulāb	دولاب
around	'inda	عِنْدَ
arrival	wuSūl	وُصول
arrive	waSal (yaSil)	وَصَل (يَصِل)
as	kamā	كَما
as for	amā bi n-nisba li . . .	أَما بِالنِّسْبَة لِـ...
as well	kamā	كَما
Aswan	aswān	أَسْوان
at	'inda, bi, lada	عِنْدَ؛ بِـ؛ لَدى
athletic	riyāDī	رِياضي
August	ughustus, āb	أَغُسْطُس؛ آبْ
available (v.) (to be available)	tawāfar	تَوافَر
award (v.) (to be awarded)	HaSal 'alā (u)	حَصَل عَلى

518

B

B.A.	līsans	ليسانْس
back	DHahr	ظَهْر
bad	sayyi'	سَيِّئ
bag	Haqība (Haqā'ib)	حَقِيبة (حَقَائِب)
baggage claim	Sālat al-Haqā'ib	صَالة الحَقَائِب
Bahrain	al-baHrayn	البَحْرَيْن
balcony	shurfa	شُرْفَة
ball	kura	كُرَة
band	firqa	فِرْقَة
bank (n.)	bank (bunūk)	بَنْك (بُنُوك)
bathroom	Hammām	حمّام
be (v.)	kān (yakūn)	كان (يكون)
be able	istaTā' (yastaTī'); amkan (yumkin)	اسْتَطاع (يَسْتَطِيع)، أمْكَن (يُمْكِن)
be afflicted with	uSib bi	أُصِيب بِ
be found	awjad (yūjid)	أوجَد (يوجِد)
be necessary (to)	wajab (yajib) an	وَجَب (يَجِب) أن
be sad	Hazin	حَزِن
be sorry	a'sif (a)	أَسِف
beach	shāTi' al-baHr	شاطِئ البَحْر
beautiful	jamīl	جَمِيل
because	li'anna	لأنّ
become	aSbaH (yuSbiH), Sāra (yaSīr)	أصْبَح (يُصْبِح)؛ صار (يَصِير)
bed	sarīr (asirra)	سَرِير (أسِرَّة)
before	qabl	قَبْل
begin	bada' (a)	بَدَأ
beginning	bidāya	بِدَاية
Beirut	bayrūt	بَيْروت

believe (that)	Saddaq anna, i'taqad anna	صَدَّق أنّ؛ اِعْتَقَد أنّ
beside	bijānib	بِجانِب
besides	thumma inna	ثمّ إنّ
better	afDal	أفْضَل
getting better (n.)	taHassun	تَحَسُّن
between	bayn	بَيْن
big	kabīr (kibār, m. pl.) (kubrā, f. pl.)	كَبِير (كِبار) (كُبْرى)
black	asuad	أسْوَد
bloc	takattul	تَكَتُّل
blossom	zahra	زهْرَة
blue	azraq	أزْرَق
boy	walad (awlād)	وَلَد (أوْلاد)
bread	khubz	خُبْز
bride	'arūs	عَروس
brown	bunnī	بُنِّي
build	bana (yabnī)	بَنَى (يَبْني)
building (n.)	mabna (mabān)	مَبنىَ (مَبان)
bulgur wheat	burghul	بُرْغُل
bureaucrat	muwaDHDHaf	مُوَظَّف
burnt	maHrūq	مَحْروق
bus	Hāfila	حافِلَة
businessperson	rajul a'māl	رَجُل أعْمَال
busy	mashghūl	مَشْغول
but	lākin, walākin	لكِن؛ وَلَكِن
buy	ishtara (yashtarī)	اِشْتَرَى (يَشْتَري)
by	lada	لَدَى
by means of	bi	بِ

C

Cairo	al-qāhira	القاهِرة
candidate	murashshaH	مُرَشَّح
capital city	'āSima (awāSim)	عاصِمَة (عَواصِم)

carry	Hamal (i)	حَمَل
carrying	Haml	حَمْل
case	Hāla	حالَة
case	al-Hāla	الحالَة
in that case	fi hādhihi l-Hāla	في هٰذِهِ الحالَة
cassette	kāsit	كاسيت
cent	sint	سِنْت
certain	mu'akkad	مُؤَكَّد
it is certain that	min al-mu'akkad anna	مِنْ المُؤَكَّد أنَّ
certainly	Tab'an, biT-Tab'	طَبْعاً ؛ بِالطَبْع
chain(s) (n.)	silsila (salāsil)	سِلْسِلة (سَلاسِل)
chair	kursi (karāsi)	كُرْسي (كراسي)
change (v.)	ghayyar	غَيَّر
to change oneself	taghayyar	تَغَيَّر
channel	qanā (qanawāt)	قناة (قَنَوات)
characteristics	muwāSafāt	مُواصَفات
cheap	rakhīS	رَخيص
cheaper	arkhaS	أرْخَص
chickpeas	HumuS	حُمُّص
chicken	dajāj	دَجاج
choice	ikhtiyār	اخْتِيار
choose	ikhtār	إخْتار
cigarette	sijāra (sajā'r)	سيجارة (سَجائِر)
cinnamon	qirfa	قِرْفَة
city	madīna (mudun)	مَدينة (مُدُن)
client	zabūn (zabā'in)	زَبون (زَبائِن)
close (adj.)	qarīb	قَريب
closet	dulāb	دولاب
clothing	malābis	مَلابِس
coffee grounds	bunn	بُنّ

coffee shop	maqhā (maqāhi)	مَقْهى (مَقاه)
colleague	zamīl	زَميل
collective	jamā'ī	جَماعي
come	atā (ya'ti)	أتَى (يَأْتي)
coming	qādim	قادِم
compose (v.) (be composed of)	takawwan min	تَكَوَّن مِن
computer	kumbiyūtar	كُمْبيوتر
condition	Hāl, Hāla	حال ؛ حالَة
conservatism	muHāfaDHa	مُحافَظة
consult	tashāwar	تَشاوَر
continent	qārra	قارَّة
continue	istamarr	إسْتَمَر
contract (n.)	'aqd ('uqūd)	عَقْد (عُقود)
control (v.)	taHakkam	تَحَكَّم
convening	'aqd	عَقْد
copy (v.)	iktatab	اكْتَتَب
copying	taSwīr	تَصْوير
correspond	kātab	كاتَب
corridor	mamarr	مَمَرّ
cost (v.)	kallaf (i)	كَلَّف
county	muHāfaZa	مُحافَظة
cover (v.)	ghaTTā (yughaTTi)	غَطَّى (يُغَطّي)
crowded	muzdaHim	مُزْدَحِم
cucumbers	khiyār	خِيار
currency	'umla	عُمْلَة
currency exchange	Sirāfa	صِرافة
customer	zabūn (zabā'in)	زَبون (زَبائِن)

D

daily	yawmiyyan	يَوْمياً
Damascus	dimashq	دِمَشْق
daughter	bint	بِنْت
day	yawm	يَوْم

dear	'azīz	عَزِيز
December	disambir, kānūn al-awwal	ديسَمِبر ؛ كانون الأوَّل
decide	qarrar	قَرَّر
degree (extent)	daraja	دَرَجَة
delay	ta'khīr	تَأْخير
delicious	ladhīdh, Tayyib	لَذيذ ؛ طَيِّب
demanded	maTlūb	مَطْلوب
desert	SaHarā'	صَحْراء
desserts	Halawayāt	حَلَويات
dialect	lahja	لَهْجَة
die (v.)	māt (yamūt)	مات (يَموت)
difference	farq (furūq), khilāf	فَرْق (فُروق) ؛ خِلاف
director	mudīr	مُدير
discussion	munāqasha	مُناقَشَة
dish	Tabaq (aTbāq)	طَبَق (أطْباق)
distance	masāfa	مَسافة
division	khilāf	خِلاف
do	fa'al (a)	فَعَل
doctor	duktōr, Tabib (aTibbā')	دُكْتور ؛ طَبيب (أطِبَّاء)
doctoral degree	shihādat doctōrā	شَهادَة دكتوراة
dollar	dulār	دولار
downtown	wasaT al-balad	وَسَط البَلَد
drink (v.)	sharib (a)	شَرِب
drinks	mashrūbāt	مَشْروبات

E

ear	udhun (udhunān)	أُذُن (أُذْنان)
earn	HaSal 'alā (u)	حَصَل عَلى
East	mashriq	مَشْرِق شَرْق
easy	sahl	سَهْل
eat	akal (u); tanāwal	أكَل تَناوَل

editor	muHarrir	مُحَرِّر
editor-in-chief (f.)	ra'īsat at-taHarīr	رَئيسَة التَّحْرير
eggplant	bādhinjān	باذِنْجان
Egypt	misr	مِصْر
eight	thamānia	ثَمانية
eight hundred	thamānimi'a	ثَمانِمائة
eighteen	thamāniat 'ashara	ثَمانية عَشَرَ
eighth	thāmin	ثامِن
elevator	miS'ad	مِصْعَد
eleven	aHad 'ashara	أحَدَ عَشَرَ
eleventh	Hādī 'ashar	حادي عَشَر
employee	muwaDHDHaf	مُوَظَّف
end	nihāya	نِهايَة
endowed with	dhū (dhāt)	ذو (ذات)
engineer	muhandis	مُهَنْدِس
engineering	handasa	هَنْدَسَة
Enjoy your meal!	wajba Tayyiba!	وَجْبَة طَيِّبَة
enough	kāfi	كافي
enter	dakhal	دَخَل
enthusiast	'āshiq	عاشِق
equivalent to	'ibāra 'an	عِبارَة عَن
era	'aSr, 'ahd	عَصْر؛ عَهْد
Ethernet	itharnit	إيثَرنِت
even (adv.)	Hattā	حَتّى
and even	bal	بَل
evening(s)	masā' (amāsi)	مَساء (أماسي)
event	wāqi'	واقِع
every	kull	كُلّ
exactly	bi D-DabT	بالضَّبْط
exam	imtiHān	امْتِحان
exceed	zād (yazīd) 'an	زاد (يَزيد) عَن
your excellence	HaDratak	حَضْرَتَك

except	illa	إلا
exception	istithnā'	اِسْتِثْناء
exchange (currency)	Sarf	صَرْف
exchange rate	si'r Sarf	سِعْر صَرْف
exercise	tamrīn	تَمْرين
expect	tawaqqa'	تَوَقَّع
expensive	ghālī (aghlā, comp./sup.)	غالي (أغْلَى)
experience	khibra	خِبْرَة
extent	daraja	دَرَجَة
eye(s)	'ayn ('aynān)	عَيْن (عَيْنان)

F

fact	wāqi'	واقِع
failure	fashal	فَشَل
fall (n.)	kharīf	خَرِيف
family	ahl, 'ā'ila, usra (usar)	أهْل ؛ عائِلَة ؛ أُسْرة (أُسَر)
far away	ba'īd	بعيد
fare	ujra	أُجْرَة
father	wālid	والِد
fault	khaTa' (akhTā')	خَطَأ (أخْطاء)
fax	fāks	فاكْس
fear (v.)	khāf (yakhāf) an	خاف (يَخاف) أنْ
February	fibrāyir, shubāT	فِبْرايِر؛ شُباط
feel (v.)	sha'ar (u)	شَعَر (يَشْعُر)
fifteen	khamsat 'ashara	خَمْسَة عَشَر
fifth	khāmis	خامِس
file	malaff	مَلَفّ
fill (v.) (to be filled with)	imtala'	اِمْتَلأ
find	wajad	وَجَد
finding	ijād	إيجاد

first	awwal	أوَّل
five	khamsa	خَمْسَة
five hundred	khamsumi'a	خَمْسُمائة
flute (Arab)	mizmār	مِزْمار
flying	Tayarān	طَيَران
food	akl, Ta'ām	أكْل ؛ طَعام
football	kurat al-qadam	كُرَة القَدَم
for	lī	لِـ
for the sake of	min ajal	مِنْ أجْل
forbidden	Harām	حَرام
force (v.) (to be forced to)	iDTurr an	اِضْطُرّ أن
foreign	ajnabī, khārijī	أجْنَبي ؛ خارِجي
four	arba'a	أرْبَعَة
four hundred	arba'umi'a	أرْبَعُمائة
fourteen	arba'at 'ashara	أرْبَعَة عَشَر
fourth	rābi'	الرابِع
freedom	Hurrīya	حُرِّية
Friday	yūm al-jum'a	يَوْم الجُمْعَة
friend	Sadīq (aSdiqā')	صَديق (أصْدِقاء)
from	min, 'an	مِنْ ؛ عَن
full (adj.)	mali'	مَلِيء
furnishings	athāth	أثاث
future	mustaqbal	مُسْتَقْبَل

G

gain (v.)	iktasab	اِكْتَسَب
garden	Hadīqa	حَديقَة
gender	jins	جِنْس
get (v.)	HaSal 'alā (u)	حَصَل عَلى
gift	hadiyya	هَدِيَّة
girl	bint	بِنْت
give	a'Tā (yu'Tī)	أعْطَى (يُعْطي)

giving	i'Tā'	إعْطاء
go	dhahab (a)	ذَهَب
God	allāh	الله
God willing!	inn shā'allah!	إن شاء الله
golden	dhahabī	ذَهَبِيّ
gold	dhahab	ذَهَب
good	jayyid, ladhīdh, Tayyib	جَيِّد ؛ لَذيذ ؛ طَيِّب
Good-bye!	ma'a as-salāma!	مَعَ السَّلامَة
Good morning!	SabāH al-khayr! (greeting), SabāH an-nūr! (response)	صَباح الخَيْر؛ صَباح النّور
government	Hukūma	حُكومة
graduate (v.)	takharraj	تَخَرَّج
graduation	takharruj	تَخَرُّج
grandmother	jadda	جَدَّة
grapes	'inab	عِنَب
green	akhDar	أخْضَر
greetings	taHiyya	تَحِيَّة
groom (n.)	'arīs	عَريس
ground (adj.)	mafrūm	مَفْروم
guest	Dayf (Duyūf)	ضَيْف (ضُيوف)
guidebook	dalīl siyāHī	دَليل سِياحي
gym	Sālat at-tamrīnāt ar-riyāDiyya	صالة التَّمْرينات الرياضيَّة

H

hair	sha'r	شَعْر
half	niSf	نِصْف
hamburger	hāmburgar	هامْبورجَر
hand (n.)	yadd (yadān)	يَدّ (يَدان)
have	lada, 'inda, lī	لَدَى ؛ عِنْدَ ؛ لِ
having	dhū (dhāt)	ذو (ذات)
head	ra's	رَأْس

headquarters	maqarr (maqārr)	مَقَرّ (مَقارّ)
heart	qalb	قَلْب
heart attack	azma qalbiyya	أزْمَة قَلبِيَّة
Hello! (on the phone)	alū!	ألو
help (v.)	sā'ad 'alā	ساعَد عَلَى
here	hunā	هُنا
honor (v.) (to be honored)	tasharraf	تَشَرَّف
hope (v.) (that)	rajā (yarjū) an	رَجا (يَرْجو) أن
hospital	mustashfa	مُسْتَشْفَى
hot	Hārr	حارّ
hotel	funduq (fanādiq)	فُنْدُق (فَنادِق)
hour	sā'a	ساعَة
house	bayt (biyūt)	بَيْت (بيوت)
how	kayfa	كَيْفَ
how many	kam	كَمْ
how much	bi kam	بِكَمْ
however	bal	بَلْ
hundred	mi'a	مائة
one hundred percent	mi'a bi l-mi'a	مائة بالمائة
hunger	jū'	جوع
hungry	jaw'ān	جَوْعان
husband	zawja (azwāj)	زَوْج (أزْواج)

I

I	ana	أنا
if	idhā, law	إذا ؛ لَو
importance	ahamiyya	أهَمِيَّة
important	hāmm	هامّ
in	bi, fī	بِ ؛ في
in the manner of	'ala	عَلَى

increase (v.)	irtafa'	اِرْتَفَع	lead to	addā (yu'addī) ilā	أَدّى (يُؤَدّي) إلى
information	isti'lāmāt	اِسْتِعْلامات	leaf	waraq (awrāq)	وَرَق (أَوْراق)
information	ma'lūmāt	مَعْلومات	learn	ta'allam	تَعَلَّم
inside	dākhil	داخِل	least	aqall	أَقَلّ
international	'ālamī, dawlī	عالَمي ؛ دَوْلي	at least	'ala l-aqall	عَلَى الأَقَلّ
Internet	intarnit	إِنْتَرْنت	Lebanese	lubnānī	لُبْناني
it is possible that	min al-mumkin an	مِنْ المُمْكِن أَنْ	left (side)	yusrā, yāsār	يُسْرىَ ؛ يَسار
			leg	sāq (sāqān)	ساق (ساقان)

J

January	yanāyir, kānūn ath-thānī	يَناير ؛ كانون الثّاني
journalism	SaHāfa	صَحافة
journalist	SaHāfiyyīn	صَحَفي
journey	safar	سَفَر
July	yulyah, tammūz	يوليَة ؛ تَمّوز
jumping	qafz	قَفْز
June	yunyah, Hazayrān	يونْيَة ؛ حَزيران

length	Tūāl	طَول
less	aqall	أَقَلّ
to be less than	qall (yaqill)	قَلّ عن
lessen	qallal min	قَلَّل مِن
Libyan	lībī	ليبي
life	Hayā	حَياة
lift (v.)	Hamal (i)	حَمَل
lifting	Haml	حَمْل
like	aHabb (v.), a'jab (v.), mithl (adv.)	أَحَبّ ؛ أَعْجَب ؛ مِثل

K

kind	naw'	نَوع
kitchen	maTbakh (maTābikh)	مَطْبَخ (مَطابِخ)
knee	rukba (rukab)	رُكْبَة (رُكَب)
know	'alim (a), 'araf (i)	عَلِم ؛ عَرَف
getting to know (n.)	ta'āruf	تَعارُف
get to know	ta'arraf 'alā	تَعَرَّفَ عَلَى
knowledge	'ilm	عِلْم
Kuwait	al-kuwayt	الكُوَيْت

listen	istama' ilā	اِسْتَمَع إِلَى
little	qalīl	قَليل
a little of	qalīl min	قَليل مِن
live	sakan (u)	سَكَن
living room	Sāla	صالة
loaf (n.)	raghīf (arghifa)	رَغيف (أَرْغِفَة)
local	maHallī	مَحَلّي
look (at)	naDHar (u) ilā	نَظَر إلى
lover (of)	'āshiq	عاشِق
love (v.)	aHabb	أَحَبّ
luggage	amti'a	أَمْتِعَة
lunch	ghadā'	غَداء

L

land	arD (arāD)	أَرْض (أَراض)
language	lugha	لُغَة
later	lāHiq	لاحِق
lead (v.)	qād (yaqūd)	قاد (يَقود)

M

machine	mākina	ماكينة
main	ra'isi	رَئيسي
majority	mu'Zam	مُعْظَم
make (v.) (to be made up of)	takawwan min	تَكَوَّن مِن
man	rajul (rijāl)	رَجُل (رِجال)
many	kathīr	كَثير
March	māris, ādhār	مارِس ؛ آذار
market	sūq (aswāq)	سُوق (أسواق)
marriage	zawāj	زواج
matchmaker	khāTiba	خاطِبة
May	mayū, ayyār	مايو ؛ أيّار
maybe	rubbamā	رُبَّما
mean (v.)	'anā (ya'ni)	عَنَى (يَعْني)
means	wasīla (wasā'il)	وَسيلة (وَسائل)
means of transport	wasā'il an-naql	وَسائل النقْل
meat	laHm	لَحْم
meat (grilled)	mashwiyyāt	مَشْوِيّات
spiced meat on a skewer	kabāb	كَباب
spiced ground meat	kufta	كُفْتة
meatballs	kibbi, kubayba	كِبّة ؛ كُبَيْبة
Mediterranean Sea	al-baHar al-mutawassiT	البَحْر المُتَوَسِّط
meet (be acquainted with)	ta'arraf 'alā	تَعَرَّف عَلَى
member	'uDw (a'Dā')	عُضْو (أعْضاء)
meter	'addād	عَدّاد
midday	DHuhr	ظُهْر
Middle East	ash-sharq al-awsaT	الشَّرْق الأوْسَط

minister	wazīr (wuzarā')	وَزير (وُزَراء)
minute	daqiqa (daqā'iq)	دَقيقة (دَقائق)
mistake	khaTa' (akhTā')	خَطَأ (أخْطَاء)
modern	Hadīth	حَديث
Monday	yūm al-'ithnayn	يوم الإثْنَيْن
monitor	shāsha	شاشة
month	shahr (shuhūr)	شَهْر (شُهور)
more	akthar	أكْثَر
Moroccan	maghribī	مَغْرِبي
Morocco	al-maghrib	المَغْرِب
most	mu'DHam	مُعْظَم
mother	wālida	والِدة
mouse	fa'ra	فَأْرة
move (v.)	tanaqqal	تَنَقَّل
movement	Haraka	حَرَكة
moving	naql	نَقْل
museum	matHaf	مَتْحَف
musical	mūsiqi	موسيقيّ

N

nail	mismār	مِسْمار
nails	aZāfir	أظافِر
name (n.)	ism (asmā')	إسْم (أسْماء)
narrow (f.)	Dayyiqa	ضَيِّقة
necklace	'iqd ('uqūd)	عِقْد (عُقود)
need (v.)	iHtāj	إحْتاج
net	shabaka	شَبَكة
new	jadīd (judud)	جَديد (جُدُد)
news	khabar (akhbār)	خَبَر (أخْبار)
next (f.)	qādima	قادِمة
nice	Hulw	حُلْو
night	layla (layāli)	لَيْلة (لَيالي)
nightgown	jalābiyya	جَلابِيّة
nightingale	bulbul	بُلْبُل

nine	tis'a	تِسْعَة
nine hundred	tis'umi'a	تِسْعُمِائة
nineteen	tis'at 'ashara	تِسْعَة عَشَر
ninth	tāsi'	تاسِع
no	lā	لا
nose	anf	أنْف
not	lā, ghayr	لا ؛ غَيْر
to not be	laysa	لَيْسَ
will not	lan	لَنْ
November	nuvambir, tishrīn ath-thāni	نوفَمْبِر؛ تِشْرين الثّاني
now	al-ān	الآن
number (of)	'adad	عَدَد
number	raqam (arqām)	رَقَم (أَرْقام)
nurse	mumarriD	مُمَرِّض

O

obtaining	HuSūl 'ala	حُصول عَلى
occupation	iHtilāl	اِحْتِلال
October	uktūbar, tishrīn al-awwal	أُكْتوبَر؛ تِشْرين الأوّل
office	maktab (makātib)	مكْتَب (مَكاتِب)
official (adj.)	rasmī	رَسْمي
old	qadīm	قَديم
on	'ala	عَلَى
one	wāhid	واحِد
only	faqaT (adv.), waHīd (adj.)	فَقَط ؛ وَحيد
opinion	ra'y	رَأْي
opponent	mu'āriD	مُعارِض
opposed (adv.) (as opposed to)	bikhilāf	بِخِلاف
or	aw, am	أوْ ؛ أمْ
orange (color)	burtuqālī	بُرتقالي

orange (fruit)	burtuqāla	بُرتُقالة
order	Talab (u) (v.), Talab (n.)	طَلَب ؛ طَلَب
in order to	lī	لِ
ordinary	'ādiyya	عادِيّة
organize	naDHDHam	نَظِّم
origin	aSl	أصْل
other (f.)	ākhar (ūkhrā)	آخَر (أُخْرَى)
over (to go over)	zād (yazīd) 'an	زاد (يَزيد) عَن
overlook	aTall 'ala	أطَلَّ عَلَى
owner	SāHib (aSHāb)	صاحِب (أصْحاب)

P

pain	alam (ālām)	ألَم (آلام)
partake (in)	ishtarak fī	اِشْتَرَك في
participate (in)	ishtarak fī	اِشْتَرَك في
partner	sharīk (shurakā')	شَريك (شُرَكاء)
party (n.)	Hafla	حَفْلَة
passport	jawāz as-safar	جَواز السَفَر
past	māDī	مَاضي
pay (v.)	dafa'a (a)	دَفَع
pen (n.)	qalam (aqlām)	قَلَم (أَقْلام)
penny	fals (fulūs)	فَلْس (فُلوس)
people	nās	ناس
perform (v.) (to be performed)	ujriya	أُجْرِيَ
period (of time)	mudda	مُدَّة
for a period of	limuddat	لِمُدَّة
person	shakhS (ashkhāS)	شَخْص (أَشْخَاص)
petroleum	bitrūl	بِتْرول

phenomenon	DHāhira	ظاهِرَة	
physician	Tabīb (aTibbā')	طَبيب (أطِبَّاء)	
pink	zahrī	زَهْري	
place(s)	makān (amākin)	مكان (أَماكِن)	
plate	Tabaq (aTbāq)	طَبَق (أطْباق)	
please (v.)	a'jab	أعْجَب	
Please!	min faDlik!	مِن فَضْلِك	
If you please!	tafaDDal!	تَفَضَّل	
politeness	dhawq	ذَوْقُ	
political	siyāsī	سياسي	
postpone	ajjal (yu'ajjil)	أجَّل (يُؤَجِّل)	
postponement	ta'jīl	تَأْجيل	
pot	wa'ā' (aw'iya)	وِعاء (أوْعِيَة)	
pound	līrā (weight), junayh (currency)	ليرَة ؛ جُنَيْه	
practice (v.)	māras	مارَس	
prefer	faDDal	فَضَّل	
preferable	afDal	أفْضَل	
pregnancy	Haml	حَمْل	
press	SaHāfa	صَحافَة	
pretty	Hulw	حُلْو	
price (n.)	thaman (athmān), si'r (as'ār)	ثَمَن (أثْمان)؛ سِعْر (أسْعَار)	
principal	ra'īsī	رَئيسي	
privacy	khuSūSiyya	خُصوصيَّة	
private	khāSS	خاصّ	
problem	mushkila (mashākil)	مُشْكِلَة (مَشاكِل)	
professor	ustādh (asātidha)	أُسْتاذ (أَساتِذة)	
punishment	mu'āqaba	مُعاقَبَة	

Q

qualification	mu'ahhil	مُؤَهِّل
qualify (v.)	ahhala (yu'ahil)	أهَّلَ (يُؤَهِّل)

R

rate(s) (n.)	si'r (as'ār)	سِعْر (أسْعَار)
rather	bal	بَلْ
reading	qirā'a	قِراءَة
real	wāqi'	واقِع
Really?	wa-llāhi?	والله؟
reason (n.)	sabab (asbāb)	سَبَب (أسْباب)
for that reason	li dhālik	لِذَلِك
reception	istiqbāl	إسْتِقْبال
red	aHmar	أحْمَر
reform (n.)	iSlāH	إصْلاح
region	minTaqa (manāTiq)	مِنْطَقة (مَناطِق)
regretful	āsif	آسِف
relative	qarīb (uqārlb)	قَريب (أقارِب)
rent	ajjar (yu'ajjir) (v.), ijār (n.)	أجَّر (يُؤَجِّر) ؛ إيْجار
required	maTlūb	مَطْلوب
researcher	bāHith	باحِث
reservation	Hajz	حَجْز
reside	sakan (u)	سَكَن
resident	sākin (sukkān)	ساكِن (سُكّان)
residential	sakanī	سَكَني
responsible	mas'ūl	مَسْؤُول
restaurant	maT'am (maTā'im)	مَطْعَم (مَطاعِم)
result in	addā (yu'addī) ilā	أدَّى (يُؤَدِّي) إلى
return (v.)	'ād (ya'ūd)	عاد (يَعود)
rial	riāl	ريال
rice	urz	أُرْز
right (side)	yamīn	يَمين
right(s) (n.)	Haqq (Huqūq)	حَقّ (حُقوق)
Right?	a laysa kadhālik?	ألَيْسَ كَذَلِك؟

527

robe	jallābiyya	جَلَّابِيَّة	shame	Harām	حَرام
room(s)	ghurfa (ghuraf); Hujra	غُرْفَة (غُرَف)؛ حُجْرَة	What a shame!	yā Harām!	يا حَرام!
running	jary	جَرْي	share (v.)	ishtarak fī	إِشْتَرَك في
			sheet (of paper)	waraq (awrāq)	وَرَق (أَوْراق)
S			shine (v.)	lama' (yalma')	لَمَع (يَلْمَع)
sadness	Hazan	حَزَن	shop	maHall	مَحَلّ
safari	safārī	سَفاري	short	qaSīr	قَصير
salad	salaTa	سَلَطَة	show (v.)	arā (yurī)	أرى (يُري)
San'a	San'ā' (capital of Yemen)	صَنْعاء	silver (adj.)	fiDDī (adj.), fiDDa (n.)	فِضِيّ؛ فِضَّة
sandwich	shaTīra	شَطيرَة	similarly	kamā	كَما
satellite	faDā'iya	فَضائِيَّة	Sinai Peninsula	saynā'	سَيْناء
Saturday	yawm as-sabt	يَوْم السَّبْت	single (adj.)	'a'zab ('uzzāb)	أعْزَب (عُزّاب)
Saudi Arabia	as-sa'udiya	السَعُودِيَّة	Sir	ustādh (asātidha)	أُسْتاذ (أَساتِذة)
Saudi Arabian	sa'ūdi	سَعُودي	sister	ukht (akhawāt)	أُخْت (أخَوات)
Saudi Aramco	arāmkū asa'ūdiyya	أرامْكو السَعُودِيَّة	situation	Hāl, Hāla	حال؛ حالَة
school(s)	madrasa (madāris)	مَدْرَسَة (مَدارِس)	six	sitta	سِتَّة
search (for) (v.)	baHath 'an	بَحَث عَن	six hundred	sittumi'a	سِتُّمِائة
			sixteen	sittat 'ashara	سِتَّة عَشَر
season	faSl	فَصْل	sixth	sādis	سادِس
second	thānī	ثاني	sky (f.)	samā'	سَماء
see	ra'ā	رَأى (يَرَى)	smoke	dakhkhan	دَخِّن
seem	bada (yabdū)	بَدا (يَبْدو)	so	thumma	ثُمَّ
seller	bā'i'	بائِع	software	suftwīr	سوفْتوير
semester	faSl	فَصْل	some	ba'D	بَعْض
separation	faSl	فَصْل	son	ibn	إبْن
September	sibtambir, aylūl	سِبْتَمْبِر؛ أَيْلول	sorry	āsif	آسِف
serve (v.)	khadam (i)	خَدَم	source	maSdar (maSādir)	مَصْدَر (مَصادِر)
seven	sab'a	سَبْعَة	speak (v.)	tahadath, takallam	تَحَدَّث؛ تَكَلَّم
seven hundred	saba'umi'a	سَبْعُمائة			
seventeen	sab'at 'ashara	سَبْعَة عَشَر	special	khāSS	خاصّ
seventh	sābi'	سابِع	specialist	akhiSSā'ī	أخِصّائي
sex	jins	جِنْس	specific	khāSS	خاصّ

spend	anfaq	أَنْفَق
exchange currency (v.)	Saraf (i)	صَرَف
spice	buhār	بُهار
spring (n.) (season)	rabī'	رَبيع
star	najma (nujūm)	نَجْمة (نُجوم)
stay (v.)	baqiya (yabqā)	بَقِيَ (يَبْقى)
still (adv.)	mā zāl	ما زال
stomach	mi'dda	مِعْدة
story (of a building)	Tābiq (Tawābiq)	طابِق (طَوابِق)
struggle	Sirā'	صِراع
student	Tālib (Tulāb)	طالِب (طُلّاب)
study (v.)	daras (u), dhākar	دَرَس ؛ ذاكَر
summer	Sayf	صَيْف
summit	qimma	قِمّة
Sunday	yawm al-aHad	يَوْم الأحَد
sunset	maghrib	مَغْرِب
sure	muta'akkid	مُتَأكِّد
to make sure of	ta'akkad min	تَأكَّد مِن
surgery	'amaliyya jirāHiyya	عَمَلِيّة جِراحِيّة
surrounding	Hawl	حَوْل
sweet	Hulw	حُلْو
sweets	Halawayāt	حَلَوَيات
swim (v.)	sabaH (a)	سَبَح
sympathize (with)	ashfaq 'alā	أشْفَق على
Syria	sūriyā	سُوريا
Syrian	sūrī	سوري

T

tabouli (salad)	tabbūli	تبُولة
Tahrir Square	maydān at-taHrīr	مَيْدان التَحْرير

take (v.)	akhadh (u)	أخَذ
tall	Tawil	طَويل
taste (n.)	dhawq	ذَوْق
taxi	tāksī	تاكْسي
tea	shāy	شاي
teacher	mudarris	مُدَرّس
technology	tiknulujya	تِكْنولوجيا
telephone	tilifūn	تِليفون
television	tilifizyūn	تِليفِزْيون
tell	Hakā (yaHkī)	حَكى (يَحْكي)
ten	ashara	عَشَرة
tenth	'āshir	عاشِر
testimony	shahāda	شَهادة
Thank God!	al-Hamdulillāh!	الحَمْد لله
Thank you.	shukran.	شُكْراً
that (f. sg.)	tilka	تِلكَ
that (m. sg.)	dhalik	ذَلِك
that which	mā	ما
that (sub. conj.)	anna	أنَّ
the same	nafs	نَفْس
then	thumma	ثُمَّ
there	hunāk	هُناك
there is/are	awjad (yūjid)	أوجَد (يوجِد)
these	hā'ula'i	هَؤُلاء
thing	shay' (ashyā')	شَيْء (أشْياء)
think	i'taqad anna	اعْتَقَد أنَّ
to think about	fakkar fī	فَكَّر في
thinking	tafkīr	تفْكير
third	thālith	ثالِث
thirteen	thalāthat 'ashara	ثَلاثة عَشَر
this (f.)	hadhihi	هَذِه
this (m.)	hadha	هَذا
those	ulā'ika	أوْلئِكَ

thousand	alf (ālf)	أَلْف (آلاف)
three	thalātha	ثَلاثَة
three hundred	thalāthumi'a	ثَلاثُمائة
throat	zawr	زَوْر
through	khilāl	خِلال
Thursday	yawm al-khamīs	يَوْم الخَميس
ticket(s)	tadhkara (tadhakir)	تَذْكَرَة (تَذاكِر)
time(s)	waqt (awqāt)	وَقْت (أَوقات)
to (prep.)	ilā, lī	إلى ؛ لِـ
in order to	likayy	لِكَيْ
(followed by a verb)	an	أَنْ
tomorrow	ghadan	غَداً
tool	adā (adawāt)	أداة (أَدَوات)
tourism	siyāHa	سِياحَة
tourist	sā'iH	سائِحَ
toward	'ila	إلى
traditional	taqlīdī	تَقْليدي
traffic	murūr	مُرور
train	qiTār	قِطار
training	tadrīb	تَدْريب
transportation	tanaqqul	تَنَقُّل
travel (v.)	sāfar	سافَر
traveler	musāfir	مُسافِر
traveling	safar	سَفَر
trip	riHla, safar	رِحْلَة ؛ سَفَر
true	SaHīH	صَحيح
truly	fi'lan	فِعْلاً
try (v.)	Hāwal	حاوَل
Tuesday	yawm ath-thulāthā'	يَوْم الثُلاثاء
Tunisian	tūnisī	تونِسي
twelfth	thānī 'ashar	ثاني عَشَر
two	ithnān (ithnatn)	إِثْنان (اثْنَتان)

typing	Tibā'a	طِباعَة

U

uncle (maternal)	khāl	خال
unfortunately	li l-'āsaf	لِلأَسَف
university	jāmi'a	جامِعَة
upper	'ulwī	عُلْوي
use (v.)	istakhdam	اسْتَخْدَم
usual	'āda	عادَة
usually	fi l-'āda	في العادَة
utensil	adā (adawāt)	أداة (أَدَوات)

V

vacation	ijāza	إجازَة
veil(s) (n.)	Hijāb (aHjiba)	حِجاب (أَحْجِبة)
Venezuela	finizwīlā	فِنِزويلا
very	jiddan	جِداً
visit (n.)	ziyāra	زِيارَة
visitor	zā'ir (zuwwār)	زائِر (زوّار)
wait (v.)	intaDHar	اِنْتَظَر

W

walk (v.)	mashā (yamshi)	مَشَى (يَمْشي)
want (v.)	arād (yurīd)	أراد (يُريد)
Washington	wāshinTun	واشِنْطُن
watch (v.)	shahad	شاهَد
wear (v.)	irtada	اِرْتَدَي
weather	jaww	جَوّ
Web site	mawqi' 'ala sh-shabaka	مَوقِع عَلى الشَبَكة
Wednesday	yawm al-arba'ā'	يوم الأَرْبَعاء
week(s)	usbū' (asābi')	أُسْبوع (أَسابيع)
weight(s) (n.)	thiql (athqāl)	ثِقْل (أَثْقال)

welcome (n.)	istiqbāl	إِسْتِقْبال
Welcome!	marHaban bikl, ahlan!, ahlan wa-sahlan!	مَرْحَباً بِك ؛ أهلاً ؛ أهْلاً وَسَهْلاً
well	jayyid	جَيّد
well-known	ma'rūf	مَعْرُوف
well-being	khayr	خَيْر
West	maghrib	مَغْرِب
Western	gharbī	غَرْبي
what	mā, mādhā	ما ؛ ماذا
when	'indama, matā	عِنْدَمَا ؛ مَتَى
where	ayna	أَيْنَ
which (m.)	alladhī	الذَي
which (f.)	allatī	الّتي
while	baynamā	بَيْنَما
white	abyaD	أَبْيَض
why	limādhā	لِمَاذا
wide	wāsi'	واسِع
wife	zawja (zawj)	زَوْجَة
will (v.)	sawfa	سَوْفَ
winter	shitā'	شِتاء

with	ma'a, lada	مَعَ ؛ لَدَى
without	bidūn, dūn	بِدون ؛ دُون
woman	imrā'a (nisā')	إمْرأة (نِساء)
work (v.)	'amil (a)	عَمِل
worker	'āmil	عامِل
world	'ālam	عالَم

Y

year	sana (sinīn), 'ām (a'wām)	سَنَة (سِنين) ؛ عام (أَعْوام)
yellow	aSfar	أَصْفَر
Yemen	al-yaman	اليَمَن
yes	na'am	نَعَمْ
yesterday	ams	أَمْس
you (f.)	anti	أَنْتِ
you (m.)	anta	أَنْتَ
your excellence	HaDratak	حَضْرَتَك

Z

zero	Sifr	صِفْر

INDEX OF GRAMMAR TOPICS

Numbers in this index refer to lessons in which topics are discussed, not page numbers. For Lessons 1 to 15, only the lesson number is indicated in the index. For Lessons 16 to 35, the lesson number is followed by the capital letter in parentheses indicating the dialect: E (Egyptian), I (Iraqi), L (Lebanese), or S (Saudi).

N

O

P

Q

Learn to Speak, Read, and Write in Arabic.

In response to the **high demand** for courses in Arabic, the experts at Living Language® have developed several courses to meet a variety of language learning needs.

Complete Arabic: The Basics

Our best-selling program helps beginner-level language learners master fundamental vocabulary, grammar, and cultural concepts.

Comes complete with 3 CDs and a coursebook, including a comprehensive two-way glossary.
$25.00/C$35.00 • ISBN: 1-4000-2123-5

In-Flight Arabic

This essential one-hour program helps travelers learn enough to get by in every travel situation.

Comes complete with one CD and an audioscript.
$13.95/C$21.00 • ISBN: 0-609-81064-2

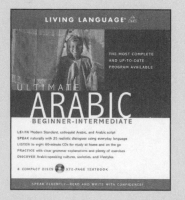

Ultimate Arabic

This comprehensive program helps serious language learners achieve fluency. It covers Modern Standard Arabic as well as the four most commonly spoken dialects: Egyptian, Iraqi, Lebanese, and Saudi.

Comes complete with 8 CDs and a coursebook, including a comprehensive two-way glossary.
$79.95/C$110.00 • ISBN: 1-4000-2082-4

Available at bookstores everywhere.   *www.livinglanguage.com*